Logics for Computer Science

Second Edition

Arindama Singh
Department of Mathematics
Indian Institute of Technology Madras

PHI Learning Private Limited
Delhi-110092
2025

In fond memory of ***Shri Asoke K. Ghosh*** *(October 1942 – February 2024), Founder Chairman and Managing Director of PHI Learning, whose vision endlessly inspires.*

The Legacy Continues....

Published by Pushpita Ghosh, PHI Learning Private Limited, Rimjhim House, 111, Patparganj Industrial Estate, Delhi-110092 and Printed by Syndicate Binders, A-20, Hosiery Complex, Noida, Phase-II Extension, Noida-201305 (N.C.R. Delhi).

₹850.00

LOGICS FOR COMPUTER SCIENCE, Second Edition
Arindama Singh

ISBN-978-93-87472-43-3 (Print Book)
ISBN-978-93-87472-44-0 (e-Book)

The export rights of the book are vested solely with the publisher.

Contents

Preface

The first edition of this book was used by many academicians; and their comments and suggestions had to be implemented sooner or later. For instance, Prof. Norman Foo of University of New South Wales (UNSW) said:

> "This is the best book available in the market that suits my course on logic for CS masters students."

However, one of his colleagues reported that he had to refer to other books for applications of compactness. Now, it becomes somewhat obligatory on my part to discuss applications of compactness in this edition.

In this revised version, the circularity in presenting logic via formal semantics is brought to the fore in a very elementary manner. Instead of developing everything from semantics, we now use an axiomatic system to model reasoning. Other proof methods are introduced and worked out later as alternative models.

Elimination of the equality predicate via equality sentences is dealt with semantically even before the axiomatic system for first order logic is presented. The replacement laws and the quantifier laws are now explicitly discussed along with the necessary motivation of using them in constructing proofs in mathematics. Adequacy of the axiomatic system is now proved in detail. An elementary proof of adequacy of Analytic Tableaux is now included.

Special attention is paid to the foundational questions such as decidability, expressibility, and incompleteness. These important and difficult topics are dealt with briefly and in an elementary manner.

The material on Program Verification, Modal Logics, and Other Logics in Chapters 9, 11 and 12 have undergone minimal change. Attempt has been made to correct all typographical errors pointed out by the readers. However, rearrangement of the old material and the additional topics might have brought in new errors. Numerous relevant results, examples, exercises and problems have been added. The correspondence of topics to chapters and sections have changed considerably, compared to the first edition. A glance through the table of contents will give you a comprehensive idea.

The book now contains enough material to keep students busy for two semesters. However, by carefully choosing the topics, the essential portion of the book can be covered in a single semester. The core topics are discussed in Chapters 1, 2, 5, 6, 10, and Sections 3.1–3.5 and 7.1–7.2. As an alternative to the axiomatic system, one may replace Chapters 2 and 6 with Sections 4.4–4.5, 8.4–8.5, 2.5 and 6.4. Topics from other chapters may be discussed depending on the requirement of the students.

I cheerfully thank all those whose suggestions were the driving force in bringing out this edition. I thank all those students who wanted me to relate to them the rigorous foundation of mathematics. I acknowledge the trouble taken by

Norman Foo of UNSW, S. H. Kulkarni, Sounaka Mishra, Kalpana Mahalingam of IIT Madras, Balasubramaniam Jayaram of IIT Hyderabad, and my long-time friend Biswa R. Patnaik of Toronto, in carefully reading the earlier drafts, finding mistakes, and suggesting improvements.

Most part of this edition was drafted during my three months stay at Fayetteville, Arkansas with my family. The pleasure of working on the book was doubled due to frequent get together arranged by Brajendra Panda of University of Arkansas, and his wife Rashmi; I thank them profusely. I thank the administrators of IIT Madras for granting me sabbatical so that I could devote full time on the book. I also thank the publisher, PHI Learning, Delhi and their production team for timely help in typesetting.

Arindama Singh

Preface to the First Edition

Each chapter in this book has an introduction, the first section. But there is no introduction to the book itself. So, let me use the mask of the Preface for this purpose. Of course, a plain introduction to the book is just to place the book in your hand; but while you are reading it, you yourself have already done that. Well done!

This is the way I will be talking to you throughout. I will ask you to do exercises on the spot, often waiting for you up to some point, and then give you a hint to proceed. It is something like the following commercial for the book:

> I would like to ask you three questions, would you answer them with a plain 'Yes' or 'No'?
>
> Good, you have answered 'Yes', whatever be the reason. But see, that was my first question. Would you answer the same to the second as to the third?
>
> Very good, you have answered 'Yes' again; of course, it does not matter. If you have not bought a copy of this book, are you going to buy it soon?
>
> Look, if you have answered 'Yes' to the second question, you are also answering 'Yes' to the third, and if you have answered 'No' to the second, you are not answering 'No' to the third, i.e., your answer to the third is undoubtedly, 'Yes'. Excellent. That is the end of the commercial.

You have participated well in the commercial; I hope you will be with me throughout. It is easy to learn logic and easier to teach it; that is the spirit of this book. I would not reveal what is logic; you will discover it eventually. My aim is to equip you with the logical methods so that when you take up computer science as your profession, you will feel like a fish in water. A warning: though the book is ideal for self-learning, it would not replace a teacher. At least on one count: you can ask a question to your teacher and, hopefully, he[1] will give you an answer, or you will be inspired by him for finding your own answer; the book cannot do that always.

If you are a teacher, you may not need to learn all the topics, for you had probably learnt them. But you can really teach logic better by helping your students in the exercises. You can supplement the book with more computer science applications

[1]The masculine gender is used throughout the book not because of some chauvinistic reasons, as it is easy to do that. It is easy to write 'he' rather than 'she' or 'one' or 'a person' or 'a human being' etc. You need not be offended by it.

which I had to omit, for it is already a somewhat lengthy book. It is ideal for a two-semester course for not so advanced students. But you can cover it in one semester[2] by omitting certain proof procedures.

In Chapter 1, you will find the logic of statements. The approach is semantic. The semantic considerations give rise to the calculational method of proof quite naturally. Calculations have been used very informally for proving valid formulas just as you solve problems in school algebra. All the metaresults have been discussed except compactness. That is done via proof theory, again, for ease. In Chapter 2, a similar approach is taken for the logic of predicates or relations, more commonly known as the first order logic. The first order logic discussed here includes the equality relation, and no preference is given to one without equality, because applications demand it. This chapter also deals with the Herbrand's theorems without waiting for the resolution method. The resolution method is the topic of Chapter 3. Chapter 4 is exclusively meant for various proof techniques. In a one-semester course, you may go for only one proof method. Or, you may do one of the proof methods formally in detail and present others in one lecture each.

In Chapter 5, you come across a fundamental area of computer science, the program verification. It is also one of the most useful applications of first order logic. You should not stop just after that; you must hunt for some more materials and pursue the topic a bit further. You must have a similar approach to the model checking algorithms that have been introduced in Chapter 6 as an application of modal logics. This chapter gives a very comprehensive account of modal logics used in computer science. It does cover the essential ingredients leaving one: decidability issues, for which you may look through the References. Similarly, Chapter 7 introduces the so-called nonstandard logics which are upcoming, but not entirely new. We discuss only those nonstandard logics that have general frameworks yet; the list is not exhaustive. You are led through the chapters towards logic engineering, an activity that is becoming increasingly important in current research in computer science.

The approach of the book is mathematical, in the sense that it involves a continual interplay between the abstract and the concrete. The yearning for understanding the concrete phenomena gives rise to abstractions and to understand the abstract, concrete phenomena are a necessity. The typical feeling in any concrete problem is that when you abstract it, an existence of a solution is an opaque mystery. The concrete problems do not come with a label that such and such method would be applicable. It is you who may think of applying an existing method to solve it. Often, patient and continuous involvement with the problems help you to gradually gain insight, leading to a solution. So, be patient and persistent, rely on yourself as far as possible; start the journey now.

I have to pause here for a second. I would like to thank all those who have made this happy journey of yours possible. Though the book has taken shape now, there has been a continual effort throughout. There must be many good reasons for this, the

[2]It takes around 60 lectures to complete the book. In fact, it is developed from my notes for a logic course offered to Engineering undergraduates at IIT Madras taking theoretical computer science as their minor subject. Some of the postgraduate students in Mathematics also credit the course as an elective.

most basic of all these being my interest in higher studies. I thank my parents and my school teacher Mr. Rupakar Sarangi who nourished me physically and mentally by keeping me fit for higher studies. I thank my wife Archana for continuing in a similar vein after our marriage. She, along with my children, Anindya Ambuj and Ananya Asmita, did suffer a lot due to my post-marriage engagement with this book. I thank them for their patience and encouragement. I am indebted to my friend and logic tutor Professor Chinmoy Goswami of the University of Hyderabad. My students helped me considerably to learn logic; in a way, this book is a reward for that. I thank my colleague Dr. M. Thamban Nair of IIT Madras for encouraging me to bring out the book from some scratches on a note book. I also thank the Publishers, Prentice Hall of India, particularly, Mr. K. C. Devasia for his expert guidance and the production team for their assistance.

Any constructive suggestions for improving the contents would be most welcome. These may be emailed to me at asingh@iitm.ac.in.

Arindama Singh

Chapter 1

Propositional Logic

1.1 INTRODUCTION

Our goal is to model *reasoning* as it is used in Mathematics and Computer science, taking cue from that found in day to day communication. We start with the simplest kind of reasoning, called the reasoning with propositions and connectives. Here are some propositions:

Bapuji was a Mahatma.
No bachelor is married.
Some unmarried men get married.
Five men cannot have eleven eyes.
Buddha's original name was Arindama.
Alexander the great did not set foot in India.
The title of a book on logic could be misspelt.
The woman who committed the crime did not have three legs.

Propositions are declarative sentences which may be asserted to be true or false. It is quite possible that you may not be able to say for certain whether a given proposition is true or false, without going to its meanings or external factors. The conjectures or open problems are propositions, the truth of which we do not know yet. For example,

Goldbach : Every even number bigger than 2 is a sum of two prime numbers.

$\mathscr{P} \neq \mathscr{NP}$: There is at least one non-deterministic polynomial time solvable problem which is not deterministic polynomial time solvable.

As of now, we do not have any way of showing the truth or falsity of these propositions. However, each of them is either true or false.

We are not defining here what a proposition is. We are only getting familiarized with the kind of objects in question. A safer way to describe a proposition is to see whether the question "Is it true that X?" is meaningful or not. If it is, then X is a proposition, else, X is not a proposition.

The sentences which are not propositions include questions, orders, exclamations, etc., for which we may not like to associate a truth value. We do not know how to say whether "Is the night sky beautiful?" is true or false. Similarly, we may not assert that "How beautiful is the morning sky!" is true or false.

Our building blocks here are propositions; we will not try to go beyond them. It is not our concern to determine whether really "each bachelor is married", for we pretend not knowing the meanings of the words uttered in the proposition. Our units here are propositions, nothing less and nothing more. However, we seem to know that two propositions such as "I know logic" and "You know logic" can be composed to get another proposition such as "I and you know logic".

We are only interested in propositions and how they are composed to yield other propositions. This is what we mean when we say that propositions are our building blocks. Thus we are interested in the forms rather than the meanings of propositions. Since propositions can be true or false, we must know how to assign truth values to the compound propositions.

If indeed I like logic and you like logic, then we must agree that the proposition "I and you like logic" is true. But what about the proposition

I like logic and you like logic or you do not like logic?

This is problematic, for we do not know exactly how this compound proposition has been composed of or formed. Which of the following ways we must parse it?

(I like logic and you like logic) or (you do not like logic)
(I like logic) and (you like logic or you do not like logic)

We will use parentheses for disambiguating compound propositions. Moreover, we will start with some commonly used connectives; and if need arises, we will enrich our formalization by adding new ones. Of course, we will explain what 'follows from' means.

In the sequel, we will shorten the phrase 'if and only if' to 'iff', and denote the set of natural numbers $\{0,1,2,3,\ldots\}$ by $\mathbb{N}$.

Exercises for § 1.1

1. Do the following pairs of sentences mean the same thing? Explain.
   (a) Healthy diet is expensive. Expensive diet is healthy.
   (b) Children and senior citizens get concession.
   Children or senior citizens get concession.
2. In *Smullyan's island*, there are two types of people; knights, who tell the truth, and knaves, who always lie. A person there asserts: "This is not the first time I have said what I am now saying". The person is a knight or a knave?
3. In Smullyan's island, a person says *A and B* where *A* and *B* are two separate sentences. (For instance, *A* is 'I have a brother' and *B* is 'I have a sister'.) The same person later asserts *A*, and then after a minute, asserts *B*. Did he convey the same as earlier?
4. Is the sentence "This sentence is true" a proposition?
5. Is the sentence "This sentence is false" a proposition?

1.2 SYNTAX OF PL

For any simple proposition, called a **propositional variable**, we will use any of the symbols $p_0, p_1, \ldots$ For **connectives** 'not', 'and', 'or', 'if ... then ...', '... if and only if ...', we use the symbols $\neg, \wedge, \vee, \rightarrow, \leftrightarrow$, respectively; their names are negation, conjunction, disjunction, conditional, biconditional. We use the parentheses ')' and '(' as punctuation marks. We also have the special propositions $\top$ and $\bot$, called **propositional constants**; they stand for propositions which are 'true' and 'false', respectively. Read $\top$ as top, and $\bot$ as bottom or falsum. Both propositional variables and propositional constants are commonly called **atomic propositions** or **atoms**. So, the **alphabet** of Propositional Logic, **PL**, is the set

$$\{),\ (,\ \neg,\ \wedge,\ \vee,\ \rightarrow,\ \leftrightarrow,\ \top,\ \bot,\ p_0,\ p_1,\ p_2,\ \ldots\}.$$

Any **expression** over this alphabet is a string of symbols such as

$$(\neg p_0 \rightarrow () \wedge p_1 \vee, \quad \neg p_{100})(\rightarrow \vee, \quad (\neg p_0 \rightarrow p_1).$$

(Do not read the commas and dots.) Only the last one of these is a propositional formula or a proposition. In fact, we are interested only in such expressions. The propositions (in PL) are defined by the following grammar:

$$w ::= \top \mid \bot \mid p \mid \neg w \mid (w \wedge w) \mid (w \vee w) \mid (w \rightarrow w) \mid (w \leftrightarrow w)$$

Here p stands for any generic propositional variable, and w stands for any generic **proposition**. The symbol $::=$ is read as 'can be'; and the vertical bar '$\mid$' describes alternate possibilities (read it as 'or'). The same symbol w may be replaced by different propositions; that is what the word "generic" means. This way of writing the grammatical rules is called the **Bacus-Naur form** or **BNF**, for short. The grammar can be written in terms of the following **formation rules** of propositions:

1. $\top$ and $\bot$ are propositions.
2. Each p_i is a proposition, where $i \in \mathbb{N}$.
3. If x is a proposition, then $\neg x$ is a proposition.
4. If x, y are propositions, then $(x \wedge y), (x \vee y), (x \rightarrow y), (x \leftrightarrow y)$ are propositions.
5. Nothing is a proposition unless it satisfies some or all of the rules (1)-(4).

The set of all propositions is written as PROP. The formation rule (5) is called the *closure rule*. It states that "PROP is the smallest set that satisfies (1)-(4)". The 'smallest' is in the sense that "A is smaller than B iff $A \subseteq B$".

Propositions are also called **PL-formulas** and **well-formed formulas**, **wff** for short. The non-atomic propositions are also called **compound propositions**.

EXAMPLE 1.1. The following are propositions:

$$p_0, (p_5 \rightarrow \top),\ ((p_{100} \leftrightarrow \bot) \wedge \neg p_7),\ (p_8 \rightarrow ((\neg p_4 \vee p_9) \leftrightarrow (p_2 \wedge (\top \rightarrow \bot)))).$$

Whereas the following are not propositions:

$$p_0 \wedge p_1,\ p_0 \rightarrow \bot),\ (\neg\neg(p_0 \vee p_1)),\ (p_8 \rightarrow ((\neg p_4 \vee p_9) \leftrightarrow (p_2 \wedge (\top \rightarrow \bot))).$$

In $p_0 \wedge p_1$, a surrounding pair of parentheses is required; in $(\neg\neg(p_0 \vee p_1))$ there is an extra pair of parentheses; etc.

The key fact is that any object that has been formed (generated) by this grammar can also be parsed. That is, you can always find out the last rule that has been applied to form a proposition and then proceed backward. Such an unfolding of the formation of a proposition can be depicted as a tree, called a **parse tree**.

EXAMPLE 1.2. Construct a parse tree for the proposition

$$\neg((p_0 \wedge \neg p_1) \rightarrow (p_2 \vee (p_3 \leftrightarrow \neg p_4))).$$

For the given proposition, the last rule applied was $w ::= \neg w$. This means that it is a proposition if the expression $((p_0 \wedge \neg p_1) \rightarrow (p_2 \vee (p_3 \leftrightarrow \neg p_4)))$ is also a proposition. Look at the root and its child in the left tree of Figure 1.1.

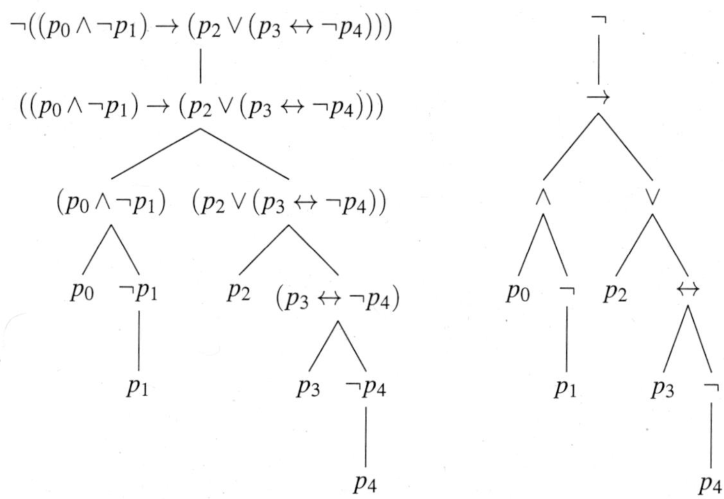

Figure 1.1: Parse tree for Example 1.2 and its abbreviation

Further, $((p_0 \wedge \neg p_1) \rightarrow (p_2 \vee (p_3 \leftrightarrow \neg p_4)))$ is a proposition if both the expressions $(p_0 \wedge \neg p_1)$ and $(p_2 \vee (p_3 \leftrightarrow \neg p_4))$ are propositions (the rule $w ::= (w \rightarrow w)$). If you proceed further, you would arrive at the left parse tree in Figure 1.1. The corresponding abbreviated tree is on the right.

EXAMPLE 1.3. Consider the string $(\vee(p_1 \wedge p_2) \rightarrow (\neg p_1 \leftrightarrow p_2))$. We cannot apply the rule for $\vee$, since to its left is just a parenthesis. But we find that by taking x as $\vee(p_1 \wedge p_2)$ and y as $(\neg p_1 \leftrightarrow p_2)$, the string appears as $(x \rightarrow y)$, which can be parsed. Look at the left tree in Figure 1.2. We cannot parse $\vee(p_1 \wedge p_2)$ any further.

Similarly, the string $(\vee \rightarrow \neg p_1 \leftrightarrow p_2)$ can be parsed in two ways; first with $\rightarrow$, and next with $\leftrightarrow$. Look at the middle and the right trees in Figure 1.2. Neither can we parse $\vee$, $\neg p_1 \leftrightarrow p_2$ nor $\vee \rightarrow \neg p_1$.

Notice that the leaves of the trees of Figure 1.1 are atomic propositions, while the leaves of the trees in Figure 1.2 are not. The corresponding expressions in the latter cases are not propositions.

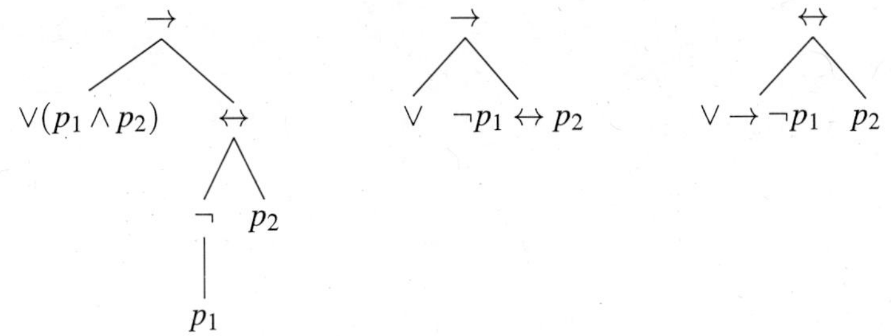

Figure 1.2: Parse trees for Example 1.3

The first task by a parser will be to determine whether the string is in one of the forms $\neg x$ or $(x * y)$. Then it parses x in the former case, and both x and y in the latter case. It continues the process until it is not able to parse further. If a parser starts with a proposition, it would end with an atom. Thus, the leaves of a parse tree of a proposition will be atomic propositions from which the proposition has been built. On the other hand, If the given string is not a proposition, there is confusion in parsing; and the parser will stop with leaves as non-atomic expressions.

Remark 1.1. There are other ways of defining the set PROP. In the *declarative version*, we say that PROP, the set of all propositions, is the smallest set of expressions satisfying the following conditions

1. $\{\top,\ \bot,\ p_0,\ p_1,\ \ldots\} \subseteq$ PROP.
2. If $x,\ y \in$ PROP, then $\neg x,\ (x \wedge y),\ (x \vee y),\ (x \to y),\ (x \leftrightarrow y) \in$ PROP.

The second alternative employs an *inductive construction* of PROP. It is as follows.

1. PROP$(0) = \{\top,\ \bot\} \cup \{p_0,\ p_1,\ \ldots\}$.
2. PROP$(i+1) = \{\neg x,\ (x \circ y),: x,\ y \in$ PROP$(k),\ \circ \in \{\wedge, \vee, \to, \leftrightarrow\},\ 0 \le k \le i\}$.
3. PROP $= \cup_{i \in \mathbb{N}}$ PROP(i).

You may prove that each of these two alternatives define the same set PROP.

Exercises for § 1.2

1. Which of the following strings are in PROP and which are not? Why?
   (a) $p_0 \vee (p_1 \to \neg p_2)$
   (b) $((p_3 \leftrightarrow p_4) \wedge \neg p_1)$
   (c) $((p_5) \to (p_2 \leftrightarrow p_3))$
   (d) $((p_3 \leftrightarrow p_4) \wedge \neg p_1)$
   (e) $(((p_0 \wedge \neg(p_1 \vee p_2)) \to (p_3 \leftrightarrow \neg p_4)) \vee (\neg(p_5 \to p_4) \to \neg p_1) \wedge p_2)$
   (f) $((p_1 \wedge \neg p_1) \vee (p_0 \to p_1)) \wedge (\neg(p_0 \wedge \neg\neg p_1) \to ((\neg p_3 \vee \neg p_1) \leftrightarrow p_2))$
2. Construct parse trees for the following propositions:
   (a) $(\neg((p_0 \wedge \neg p_1) \to (p_0 \to p_1)) \leftrightarrow \neg(p_1 \vee p_2))$
   (b) $((p_3 \vee (p_4 \leftrightarrow \neg(p_3 \wedge p_1))) \wedge \neg(p_2 \to p_5))$
   (c) $(\neg(\neg(p_1 \to p_2) \wedge \neg(p_3 \vee p_4)) \leftrightarrow (p_5 \leftrightarrow \neg p_6))$

3. Construct parse trees for the following strings, and then determine which of them are propositions.
   (a) $(\neg((p_0 \wedge \neg p_1) \to (p_0 \to p_1))) \leftrightarrow \neg(p_1 \vee p_2)$
   (b) $(\neg(((p_0 \wedge \neg p_1) \to (p_0 \to p_1)) \leftrightarrow \neg p_1 \vee p_2))$
   (c) $(\neg((p_0 \wedge \neg p_1) \to p_0) \to p_1) \leftrightarrow (\neg(p_1 \vee p_2))$
   (d) $((p_0 \to p_1) \vee (p_2 \to (\neg p_1 \wedge (p_0 \leftrightarrow \neg p_2))))$
   (e) $((p_0 \to p_1) \vee (p_2 \to (\neg p_1 \wedge (p_0 \leftrightarrow \neg p_2))) \leftrightarrow (p_3 \to p_5)))$
   (f) $(((p_5 \to (p_6 \vee p_8)) \leftrightarrow (p_3 \wedge \neg p_2)) \vee (\neg(p_1 \leftrightarrow p_3) \to p_{10}))$
   (g) $(((p_5 \to p_6 \vee p_8) \leftrightarrow (p_3 \wedge \neg p_2)) \vee (\neg(p_1 \leftrightarrow p_3 \to p_{10})))$
4. List all propositions in PROP that can be built using one propositional variable p_0, two occurrences of connectives, and no propositional constant.
5. List all propositions in PROP that can be built from two propositional variables p_1, p_2 using only the connective $\wedge$, and using no propositional constant.

1.3 IS IT A PROPOSITION?

Given a proposition, can we determine in which way it has been formed? If the proposition is of the form $\neg x$, then obviously the x here is uniquely determined from the proposition. If it is in the form $(x \vee y)$ for propositions x and y, can it also be in the form $(z \wedge u)$ for some (other) propositions z and u? Consider the proposition

$$w = ((p_1 \to p_2) \wedge (p_1 \vee (p_0 \leftrightarrow \neg p_2))).$$

We see that $w = (x \wedge y)$, where $x = (p_1 \to p_2)$ and $y = (p_1 \vee (p_0 \leftrightarrow \neg p_2))$. If we write it in the form $(z \vee u)$, then $z = (p_1 \to p_2) \wedge (p_1$ and $u = (p_0 \leftrightarrow \neg p_2))$. Here, z and u are not propositions. You can try to break at the connectives $\to$ or $\leftrightarrow$ similarly and see that the obtained substrings are not propositions.

Recall that *prefix* of a string means reading the string symbol by symbol from left to right and stopping somewhere. The prefixes of w above are

$$(,\ ((,\ ((p_1,\ ((p_1 \to,\ ((p_1 \to p_2,\ ((p_1 \to p_2),\ ((p_1 \to p_2)\wedge,\ \ldots$$

We see that none of these is a proposition except w itself, since the condition of matching parentheses is not met. Similar situation occurs when a proposition starts with one or more occurrences of $\neg$. That is, a proper prefix of a proposition is never a proposition. We express this fact in a bit different way, which may be proved by using induction on the number of occurrences of connectives in a proposition.

Observation 1.1. *Let u and v be propositions. If u is a prefix of v, then $u = v$.*

Theorem 1.1 (Unique parsing). *Let w be a proposition. Then exactly one of the following happens:*

(1) $w \in \{\top, \bot, p_0, p_1, \ldots\}$.
(2) $w = \neg x$ *for a unique* $x \in$ PROP.
(3) $w = (x \circ y)$ *for a unique* $\circ \in \{\wedge, \vee, \to, \leftrightarrow\}$ *and unique* $x, y \in$ PROP.

Proof. Due to the formation rules of a proposition, either w is atomic, or it is in one of the forms $\neg x$ or $(x \circ y)$. We must show that in the two latter cases, the propositions x and y are unique.

In the first case, suppose that $w = \neg x$. The first symbol of w is $\neg$. So, w is neither atomic nor is in the form $(y * z)$. However, w can be equal to $\neg z$ for some z. In that case, $\neg x = \neg z$ forces $x = z$. That is, x is a unique proposition determined from w.

In the second case, suppose $w = (x \circ y)$ for some $\circ \in \{\wedge, \vee, \rightarrow, \leftrightarrow\}$ and some propositions x and y. The first symbol of w is the left parenthesis (. Hence w is neither atomic nor in the form $\neg z$. So, suppose that $w = (u * v)$ for some propositions u, v and connective $* \in \{\wedge, \vee, \rightarrow, \leftrightarrow\}$. Then $x \circ y) = u * v)$. Now, x is a prefix of u or u is a prefix of x. Observation 1.1 implies that $x = u$. Then $\circ y) = *v)$. It gives $\circ = *$ and then $y = v$. ♦

The theorem is so named because it asserts that each proposition has a unique parse tree, which demonstrates how it has been formed by applying the rules of the grammar. Of course, unique parsing does not give any clue as to how to determine whether a given string over the alphabet of PROP is a proposition or not.

For example, $p_1 \rightarrow p_2$ is not a proposition; you need a pair of parentheses. Similarly, $(p_0 \wedge p_1 \rightarrow p_2)$ is also not a proposition. But that is not the question. The question is: Can you give a procedure to do this for all possible expressions?

Observe that the unique parse tree for a proposition has only atomic propositions on its leaves. Whereas if an expression is not a proposition, in any parse tree for the expression some leaf will contain an expression other than an atomic proposition.

Look at the second leaf from the left in the the abbreviated parse tree of Figure 1.1; it is a node labelled p_1. There is a subtree with parent node $\neg$ whose only child is this p_1. It corresponds to the proposition $\neg p_1$. You can replace this subtree, say, by p_1. You thus obtain the tree T_1 in Figure 1.3.

Do not be confused while replacing $\neg p_1$ by p_1; we have not yet assigned any meaning to the symbol $\neg$. We are only playing with symbols.

In T_1, there is again a subtree with parent node $\wedge$, whose children are p_0 and p_1. This corresponds to the proposition $(p_0 \wedge p_1)$. You can replace this subtree, say by p_0. In the new tree T_2, you have a leaf p_4 which is the sole child of the node $\neg$. So, first replace $\neg p_4$ by p_4, then replace the subtree corresponding to the proposition $(p_3 \leftrightarrow p_4)$, by p_3. As you continue this replacements, you get the sequence of trees $T_0, \ldots, T_7$, in Figure 1.3, where the tree T_0 is the left tree of Figure 1.1.

The expressions corresponding to the sequence of parse trees $T_0, \ldots, T_7$ are:

$$\begin{aligned}
T_0 &: \quad \neg((p_0 \wedge \neg p_1) \rightarrow (p_2 \vee (p_3 \leftrightarrow \neg p_4)))\\
T_1 &: \quad \neg((p_0 \wedge p_1) \rightarrow (p_2 \vee (p_3 \leftrightarrow \neg p_4)))\\
T_2 &: \quad \neg(p_0 \rightarrow (p_2 \vee (p_3 \leftrightarrow \neg p_4)))\\
T_3 &: \quad \neg(p_0 \rightarrow (p_2 \vee (p_3 \leftrightarrow p_4)))\\
T_4 &: \quad \neg(p_0 \rightarrow (p_2 \vee p_3))\\
T_5 &: \quad \neg(p_0 \rightarrow p_2)\\
T_6 &: \quad \neg p_0\\
T_7 &: \quad p_0
\end{aligned}$$

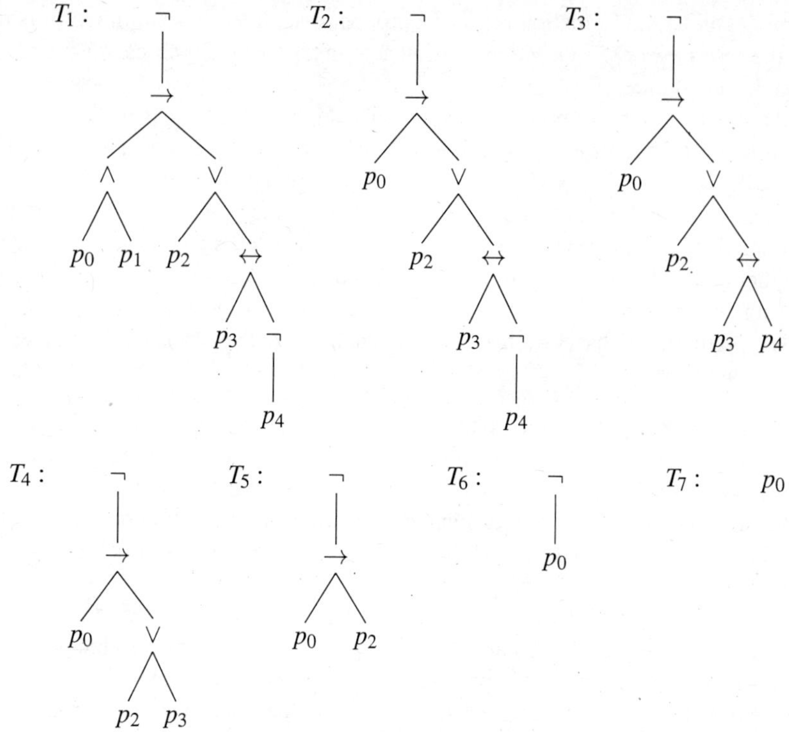

Figure 1.3: Sequence of parse trees for the tree in Figure 1.1

To obtain the second expression from the first, you simply had to replace the proposition $\neg p_1$ by p_1. In the second expression, replace the proposition $(p_0 \wedge p_1)$ by p_0 to get the third, and so on. The construction can be written as a procedure to determine whether a given expression is a proposition or not.

PROCEDURE ***PropDet***

Input: Any string x over the alphabet of PL.
Output: 'yes', if x is a proposition, else, 'no'.

1. If x is a (single) symbol and $x \notin \{\ ),\ (,\ \neg,\ \wedge,\ \vee,\ \rightarrow,\ \leftrightarrow \}$, then report 'yes'; else, report 'no'; and stop.
2. Otherwise, scan x from left to right to get a substring w in one of the forms
$$\neg p,\ (p \wedge q),\ (p \vee q),\ (p \rightarrow q),\ (p \leftrightarrow q);$$
where p, q are symbols not in the set $\{\ ),\ (,\ \neg,\ \wedge,\ \vee,\ \rightarrow,\ \leftrightarrow \}$.
3. If not found, then report 'no'; and stop.
4. If found, then replace w by p_0; go to Step 1.

EXAMPLE 1.4. We apply *PropDet* on the strings $(\vee(p_1 \wedge p_2) \rightarrow (\neg p_1 \leftrightarrow p_2))$ and $(\vee \rightarrow \neg p_1 \leftrightarrow p_2)$.

In $(\vee(p_1 \wedge p_2) \to (\neg p_1 \leftrightarrow p_2))$ the substring $(p_1 \wedge p_2)$ is replaced by p_0 resulting in the string $(\vee p_0 \to (\neg p_1 \leftrightarrow p_2))$.

Next, the substring $\neg p_1$ is replaced by p_0; and then $(p_0 \leftrightarrow p_2)$ is replaced by p_0. We obtain $(\vee p_0 \to p_0)$.

The algorithm stops here reporting 'no'. It means $(\vee(p_1 \wedge p_2) \to (\neg p_1 \leftrightarrow p_2))$ is not a proposition.

Similarly, in $(\vee \to \neg p_1 \leftrightarrow p_2)$, the proposition $\neg p_1$ is replaced by p_0 resulting in $(\vee \to p_0 \leftrightarrow p_2)$. No more replacements can be done.

Since $(\vee \to p_1 \leftrightarrow p_2)$ is not a symbol, the original string $(\vee \to \neg p_1 \leftrightarrow p_2)$ is not a proposition.

PropDet works by identifying a substring of the given string as a proposition, and then replacing the substring by a propositional variable, p_0. Thus, if it starts from a proposition it must end with one. The invariance of the loop executed by *PropDet* is the proposition-hood of the string. Moreover, by any such replacement, *PropDet* reduces the length of the string. Thus, the given string is a proposition iff the final string of length 1, is p_0, which is also a proposition. This criterion is checked in Step 1. This completes the correctness proof of *PropDet*. You can construct a formal proof of correctness of *PropDet* using induction on the height of the parse tree.

Due to unique parsing, we define the **main connective** and the **immediate sub-propositions** of a non-atomic proposition w as follows:

1. The main connective of $\neg x$ is $\neg$, and
   the immediate sub-proposition of $\neg x$ is x.
2. For any $\circ \in \{\wedge, \vee, \to, \leftrightarrow\}$, the main connective of $(x \circ y)$ is $\circ$, and
   the immediate sub-propositions of $(x \circ y)$ are x and y.

A **sub-proposition** of a proposition w is any substring of w which is itself a proposition. It turns out that a sub-proposition of w is either w or one of its immediate sub-propositions, or a sub-proposition of an immediate sub-proposition of w.

EXAMPLE 1.5. The immediate sub-proposition of the proposition

$$\neg\neg(\top \vee ((p_2 \to (p_3 \leftrightarrow p_4)) \to (\bot \wedge (p_2 \wedge \neg p_3))))$$

is the proposition $\neg(\top \vee ((p_2 \to (p_3 \leftrightarrow p_4)) \to (\bot \wedge (p_2 \wedge \neg p_3))))$.

The immediate sub-propositions of $((p_2 \to (p_3 \leftrightarrow p_4)) \to (\bot \wedge (p_2 \wedge \neg p_3)))$ are $(p_2 \to (p_3 \leftrightarrow p_4))$ and $(\bot \wedge (p_2 \wedge \neg p_3))$.

The sub-propositions of $(\bot \wedge (p_2 \wedge \neg p_3))$ are $\bot$, $(p_2 \wedge \neg p_3)$, p_2, $\neg p_3$, and p_3.

The sub-propositions of $(p_2 \to (p_3 \leftrightarrow p_4))$ are p_2, $(p_3 \leftrightarrow p_4)$, p_3 and p_4.

Using the notion of the main connective, we see that any proposition can be in one of the following forms: (Here, p_i is a propositional variable, and x, y are propositions.)

$$\top,\ \neg\top,\ \bot,\ \neg\bot,\ p_i,\ \neg p_i,\ \neg\neg x,\ (x \wedge y),\ \neg(x \wedge y),$$
$$(x \vee y),\ \neg(x \vee y),\ (x \to y),\ \neg(x \to y),\ (x \leftrightarrow y),\ \neg(x \leftrightarrow y).$$

After understanding what parsing is all about, we put some conventions so that writing propositions will become easier.

Convention 1.1. Instead of writing $p_0, p_1, p_2, \ldots$ we write propositional variables as $p, q, r, s, t, \ldots$. We write $u, v, w, x, \ldots$ for propositions. Sometimes we may write $p, q, r, s, t, \ldots$ for propositions also provided no confusion arises.

To *write less,* we put down some **precedence rules** and omit the outer parentheses. Recall the precedence rule that multiplication has higher precedence than addition. It means that the expression $x \times y + z$ is to be rewritten as $((x \times y) + z)$, and not as $((x \times (y + z))$.

Convention 1.2. Our precedence rules are the following:

$\neg$ has the highest precedence.
$\wedge, \vee$ have the next precedence, their precedence being equal.
$\to, \leftrightarrow$ have the lowest precedence, their precedence being equal.

Using precedence rules, the proposition $((p_1 \vee (p_3 \wedge p_6)) \to (p_{100} \leftrightarrow \neg p_1))$ can be abbreviated to $p_1 \vee (p_3 \wedge p_6) \to (p_{100} \leftrightarrow \neg p_1)$. Using abbreviations p, q, r, s for p_1, p_3, p_6, p_{100}, respectively, the abbreviated proposition is $p \vee (q \wedge r) \to (s \leftrightarrow \neg p)$.

However, you must not stretch too much the notion of abbreviated propositions. For instance $p_0 \to p_1$ is not a sub-proposition of $(p_0 \to (p_1 \wedge p_2))$. Reason: the abbreviated proposition in full form looks like $(p_0 \to (p_1 \wedge p_2))$. The propositions $p_0 \to p_1$ and $(p_0 \to p_1)$ are not even substrings of $(p_0 \to (p_1 \wedge p_2))$.

Exercises for § 1.3

1. Parentheses in a string can be matched in the following way:
   (a) Pick any occurrence of (. Start a counter with 1.
   (b) While proceeding to the right, increase the counter by 1 if (is met; and decrease the counter by 1 if) is met.
   (c) At any time, if the counter is 0, then that instance of) is the right parenthesis corresponding to the left parenthesis picked.

   Using this algorithm, find the corresponding occurrence of) to each occurrence of (in the following strings:
   (i) $((p \to (\neg q \vee r)) \leftrightarrow (\neg p \vee r))$
   (ii) $((\neg p \leftrightarrow (\neg q \wedge r)) \to (\neg p \to (r \to s)))$
   (iii) $(((\neg p \leftrightarrow (\neg q \wedge r))) \to (\neg p \to ((r \to s) \leftrightarrow \neg q)))$
2. Apply *PropDet* on the strings given in Exercise 1:(i)-(iii).
3. Find all sub-propositions of the following propositions:
   (a) $(\neg\neg\neg p_3 \wedge (\neg p_2 \vee \neg(p_1 \vee p_3)))$
   (b) $\neg(p_1 \vee (p_2 \wedge (p_3 \vee p_4) \wedge (p_2 \wedge (p_1 \wedge (p_3 \to \neg p_2) \vee (p_3 \leftrightarrow p_1)))))$
   (c) $(((\neg p_5 \vee (\neg p_3 \wedge \neg p_2)) \to (r_5 \to p_2)) \wedge \neg(p_1 \leftrightarrow \neg(p_3 \wedge \neg p_4)))$
   (d) $(((p_3 \to (p_2 \vee p_6)) \leftrightarrow (p_6 \wedge \neg q_3)) \vee (\neg(p_6 \leftrightarrow r_5) \to p))$
4. Insert parentheses at appropriate places using the precedence rules so that the following strings become propositions. Also find their sub-propositions.
   (a) $(p \to q) \wedge \neg(r \vee q \leftrightarrow p) \leftrightarrow (\neg p \vee q \to r)$
   (b) $(p \to q) \leftrightarrow (r \to t \vee p) \wedge (p \vee q \to \neg p \wedge t)$
   (c) $p \vee (\neg q \leftrightarrow r \wedge p) \leftrightarrow (p \vee p \to \neg q)$
   (d) $\neg(p \vee (q \to r \vee s) \leftrightarrow (q \leftrightarrow (p \wedge r \wedge \neg q) \vee (r \vee p)))$

1.4 INTERPRETATION

The meaning associated with any proposition is of two kinds, called *true* and *false*, for convenience. In what follows we write 0 for *false*, and 1 for *true*. These two tokens, true and false, or 0 and 1, are called the *truth values*. Propositions are built from the atomic propositions with the help of connectives. The propositional constants are special; $\top$ always receives the truth value true, and $\bot$ always receives the truth value false. Depending on situations, the propositional variables may receive either of the truth values. We must then prescribe how to deal with connectives.

The common sense meaning of the connectives $\neg, \wedge, \vee, \rightarrow$ and $\leftrightarrow$ are respectively, *not, and, or, implies,* and *if and only if*. It means, $\neg$ reverses the truth values. That is, if x is true, then $\neg x$ is false; and if x is false, then $\neg x$ is true. When both x and y are true, $x \wedge y$ is true; and when at least one of x or y is false, $x \wedge y$ is false. If at least one of x or y is true, then $x \vee y$ is true; and if both x and y are false, $x \vee y$ is false. Similarly, $x \leftrightarrow y$ is true when x and y are true together, or when x and y are false together; $x \leftrightarrow y$ is false if one of x, y is true and the other is false. The problematic case is $x \rightarrow y$. We will consider some examples to see what do we mean by this phrase 'implies', or as is commonly written 'if ..., then ....

The sentence *if x then y* is called a conditional sentence with antecedent as x and consequent as y. In main stream mathematics, the meaning of a conditional sentence is fixed by accepting it as false only when its antecedent is true but its consequent is false. It is problematic in the sense that normally people think of a conditional statement expressing causal connections; but this view does not quite go with that. However, this meaning of the conditional statement is not so counter intuitive as is projected by the philosophers. Let us take some examples.

Your friend asks you whether you have got an umbrella, and you answer, "If I have got an umbrella, then I would not have been wet". Suppose, you do not have an umbrella. Then is your statement true or false? Certainly it is not false if you had been really wet. It is also not false even if you had not been wet since it did not rain at all. That is, the statement is not false whenever its antecedent "I have got an umbrella" is false.

Since it is tricky, we consider one more example. At the bank, you asked me for a pen to fill up a form. Before searching I just replied "If I have a pen, I will oblige you." I searched my pockets and bag, but could not find a pen. Looking around I spotted a friend, and borrowed a pen from him for you. Did I contradict my own statement? Certainly not. I would have done so had I got a pen and I did not lend it to you. Even if I did not have a pen, I obliged you; and that did not make my statement false. That is, the sentence "if x then y" is true, if its antecedent x is false.

Let us consider another statement, which is assumed to be true:

> To receive the merit scholarship, one must secure at least eighty percent of marks in at least five subjects.

Suppose that Rahul has received the merit scholarship. Then it follows that he has secured at least eighty percent of marks in at least five subjects. The sentence is equivalent to

> If one receives the merit scholarship, then s/he has secured at least eighty percent of marks in at least five subjects.

It does not mean that securing at least eighty percent of marks in at least five subjects is the only requirement for receiving the merit scholarship.

One more situation: your friend promises to buy you the book *Logics for Computer Science* provided you help him in solving some problems. Certainly he had not broken his promise, when he bought you the book in spite of the fact that you did not actually help him solve those problems. That is, the statement is not false, when the consequent "I will buy you the book" is true.

Thus we accept this meaning of the conditional statement. The proposition $x \to y$ is false only when x is true and y is false; in all other cases, $x \to y$ is true. The true cases of $x \to y$ are when x is false, or when y is true. The former case, that is, when x is false, the conditional statement $x \to y$ looks vacuous; consequently, philosophers call the connective $\to$ as *material implication*. A rose is a rose, with whatever name you call it!

Formally, the assumed association of truth values to the propositional variables is called a truth assignment. That is, a **truth assignment** is any function from $\{p_0, p_1, \ldots\}$ to $\{0,1\}$. An extension of a truth assignment to the set of all propositions that evaluates the connectives in the above manner is called an interpretation. That is, An **interpretation** is any function $i : \text{PROP} \to \{0,1\}$ satisfying the following properties for all $x, y \in \text{PROP}$:

1. $i(\top) = 1$.
2. $i(\bot) = 0$.
3. $i(\neg x) = 1$ if $i(x) = 0$, else, $i(\neg x) = 0$.
4. $i(x \wedge y) = 1$ if $i(x) = i(y) = 1$, else, $i(x \wedge y) = 0$.
5. $i(x \vee y) = 0$ if $i(x) = i(y) = 0$, else, $i(x \vee y) = 1$.
6. $i(x \to y) = 0$ if $i(x) = 1, i(y) = 0$, else, $i(x \to y) = 1$.
7. $i(x \leftrightarrow y) = 1$ if $i(x) = i(y)$, else, $i(x \leftrightarrow y) = 0$.

The same conditions are also exhibited in Table 1.1, where the symbols u, x, y stand for propositions. The conditions are called **boolean conditions**; and such a table is called a **truth table.** You must verify that these conditions and the truth table convey the same thing.

Table 1.1: Truth table for connectives

$\top$	$\bot$	u	$\neg u$	x	y	$x \wedge y$	$x \vee y$	$x \to y$	$x \leftrightarrow y$
1	0	1	0	1	1	1	1	1	1
		0	1	1	0	0	1	0	0
				0	1	0	1	1	0
				0	0	0	0	1	1

Alternatively, the boolean conditions can be specified in the following way. Verify that it is indeed the case.

1. $i(\top) = 1$.
2. $i(\bot) = 0$.
3. $i(\neg x) = 1 - i(x)$.

4. $i(x \wedge y) = \min\{i(x), i(y)\}$.
5. $i(x \vee y) = \max\{i(x), i(y)\}$.
6. $i(x \to y) = \max\{1 - i(x),\, i(y)\}$.
7. $i(x \leftrightarrow y) = 1 - |i(x) - i(y)|$.

An interpretation is also called a *valuation*, a *boolean valuation*, a *state*, a *situation*, a *world*, or a *place*.

We view an interpretation the bottom-up way. We start with any function $i : \{p_0, p_1, \ldots\} \to \{0,1\}$. Then following the above rules, we extend this i to a function from PROP to $\{0,1\}$. Is the bottom-up way of extending a function from propositional variables to all propositions well defined by the required properties? Can there be two different interpretations that agree on all propositional variables?

Theorem 1.2. *Let $f : \{p_0, p_1, \ldots,\} \to \{0,1\}$ be any function. There exists a unique interpretation g such that $g(p_j) = f(p_j)$ for each $j \in \mathbb{N}$.*

Proof. Let $n(x)$ denote the number of occurrences of connectives in a proposition x. We define $g(x)$ by induction on $n(x)$. If $n(x) = 0$, then x is an atom. So, $x = \top$, $x = \bot$, or $x = p_j$ for some $j \in \mathbb{N}$. In this case, we define

$$g(\top) = 1, \quad g(\bot) = 0, \quad g(p_j) = f(p_j) \text{ for each } j \in \mathbb{N}$$

For the inductive definition, assume that for all propositions w, if $n(w) < m$, then $g(w)$ has been defined. For a proposition x with $n(x) = m$, we see that either $x = \neg u$ or $x = (u \circ v)$ for $\circ \in \{\wedge, \vee, \to, \leftrightarrow\}$, u, v are propositions with $n(u) < m$, and $n(v) < m$. Then we define $g(x)$ as follows:

1. For $x = \neg u$, $g(x) = 1 - g(u)$.
2. For $x = (u \wedge v)$, $g(x) = \min\{g(u), g(v)\}$.
3. For $x = (u \vee v)$, $g(x) = \max\{g(u), g(v)\}$.
4. For $x = (u \to v)$, $g(x) = \max\{1 - g(u),\, g(v)\}$.
5. For $x = (u \leftrightarrow v)$, $g(x) = 1 - |g(u) - g(v)|$.

This proves the existence of an interpretation g that agrees with f on all p_i.

For uniqueness, suppose h is another interpretation that agrees with f on the propositional variables. Let $x \in$ PROP. In the basis case, when $n(x) = 0$, we see that $h(x) = g(x)$. Let $m \geq 1$. Assume the induction hypothesis that whenever $n(x) < m$, $h(x) = g(x)$. If $n(x) = m$, then by the Unique parsing theorem, either $x = \neg u$ or $x = (u \circ v)$ for unique $u, v \in$ PROP and unique connective $\circ \in \{\wedge, \vee, \to, \leftrightarrow\}$. Notice that $n(u) < m$ and $n(v) < m$. By the induction hypothesis, $h(u) = g(u)$ and $h(v) = g(v)$. Now, both g and h satisfy the boolean conditions.

If $x = \neg u$, then $g(x) = g(\neg u) = 1 - g(u) = 1 - h(u) = h(\neg u) = h(x)$. Similarly, other connectives are tackled to show that $g(x) = h(x)$. ♦

Convention 1.3. Due to Theorem 1.2, we write the interpretation that agrees with a truth assignment i as i itself.

The following result implies that if a propositional variable does not occur in a proposition, then changing the truth value of that propositional variable does not change the truth value of that proposition.

Theorem 1.3 (Relevance Lemma). *Let w be a proposition. Let i and j be two interpretations. If $i(p) = j(p)$ for each propositional variable p occurring in w, then $i(w) = j(w)$.*

Proof. Suppose $i(p) = j(p)$ for each propositional variable p occurring in w. We use induction on $n(w)$, the number of occurrences of connectives in w. In the basis case, suppose $n(w) = 0$. Then w is either $\top$, $\bot$, or a propositional variable. If $w = \top$, then $i(w) = 1 = j(w)$. If $w = \bot$, then $i(\bot) = 0 = j(\bot)$. If w is a propositional variable, then of course, $i(w) = j(w)$. In all cases, $i(w) = j(w)$.

Lay out the induction hypothesis that for all propositions z with $n(z) < m$, the statement holds. If w is a proposition with $n(w) = m$, then either $w = \neg x$ or $w = (x \circ y)$ for unique propositions x, y and a unique connective $\circ \in \{\wedge, \vee, \to, \leftrightarrow\}$ with $n(x) < m$ and $n(y) < m$. By the induction hypothesis, $i(x) = j(x)$ and $i(y) = j(y)$. Due to the boolean conditions that both i and j satisfy, it follows that $i(w) = j(w)$. For instance, if $w = (x \wedge y)$, then

$$i(w) = i(x \wedge y) = \min\{i(x), i(y)\} = \min\{j(x), j(y)\} = j(x \wedge y) = j(w).$$

Similarly, other cases are tackled. ♦

The relevance lemma shows that in order to assign a truth value to a proposition it is enough to know how an interpretation assigns the truth values to the propositional variables occurring in it. We do not need to assign truth values to the propositional variables which do not occur in the proposition.

Given any proposition w, and the truth values of the propositional variables occurring in it, Table 1.1 can be used to compute the truth value of w. If no specific truth values for the propositional variables are known, then all possible truth values of the proposition may be generated.

If a proposition w is built up from n number of propositional variables, say, $q_1, \ldots, q_n$, then due to the relevance lemma, an interpretation of w will be depending only on the truth values assigned to $q_1, \ldots, q_n$. Since each q_i may be assigned 0 or 1, there are 2^n possible (relevant) interpretations of w in total. A *truth table for w* will thus have 2^n rows, where each row represents an interpretation.

EXAMPLE 1.6. The truth table for $(p \to (\neg p \to p)) \to (p \to (p \to \neg p))$ is shown in Table 1.2, where we write $u = p \to (\neg p \to p)$, $v = p \to (p \to \neg p)$, and the given proposition as $u \to v$.

Table 1.2: Truth Table for Example 1.6

p	$\neg p$	$p \to \neg p$	$\neg p \to p$	u	v	$u \to v$
0	1	1	0	1	1	1
1	0	0	1	1	0	0

The first row is the interpretation that extends the truth assignment i with $i(p) = 0$ to the propositions $\neg p$, $p \to \neg p$, $\neg p \to p$, u, v, $u \to v$. The second row is the interpretation j with $j(p) = 1$. We see that $i(u \to v) = 1$ while $j(u \to v) = 0$.

EXAMPLE 1.7. The truth table for $u = \neg(p \wedge q) \rightarrow (p \vee (r \leftrightarrow \neg q))$ is given in Table 1.3. The first row is the assignment i with $i(p) = i(q) = i(r) = 0$. This is extended to the interpretation i where $i(\neg q) = 1$, $i(p \wedge q) = 0$, $i(\neg(p \wedge q)) = 1$, $i(r \leftrightarrow \neg q) = 0$, $i(p \vee (r \leftrightarrow \neg q)) = 0$, and $i(u) = 0$. Similarly, other rows are constructed.

Table 1.3: Truth Table for $u = \neg(p \wedge q) \rightarrow (p \vee (r \leftrightarrow \neg q))$

p	q	r	$\neg q$	$p \wedge q$	$\neg(p \wedge q)$	$r \leftrightarrow \neg q$	$p \vee (r \leftrightarrow \neg q)$	u
0	0	0	1	0	1	0	0	0
1	0	0	1	0	1	0	1	1
0	1	0	0	0	1	1	1	1
1	1	0	0	1	0	1	1	1
0	0	1	1	0	1	1	1	1
1	0	1	1	0	1	1	1	1
0	1	1	0	0	1	0	0	0
1	1	1	0	1	0	0	1	1

Boolean valuations can also be computed using parse trees.

EXAMPLE 1.8. The parse tree for $u = \neg(p \wedge q) \rightarrow (p \vee (r \leftrightarrow \neg q))$ is the left tree in Figure 1.4.

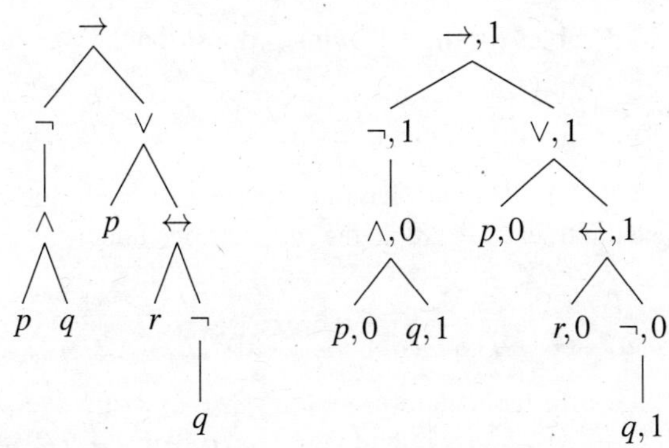

Figure 1.4: Interpretation in a parse tree for Example 1.8

The truth assignment j with $j(p) = 0$, $j(q) = 1$, $j(r) = 0$ is shown by mentioning the truth values to the right of the corresponding leaves. Then we travel upwards in the tree for evaluating the connectives following the truth table rules. The interpretation is given on the right hand tree in Figure 1.4. Work it out. Compare it with the third row in Table 1.3.

Suppose that you have a truth table for a proposition $u = (p \vee q)$ and you have another for the proposition $w = (q \vee r)$. How do you talk about a truth table for $u \wedge w$? The rows in the truth table for u may not assign any truth value to r, and similarly, the rows in a truth table for w may not assign a truth value to p. You must extend the truth tables by adding corresponding rows to the truth tables. In case of interpretations, our assumption is that already some truth value has been assigned to all variables. We only show the relevant ones in a truth table.

Formally, such a context with only the appropriate propositional variables is captured by a propositional language. A **propositional language** has an alphabet which is a subset of the alphabet of PL including all the connectives, the punctuation marks and the constants $\top$ and $\bot$. In such a case, the suitable connectives, the punctuation marks, and the symbols $\top, \bot$ are called the **logical constants** and the propositional variables are called the **nonlogical constants**. The set of appropriate nonlogical constants is called the **signature** of the propositional language.

A propositional language is characterized by its signature. Then an interpretation is said to be an interpretation of the propositional language. When we have another language containing all the nonlogical constants of a given language, then any interpretation of the bigger language is again considered as an interpretation of the smaller one. We do not use this terminology here, but you must be able to read and understand this terminology if used elsewhere.

Exercises for § 1.4

1. For the interpretation i with $i(p) = 1,\ i(q) = 0,\ i(r) = 0,\ i(s) = 1$, compute

   (a) $i(r \leftrightarrow p \vee q)$ (b) $i(p \vee q) \rightarrow (r \wedge \neg s)$ (c) $i(r \rightarrow p \vee s)$
   (d) $i(\neg s \vee q) \leftrightarrow (r \vee p)$ (e) $i(p \vee \neg q \vee s \leftrightarrow s \vee \neg s)$ (f) $i(r \leftrightarrow (p \rightarrow \neg r))$

2. Construct truth tables for the following propositions:

   (a) $p \rightarrow (q \rightarrow (p \rightarrow q))$ (b) $\neg p \vee q \rightarrow (q \rightarrow p)$ (c) $\neg(p \leftrightarrow q)$
   (d) $(p \leftrightarrow q) \leftrightarrow (p \rightarrow q)$ (e) $p \rightarrow (p \rightarrow q)$ (f) $(p \rightarrow \bot) \leftrightarrow \neg p$

3. Let $i(p) = i(q) = 1,\ i(r) = 0$. Draw parse trees of the following propositions, and then use the trees to evaluate the propositions under i.

   (a) $\neg(p \vee \neg(p \vee \neg(q \leftrightarrow r)))$ (b) $(p \leftrightarrow \neg q) \rightarrow (r \rightarrow p \wedge q)$
   (c) $(\neg p \vee \neg q) \leftrightarrow (\neg r \vee (p \rightarrow q))$ (d) $(p \wedge (q \vee \neg p)) \vee (p \wedge (q \vee p))$

4. Construct the truth tables and draw the parse trees for the propositions $v = \neg(p \wedge q) \vee r \rightarrow \neg p \vee (\neg q \vee r)$ and $w = (p \wedge q \rightarrow r) \leftrightarrow p \wedge (q \wedge \neg r)$. See how a row in the truth table evaluates the proposition v (and also w) via the corresponding parse tree.

5. For an interpretation i, we know that $i(p) = 1$. Then which of the following can be determined uniquely by i with this information only?

   (a) $(p \rightarrow q) \leftrightarrow (r \rightarrow \neg p)$ (b) $(q \rightarrow r) \rightarrow (q \rightarrow \neg p)$
   (c) $p \rightarrow (q \leftrightarrow (r \rightarrow p))$ (d) $p \leftrightarrow (q \rightarrow (r \leftrightarrow p))$

6. Using the vocabulary – p: It is normal, q: It is cold, r: It is hot, and s: It is small, translate the following into acceptable English.

   (a) $p \vee q \wedge s$ (b) $p \leftrightarrow q$ (c) $p \rightarrow \neg(q \vee r)$
   (d) $p \vee (s \rightarrow q)$ (e) $p \rightarrow \neg(q \wedge r)$ (f) $p \leftrightarrow ((q \wedge \neg r) \vee s)$

1.5 MODELS

The proposition $p \vee \neg p$ is always evaluated to 1 and $p \wedge \neg p$ always to 0. Whereas the proposition u in Table 1.3 is evaluated to 0 in some interpretations and to 1 in some other interpretations. It is one of the aims of semantics to categorize propositions according to their truth values under all or some interpretations.

Let w be a proposition. A **model** of w is an interpretation i with $i(w) = 1$. The fact that i is a model of w is written as $i \vDash w$. It is also read as i **verifies** w; and i **satisfies** w. The fact that i is not a model of w is written as $i \nvDash w$; and is also read as, i does not satisfy w, i does not verify w, and i **falsifies** w.

EXAMPLE 1.9. In Table 1.3, let i be the interpretation as given in the first row. That is, $i(p) = i(q) = i(r) = 0$. The table says that $i \nvDash u$. Check that

$$i \vDash \neg(p \wedge q) \vee r \to \neg p \vee (\neg q \vee r), \quad i \nvDash (p \wedge q \to r) \leftrightarrow p \wedge (q \wedge \neg r).$$

The interpretation j with $j(p) = 1, j(q) = j(r) = 0$ is a model of u. Which line in Table 1.3 is the interpretation j?

A proposition w is called

valid, written as $\vDash w$, iff each interpretation of w is its model;

invalid iff it is not valid, and we write $\nvDash w$;

satisfiable iff it has a model;

unsatisfiable iff it is not satisfiable;

contingent iff it is both invalid and satisfiable;

the proposition $\top$ is defined to be satisfiable;

the proposition $\bot$ is defined to be invalid.

Valid propositions are also called *tautologies*, and unsatisfiable propositions are called *contradictions*.

Notice that $\top$ is both valid and satisfiable whereas $\bot$ is both unsatisfiable and invalid; each propositional variable is contingent.

EXAMPLE 1.10. The proposition $p \vee \neg p$ is valid, i.e., $\vDash p \vee \neg p$, since each interpretation evaluates it to 1. Each of its interpretations is its model.

The proposition $p \wedge \neg p$ is unsatisfiable since each interpretation evaluates it to 0. No interpretation is its model.

Let $u = \neg(p \wedge q) \to (p \vee (r \leftrightarrow \neg q))$. Look at Table 1.3. Let i, j be interpretations of u with $i(p) = 1$, $i(q) = i(r) = 0$ and $j(p) = j(q) = j(r) = 0$. it is clear that $i \vDash u$ whereas $j \nvDash u$. Therefore, u is contingent.

EXAMPLE 1.11. Categorize the following propositions into valid, invalid, satisfiable, and unsatisfiable:

(a) $(p \to (q \to r)) \to ((p \to q) \to (p \to r))$

(b) $((p \to q) \to (p \to r)) \wedge \neg(p \to (q \to r))$

You can construct a truth table to answer both (a)-(b). Here is an approach that avoids the construction of a truth table.

(a) Suppose $i((p \to (q \to r)) \to ((p \to q) \to (p \to r))) = 0$, for an interpretation i. Then, $i((p \to (q \to r)) = 1$ and $i((p \to q) \to (p \to r)) = 0$. The last one says that $i(p \to q) = 1$ and $i(p \to r) = 0$. Again, $i(p \to r) = 0$ gives $i(p) = 1$ and $i(r) = 0$. Now, $i(p) = 1 = i(p \to q)$ implies that $i(q) = 1$. Then $i(p) = 1,\ i(q \to r) = 0$ gives $i((p \to (q \to r)) = 0$. It contradicts $i((p \to (q \to r)) = 1$.

Hence, $i((p \to (q \to r)) \to ((p \to q) \to (p \to r))) = 1$, whatever be the interpretation i. Thus, $\vDash (p \to (q \to r)) \to ((p \to q) \to (p \to r))$. It is also satisfiable, since it has a model, e.g., the interpretation that assigns each of p, q, r to 0.

(b) Suppose $i(((p \to q) \to (p \to r)) \wedge \neg(p \to (q \to r))) = 1$, for an interpretation i. Then, $i((p \to q) \to (p \to r)) = 1 = i(\neg(p \to (q \to r)))$. The last one says that $i(p) = 1, i(q) = 1$, and $i(r) = 0$. Then, $i(p \to q) = 1, i(p \to r) = 0$; consequently, $i((p \to q) \to (p \to r)) = 0$, which is not possible.

Therefore, $i(((p \to q) \to (p \to r)) \wedge \neg(p \to (q \to r))) = 0$ for each interpretation i. That is, the proposition is unsatisfiable. It is also invalid, e.g., the interpretation that assigns each of p, q, r to 0 falsifies the proposition.

In general, each valid proposition is satisfiable and each unsatisfiable proposition is invalid. Validity and unsatisfiability are dual concepts. Further, if i is an interpretation, then $i(w) = 1$ iff $i(\neg w) = 0$. This proves the following statement.

Theorem 1.4. *A proposition is valid iff its negation is unsatisfiable. A proposition is unsatisfiable iff its negation is valid.*

Remark 1.2. The concepts of interpretations and models can be presented in at least three ways other than the one we adopt.

In the first alternative view, a truth assignment is considered as a mapping of voltages on a wire, either high or low; the wires represent propositional variables. Any proposition is thought of as a function, a circuit or a gate as is called by electrical engineers, that maps a truth assignment to $\{0,1\}$. For example, if i assigns p to 0 and q to 1, then the proposition $p \wedge \neg q$ takes i to 0. A formalization of this view would use the notation $p(i)$ instead of $i(p)$, $\neg x(i)$ instead of $i(\neg x)$, and $(x \circ y)(i)$ instead of $i(x \circ y)$, etc. Thus connectives are taken as **truth functions**, i.e., functions that map 0's and 1's to 0's and 1's. In this view, $\neg$ is the function $\neg : \{0,1\} \to \{0,1\}$ with $\neg(0) = 1$ and $\neg(1) = 0$. Similarly, $\wedge : \{0,1\} \times \{0,1\} \to \{0,1\}$ with $\wedge(0,0) = \wedge(0,1)$ $= \wedge(1,0) = 0$ and $\wedge(1,1) = 1$.

There are 2^2 functions from $\{0,1\}$ to $\{0,1\}$. These functions are called unary truth functions. Among these, $\top$ and $\bot$ are the constant unary truth functions. Similarly, there are 2^4 functions from $\{0,1\} \times \{0,1\}$ to $\{0,1\}$. These functions are called binary truth functions. Out of the sixteen binary truth functions, we have considered only seven; the three unary and the four binary. In general, there are 2^n elements in the set $\{0,1\}^n$. Thus, there are 2^{2^n} number of n-ary truth functions. We will discuss truth functions later in a different context.

In the second alternative view of semantics, a proposition is seen as a set of truth assignments. Writing $\mathbb{M}(x)$ for the set of models of a proposition x, the driving idea is to define $\mathbb{M}(x)$ in an alternate way. Due to compositionality, the whole idea rests on the sets of models of propositional variables. Denote by $\mathbb{T}$ the set of all possible truth assignments, by i any truth assignment in $\mathbb{T}$, by p any propositional variable, and by x, y any propositions. Then the sets of models are defined to satisfy the following properties:

$$\mathbb{M}(\top) = \mathbb{T},\ \mathbb{M}(\bot) = \varnothing,\ \mathbb{M}(p) = \{i : i(p) = 1\},\ \mathbb{M}(\neg x) = \mathbb{T} \setminus \mathbb{M}(x),$$
$$\mathbb{M}(x \wedge y) = \mathbb{M}(x) \cap \mathbb{M}(y),\ \mathbb{M}(x \vee y) = \mathbb{M}(x) \cup \mathbb{M}(y),$$
$$\mathbb{M}(x \to y) = (\mathbb{T} \setminus \mathbb{M}(x)) \cup \mathbb{M}(y),$$
$$\mathbb{M}(x \leftrightarrow y) = (\mathbb{M}(x) \cap \mathbb{M}(y)) \cup ((\mathbb{T} \setminus \mathbb{M}(x)) \cup (\mathbb{T} \setminus \mathbb{M}(y))).$$

In the third alternative view, one tries to see each model as a set of **literals**, i.e., propositional variables or their negations. For example, all models of the proposition $p \vee q$ are the truth assignments i, j, k, where $i(p) = 1, i(q) = 1$; $j(p) = 0$, $j(q) = 1$; and $k(p) = 1, k(q) = 0$. Then the models i, j, k, in this view, correspond to the sets $\{p,q\}, \{\neg p, q\}, \{p, \neg q\}$, respectively. Any set of literals is a model of $\top$; and the set of all models of $\bot$ is $\varnothing$. In general, this view rests on the observation that each truth assignment i is associated to the set $\mathscr{M}_i$ the following way:

$$i(p) = \begin{cases} 1 & \text{iff } p \in \mathscr{M}_i \\ 0 & \text{iff } \neg p \in \mathscr{M}_i \end{cases}$$

There is also a slight variation on this theme, which assigns each interpretation i of a proposition to a subset of propositional variables only, negations of them being removed. It rests on the convention that whichever propositional variable is absent in such a set is in fact negated. For example, let u be a proposition built up from the propositional variables p and q. If $\mathscr{M}_i = \{p, \neg q\}$, then abbreviate $\mathscr{M}_i$ to $\{p\}$. The truth assignment is constructed from such a subset of propositional variables by its characteristic function.

For instance, let $w = (p \to q) \vee (r \leftrightarrow s \vee t)$. Write $V_w = \{p,q,r,s,t\}$, the set of propositional variables occurring in w. The interpretation i with $i(p) = i(r) = i(s) = 1$, $i(q) = i(t) = 0$ is represented by the set $\{p, r, s\}$. Note that the characteristic function of the set $\{p, r, s\}$ as a subset of V_w is the interpretation i.

Exercises for § 1.5

1. Categorize the following propositions into valid, invalid, satisfiable, and unsatisfiable:

(a) $p \to (q \to p)$ (b) $(p \to (q \to r)) \to ((p \to q) \to (p \to r))$

(c) $p \wedge (p \to q) \to q$ (d) $(\neg p \to \neg q) \to ((\neg p \to q) \to p)$

(e) $p \vee q \leftrightarrow ((p \to q) \to q)$ (f) $p \wedge q \leftrightarrow ((q \to p) \to q)$

(g) $(\neg p \vee q) \to ((p \vee r) \leftrightarrow r)$ (h) $(p \wedge q \leftrightarrow p) \to (p \vee q \leftrightarrow q)$

(i) $(p \vee q \to p) \to (q \to p \wedge q)$ (j) $(\neg p \to \neg q) \leftrightarrow (\neg p \vee q \to q)$

(k) $(q \to p) \to p$ (l) $((p \leftrightarrow q) \leftrightarrow r) \leftrightarrow ((p \leftrightarrow q) \wedge (q \leftrightarrow r))$

(m) $((p \wedge q) \leftrightarrow p) \to q$ (n) $\neg((\neg(p \wedge q) \wedge (p \leftrightarrow \bot)) \leftrightarrow (q \leftrightarrow \bot))$

(o) $(p \wedge q \to r) \wedge (p \wedge \neg q \to r)$ (p) $(p \leftrightarrow \neg(q \leftrightarrow r)) \leftrightarrow (\neg(p \leftrightarrow q) \leftrightarrow r)$

(q) $(p \to q) \vee (q \to p)$ (r) $((p \to q) \to p) \to p$

2. For $n \in \mathbb{N}$, define A_n by $A_0 = p \to q$, and $A_{m+1} = A_m \to p$. For which values of n, is A_n valid?
3. Why have we defined $\top$ to be satisfiable and $\bot$ to be invalid?
4. Draw a Venn diagram depicting the sets of valid, invalid, satisfiable, and unsatisfiable propositions in the set of all propositions.

1.6 EQUIVALENCES AND CONSEQUENCES

In the context of reasoning, it is important to determine whether saying this is same as saying that. It is the notion of equivalence. Along with this we must also specify the meaning of *follows from.*

Propositions u and v are called **equivalent**, written as $u \equiv v$, iff each model of u is a model of v, and each model of v is also a model of u. We write $u \not\equiv v$ when u is not equivalent to v.

EXAMPLE 1.12. To determine whether $p \vee q \equiv (p \to q) \to q$, let i be an interpretation. If $i(p \vee q) = 0$, then $i(p) = i(q) = 0$; thus $i((p \to q) \to q) = 0$.

Conversely, if $i((p \to q) \to q) = 0$, then $i(p \to q) = 1$ and $i(q) = 0$. So, $i(p) = i(q) = 0$. Hence $i(p \vee q) = 0$.

That is, $i(p \vee q) = 0$ iff $i((p \to q) \to q) = 0$. So, $i \vDash p \vee q$ iff $i \vDash (p \to q) \to q$. Therefore, $p \vee q \equiv (p \to q) \to q$.

To show that $p \to (q \to r) \not\equiv (p \to q) \to r$, consider the interpretation i with $i(p) = 0, i(q) = 1$, and $i(r) = 0$. Now, $i(q \to r) = 0$ and $i(p \to q) = 1$. Consequently, $i(p \to (q \to r)) = 1$ and $i((p \to q) \to r) = 0$. Therefore, $p \to (q \to r) \not\equiv (p \to q) \to r$.

A consequence is a formalization of an argument found in ordinary discourse. A typical argument goes as follows:

$w_1, w_2, \ldots, w_n$. Therefore, w.

The propositions w_i may not be valid. The argument compels us to imagine a world where all of $w_1, w_2, \ldots, w_n$ become true. In any such world, it is to be checked whether w is also true. In order that the argument is declared correct, all those interpretations which are simultaneously satisfying all the propositions $w_1, w_2, \ldots, w_n$ must also satisfy w.

Let Σ be a set of propositions, and w a proposition. An interpretation i is called a **model** of Σ, written $i \vDash \Sigma$, iff i is a model of each proposition in Σ. Every interpretation is taken as a model of the empty set $\varnothing$, as a convention.

The set Σ is called **satisfiable** iff Σ has a model. Σ **semantically entails** w, written as $\Sigma \vDash w$, iff each model of Σ is a model of w. $\Sigma \vDash w$ is also read as "w follows from Σ" and also as "the consequence $\Sigma \,!\!\vdash w$ is valid". For a consequence $\Sigma \,!\!\vdash w$, the propositions in Σ are called the **premises** or **hypotheses**, and w is called the **conclusion**.

The abstract notion of a consequence $\Sigma \,!\!\vdash w$ refers to an argument which may or may not be valid. Once $\Sigma \,!\!\vdash w$ is valid, we write $\Sigma \vDash w$. For a finite set of premises

$\Sigma = \{w_1, \ldots, w_n\}$, we write the consequence $\Sigma \mathrel{!\vdash} w$ as $w_1, \ldots, w_n \mathrel{!\vdash} w$, and $\Sigma \vDash w$ as $w_1, \ldots, w_n \vDash w$, without the braces.

Thus, $\Sigma \vDash w$ iff for each interpretation i, if i falsifies w then i falsifies some proposition from Σ. Moreover, $\{w_1, \ldots, w_n\} \vDash w$ iff $w_1 \wedge \cdots \wedge w_n \vDash w$. It also follows that $x \equiv y$ iff $x \vDash y$ and $y \vDash x$.

EXAMPLE 1.13. Is the consequence $p \to q,\ \neg q \mathrel{!\vdash} \neg p$ valid?

We try out each model of the set of premises and check whether it is also a model of the conclusion. So, let $i \vDash p \to q$ and $i \vDash \neg q$. We see that $i(q) = 0$. Since $i(p \to q) = 1$, we have $i(p) = 0$. The only model of all premises is the interpretation i with $i(p) = i(q) = 0$. Now, this i is also a model of $\neg p$. Therefore, the consequence is valid. So, we write $p \to q,\ \neg q \vDash \neg p$.

Translation of natural language arguments into PL-consequences involves identifying simple declarative sentences as propositional variables. This identification sometimes requires to determine the connectives, or the words which look like connectives. A brief guideline for identifying connectives follows.

1. The proposition $\neg p$:

   Not p. It is not the case that p.
   p does not hold. p is false. p is not true.

2. The proposition $p \wedge q$:

   Both p and q. Not only p but also q. p although q.
   p yet q. p while q. p despite q.

3. The proposition $p \vee q$:

   p or q or both. p and/or q. Either p or q.
   p unless q. p except when q. p otherwise q.

4. The proposition $p \to q$:

   If p then q. q if p p only if q.
   q when p. When p, q. p only when q.
   In case p, q. q in case p. p only in case q.
   p is sufficient for q. q is necessary for p. p implies q.
   q provided that p. From p we get q. p gives q.
   p yields q. p produces q. From p we obtain q.

5. The proposition $p \leftrightarrow q$:

   p iff q. p if and only if q.
   p and q are equivalent. p implies q, and q implies p.
   If p, then q; and conversely. p is necessary and sufficient for q.
   p exactly when q. p if q, and q if p.
   p just in case q. p gives q and q gives p.

The last three reading of $\neg p$ in (1) do mess up with truth, which is not the intent of the connective $\neg$. However, sometimes a translation of these three is also done as $\neg p$, depending on context. This comment applies to other connectives also; these are no strict rules, but only guidelines!

The connective "Either – or" is sometimes used in the sense of 'inclusive or', and sometimes in the sense of 'exclusive or'; it depends on the context. The 'exclusive or' sense of the connective 'either – or' is translated as as $(p \vee q) \wedge \neg(p \wedge q)$ or as $\neg(p \leftrightarrow q)$. This is also read in English as "p or else q", and also as "p or q but not both".

Similarly, "neither p nor q" is translated as $\neg(p \vee q)$.

EXAMPLE 1.14. Show that the following argument is correct (Stoll (1963)):

> If the band performs, then the hall will be full provided that the tickets are not too costly. However, if the band performs, the tickets will not be too costly. Therefore, if the band performs, then the hall will be full.

We identify the simple declarative sentences in the above argument and build a vocabulary for translation:

p: the band performs
q: the hall is (will be) full
r: tickets are not too costly

Then the hypotheses are the propositions $p \to (r \to q)$, $p \to r$, and the conclusion is $p \to q$. We check the following consequence for validity:

$$p \to (r \to q),\ p \to r \,!\!\vDash p \to q.$$

Since there are only three propositional variables, by the Relevance Lemma, there are $2^3 = 8$ interpretations. These are given in second, third, and fourth columns of Table 1.4.

Table 1.4: Truth Table for Example 1.14

Row No.	p	q	r	$p \to r$	$r \to q$	$p \to (r \to q)$	$p \to q$
1	0	0	0	1	1	1	1
2	1	0	0	0	1	1	0
3	0	1	0	1	1	1	1
4	1	1	0	0	1	1	1
5	0	0	1	1	0	1	1
6	1	0	1	1	0	0	0
7	0	1	1	1	1	1	1
8	1	1	1	1	1	1	1

For the time being do not read the column for $p \to q$ in Table 1.4. You must find out all (common) models of both $p \to (r \to q)$ and $p \to r$. They are in rows 1, 3, 5, 7, and 8. In order that the argument is correct, you must check whether $p \to q$ is true (evaluated to 1) in all these rows. This is the case.

Therefore, $p \to (r \to q),\ p \to r \vDash p \to q$; the argument is correct.

In Example 1.14, you need not evaluate $p \to q$ in the rows 2, 4, 6 since it does not matter whether $p \to q$ receives the truth value 0 or 1 in these cases. But if one of the rows 1, 3, 5, 7, 8 had 0 for $p \to q$, then the consequence would not be valid.

Thus, the alternative way to show $\Sigma \vDash w$ is to search for an interpretation i with $i(w) = 0$, and $i(x) = 1$ for each $x \in \Sigma$. If the search fails, then $\Sigma \vDash w$. If the search succeeds in finding one such interpretation, then $\Sigma \nvDash w$.

To apply this method on Example 1.14, look at Table 1.4. The interpretations which assign 0 to $p \to q$ are in rows 2 and 6. Row 2 assigns 0 to $p \to r$ and row 6 assigns 0 to $p \to (r \to q)$, that is, whenever the conclusion is falsified, at least one of the premises is also falsified. Hence the consequence is valid. Another instance of this procedure is employed in Example 1.11, though in a different context.

Further, employing this method prempts construction of a truth table. For, suppose $i(p \to q) = 0$. Then $i(p) = 1$ and $i(q) = 0$. Now, if $i(r) = 0$, then $i(p \to r) = 0$. And, if $i(r) = 1$, then $i(r \to q) = 0$ yielding $i(p \to (q \to r)) = 0$. That is, falsity of the conclusion ensures falsity of at least one premise.

EXAMPLE 1.15. Let Σ be a set of propositions; $x \in \Sigma$; and y a proposition. Assume that $\vDash x$ and $\Sigma \vDash y$. Show that $\Sigma \setminus \{x\} \vDash y$.

Let i be a model of $\Sigma \setminus \{x\}$. As $\vDash x$, $i \vDash x$. So, $i \vDash \Sigma$. Since $\Sigma \vDash y$, $i \vDash y$. Therefore, $\Sigma \setminus \{x\} \vDash y$.

Example 1.15 says that valid propositions have no information content. Valid propositions have to be asserted and unsatisfiable propositions have to be negated, whatever be the context. Whereas, declaring a contingent proposition to be true (or false) in a context really supplies some information.

EXAMPLE 1.16. We show that for all propositions x and y, $\{x,\ x \to y\} \vDash y$.

Of course, we should use the definition of $\vDash$. So, let i be a model of x and also of $x \to y$. If i is not a model of y, then $i(x) = 1$ and $i(y) = 0$. Consequently, $i(x \to y) = 0$, which is not possible. Therefore, i is a model of y. Hence, $\{x,\ x \to y\} \vDash y$.

Remark 1.3. We have used the symbol $\vDash$ in three different ways. They are

$i \vDash w$: i is a model of w
$\vDash w$: w is valid
$\Sigma \vDash w$: the consequence $\Sigma\, !\!\vdash w$ is valid.

As in the third view of semantics, where a model is identified with the set of literals that are true under the model, we see that the first use is same as the third. Next, the second one is a particular case of the third, namely, when $\Sigma = \varnothing$.

Equivalences are useful in obtaining other equivalences, and also they can be used in consequences, as the following theorem shows.

Exercises for § 1.6

1. Show the following equivalences:

(a) $p \vee q \equiv \neg p \to q$ (b) $p \wedge q \equiv \neg(p \to \neg q)$
(c) $p \leftrightarrow q \equiv (p \to q) \wedge (q \to p)$ (d) $p \wedge (p \to q) \equiv p \wedge q$
(e) $\neg(p \wedge q) \equiv \neg p \vee \neg q$ (f) $\neg p \to \neg q \equiv q \to p$
(g) $\neg(p \leftrightarrow q) \equiv (\neg p \leftrightarrow q)$ (h) $p \leftrightarrow (q \leftrightarrow r) \equiv (p \leftrightarrow q) \leftrightarrow r$

2. Simplify the following propositions using equivalences:
(Of course, 'to simplify' here is subjective.)

   (a) $(p \vee \top) \to q$ (b) $p \wedge (\neg p \to p)$
   (c) $\neg q \to \neg(q \to \neg p)$ (d) $\neg p \wedge q \wedge (p \to (q \vee \neg r))$
   (e) $((p \vee (p \wedge q)) \to (p \wedge (p \vee q)))$ (f) $(p \wedge (q \vee \neg p)) \vee q \vee (p \wedge (q \vee p))$
   (g) $((p \leftrightarrow q) \leftrightarrow r) \leftrightarrow ((p \leftrightarrow q) \wedge (q \leftrightarrow r))$
   (h) $((\top \to p) \wedge (q \vee \bot)) \to (q \to \bot) \vee (r \wedge \top))$

3. Are the following sets of propositions satisfiable?

   (a) $\{p \to (p \to q),\ p \vee q,\ p \to \bot\}$
   (b) $\{\neg p \vee \neg(q \wedge r),\ s \vee t \to u,\ u \to \neg(v \vee w),\ r \wedge v\}$
   (c) $\{p \vee q \to r \wedge s,\ s \vee t \to u,\ p \vee \neg u,\ p \to (q \to r)\}$
   (d) $\{p \to q \wedge r,\ q \to s,\ d \to t \wedge u,\ q \to p \wedge \neg t,\ q \to t\}$
   (e) $\{p \to q \wedge r,\ q \to s,\ d \to t \wedge u,\ q \to p \wedge \neg t,\ \neg q \to t\}$
   (f) $\{p \to q,\ r \to s,\ q \to s,\ \neg r \to p,\ t \to u,\ u \to \neg s,\ \neg t \to t\}$
   (g) $\{p \to q \wedge r,\ s \to q \wedge t,\ u \to \neg p,\ (v \to w) \to u \wedge s,\ \neg(\neg r \to t)\}$

4. Determine whether the following consequences are valid:

   (a) $p \vee q \to r,\ q \wedge r\ !\vdash p \to r$
   (b) $p \vee (q \wedge \neg q),\ p\ !\vdash \neg(p \wedge \neg p)$
   (c) $p \wedge q \to r\ !\vdash (p \to r) \vee (q \to r)$
   (d) $p \to (q \vee r),\ q \wedge r \to \neg p\ !\vdash \neg p$
   (e) $p \vee q \to p \wedge q,\ \neg p \to q\ !\vdash p \wedge q$
   (f) $p \vee q \vee (p \wedge q),\ \neg(p \to q)\ !\vdash p \vee q$
   (g) $p \vee q \to p \wedge q,\ \neg p \to q\ !\vdash \neg(p \vee q)$
   (h) $p \vee q \to p \wedge q,\ \neg p \wedge \neg q\ !\vdash \neg(p \wedge q)$
   (i) $p \leftrightarrow q\ !\vdash \neg((p \to q) \to \neg(q \to p))$
   (j) $p \vee q \to r,\ r \to p \wedge q\ !\vdash p \wedge q \to p \vee q$
   (k) $\neg((p \to q) \to \neg(q \to p))\ !\vdash (\neg p \vee q) \wedge (p \vee \neg q)$
   (l) $(p \leftrightarrow (q \leftrightarrow r))\ !\vdash ((p \wedge q) \wedge r) \vee (\neg p \wedge (\neg q \wedge \neg r))$
   (m) $((p \wedge q) \wedge r) \vee (\neg p \wedge (\neg q \wedge \neg r))\ !\vdash (p \leftrightarrow (q \leftrightarrow r))$

5. Translate the following into PL consequences; and check their validity:

   (a) If he is innocent, then he will be hurt unless appreciated. He is not appreciated. Therefore, he is not innocent.
   (b) He cannot come to office unless he sleeps well the previous night. If he sleeps well the previous night, then he cannot come to office. Therefore, he cannot come to office.
   (c) If he knows magic then he can create a rock that he cannot lift. If he cannot lift the rock he has made, then he does not know magic. Therefore, he does not know magic.
   (d) Labour is stubborn but management is not. The strike will be settled; the government obtains an injunction; and troops are sent into the mills. Therefore, If either management or labour is stubborn, then the strike will be settled if and only if the government obtains an injunction, but troops are not sent into the mills.

1.7 MORE ABOUT CONSEQUENCES

In the following, we prove some facts which are used in almost every mathematical argument, without mention.

Since $\varnothing$ contains no propositions; no interpretation can succeed in falsifying some proposition from $\varnothing$. That is, every interpretation is a model of $\varnothing$. Vacuously, each interpretation verifies each premise here (there is none). This justifies (2) in the following theorem; others are easier to prove.

Theorem 1.5. *Let u and v be propositions. Then the following are true:*

(1) $u \equiv v$ *iff* $\vDash u \leftrightarrow v$ *iff* ($u \vDash v$ *and* $v \vDash u$).

(2) $\vDash u$ *iff* $u \equiv \top$ *iff* $\top \vDash u$ *iff* $\varnothing \vDash u$ *iff* $\neg u \equiv \bot$.

(3) *u is unsatisfiable iff* $u \equiv \bot$ *iff* $u \vDash \bot$ *iff* $\neg u \equiv \top$.

The following limiting case implies that from a contradiction everything follows.

Theorem 1.6 (Paradox of Material Implication). *A set of propositions Σ is unsatisfiable iff $\Sigma \vDash w$ for each proposition w.*

Proof. Suppose Σ has no model. Then it is not the case that there exists an interpretation, which satisfies the propositions in Σ and falsifies any given proposition w. Thus, $\Sigma \nvDash w$ never holds; which means $\Sigma \vDash w$.

Conversely, if $\Sigma \vDash w$ for each proposition w, then in particular, $\Sigma \vDash \bot$. Then Σ is unsatisfiable. ♦

EXAMPLE 1.17. The hatter says that if he has eaten the cake, then he cannot eat it. Therefore, he has not eaten the cake. Is the hatter's argument correct, in PL?

In PL, 'has not' and 'cannot' are same as 'not'. Writing p for the statement "The hatter has eaten the cake", his first statement is symbolized as $p \to \neg p$. His conclusion is $\neg p$. Thus the consequence to be checked for validity is

$$p \to \neg p \,!\!\vdash \neg p.$$

Let i be any interpretation, which is a model of $p \to \neg p$. Now, if $i(\neg p) = 0$ then $i(p \to \neg p) = 0$. This is not possible. So, $i(\neg p) = 1$. Therefore, $p \to \neg p \vDash \neg p$.

However, if we consider "the hatter has eaten the cake" as the proposition p and "the hatter cannot eat the cake" as the proposition q, different from p and $\neg p$, then the consequence would be symbolized as $p, q \,!\!\vdash \neg p$. This consequence is invalid. For instance, the interpretation i with $i(p) = 1, i(q) = 1$ satisfies the premises but falsifies the conclusion.

Theorem 1.7 (M: Monotonicity). *Let Σ and Γ be sets of propositions, $\Sigma \subseteq \Gamma$, and let w be a proposition.*

(1) *If Σ is unsatisfiable, then Γ is unsatisfiable.*

(2) *If $\Sigma \vDash w$, then $\Gamma \vDash w$.*

Proof. Let $i \vDash \Gamma$. This means i satisfies each proposition in Γ. If $y \in \Sigma$, then $y \in \Gamma$; so $i \vDash y$. Hence, $i \vDash \Sigma$. Thus, each model of Γ is also a model of Σ.

(1) If Σ has no model, then Γ has no model.

(2) Suppose $\Sigma \vDash w$. Let $i \vDash \Gamma$. Then $i \vDash \Sigma$. Since $\Sigma \vDash w$, $i \vDash w$. So, $\Gamma \vDash w$. ♦

In day to day life, you will have many situations where the consequence relation is not monotonic; especially when there are hidden common knowledge as premises. The nonmonotonic logics tackle such situations. However, when all premises are spelled out explicitly, as in mathematics, monotonicity holds.

Along with monotonicity, the consequence relation in PL allows a very commonly used proof method: proof by contradiction. Informally, it is stated as

If from $\neg S$ follows a contradiction, then S must be true.

It says that along with some given assumptions, if we use the extra assumption $\neg S$ and are able to conclude a contradiction, then the given assumptions must imply S. Notice its connection with the paradox of material implication.

Theorem 1.8 (RA: Reductio ad Absurdum). *Let Σ be a set of propositions, and let w be a proposition.*

(1) $\Sigma \vDash w$ *iff* $\Sigma \cup \{\neg w\}$ *is unsatisfiable.*

(2) $\Sigma \vDash \neg w$ *iff* $\Sigma \cup \{w\}$ *is unsatisfiable.*

Proof. (1) Let $\Sigma \vDash w$. Let i be any interpretation. If $i \vDash \Sigma$, then $i \vDash w$. So, $i \nvDash \neg w$. Thus, $i \nvDash \Sigma \cup \{\neg w\}$. If $i \nvDash \Sigma$, then $i \nvDash x$ for some $x \in \Sigma$; hence $i \nvDash \Sigma \cup \{\neg w\}$. In any case, $i \nvDash \Sigma \cup \{\neg w\}$. That is, $\Sigma \cup \{\neg w\}$ is unsatisfiable.

Conversely, let $\Sigma \cup \{\neg w\}$ be unsatisfiable. Let $i \vDash \Sigma$. Then $i \nvDash \neg w$; that is, $i \vDash w$. Therefore, $\Sigma \vDash w$.

(2) Take w instead of $\neg w$, and $\neg w$ instead of w in the proof of (1). ♦

Another important principle, found in almost every mathematical proof, says that to prove $p \to q$, it is enough to assume the truth of p and then conclude the truth of q. In our notation, $\vDash p \to q$ iff $p \vDash q$. A generalized version of this principle follows.

Theorem 1.9 (DT: Deduction Theorem). *Let Σ be a set of propositions, and let x, y be propositions. Then,* $\Sigma \vDash x \to y$ *iff* $\Sigma \cup \{x\} \vDash y$.

Proof. Suppose $\Sigma \vDash x \to y$. Let $i \vDash \Sigma \cup \{x\}$. Then $i \vDash \Sigma$, and $i \vDash x$. If $i \nvDash y$, then $i(x) = 1$ and $i(y) = 0$. That is, $i(x \to y) = 0$; so $i \nvDash x \to y$. This contradicts $\Sigma \vDash x \to y$. Thus, $i \vDash y$. Therefore, $\Sigma \cup \{x\} \vDash y$.

Conversely, suppose $\Sigma \cup \{x\} \vDash y$. Let $i \vDash \Sigma$. If $i \nvDash x \to y$, then $i(x) = 1$ and $i(y) = 0$. That is, $i \vDash \Sigma \cup \{x\}$ and $i \nvDash y$; this contradicts $\Sigma \cup \{x\} \vDash y$. So, $i \vDash x \to y$. Therefore, $\Sigma \vDash x \to y$. ♦

EXAMPLE 1.18. We use Monotonicity, Reductio ad Absurdum and/or Deduction Theorem to justify the argument in Example 1.14.

Solution 1. Due to DT, $\{p \to (r \to q),\ p \to r\} \vDash p \to q$ iff $\{p \to r,\ p \to (r \to q),\ p\} \vDash q$. We show the latter.

Let i be an interpretation such that $i(p \to r) = 1$, $i(p \to (r \to q)) = 1$ and $i(p) = 1$. If $i(r) = 0$, then it will contradict $i(p \to r) = 1$. So, $i(r) = 1$. Similarly, from second and third, we have $i(r \to q) = 1$. Then $i(q) = 1$. Therefore, the consequence is valid.

Solution 2. Due to RA, we show that $\{p \to r,\ p \to (r \to q),\ p,\ \neg q\}$ is unsatisfiable. If the set is satisfiable, then there is an interpretation i such that

$$i(p \to r) = i(p \to (r \to q)) = i(p) = i(\neg q) = 1.$$

Now, $i(p) = 1$ and $i(p \to r) = 1$ force $i(r) = 1$. Then $i(q) = 0$ gives $i(q \to r) = 0$. It follows that $i(p \to (r \to q)) = 0$ contradicting $i(p \to (r \to q)) = 1$. So, there exists no such i. That is, $\{p \to r,\ p \to (r \to q),\ p,\ \neg q\}$ is unsatisfiable.

Solution 3. Due to Example 1.16, $\{p \to r,\ p\} \vDash r$ and $\{p \to (r \to q),\ p\} \vDash r \to q$. Again, $\{r,\ r \to q\} \vDash q$. Using monotonicity, we have $\{p \to r,\ p \to (r \to q),\ p\} \vDash q$. Is this solution complete?

Exercises for § 1.7

1. Determine whether the following consequences are valid:
   (a) $\neg(r \wedge \neg\neg q)\ !\vdash (\neg q \vee \neg r)$
   (b) $p \vee \neg q,\ p \to \neg r\ !\vdash q \to \neg r$
   (c) $p \vee q \to r \wedge s,\ t \wedge s \to u\ !\vdash p \to u$
   (d) $p \vee q \to r \wedge s,\ s \vee t \to u,\ p \vee \neg u\ !\vdash p \to (q \to r)$
   (e) $p \to q \wedge r,\ q \to s,\ d \to t \wedge u,\ q \to p \wedge \neg t\ !\vdash q \to t$
   (f) $p,\ \neg r \to \neg p,\ (p \to q) \wedge (r \to s),\ (s \to u) \wedge (q \to t),\ s \to \neg t\ !\vdash \bot$
2. Translate to PL and then decide the validity of the following argument:

   The Indian economy will decline unless cashless transaction is accepted by the public. If the Indian economy declines, then Nepal will be more dependent on China. The public will not accept cashless transaction. So, Nepal will be more dependent on China.

1.8 SUMMARY AND PROBLEMS

Logic is concerned with methods of reasoning involving issues such as validity of arguments and formal aspects of truth and falsehood. Propositional Logic addresses these issues by starting with atomic propositions and gradually building up more propositions using the connectives such as $\neg$ (not), $\wedge$ (and), $\vee$ (or), $\to$ (implies), and $\leftrightarrow$ (if and only if). The meanings of these connectives are defined by means of truth tables. The meanings are unambiguous because the compound propositions are formed from the basic ones in an unambiguous manner by a formal construction of the language of PL. Such a formal construction, where no concept of truth is attached to the constructs is termed as the *syntax* of PL. Giving meanings to the propositions by way of truth values is termed as the *semantics* of PL.

In semantics, we attach truth values to the propositions by way of interpretations. A model is defined as an interpretation that evaluates a proposition to 1 (true).

Propositions of which each interpretation is a model are called valid propositions (also tautologies). A satisfiable proposition is one which has a model. The concept of models has been used to define a valid consequence which formalizes the notion of a correct argument. A consequence is valid if it is never the case that the premises are true and the conclusion is false.

Though propositional logic has a long history of more than 2000 years, the truth value semantics as discussed here was invented by Boole (1951) in the form of an algebra, now called boolean algebra. The truth table had been used by Frege (1934) in a somewhat awkward fashion. The modern form of the truth table semantics was popularized by Post (1921) and Wittgenstein (1922). There had been debates about how well the *material implication* as given through the semantics of $\rightarrow$ represents the *implication* as found in natural languages. See Epstein (2001) and Mates (1972) for such discussions and other philosophical issues related to propositional logic. Some of the story problems below are taken from Backhouse (1986), Smullyan (1968, 1978), and Smullyan (1983).

Problems for Chapter 1

1. Construct propositions x, y and strings u, v such that $(x \leftrightarrow y) = (u \leftrightarrow v)$, where $x \neq u$.
2. Show that $n(w)$, the number of occurrences of connectives in a proposition w can be defined the following way:

   If w is a propositional variable, or $\top$, or $\bot$, then $n(w) = 0$.
   If $w = \neg x$, then $n(w) = n(x) + 1$.
   If $w = (x \circ y)$, for $\circ \in \{\wedge, \vee, \rightarrow, \leftrightarrow\}$, then $n(w) = n(x) + n(y) + 1$.
3. Prove by induction that the number of occurrences of binary connectives in a proposition is equal to the number of left parentheses, and is also equal to the number of right parentheses.
4. Prove that the three alternative ways of defining PROP such as the grammar, the declarative version, and the inductive construction, define the same set PROP.
5. Show that no proposition can be a string of negation symbols.
6. Show that a proper prefix of a proposition is either a string of negation symbols or has more left than right parentheses.
7. Show that the set PROP(i) consists of all propositions whose parse trees have height at most k.
8. Let x, y, z be nonempty strings over the alphabet of PROP such that y and z are prefixes of x. Prove that y is a prefix of z or z is a prefix of y.
9. Is it true that in a proposition the number of left parentheses plus the number of occurrences of the symbol $\neg$ is equal to the height of the parse tree of the proposition?
10. Let A be a proposition where $\neg$ does not appear. Show that the number of occurrences of atomic propositions in A is at least a quarter of the length of A; and the length of A is odd. [Hint: Length of A is $4k + 1$ and the number of occurrences of atomic propositions is $k + 1$.]

11. Let x, y, z be any three nonempty strings over the alphabet of PROP. Show that at most one of xy and yz is a proposition.
12. Let us say that a *statement* is obtained from a proposition by omitting all left parentheses. Show that unique parsing holds for statements.
13. Define the main connective of a proposition without using parse trees. Write a procedure to get the main connective of a proposition.
14. Our algorithm of *PropDet* starts by identifying a leftmost innermost proposition. Describe another procedure that may start by identifying a possible outermost proposition.
15. Show that PROP is a denumerable set.
16. Write a procedure to determine in which of the forms $\top$, $\neg\top$, $\bot$, $\neg\bot$, p_i, $\neg p_i$, $\neg\neg x$, $(x\wedge y)$, $\neg(x\wedge y)$, $(x\vee y)$, $\neg(x\vee y)$, $(x\rightarrow y)$, $\neg(x\rightarrow y)$, $(x\leftrightarrow y)$, or $\neg(x\leftrightarrow y)$ a given proposition is.
17. Prove Observation 1.1 by induction on the number of occurrences of connectives in the given proposition.
18. Suppose that we replace both (and) with $|$. Will the unique parsing still hold?
19. Replace the formation rules of propositions by: if u, v are propositions, then $\neg(u)$, $(u)\wedge(v)$, $(u)\vee(v)$, $(u)\rightarrow(v)$, $(u)\leftrightarrow(v)$ are propositions. Show that the unique parsing theorem holds with such a definition.
20. Show that unique parsing holds for the following grammar of propositions: $w ::= \top \mid \bot \mid p \mid (\neg w) \mid (w\wedge w) \mid (w\vee w) \mid (w\rightarrow w) \mid (w\leftrightarrow w)$
21. In *outfix notation*, we write $(p\vee q)$ as $\vee(p,q)$. Similarly, we write the proposition $(\neg p\rightarrow(q\vee(r\wedge s)))$ as $\rightarrow(\neg p,\vee(q,\wedge(r,s)))$. If you omit the commas and parentheses, the latter will look like $\rightarrow\neg p\vee q\wedge rs$. Can you see how to put commas and parentheses into this expression and then rewrite so that you obtain the usual infix notation? Taking clues from this, define a language of propositional logic without parentheses. Show that unique parsing still holds. (This is the *Polish* notation.)
22. Sometimes, Polish notation uses writing connectives on the right, instead of writing on the left. Using this, the proposition $((p\rightarrow q)\leftrightarrow(\neg p\wedge\neg q))$ is written as $q\neg p\neg\wedge qp\rightarrow\leftrightarrow$. Give a formal definition of the set of all propositions using this notation and then prove unique parsing.
23. Give two parse trees that do not correspond to propositions, such that
    (a) one of them could be extended, by adding subtrees at the leaves, to a parse tree which would correspond to a proposition.
    (b) whatever way you extend the other, by adding subtrees at the leaves, it cannot correspond to a proposition; it is inherently ill formed.
24. Prove by induction on the length of a string that the procedure *PropDet* works correctly.
25. Give a formal proof of correctness of *PropDet* by using induction on the height of a parse tree.
26. The procedure *PropDet* is a recursive procedure. Give an iterative procedure for determining whether an arbitrary string over the alphabet of PL is a proposition or not.

27. Write another algorithm for determining whether a given string over the alphabet of PROP is a proposition or not, by using the procedure for computing the main connective.

28. Identify the set $sp(w)$ for a proposition w, where

    $sp(p) = \{p\}$, for any atomic proposition p.
    $sp(\neg w) = sp(w) \cup \{\neg w\}$, for any proposition w.
    $sp(u \circ v) = sp(u) \cup sp(v) \cup \{(u \circ v)\}$, for any propositions u, v, and any binary connective $\circ \in \{\wedge, \vee, \rightarrow, \leftrightarrow\}$.

29. Define the *degree* of a proposition $d(w)$ recursively by:

    $d(p) = 0$, for any atomic proposition p.
    $d(\neg w) = 1 + d(w)$, for any proposition w.
    $d((u \circ v)) = 1 + \max\{d(u), d(v)\}$, for any propositions u, v, and any binary connective $\circ \in \{\wedge, \vee, \rightarrow, \leftrightarrow\}$.

    Does $d(w)$ coincide with the height of the parse tree for w?

30. Recall that any proposition is in one of the forms $\top$, $\neg\top$, $\bot$, $\neg\bot$, $p_i, \neg p_i, \neg\neg x$, $(x \wedge y)$, $\neg(x \wedge y)$, $(x \vee y)$, $\neg(x \vee y)$, $(x \rightarrow y)$, $\neg(x \rightarrow y)$, $(x \leftrightarrow y)$, or $\neg(x \leftrightarrow y)$. Using this, we define the *rank* of a proposition $r(w)$ as follows.

    $r(w) = 0$ if w is one of $\top$, $\neg\top$, $\bot$, $\neg\bot$, p_i, $\neg p_i$.
    $r(\neg\neg x) = r(x) + 1$.
    $r(w) = r(x) + r(y) + 1$, otherwise.

    To connect the rank with the degree defined in the previous problem, show the following:

    (a) For any proposition w, $r(w) + 1 \leq 2^{d(w)}$.
    (b) For any positive integer n, there exists a proposition w such that $d(w) = n$ and $r(w) + 1 = 2^n$.

31. Let w be any proposition. View it as a truth function; that is, a function from $\{0,1\}^n$ to $\{0,1\}$ for some n. Show by induction on the number of occurrences of connectives in w that for any truth assignment i, $i \vDash w$ iff $w(i) = 1$.

32. Let w be any proposition. For any interpretation i, show by induction on the number of occurrences of connectives in w, that $i \vDash w$ iff $i \in \mathbb{M}(w)$. (See Remark 1.2.)

33. For any truth assignment i, let $\mathscr{M}_i = \{p : i(p) = 1\} \cup \{\neg p : i(p) = 0\}$. Show that corresponding to each interpretation i of a proposition w, the set $\mathscr{M}_i$ is unique.

34. In continuation of the previous problem, let A_w be the set of all propositional variables occurring in w, and let M be any subset of $A_w \cup \{\neg p : p \in A_w\}$ such that for each $p \in A_w$, either $p \in M$ or $\neg p \in M$. Show that there is a unique interpretation i of w such that $M = \mathscr{M}_i$.

35. Define an interpretation of any proposition w starting from a truth assignment given as a subset of the set of propositional variables occurring in w and then define valid and satisfiable propositions.

36. The semantics of PL can be defined in another way via the satisfaction relation $\vDash$. Let p stand for any propositional variable, and x, y for any proposition(s). An interpretation is a symbol i that satisfies the following properties:

    Either $i \vDash p$ or $i \nvDash p$.
    $i \vDash \top$.
    $i \nvDash \bot$.
    $i \vDash (x \wedge y)$ iff both $i \vDash x$ and $i \vDash y$ hold.
    $i \vDash (x \vee y)$ iff at least one of $i \vDash x$ or $i \vDash y$ holds.
    $i \vDash (x \to y)$ iff at least one of $i \nvDash x$ or $i \vDash y$ holds.
    $i \vDash (x \leftrightarrow y)$ iff both $i \vDash x$ and $i \vDash y$ hold, or both $i \nvDash x$ and $i \nvDash y$ hold.

    Show that this definition is equivalent to one we have adopted.
37. Instead of using truth tables, an arithmetic procedure can be used. The basis for this is the following representation of the connectives: $\neg w$ is represented as $1+w$, $u \wedge v$ as $u+v+uv$, $u \vee v$ as uv, $u \to v$ as $(1+u)v$ and $u \leftrightarrow v$ as $u+v$. The constants $\top$ and $\bot$ are taken as 0 and 1, respectively. In this representation, each propositional variable is treated as a variable over the set $\{0,1\}$. The arithmetic operations of addition and multiplication are taken as usual with one exception, that is, $1+1=0$. Thus tautologies are those propositions which are identically 0 and contradictions become identically equal to 1. See that in this algebra, you have $2x=0$ and $x^2=x$. Justify the procedure. [This is the starting point for boolean algebra.]
38. See Problem 37. Give another arithmetic representation of the connectives where $\top$ is represented as 1 and $\bot$ as 0.
39. Let w be a proposition having the only connective as $\leftrightarrow$; and having no occurrence of $\top$ or $\bot$. Show that $\vDash w$ iff each propositional variable occurring in w occurs an even number of times. What happens if $\top$ or $\bot$ occurs in w?
40. An advertisement on a sports magazine reads: "If I am not playing cricket, then I am watching it; if I am not watching it, then I am talking about it." If the speaker does not do more than one of these activities at a time, then what is he doing?
41. Assume that any politician is either honest or dishonest. An honest politician, by definition, always tells the truth, and a dishonest politician always lies. In a campaign rally, politician A declares "I am honest iff my opponent is honest". Let p be "A is honest", and q be "The opponent of A is honest".
    (a) Explain why $p \leftrightarrow (p \leftrightarrow q)$ holds.
    (b) Is A honest?
    (c) Is the opponent of A honest?
    (d) Later the opponent of A declares, "If I am honest, so is my opponent". What new propositions now become true?
    (e) Using the statements of both the politicians, answer (b) and (c).
42. Explain why you are trapped in the commercial for this book mentioned at the beginning of *Preface to First Edition*.
43. In Smullyan's island, there are two types of people: knights, who always tell the truth, and knaves, who always lie. We write A, B, C for three inhabitants of the island. Answer the following questions.

(a) Assume that if A is a knight, then B is a knight; and if C is a knave, then B is a knight. Is it true that if A is a knight or C is a knave, then B is a knight?

(b) Suppose that if A is a knave, then B is a knave; and if C is a knight, then B is a knave. Does it mean that if A is a knave and C is a knight, then B is a knave?

(c) You find A, B, C standing together. You asked A, "Are you a knight or a knave?" You could not hear the low voice of A. You asked B, "What did A say?" B replied, "A said that he was a knave." Then C said, "Do not believe B, he is lying." Then what are they, knights or knaves?

(d) While A, B, C are nearby, you asked A, "How many knights are among you?" Again you could not listen to A. You asked B, "What did A say?" B replied, "A said, there was only one knight among us." C said, "Do not believe B, he is lying." Then what are they, knights or knaves?

(e) A, B, C were the suspects for a crime. Each of them told he did not commit the crime. It is known that two of them told truth and the third one lied. Besides they told something else. A said "The victim was a friend of B, and an enemy of C." B said, "I did not know the victim; and I was out of town throughout the day." C said, "I saw A and B with the victim in the town that day; one of them must have done it." Who committed the crime?

44. In *Merchant of Venice*, Portia takes three caskets: gold, silver, and lead. Inside one of the caskets, she puts her portrait, and on each of the locked caskets, she writes an inscription. She explains to her suitors that each inscription could be either true or false. But on the basis of the inscriptions, one has to choose the casket containing the portrait. We will have two variations of the puzzle here.

    (a) Suppose that Portia writes the inscriptions as
    Gold: The portrait is in here.
    Silver: The portrait is in here.
    Lead: At least two caskets bear false inscriptions.
    Which casket should the suitor choose? Find the answer by trying to see which of the facts such as the portrait is in the Gold, Silver, or Lead casket goes well with the situation.

    (b) This time Portia says that one has to choose a casket *not* containing the portrait, basing on the following inscriptions:
    Gold: The portrait is in here.
    Silver: The portrait is not in here.
    Lead: At most one casket bears a true inscription.
    Find an answer. Prove that your answer is correct.

45. Prove or give a counter example:

    (a) If $x \wedge y$ is satisfiable, then x is satisfiable and y is satisfiable.
    (b) If $x \vee y$ is satisfiable, then x is satisfiable or y is satisfiable.
    (c) If $x \to y$ is valid and x is valid, then y is valid.
    (d) If $x \to y$ is satisfiable, and x is satisfiable, then y is satisfiable.
    (e) If $x \wedge y$ is valid, and x is satisfiable then y is satisfiable.

(f) If $\vDash x$, then x must have at least two atomic propositions.
(g) If $\vDash x$, and x has an occurrence of a propositional variable, then x has at least two occurrences of a propositional variable.
(h) If x is a contradiction, then the main connective of x must be $\neg$ or $\wedge$.

46. Give models for each of the following sets of propositions:
   (a) $\{p_i \vee p_{i+1}, \neg(p_i \wedge p_{i+1}) : i \in \mathbb{N}\}$
   (b) $\{(p_i \vee p_{i+1}), (p_i \to \neg(p_{i+1} \wedge p_{i+2})), (p_i \leftrightarrow p_{i+3}) : i \in \mathbb{N}\}$
   (c) $\{\neg p_1, p_2\} \cup \{(p_i \wedge p_j \leftrightarrow p_{i.j}) : 1 < i, j\}$
47. Let w be any proposition that uses the connectives $\wedge$ and $\vee$ only. Let i and j be two interpretations such that for each propositional variable p, we have "if $i(p) = 1$, then $j(p) = 1$." Show that if $i(w) = 1$, then $j(w) = 1$. Is it true that if $j(w) = 1$, then $i(w) = 1$?
48. Show that on the set of all propositions, $\equiv$ is an equivalence relation.
49. An equivalence relation on a set decomposes the set into equivalence classes. What are the equivalence classes of $\equiv$ on the set of all propositions built up from two propositional variables p and q?
50. *Transitivity*: Let Σ and Γ be sets of propositions, and let w be a proposition. Let $\Sigma \vDash x$ for each $x \in \Gamma$. Show that if $\Gamma \vDash w$, then $\Sigma \vDash w$.
51. Show that a set Σ of propositions is satisfiable iff there exists no contradiction C such that $\Sigma \vDash C$ iff $\Sigma \nvDash \bot$.
52. Let Σ be a set of propositions, and let p, q be propositions. Prove or refute the following:
   (a) If $\Sigma \vDash p \vee q$, then $\Sigma \vDash p$ or $\Sigma \vDash q$.
   (b) If $\Sigma \vDash p$ or $\Sigma \vDash q$, then $\Sigma \vDash p \vee q$.
53. For each $i \in \mathbb{N}$, let x_i be a proposition; and let $\Sigma = \{x_i \to x_{i+1} : i \in \mathbb{N}\}$. Show that $\Sigma \vDash x_0 \to x_n$ for each $n \in \mathbb{N}$.
54. Let A be a proposition built from propositional variables $p_1, \ldots, p_n$, and $\leftrightarrow$, but nothing else. Show the following:
   (a) If p_k occurs in A, then an interpretation i satisfies A iff $i(p_k) = 0$ for an even number of ks.
   (b) If A is not equivalent to $\top$, then A is equivalent to some proposition B, where if p_k occurs at all, then p_k occurs an odd number of times.
   (c) There exists a proposition B equivalent to A where any p_k occurs at most once.
55. Let Σ be an unsatisfiable set of propositions. Give examples of Σ meeting the following condition:
   (a) Each set $\{x\}$ is satisfiable for $x \in \Sigma$.
   (b) Each set $\{x, y\}$ is satisfiable for $x, y \in \Sigma$, $x \neq y$.
   (c) Each set $\{x, y, z\}$ is satisfiable for $x, y, z \in \Sigma$ and $x \neq y$, $y \neq z$, $z \neq x$.
56. Give a proof of Deduction Theorem by using RA.
57. Give a proof of RA by using Deduction Theorem. [Hint: $\neg w \equiv (w \to \bot)$.]
58. Let Σ and Γ be sets of propositions, and let w be a proposition. Show that if $\Sigma \cup \{w\}$ and $\Gamma \cup \{\neg w\}$ are unsatisfiable, then $\Sigma \cup \Gamma$ is unsatisfiable.

59. Let Σ be a set of propositions, and let w be a proposition. Prove or refute the following:
    (a) $\Sigma \cup \{w\}$ is satisfiable or $\Sigma \cup \{\neg w\}$ is satisfiable.
    (b) $\Sigma \cup \{w\}$ is unsatisfiable or $\Sigma \cup \{\neg w\}$ is unsatisfiable.
    (c) if $\Sigma \cup \{w\}$ and $\Sigma \cup \{\neg w\}$ are unsatisfiable, then Σ is unsatisfiable.
60. A set of propositions Σ_1 is called *equivalent to* a set of propositions Σ_2 iff for each proposition x, $\Sigma_1 \vDash x$ iff $\Sigma_2 \vDash x$. A set of propositions Σ is called *independent* iff for each $x \in \Sigma$, $\Sigma \setminus \{x\} \nvDash x$. Prove or refute the following:
    (a) Each finite set of propositions has an independent subset equivalent to the set.
    (b) An infinite set of propositions need not have an independent subset equivalent to the set.
    (c) Corresponding to each set of propositions Σ, there exists an independent set equivalent to Σ.

Chapter 2

A Propositional Calculus

2.1 AXIOMATIC SYSTEM PC

We give meaning to the connective $\wedge$ by saying that the proposition $p \wedge q$ is assigned to 1 when both p, q are assigned to 1. Here, we assume that we know the meaning of *both* p, q *are assigned to* 1. Look at the italicized phrase. It presupposes the meaning of *and*. To understand *and* we have created the symbol $\wedge$, and then we are interpreting $\wedge$ as *and*!

Of course, we may use the alternate definition, where $i(x \wedge y) = \min\{i(x), i(y)\}$. It involves the implicit meaning of *taking minimum*. That looks better. But it assumes that $\min\{1,1\} = 1$, $\min\{0,1\} = 0$, $\min\{1,0\} = 0$, and $\min\{0,0\} = 0$. It is same thing as the truth table for $\wedge$. In the truth table for $\wedge$, consider a row, where p is assigned 1 and q is assigned 1. Here, we say $p \wedge q$ is assigned 1, when *both* p, q *are assigned* 1. We are again back to where we have started.

In general, we wish to introduce and model the process of reasoning; and our way of doing it involves reasoning itself. How can we meaningfully analyse logical patterns when the analysis itself uses some such pattern as a method? For instance, look at the proof of Theorem 1.8. We use some sort of reasoning in the proof. How can one accept the proof if he doubts (does not know) the reasoning process itself? Is it not circular to use reasoning to explain reasoning?

The basic questions are the following. How can we analyse truth and falsity by using the notion of truth and falsity? How can we analyse meaningfully the logical patterns using the same logical patterns?

A solution was proposed by D. Hilbert. Imagine, the language PL as a language of some computer. Suppose that executing a computer program one may determine whether the symbols are joined together in a permissible way. In fact, such a program is the grammar of PL. Again, in which way these constructs of PL give rise to correct logical arguments is also governed by some computer program. To talk about these programs and to determine whether a program does its job correctly or not, we need another language. The mathematical English serves as the *metalanguage* for PL. We assume that we know the meanings of the words 'not' and 'and', etc. in this metalanguage. This hierarchy of languages prevents circularity.

However, it raises another question: why does one need to create such a computer language if we already know the meanings of the connectives? It looks that the meanings of connectives are carried over to the language of PL from the metalanguage. Moreover, these meanings presuppose our knowledge of what is *true* and what is *false*. Can we have an alternative for truth and falsity? Can we have a mechanical process instead of the assumed validity or truth? In this chapter, our goal is to demonstrate that the notion of validity which involves meaning or which presupposes the knowledge of truth and falsity can be replaced by a completely mechanical process called *provability*.

A proof starts with some well known facts and proceeds towards the result using the allowed inferences. The accepted facts are called *axioms*. The allowed inferences are called the *rules of inference*, which link one or more propositions to another. A *proof* is then a sketch of how we reach the final proposition from the axioms by means of the inference rules. Notice that anything which is proved this way has nothing to do with *truth* or *falsity*. The trick is to select the axioms and inference rules in such a way that validity and provability may be on par.

To keep the matter simple, we plan to work with a subset of connectives. We choose the subset $\{\neg, \to\}$. We may introduce other connectives by way of definitions later. We thus choose our language for *propositional calculus* (PC, for short) as the fragment of PROP having all propositional variables and the connectives $\neg$ and $\to$. In PC, right now, we do not have the propositional constants $\top$ and $\bot$; and we do not have the connectives $\wedge, \vee$ and $\leftrightarrow$. Again, we use the grammar of PROP appropriate for this fragment. We also use the precedence rules to abbreviate our PC-propositions with usual conventions of omitting brackets and subscripts in the propositional variables. Moreover, we use capital letters $A, B, C, \ldots$ as generic symbols for propositions.

The **axiom schemes** of PC are:

(A1) $A \to (B \to A)$

(A2) $(A \to (B \to C)) \to ((A \to B) \to (A \to C))$

(A3) $(\neg A \to \neg B) \to ((\neg A \to B) \to A)$

An **axiom** is any instance of an axiom scheme, obtained by replacing throughout the letters A, B, C by propositions. For example, $p \to (q \to p)$ is an axiom as it is obtained from A1 by replacing A by p and B by q throughout. We thus refer to $p \to (q \to p)$ as A1. Similarly, $(p \to q) \to ((q \to p) \to (p \to q))$ is also A1.

In addition to the axioms, PC has a **rule of inference**; it is as follows:

(MP) $$\frac{A \qquad A \to B}{B}$$

The inference rule MP is an incarnation of the valid consequence Modus Ponens: $\{A, A \to B\} \vDash B$. Since in an axiomatic system there is no truth or falsity, we simply write the consequence as a fraction. You may read the rule MP as

From A and $A \to B$, derive B.

This is again a rule scheme in the sense that any instance of this scheme is a rule. That is, if you have already (derived) the propositions p and $p \to q$, then the rule allows you to derive q. Deriving $q \to r$ from $p \to q$ and $(p \to q) \to (q \to r)$ is an application of the rule MP. Informally, the word 'derive' signals deductions; formally, it just allows to write the propositions one after another.

The axiomatic system **PC** has all the propositions having the only connectives as $\neg$ and $\to$. PC has axiom schemes A1, A2, A3, and the inference rule MP. A **proof in PC** is defined to be a finite sequence of propositions, where each one is either an axiom or is obtained (derived) from earlier two propositions by an application of MP. The last proposition of a proof is called a **theorem of PC**; the proof is said to prove the theorem. The fact that "A is a theorem in PC" is written as $\vdash_{PC} A$. We also read $\vdash_{PC} A$ as "A is **provable** in PC". If no other axiomatic system is in sight, we may abbreviate $\vdash_{PC}$ to $\vdash$ without the subscript PC. In that case, the phrases 'proof in PC', 'PC-proof', and 'proof' mean the same thing.

The symbol $\vdash$ will have the least precedence. For example, $\vdash p \to p$ is a shorthand for writing $\vdash (p \to p)$; and $\vdash \neg p \to (p \to q)$ abbreviates $\vdash (\neg p \to (p \to q))$.

EXAMPLE 2.1. The following is a proof of $\vdash_{PC} r \to (p \to (q \to p))$.

1.	$(p \to (q \to p)) \to (r \to (p \to (q \to p)))$	A1, $A := p \to (q \to p), B := r$
2.	$p \to (q \to p)$	A1, $A := p, B := q$
3.	$r \to (p \to (q \to p))$	1, 2, MP

The documentation on the right says why the propositions in lines 1 and 2 are axioms, instances of A1. The proposition on the third line is derived from the propositions in lines 1 and 2 by an application of the inference rule MP. In this application of MP, we have taken

$$A = p \to (q \to p), \quad B = (r \to (p \to (q \to p))).$$

The line numbers on the first column help us in book keeping. The third column shows why a particular proposition is entered in that line. The actual proof is in the middle column.

EXAMPLE 2.2. Show that $\vdash p \to p$.

It is a ridiculously simple theorem to be proved; but which axiom do we start with, A1, A2, or A3?

A1 is $A \to (B \to A)$. We have $p \to (p \to p)$, as one of its instances. If somehow we are able to eliminate the first p, then we are through. The only way of elimination is the inference rule MP. It would require p so that from p and $p \to (p \to p)$ we will arrive at $p \to p$. But it seems we cannot derive p.

An instance of A2 looks like: $(p \to (q \to r)) \to ((p \to q) \to (p \to r))$. If we plan to apply MP, we may derive $p \to r$, provided we have already the propositions: $p \to (q \to r)$ and $p \to q$. But towards reaching $p \to p$, we have to take r as p. Thus, we must have the two propositions (replace r by p): $p \to (q \to p)$ and $p \to q$. Now, the first of these propositions, i.e., $p \to (q \to p)$ is simply A1. Some progress has been made.

At this stage, we plan to have A2 as $(p \to (q \to p)) \to ((p \to q) \to (p \to p))$, A1 as $p \to (q \to p)$, and apply MP to get $(p \to q) \to (p \to p)$. Fine, but then how to eliminate $p \to q$? We have again A1 as $p \to (q \to p)$. Thus, instead of q if we had

$p \to q$, then we would have been through. Well, then replace q by $p \to q$ throughout. That is, we would start with A2, where we replace r by p and q by $p \to q$, and start all over again.

We take A2 as $(p \to ((q \to p) \to p)) \to ((p \to (q \to p)) \to (p \to p))$, A1 as $p \to ((q \to p) \to p)$, and conclude by MP that $(p \to (q \to p)) \to (p \to p)$. Next, we use A1 as $p \to (q \to p)$ and apply MP to conclude $p \to p$. Find appropriate replacements in the proof given below.

1.	$p \to ((q \to p) \to p)$	A1
2.	$(p \to ((q \to p) \to p)) \to ((p \to (q \to p)) \to (p \to p))$	A2
3.	$(p \to (q \to p)) \to (p \to p)$	1, 2, MP
4.	$p \to (q \to p)$	A1
5.	$p \to p$	3, 4, MP

Can you construct a proof of $\vdash p \to p$ without using q?

In an axiomatic system such as PC, the notion of a proof is *effective*, i.e., if it is claimed that some object is a proof of a theorem, then it can be checked whether the claim is correct or not in an algorithmic manner. However, construction of a proof may not be effective; there may or may not be an algorithm to construct a proof of a given theorem.

Of course, proofs can be generated mechanically by following the specified rules. The problem comes when a proof is targeted towards proving a given theorem. We will see by way of examples how to do it. We may have to rely on our intuition in constructing proofs.

EXAMPLE 2.3. Show that $\vdash q \to (p \to p)$.

Look at Examples 2.1 and 2.2. Do they suggest anything? In Example 2.2, we have proved $p \to p$. We will append an appropriate copy of Example 2.1 to that proof. Here it is:

1.	$p \to ((q \to p) \to p)$	
	$\vdots$	
5.	$p \to p$	Example 2.2
6.	$(p \to p) \to (q \to (p \to p))$	A1
7.	$q \to (p \to p)$	5, 6, MP

Just like axiom schemes and inference rules, theorems are *theorem schemes.* Once you have a proof of $p \to p$, you can have a proof of $(p \to q) \to (p \to q)$. It is simple; just replace p by $p \to q$ throughout the proof. Thus known theorems can be used in proving new theorems. We will mention 'Th' on the rightmost column of a proof, when we use an already proved theorem. The proof in Example 2.3 can be rewritten as

1.	$p \to p$	Th
2.	$(p \to p) \to (q \to (p \to p))$	A1
3.	$q \to (p \to p)$	1, 2, MP

EXAMPLE 2.4. Show that $\vdash (\neg q \to q) \to q$.

The following proof uses $\vdash p \to p$ as a theorem scheme.

1. $\neg q \to \neg q$ Th
2. $(\neg q \to \neg q) \to ((\neg q \to q) \to q)$ A3
3. $(\neg q \to q) \to q$ 1, 2, MP

We extend our definition of proofs and theorems to take care of consequences. If a proof uses premises as axioms, and derives the conclusion, then the consequence is proved.

Let Σ be a set of propositions, and let w be any proposition. A **proof of the consequence** $\Sigma \,!\!\vdash w$ **in PC** is defined to be a finite sequence of propositions where each proposition is either an axiom, a proposition in Σ, or is obtained from earlier two propositions by an application of MP; and the last proposition in the sequence is w. In the consequence $\Sigma \,!\!\vdash w$, each proposition from Σ is called a **premise**, and w is called the **conclusion**.

We write $\Sigma \vdash_{PC} w$ to say that there exists a proof of the consequence $\Sigma \,!\!\vdash w$ in PC. This fact is also expressed as "the consequence $\Sigma \,!\!\vdash w$ is provable in PC." Informally, a proof of $\Sigma \,!\!\vdash w$ is also called a *proof of* $\Sigma \vdash_{PC} w$. When $\Sigma = \{w_1, \ldots, w_n\}$, a finite set, we write $\Sigma \vdash_{PC} w$ as $w_1, \ldots, w_n \vdash_{PC} w$. As earlier we will write $\Sigma \vdash w$ if no confusion arises.

We observe that when $\Sigma = \varnothing$, $\Sigma \vdash w$ boils down to $\vdash w$. Moreover, it is not mandatory that a proof uses all axioms; similarly, a proof of a consequence need not use all given premises.

Proofs of consequences are written in three columns, like proofs of theorems. We mention the letter 'P' in the documentation to say that the proposition used in that line of the proof is a premise.

EXAMPLE 2.5. Construct a proof to show that $\neg p,\ p \vdash q$.

Look at A3. If we can have $\neg q \to \neg p$ and $\neg q \to p$, then with two applications of MP, we can conclude q. Again, due to A1 as $\neg p \to (\neg q \to \neg p)$, we can derive $\neg q \to \neg p$ from $\neg p$, as in Example 2.1. Similarly, from p, we can derive $\neg q \to p$.

Here is the proof:

1. p P
2. $p \to (\neg q \to p)$ A1
3. $\neg q \to p$ 1, 2, MP
4. $\neg p$ P
5. $\neg p \to (\neg q \to \neg p)$ A1
6. $\neg q \to \neg p$ 4, 5, MP
7. $(\neg q \to \neg p) \to ((\neg q \to p) \to q)$ A3
8. $(\neg q \to p) \to q$ 6, 7, MP
9. q 3, 8, MP

EXAMPLE 2.6. Show that $p \to q,\ q \to r \vdash p \to r$.

We can start from a premise, say, $p \to q$. To arrive at $p \to r$, we should have $(p \to q) \to (p \to r)$. A look at A2 says that this new proposition matches with its second part. The first part $p \to (q \to r)$ should have been derived. Well, this can be derived from the other premise $q \to r$ by using A1.

Here is the proof:

1.	$q \to r$	P
2.	$(q \to r) \to (p \to (q \to r))$	A1
3.	$p \to (q \to r)$	1, 2, MP
4.	$(p \to (q \to r)) \to ((p \to q) \to (p \to r))$	A2
5.	$(p \to q) \to (p \to r)$	3, 4, MP
6.	$p \to q$	P
7.	$p \to r$	6, 5, MP

Theorems can be used as *new axioms*. The same way, already derived consequences can be used as new inferences rules. The reason: proof of such a consequence can be duplicated with necessary replacements. Such new inference rules are referred to as **derived rules** of inference.

The consequence $\{p \to q, q \to r\} \vdash p \to r$ in Example 2.6 is rewritten as the derived rule of Hypothetical Syllogism:

(HS) $$\frac{A \to B \qquad B \to C}{A \to C}$$

EXAMPLE 2.7. Show that $\neg q \to \neg p \vdash p \to q$.

We use the derived rule HS in the following proof.

1.	$\neg q \to \neg p$	P
2.	$(\neg q \to \neg p) \to ((\neg q \to p) \to q)$	A3
3.	$(\neg q \to p) \to q$	1, 2, MP
4.	$p \to (\neg q \to p)$	A1
5.	$p \to q$	4, 3, HS

EXAMPLE 2.8. Show that $\vdash \neg\neg p \to p$.

1.	$\neg\neg p \to (\neg p \to \neg\neg p)$	A1
2.	$(\neg p \to \neg\neg p) \to ((\neg p \to \neg p) \to p)$	A3
3.	$\neg\neg p \to ((\neg p \to \neg p) \to p)$	1, 2, HS
4.	$(\neg\neg p \to ((\neg p \to \neg p) \to p)) \to$ $((\neg\neg p \to (\neg p \to \neg p)) \to (\neg\neg p \to p))$	A3
5.	$(\neg\neg p \to (\neg p \to \neg p)) \to (\neg\neg p \to p)$	3, 4, MP
6.	$\neg p \to \neg p$	Th
7.	$(\neg p \to \neg p) \to (\neg\neg p \to (\neg p \to \neg p))$	A1
8.	$(\neg\neg p \to (\neg p \to \neg p))$	6, 7, MP
9.	$\neg\neg p \to p$	8, 5, MP

Exercises for § 2.1

Try to construct PC-proofs of the following consequences:

1. $p \to q,\ q \to r,\ p \vdash r$
2. $\neg q \to \neg p,\ p \vdash q$
3. $p \to q,\ \neg q \vdash \neg p$
4. $p \vdash \neg\neg p$
5. $\{p, \neg q\} \vdash \neg(p \to q)$
6. $\neg(p \to q) \vdash p$
7. $\neg(p \to q) \vdash \neg q$
8. $p \to (q \to r),\ q \vdash p \to r$
9. $\vdash (p \to q) \to (\neg q \to \neg p)$
10. $\vdash \neg q \to ((p \to q) \to \neg p)$

2.2 FOUR THEOREMS ABOUT PC

To prove "if x then y" we assume x and derive y. It is accepted in each branch of mathematics. Since we are questioning the process of reasoning itself, can we accept it in PC? We should rather prove this principle.

Theorem 2.1 (DT: Deduction Theorem). *Let Σ be a set of propositions, and let p, q be propositions. Then, $\Sigma \vdash p \to q$ iff $\Sigma \cup \{p\} \vdash q$.*

Proof. Suppose that $\Sigma \vdash p \to q$. To show $\Sigma \cup \{p\} \vdash q$, take the proof of $\Sigma \vdash p \to q$, adjoin to it the lines (propositions) p, q. It looks like:

1.	$\cdots$	
2.	$\cdots$	
	$\vdots$	
n.	$p \to q$	Proof of $\Sigma \vdash p \to q$
$n+1$.	p	P
$n+2$.	q	$n+1, n$, MP

This is a proof of $\Sigma \cup \{p\} \vdash q$.

Conversely, suppose that $\Sigma \cup \{p\} \vdash q$; we have a proof of it. We construct a proof of $\Sigma \vdash p \to q$ by induction on the number of propositions (number of lines) used in the proof of $\Sigma \cup \{p\} \vdash q$.

In the basis step, suppose that the proof of $\Sigma \cup \{p\} \vdash q$ has only one proposition. Then this proposition has to be q. Now, why is this a proof of $\Sigma \cup \{p\} \vdash q$? There are three possibilities:

(a) q is an axiom (b) $q \in \Sigma$ (c) $q = p$

In each case, we show how to get a proof of $\Sigma \vdash p \to q$.

(a) In this case, our proof is:

1.	q	An axiom
2.	$q \to (p \to q)$	A1
3.	$p \to q$	1, 2, MP

It is a proof of $\Sigma \vdash p \to q$ since it uses no proposition other than axioms.

(b) In this case the above proof still works, only the first line would be documented as 'P', a premise in Σ, rather than an axiom.

(c) Here, $q = p$. We just repeat the proof given in Example 2.2:

1.	$\cdots$	
	$\vdots$	
5.	$p \to p$	MP

For the induction step, lay out the induction hypothesis:

> If there exists a proof of $\Sigma \cup \{p\} \vdash q$ having less than n propositions in it (in the proof), then there exists a proof of $\Sigma \vdash p \to q$.

Suppose now that we have a proof P of $\Sigma \cup \{p\} \vdash q$ having n propositions in it. Observe that we have four cases to consider basing on what q is. They are

(i) q is an axiom (ii) $q \in \Sigma$ (iii) $q = p$
(iv) q has been derived by an application of MP in the proof P

We will construct a proof of $\Sigma \vdash p \to q$ in all the four cases. The cases (i)-(iii) are similar to the basis case. In the case (iv), the proof P looks like:

$$
\begin{array}{lll}
\text{P}: 1. & \cdots & \\
2 & \cdots & \\
 & \vdots & \\
m. & r & \\
 & \vdots & \\
m+k. & r \to q & \\
 & \vdots & \\
n. & q & m, m+k, \text{MP}
\end{array}
$$

where $m < n$, $m+k < n$, and r is some proposition. The proof segment

P1 : lines 1 through m proves $\Sigma \cup \{p\} \vdash r$
P2 : lines 1 through $m+k$ proves $\Sigma \cup \{p\} \vdash r \to q$

The proofs P1, P2 have less than n number of propositions. By induction hypothesis, corresponding to P1, P2, there exist proofs P3, P4 such that

P3 proves $\Sigma \vdash p \to r$
P2 proves $\Sigma \vdash p \to (r \to q)$

Suppose that P3 has i number of propositions and P4 has j number of propositions. We use the two proofs P3, P4 to construct a proof P5 of $\Sigma \vdash p \to q$. The proof P5 is constructed by adjoining P4 to P3, and then some more propositions:

$$
\begin{array}{lll}
\text{P5}: 1. & \cdots & \text{P3 begins} \\
 & \vdots & \\
i. & p \to r & \text{P3 ends} \\
i+1. & \cdots & \text{P4 begins} \\
 & \vdots & \\
i+j. & p \to (r \to q) & \text{P4 ends} \\
i+j+1. & (p \to (r \to q)) \to ((p \to r) \to (p \to q)) & \text{A2} \\
i+j+2. & (p \to r) \to (p \to q) & i+j, i+j+1, \text{MP} \\
i+j+3. & p \to q & i, i+j+2, \text{MP}
\end{array}
$$

Now, P5 is a proof of $\Sigma \vdash p \to q$ since the premises used in it are either axioms or propositions from Σ. ♦

We introduce a notion parallel to unsatisfiability. Let Σ be a set of propositions. We say that Σ is **inconsistent** iff there exists a proposition w such that $\Sigma \vdash w$ and $\Sigma \vdash \neg w$. That is, Σ is inconsistent iff there exists a proof, possibly using premises from Σ, where some proposition and its negation both occur. We say that Σ is **consistent** iff Σ is not inconsistent.

In case of consequences, each premise is also a conclusion since it has a one line proof, with the justification that it is a premise. Similarly, any conclusion that has been derived from a set of premises can still be derived if some more premises are added. This is monotonicity.

Theorem 2.2 (M: Monotonicity). *Let Σ and Γ be sets of propositions, $\Sigma \subseteq \Gamma$, and let w be a proposition.*

(1) *If $\Sigma \vdash w$, then $\Gamma \vdash w$.*

(2) *If Σ is inconsistent, then Γ is inconsistent.*

Proof. (1) Let $\Sigma \vdash w$. We then have a proof where some (or all) of the premises from Σ are used to have its last line as w. The same proof shows that $\Gamma \vdash w$.

(2) If Σ is inconsistent, then there exists a proposition p such that $\Sigma \vdash p$ and $\Sigma \vdash \neg p$. By (1), $\Gamma \vdash p$ and $\Gamma \vdash \neg p$. Therefore, Γ is inconsistent. ♦

Theorem 2.3 (RA: Reductio ad Absurdum). *Let Σ be a set of propositions, and let w be a proposition.*

(1) *$\Sigma \vdash w$ iff $\Sigma \cup \{\neg w\}$ is inconsistent.*

(2) *$\Sigma \vdash \neg w$ iff $\Sigma \cup \{w\}$ is inconsistent.*

Proof. (1) Suppose that $\Sigma \vdash w$. By monotonicity, $\Sigma \cup \{\neg w\} \vdash w$. With a one-line proof, $\Sigma \cup \{\neg w\} \vdash \neg w$. Therefore, $\Sigma \cup \{\neg w\}$ is inconsistent.

Conversely, suppose that $\Sigma \cup \{\neg w\}$ is inconsistent. Then there is a proposition, say p, such that $\Sigma \cup \{\neg w\} \vdash p$ and $\Sigma \cup \{\neg w\} \vdash \neg p$. By the deduction theorem, $\Sigma \vdash \neg w \to p$ and $\Sigma \vdash \neg w \to \neg p$. Suppose P1 is a proof of $\Sigma \vdash \neg w \to \neg p$ containing m propositions and P2 is a proof of $\Sigma \vdash \neg w \to p$ containing n propositions. Construct a proof P of $\Sigma \vdash w$ as follows:

P:		
1.	$\cdots$	P1 begins
	$\vdots$	
$m.$	$\neg w \to \neg p$	P1 ends
$m+1.$	$\cdots$	P2 begins
	$\vdots$	
$m+n.$	$\neg w \to p$	P2 ends
$m+n+1.$	$(\neg w \to \neg p) \to ((\neg w \to p) \to w)$	A3
$m+n+2.$	$(\neg w \to p) \to w$	$m, m+n+1$, MP
$m+n+3.$	w	$m+n, m+n+2$, MP

(2) If $\Sigma \vdash \neg w$, then by monotonicity, $\Sigma \cup \{w\} \vdash \neg w$. Also, $\Sigma \cup \{w\} \vdash w$, trivially. Hence, $\Sigma \cup \{w\}$ is inconsistent.

Conversely, suppose that $\Sigma \cup \{w\}$ is inconsistent. We show that $\Sigma \cup \{\neg\neg w\}$ is also inconsistent. Now, inconsistency of $\Sigma \cup \{w\}$ implies that there exists a proposition p such that $\Sigma \cup \{w\} \vdash p$ and $\Sigma \cup \{w\} \vdash \neg p$. So, there exist proofs P1 and P2 such that

P1 proves $\Sigma \cup \{w\} \vdash p$
P2 proves $\Sigma \cup \{w\} \vdash \neg p$

Observe that $\Sigma \cup \{\neg\neg w, \neg w\} \vdash \neg\neg w$ and $\Sigma \cup \{\neg\neg w, \neg w\} \vdash \neg w$. That is, $\Sigma \cup \{\neg\neg w, \neg w\}$ is inconsistent. By (1), we obtain $\Sigma \cup \{\neg\neg w\} \vdash w$. Then there exists a proof P3 such that

P3 proves $\Sigma \cup \{\neg\neg w\} \vdash w$

Now, construct a proof P4 by taking P3 followed by P1. Further, if w is actually used in P1, then it is mentioned as 'P' in it. In P4, mention it as 'Th'. It is justified, since in the P3 portion, w has been proved. The proof P4 is a proof of $\Sigma \cup \{\neg\neg w\} \vdash p$. If w is not used in P1, then as it is P4 is a proof of $\Sigma \cup \{\neg\neg w\} \vdash p$.

Similarly, construct the proof P5 by taking P3 followed by P2, and change the justification corresponding to the line $\neg w$ in the P2 portion to 'Th', if necessary. Now, P5 is a proof of $\Sigma \cup \{\neg\neg w\} \vdash \neg p$.

Therefore, $\Sigma \cup \{\neg\neg w\}$ is inconsistent. By (1), we conclude that $\Sigma \vdash \neg w$. ♦

Do you now see the rationale behind choosing the three axioms? The proof of DT uses A1 and A2 while that of RA uses A3 explicitly. Notice that DT, M, and RA are not theorems of PC; they speak something about PC, and as such, are called metatheorems for PC.

The next metatheorem for PC follows from the definition of a PC-proof.

Theorem 2.4 (Finiteness). *Let Σ be a set of propositions, and let w be a proposition. Then the following are true:*

(1) *If $\Sigma \vdash w$, then there exists a finite subset Γ of Σ such that $\Gamma \vdash w$.*

(2) *If Σ is inconsistent, then there exists a finite inconsistent subset of Σ.*

Proof. (1) Suppose $\Sigma \vdash w$. Then there exists a proof P with its last proposition as w. Let Γ be the set of all propositions from Σ that occur in P. Since P contains finitely many propositions, Γ is a finite subset of Σ. The same P is a proof of $\Gamma \vdash w$.

(2) Suppose that Σ is inconsistent. There exists a proposition w such that $\Sigma \vdash w$ and $\Sigma \vdash \neg w$. By (1), there exist finite subsets Γ_1, Γ_2 of Σ such that $\Gamma_1 \vdash w$ and $\Gamma_2 \vdash \neg w$. Take $\Gamma = \Gamma_1 \cup \Gamma_2$. Then Γ is a finite subset of Σ. By Monotonicity, $\Gamma \vdash w$ and $\Gamma \vdash \neg w$. That is, Γ is inconsistent. ♦

Inconsistency yields everything, and hence vacuousness.

Theorem 2.5 (Paradox of material Implication). *Let Σ be a set of propositions. Then, Σ is inconsistent iff $\Sigma \vdash x$ for each proposition x.*

Proof. If $\Sigma \vdash x$ for each proposition x, then $\Sigma \vdash p$ and also $\Sigma \vdash \neg p$ for some (each) propositional variable p. Thus Σ is inconsistent.

Conversely, if Σ is inconsistent, then by Monotonicity, $\Sigma \cup \{\neg x\}$ is inconsistent. By RA, $\Sigma \vdash x$. ♦

Logic is used to derive information about the real world from simple assumptions in a scientific model. According to Theorem 2.5, if our model is inconsistent, then it would lead to a situation where every sentence about the world relevant to the model can be derived. However, every such sentence cannot be true in the world. Thus there will be a mismatch between our formal method of derivation and the truth in the world. This will render our model useless.

Exercises for § 2.2

1. Assume that $\vdash \neg x \to (x \to y)$. Prove Deduction Theorem by using RAA.
2. Let Σ be a set of propositions. Show that Σ is consistent iff there is a proposition w such that $\Sigma \nvdash w$.
3. Construct a set of propositions Σ and propositions p, q to show that $\Sigma \nvdash p$, $\Sigma \nvdash q$ but $\Sigma \vdash p \vee q$.
4. *Transitivity*: Let Σ be a set of propositions, and let x, y be propositions. Show that if $\Sigma \vdash x$ and $x \vdash y$, then $\Sigma \vdash y$.
5. Let Σ and Γ be sets of propositions, and let w be a proposition. Let $\Sigma \vdash x$ for each $x \in \Gamma$. Show that if $\Sigma \cup \Gamma \vdash w$, then $\Sigma \vdash w$.
6. Let Σ be a set of propositions, and let x, y, z be propositions. Show that if $\Sigma \cup \{x\} \vdash z$ and $\Sigma \cup \{y\} \vdash z$, then $\Sigma \cup \{x \vee y\} \vdash z$.
7. Here is an application of deduction theorem:

   Let A be the sentence *There is no life on earth.*
   Let B be the sentence *If* B, *then* A.
   Assume B. Then we have B and $B \to A$.
   By Modus Ponens, we obtain A.
   Notice that by assuming A, we have obtained B.
   Therefore, by deduction theorem, $B \to A$ has been proved.
   Since B is simply $B \to A$, we have proved both B and $B \to A$.
   Again, by Modus Ponens, we get A.
   Therefore, *There is no life on earth.*

   In this proof of *There is no life on earth,* what is wrong?

2.3 USING THE METATHEOREMS

The metatheorems can be used for showing the existence of a proof rather than constructing an actual proof. As expected, it will ease our work. For example, in the proof of RA(2), you have already used RA(1) showing $\neg\neg p \vdash p$. This avoided using Example 2.8. As in PL, the deduction theorem is especially useful for propositions involving serial implications. See the following examples.

EXAMPLE 2.9. Show that $\Sigma \cup \{A\}$ is consistent iff $\Sigma \cup \{\neg\neg A\}$ is consistent.

In the proof of RA(2), we proved one part; now using RA, we prove both:

$$\Sigma \cup \{A\} \text{ is inconsistent iff } \Sigma \vdash \neg A \text{ iff } \Sigma \cup \{\neg\neg A\} \text{ is inconsistent.}$$

EXAMPLE 2.10. Show that $\vdash \neg\neg p \to p$ and $\vdash p \to \neg\neg p$.

Due to the deduction theorem and RA(1),

$$\vdash \neg\neg p \to p \text{ iff } \neg\neg p \vdash p \text{ iff } \{\neg\neg p, \neg p\} \text{ is inconsistent.}$$

The last one holds as $\{\neg\neg p, \neg p\} \vdash \neg p$ and $\{\neg\neg p, \neg p\} \vdash \neg\neg p$.

Similarly, by the deduction theorem and RA(2),

$$\vdash p \to \neg\neg p \text{ iff } p \vdash \neg\neg p \text{ iff } \{p, \neg p\} \text{ is inconsistent.}$$

Example 2.10 gives following theorems and the derived rules of *double negation:*

(DN) $\vdash A \to \neg\neg A$ $\quad \vdash \neg\neg A \to A$ $\quad \dfrac{\neg\neg A}{A}$ $\quad \dfrac{A}{\neg\neg A}$

EXAMPLE 2.11. $(\neg p \to q) \to ((q \to \neg p) \to p), (\neg p \to q) \to (q \to \neg p), \neg p \to q \vdash p$.

1.	$\neg p \to q$	P
2.	$(\neg p \to q) \to (q \to \neg p)$	P
3.	$q \to \neg p$	1, 2, MP
4.	$(\neg p \to q) \to ((q \to \neg p) \to p)$	P
5.	$(q \to \neg p) \to p$	1, 4, MP
6.	p	3, 5, MP

EXAMPLE 2.12. Show that $\vdash \neg q \to ((p \to q) \to \neg p)$.

By the deduction theorem and RA, we see that

$$\vdash \neg q \to ((p \to q) \to \neg p) \text{ iff } \neg q \vdash ((p \to q) \to \neg p) \text{ iff } \{\neg q, p \to q\} \vdash \neg p$$
$$\text{iff } \{\neg q, p \to q, p\} \text{ is inconsistent iff } \{p \to q, p\} \vdash q.$$

The last one is proved by an application of MP.

Example 2.12 brings up another familiar rule. We write it as the derived rule of Modus Tolens:

(MT) $\dfrac{\neg B \qquad A \to B}{\neg A}$

EXAMPLE 2.13. Show that $\vdash (p \to q) \to (\neg q \to \neg p)$.

By the deduction theorem,

$$\vdash (p \to q) \to (\neg q \to \neg p) \text{ iff } \{p \to q, \neg q\} \vdash \neg p.$$

An application of MT does the job.

Due to Examples 2.7 and 2.13, we have the following theorems and the derived rules of *contraposition*:

(CN) $\vdash (\neg B \to \neg A) \to (A \to B)$ $\quad \vdash (A \to B)(\neg B \to \neg A)$

(CN) $\dfrac{\neg B \to \neg A}{A \to B}$ $\quad \dfrac{A \to B}{\neg B \to \neg A}$

EXAMPLE 2.14. Show that $\vdash \neg p \to (p \to q)$.

By the deduction theorem, $\vdash \neg p \to (p \to q)$ iff $\{\neg p,\ p\} \vdash q$. Now, $\{\neg p,\ p\}$ is inconsistent. By monotonicity, $\{\neg p,\ p,\ \neg q\}$ is inconsistent. By RA, $\{\neg p,\ p\} \vdash q$. Below is another alternative proof of the theorem:

1.	$\neg p$	P
2.	$\neg p \to (\neg q \to \neg p)$	A1
3.	$\neg q \to \neg p$	1, 2, MP
4.	$p \to q$	3, CN

EXAMPLE 2.15. Show that $\vdash p \to (\neg q \to \neg(p \to q))$.

$\vdash p \to (\neg q \to \neg(p \to q))$ iff $\{p, \neg q\} \vdash \neg(p \to q)$ iff $\{p, \neg q, p \to q\}$ is inconsistent iff $\{p, p \to q\} \vdash q$, which is MP.

Notice that the deduction theorem on MP proves $\vdash p \to ((p \to q) \to q)$. We use this as a theorem in the following alternative proof of $p \vdash \neg q \to \neg(p \to q)$:

1. p	P
2. $p \to ((p \to q) \to q)$	Th (From MP)
3. $(p \to q) \to q$	1, 2, MP
4. $\neg q \to \neg(p \to q)$	3, CN

EXAMPLE 2.16. Show that $\vdash (\neg q \to q) \to q$.

$\vdash (\neg q \to q) \to q$ iff $\neg q \to q \vdash q$ iff $\{\neg q \to q, \neg q\}$ is inconsistent. Look at lines 1 and 3 in the following proof:

1. $\neg q$	P
2. $\neg q \to q$	P
3. q	1, 2, MP

Compare this proof with that in Example 2.4.

EXAMPLE 2.17. Show that $p \to q, \neg p \to q \vdash q$.

1. $p \to q$	P
2. $\neg q$	P
3. $\neg p$	1, 2, MT
4. $\neg p \to q$	P
5. q	3, 4, MP

The consequence in Example 2.17 is the familiar 'argument by cases'. Try constructing another proof using Examples 2.13 and 2.16 instead of MT.

To keep the axiomatic system simple, we have used only two connectives. The other connectives can be introduced with definitions. Remember that the definitions are, in fact, definition schemes. In the following, we use the symbol $\triangleq$ for the expression "equal to by definition".

(D1) $p \wedge q \triangleq \neg(p \to \neg q)$

(D2) $p \vee q \triangleq \neg p \to q$

(D3) $p \leftrightarrow q \triangleq \neg((p \to q) \to \neg(q \to p))$

(D4) $\top \triangleq p \to p$

(D5) $\bot \triangleq \neg(p \to p)$

We also require some inference rules to work with the definitions. They would provide us with ways of how to use the definitions. We have the two rules of definition, written as one, as follows:

(RD) $\dfrac{X \triangleq Y \qquad Z}{Z[X := Y]} \qquad \dfrac{X \triangleq Y \qquad Z}{Z[Y := X]}$

The notation $Z[Y := X]$ is the **uniform replacement** of Y by X in Z. The proposition $Z[Y := X]$ is obtained from the proposition Z by replacing each occurrence of the proposition Y by the proposition X. The rule RD says that if X and Y are equal by definition, then one can be replaced by the other wherever we wish. For instance, from $(p \vee q) \to r$ we can derive $(\neg p \to q) \to r$, and from $(\neg p \to q) \to r$, we may derive $(p \vee q) \to r$. In fact, given any consequence, we may apply this rule recursively replacing expressions involving connectives other than $\neg$ and $\to$ with the ones having only these two. Then the axiomatic system PC takes care of the consequence. Of course, the definitions and the rule RD do the job of eliminating as also introducing the other connectives.

EXAMPLE 2.18. (a) $\vdash p \wedge q \to p$ (b) $\vdash p \wedge q \to q$ (c) $\vdash (p \to (q \to (p \wedge q)))$

(a)	1.	$\neg p \to (p \to q)$	Th, Example 2.14
	2.	$\neg(p \to q) \to \neg\neg p$	1, CN
	3.	$\neg\neg p \to p$	DN
	4.	$\neg(p \to q) \to p$	2, 3, HS
	5.	$p \wedge q \to p$	4, RD

(b)	1.	$\neg q \to (p \to \neg q)$	A1
	2.	$\neg(p \to \neg q) \to \neg\neg q$	1, CN
	3.	$\neg\neg q \to q$	DN
	4.	$\neg(p \to \neg q) \to q$	2, 3, HS
	5.	$p \wedge q \to q$	4, RD

(c)	1.	p	P
	2.	q	P
	3.	$p \to \neg q$	P
	4.	$\neg q$	1, 3, MP

Thus $\{p, q, p \to \neg q\}$ is inconsistent. By RA, $p, q \vdash \neg(p \to \neg q)$. Due to D1 and RD, $p, q \vdash (p \wedge q)$. By DT, $\vdash (p \to (q \to (p \wedge q)))$.

EXAMPLE 2.19. Show that $\vdash (p \to q) \to ((p \vee r) \to (q \vee r))$.

1.	$p \to q$	P
2.	$\neg q$	P
3.	$\neg p$	1, 2, MT
4.	$\neg p \to r$	P
5.	r	MP

Hence $p \to q, \neg p \to r, \neg q \vdash r$. By DT, $\vdash (p \to q) \to ((\neg p \to r) \to (\neg q \to r))$. By D1 and RD, we conclude that $\vdash (p \to q) \to ((p \vee r) \to (q \vee r))$.

EXAMPLE 2.20. (a) $\vdash p \to (p \vee q)$ (b) $\vdash q \to (p \vee q)$

(a)	1.	$p \to \neg\neg p$	DN
	2.	$\neg\neg p \to (\neg p \to q)$	Th
	3.	$p \to (\neg p \to q)$	1, 2, HS
	4.	$p \to (p \vee q)$	3, RD

(b) 1. $q \to (\neg p \to q)$ A1
2. $q \to (p \vee q)$ 1, RD

EXAMPLE 2.21. $p \to r,\ q \to r \vdash p \vee q \to r$.

1. $p \to r$ P
2. $q \to r$ P
3. $p \vee q$ P
4. $\neg r$ P
5. $\neg r \to \neg p$ 1, CN
6. $\neg p$ 4, 5, MP
7. $\neg p \to q$ 3, RD
8. q 6, 7, MP
9. r 8, 2, MP

Lines 4 and 9 show that $\{p \to r,\ q \to r,\ p \vee q,\ \neg r\}$ is inconsistent. By RA and DT it follows that $p \to r,\ q \to r \vdash p \vee q \to r$.

EXAMPLE 2.22. Show that $\vdash \neg(p \wedge q) \to (\neg p \vee \neg q)$.

1. $\neg(p \wedge q)$ P
2. $\neg\neg(p \to \neg q)$ RD
3. $p \to \neg q$ DN
4. $\neg\neg p \to p$ DN
5. $\neg\neg p \to \neg q$ 4, 3, HS
6. $\neg p \vee \neg q$ RD

Thus $\neg(p \wedge q) \vdash (\neg p \vee \neg q)$. An application of DT completes the proof.

EXAMPLE 2.23. Prove: Σ is inconsistent iff $\Sigma \vdash \bot$, for any set of propositions Σ.

Let Σ be inconsistent. Then $\Sigma \vdash p$ and $\Sigma \vdash \neg p$ for some proposition p. Now, construct a proof by adjoining the proofs of $\Sigma \vdash p$, of $\Sigma \vdash \neg p$, and of $\{p, \neg p\} \vdash \neg(p \to p)$ (See Example 2.5.), in that order. Next, use D5 with RD to derive $\bot$.

Conversely, suppose $\Sigma \vdash \bot$. By D5 and RD, $\Sigma \vdash \neg(p \to p)$. Adjoin to its proof the proof $\vdash p \to p$. The new proof proves both $p \to p$ and $\neg(p \to p)$. Thus, Σ is inconsistent.

The result of Example 2.23 can be summarized as a derived inference rule, called the rule of *Inconsistency*.

(IC): $$\frac{A \qquad \neg A}{\bot}$$

Then the second part of Monotonicity can be restated as

If $\Sigma \subseteq \Gamma$ and $\Sigma \vdash \bot$, then $\Gamma \vdash \bot$.

And, RA can be restated as follows:

(1) $\Sigma \vdash w$ iff $\Sigma \cup \{\neg w\} \vdash \bot$.
(2) $\Sigma \vdash \neg w$ iff $\Sigma \cup \{w\} \vdash \bot$.

Sometimes using $\Sigma \vdash \bot$ instead of writing "Σ is inconsistent" improves elegance. For instance, in the proof of Example 2.18, instead of asking you to look at the lines 2 and 4, I could have added the fifth line having $\bot$ in it; giving justification as "2,4,IC".

EXAMPLE 2.24. Let Σ be a set of propositions, and let p, q be propositions. Show that $\Sigma \vdash \neg(p \to q)$ iff $\Sigma \vdash p$ and $\Sigma \vdash \neg q$.

We show that (a) $\neg(p \to q) \vdash p$, (b) $\neg(p \to q) \vdash \neg q$, (c) $p, \neg q \vdash \neg(p \to q)$.

(a) By RA and DT, $\neg(p \to q) \vdash p$ iff $\{\neg(p \to q), \neg p\} \vdash \bot$ iff $\neg p \vdash p \to q$ iff $\{\neg p, p\} \vdash q$, which holds due to the paradox of material implication.

(b) Similarly, $\neg(p \to q) \vdash \neg q$ iff $\{\neg(p \to q), q\} \vdash \bot$ iff $q \vdash p \to q$ iff $\{q, p\} \vdash q$, which holds.

(c) Again, by DT and RA, $p, \neg q \vdash \neg(p \to q)$ iff $\{p, \neg q, p \to q\} \vdash \bot$, which holds since $p, p \to q \vdash q$ by MP.

Now if $\Sigma \vdash \neg(p \to q)$, then using (a) and (b), we have $\Sigma \vdash p$ and $\Sigma \vdash q$. Similarly, using (c), we conclude that if $\Sigma \vdash p$ and $\Sigma \vdash q$, then $\Sigma \vdash \neg(p \to \neg q)$.

Exercises for § 2.3

1. Show the following.

   (a) $\vdash p \to \neg\neg p$ (b) $\vdash (p \to q) \to (\neg q \to \neg p)$
   (c) $\vdash (p \vee q) \to (p \to q) \to q$ (d) $\vdash ((p \to q) \to q) \to (p \vee q)$
   (e) $\vdash (p \to \neg q) \to (q \to \neg p)$ (f) $\vdash (\neg p \to q) \to (\neg q \to p)$
   (g) $\vdash (p \to \neg q) \to ((p \to q) \to \neg p)$ (h) $\vdash (q \to \neg p) \to ((p \to q) \to \neg p)$
   (i) $\vdash (p \to r) \to ((q \to r) \to (p \vee q \to r))$
   (j) $\vdash (p \to q) \to ((p \to r) \to (p \to q \wedge r))$

2. For each $i \in \mathbb{N}$, let x_i be a proposition; and let $\Sigma = \{x_i \to x_{i+1} : i \in \mathbb{N}\}$. Show that $\Sigma \vdash x_0 \to x_n$ for each $n \in \mathbb{N}$.

2.4 ADEQUACY OF PC TO PL

We must see that the syntactic notion of proof matches with the semantic notion of validity. This is called the *adequacy* of PC to PL. Similarly, we would like to see that provability of consequences matches with the validity of consequences. This is called the *Strong adequacy* of PC to PL.

The matching is two way: each valid consequence has a proof and each provable consequence is valid. The former property is called the *strong completeness* of PC and the latter property is called the *strong soundness* of PC with respect to PL. The adjective *strong* is used to say that the property holds for consequences and not only for theorems.

Observe that strong soundness of PC implies its soundness; strong completeness implies completeness; and strong adequacy implies adequacy. We thus prove strong soundness and strong completeness.

Notice that the axioms and the rules of inference of PC uses only $\neg$ and $\to$. The other connectives are introduced to PC by way of definitions. For convenience, we will restrict PL to the fragment of PROP where we do not have the symbols $\top, \bot, \wedge, \vee$, and $\leftrightarrow$. Later, you will be able to see that strong adequacy holds for the full PL as well.

Theorem 2.6 (Strong Soundness of PC to PL). *Let Σ be a set of propositions, and let w be a proposition.*

(1) *If $\Sigma \vdash w$ in PC, then $\Sigma \vDash w$.*

(2) *If Σ is satisfiable, then Σ is PC-consistent.*

Proof. (1) We apply induction on the lengths of proofs. In the basis step, if a proof of $\Sigma \vdash w$ has only one proposition, then it must be w. Now, w is either an axiom or a premise in Σ. Since the axioms are valid propositions (Check it.), $\Sigma \vDash w$.

Lay out the induction hypothesis that for every proposition v, if $\Sigma \vdash v$ has a proof of less than m propositions, then $\Sigma \vDash v$. Let P be a proof of $\Sigma \vdash w$ having m propositions. If w is again an axiom or a premise in Σ, then clearly $\Sigma \vDash w$ holds. Otherwise,

w has been obtained in P by an application of MP.

Then, there are propositions v and $v \rightarrow w$ occurring earlier to w in P. By the induction hypothesis, $\Sigma \vDash v$ and $\Sigma \vDash v \rightarrow w$. Since $\{v, v \rightarrow w\} \vDash w$, $\Sigma \vDash w$.

(2) Let Σ be inconsistent, then $\Sigma \vdash u$ and $\Sigma \vdash \neg u$ for some proposition u. By (1), $\Sigma \vDash u$ and $\Sigma \vDash \neg u$. Hence, any model of Σ is a model of both u and $\neg u$. This is impossible since the same interpretation cannot be a model of both u and $\neg u$. Therefore, Σ does not have a model; Σ is unsatisfiable. ♦

Notice that when $\Sigma = \varnothing$, soundness implies that the axioms taken together form a consistent set.

Similar to strong soundness, we can formulate strong completeness in two ways: by connecting validity and provability, or by connecting satisfiability and consistency. Let us try the second alternative:

Every consistent set is satisfiable.

For a consistent set Σ and a propositional variable p, if it so happens that $\Sigma \vdash p$, then clearly $\Sigma \nvdash \neg p$. Therefore, while constructing a model of Σ, we may safely assign p to 1. Similarly, for a propositional variable q, if $\Sigma \vdash \neg q$, then we assign q to 0 in our intended model. Difficulty arises when for a propositional variable r, neither $\Sigma \vdash r$ nor $\Sigma \vdash \neg r$ happens. In this case, both $\Sigma \cup \{r\}$ and $\Sigma \cup \{\neg r\}$ are consistent. We may consider one of them and continue to build our model.

In the following, we use this heuristic in a formal way. In fact, instead of considering only propositional variables, p, q, r etc, we consider all propositions directly. Moreover, we use the notion of maximal consistency. A set of propositions is called a **maximally consistent** set iff it is consistent and each proper superset of it is inconsistent.

The set of all propositions (now, without $\vee, \wedge, \leftrightarrow, \top, \bot$) is countable. Suppose the following is an enumeration of it:

$$w_0, w_1, w_2, \ldots, w_n, \ldots$$

Let Σ be a consistent set of propositions. Define a sequence of sets of propositions Σ_m inductively by

$$\Sigma_0 = \Sigma; \quad \Sigma_{n+1} = \begin{cases} \Sigma_n & \text{if } \Sigma_n \cup \{w_n\} \text{ is inconsistent} \\ \Sigma_n \cup \{w_n\} & \text{if } \Sigma_n \cup \{w_n\} \text{ is consistent} \end{cases}$$

We see that each Σ_i is consistent and that if $i < j$, then $\Sigma_i \subseteq \Sigma_j$. Next, take

$$\Sigma' = \cup_{m \in \mathbb{N}} \Sigma_m = \Sigma_0 \cup \Sigma_1 \cup \Sigma_2 \cup \cdots .$$

The following lemma lists some interesting properties of Σ'.

Lemma 2.1. *Let Σ be a consistent set of propositions. Let Σ' be the set as constructed earlier; and let p, q be propositions.*

(1) *If $\Sigma' \vdash p$, then there exists $m \in \mathbb{N}$ such that $\Sigma_m \vdash p$.*
(2) *Σ' is consistent.*
(3) *Σ' is maximally consistent.*
(4) *$q \in \Sigma'$ iff $\Sigma' \vdash q$.*
(5) *Either $q \in \Sigma'$ or $\neg q \in \Sigma'$.*
(6) *If $q \in \Sigma'$, then $p \to q \in \Sigma'$.*
(7) *If $p \notin \Sigma'$, then $p \to q \in \Sigma'$.*
(8) *If $p \in \Sigma'$ and $q \notin \Sigma'$, then $p \to q \notin \Sigma'$.*

Proof. (1) Suppose $\Sigma' \vdash p$. By finiteness (Theorem 2.4), there exists a finite subset Γ of Σ' such that $\Gamma \vdash p$. If Γ has ℓ number of propositions, then we may write $\Gamma = \{w_{i_1}, \ldots, w_{i_k}\}$, where $i_1 < i_2 < \cdots < i_\ell$. Observe that $\Sigma_{i_1} \subseteq \Sigma_{i_2} \subseteq \cdots$. Hence

$$w_{i_1} \in \Sigma_{i_1};\ w_{i_1}, w_{i_2} \in \Sigma_{i_2};\ \ldots\ ;\ w_{i_1}, \ldots, w_{i_\ell} \in \Sigma_{i_\ell}.$$

Write $i_\ell = m$. Then $\Gamma \subseteq \Sigma_m$. By monotonicity it follows that $\Sigma_m \vdash p$.

(2) If Σ' is inconsistent, then $\Sigma' \vdash u$ and $\Sigma' \vdash \neg u$ for some proposition u. By (1), $\Sigma_i \vdash u$ and $\Sigma_j \vdash \neg u$ for some $i, j \in \mathbb{N}$. Take $k = \max\{i, j\}$. Then, $\Sigma_i \subseteq \Sigma_k$ and $\Sigma_j \subseteq \Sigma_k$. By monotonicity, $\Sigma_k \vdash u$ and $\Sigma_k \vdash \neg u$. This contradicts the fact that each Σ_k is consistent. Hence Σ' is consistent.

(3) In (2), we have already shown that Σ' is consistent. Let r be a proposition such that $r \notin \Sigma'$. Suppose $\Sigma' \cup \{r\}$ is consistent. Due to the enumeration $w_0, w_1, w_2, \ldots$ of the set of all propositions, $r = w_n$ for some $n \in \mathbb{N}$. Since $\Sigma' \cup \{r\}$ is consistent, by monotonicity, $\Sigma_n \cup \{r\}$ is consistent. It then follows that $q = w_n \in \Sigma_{n+1} \subseteq \Sigma'$, contradicting the fact that $r \notin \Sigma'$. Thus $\Sigma' \cup \{r\}$ is inconsistent. This proves that Σ' is maximally consistent.

(4) If $q \in \Sigma'$, then clearly $\Sigma' \vdash q$. Conversely, if $q \notin \Sigma'$, then by (3), $\Sigma' \cup \{q\}$ is inconsistent. By RA, $\Sigma' \vdash \neg q$. Since Σ' is consistent, $\Sigma' \nvdash q$.

(5) Since Σ' is consistent, if $q \in \Sigma'$, then $\neg q \notin \Sigma'$. On the other hand, if $q \notin \Sigma'$, then due to (3), $\Sigma' \cup \{q\}$ is inconsistent. By RA, $\Sigma' \vdash \neg q$. By (4), $\neg q \in \Sigma'$.

(6) Let $q \in \Sigma'$. By monotonicity, $\Sigma' \cup \{p\} \vdash q$. By the deduction theorem, $\Sigma' \vdash p \to q$. Due to (4), $p \to q \in \Sigma'$.

(7) Let $p \notin \Sigma'$. By (3), $\Sigma' \cup \{p\}$ is inconsistent. By monotonicity, $\Sigma' \cup \{p, \neg q\}$ is inconsistent. By RA, $\Sigma' \cup \{p\} \vdash q$. By the deduction theorem, $\Sigma' \vdash p \to q$. Due to (4), $p \to q \in \Sigma'$.

(8) Suppose $p \in \Sigma'$ and $q \notin \Sigma'$. If $p \to q \in \Sigma'$, then by MP, $\Sigma' \vdash q$. By (4), $q \in \Sigma'$, a contradiction. Hence, $p \to q \notin \Sigma'$. ♦

Properties (1)-(3) are the basic properties of Σ'; these have been used to prove the others. Property (4) says that the set Σ' is its own *deductive closure.* Properties (5)-(8) capture the meanings of the connectives $\neg$ and $\to$.

Any set having Properties (2)-(8) listed in Lemma 2.1 is called a *Hintikka set* after the logician J. Hintikka. By Lemma 2.1, we have simply shown the existence of a Hintikka set. The fact that any consistent set can be extended to a maximally consistent set is referred to as *Lindenbaum Lemma,* which is captured in Property (3).

Remark 2.1. In fact, Lindenbaum Lemma can be proved even for propositional languages having uncountable number of propositional variables, using Zorn's lemma. In the following, we give such a proof with the disclaimer that in your first reading, you can safely ignore it.

Lemma 2.2 (Lindenbaum). *Each consistent set of propositions has a maximally consistent extension.*

Proof. Let Σ be a consistent set of propositions. Consider $\mathscr{C}$ as the set of all consistent supersets of Σ. Notice that $\mathscr{C} \neq \varnothing$ since $\Sigma \in \mathscr{C}$. This nonempty set $\mathscr{C}$ is partially ordered by the relation $\subseteq$. Let H be any chain in this partially ordered set. That is, for any $A, B \in H$, at least one of $A \subseteq B$ or $B \subseteq A$ is true. Write $K = \cup\{X : X \in H\}$. Is K consistent?

If K is inconsistent, then $K \vdash p$ and $K \vdash \neg p$ for some proposition p. Due to Theorem 2.4, we have finite subsets K_1, K_2 of K such that $K_1 \vdash p$ and $K_2 \vdash \neg p$. Then we have a finite subset of K, namely, $K_0 = K_1 \cup K_2$ such that $K_0 \vdash p$ and $K_0 \vdash \neg p$. That is, K_0 is inconsistent.

Suppose, $K_0 = \{x_1, \ldots, x_n\}$ for propositions x_i, $1 \le i \le n$. Now, each $x_i \in K$. Therefore, each x_i is in some set Y_i, which is a member of the chain H. Let Y be the biggest of the sets $Y_1, \ldots, Y_n$. It means that $Y_i \subseteq Y$ for each i. Also, since H is a chain, Y is one of $Y_1, \ldots, Y_n$. Then $K_0 \subseteq Y$ and $Y \in H$. By monotonicity, it follows that $Y \vdash p$ and $Y \vdash \neg p$. This is a contradiction since each set in H is consistent. Therefore, we conclude that K is consistent.

It then follows that each chain in $\mathscr{C}$ has an upper bound. Then Zorn's lemma implies that $\mathscr{C}$ has a maximal element. Call it Σ'. This Σ' is a maximally consistent set containing Σ. ♦

Now that Lindenbaum lemma holds for all types of propositional languages, the countability of the set of propositional variables is no more needed. For this, we require Zorn's lemma which is equivalent to the axiom of choice. We resort to this approach only when our propositional language contains an uncountable number of propositional variables. Otherwise, we continue with the constructive Lemma 2.1.

Theorem 2.7 (Model Existence Theorem for PC). *Every PC-consistent set of propositions has a model.*

Proof. Let Σ be a consistent set of propositions. Let Σ' be the maximally consistent set of Lemma 2.1 (or as in Lemma 2.2). Define a function i from the set of all propositions to $\{0,1\}$ by $i(p) = 1$ if $p \in \Sigma'$, else, $i(p) = 0$. The function i is a boolean valuation due to Lemma 2.1(5)-(8). Obviously, i is a model of Σ'. Since $\Sigma \subseteq \Sigma'$, i is a model of Σ as well. ♦

Model existence theorem says that every consistent set is satisfiable, or that every unsatisfiable set is inconsistent. Then, RA (in PC and in PL) gives the following result.

Theorem 2.8 (Strong Completeness of PC to PL). *Let Σ be a set of propositions, and let w be any proposition. If $\Sigma \models w$ then $\Sigma \vdash_{PC} w$.*

With this we have proved the Strong Adequacy of PC to PL. Thus the inherent circularity in the semantic method is eliminated. We may, then, approach any problem in PL through semantics or through the PC-proofs.

If a proposition is a theorem, we may be able to show it by supplying a PC-proof of it. If it is not a theorem, then the mechanism of PC fails to convince us. Reason: I am not able to construct a proof does not mean there exists no proof! In a such a case, we may resort to the truth tables and try to supply a falsifying interpretation. That would succeed, at least theoretically, if the given proposition is not a theorem.

From adequacy of PC and Theorem 2.5 it follows that the set of all axioms of PC is consistent. For otherwise, each proposition would be a theorem of PC. And then each proposition would be satisfiable. But this is not the case; for instance, $\neg(p \to p)$ is unsatisfiable.

Exercises for § 2.4

1. Let Σ be a set of propositions, and let x, y, z be propositions. Show that if $\Sigma \vdash y \to z$, then $\Sigma \vdash ((x \to y) \to (x \to z))$.
2. A set Σ of propositions is called *negation complete* iff for each proposition w, either $\Sigma \vdash w$ or $\Sigma \vdash \neg w$. Show that each consistent set of propositions is a subset of a negation complete set.
3. Show that a consistent set of propositions is maximally consistent iff it is negation complete.
4. Lindenbaum Lemma tells that a consistent set of propositions can always be extended to a maximally consistent set. Is such a maximally consistent set unique? Give an example to illustrate your point.
5. Call a set of propositions *finitely satisfiable* iff every finite subset of it is satisfiable. Without using compactness, prove that if Σ is a finitely satisfiable set of propositions, and A is any proposition, then one of the sets $\Sigma \cup \{A\}$ or $\Sigma \cup \{\neg A\}$ is finitely satisfiable.

2.5 COMPACTNESS OF PL

Each finite subset of the set of natural numbers $\mathbb{N}$ has a minimum. Also, $\mathbb{N}$ itself has a minimum. However, each finite subset of $\mathbb{N}$ has a maximum but $\mathbb{N}$ does not have a maximum. The properties of the first type, which holds for an infinite set whenever it holds for all finite subsets of the infinite set, are called compact properties. For example, in a vectors space, if all finite subsets of a set of vectors are linearly independent, then the set of vectors itself is linearly independent. Thus linear independence is a compact property. In PC, consistency is a compact property due to Theorem 2.4. We use this to show that satisfiability in PL is also a compact property.

Theorem 2.9 (Compactness of PL). *Let Σ be an infinite set of propositions, and let w be a proposition.*

(1) *$\Sigma \vDash w$ iff Σ has a finite subset Γ such that $\Gamma \vDash w$.*

(2) *Σ is unsatisfiable iff Σ has a finite unsatisfiable subset.*

(3) *Σ is satisfiable iff each nonempty finite subset of Σ is satisfiable.*

Proof. (1) Let $\Sigma \vDash w$. By the strong completeness of PC, $\Sigma \vdash_{PC} w$. By finiteness, there exists a finite subset Γ of Σ such that $\Gamma \vdash w$. By the strong soundness of PC, $\Gamma \vDash w$. Conversely, if there exists a finite subset Γ of Σ such that $\Gamma \vDash w$, then by Monotonicity, $\Sigma \vDash w$.

(2) In (1), take $w = p_0$ and then take $w = \neg p_0$. We have finite subsets Γ_1 and Γ_2 of Σ such that $\Gamma_1 \vDash p_0$ and $\Gamma_2 \vDash \neg p_0$. By monotonicity, $\Gamma \vDash p_0$ and $\Gamma \vDash \neg p_0$, where $\Gamma = \Gamma_1 \cup \Gamma_2$ is a finite subset of Σ. Now, Γ is inconsistent.

(3) This a is a re-statement of (2). ♦

Compactness, in its full generality, is a consequence of axiom of choice as our proof of Lindenbaum's lemma shows. It is known that the axiom of choice is equivalent to the well ordering principle that every set can be well ordered. In turn, compactness implies that each set can be totally ordered; see the following example.

EXAMPLE 2.25. Let S be any nonempty set. For each ordered pair $(a,b) \in S \times S$, introduce a propositional variable, say, $p_{a,b}$. Define the set Σ as the union of the following three sets:

$$\{\neg p_{a,a} : a \in S\},\ \{p_{a,b} \wedge p_{b,c} \to p_{a,c} : a,b,c \in S\},\ \{p_{a,b} \vee p_{b,a} : a,b \in S,\ a \neq b.\}.$$

Let $S_0 \subseteq S$ be a finite set. Write $S_0 = \{x_1, \ldots, x_n\}$. Define the ordering $<$ on S_0 by

$$x_i < x_j \text{ iff } i < j.$$

This ordering is a total order on S_0. Let Σ_0 be the union of three sets written above, where $a,b,c \in S_0$ instead of S. Define an interpretation i of Σ_0 by

$$i(p_{a,b}) = 1 \text{ iff } a < b \quad \text{for } a,b \in S_0.$$

Such an interpretation is a model of Σ_0 since $<$ is a total order on S_0.

We conclude that each finite subset of Σ is satisfiable. By the compactness theorem, it follows that Σ is satisfiable. Then let j be a model of Σ. We define a relation on $S \times S$ as in the above; that is,

$$a < b \text{ iff } j(p_{a,b}) = 1 \quad \text{for } a, b \in S.$$

Since Σ is satisfiable, the order $<$ is a total order on S.

Using the *four colour theorem* and compactness theorem, it can be shown that every infinite simple planar graph is four colourable. A general form of the colourability theorem for infinite graphs is illustrated in the following example.

EXAMPLE 2.26. (*Erdös-Rado*) Let $G = (V, E)$ be a simple graph. This means that $E \subseteq V \times V$ is an irreflexive and symmetric relation. Thus, instead of ordered pairs, we may write the elements of E as two-elements sets. We say that G is k-colourable iff there exists an onto function $V \to \{1, 2, \ldots, k\}$ such that if $\{a, b\} \in E$, then $f(a) \neq f(b)$. We show that if each finite subgraph of a simple graph with denumerable number of vertices is k-colourable, then $G = (V, E)$ itself is k-colourable. The technique is the same as in the previous example.

For each $a \in V$ and $i \in \{1, 2, \ldots, k\}$, we introduce a propositional variable $p_{a,i}$ and define the set Σ as the union of the three sets

$$\{p_{a,1} \vee \cdots \vee p_{a,k} : a \in V\}, \quad \{\neg(p_{a,i} \wedge p_{a,j}) : a \in V,\, 1 \leq i < j \leq n\},$$
$$\{\neg(p_{a,i} \wedge p_{b,i}) : \{a, b\} \in E,\, 1 \leq i \leq n\}.$$

We associate a model v of Σ to the function $f : V \to \{1, 2, \ldots, k\}$ the following way:

$$v(p_{a,i}) = 1 \text{ iff } f(a) = i.$$

Assume that each finite subgraph G_0 of G is k-colourable. Then a corresponding set Σ_0 of propositions is satisfiable. (Work out the details.) By the compactness theorem, we conclude that Σ itself is satisfiable. And then we see that G is k-colourable.

In a directed rooted tree, if the number of children of any node is some natural number, then the tree is called a *finitely generated tree.* Notice that this number may vary when nodes vary. A *path* in a directed rooted tree is any sequence of nodes $x_1, \ldots, x_n, \ldots$ such that the first node x_1 is the root, and x_{i+1} is a child of x_i for each $i \geq 1$. *König's lemma* asserts that in any finitely generated infinite tree, there exists an infinite path. It is usually proved by induction; and we will do that later while discussing Analytic Tableaux. For now, we will derive König's lemma from the compactness theorem.

EXAMPLE 2.27. (*König*) Let T be a finitely generated rooted infinite tree. We take the level of the root as 0 and level of a child is one plus the level of its parent. Each level of T has only a finite number of nodes; and T has countably infinite number of nodes. Corresponding to each node n in T we introduce a propositional variable p_n. The set of all nodes of T can be written as a disjoint union of nodes in each level. If $m_1, \ldots, m_n$ are the nodes in level ℓ of the tree, then corresponding to this level, we define a proposition w_ℓ and a set of propositions S_ℓ as follows:

$$w_\ell = p_{m_1} \vee \cdots \vee p_{m_n}, \quad S_\ell = \{\neg(p_{m_i} \wedge p_{m_j}) : 1 \leq i < j \leq n\}.$$

Next, we construct the set of propositions Σ as follows:

$$\Sigma = \cup_{\ell \in \mathbb{N}} (\{w_\ell\} \cup S_\ell) \cup \{p_b \to p_a : a \text{ is the parent of } b\}.$$

The intention behind the above construction is as follows. Any model v of w_ℓ must satisfy one of the propositions that correspond to the nodes in level ℓ. If such a model v is also a model of S_ℓ, then it makes only one of those propositional variables true. So, suppose b is such a node in level ℓ of which v is a model. Since $p_b \to p_a$ is true, v is also a model of a. According to the construction of Σ, this a is the parent node of b. That is, a model of Σ would pin-point a path starting from the root and passing through all levels.

Let Γ be a finite subset of Σ. Let k be the maximum index such that p_k occurs in a proposition of Γ. Let Σ_0 be constructed as Σ except that we restrict ℓ to $0 \le \ell \le m$. Then $\Gamma \subseteq \Sigma_0$, and Σ_0 is a finite subset of Σ. Choose any node from level k; call it α. Look at the path joining the root to this node α. Define an interpretation v by assigning each propositional variable corresponding to the node that occurs in this path to 1. Since the propositional variables are all distinct, v is an interpretation. Further, this v is a model of Σ_0. Hence, v is a model of Γ.

Since each finite subset Γ of Σ is satisfiable, by the compactness theorem, Σ is satisfiable. Now, a model that satisfies Σ gives rise to a path that starts at the root and passes through a vertex in each level. Such a path is an infinite path.

Compactness helps in treating an infinite set provided all its finite subsets can be treated for satisfying a certain property. For another application, consider the word-meaning pairing. A word may have several meanings. Thus given a set of words and given that each word has only a finite number of meanings, can an assignment be made so that each word gets its meaning? It has an affirmative answer provided that for each k, meanings of each subset of k words form a subset of at least k elements.

The same problem is formulated in terms of bipartite graphs. Suppose G is a bipartite graph with partition of its vertices as A and B. We assume that each vertex in A is adjacent to finitely many vertices in B, and that for any k-elements subset of A, the set of all vertices from B which are adjacent to vertices from the subset has at least k elements. Then the problem is to determine whether there is a matching from A to a subset of B.

We would like to formulate the problem in terms of relations and functions. Suppose R is a relation from a nonempty set A to a nonempty set B. For any subset X of A, write

$$R(X) = \{y \in B : (x,y) \in R \text{ for some } x \in X\}.$$

We write $|B|$ for the cardinality or the number of elements in a set B. Assume that for each $a \in A$, $R(\{a\})$ is a nonempty finite set. Further, assume that R satisfies the **marriage condition,** that is,

$$|X| \le |R(X)| \quad \text{for each } X \subseteq A.$$

Then the problem is to determine whether the relation R contains a one-one function.

If A is a nonempty finite set, then the answer is affirmative. We show it by induction on the cardinality of A. If A is a singleton, say, $A = \{a\}$, then choose one $b \in R(\{a\})$. The set $\{(a,b)\}$ is the required one-one function from A to B.

Lay out the induction hypothesis that the statement is true for all sets A with $|A| \leq n$. Let A be a set of cardinality $n+1$. We break our argument into two cases.

Case 1: Suppose that for each subset S of A, $|S| < |R(S)|$. In this case, choose an $a \in A$ and $b \in R(\{a\})$. If $S \subseteq A \setminus \{a\}$ has k elements, then $R(S) \setminus \{b\}$ has at least $k+1-1=k$ elements. Thus the restricted relation R from $A \setminus \{a\}$ to $B \setminus \{b\}$ satisfies the marriage condition. By the induction hypothesis, this restricted relation contains a one-one function. We combine with this function the ordered pair (a,b) to obtain the required one-one function from A to B.

Case 2: Suppose that A has a subset S such that $|S| = |R(S)| = k$, where $1 \leq k \leq n$. Then the restriction of R from S to $R(S)$ satisfies the marriage condition. By the induction hypothesis, this restricted relation contains a one-one function. Call this function $f : S \to R(S)$.

Consider the remaining subset $A \setminus S$; it has $n+1-k \leq n$ number of elements. We want to apply the induction hypothesis on this set. So, we must verify that the relation R restricted to $A \setminus S$ and $B \setminus R(S)$ satisfies the marriage condition. Towards this, let $E \subset A \setminus S$. Let

$$G = \{y : x \in E,\ (x,y) \in R(A \setminus S),\ y \notin R(S)\}.$$

Notice that $R(E \cup S) = G \cup R(S)$. Also, $E \cap S = \varnothing = G \cap R(S)$. Now, the marriage condition implies that

$$|E| + |S| = |E \cup S| \leq |R(E \cup S)| = |G \cup R(S)| = |G| + |R(S)|.$$

Since $|S| = |R(S)|$, we conclude that $|E| \leq |G|$. As $G \subseteq R(E)$, we see that

$$|E| \leq |R(E)|.$$

That is, the restriction of R to $A \setminus S$ and $R(A \setminus S)$ satisfies the marriage condition. By the induction hypothesis, this restriction of R contains a one-one function; call this function $g : A \setminus S \to R(A \setminus S)$. Combining the two functions f and g, we obtain a one-one function from A to $R(A) \subseteq B$, which is contained in the relation R.

The result we have just proved is termed as *Hall's marriage theorem*; and it is stated as follows:

> Let R be any relation from a nonempty finite set A to a nonempty set B such that each element of A is related by R to at least one element in B. If R satisfies the marriage condition, then R contains a one-one function from A to B.

In the following example, we extend Hall's marriage theorem to infinite sets.

EXAMPLE 2.28. Let A and B be any infinite sets and et $R \subseteq A \times B$ be such that $R(\{x\})$ is a finite set for each $x \in A$. Suppose that for each finite subset X of A, $|X| \leq |R(X)|$.

Corresponding to each ordered pair $(a,b) \in A \times B$, introduce a propositional variable $p_{a,b}$. For each $a \in A$, construct sets of propositions S_a and N_a by

$$S_a = \{p_{a,b_1} \vee \cdots \vee p_{a,b_k} : R(\{a\}) = \{b_1, \ldots, b_k\} \subseteq B\},$$
$$N_a = \{\neg(p_{a,b} \wedge p_{a,c}) : b, c \in B,\ b \neq c\}.$$

Let $\Sigma = \cup_{a \in A}(S_a \cup N_a)$. Now, S_a has a model means that a is related to $b_1, \ldots, b_k$. If the same model is also a model of N_a, then it would imply that a is related to exactly one element from B.

Let $\Gamma \subseteq \Sigma$ be a finite set. Consider all propositional variables occurring in Γ. From this we construct the set $A_0 = \{a : p_{a,b} \text{ occurs in } \Gamma\}$. Construct Σ_0 from A_0 as we have constructed Σ from A above, by restricting $a \in A_0$. Now, $\Gamma \subseteq \Sigma_0$. By the discussion we had prior to this example, there exists a one-one function contained in the relation R restricted to $A_0 \times B$. Hence, Σ_0 is satisfiable. By monotonicity, Γ is satisfiable.

That is, each finite subset of Σ is satisfiable. By the compactness theorem, Σ itself is satisfiable. Then it follows that the relation R from A to B contains a one-one function from A to B.

We discuss another application of compactness. Let $\mathscr{C}$ be a nonempty collection of subsets of a nonempty set A. We say that $\mathscr{C}$ is an *ultrafilter* on A if the following conditions are satisfied for all subsets X, Y of A:

$$(X \in \mathscr{C} \text{ and } Y \in \mathscr{C}) \text{ iff } X \cap Y \in \mathscr{C}, \quad A \setminus X \in \mathscr{C} \text{ iff } X \notin \mathscr{C}.$$

Using the compactness theorem we show that every nonempty collection of subsets of a nonempty set can be extended to an ultrafilter on the set. This is referred to as the *ultrafilter theorem*.

EXAMPLE 2.29. Let A be a nonempty set. Let $\mathscr{C}$ be a nonempty collection of subsets of A. Corresponding to each $X \subseteq A$, introduce propositional variables P_X and $P_{\overline{X}}$. Also corresponding to each ordered pair (X, Y) of subsets $X, Y \subseteq A$, introduce a propositional variable $P_{X,Y}$. (We write capital P so that capital letter as subscripts become visible.) Then construct the set of propositions

$$\Sigma = \{P_{X,Y} \leftrightarrow (P_X \cap P_Y) : X, Y \subseteq A\} \cup \{P_{\overline{X}} \leftrightarrow \neg P_X : X \subseteq A\} \cup \{P_X : X \in \mathscr{C}\}.$$

Observe that if i is a model of Σ, then the conditions of the ultrafilter are satisfied for the collection $\mathscr{F} = \{X \subseteq A : i \vDash P_X\}$; and $\mathscr{F}$ becomes an ultrafilter containing $\mathscr{C}$.

Let Γ be a finite subset of Σ. Let A_0 be the set of all propositional variables appearing in Γ. The set of all those subsets X of A such that $P_X \in A_0$ form a finite collection, say $\mathscr{C}_0$. If $\mathscr{C}_0 = \{B_1, \ldots, B_n\}$, then construct

$$\mathscr{F} = \{X \subseteq A : X \supseteq B_1 \cap \cdots \cap B_n\}.$$

That is, if we write $I = B_1 \cap \cdots \cap B_n$; then $\mathscr{F}$ is the collection of all supersets of I. Obviously, it contains each of $B_1, \ldots, B_n$. Moreover, if $X, Y \in \mathscr{F}$, then $X \cap Y \supseteq I$; thus $X \cap Y \in \mathscr{F}$. And, if $Z \notin \mathscr{F}$, then there exists $z \in I$ such that $z \notin Z$. Then each such $z \in I$ is in $A \setminus Z$. That is, $I \subseteq A \setminus Z$. Thus, $A \setminus Z \in \mathscr{F}$. Therefore, $\mathscr{F}$ is an ultrafilter containing $\mathscr{C}_0$.

It then follows that Σ_0 is satisfiable; by monotonicity, Γ is satisfiable. That is, each finite subset of Σ is satisfiable. By the compactness theorem, Σ itself is satisfiable. Therefore, there exists an ultrafilter containing $\mathscr{C}$.

Exercises for § 2.5

1. Let $\Sigma = \{w_1, w_2, w_3, \ldots\}$ be a denumerable set of propositions. Prove that for each $n \geq 1$, $\{w_1, \ldots, w_n\}$ is satisfiable iff each finite subset of Σ is satisfiable.
2. Let Σ be a set of propositions, and let X be a proposition. Show that if some finite subset of $\Sigma \cup \{X\}$ is unsatisfiable, and some finite subset of $\Sigma \cup \{\neg X\}$ is unsatisfiable, then some finite subset of Σ is unsatisfiable.
3. Let Σ be such a set of propositions that given any interpretation i, there exists a proposition $w \in \Sigma$ such that $i \vDash w$. Prove that there are propositions $x_1, \ldots, x_n$ in Σ such that $x_1 \vee \cdots \vee x_n$ is valid, for some $n \in \mathbb{N}$.
4. Let Σ and Γ be sets of propositions such that $\Gamma \neq \varnothing$, and $\Sigma \cup \{\neg X : X \in \Gamma\}$ is inconsistent. Show that there exist $x_1, \ldots, x_n \in \Gamma$ for some natural number n such that $\Sigma \vDash x_1 \vee \cdots \vee x_n$.

2.6 REPLACEMENT LAWS

Now that our trust in the semantic method is restored, we go back to discussing consequences and their proofs. In this context, we will develop some meta-laws like replacements laws, though we will call them laws as usual. And, we will also mention (you can prove) some laws which will be of help in tackling consequences.

We know that the proposition $p \leftrightarrow p$ is valid. Does it imply that the proposition $(p \to q) \leftrightarrow (p \to q)$ is also valid? Alternatively, in our axiomatic system PC, we would ask whether the knowledge of $\vdash p \leftrightarrow p$ guarantees $\vdash (p \to q) \leftrightarrow (p \to q)$? To answer this question, we use *uniform replacement.*

Let p be a propositional variable, x any proposition having at least one occurrence of p, and y any proposition. Recall that $x[p := y]$ denotes the proposition obtained from x by replacing each and every occurrence of p with y. If p does not occur in x, then we take $x[p := y] = x$. Read the symbol $:=$ as **uniformly replaced with**. For instance, if $x = (p \to q) \wedge (\neg p \vee (p \leftrightarrow p \vee q))$ and $y = p \to \neg q$, then

$$x[p := y] = ((p \to \neg q) \to q) \wedge (\neg(p \to \neg q) \vee ((p \to \neg q) \leftrightarrow (p \to \neg q) \vee q)).$$

In fact any finite number of propositional variables can be replaced with that many number of propositions simultaneously. For instance, suppose p, q are propositional variables, and $x = \neg p \vee (p \leftrightarrow p \vee q)$, $y = p \to \neg q$, $z = p \to q$ are propositions. Then

$$x[p := y, q := z] = \neg(p \to \neg q) \vee ((p \to \neg q) \leftrightarrow (p \to \neg q) \vee (p \to q)).$$

Theorem 2.10 (Uniform Replacement). *Let $p_1, \ldots, p_n$ be propositional variables; $y_1, \ldots, y_n$ propositions. Let $w[p_1 := y_1, \ldots, p_n := y_n]$ denote the proposition obtained from a proposition w by replacing each occurrence of p_i with y_i for $i \in \{1, \ldots, n\}$, simultaneously. Then, for all propositions u, v, the following are true:*

(1) *If $\vDash u$, then $\vDash u[p_1 := y_1, \ldots, p_n := y_n]$.*
(2) *If $u \equiv v$, then $u[p_1 := y_1, \ldots, p_n := y_n] \equiv v[p_1 := y_1, \ldots, p_n := y_n]$.*
(3) *If $u \vDash v$, then $u[p_1 := y_1, \ldots, p_n := y_n] \vDash v[p_1 := y_1, \ldots, p_n := y_n]$.*

Proof. (1) In the truth table for $w[p_1 := y_1, \ldots, p_n := y_n]$, there is a column for each y_i. The individual entries in this column may be 0 or 1. These truth values are used to evaluate $w[p_1 := y_1, \ldots, p_n := y_n]$, whereas w is evaluated by using the truth values of p_i, which are either 0 or 1. Since all the entries in the column for w are 1, so are the entries in the column for $w[p_1 := y_1, \ldots, p_n := y_n]$.

Alternatively, we may use PC to show the following:

$$\text{if } \vdash u, \text{ then } \vdash u[p_i := y_1, \ldots, p_n := y_n].$$

For this, suppose P is a proof of u. In P, replace each occurrence of p_i with y_i for $1 \le i \le n$. It is easy to see that the new sequence of propositions is again a proof; and, it is a proof of $u[p_i := y_1, \ldots, p_n := y_n]$.

The statement (2) follows from (1), since $u \equiv v$ iff $\vDash (u \leftrightarrow v)$. Similarly, (3) follows from (1) as $u \vDash v$ iff $\vDash (u \to v)$. ♦

Since PC is adequate to PL, we treat $\vDash$ and $\vdash$ on par. Similarly, $A \equiv B$ may be seen as $A \vdash B$ and $B \vdash A$. We illustrated both PL and PC machinery in the proof of Theorem 2.10, while any one of them is enough.

We may require another kind of replacement. For instance, $\neg(p \to q) \equiv (p \wedge \neg q)$. To show that $(p \to q) \vee (p \wedge \neg q) \equiv \top$, you may proceed as follows:

$$(p \to q) \vee (p \wedge \neg q) \;\equiv\; (p \to q) \vee (\neg(p \to q)) \;\equiv\; \top.$$

In so doing, you have substituted $\neg(p \to q)$ in place of $p \wedge \neg q$ and you have apparently claimed that this replacement preserves equivalence.

Let x, y and w be propositions. The expression $w[x :=_e y]$ denotes any proposition obtained from w by replacing some (or all or no) occurrences of x with y. Read the symbol $:=_e$ as **equivalently replaced with.**

For example, if $w = p \wedge q \wedge \neg r \to \neg p \vee q$, then $w[p :=_e p] = w$, and $w[s :=_e p] = w$. Whereas $w[p :=_e q]$ can be any one of the following propositions

$$w, \quad q \wedge q \wedge \neg r \to \neg p \vee q, \quad p \wedge q \wedge \neg r \to \neg q \vee q, \quad q \wedge q \wedge \neg r \to \neg q \vee q.$$

The following theorem approves the use of the Euclidean principle of substituting equals by equals.

Theorem 2.11 (Equivalence Replacement). *Let u, v, x and y be propositions. For any proposition w, let $w[x :=_e y]$ denote a proposition obtained from w by replacing some or all or no occurrences of x with y. If $x \equiv y$, then the following are true:*

(1) $u \equiv u[x :=_e y]$.

(2) *If* $u \equiv v$, *then* $u[x :=_e y] \equiv v[x :=_e y]$.

(3) *If* $u \vDash v$, *then* $u[x :=_e y] \vDash v[x :=_e y]$.

Proof. Since the relation of equivalence is involved, it is convenient to use the semantic method. Let i be an interpretation. (Imagine a truth table for u and $u[x :=_e y]$, where i is simply a row.) Since $x \equiv y$, $i(x) = i(y)$. For computing $i(u)$, what matters is $i(x)$ and/or $i(y)$, but not the particular sub-propositions x, y. So, $i(u) = i(u[x :=_e y])$. This completes the proof of (1). Both (2) and (3) follow from (1). ♦

Notice that if x does not occur in u, then $u[x :=_e y] = u$, and then Theorem 2.11 is obvious. If x occurs in u, and u is atomic, then $u = x$, x is atomic, and then either $u[x :=_e y] = u$ or $u[x :=_e y] = y$. In any case, Theorem 2.11 is clear. Taking this observation as the basis step, you can give an induction proof of Theorem 2.11. Moreover, you can use PC-proofs instead of PL-models.

Observe the difference between $w[x := y]$ and $w[x :=_e y]$. In obtaining $w[x := y]$ from w, you must substitute *each* occurrence of x by y in w, while in obtaining $w[x :=_e y]$ you may substitute *some* of the occurrences of x by y in w, according to your convenience. Moreover, x in $w[x := y]$ must be a propositional variable; while in $w[x :=_e y]$, x can be any proposition. The law of uniform replacement cannot be generalized to include the case that x can be any proposition; see the following example.

EXAMPLE 2.30. Consider $u = (\neg p \to p) \to p$, where p is a propositional variable. Take $x = \neg p$ and $y = p$. Then

$$u[x := y] = ((\neg p \to p) \to p)[\neg p := p] = (p \to p) \to p \equiv p.$$

Notice that u is valid but $u[x := y]$ is invalid.

We will refer to both the uniform replacement of Theorem 2.10 and equivalence replacement of Theorem 2.11 as the **rule of Leibniz**. The usage of these replacement theorems require some other equivalences and consequences. Some of the most used laws are given in the following theorem. Sometimes a law is written as $x \equiv \top$ instead of the equivalent expression $\vDash x$. Similarly, $x \vDash y$ is written as $x \to y \equiv \top$. There is no need to put effort in memorizing them; they should be internalized by their use.

Theorem 2.12 (Laws of PL). *Let x, y and z be propositions. Then the following laws hold in PL.*

(1) ABSORPTION $\quad x \wedge (x \vee y) \equiv x, \qquad x \vee (x \wedge y) \equiv x.$

(2) ASSOCIATIVITY $\quad x \wedge (y \wedge z) \equiv (x \wedge y) \wedge z, \qquad x \vee (y \vee z) \equiv (x \vee y) \vee z,$
$x \leftrightarrow (y \leftrightarrow z) \equiv (x \leftrightarrow y) \leftrightarrow z.$

(3) BICONDITIONAL $\quad x \leftrightarrow y \equiv (x \to y) \wedge (y \to x),$
$x \leftrightarrow y \equiv (x \vee \neg y) \wedge (\neg x \vee y), \qquad x \leftrightarrow y \equiv (x \wedge y) \vee (\neg x \wedge \neg y),$
$\neg(x \leftrightarrow y) \equiv \neg x \leftrightarrow y, \qquad \neg(x \leftrightarrow y) \equiv x \leftrightarrow \neg y,$
$\neg(x \leftrightarrow y) \equiv (x \wedge \neg y) \vee (\neg x \wedge y), \qquad \neg(x \leftrightarrow y) \equiv (x \vee y) \wedge (\neg x \vee \neg y).$

(4) CASES $\quad$ *If $x \vDash z$ and $y \vDash z$, then $x \vee y \vDash z$.*

(5) CLAVIUS $\quad \neg x \to x \equiv x.$

(6) COMMUTATIVITY $\quad x \wedge y \equiv y \wedge x, \qquad x \vee y \equiv y \vee x, \qquad x \leftrightarrow y \equiv y \leftrightarrow x.$

(7) CONSTANTS $\quad \neg\top \equiv \bot, \qquad \neg\bot \equiv \top, \qquad x \wedge \top \equiv x, \qquad x \wedge \bot \equiv \bot,$
$x \vee \top \equiv \top, \qquad x \vee \bot \equiv x, \qquad x \to \top \equiv \top, \qquad x \to \bot \equiv \neg x,$
$\top \to x \equiv x, \qquad \bot \to x \equiv \top, \qquad x \leftrightarrow \top \equiv x, \qquad x \leftrightarrow \bot \equiv \neg x.$

(8) CONTRADICTION $x \wedge \neg x \equiv \bot, \quad x \leftrightarrow \neg x \equiv \bot,$
$(\neg x \to \neg y) \to ((\neg x \to y) \to x) \equiv \top.$

(9) CONTRAPOSITION $x \to y \equiv \neg y \to \neg x, \quad \neg x \to y \equiv \neg y \to x,$
$x \to \neg y \equiv y \to \neg x.$

(10) DE MORGAN $\neg(x \wedge y) \equiv \neg x \vee \neg y, \quad \neg(x \vee y) \equiv \neg x \wedge \neg y.$

(11) DISJUNCTIVE SYLLOGISM $\{x \vee y\ \neg x\} \vDash y.$

(12) DISTRIBUTIVITY
$x \wedge (y \vee z) \equiv (x \wedge y) \vee (x \wedge z), \quad x \vee (y \wedge z) \equiv (x \vee y) \wedge (x \vee z),$
$x \vee (y \to z) \equiv (x \vee y) \to (x \vee z), \quad x \vee (y \leftrightarrow z) \equiv (x \vee y) \leftrightarrow (x \vee z),$
$x \to (y \wedge z) \equiv (x \to y) \wedge (x \to z), \quad x \to (y \vee z) \equiv (x \to y) \vee (x \to z),$
$x \to (y \to z) \equiv (x \to y) \to (x \to z), \quad x \to (y \leftrightarrow z) \equiv (x \to y) \leftrightarrow (x \to z).$

(13) DOUBLE NEGATION $\neg\neg x \equiv x.$

(14) ELIMINATION $x \wedge y \vDash x, \quad x \wedge y \vDash y.$

(15) EXCLUDED MIDDLE $x \vee \neg x \equiv \top.$

(16) EXPORTATION $x \to (y \to z) \equiv (x \wedge y) \to z,$
$x \to (y \to z) \equiv y \to (x \to z).$

(17) GOLDEN RULE $x \leftrightarrow y \leftrightarrow (x \wedge y) \leftrightarrow (x \vee y) \equiv \top.$

(18) HYPOTHESIS INVARIANCE $x \to (y \to x) \equiv \top.$

(19) HYPOTHETICAL SYLLOGISM $\{x \to y\ y \to z\} \vDash x \to z.$

(20) IDEMPOTENCY $x \wedge x \equiv x, \quad x \vee x \equiv x.$

(21) IDENTITY $x \equiv x, \quad x \leftrightarrow x \equiv \top, \quad x \to x \equiv \top.$

(22) IMPLICATION $x \to y \equiv \neg x \vee y, \quad \neg(x \to y) \equiv x \wedge \neg y,$
$x \to y \equiv x \leftrightarrow x \wedge y, \quad x \to y \equiv x \vee y \leftrightarrow y.$

(23) INTRODUCTION $\{x,\ y\} \vDash x \wedge y, \quad x \vDash x \vee y, \quad y \vDash x \vee y.$

(24) MODUS PONENS $\{x,\ x \to y\} \vDash y, \quad x \wedge (x \to y) \equiv x \wedge y.$

(25) MODUS TOLLENS $\{x \to y,\ \neg y\} \vDash \neg x, \quad (x \to y) \wedge \neg y \equiv \neg x \wedge \neg y.$

(26) PIERCE $(x \to y) \to x \equiv x, \quad (x \to y) \to y \equiv x \vee y.$

You can prove the laws in Theorem 2.12 either using PL, or using PC. If you use PC, then each equivalence of the form $x \equiv y$ will require proofs of $x \vdash y$ and $y \vdash x$.

With the help of replacement laws, you can now prove the strong adequacy of PC to PL, in its totality. This is left to you as an exercise.

Exercises for § 2.6

1. Using associativity and commutativity of $\leftrightarrow$, write all possible forms of the Golden Rule.
2. Prove some of the laws in Theorem 2.12 by using truth tables, and then derive others from those already proved.
3. Formulate simultaneous equivalence replacement theorem where more than one sub-proposition are replaced by the corresponding equivalent propositions.
4. Prove Theorem 2.11 by using PC instead of PL.
5. Show that each proposition is equivalent to either $\top$, or $\bot$, or to one having no occurrence of $\top$ or $\bot$.
6. Let $p_1, \ldots, p_n$ be propositional variables; $y_1, \ldots, y_n$ propositions; and Σ a set of propositions. Define

$$\Sigma[p_1 := y_1, \ldots, p_n := y_n] = \{w[p_1 := y_1, \ldots, p_n := y_n] : w \in \Sigma\}.$$

   Prove the law of *uniform replacement*: For any proposition x, if $\Sigma \vDash x$, then $\Sigma[p_1 := y_1, \ldots, p_n := y_n] \vDash x[p_1 := y_1, \ldots, p_n := y_n]$.
7. For $1 \le i \le n$, let x_i, y_i be propositions with $x_i \equiv y_i$. Let z be a proposition; and Σ a set of propositions. For any proposition w, denote by $w[x_1 :=_e y_1, \ldots, x_n :=_e y_n]$ as any proposition obtained from w by replacing some (or all or no) occurrences of x_i by y_i for $1 \le i \le n$. Define

$$\Sigma[x_1 :=_e y_1, \ldots, x_n :=_e y_n] = \{w[x_1 :=_e y_1, \ldots, x_n :=_e y_n] : w \in \Sigma\}.$$

   Prove the law of *Equivalence replacement*: For any proposition z, if $\Sigma \vDash z$, then $\Sigma[x_1 :=_e y_1, \ldots, x_n :=_e y_n] \vDash z[x_1 :=_e y_1, \ldots, x_n :=_e y_n]$.
8. Prove that PC is strongly adequate to PL.

2.7 QUASI-PROOFS IN PL

The laws mentioned in Theorem 2.12 give rise to derived rules with the help of the replacement laws. Using these we may create **quasi-proofs**. Like proofs, quasi-proofs are finite sequences of propositions which are either valid propositions mentioned in the laws, or are derived from earlier propositions by using some laws. From a quasi-proof a formal PC-proof can always be developed.

We write a quasi-proof in three columns; the first column contains the line numbers, the third column is the justification column documenting the laws that have been used to derive the proposition in that line, and the second column is the actual quasi-proof. In the third column, we will write 'P' for a premise, and sometimes 'T' for a law, for hiding details.

Moreover, the deduction theorem can be used inside a quasi-proof rather than outside. To prove $X \to Y$, we simply introduce X anywhere in the quasi-proof and mark its introduction by DTB abbreviating an application of the deduction theorem begins here.

When we deduce Y latter in the quasi-proof, the next line will have $X \to Y$, and it will be marked as DTE abbreviating

the application of the deduction theorem ends here.

It says that the extra assumption X has been removed as an assumption, and by the deduction theorem, the formula $X \to Y$ has been obtained.

The deduction theorem can be applied many times in a quasi-proof and the pairs of DTB-DTE must be nested like parentheses. In such a case, we may write DTB1-DTE1, DTB2-DTE2, and so on.

Similarly, reductio ad absurdum can be used inside a quasi-proof by introducing a formula $\neg X$ anywhere in the quasi-proof. We document it as RAB abbreviating

an application of a proof by reductio ad absurdum begins here,

and then by deducing $\bot$ later. The next line to the $\bot$ would be X and the documentation would include RAE abbreviating

the application of the proof by reductio ad absurdum ends here.

Thereby the conditionality of the extra premise $\neg X$ is considered over. Again, many applications of reductio ad absurdum are nested like parentheses. We will mark the pairs as RAB1-RAE1, RAB2-RAE2, etc.

When both the deduction theorem and reductio ad absurdum are used in a quasi-proof, the pairs DTBm-DTEm and RABn-RAEn will be used as parentheses of different types. They can nest but the nesting must not intersect.

If a quasi-proof employs premises from a set of propositions Σ and its last proposition is w, then we say that it is a **quasi-proof of** $\Sigma \vDash w$. When $\Sigma = \varnothing$, the quasi-proof does not use any premise; thus its last proposition is valid. The validity of such a proposition follows from the adequacy of PC. Also, a quasi-proof for $\top \vDash w$ proves the validity of w.

EXAMPLE 2.31. Construct a quasi-proof to show that

$$\{p \to \neg q,\ r \to s,\ \neg t \to q,\ s \to \neg u,\ t \to \neg v,\ \neg u \to w\} \vDash p \wedge r \to \neg(w \to v).$$

In the quasi-proof below, note the nesting for RA in Lines 17 and 21, and that of DT in Lines 1 and 22. We also mention the line number of RAB while writing its corresponding RAE, and that of DTB while writing DTE, for better readability.

1.	$p \wedge r$	DTB
2.	p	1, T
3.	$p \to \neg q$	P
4.	$\neg q$	2, 3, T
5.	$\neg t \to q$	P
6.	$\neg\neg t$	4, 5, T
7.	t	6, T
8.	$t \to \neg v$	P
9.	$\neg v$	7, 8, T
10.	r	1, T

11.	$r \to s$	P
12.	s	10, 11, T
13.	$s \to \neg u$	P
14.	$\neg u$	12, 13, T
15.	$\neg u \to w$	P
16.	w	14, 15, T
17.	$\neg\neg(w \to v)$	RAB
18.	$w \to v$	17, T
19.	v	16, 18, T
20.	$\bot$	9, 19, T
21.	$\neg(w \to v)$	17, 20, RAE
22.	$p \wedge r \to \neg(w \to v)$	1, 21, DTE

Document all instances of 'T' in the above quasi-proof by writing the exact law. For instance, the 'T' in Line 6 is Modus Ponens.

In a quasi-proof the replacement laws work implicitly. They give rise to the instances of other laws mentioned as 'T'. Since a PC-proof can be constructed from a quasi-proof, we regard quasi-proofs as intermediary steps towards construction of a formal PC-proof.

Exercises for § 2.7

Give quasi-proofs of the following valid propositions:

1. $((p \leftrightarrow q) \leftrightarrow (q \leftrightarrow p))$
2. $((p \to q) \leftrightarrow (p \leftrightarrow (p \wedge q)))$
3. $((p \to q) \leftrightarrow (q \leftrightarrow (p \vee q)))$
4. $(((p \leftrightarrow q) \leftrightarrow (p \vee q)) \leftrightarrow (p \leftrightarrow q))$
5. $(((p \leftrightarrow q) \leftrightarrow r) \leftrightarrow (p \leftrightarrow (q \leftrightarrow r)))$
6. $((p \to r) \wedge (q \to r) \to (p \vee q \to r))$
7. $((p \to q) \wedge (p \to r) \to (p \to q \wedge r))$
8. $((p \wedge q \to r) \wedge (p \to q \vee r) \to (p \to r))$
9. $(((p \to q) \to (p \to r)) \to (p \to (q \to r)))$

2.8 SUMMARY AND PROBLEMS

The axiomatic system PC, the propositional calculus, has three axiom schemes and one inference rule. It uses the connectives $\neg$ and $\to$. Other connectives are introduced through definitions. The axiom schemes have been constructed in such a way that the deduction theorem and reductio ad absurdum become easier to prove. A proof has been defined as a finite sequence of propositions where each proposition in it is either an axiom, a premise, or is obtained by an application of the inference rule on some earlier formulas. Then a conclusion of the premises is defined as the last proposition in a proof.

PC is strongly adequate to PL. The method of deduction used in PC truly captures the notion of entailment in PL. Since finiteness of proofs is a matter of definition and the system is adequate, the compactness theorem for PL follows from the adequacy of PC. It says that if a conclusion follows from an infinite number of premises, then it also follows from some finite number of those premises.

Since the concept of provability is effective, the notion of truth becomes effective. However, construction of a proof need not be effective. This negative feeling is very much evidenced in PC. You have seen how difficult it is to construct proofs of trivial looking valid propositions. This is remedied by quasi-proofs which use many derived rules as laws. Formal proofs can be developed from the quasi-proofs.

You can find the axiomatic system PC in almost all texts on logic, though in different incarnations; see for example, Barwise & Etchemendy (1999), Enderton (1972), Ershov & Palyutin (1984), Mates (1972), Mendelson (1979), and Singh & Goswami (1998). The one presented here is taken from Bilaniuk (1999). The completeness proof for PC as presented here follows the ideas of J. Hintikka and A. Lindenbaum. The relevant works can be found in van Heijenoort (1967). For a topological proof of compactness, you may see Rasiowa & Sikorski (1970).

Problems for Chapter 2

1. Formulate a definition of the substitution $w[x := y]$, where x is a sub-proposition of w. Show that it is not very useful by constructing propositions w, y and identifying a sub-proposition x of w for each of the following cases.

   (a) w is valid but $w[x := y]$ is invalid.
   (b) w is invalid but $w[x := y]$ is valid.
   (c) w is satisfiable but $w[x := y]$ is unsatisfiable.
   (d) w is unsatisfiable but $w[x := y]$ is satisfiable.

2. Without using the deduction theorem, construct a proof of

$$\vdash ((\neg p \to q) \to ((q \to \neg p) \to p)) \to (((\neg p \to q) \to (q \to \neg p)) \to ((\neg p \to q) \to p))$$

3. Given a set of propositions Σ and a proposition w, how do you prove that $\Sigma \nvdash w$?

4. Recall that a set of propositions is called *finitely satisfiable* iff every finite subset of it is satisfiable. Using compactness, prove that if Σ is a finitely satisfiable set of propositions, and A is any proposition, then one of the sets $\Sigma \cup \{A\}$ or $\Sigma \cup \{\neg A\}$ is finitely satisfiable.

5. Using the previous exercise, prove that if Σ is finitely satisfiable, then there exists a superset Γ of Σ such that (a) Γ is finitely satisfiable, and (b) every proper superset of Γ fails to be finitely satisfiable. [You may have to extend Σ as in the proof of completeness of PC.]

6. Given a finitely satisfiable set Σ of propositions, use the previous exercise to define a function f on all propositions by $f(w) = 1$ if $w \in \Gamma$; otherwise, $f(w) = 0$. Show that such a function is a boolean valuation. Conclude that Σ is satisfiable. [This is a direct proof of compactness.]

7. In a proposition w, replace each occurrence of a propositional variable p by $\neg p$ to obtain the proposition $\bar{w}$. Show that w is valid iff $\bar{w}$ is valid.

8. The axioms of PC do not say that they must be interpreted in the set $\{0, 1\}$. We fix the following conditions for interpreting $\to$ in the set $\{0, 1/2, 1\}$.

If x is a propositional variable, then $i(x) \in \{0, 1/2, 1\}$.
If $i(x) \neq 0$ and $i(y) = 0$, then $i(x \to y) = 0$.
If $i(x) = 1$ and $i(y) = 1/2$, then $i(x \to y) = 1/2$.
In all other cases, $i(x \to y) = 1$.

For a set Σ of propositions, take $i(\Sigma) = \min\{i(X) : X \in \Sigma\}$ with $i(\varnothing) = 1$. In this semantic system, we say that Σ entails w, and write $\Sigma \vDash w$, iff for each interpretation i, $i(\Sigma) \leq i(w)$. Here, we say that the propositions in Σ are premises and w is a conclusion.

Prove that by taking all instances of Axiom schemes A1 and A2 as premises, we would never obtain $((x \to y) \to x) \to x)$ as a conclusion. Conclude that A3 is independent of A1 and A2.

9. Interpret the connective $\neg$ in the set $\{0, 1/2, 1\}$ in such a way that taking all instances of Axiom schemes A1 and A2 as premises, we would never have conclusion as all instances of A3.
10. To show that Axiom A3 does not follow from A1 and A2, interpret $\to$ the usual way, but use $\neg 0 = \neg 1 = 1$; see that for some choice of values of A, B, C, first two axioms (schemes) become 1 whereas third becomes 0.
11. The previous three exercises show that Axiom A3 cannot be derived from A1 and A2. Similarly, prove that A1 cannot be derived from A2 and A3; and A2 cannot be derived from A1 and A3. [Thus we say that axioms of PC are *independent*.]
12. Instead of choosing our basic connectives as $\neg$ and $\to$, suppose we choose $\to$ and $\bot$. We replace A3 with $((A \to \bot) \to \bot) \to A$. Show that this new system is also complete. [Hint: Give a derivation of A3 in the new system.]
13. In PC, if we replace A3 by $\neg\neg A \to A$, will the new system be complete?
14. Let Σ be a set of propositions, and let w be a proposition. Show that if $\Sigma \cup \{w\}$ and $\Sigma \cup \{\neg w\}$ are inconsistent, then Σ is inconsistent.
15. Let Σ and Γ be sets of propositions, and let w be a proposition. Show that if $\Sigma \cup \{w\}$ and $\Gamma \cup \{\neg w\}$ are inconsistent, then $\Sigma \cup \Gamma$ is inconsistent.
16. For a set of propositions Σ, define its *deductive closure* as $\bar{\Sigma} = \{w : \Sigma \vdash w\}$. Prove that if Σ is consistent, then so is $\bar{\Sigma}$.
17. A set Γ of propositions is called *deductively closed* iff "for each proposition w, $\Gamma \vdash w$ iff $w \in \Gamma$". Show the following:
    (a) The set of all propositions is deductively closed.
    (b) The set of all theorems is deductively closed.
    (c) Intersection of two deductively closed sets is deductively closed.
    (d) For any set of propositions Σ, the intersection of all deductively closed supersets of Σ is deductively closed.
    (e) For any set of propositions Σ, the minimal deductively closed set containing Σ is deductively closed.
    (f) The deductive closure of Σ, i.e., the set $\{w : \Sigma \vdash w\}$, is deductively closed.
    (g) Any maximally consistent extension of Σ is deductively closed.
    (h) There exists a deductively closed set which is not maximally consistent.

(i) (*Tarski*) A consistent deductively closed set is the intersection of all its consistent supersets which are negation complete. (See Exercise 2 in § 2.4 for negation completeness.)

18. Attempt proofs of all statements in Lemma 2.1 by using the deductive closure $\bar{\Sigma}$ instead of Σ^*.

19. Translate the following arguments into PL-consequences; and then determine whether they are valid. For valid ones, construct quasi-proofs.

    (a) Either the program does not terminate or m is eventually 0. If n is eventually 0, then m also becomes eventually 0. The program is known not to terminate. Hence m is eventually 0.

    (b) All of x, y, z cannot be negative. If they were, then x would be less than both y and z. Hence x is not less than one of y or z.

    (c) If the initialization is correct and the loop terminates, then the required output is obtained. The output has been obtained. Therefore, if the initialization is correct, the loop must terminate.

    (d) If 2 is a prime, then it is the least prime. If 1 is a prime, then 2 is not the least prime. The number 1 is not a prime. Therefore, 2 is the least prime.

20. Let w be a PC-proposition. Let $p_1, \ldots, p_k$ be all distinct propositional variables that occur in w. Let i be an interpretation of w. Define propositions $q_1, \ldots, q_k, x$ by the following:

    If $i(p_j) = 1$, then $q_j = p_j$; else, $q_j = \neg p_j$ for $1 \leq j \leq k$.
    If $i(w) = 1$, then $x = w$; else, $x = \neg w$.

    Show that $\{q_1, \ldots, q_k\} \vdash_{PC} x$.

Chapter 3

Normal Forms and Resolution

3.1 TRUTH FUNCTIONS

There exist exactly two propositions having no propositional variables; $\top$ and $\bot$, up to equivalence. What about propositions that use a single propositional variable? Suppose x is a proposition built from the only propositional variable p. There are only two (relevant) interpretations of x, namely, when p is 0, and when p is 1. In these two interpretations, x can take any of the two values 0 or 1. Table 3.1 shows all possibilities for x.

Table 3.1: Propositions with one variable

p	x	x	x	x
0	0	0	1	1
1	0	1	0	1

The second column shows that $x \equiv \bot$. The third column: $x \equiv p$, the fourth column: $x \equiv \neg p$, and the fifth column shows that $x \equiv \top$. Thus all propositions that can be built from a single propositional variable p, up to equivalence, are

$$\bot, \quad \top, \quad p, \quad \neg p.$$

We accept $\bot$ and $\top$ as propositions built from p since $\bot \equiv p \wedge \neg p$ and $\top \equiv p \vee \neg p$. In fact, when we say that a proposition y is built from the propositional variables $p_1, \ldots, p_k$, it means that the set of propositional variables occurring in y is a subset of $\{p_1, \ldots, p_n\}$.

Any function $f : \{0,1\}^m \to \{0,1\}$ is called an m-ary *truth function*. Such a truth function having the m variables $q_1, \ldots, q_m$ may be written as $f(q_1, \ldots, q_m)$. The independent variables $q_1, \ldots, q_m$ are called the **boolean variables** on which the truth function f depends. For instance, Table 3.1 shows four unary (1-ary) truth functions.

It is obvious that any truth function $f(q_1, q_2, \ldots, q_m)$ can be represented by a truth table by specifying explicitly its value for the corresponding values of the arguments

$q_1, q_2, \ldots, q_m$. Such a truth table will have 2^m rows, where each row is such an assignment of values to the arguments. Corresponding to each such row, f may be assigned one of the values 0 or 1. Therefore, there exist 2^{2^m} number of m-ary truth functions.

For $m = 1$, we have seen that each truth function (each possibility for x in Table 3.1) is represented as a proposition. What about the case $m = 2$? There are 16 truth functions with two propositional variables p and q. They are given in Table 3.2.

Table 3.2: Binary truth functions

p	q	x_1	x_2	x_3	x_4	x_5	x_6	x_7	x_8	x_9	x_{10}	x_{11}	x_{12}	x_{13}	x_{14}	x_{15}	x_{16}
0	0	0	0	0	0	1	0	0	1	0	1	1	0	1	1	1	1
1	0	0	0	0	1	0	0	1	0	1	0	1	1	0	1	1	1
0	1	0	0	1	0	0	1	0	0	1	1	0	1	1	0	1	1
1	1	0	1	0	0	0	1	1	1	0	0	0	1	1	1	0	1

Observe that the unary truth functions p, q, $\neg p$ and $\neg q$ are also listed as binary truth functions. You may read the unary truth function x_7, which is p, as

p regardless of q.

Similarly, the unary truth function x_{16}, which is $\top$, is read as

$\top$ regardless of p and q.

Other unary and 0-ary truth functions can now be read as binary truth functions in an analogous way. The sixteen truth functions x_1 to x_{16} can be represented as follows:

$x_1 \equiv \bot$ $\quad x_2 \equiv p \land q$ $\quad x_3 \equiv \neg(q \to p)$ $\quad x_4 \equiv \neg(p \to q)$
$x_5 \equiv \neg(p \lor q)$ $\quad x_6 \equiv q$ $\quad x_7 \equiv p$ $\quad x_8 \equiv p \leftrightarrow q$
$x_9 \equiv \neg(p \leftrightarrow q)$ $\quad x_{10} \equiv \neg p$ $\quad x_{11} \equiv \neg q$ $\quad x_{12} \equiv p \lor q$
$x_{13} \equiv p \to q$ $\quad x_{14} \equiv q \to p$ $\quad x_{15} \equiv \neg(p \land q)$ $\quad x_{16} \equiv \top$

Observe that m-ary truth functions include $(m-1)$-ary truth functions also. Can all m-ary truth functions be represented by propositions in PROP?

Exercises for § 3.1

1. For the proposition $w = (((p \land q) \lor (p \lor r \lor q)) \land (\neg p \land \neg r \land q))$, show that $\neg w \equiv (((\neg p \lor \neg q) \land (\neg p \land \neg r \land \neg q)) \lor (p \lor r \lor \neg q))$. Generalize this exercise for computing negation of a proposition having no occurrence of $\to$ and $\leftrightarrow$.
2. The equivalence $(p \lor q) \equiv (\neg p \to q)$ says that $\lor$ can be expressed through $\neg$ and $\to$. Show the following equivalences and read them that way.

   (a) $(p \land q) \equiv (p \leftrightarrow (p \to q))$ (b) $(p \land q) \equiv ((p \lor q) \leftrightarrow (p \leftrightarrow q))$
   (c) $(p \lor q) \equiv (q \leftrightarrow (p \to q))$ (d) $(p \lor q) \equiv ((p \land q) \leftrightarrow (p \leftrightarrow q))$
   (e) $(p \lor q) \equiv ((p \to q) \to q)$ (f) $(p \to q) \equiv (p \leftrightarrow (p \land q))$
   (g) $(p \to q) \equiv (q \leftrightarrow (p \lor q))$ (h) $(p \leftrightarrow q) \equiv ((p \land q) \lor (\neg p \land \neg q))$
   (i) $(p \leftrightarrow q) \equiv ((p \lor \neg q) \land (\neg p \lor q))$

3.2 CNF AND DNF

To see that any m-ary truth function can be represented by a proposition in PROP, we start with some terminology.

A **literal** is either a propositional variable, negation of a propositional variable, $\top$, or $\bot$. For any propositional variable p, the literals p and $\neg p$ are called **complementary literals** (complementary to each other). Also, $\top$ and $\bot$ are complementary to each other. A **conjunctive clause** is a conjunction of literals; a **disjunctive clause** is a disjunction of literals. A conjunctive normal form proposition (**cnf**) is a conjunction of disjunctive clauses; a disjunctive normal form proposition (**dnf**) is a disjunction of conjunctive clauses.

For example, let p and q be propositional variables. Then

$\top,\ \bot,\ p,\ \neg p,\ q,\ \neg q$ are literals;
$\top,\ \bot,\ p,\ \neg q,\ p\wedge q,\ p\wedge\neg p,\ q\wedge p,\ p\wedge\neg q,$ are conjunctive clauses;
$\top,\ \bot,\ p,\ \neg p,\ p\vee q,\ \neg q\vee q,\ \neg q\vee p,\ q\vee\neg q,$ are disjunctive clauses;
$\top,\ \bot,\ p,\ q,\ \neg p,\ p\wedge q,\ p\vee q,\ (p\wedge q)\vee(p\wedge\neg q)$ are dnfs; and
$\top,\ \bot,\ p,\ \neg q,\ p\wedge q,\ \neg p\vee q,\ (p\wedge q)\vee(\neg q\wedge p)\vee(\neg p\wedge\neg q)$ are cnfs.

Of course, the lists above are not complete. For instance, $q\wedge\neg p$ is also a conjunctive clause not listed above.

Theorem 3.1 (Normal Form). *Each truth function is equivalent to a proposition in dnf, and also to one in cnf.*

Proof. Observe that $\top$ and $\bot$ are already in cnf as well as in dnf. Let w be an m-ary truth function, say $w = f(q_1,\ldots,q_m)$ for $m \geq 1$. Specify w in a tabular form; the table now has 2^m rows, each row specifies values 0 or 1 to each of the variables $q_1,\ldots,q_m$ and a value to w, again from $\{0,1\}$. If w receives the value 0 in each row, then its dnf representation is $\bot$. Otherwise, suppose w receives the value 1 in the rows numbered $r_1, r_2, \ldots, r_n$, $n \geq 1$, and it receives the value 0 at other rows. Corresponding to each such row numbered r_j, we construct a conjunctive clause C_j, and then the dnf w' as in the following:

If q_k has the value 1 in the r_jth row, then take $\ell_{jk} = q_k$; else, take $\ell_{jk} = \neg q_k$.
Take $C_j = \ell_{j1}\wedge\ell_{j2}\wedge\cdots\wedge\ell_{jm}$.
Finally, take $w' = C_1\vee C_2\vee\cdots\vee C_n$.

We show that w' represents w, which means that in each row of the table, both w and w' receive the same value. Notice that the table is a truth table for w' also. Consider any row R in the table.

Suppose w is evaluated to 1 in R. Then R is one of the rows numbered $r_1,\ldots,r_n$. If R is the r_jth row, then all the literals $\ell_{j1},\ \ell_{j2},\ \cdots,\ \ell_{jm}$ are assigned the value 1. Thus C_j is evaluated to 1. It follows that w' is evaluated to 1 in the row R.

Conversely, suppose w' has the value 1 in R. Then at least one of the clauses $C_1,\ldots,C_n$ is assigned 1 in R. Suppose C_j has value 1 in R. Then all the literals $\ell_{j1},\ \ell_{j2},\ \cdots,\ \ell_{jm}$ are assigned the value 1 in R. Then R is the r_jth row in the truth table. It follows that R evaluates w to 1.

Since w' is in dnf, use distributivity on w' to get an equivalent cnf w''. ♦

When a truth function is already given as a proposition w, the construction in the proof of Theorem 3.1 amounts to considering all models of w. Each such model is then represented as a conjunctive clause. Finally, the conjunctive clauses are $\vee$-ed together to form the required equivalent dnf. The proof also shows that a dnf explicitly exhibits all the models of a proposition.

Similarly, you can see that a cnf displays all non-models of a proposition. In fact, corresponding to each non-model, a row that evaluates w to 0, we look at the assignments of variables. A variable which is assigned 0 is taken as it is; and a variable assigned to 1 is negated. Then all the resulting literals are $\vee$-ed together to form a disjunctive clause. Finally, all such disjunctive clauses (formed from each row) are $\wedge$-ed together to represent w by a cnf.

EXAMPLE 3.1. Construct a dnf and a cnf equivalent to the proposition $\neg(p \leftrightarrow q)$.

Let $w = \neg(p \leftrightarrow q)$. We find all possible models of w. From the truth table for w (construct it), you see that the models are i and j, where $i(p) = 1$, $i(q) = 0$ and $j(p) = 0$, $j(q) = 1$. The conjunctive clause corresponding to i is $p \wedge \neg q$, and one that corresponds to j is $\neg p \wedge q$. So, the dnf representation of w is

$$(p \wedge \neg q) \vee (\neg p \wedge q).$$

By distributing $\vee$ over $\wedge$, the cnf is $(p \vee \neg p) \wedge (p \vee q) \wedge (\neg q \vee \neg p) \wedge (\neg q \vee q)$. Due to the laws of constants, the later proposition is equivalent to the cnf

$$(p \vee q) \wedge (\neg q \vee \neg p).$$

To construct the cnf directly from the truth table, we look at the non-models of w. They are $\ell(p) = 1$, $\ell(q) = 1$; and $k(p) = 0$, $k(q) = 0$. The disjunctive clause corresponding to ℓ is $\neg p \vee \neg q$; and the one that corresponds to k is $p \vee q$. Thus the cnf is $(\neg p \vee \neg q) \wedge (p \vee q)$, as earlier.

The construction in the proof of Theorem 3.1 demands a truth table with 2^m rows if there are m propositional variables in w. It is inefficient, and becomes unmanageable once m exceeds five. The following procedure, called *NorFor* uses equivalences instead of truth tables.

PROCEDURE ***NorFor***

Input: Any proposition w of PL

Output: A dnf and a cnf equivalent to w

1. Eliminate the connectives $\rightarrow, \leftrightarrow$ by using the laws of Implication and Biconditional.
2. Use De Morgan to take $\neg$ close to the atomic propositions.
3. Use Double Negation to have at most one $\neg$ with any atomic proposition.
4. Replace $\neg\top$ with $\bot$, and $\neg\bot$ with $\top$.
5. Use the laws of Commutativity, Associativity and Distributivity to get the required dnf or cnf.

You can use the laws of absorption and constants for simplifying the normal forms further.

EXAMPLE 3.2. Represent $(p \to q) \to (p \vee r \to q \wedge s)$ by a dnf.

$$\begin{aligned}
&(p \to q) \to (p \vee r \to q \wedge s)\\
&\equiv \neg(p \to q) \vee (p \vee r \to q \wedge s)\\
&\equiv (p \wedge \neg q) \vee (\neg(p \vee r) \vee (q \wedge s))\\
&\equiv (p \wedge \neg q) \vee ((\neg p \wedge \neg r) \vee (q \wedge s))\\
&\equiv (p \wedge \neg q) \vee (\neg p \wedge \neg r) \vee (q \wedge s).
\end{aligned}$$

EXAMPLE 3.3. Convert $(p \to (\neg q \to r)) \wedge (p \to \neg q)$ to a cnf and also to a dnf.

$$\begin{aligned}
&(p \to (\neg q \to r)) \wedge (p \to \neg q)\\
&\equiv (\neg p \vee (\neg q \to r)) \wedge (\neg p \vee \neg q)\\
&\equiv (\neg p \vee (\neg\neg q \vee r)) \wedge (\neg p \vee \neg q)\\
&\equiv (\neg p \vee q \vee r) \wedge (\neg p \vee \neg q)
\end{aligned}$$

The last proposition is in cnf. Using distributivity and simplifying we obtain:

$$\begin{aligned}
&(\neg p \vee q \vee r) \wedge (\neg p \vee \neg q)\\
&\equiv (\neg p \wedge \neg p) \vee (\neg p \wedge \neg q) \vee (q \wedge \neg p) \vee (q \wedge \neg q) \vee (r \wedge \neg p) \vee (r \wedge \neg q)\\
&\equiv \neg p \vee (\neg p \wedge \neg q) \vee (q \wedge \neg p) \vee (r \wedge \neg p) \vee (r \wedge \neg q), \text{ a dnf.}
\end{aligned}$$

The normal forms can be used to decide whether a proposition is valid, invalid, satisfiable, or unsatisfiable, relatively easily. For example, the proposition

$$(p \vee \neg p \vee q) \wedge (q \vee \neg q \vee r).$$

is valid. But the proposition $(p \vee q) \wedge (\neg p \vee p \vee r)$ is invalid since the interpretation i, with $i(p) = i(q) = i(r) = 0$, falsifies it. Similarly, $(p \wedge \neg p \wedge q) \vee (q \wedge \neg q \wedge r)$ is unsatisfiable while $(p \wedge q) \vee (\neg p \wedge p \wedge r)$ is satisfiable.

Theorem 3.2. *A dnf is unsatisfiable iff each conjunctive clause in it contains $\bot$, or a pair of complementary literals. A cnf is valid iff each disjunctive clause in it contains $\top$, or a pair of complementary literals.*

Proof. Let $w = C_1 \vee \cdots \vee C_n$ be a proposition in dnf. Suppose each conjunctive clause C_j contains $\bot$, or a pair of complementary literals. Then each clause C_j is equivalent to $\bot$. Hence, w is unsatisfiable.

Conversely, suppose $w = C_1 \vee \cdots \vee C_n$ is in dnf and a conjunctive clause, say, C_j contains neither $\bot$ nor a pair of complementary literals. Write $C_j = \ell_{j1} \wedge \cdots \ell_{jm}$. Define a map t by taking $t(\ell_{j1}) = \cdots = t(\ell_{jm}) = 1$. Since for no literal ℓ_{jk}, its negation is in C_j, the (boolean extension of the) map t is indeed an interpretation. Now, $t(C_j) = 1$; hence w is satisfiable.

Similarly, validity of a cnf is proved. ♦

It is sometimes advantageous to simplify the normal forms whenever possible using the laws of constants. In such a case, a valid proposition would be simplified to $\top$, and an unsatisfiable proposition will be simplified to $\bot$.

EXAMPLE 3.4. Categorize the following propositions into valid, invalid, satisfiable, or unsatisfiable by converting into a suitable normal form:

(a) $(p \to q) \lor (q \to \neg r) \lor (r \to q) \to \neg(\neg(q \to p) \to (q \leftrightarrow r))$

(b) $\neg((p \to q) \land (q \to r) \to (q \to r))$

(c) $(p \to (\neg q \to r)) \land (p \to \neg q) \to (p \to r)$

(a) $(p \to q) \lor (q \to \neg r) \lor (r \to q) \to \neg(\neg(q \to p) \to (q \leftrightarrow r))$
$\equiv (p \to q) \lor (q \to \neg r) \lor (r \to q) \to (\neg(q \to p) \land \neg(q \leftrightarrow r))$
$\equiv (p \to q) \lor (q \to \neg r) \lor (r \to q) \to (q \land \neg p \land ((q \land \neg r) \lor (\neg q \land r)))$
$\equiv (\neg p \lor q \lor \neg q \lor \neg r \lor \neg r \lor q) \to ((q \land \neg p \land q \land \neg r) \lor (q \land \neg p \land \neg q \land r))$
$\equiv \neg(\neg p \lor q \lor \neg q \lor \neg r \lor \neg r \lor q) \lor (q \land \neg p \land q \land \neg r) \lor (q \land \neg p \land \neg q \land r)$
$\equiv (p \land \neg q \land q \land r \land r \land \neg q) \lor (q \land \neg p \land q \land \neg r) \lor (q \land \neg p \land \neg q \land r)$
$\equiv (p \land \neg q \land q \land r) \lor (\neg p \land q \land \neg r) \lor (\neg p \land q \land \neg q \land r)$

In the first and third clauses, q and $\neg q$ occur; while in the second, $\neg p$ occurs but not p; q occurs but not $\neg q$; and $\neg r$ occurs but not r. This is in dnf, having at least one conjunctive clause which does not have a pair of complementary literals. Thus it is satisfiable.

For validity, you have to convert it to a cnf, say, by distributing the $\lor$'s over $\land$'s in the dnf. However, there is a shorter approach here. Since both the first and the third clauses have a pair of complementary literals, they are each equivalent to $\bot$. Moreover, $\bot \lor x \equiv x$. Therefore, the above dnf is equivalent to the second clause only, i.e., it is equivalent to:

$$\neg p \land q \land \neg r$$

which is in both cnf and dnf. The cnf has now three clauses, namely, $\neg p, q, \neg r$. Neither contains a pair of complementary literals. Thus the proposition is invalid.

(b) $\neg((p \to q) \land (q \to r) \to (q \to r))$
$\equiv (p \to q) \land (q \to r) \land \neg(q \to r)$
$\equiv (\neg p \lor q) \land (\neg q \lor r) \land q \land \neg r$

This is in cnf, and you may conclude that it is invalid. Is it satisfiable? We need a dnf. Distribute to get

$$(\neg p \land \neg q \land q \land \neg r) \lor (\neg p \land r \land q \land \neg r) \lor (q \land \neg q \land q \land \neg r) \lor (q \land r \land q \land \neg r).$$

Each clause in this dnf contains a pair of complementary literals; thus the proposition is unsatisfiable.

Alternatively, $x \land y \to y \equiv \top$. So, $(p \to q) \land (q \to r) \to (q \to r) \equiv \top$. Hence, $\neg((p \to q) \land (q \to r) \to (q \to r)) \equiv \neg\top \equiv \bot$.

(c) $(p \to (\neg q \to r)) \land (p \to \neg q) \to (p \to r)$
$\equiv \neg((p \to (\neg q \to r)) \land (p \to \neg q)) \lor (p \to r)$
$\equiv \neg(p \to (\neg q \to r)) \lor \neg(p \to \neg q) \lor (p \to r)$
$\equiv (p \land \neg(\neg q \to r)) \lor (p \land \neg\neg q) \lor (\neg p \lor r)$
$\equiv (p \land \neg q \land \neg r) \lor (p \land q) \lor \neg p \lor r$

This is in dnf having at least one clause, say, the last one, r, which does not have a pair of complementary literals. Hence the proposition is satisfiable. But is it valid? By distributing and simplifying, you find that

$$\begin{aligned}
&(p\wedge\neg q\wedge\neg r)\vee(p\wedge q)\vee\neg p\vee r\\
&\equiv (p\wedge\neg q\wedge\neg r)\vee((p\vee\neg p\vee r)\wedge(q\vee\neg p\vee r))\\
&\equiv (p\wedge\neg q\wedge\neg r)\vee(\top\wedge(q\vee\neg p\vee r))\\
&\equiv (p\wedge\neg q\wedge\neg r)\vee(q\vee\neg p\vee r)\\
&\equiv (p\vee q\vee\neg p\vee r)\wedge(\neg q\vee q\vee\neg p\vee r)\wedge(\neg r\vee q\vee\neg p\vee r)
\end{aligned}$$

Each clause in the cnf has a pair of complementary literals. Therefore, the original proposition is valid.

Normal forms are used for storing and arguing with knowledge. For example, in diagnosing a disease from the symptoms, we can have a data base, where information regarding a disease is stored as propositions. The task is to determine whether a particular set of symptoms points to a certain disease. In such cases, the data base is called a knowledge base, a **propositional knowledge base**, and the set of all conclusions that can be drawn from the base is called a **propositional theory**.

When a case is presented to the theory, it is required to ascertain whether a particular proposition follows from the knowledge base. It may take a considerable amount of time to see whether such a consequence is valid. Thus the knowledge base, instead of just being stored, is first transformed to a better form so that particular consequences will be easier to decide. Such a transformation is done off-line, that is, before any conclusion is suggested. Such an off-line transformation of the knowledge base is called **knowledge compilation**.

Methods of knowledge compilation depend upon the nature of the theory and the requirement of on-line inference procedure. For example, a common approach to the knowledge compilation is to transform a set of propositions (the knowledge base) to the set of its prime implicants. A **prime implicant** of a proposition is a conjunctive clause that implies the proposition with the property that no subclause of the clause implies the proposition. It can be proved that the set (disjunction) of all prime implicants of a proposition is equivalent to the proposition.

Analogously, and dually, a *prime implicate* of a proposition is defined as a disjunctive clause that is implied by the proposition, and no subclause of which is implied by the proposition. It can also be proved that the set (conjunction) of prime implicates of a proposition is equivalent to the proposition.

Once the prime implicants of a propositional theory is obtained, any conclusion that can be drawn from the theory can equivalently be drawn from the set of prime implicants. However, drawing a conclusion from the set of prime implicants is easy, in the sense that a conclusion as a clause must have a subclause which is an element of the set of prime implicants. This activity of drawing an inference from a compiled knowledge base is an on-line activity. If we have to use some other on-line methods instead of checking for subclauses, then some other way of knowledge compilation or an off-line activity should be chosen, for efficiency.

Exercises for § 3.2

Categorize the following propositions into valid, invalid, satisfiable, or unsatisfiable, by converting to cnf and dnf.

(a) $((p\to q)\to p)\to p$ (b) $\neg(\neg(p\leftrightarrow q)\leftrightarrow\neg(q\leftrightarrow p))$

(c) $(p \to \top) \wedge (q \to p) \to (q \to \top)$ (d) $(p \to \bot) \wedge (q \to p) \to (q \to \bot)$
(e) $\neg(\neg(p \leftrightarrow q) \leftrightarrow r) \leftrightarrow \neg(p \leftrightarrow \neg(q \leftrightarrow r))$
(f) $((p \to q) \vee (q \to r)) \wedge ((r \to q) \vee (q \to p))$

3.3 LOGIC GATES

From Theorem 3.1 it follows that every truth function (also every proposition) can be expressed as a proposition using the only connectives $\neg, \wedge, \vee$. This fact is often expressed by saying that the set $\{\neg, \wedge, \vee\}$ is an *adequate set of connectives* or that the set $\{\neg, \wedge, \vee\}$ is **truth functionally complete**. Due to De Morgan's laws, $\vee$ can be expressed through $\neg$ and $\wedge$. So, $\{\neg, \wedge\}$ is a truth functionally complete set of connectives.

Can we further reduce the sizes of truth functionally complete sets? Is $\{\neg\}$ truth functionally complete? That is, can you define $\wedge$ in terms of $\neg$ alone? In PL, we have the propositional variables $p_0, p_1, \ldots$. If $\neg$ is the only connective to be used, we would generate the formulas:

$$p_0, p_1, p_2, \cdots, \neg p_0, \neg p_1, \neg p_2, \ldots, \neg\neg p_0, \neg\neg p_1, \neg\neg p_2, \ldots$$

Up to equivalence, the propositions reduce to

$$p_0, p_1, p_2, p_3, \cdots, \neg p_0, \neg p_1, \neg p_2, \neg p_3, \ldots, \ldots$$

Now, is any of these propositions equivalent to $p_0 \wedge p_1$? Due to relevance lemma, it is enough to consider the following propositions from the above list:

$$p_0, \ p_1, \ \neg p_0, \ \neg p_1$$

Definitely $p_0 \wedge p_1$ is not equivalent to any of the four. For instance, the interpretation i with $i(p_0) = 1, i(p_1) = 0$ is a model of p_0, but not a model of $p_0 \wedge p_1$. Thus $p_0 \wedge p_1 \not\equiv p_0$. Similarly, other three non-equivalences can be shown,

The connective $\wedge$ does not form a truth functionally complete set since $\neg p$ is not equivalent to any of $p, \ p \wedge p, \ p \wedge p \wedge p$, etc.

Since $p \wedge q \equiv \neg(\neg p \vee \neg q)$, the set $\{\neg, \vee\}$ is truth functionally complete. We already know that $\{\neg, \to\}$ is truth functionally complete. Since

$$\neg p \equiv p \to \bot, \quad p \vee q \equiv \neg p \to q$$

we conclude that $\{\bot, \to\}$ is truth functionally complete. It is a matter of which truth functions can be expressed by what. Both $\wedge$ and $\vee$ can be expressed by $\to$ and $\leftrightarrow$ as follows:

$$(p \wedge q) \equiv (p \leftrightarrow (p \to q)), \quad (p \vee q) \equiv (q \leftrightarrow (p \to q))$$

Of course, due to Pierce law, $\vee$ can be expressed through $\to$ alone. In fact, each binary truth function can be expressed through x_5 alone; see Table 3.2. Similar is the case for x_{15}. We give special symbols to these truth functions and reproduce their truth tables in Table 3.3. Here, x_5 is written as $\downarrow$ and x_{15} is written as $\uparrow$.

Table 3.3: NOR and NAND

p	q	$p\downarrow q$	$p\uparrow q$
0	0	1	1
1	0	0	1
0	1	0	1
1	1	0	0

Since $p\downarrow q\equiv\neg(p\vee q)$ and $p\uparrow q\equiv\neg(p\wedge q)$, we call $\downarrow$ as NOR, and $\uparrow$ as NAND. Observe that

$$\neg p\equiv p\downarrow p, \quad p\vee q\equiv\neg\neg(p\vee q)\equiv\neg(p\downarrow q)\equiv(p\downarrow q)\downarrow(p\downarrow q).$$

Since $\{\neg,\vee\}$ is a truth functionally complete set, so is $\{\downarrow\}$. Similarly,

$$\neg p\equiv p\uparrow p, \quad p\wedge q\equiv(p\uparrow q)\uparrow(p\uparrow q).$$

Therefore, $\{\uparrow\}$ is also a truth functionally complete set.

It means that any binary truth function, that is, any function from $\{0,1\}\times\{0,1\}$ to $\{0,1\}$, can be expressed as a (serial) composition of $\uparrow$ alone. Curiously enough, out of the 16 truth functions, $\uparrow$ and $\downarrow$ are the only truth functions, each of which forms a truth functionally complete set. That is how they are special.

In another terminology, the set $\{0,1\}$ is named as BOOL. A **boolean variable** is a variable taking values in $\{0,1\}$. A **boolean function** is any function from $\{0,1\}^n$ to $\{0,1\}$; the positive integer n is the arity of the boolean function. Thus boolean variables are the propositional variables, and boolean functions are truth functions. The unary boolean function **complement** ($^-$), the binary boolean functions **sum** ($+$), **product** ($\cdot$), and **exclusive sum** ($\oplus$) are defined as follows:

$\overline{0}=1,\ \overline{1}=0;$

$x+y=0$ if $x=0=y$, else $x+y=1;$

$x\cdot y=1$ if $x=1=y$, else $x\cdot y=0.$

$x\oplus y=1$ if $x\neq y$, else $x\oplus y=0.$

Usually, boolean variables are denoted by $x,y,z,\ldots,x_1,x_2,x_3,\ldots$ and boolean functions by $f,g,h,\ldots,f_1,f_2,f_3,\ldots$. To show the arguments of a boolean function explicitly we write a boolean function f of arity n as $f(x_1,x_2,\cdots,x_n)$, or sometimes as $f(v)$, where v is a list of n boolean variables.

Obviously, the connective $\neg$ is the complement, $\vee$ is the sum, and $\wedge$ is the product. The boolean function $\oplus$ is also called XOR, exclusive or; it is same as the negation of the biconditional, the truth function x_9 in Table 3.2.

Normal Form Theorem (Theorem 3.1) says that any boolean function can be expressed as a sum of products and also as a product of sums of boolean variables. For example, $(x\oplus y)=(\overline{x}\cdot y)+(x\cdot\overline{y})$. We can even eliminate one of sum or product due to De Morgan's law, which may now be expressed as

$$\overline{(x+y)}=\overline{x}\cdot\overline{y}, \quad \overline{x\cdot y}=\overline{x}+\overline{y}.$$

Truth functions are also written as logic gates, another alternative symbolism. The gates for the corresponding basic truth functions $\neg, \wedge, \vee, \uparrow, \downarrow$ as symbolized by hardware engineers are depicted in Figure 3.1.

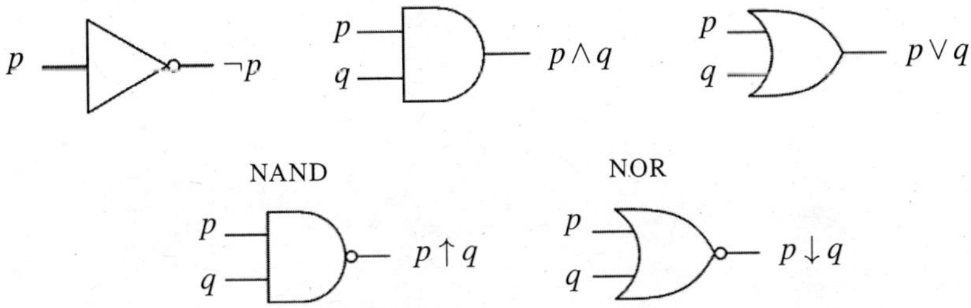

Figure 3.1: Basic logic gates

The NOT-gate means that if a wire carries a large amount of voltage, then the gate outputs a small amount, and vice versa. Similarly, the AND-gate means that if two wires carry some voltage p, q, then the gate outputs $\min(p, q)$. Similarly, the OR-gate outputs $\max(p, q)$. The voltage p, q represent either a 'small' or a 'large' amount of voltage, and are modelled by the truth values 0 and 1, respectively. Similar explanations go for the NAND and NOR gates.

These gates are combined to form bigger circuits which can perform many complicated jobs such as doing arithmetic and taking control jobs. See Figure 3.2.

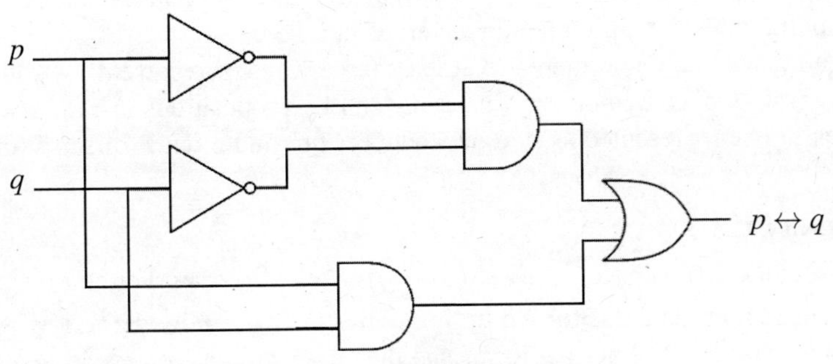

Figure 3.2: Circuit for $\leftrightarrow$

The circuit in Figure 3.2 employs the dnf representation

$$p \leftrightarrow q \equiv (p \wedge q) \vee (\neg p \wedge \neg q).$$

Normal Form Theorem implies that every logic gate can be represented as a combination of the basic gates for $\neg, \wedge, \vee$. For example, consider the truth function w as given in Table 3.4.

Table 3.4: A truth function

p	q	r	$w(p,q,r)$
0	0	0	0
1	0	0	1
0	1	0	1
1	1	0	1
0	0	1	1
1	0	1	1
0	1	1	1
1	1	1	0

The construction used in the proof of the normal form theorem gives:

$$w \equiv (p \wedge \neg q \wedge \neg r) \vee (\neg p \wedge q \wedge \neg r) \vee (p \wedge q \wedge \neg r) \vee (\neg p \wedge \neg q \wedge r) \vee \\ (p \wedge \neg q \wedge r) \vee (\neg p \wedge q \wedge r).$$

This dnf representation can be used for drawing the circuit diagram of w. But you can have a smaller circuit to do the same job as w. Grouping together the first and third clauses, second and sixth, and fourth and fifth, and using the laws, you get

$$w \equiv (p \vee q \vee r) \wedge (\neg p \vee \neg q \vee \neg r).$$

Since circuits are implemented by metallic prints, it is preferable to have a circuit of smaller size which might do the same work than a crude one. This gives rise to the problem of *minimization of boolean circuits.* There are many methods to do it; we will point out some bibliographic materials later.

For now, we know that there are at least three ways of representing truth functions: by truth tables, by boolean functions, and by propositions in PL. Also, truth functions can be represented as sum of products (dnf) and product of sums (cnf).

Exercises for § 3.3

1. Using the equivalence $p \leftrightarrow q \equiv (p \vee \neg q) \wedge (\neg p \vee q)$ draw a circuit for $p \leftrightarrow q$.
2. Construct cnf and dnf for the truth functions u, v given by the following truth table. Simplify the normal forms and then draw circuits representing u and v.

p	q	r	u	v
0	0	0	0	0
0	0	1	0	1
0	1	0	0	1
0	1	1	1	1
1	0	0	0	0
1	0	1	1	0
1	1	0	1	0
1	1	1	1	1

3. A boolean circuit with n inputs is called *monotone* iff changing the value of any of the inputs from 0 to 1 may change the output of the circuit from 0 to 1, but never from 1 to 0.
   (a) Give an example of a truth table representing a monotone circuit with three inputs.
   (b) Show that your truth table can be represented by a monotone circuit.
   (c) Prove that a circuit made of AND and OR-gates is monotone.
   (d) Prove: any monotone circuit can be built using only AND and OR-gates.

3.4 SATISFIABILITY PROBLEM

Suppose after converting a proposition to cnf, you find that the cnf is invalid. It may quite well happen that the proposition is, in fact, unsatisfiable. To determine whether it is so, you may have to get a dnf conversion. Similarly, from a dnf conversion you conclude that a proposition is satisfiable, whereas it could be valid. And now, you may need a cnf conversion. Instead of a fresh conversion, you may like to use distributivity of $\wedge$ over $\vee$, and of $\vee$ over $\wedge$.

But, distribution of $\wedge$ over $\vee$ (or of $\vee$ over $\wedge$) is *costly*. Suppose that we have a cnf with m clauses, and there are ℓ_i number of literals in the ith clause. An application of distributivity leads to writing out the $n = \ell_1 \times \cdots \times \ell_m$ conjunctive clauses where each clause has m literals. Then, you check for the presence of pair of complementary literals in each of these n clauses. In the worst case, it would require an exponential number (with respect to the number of propositional variables in the cnf) of checks to determine satisfiability. So, it is no better than the truth table method.

The problem of determining whether a given cnf is satisfiable is denoted by **SAT**. Many smart ways have been devised to tackle SAT. Though they work better than exponential in most cases, the worst cases still require an exponential amount of labour, like the truth table method. We do not yet have an algorithm which would take a polynomial (in the length of the cnf) time for solving SAT. The collection of problems for which there is an algorithm to solve any instance in a polynomial time is denoted by $\mathscr{P}$. And we do not yet know whether SAT is in $\mathscr{P}$.

In contrast, if you are given an interpretation and it is claimed that the interpretation is a model of the given cnf, you can check the claim in a polynomial time. You just have to evaluate the cnf under the interpretation. This class of problems, called $\mathscr{NP}$, includes all those problems for which a suggested solution can be verified in a polynomial time.

Intuitively, $\mathscr{P}$ consists of problems that can be solved in polynomial time, whereas for a problem in $\mathscr{NP}$, a suggested solution can be checked for its correctness in polynomial time. It is clear that SAT is in $\mathscr{NP}$, but it is not yet clear whether SAT is in $\mathscr{P}$. Moreover, a fundamental fact with SAT is that if it is found to be in $\mathscr{P}$, then both $\mathscr{P}$ and $\mathscr{NP}$ will coincide. Such problems, like SAT, are called $\mathscr{NP}$-complete problems.

There is a related problem, called kSAT. A k**cnf** is a cnf in which each disjunctive clause has no more than k literals. The problem kSAT is the following:

Given a $k$cnf, determine whether it is satisfiable.

It can be shown that corresponding to each cnf X, there exists a 3cnf Y such that X is satisfiable iff Y is satisfiable. (Sometimes we use capital letters for propositions for ease in reading.)

EXAMPLE 3.5. The proposition $X = (p \vee q \vee r \vee s)$ is true when $(p \vee q \vee x)$ is true and $x \leftrightarrow r \vee s$ is true. That means, by extending a model i of X with $i(x) = i(r \vee s)$, we obtain a model of $Z = (p \vee q \vee x) \wedge (x \leftrightarrow r \vee s)$. Conversely, any model j of Z will assign the same truth value to both x and $r \vee s$, and consequently, is a model of X. Since $(x \leftrightarrow r \vee s) \equiv (\neg x \vee r \vee s) \wedge (x \vee \neg r) \wedge (x \vee \neg s)$, we have

$$Z \equiv (p \vee q \vee x) \wedge (\neg x \vee r \vee s) \wedge (x \vee \neg r) \wedge (x \vee \neg s).$$

This is a 3cnf. Thus X is satisfiable iff this 3cnf is satisfiable.

We observe that by neglecting the last two disjunctive clauses in the 3cnf, we loose nothing. For, suppose $i(X) = 1$. We extend i to x by taking $i(x) = i(r \vee s)$. Then i is a model of Y, where $Y = (p \vee q \vee x) \wedge (\neg x \vee r \vee s)$. Conversely, if j is a model of Y then j is also a model of X.

Example 3.5 suggests a method to construct a 3cnf corresponding to each cnf preserving satisfiability. Moreover, the length of the 3cnf is a constant times that of the original cnf. Here, **length** of a proposition is the number of occurrences of symbols in it.

Theorem 3.3. *For each cnf X, there exists a 3cnf Y such that length of Y is a constant times the length of X, and that X is satisfiable iff Y is satisfiable.*

Proof. For $C = p_1 \vee p_2 \vee p_3 \vee p_4$, take $C' = (p_1 \vee p_2 \vee z_1) \wedge (p_3 \vee p_4 \vee \neg z_1)$. For $C = p_1 \vee p_2 \vee \cdots \vee p_m$, where $m \geq 5$, construct

$$\begin{aligned} C' = {} & (p_1 \vee p_2 \vee z_1) \wedge (p_3 \vee \neg z_1 \vee z_2) \wedge (p_4 \vee \neg z_2 \vee z_3) \\ & \wedge \cdots \wedge (p_{m-2} \vee \neg z_{m-4} \vee z_{m-3}) \wedge (p_{m-1} \vee p_m \vee \neg z_{m-3}). \end{aligned}$$

by introducing new propositional variables $z_1, \ldots, z_{m-3}$. We first show that C is satisfiable iff the cnf C' is satisfiable. To show this, take an interpretation i such that $i(C') = 1$. If $i(C) = 0$, then $i(p_j) = 0$ for each j with $1 \leq j \leq m$. Looking at individual clauses of C', we find that if $i(z_1) = 1$, then $i(z_2) = 1$. Continuing further, we see that $i(z_3) = i(z_4) = \cdots = i(z_{m-3}) = 1$. Then i of the last clause $(p_{m-1} \vee p_m \vee \neg z_{m-3})$ in C' is 0. This contradicts $i(C') = 1$. Therefore, $i(C) = 1$.

Conversely, suppose that $i(C) = 1$. Since C' contains new literals (the z's), we construct an extension of i, which we write as i again taking care of these zs where $i(p_j)$s remain the same. Since $i(C) = 1$, not all p_js are 0 under i. Let k be the smallest index such that $i(p_k) = 1$. Then, we set

$$i(z_1) = i(z_2) = \cdots = i(z_{k-1}) = 1, \; i(z_k) = i(z_{k+1}) = \cdots = i(z_{m-3}) = 0.$$

It is easy to verify that under this (extended) interpretation i, each of the clauses in C' is evaluated to 1. Therefore, $i(C') = 1$ as desired.

The reduction of SAT to 3SAT first replaces each clause C having more than 3 literals in the cnf X by the corresponding 3cnf C' thus obtaining a 3cnf Y. Clearly X

is satisfiable iff Y is satisfiable. Notice that if C has m occurrences of literals, then C' has at the most $3m$ occurrences of literals. (Exactly how many?) Hence the length of the corresponding 3SAT instance Y is at the most a constant times the length of the original cnf X. ♦

With this result, we would then have: SAT is in $\mathscr{P}$ iff 3SAT is in $\mathscr{P}$. Moreover, 3SAT is also $\mathscr{NP}$-complete. Thus for deciding whether $\mathscr{P} = \mathscr{NP}$, it is enough to concentrate on 3SAT.

Exercises for § 3.4

1. In Example 3.5, are the propositions X and Z equivalent?
2. For the cnf $X = (p \vee q \vee \neg r \vee s) \wedge (\neg p \vee q \vee r \vee t)$, construct a 3cnf Z following the proof of Theorem 3.3 so that X is satisfiable iff Z is satisfiable.

3.5 2SAT AND HORN-SAT

There are many subclasses of propositions for which polynomial time algorithms exist for checking satisfiability. We review two such subclasses of SAT.

Unlike 3SAT, the class of problems 2SAT is in $\mathscr{P}$; the following algorithm for "determining whether a given 2SAT instance is satisfiable" shows it.

PROCEDURE ***TwoSat***
Input: Any 2cnf x
Output: "x is satisfiable" when it is; otherwise, "x is unsatisfiable"

Stage 1 : Scan the clauses in x for a single-literal clause. If x contains no single-literal clause, then perform Stage 2. Otherwise, let p be a single-literal clause of x. Scan further for the single-literal clause $\neg p$. If $\neg p$ is also a clause of x, then report that x is unsatisfiable. If $\neg p$ is not a clause of x, then scan x from the beginning. Drop each clause that contains p and drop $\neg p$ from each clause that contains $\neg p$. That is, update x by deleting all clauses of the form $p \vee y$ and by replacing each clause of the form $\neg p \vee y$ by y.

Repeat Stage 1 as long as possible. If the result is empty, i.e., every clause has been deleted in the process, then report that x is satisfiable. Otherwise, the result is a 2cnf A, each clause of which has exactly two literals. Then perform Stage 2.

Stage 2 : Take the first literal in the first clause of A; say p, in the first clause $p \vee q$ of A. Scan A from the beginning. Drop the literal p from each clause that contains p, and drop each clause that contains $\neg p$, from A. That is, update A by replacing each clause of the form $p \vee q$ by q, and by deleting each clause of the form $\neg p \vee q$. Call the updated 2cnf as B. Execute Stage 1 repeatedly on the updated 2cnf. This will result in one of the following three cases:

(a) reporting that B is unsatisfiable
(b) an empty cnf
(c) a cnf C having only two-literals clauses

In the case (a), execute Stage 3 on A as given below. In the case (b), report that x is satisfiable. In the case (c), repeat Stage 2 on C.

Stage 3 : Go back to the 2cnf A. Let $p \vee q$ be the first clause of A. Scan each clause of A. Update A to D by dropping each clause of the form $p \vee r$. Scan D for an occurrence of the literal $\neg p$. If $\neg p$ does not occur in D, then execute Stage 2 on D. Otherwise, update D to E by dropping the literal $\neg p$ from each clause of the form $\neg p \vee r$. Now, E has at least one single-literal clause. Execute Stage 1 on E repeatedly. This will halt resulting in one of the following cases:

(a) reporting that E is unsatisfiable

(b) an empty cnf

(c) a cnf F having only two-literals clauses

In the case (a), report that x is unsatisfiable. In the case (b), report that x is satisfiable. In the case (c), execute Stage 2 on F.

Stage 1 of the procedure eliminates at least one atomic proposition, and Stages 2 and 3 together eliminate one. Moreover, unsatisfiability of the 2cnf x is reported while executing Stage 1. The worst case scenario corresponds to the case, when all atomic propositions are eliminated one by one in Stage 2 followed by an execution of Stage 3, and when finally, x is found to be satisfiable. Initially, the 2cnf is scanned for checking for a possible application of Stage 1, anyway.

Suppose n is the length of the 2cnf. Initial scanning of the 2cnf for a single literal clause takes an $O(n)$ time. Repeated execution of Stage 1 can take, at the most, an $O(n^2)$ time. Thus, executing Stage 3 for a literal, which turns out to be an unsuccessful attempt, takes an $O(n^2)$ time. It is followed by an execution of Stage 2, which again takes an $O(n^2)$ time. So, finally a literal is eliminated in $O(n^2)$ time. At the worst, each literal is eliminated; thus the maximum time amounts to an $O(n^3)$. This proves that

$$2\text{SAT} \in \mathscr{P}.$$

An alternative procedure to solve 2SAT is based on the observation that each clause $p \vee q$ is equivalent to both $\neg p \to q$ and $\neg q \to p$; see Problem 34.

Another important subclass of SAT comprises the *Horn clauses,* so called after the logician A. Horn. An arbitrary disjunctive clause in a cnf may have some literals with $\neg$, and others without $\neg$. While in a Horn clause, there is at most one literal which is un-negated.

For example, $\neg p \vee \neg q$, r, $\neg p \vee \neg q \vee r$ are Horn clauses, while $\neg p \vee \neg q \vee r \vee s$ and $r \vee s$ are not Horn clauses. Conventionally, Horn clauses are not written as disjunctive clauses since they can be written in another more suggestive way. For example, we use the equivalences $\neg p \vee \neg q \equiv p \wedge q \to \bot$, $\neg p \vee \neg q \vee r \equiv p \wedge q \to r$ and $r \equiv \top \to r$ to rewrite these Horn clauses.

A **Horn clause** is a proposition of the form $q_1 \wedge q_2 \wedge \cdots \wedge q_m \to q$, where $q_1, \ldots, q_m$ and q are atomic propositions. A **Horn formula** is a conjunction of Horn clauses, written often as a set of Horn clauses.

EXAMPLE 3.6. Is the following Horn formula satisfiable?

$$w = \{\top \to q,\ \top \to u,\ \top \to t,\ t \to p,\ u \to v,\ p \wedge q \wedge r \to \bot\}$$

Let us try to construct a model i of w. Since $\top \to q, \top \to u$ and $\top \to t$ are clauses, we must have $i(q) = i(u) = i(t) = 1$. Next, we have the clauses $t \to p$ and $u \to v$. If i is a model of these clauses, we must have $i(p) = i(v) = 1$. The clause $p \wedge q \wedge r \to \bot$ is satisfied by taking $i(r) = 0$. Hence the interpretation i with $i(p) = i(q) = i(t) = i(u) = i(v) = 1$ and $i(r) = 0$ satisfies w.

While we try constructing a model by assigning truth values to some of the propositional variables present in a given Horn formula x, we observe the following.

1. If $\top \to q$ is a clause in x, then in any model of x, q is true.
2. If $q_1 \wedge \cdots \wedge q_m \to \bot$ is a clause in x, and each of $q_1, \ldots, q_m$ has been assigned to 1, then the clause cannot have a model. Thus x is unsatisfiable.
3. If there is a clause $q_1 \wedge \cdots \wedge q_m \to q$ in x, with $q \neq \bot$, and $q_1, \ldots, q_m$ have been assigned to 1, then q must be assigned to 1.

If our interest is in determining satisfiability, then we simplify the above model construction, and use only a marking scheme.

For instance, in Example 3.6, looking at the first three clauses, we just mark the propositional variables q, u, t. Marking a variable here means that we assign it to 1, though explicitly, we do not need to do it. Since, t has been marked, using the fourth clause, we mark p. Finally, we find that the last clause having consequence $\bot$ contains an unmarked propositional variable. Then, we declare that w is satisfiable. The following procedure, *HornSat*, does just this.

PROCEDURE ***HornSat***
Input: A Horn formula w
Output: w is satisfiable or w is not satisfiable

> mark all propositional variables p where $\top \to p$ is a clause in w
> while there is a clause $p_1 \wedge p_2 \wedge \cdots \wedge p_k \to q$ in w such that all of $p_1, p_2, \ldots p_k$ have been marked but q is not, do:
>> if $q = \bot$, then report that w is unsatisfiable,
>> else, mark q for all such clauses in w
>
> report w is satisfiable

Exercises for § 3.5

1. Which of the following are Horn clauses and why? Which of the Horn clauses are satisfiable?
   (a) $(\top \to p \wedge q) \wedge (\bot \to \top)$
   (b) $\{p \wedge q \wedge r \to \neg s,\ s \to \bot\}$
   (c) $\{p \wedge q \to s,\ p \wedge r \to p,\ r \to p \wedge t\}$
   (d) $(p \wedge q \wedge r \to \top) \wedge (p \wedge r \to s) \wedge (s \to \bot)$
   (e) $(p \wedge q \wedge r \to s) \wedge (\top \to s) \wedge (p \wedge q \to \bot)$
   (f) $(p \wedge q \wedge r \to \bot) \wedge (\neg p \wedge q \to r) \wedge (\bot \to s)$
2. Apply *HornSat* to the following Horn formulas:
   (a) $\{p \to q,\ r \wedge s \wedge t \to u,\ \top \to t,\ t \wedge q \to \bot\}$
   (b) $\{p \wedge q \wedge s \to p,\ q \wedge r \to p,\ p \wedge s \to s,\ s \wedge r \to t\}$
   (c) $\{p \wedge q \wedge r \to \bot,\ s \to p,\ t \to \bot,\ \top \to s,\ \top \to q,\ u \to v,\ \top \to u\}$

3. Write the procedure *HornSat* in a step-by-step fashion. Apply *HornSat* on each Horn clause in Exercise 1, and determine their satisfiability.

3.6 RESOLUTION IN PL

Recall that dnfs can be used to determine satisfiability and cnfs can be used to determine validity. Determining validity of a dnf or satisfiability of a cnf are dual to each other, and are equally difficult. We consider the latter problem. Our goal is to develop a mechanical strategy for checking satisfiability of a cnf that possibly avoids distribution of $\wedge$ over $\vee$, and that of $\vee$ over $\wedge$.

Consider the cnf $C = (\neg p \vee r) \wedge (q \vee \neg r)$. Using distributivity, we have

$$C = (\neg p \vee r) \wedge (q \vee \neg r) \equiv (\neg p \wedge q) \vee (\neg p \wedge \neg r) \vee (r \wedge q) \vee (r \wedge \neg r) = C'.$$

Now, suppose that $i \vDash C'$. As $i \nvDash (r \wedge \neg r)$, we see that

$$\text{either} \quad i \vDash \neg p,\ i \vDash q \quad \text{or} \quad i \vDash \neg p,\ i \vDash \neg r \quad \text{or} \quad i \vDash q,\ i \vDash r.$$

This means that $i \vDash \neg p$ or $i \vDash q$, or both. That is, $i \vDash \neg p \vee q$.

Alternatively, you can also conclude directly from C that each model of C has to be a model of $\neg p \vee q$.

Now, looking at the form of C, where $C = (\neg p \vee r) \wedge (q \vee \neg r)$, we see that in one clause there is r, and in the other there is $\neg r$. If we omit this pair of complementary literals, we get $\neg p$ and we get q. We $\vee$ them together to get $\neg p \vee q$. And then any model of C *must* be a model of this proposition.

The omission of a pair of complementary literals has connection with the laws of Modus Ponens (MP) and Hypothetical Syllogism (HS) as given below.

MP: Form A and $A \to B$, derive B.
HS: From $A \to B$ and $B \to C$, derive $A \to C$.

Due to the equivalence $A \to B \equiv \neg A \vee B$, you can rewrite these laws as follows.

MP: From A and $\neg A \vee B$, derive B.
HS: From $\neg A \vee B$ and $\neg B \vee C$, derive $\neg A \vee C$.

In the first case, omitting the pair $A, \neg A$ from the premises, you reach at the conclusion B and in the second case, omitting the pair $B, \neg B$ gives the conclusion $\neg A \vee C$. Does this method of omitting a pair of complementary literals work in general?

Now that all our propositions are in cnfs, we can represent them in a set notation. For example, the clause $p \vee q$, can be rewritten as $\{p, q\}$ and the cnf $(p \vee q) \wedge (r \vee s)$ can be rewritten as $\{\{p, q\}, \{r, s\}\}$. While writing back to the original form, there will be no confusion since a set of literals is a disjunction of literals; and a set of sets (of literals) is a conjunction of disjunctions of literals.

In this notation, what does an empty set of literals represent? And, what does an empty set of clauses (sets of literals) represent?

Let p and q be propositional variables. Consider $\{p\}$ and $\{p, q\}$ as clauses. $\{p\}$ represents the clause p and $\{p, q\}$ represents the clause $p \vee q$. we see that $p \vDash p \vee q$. In general, when $A \subseteq B$, we may write $B = A \vee X$ for some clause X. Then, $A \vDash B$.

Since the empty set is a subset of every set, the empty clause entails every clause. So, what is that formula which entails every clause? A little thought shows that it must be the propositional constant $\bot$; show it.

Another way of looking at it is that a disjunctive clause is true under an interpretation only when one of its literals is true; else, it is false. But there is no literal in the empty clause to become true; so, it is false.

What about the empty set of clauses? Now, a cnf is a conjunction of clauses. A conjunction is false under an interpretation only when there is at least one clause in which it is false. But there is none. Hence, it cannot be false. That is, an empty set of clauses is always true.

Moreover, if A and B are two sets of clauses (conjunctions of those clauses) with $B \supseteq A$, we see that B is either A or $A \wedge X$ for some cnf X. Thus, $B \vDash A$. Since each set of clauses is a superset of the empty set of clauses, each cnf entails the empty cnf. Then you can see that the only such cnf which is entailed by each cnf has to be $\top$.

When p is a propositional variable, we have its negation as $\neg p$ which is obviously a literal. But then its negation, $\neg\neg p$ is not a literal. In this case, we will write the negation of the literal $\neg p$ as p itself, and generically, we will accept that $\neg q$ is a literal even when $q = \neg p$; the literal $\neg q$ being equal to p. Thus we put forth the following convention.

Convention 3.1.

If $q = \neg p$ is a literal, then its negation $\neg q$ is the literal p.
A clause is a disjunctive clause; a set of literals.
A clause is written as $\ell_1 \vee \cdots \vee \ell_k$ and also as $\{\ell_1, \ldots, \ell_k\}$, where $\ell_1, \ldots, \ell_k$ are literals.
A cnf is a set of clauses, a set of sets of literals.
A cnf is written as $D_1 \wedge \cdots \wedge D_m$ and also as $\{D_1, \ldots, D_m\}$, where $D_1, \ldots, D_m$ are clauses.
The empty clause is $\bot$.
The empty cnf is $\top$.

Our strategy may now be formalized. Let A and B be two clauses (sets of literals). If there is a literal p such that $p \in A$ and $\neg p \in B$, then the **resolvent** $res(A,B;p)$ of A and B with respect to the literal p (or $\neg p$) is the clause $(A \setminus \{p\}) \cup (B \setminus \{\neg p\})$.

In such a case, both the literals p and $\neg p$ are called **biform literals**. We say that the resolvent has been obtained by **resolving upon the literal** p. We also say that the resolvent has been obtained by *resolving upon the variable* p. The variable p is called a **biform variable**, whereas both p and $\neg p$ are biform literals. If the literal or variable p is clear from the context, we will simply write $res(A,B;p)$ as $res(A,B)$.

EXAMPLE 3.7. Let $A = \{\neg p, r\}$ and $B = \{q, \neg r\}$. By resolving upon r, we get

$$res(A,B) = res(A,B;r) = \{\neg p, q\}.$$

If $A = \{\neg p, q, r\}$ and $B = \{\neg q, \neg r\}$, then by resolving upon the biform variable q, we obtain

$$res(A,B;q) = \{\neg p, r, \neg r\}.$$

Whereas $res(A,B;r) = \{\neg p, q, \neg q\}$ is obtained by resolving upon r.

However, $res(\{\neg p,q,r\},\{\neg q,\neg r\}) \neq \{\neg p\}$ as you would have obtained by omitting both the pairs $q,\neg q$ and $r,\neg r$. You cannot cancel more than one pair at a time! Resolution does not allow it. Why is it so?

You have already seen that if $i \vDash \{\neg p,r\}$ and $i \vDash \{q,\neg r\}$, then $i \vDash \{\neg p,q\}$. Similarly, you expect that if $i \vDash \{\neg p,q,r\}$ and $i \vDash \{\neg q,\neg r\}$, then $i \vDash \{\neg p,r,\neg r\}$. But will it be that $i \vDash \neg p$? Not necessarily. The interpretation j with $j(p) = j(q) = 1$, $j(r) = 0$, is a model of $\{\neg p,q,r\}$ and also of $\{\neg q,\neg r\}$, but $j \nvDash \neg p$. (Remember $\{\neg p,q,r\}$ is, by definition, $\neg p \vee q \vee r$.)

For convenience, we write clauses as disjunctions of literals and cnfs as sets of clauses. We prove that the resolvent of two clauses is their logical consequence.

Theorem 3.4 (Resolution Principle for PL). *Let A and B be two clauses. Let p be a literal such that $p \in A$ and $\neg p \in B$. Then $\{A,B\} \vDash res(A,B;p)$.*

Proof. Let $A = \ell_1 \vee \ell_2 \vee \cdots \vee \ell_k \vee p$ and $B = m_1 \vee m_2 \vee \cdots \vee m_n \vee \neg p$, where ℓ's and m's are literals. Then

$$res(A,B;p) = \ell_1 \vee \ell_2 \vee \cdots \vee \ell_k \vee m_1 \vee m_2 \vee \cdots \vee m_n.$$

Let i be an interpretation with $i \vDash A$ and $i \vDash B$. If $i \nvDash res(A,B;p)$, then

$$i(\ell_1) = \cdots = i(\ell_k) = i(m_1) = \cdots = i(m_n) = 0.$$

Looking at A and B, we find that $i(p) = 1 = i(\neg p)$, a contradiction. ♦

EXAMPLE 3.8. Consider the cnf $\Sigma = \{\neg p \vee q,\ \neg q \vee r,\ p,\ \neg r\}$. Here,

$$res(\neg p \vee q, \neg q \vee r; q) = \neg p \vee r,\ res(\neg p \vee q, p; p) = q,\ res(\neg q \vee r, \neg r; r) = \neg q$$

By the resolution principle, $\Sigma \vDash \neg p \vee r$, $\Sigma \vDash q$, $\Sigma \vDash \neg q$. Since Σ entails each of its members, we also have

$$\Sigma \vDash \neg p \vee q,\ \Sigma \vDash \neg q \vee r,\ \Sigma \vDash p,\ \Sigma \vDash \neg r.$$

Taking further resolvents, we obtain

$$res(\neg p \vee r, \neg r; r) = \neg p,\ res(q, \neg q; q) = \bot,\ res(q, \neg q \vee r; q) = r.$$

Other resolvents do not produce new clauses. In addition to the earlier conclusions, we find that $\Sigma \vDash \neg p$, $\Sigma \vDash \bot$, $\Sigma \vDash r$.

Of all these conclusions from Σ, the special conclusion $\bot$ signifies something important. It says that if $i \vDash \Sigma$, then i must also be a model of $\bot$. But there cannot be any model of $\bot$. Therefore, Σ is unsatisfiable.

We write the resolution principle as the inference rule of **resolution for PL**:

(RPL) $\dfrac{A \quad B}{res(A,B)}$ the resolution is taken on a biform literal p.

We use the notation $cnf(u)$ for a cnf representation of a proposition u, which is also regarded as a set of clauses.

Let Σ be a set of clauses. A **resolution refutation** of Σ is a finite sequence of clauses, where each clause is either from Σ or is obtained (derived) by an application of the rule RPL from two earlier clauses, and the last clause in the sequence is $\bot$. For a set Γ of propositions and a proposition w, a **resolution proof** of the consequence $\Gamma \,!\!\vDash w$ is a resolution refutation of the set

$$\Sigma = \{cnf(u) : u \in \Gamma\} \cup \{cnf(\neg w)\}.$$

If a consequence $\Gamma \,!\!\vDash w$ has a resolution proof, we write $\Gamma \vdash_R w$.

Notice that a resolution proof of $\Sigma \,!\!\vDash w$ can be defined as a finite sequence of clauses, where each clause is either a clause in Σ or is obtained (derived) by an application of the rule RPL from two earlier clauses, and the last clause in the sequence is w. We prefer to go with the conventional resolution refutations, where reductio ad absurdum is inbuilt.

EXAMPLE 3.9. Here is the resolution refutation of $\Sigma = \{\neg p \vee q,\ \neg q \vee r,\ p,\ \neg r\}$ as worked out in Example 3.8. We also add the line numbers and the right-most column for documentation. They help in reading the refutation. The refutation is simply the sequence of clauses in the middle column read from top to bottom. An element of the set of premises Σ is documented by 'P'. Sometimes, instead of writing the full $res(1,2;p)$ as in line 3 above, we only quote the line numbers, like 1,2.

1.	$\neg p \vee q$	P
2.	p	P
3.	q	$res(1,2;p)$
4.	$\neg q \vee r$	P
5.	$\neg r$	P
6.	$\neg q$	$res(4,5;r)$
7.	$\bot$	$res(3,6;q)$

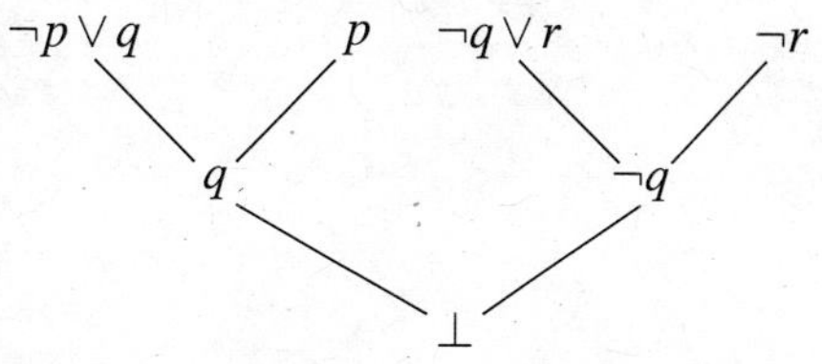

On the right, we depict the resolution refutation as a directed acyclic graph (DAG). To construct such a **resolution DAG**, we start with all premises as nodes of Level 1. Their resolvents are added as new nodes in Level 2, and so on. Resolvents of nodes of levels up to n are added as new nodes in Level $(n+1)$. The biform literal upon which the resolvent is taken is not usually mentioned in the DAG.

EXAMPLE 3.10. Show that $\{\neg p \to q, p \to r \vee s, r \to t \wedge u, u \wedge \neg s \to \neg t\} \vDash \neg s \to q$ by using resolution.

The cnf of the premises, and the cnf of the negation of the conclusion are

$$\neg p \to q \equiv p \vee q,\ p \to r \vee s \equiv \neg p \vee r \vee s,\ r \to t \wedge u \equiv (\neg r \vee t) \wedge (\neg r \vee u),$$
$$u \wedge \neg s \to \neg t \equiv \neg u \vee s \vee \neg t,\ \neg(\neg s \to q) \equiv \neg s \wedge \neg q.$$

Thus the set of premises is

$$\Sigma = \{p \vee q,\ \neg p \vee r \vee s,\ \neg r \vee t,\ \neg r \vee u,\ \neg u \vee s \vee \neg t,\ \neg s,\ \neg q\}.$$

A resolution refutation of Σ is as follows.

1.	$p \vee q$	P
2.	$\neg q$	P
3.	p	1,2
4.	$\neg p \vee r \vee s$	P
5.	$r \vee s$	3,4
6.	$\neg s$	P
7.	r	5,6
8.	$\neg r \vee t$	P
9.	t	7,8
10.	$\neg r \vee u$	P
11.	u	7,10
12.	$\neg u \vee s \vee \neg t$	P
13.	$s \vee \neg t$	11,12
14.	$\neg t$	6,13
15.	$\bot$	9,14

The proposition p on the third line is the resolution of those in lines 1 and 2; thus in the justification column, we write "1, 2". Similarly, read the line numbers mentioned in lines 5, 7, 9, 11, 13, 14 and 15. In all these cases find the biform variable on which the resolvents have been taken.

A resolution DAG of Σ is shown in Figure 3.3. Observe that the resolution refutation does not correspond to the DAG exactly. Where do they differ?

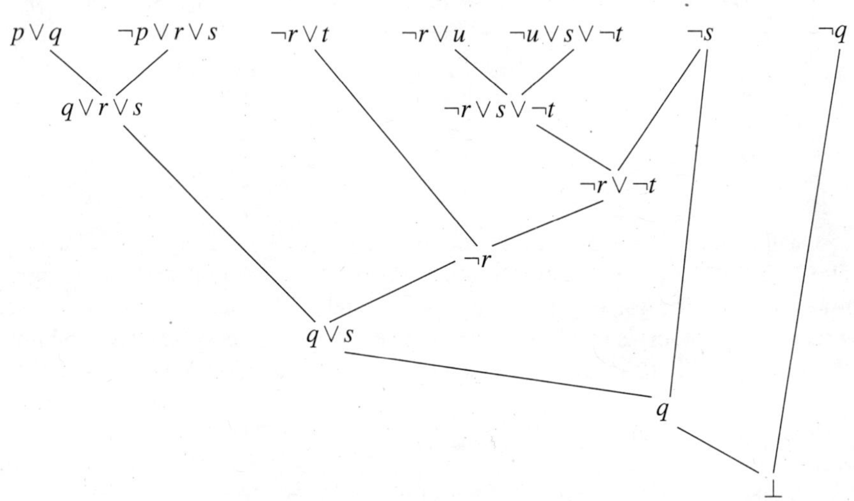

Figure 3.3: Resolution DAG for Example 3.10

Exercises for § 3.6

1. In Example 3.10, construct the resolution DAG corresponding to the resolution refutation; and construct the resolution refutation corresponding to the resolution DAG of Figure 3.3.

2. Attempt resolution proofs of the following consequences. Whenever possible, construct the resolution DAGs.

   (a) $\top \vDash p \to (q \to p)$
   (b) $\top \vDash (p \vee q) \leftrightarrow (\neg p \to q)$
   (c) $\top \vDash (p \wedge q) \leftrightarrow \neg(p \to \neg q)$
   (d) $\top \vDash (\neg q \to \neg p) \to (p \to q)$
   (e) $\top \vDash (((p \to q) \to \neg q) \to \neg q)$
   (f) $(p \leftrightarrow (q \to r)) \wedge (p \leftrightarrow q) \wedge (p \leftrightarrow \neg r) \vDash \bot$
   (g) $\top \vDash (p \to (q \to r)) \to ((p \to q) \to (p \to r))$
   (h) $\{\{p, \neg q, r\}, \{q, r\}, \{\neg p, r\}, \{q, \neg r\}, \{\neg q\}\} \vDash \bot$
   (i) $\{\{\neg p, q\}, \{\neg q, r\}, \{p, \neg r\}, \{p, q, r\}, \{\neg p, \neg q, \neg r\}\} \vDash \bot$
   (j) $\{\{p, \neg q\}, \{r, p\}, \{\neg q, r\}, \{\neg p, q\}, \{q, \neg r\}, \{\neg r, \neg p\}\} \vDash \bot$
   (k) $((p \wedge q) \vee (p \wedge r) \vee (q \wedge r)) \vee (\neg p \wedge \neg q) \vee (\neg p \wedge \neg r) \vee (\neg q \wedge \neg r) \vDash \bot$

3. Construct essentially two different resolution proofs along with the resolution DAGs of $(p \leftrightarrow q) \wedge (q \leftrightarrow r) \vDash (p \leftrightarrow r)$.

4. The truth function $\oplus$ is defined by the equivalence $x \oplus y \equiv \neg(x \leftrightarrow y)$. Give resolution proofs of the facts that $\oplus$ is commutative and associative.

3.7 ADEQUACY OF RESOLUTION IN PL

While constructing a resolution refutation, you had to select premises one after another in order that $\bot$ is derived. How can a machine do it?

A crude method is to generate all possible resolvents of the premises, add them to the premises, and then generate more resolvents until you get $\bot$. Will the procedure work? Yes, provided the original set of clauses is finite. For, in that case, resolvents, resolvents of resolvents, etc. are finite in number.

If a cnf has n number of propositional variables, then there are $2n$ number of literals, and then, since each clause is a subset of literals, there are at the most 2^{2n} number of clauses. Among them, there are trivial clauses of the form $\ell_1 \vee \cdots \vee \ell_m \vee p \vee \neg p$ which are equivalent to $\top$, and hence, can be omitted. Then you are left with 3^n number of clauses. (Either p appears, or $\neg p$ appears, or none appears.)

Then, quite mechanically, the procedure will terminate in a set of resolvents, resolvents of resolvents, etc. where no more new clauses can be obtained by using RPL. A formal description of the method follows.

For any set B of clauses (sets of literals), define

$$R(B) = B \cup \{res(C_1, C_2; p) : C_1, C_2 \in B,\ C_1 \neq C_2, \text{ are clauses in } B \text{ and } p \text{ is a biform literal}\}.$$

Let A be a given set of clauses. Define $R^*(A)$ by

$$R_0(A) = A, \quad R_{i+1}(A) = R(R_i(A)), \quad R^*(A) = \cup_{n \in \mathbb{N}} R_n(A).$$

The set $R(A)$ is the set of all clauses of A along with resolvents of all possible pairs of clauses of A that could be resolved upon some biform literal. Sets $R(R(A))$ etc. form an increasing sequence of sets of clauses:

$$A = R_0(A) \subseteq R_1(A) \subseteq R_2(A) \subseteq \cdots \subseteq R_n(A) \subseteq \cdots R^*(A).$$

The set $R^*(A)$ is called the **resolvent closure** of the cnf A. Since there are only a finite number of possible clauses which can be generated from A, there exists a natural number n such that

$$R^*(A) = R_n(A) = R_{n+1}(A).$$

Therefore, by monitoring the condition that whether new clauses are generated at a stage or not, the resolvent closure can be computed. A resolution refutation of A would then mean that $\bot \in R^*(A)$.

EXAMPLE 3.11. Let $A = (\neg p \vee q) \wedge (p \vee q) \wedge (\neg p \vee \neg q)$. To compute the resolvent closure of the cnf A we proceed as follows.

$$\begin{aligned} R_0(A) &= \{\{\neg p, q\}, \{p, q\}, \{\neg p, \neg q\}\} \\ R_1(A) &= R_0(A) \cup \{\{q\}, \{\neg p\}, \{q, \neg q\}, \{p, \neg p\}\} \\ R_2(A) &= R_1(A) \end{aligned}$$

Therefore, $R^*(A) = R_2(A) = R_1(A)$.

The property that "if $\bot$ is generated, then the given cnf is unsatisfiable" is the **soundness** of resolution. And its converse that "if the cnf is unsatisfiable, then $\bot$ is eventually generated" is the **completeness** of resolution. To study these properties, we start with the enumeration of all propositional variables:

$$p_0,\ p_1,\ p_2,\ \cdots$$

Let $A_0 = \{\bot,\ \neg\bot\}$. Let A_m denote the set of all clauses which can be formed from the first m propositional variables including the propositional constant $\bot$, up to equivalence. For instance,

$$A_1 = \{\bot,\ p_0,\ \neg p_0,\ p_0 \vee \neg p_0\}.$$

Lemma 3.1. *For $m \geq 1$, if $R^*(A) \cap A_m$ is satisfiable, then $R^*(A) \cap A_{m+1}$ is also satisfiable.*

Proof. Let $R^*(A) \cap A_m$ be satisfiable. All propositional variables that occur in this set are from $\{p_0, p_1, \ldots, p_{m-1}\}$. So, let $i : \{p_0, \ldots, p_{m-1}\} \to \{0,1\}$ be a model of all clauses in $R^*(A) \cap A_m$. Construct two more interpretations f and g by extending i to the set $\{p_0, \ldots, p_{m-1}, p_m\}$ in the following way:

$f, g : \{p_0, \ldots, p_m\} \to \{0,1\}$ with $f(p_k) = g(p_k) = i(p_k)$ for $1 \leq k \leq m-1$; and $f(p_m) = 0,\ g(p_m) = 1$.

Now suppose that $R^*(A) \cap A_{m+1}$ is unsatisfiable. Then neither f nor g satisfies all the clauses in $R^*(A) \cap A_{m+1}$. Thus, there are clauses C and $\overline{C}$ in $R^*(A) \cap A_{m+1}$ such that $f \nvDash C$ and $g \nvDash \overline{C}$.

Can it happen that neither p_m nor $\neg p_m$ is a member of C? If yes, then all the propositional variables occurring in C are from $\{p_0,\ldots,p_{m-1}\}$ and then C must be in $R^*(A)\cap A_m$. As f agrees with i on the set $\{p_0,\ldots,p_{m-1}\}$, we have $f(C)=i(C)$. Since i is a model of $R^*(A)\cap A_m$, $i\vDash C$. That is, $f\vDash C$ contradicting $f\nvDash C$. Therefore, at least one of p_m or $\neg p_m$ is in C. Similarly, $\overline{C}$ contains at least one of p_m or $\neg p_m$.

If $p_m\notin C$, then $\neg p_m\in C$. Since $f\nvDash C$, we have $f(\neg p_m)=0$. This contradicts $f(p_m)=0$. Thus, $p_m\in C$. Similarly, $\neg p_m\in\overline{C}$.

If $C=p_m$ and $\overline{C}=\neg p_m$, then their resolvent $\bot\in R^*(A)\cap A_m$. This contradicts the satisfiability of $R^*(A)\cap A_m$.

Then, C and $\overline{C}$ can be written as $C=D\vee p_m$, $\overline{C}=\overline{D}\vee\neg p_m$ for some clauses $D,\overline{D}\in R^*(A)\cap A_m$, where at least one of D or $\overline{D}$ is a nonempty clause. The clause $res(C,\overline{C};p_m)=D\vee\overline{D}\in A_m$. Moreover, $D\vee\overline{D}$ is nonempty and $D\vee\overline{D}\in R^*(A)\cap A_m$. As i is a model of $R^*(A)\cap A_m$, we have $i(D\vee\overline{D})=1$. Then $i(D)=1$ or $i(\overline{D})=1$. (Notice that the case $i(D)=1$ covers the case that $\overline{D}$ is empty, and the case $i(\overline{D})=1$ similarly covers the case that D is empty.)

The propositional variables that occur in D and $\overline{D}$ are from $\{p_0,\ldots,p_{m-1}\}$. Also i agrees with f and g on $\{p_0,\ldots,p_{m-1}\}$. Thus, if $i(D)=1$, then $f(C)=f(D\vee p_m)=1$. This contradicts $f\nvDash C$. Similarly, if $i(\overline{D})=1$, then $g(\overline{D})=1$. This again leads to a contradiction since $g\nvDash\overline{C}$.

Therefore, unsatisfiability of $R^*(A)\cap A_{m+1}$ is impossible. ♦

Lemma 3.2. *For each $n\geq 1$, if $\bot\notin R^*(A)\cap A_n$ then $R^*(A)\cap A_n$ is satisfiable.*

Proof. We use induction on n. For $n=1$, $A_1=\{\bot,p_0,\neg p_0,p_0\vee\neg p_0\}$. Assume that $\bot\notin R^*(A)\cap A_1$. Now, $R^*(A)\cap A_1$ cannot contain both p_0 and $\neg p_0$, since otherwise their resolvent, $\bot$, would also be in $R^*(A)\cap A_1$. That is, $R^*(A)\cap A_1$ can be one of

$$\varnothing,\quad \{p_0\},\quad \{\neg p_0\},\quad \{p_0,p_0\vee\neg p_0\},\quad \text{or}\quad \{\neg p_0,p_0\vee\neg p_0\}.$$

In either case, $R^*(A)\cap A_1$ is satisfiable.

Lay out the induction hypothesis: $\bot\notin R^*(A)\cap A_m$ implies that $R^*(A)\cap A_m$ is satisfiable. Suppose that $\bot\notin R^*(A)\cap A_{m+1}$. Since $R^*(A)\cap A_m\subseteq R^*(A)\cap A_{m+1}$, $\bot\notin R^*(A)\cap A_m$ either. By the induction hypothesis, $R^*(A)\cap A_m$ is satisfiable. By Lemma 3.1, $R^*(A)\cap A_{m+1}$ is satisfiable. ♦

We take help from these lemmas to prove our main results.

Theorem 3.5 (Closure Property of Resolution). *Let $R^*(A)$ be the resolvent closure of a cnf A. Then A is unsatisfiable iff $\bot\in R^*(A)$.*

Proof. If $\bot\in R^*(A)$, then by the resolution principle and induction, it is clear that $A\vDash\bot$. Thus A is unsatisfiable.

Conversely, suppose that $\bot\notin R^*(A)$. Suppose the propositional variables that occur in A are from the set $\{p_0,p_1,\ldots,p_{m-1}\}$. Then $\bot\notin R^*(A)\cap A_m$. By Lemma 3.2, $R^*(A)\cap A_m$ is satisfiable. $A\subseteq R^*(A)\cap A_m$. By monotonicity, A is satisfiable. ♦

Let us write $\Sigma\vdash_R w$ for the phrase "Σ entails w by resolution." It means that there exists a resolution refutation of $\Sigma\cup\{\neg w\}$ which uses the only rule of inference as

RPL. In case, $\Sigma = \{X_1, \ldots, X_n\}$, writing

$$A = cnf(X_1) \wedge \cdots \wedge cnf(X_n) \wedge cnf(\neg w),$$

we see that $\Sigma \vdash_R w$ iff $\bot \in R^*(A)$.

Theorem 3.6 (Strong Adequacy of Resolution). *Let Σ be a set of propositions, and let w be a proposition. $\Sigma \vDash w$ iff $\Sigma \vdash_R w$.*

Proof. First, consider the case that Σ is finite. Write $\Sigma = \{X_1, \ldots, X_n\}$, and $A = cnf(X_1) \wedge cnf(X_2) \wedge \cdots \wedge cnf(X_n) \wedge cnf(\neg w)$. Using RA, normal form theorem, and the closure property of resolution, we see that $\Sigma \vDash w$ iff $\Sigma \cup \{\neg w\}$ is unsatisfiable iff A is unsatisfiable iff $\bot \in R^*(A)$ iff $\Sigma \vdash_R w$.

If Σ is infinite, then by the compactness theorem, there exists a finite subset Γ of Σ such that $\Sigma \vDash w$ iff $\Gamma \vDash w$. By what we have just proved, this happens if and only if $\Gamma \vdash_R w$. Moreover, $\Gamma \vdash_R w$ iff $\Sigma \vdash_R w$ due to the finiteness of a resolution proof. ♦

Exercises for § 3.7

1. Let $A \subseteq B$ be sets of propositions. Show that $R_m(A) \subseteq R_m(B)$ for any $m \in \mathbb{N}$. Conclude that $R^*(A) \subseteq R^*(B)$.
2. Give resolution proofs of all axiom schemes, the rule of inference, and the definitions (as biconditionals) of PC. Does it prove adequacy of resolution?
3. Show that the resolution rule RPL is a derived rule of PC.

3.8 RESOLUTION STRATEGIES

In search of a mechanical procedure implementing resolution, we landed up at the resolvent closure. However, we require to check whether $\bot$ is ever generated by resolution or not; the whole lot of clauses in $R^*(A)$ seem wasteful. One obvious strategy to cut down wasteful generation of clauses is the following:

Once $\bot$ has been generated, do not proceed further.

For another strategy, look at Example 3.11. There, we had

$$\begin{aligned} A &= (\neg p \vee q) \wedge (p \vee q) \wedge (\neg p \vee \neg q) \\ R_0(A) &= \{\{\neg p, q\}, \{p, q\}, \{\neg p, \neg q\}\} \\ R_1(A) &= \{\{\neg p, q\}, \{p, q\}, \{\neg p, \neg q\}, \{q\}, \{\neg p\}, \{q, \neg q\}, \{p, \neg p\}\} \end{aligned}$$

While computing $R_2(A)$, we had to take resolvents of $\{p, q\}$ with the possible clauses, namely, $\{\neg p\}, \{q, \neg q\}, \{p, \neg p\}$. This gave $\{q\}, \{p, q\}, \{\neg p, q\}$. This was wasteful due to two reasons.

First, there is no need to resolve with the clauses $\{q, \neg q\}$ and with $\{p, \neg p\}$. This is because $\{\{\neg p\}, \{q, \neg q\}, \{p, \neg p\}\}$ is logically equivalent to $\{\{\neg p\}\}$.

A clause is called a **fundamental** clause (also called a **nontrivial** clause) if it does not contain a pair of complementary literals. A clause containing a pair of complementary literals is called **nonfundamental** (also called **trivial** or **tautological**). The strategy is as follows:

Delete all nonfundamental clauses.

The second source of wasteful generation emanates from keeping all the clauses $\{q\}, \{p,q\}, \{\neg p,q\}$. Notice that the clause $\{q\}$ is already a subset of other clauses. When you write $R_2(A)$ as a cnf, it will look like

$$\cdots q \wedge (p \vee q) \wedge (\neg p \vee q) \cdots$$

Now, $q \wedge (p \vee q)$ simplifies to q and $q \wedge (\neg p \vee q)$ also simplifies to q, due to the laws of Absorption. Thus it should be enough to keep only q. The strategy is

Keep only a subset (a clause) and delete all its supersets.

In Example 3.11, $R_1(A)$ would become modified to $\{\{q\}, \{\neg p\}\}$. You can check at this point that this new set is logically equivalent to the set $R_1(A)$ obtained earlier.

To express these strategies formally, let C and D be two clauses. C is said to **subsume** D if $C \subseteq D$. If A is a set of clauses, then the **residue of subsumption** of A is the set

$$RS(A) = \{C \in A : C \text{ is fundamental and } C \text{ is not subsumed by any other clause of } A\}.$$

Thus, $RS(R_1(A)) = \{\{q\}, \{\neg p\}\}$. You can also verify that $A \equiv RS(A)$ as cnfs. While generating $R^*(A)$, we can take residue of subsumption on each resolvent set $R_n(A)$ and proceed further. That is, for a set of clauses A, we compute the sequence:

$$\begin{array}{ll} A_0 = A, & B_0 = RS(A_0); \\ A_1 = R(B_0), & B_1 = RS(A_1); \\ A_2 = R(B_1), & B_2 = RS(A_2); \\ \vdots & \vdots \end{array}$$

until one of $\bot \in A_{n+1}$ or $B_{n+1} = B_n$ happens.

The termination criterion $B_{n+1} = B_n$ is bound to be met because the totality of all clauses that could be generated from the propositional variables of A are finite in number. Whenever for some n, we have $B_n = B_{n+1}$, we denote this set of clauses as $RS^*(A)$, that is,

$$RS^*(A) = B_n \quad \text{when } B_n = B_{n+1}.$$

It is easy to see that the conjunction of all clauses in $RS^*(A)$ is equivalent to the conjunction of all clauses in $R^*(A)$. Then from the adequacy of resolution it follows that $\bot \in RS^*(A)$ iff A is unsatisfiable. Moreover, $\bot \in A_{n+1}$ iff $\bot \in B_{n+1}$. Thus, in the first case of the termination criterion, A is unsatisfiable, and if the first does not happen but the second termination criterion is met, then A is satisfiable.

EXAMPLE 3.12. Using resolution with subsumption in Example 3.11, we obtain

$$\begin{array}{ll} A_0 = A = \{\{\neg p,q\}, \{p,q\}, \{\neg p, \neg q\}\} & B_0 = RS(A_0) = A_0 \\ A_1 = R(B_0) = A_0 \cup \{\{q\}, \{\neg p\}, \{q, \neg q\}, \{p, \neg p\}\} & B_1 = RS(A_1) = \{\{q\}, \{\neg p\}\} \\ A_2 = R(B_1) = \{\{q\}, \{\neg p\}\} & B_2 = RS(A_2) = \{\{q\}, \{\neg p\}\} = B_1 \end{array}$$

So, $RS^*(A) = B_1$. Since $\bot \notin B_1$, A is satisfiable

EXAMPLE 3.13. Use resolution with subsumption to show that

$$\{p \vee q \to r,\ r \to s \vee t,\ s \to u,\ \neg(\neg t \to u)\} \vDash \neg p.$$

Take negation of the conclusion and then convert each proposition to cnf. The clause set corresponding to this consequence is

$$A = \{\{\neg p, r\},\ \{\neg q, r\},\ \{\neg r, s, t\},\ \{\neg s, u\},\ \{\neg t\},\ \{\neg u\},\ \{p\}\}.$$

We notice that there is no nonfundamental clause in A and no clause subsumes another. Hence, $A_0 = A,\ B_0 = RS(A) = A$. Since

$$\begin{array}{ll} res(\{\neg p, r\}, \{p\}; p) = \{r\} & res(\{\neg p, r\}, \{\neg r, t, s\}; r) = \{\neg p, t, s\} \\ res(\{\neg q, r\}, \{\neg r, t, s\}; r) = \{\neg q, t, s\} & res(\{\neg r, t, s\}, \{\neg s, u\}; s) = \{\neg r, t, u\} \\ res(\{\neg r, t, s\}, \{\neg t\}; t) = \{\neg r, s\} & res(\{\neg s, u\}, \{\neg u\}; u) = \{\neg s\} \end{array}$$

we have

$$\begin{aligned} A_1 = R(B_0) = \{&\{\neg p, r\}, \{\neg q, r\}, \{\neg r, t, s\}, \{\neg s, u\}, \{\neg t\}, \{\neg u\}, \{p\}, \{r\}, \{\neg p, t, s\}, \\ &\{\neg q, t, s\}, \{\neg r, t, u\}, \{\neg r, s\}, \{\neg s\}\} \end{aligned}$$

Since $\{r\}$ subsumes $\{\neg p, r\}$ and $\{\neg q, r\}$, $\{\neg r, s\}$ subsumes $\{\neg r, t, s\}$, and $\{\neg s\}$ subsumes $\{\neg s, u\}$, we obtain

$$\begin{aligned} B_1 = RS(A_1) &= \{\{\neg t\}, \{\neg u\}, \{p\}, \{r\}, \{\neg p, t, s\}, \{\neg q, t, s\}, \{\neg r, t, u\}, \{\neg r, s\}, \{\neg s\}\} \\ A_2 = R(B_1) &= \{\{\neg t\}, \{\neg u\}, \{p\}, \{r\}, \{\neg p, t, s\}, \{\neg q, t, s\}, \{\neg r, t, u\}, \{\neg r, s\}, \{\neg s\}, \\ &\quad \{\neg p, s\}, \{\neg q, s\}, \{\neg r, u\}, \{\neg r, t\}, \{t, s\}, \{t, u\}, \{s\}, \{\neg p, t\}, \{\neg q, t\}, \{\neg r\}\} \\ B_2 = RS(A_2) &= \{\{\neg t\}, \{\neg u\}, \{p\}, \{r\}, \{\neg s\}, \{t, u\}, \{s\}, \{\neg p, t\}, \{\neg q, t\}, \{\neg r\}\} \\ A_3 = R(B_2) &= \{\ldots, \{\neg s\}, \ldots, \{s\}, \ldots, \bot, \ldots\} \end{aligned}$$

Therefore, A is unsatisfiable; and the consequence is valid.

Observe that each clause in $RS^*(A)$ is a logical consequence of A but no clause is a logical consequence of any other. Also, A is logically equivalent to $RS^*(A)$. That is, $RS^*(A)$ is the set of all prime implicates of A.

To repeat, let A be a cnf and let D be a disjunctive clause. D is an *implicate* of A iff $A \vDash D$. D is a *prime implicate* of A iff D is an implicate of A and there is no other implicate C of A such that $C \vDash D$. That is, no other implicate comes in between A and D with respect to the consequence relation. By way of trying to make resolution efficient, we have landed in computing all prime implicates of a cnf.

Other strategies for cutting down waste in resolution are based on the so called pure literal and unit clauses. In the context of a set A of clauses, a literal p is called a *pure literal* if p occurs in some clause of A and $\neg p$ dos not occur in any clause of A. Similarly, a unit clause of A is a clause that occurs in A and which contains a single literal. A unit clause looks like $\{p\}$ or $\{\neg p\}$ for any propositional variable p.

1. *Pure literal heuristic*: Let p be a pure literal occurring in a cnf A. Delete from A each clause that contains p to obtain A'. Then A is satisfiable iff A' is satisfiable.

2. *Unit clause heuristic*: Let $\{p\}$ be a unit clause contained in a cnf A. Delete from A every clause that contains the literal p to obtain the set of clauses A'. Next, update each clause of A' by deleting the occurrence of $\neg p$ from it, and call the new set of clauses as A''. Then A is satisfiable iff A'' is satisfiable.

The *DPLL algorithm* for checking satisfiability of cnfs uses these two heuristics recursively. Notice that these two heuristics cannot decide on their own whether a given cnf is satisfiable. DPLL algorithm first simplifies the cnf using these heuristics. When these heuristics are no more applicable, the algorithm arbitrarily selects a literal and assigns it the truth value 1 and then tries to apply the heuristics. If later, it finds that satisfiability cannot be established, the algorithm backtracks and assigns 0 to the selected literal and starts all over again.

There are also heuristics in selecting such a literal in the process leading to many refinements of the algorithm.

Exercises for § 3.8

1. Find $R^*(A)$ and $RS^*(A)$ for the following clause sets A:

   (a) $\{\{p\},\{q\},\{p,q\}\}$ (b) $\{\{p,q,\neg r\},\{\neg p,\neg q,r\}\}$
   (c) $\{\{p,\neg q\},\{p,q\},\{\neg q\}\}$ (d) $\{\{\neg p\},\{\neg p,r\},\{p,q,\neg r\}\}$
   (e) $\{\{\neg p,\neg r\},\{\neg q,\neg r\}\{p,q,r\}\}$ (f) $\{\{q,r\},\{\neg p,\neg q\},\{\neg r,\neg p\}\}$
2. Write a detailed procedure for resolution employing subsumption.
3. Show that deletion of trivial clauses does not affect the adequacy (soundness and completeness) of resolution.
4. If a clause C subsumes D, then removal of D does not affect the adequacy of resolution. Show it.

3.9 SUMMARY AND PROBLEMS

The semantics of PL led us to consider the truth functions, which map n-tuples of truth values to true or false. Each truth function could be represented by a proposition, especially by a dnf and also by a cnf. A dnf is satisfiable iff each conjunctive clause in it contains a pair of complementary literals. Similarly, a cnf is valid iff each disjunctive clause in it contains a pair of complementary literals.

In the worst case, the satisfiability of a cnf, and its dual problem of determining validity of a dnf are exponential processes. The method of resolution helps in many cases reducing the complexity. We found that the resolution method is adequate to PL. Strategies have been developed for improving the performance of resolution. Briefly, we have described the DPLL algorithm, which is an improvement over the Davis-Putnum proof procedure.

Davis-Putnum proof procedure is an earlier method closely related to resolution; see Davis & Putnam (1960). The resolution method was found by Robinson (1996). Since then it had received much attention due to its easy machine implementation. An exposition of the resolution method basing on different formal systems can be found in Robinson (1979).

The resolution method is extensively used in computing the set of prime implicants and implicates arising in minimization of boolean circuits and knowledge compilation. For knowledge compilation and its application to various reasoning activities and minimization of boolean circuits, many algorithms have been devised. The method of Karnaugh maps is one among them. The Karnaugh maps become quite involved when the number of propositional variables and the number of clauses become large. In our terminology this amounts to computing the prime implicants or prime implicates of a knowledge base. One of the oldest methods of computing prime implicants is discussed in Quine (1959). For more information on the knowledge compilation techniques, see Doyle et al. (1994), Reiter & de Kleer (1987), Selman & Kautz (1991), Singh (1999), and Tison (1967).

In the worst case, resolution takes an exponential time; see Fitting (1996). Accordingly, many refinements of resolution have been attempted. Some refinements such as linear resolution, model elimination, unit resolution, etc. have been tried keeping in view a particular class of clauses, on which they become efficient too. For these refinements, you may consult Chang & Lee (1973), Kowalski (1979), Loveland (1979), and Robinson (1979).

A linear time algorithm for checking satisfiability of Horn formulas is given in Dowling & Gallier (1984). Consult Garey & Johnson (1979) for more information on $\mathscr{NP}$-completeness and many problems including 3-SAT. As general references on these topics, see the texts Chang & Lee (1973), Du et al. (1997), Gallier (1987), Huth & Ryan (2000), and Singh & Goswami (1998).

Problems for Chapter 3

1. Prove that the construction of a cnf equivalent to a proposition by looking at the non-models works correctly.
2. Look at the laws used in the procedure *NorFor*. Do you feel that using only these laws, all the other laws in Theorem 2.12 can be derived by equivalences? If so, why? If not, what else do you require?
3. Prove that the procedure *NorFor* works as intended.
4. Construct a proposition w involving three atomic propositions p, q, r such that for any interpretation, changing any one of the truth values of p, q, or r changes the truth value of w.
5. Let $n \geq 1$. Let $f : \{0,1\}^n \to \{0,1\}$ be any truth function. Prove that f can be expressed as a composition of (a) $\uparrow$ only; (b) $\downarrow$ only.
6. Prove that except $\uparrow$ and $\downarrow$, no other binary truth function alone can express all truth functions.
7. Which pair of connectives form a truth functionally complete set? Justify your answer.
8. Let w be a proposition built from propositional variables $p_1, \ldots, p_n$, and connectives $\wedge, \vee$ and $\to$. Let i be an interpretation with $i(p_1) = \cdots = i(p_n) = 1$. Show that $i(w) = 1$. Deduce that the set $\{\wedge, \vee, \to\}$ of connectives is not truth functionally complete.
9. Is $\{\wedge, \top, \bot\}$ truth functionally complete?

10. Show that $\{\wedge, \leftrightarrow, \oplus\}$ is a truth functionally complete set, but none of its proper subsets is truth functionally complete.
11. Show that each function from $\{0,1\}^n$ to $\{0,1\}$ can be generated using the function $f : \{0,1\}^2 \to \{0,1\}$, where $f(x,y) = (1+x)(1+y)$. Can you find another function from $\{0,1\}^2$ to $\{0,1\}$ which behaves like f? [See Problems 37-38 of Chapter 1.]
12. Show that each function from $\{0,1\}^n$ to $\{0,1\}$ can be generated using the function $g : \{0,1\}^3 \to \{0,1\}$ given by $g(x,y,z) = 1+x+y+xyz$.
13. A set S of connectives is called *maximally inadequate* iff there exists a truth function f which is not expressible by using connectives from S, and for any such f, the set $S \cup \{f\}$ is adequate (truth functionally complete). Show that each of the sets $\{\wedge, \vee, \top, \bot\}$, $\{\wedge, \to\}$, and $\{\neg, \leftrightarrow\}$ is maximally inadequate.
14. Suppose that all our propositions are defined in terms of the connectives $\neg, \wedge, \vee$, without using the constants $\top$ and $\bot$. Let p stand for atomic propositions, and u, v, w for propositions.
    (a) Define the *dual* of a proposition, $dl(\cdot)$, recursively by $dl(p) = p$, and $dl(\neg w) = \neg dl(w), dl(u \wedge v) = (dl(u) \vee dl(v)), dl(u \vee v) = (dl(u) \wedge dl(v))$. Show that $x \equiv y$ iff $dl(x) \equiv dl(y)$ for all propositions x and y.
    (b) Is the dual of $(p_1 \wedge p_2) \vee (p_2 \wedge p_3) \vee (p_3 \wedge p_1)$ itself?
    (c) Let $\circ$ and $\star$ be two binary truth functions. We say that $\circ$ is *the dual of* $\star$ iff $\neg(x \star y) \equiv (\neg x \circ \neg y)$ for all propositions x and y. For example, $\wedge$ is the dual of $\vee$, and $\vee$ is the dual of $\wedge$. Show that if $\circ$ is the dual of $\star$, then $\star$ is the dual of $\circ$. For the 16 binary truth functions, determine which is the dual of which.
    (d) Define the *denial* of a proposition, $d(\cdot)$, recursively by $d(p) = \neg p$, and $d(\neg w) = \neg d(w)$, $d(u \wedge v) = (d(u) \vee d(v))$, $d(u \vee v) = (d(u) \wedge d(v))$. Show that $d(z) \equiv \neg z$ for any proposition z.
15. The *negation normal form* (nnf) is defined recursively by:

    If p is a propositional variable, then both p and $\neg p$ are in nnf.
    If u and v are in nnf, then $(u \wedge v)$ and $(u \vee v)$ are in nnf.

    Construct a grammar for nnf. Show that each proposition is equivalent to one in nnf. Give a procedure to obtain an nnf equivalent to a proposition, without using cnf or dnf conversion.
16. Write programs in any language you know to convert a proposition to a cnf and to a dnf.
17. The grammar in BNF for the set of literals can be written as $l ::= p \mid \neg p$, where p stands for atomic propositions. Give grammars in BNF for conjunctive clauses, disjunctive clauses, cnf, and dnf.
18. Recall the notation $\oplus$ for XOR, the *exclusive or*. Attempt to show that

    (a) $\oplus$ is both commutative and associative.
    (b) $w \oplus \bot \equiv w, \quad w \oplus \top \equiv \neg w, \quad w \oplus w \equiv \bot$.
    (c) $u \vee (v \oplus w) \equiv (u \vee v) \oplus (u \vee w), \quad u \wedge (v \oplus w) \equiv (u \wedge v) \oplus (u \wedge w)$.
    (d) $\{\oplus, \wedge, \top\}$ is truth functionally complete.

(e) Any of $\oplus, \wedge, \top$ can be expressed through the other two.
(f) $\{\oplus, \vee, \top\}$ is truth functionally complete.

19. Show that any proposition A that uses the connectives $\wedge$, $\oplus$, $\top$, $\bot$, and propositional variables $p_1, \ldots, p_n$ can be written uniquely in the form

$$A \equiv a_0 \oplus (a_1 \wedge p_1) \oplus (a_2 \wedge p_2) \oplus \cdots \oplus (a_n \wedge p_n)$$

where $a_i \in \{\top, \bot\}$ for $0 \le i \le n$.

20. Do the previous exercise if A is a proposition that uses the connectives
(a) $\oplus$, $\top$ (b) $\leftrightarrow$, $\bot$ (c) $\leftrightarrow$, $\neg$

21. See Problem 18. Prove that each proposition is equivalent to either $\bot$ or $\top$ or $C_1 \oplus \cdots \oplus C_m$, where each C_i is either $\top$ or a conjunction of propositional variables. This is called the *exclusive or normal form* (enf). What are the enf of valid propositions?

22. Let $x = C_1 \wedge C_2 \wedge \cdots \wedge C_m$ and $y = D_1 \wedge D_2 \wedge \cdots \wedge D_n$, where C_i, D_j are disjunctive clauses. Define $dist(x,y) = \wedge_{i,j}(C_i \vee D_j)$. Using this, a *cnf* of a proposition can be defined recursively as follows:

If w is a disjunctive clause, then $cnf(w) = w$.
If w is $x \wedge y$, then $cnf(w) = cnf(x) \wedge cnf(y)$.
If w is $x \vee y$, then $cnf(w) = dist(cnf(x), cnf(y))$.

This *recursive definition of a cnf* can easily be implemented in a functional programming language. Show that the definition correctly defines a cnf of a proposition which uses the connectives $\neg$, $\wedge$ and $\vee$.

23. Define *dnf* recursively, analogous to the recursive definition of *cnf*.

24. For each proposition x, and each propositional variable p occurring in x, let x^p be the proposition obtained from x by replacing each occurrence of p by $\top$. Similarly, let x_p be the proposition obtained from x by replacing each occurrence of p by $\bot$. Let $\bar{x}$ be the proposition $x^p \vee x_p$.Prove the following:

(a) $x \models \bar{x}$.
(b) for any proposition y, if $x \models y$ and p does not occur in y, then $\bar{x} \models y$.
(c) x is satisfiable iff $\bar{x}$ is satisfiable.

25. Let x, y be propositions having no common propositional variables. Show that if $\models x \to y$, then x is unsatisfiable or y is valid.

26. *Craig's interpolation theorem:* Let x, y be propositions having at least one propositional variable in common. A proposition z is called an *interpolant* of $x \to y$ iff $\models x \to z$, and $\models z \to y$, where all propositional variables occurring in z are from among the common propositional variables of x, y. Show that if $\models x \to y$, then x is unsatisfiable or y is valid or $x \to y$ has an interpolant.

27. For each $i \in \mathbb{N}$, let x_i be a proposition; and let $\Sigma = \{x_i \to x_{i+1} : i \in \mathbb{N}\}$. Using resolution, show that $\Sigma \models x_0 \to x_n$ for each $n \in \mathbb{N}$.

28. Let $f : \{q_1, \ldots, q_m\} \to \{0,1\}$ be a function, where $q_1, \ldots, q_m$ are distinct propositional variables. Show that there is a proposition w such that for any function $g : \{q_1, \ldots, q_m\} \to \{0,1\}$, $g \models w$ iff $f = g$.

29. Let Σ be a set of propositions. Let w be a proposition. Show that if $\Sigma \cup \{w\}$ and $\Sigma \cup \{\neg w\}$ have resolution refutations, then Σ also has a resolution refutation.
30. Let Σ and Γ be sets of propositions, and let w be a proposition. Show that if $\Sigma \cup \{w\}$ and $\Gamma \cup \{\neg w\}$ have resolution refutations, then $\Sigma \cup \Gamma$ has a resolution refutation.
31. In a set of clauses, replace simultaneously, each occurrence of p by $\neg p$, and each occurrence of $\neg p$ by p, for each propositional variable p. Show that a resolution refutation of the new set of clauses will remain essentially the same.
32. Define formally 3SAT and 2SAT.
33. Show that Procedure *TwoSat* correctly solves 2SAT. The catch is to see that in Stage 2, the 2cnf A is satisfiable if the 2cnf C is satisfiable.
34. Given a 2cnf x having n propositional variables $p_1, \cdots, p_n$, construct a directed graph G_x by taking $2n$ vertices $p_1, \neg p_1, \cdots, p_n, \neg p_n$. Corresponding to each clause of the form $p \vee q$, join an edge from the vertex $\neg p$ to q, and join another edge from the vertex $\neg q$ to p. First, show that x is unsatisfiable iff there is a vertex p in G_x such that there is a path from p to $\neg p$, and also there is a path from $\neg p$ to p. Next, show that determining whether such a vertex p exists in G_x takes polynomial time.
35. Try to show that the procedure *HornSat* correctly checks whether a given Horn formula is satisfiable. [Hint: You may have to use induction on the number of times the while loop is executed in running the procedure.]
36. Redefine a Horn clause as $q_1 \wedge q_2 \wedge \cdots \wedge q_m \to q$ admitting q_i's to be any literal. Explain why the procedure *HornSat* fails.
37. Can you specify a syntactic criterion on cnfs so that they will be equivalent to Horn formulas? If you answer 'no', why? If you answer 'yes', can you write a procedure to convert such special cnfs to Horn formulas?
38. Can you use grammars in BNF to define Horn formulas? Do you require any intermediate definitions so that this can be done?
39. Let $\mathscr{C}$ be a collection of interpretations. Define the intersection (call it I) of all interpretations in $\mathscr{C}$ by $I(p) = 1$ iff $i(p) = 1$ for each $i \in \mathscr{C}$. Show that if a Horn clause $p_1 \wedge \cdots \wedge p_n \to q$ receives the value 1 under each interpretation in $\mathscr{C}$ then it receives the value 1 under I.
40. Justify both *pure literal heuristic* and *unit clause heuristic*.
41. Let A and B be conjunctive clauses. Define $Re(A,B)$ by omitting a literal p from A and $\neg p$ from B, and then taking their conjunction. Let i be an interpretation.

    (a) Show that if $i \nvDash A$ and $i \nvDash B$, then $i \nvDash Re(A,B)$.
    (b) Give examples of A, B and i to show that $i \vDash A$, $i \vDash B$, but $i \nvDash Re(A,B)$.
42. Denote by $\pi(A)$ the set of all prime implicates of A and interpret this set as the conjunction of all its clauses as usual. For a cnf A, show the following:

    (a) $A \equiv \pi(A)$ (b) $RS^*(A) = \pi(A)$ (c) $RS^*(A) \equiv R^*(A)$
43. Write a procedure for the DPLL algorithm as described in the text. Prove that it correctly determines whether a given proposition is satisfiable or not.

44. For a clause set A, define $S_0(A) = A$, $S_{m+1}(A) = \{C : C$ is a resolvent of two clauses in $S_m(A)\}$; and then take $S^*(A) = \cup_{n\in\mathbb{N}} S_n(A)$. Give an example of a clause set A such that A is unsatisfiable but $\bot \notin S^*(A)$.
45. For a clause set A, define $U^*(A) = \cup_{n\in\mathbb{N}} U_n(A)$, where $U_0(A) = A$, $U_{m+1}(A) = U_m(A) \cup \{C : C$ is a resolvent of two clauses in $U_m(A)$ one of which is a singleton$\}$. This is called *unit resolution*. Give an example of a clause set A such that A is unsatisfiable but $\bot \notin U^*(A)$.
46. Let A be any clause set. For any set $B \subseteq A$, write $N(A,B) = A \cup \{C : C$ is a resolvent of a clause in B and a clause in $A\}$. Define $UN_n(A)$ inductively by: $UN_0(A) = A$, $UN_{m+1}(A) = N(UN_m(A), A)$. Let $UN^*(A) = \cup_{n\in\mathbb{N}} UN_n(A)$. Show that $\bot \in U^*(A)$ iff $\bot \in UN^*(A)$.
47. Let A be a clause set and $B \subseteq A$ is such that $A \setminus B$ is satisfiable. A clause in $R^*(A)$ *has B-support* iff it is in B or is a resolvent of two clauses, of which at least one has B-support. Let $R_1(A) = A \cup \{C \in R(S) : C$ has B-support$\}$. Define $R_1^*(A)$ in the usual way. Show that A is unsatisfiable iff $\bot \in R_1^*(A)$.
48. Let A be a clause set with each clause in it having at most two literals. Show that the resolution method determines the satisfiability of A in a time which is a polynomial in the length of A.
49. Let B be a clause set, each clause of which has at most three literals. Give reasons why your solution of Problem 48 may not prove that the resolution method determines satisfiability of such a clause set B in polynomial time.
50. Let p_{ij} be propositional variables for $i, j \in \{1, \ldots, n+1\}$. For $n \geq 1$, define a proposition H_n as follows:

$$H_n = \bigwedge_{i=1}^{n+1} \bigvee_{j=1}^{n} p_{ij} \to \bigvee_{k=1}^{n} \bigvee_{i=1}^{n+1} \bigvee_{j=i+1}^{n+1} (p_{ik} \wedge p_{jk})$$

Prove that H_n is valid for each n. Convince yourself that a resolution proof of validity of H_n has length as an exponential in n. [Hint: You may have to use and encode the Pigeon Hole Principle; see Haken (1985).]

Chapter 4

Other Proof Systems for PL

4.1 CALCULATION

From among many available proof systems for PL, we choose four for their different approaches. Calculations, as advocated by D. Gries, use equivalences to construct a proof. We will use equivalences as well as other laws in calculations. Both natural deduction system and the sequent calculus were advocated by G. Gentzen. And he preferred the sequent calculus due to its generality and symmetry. The other system, called the Analytic Tableau, was advocated by R. M. Smullyan. It has certain advantages over the other systems so much so that in many books, you will find this system as the major one instead of the Hilbert style axiomatic system PC. compared to other proof systems, it is easier to construct analytic tableaux.

To have a feel of calculations, consider proving $x \wedge y \equiv (x \leftrightarrow (x \vee y \leftrightarrow y))$. By Theorem 1.5, it is enough to show that $\vDash (x \wedge y \leftrightarrow (x \leftrightarrow (x \vee y \leftrightarrow y)))$. Here is an attempt:

$$
\begin{array}{ll}
x \wedge y \leftrightarrow (x \leftrightarrow (x \vee y \leftrightarrow y)) & \text{[Associativity]} \\
\equiv\ (x \wedge y \leftrightarrow x) \leftrightarrow (x \vee y \leftrightarrow y) & \text{[Implication, Commutativity]} \\
\equiv\ (x \to y) \leftrightarrow (x \to y) & \text{[Identity]} \\
\equiv\ \top &
\end{array}
$$

Again, the use of Theorem 1.5 completes the job. Moreover, the serial equivalences are permitted since $\equiv$ is transitive, i.e., if $x \equiv y$ and $y \equiv z$, then $x \equiv z$.

Look at the above series of equivalences closely. How is the first equivalence justified? In the Law of Associativity: $x \leftrightarrow (y \leftrightarrow z) \equiv (x \leftrightarrow y) \leftrightarrow z$, we take x, y, z as propositional variables. Then we uniformly substitute x as $x \wedge y$, y as x, and z as $x \vee y \leftrightarrow y$. Similarly, other equivalences hold. We can use our theorems, laws and the replacement laws for devising a proof system, where equivalences and consequences can be proved by calculations.

A **calculation** will be written as a sequence of propositions where successive propositions are linked by the symbol $\equiv$ or $\vDash$. Each step of the calculation which appears as $A \equiv B$ or as $A \vDash B$ must be justified by a law listed in Theorem 2.12, implicitly using the replacement laws. A calculation looks like: $C_0 \star C_1 \star \cdots \star C_m$, where an instance of $\star$ can be one of $\equiv$ or $\vDash$; and each step $C_{i-1} \star C_i$ must be an instance of a law $E_1 \star E_2$. The calculation **justifies** the metastatement $C_0 \otimes C_m$, where $\otimes$ is $\equiv$ if all instances of $\star$ are $\equiv$, and $\otimes$ is $\vDash$ if at least one instance of $\star$ is $\vDash$. A calculation that justifies a consequence or an equivalence is also called a **calculational proof** of that consequence or equivalence.

A calculation for $\vDash u$ can be any calculation justifying $u \equiv \top$ or $\top \vDash u$.

A calculation for $\vDash u \to v$ can be any calculation justifying $u \vDash v$ or $\top \vDash u \to v$.

A calculation for $\vDash u \leftrightarrow v$ can be any calculation justifying $\top \vDash u \leftrightarrow v$ or $u \equiv v$.

A justification for the unsatisfiability of a set $\Sigma = \{w_1, \ldots, w_n\}$ can be any calculation justifying $w_1 \wedge \cdots \wedge w_n \equiv \bot$ or $w_1 \wedge \cdots \wedge w_n \vDash \bot$; due to Theorem 1.5.

To justify $\{w_1, \ldots, w_n\} \vDash w$, we may construct a calculation for $w_1 \wedge \cdots \wedge w_n \vDash w$ or for $\vDash w_1 \wedge \cdots \wedge w_n \to w$ or for $\vDash w_1 \to ((\cdots w_2 \to \cdots (w_n \to w) \cdots)$. By RA, we may alternatively construct a calculation for $w_1 \wedge \cdots \wedge w_n \wedge \neg w \vDash \bot$.

EXAMPLE 4.1. Show by calculation that $\{p \wedge (q \wedge r), s \wedge t\} \vDash q \wedge s$.

$p \wedge (q \wedge r) \wedge (s \wedge t)$	[Associativity, Commutativity]
$\equiv\ p \wedge (r \wedge t) \wedge (q \wedge s)$	[Elimination]
$\vDash\ q \wedge s.$	

If the premises are many, we may not write down the conjunction of all the premises at a time. We rather start with a premise, and go on introducing more and more premises as we please, by using a conjunction. However, we document it writing 'P' as a shorthand for 'introducing a premise' in the documentation column.

EXAMPLE 4.2. Show that $p \to (q \to r),\ \neg r,\ p \vDash \neg q$.

$(p \to (q \to r)) \wedge p$	[Mod Pon, P]
$\vDash\ (q \to r) \wedge \neg r$	[Mod Tol]
$\vDash\ \neg q$	

The premise $\neg r$ has been introduced in the second line of the calculation; it is documented by mentioning 'P'.

EXAMPLE 4.3. Show that $(p \to q) \wedge (\neg p \to r) \equiv (p \wedge q) \vee (\neg p \wedge r)$

$(p \to q) \wedge (\neg p \to r)$	[Imp]
$\equiv (\neg p \vee q) \wedge (\neg\neg p \vee r)$	[Doub Neg, Dist]
$\equiv (\neg p \wedge p) \vee (\neg p \wedge r) \vee (q \wedge p) \vee (q \wedge r)$	[Const]
$\equiv (\neg p \wedge r) \vee (q \wedge p) \vee (q \wedge r)$	[Const]
$\equiv (\neg p \wedge r) \vee (q \wedge p) \vee ((p \vee \neg p) \wedge (q \wedge r))$	[Dist]
$\equiv (\neg p \wedge r) \vee (q \wedge p) \vee (p \wedge q \wedge r) \vee (\neg p \wedge q \wedge r)$	[Comm, Absr]
$\equiv (\neg p \wedge r) \vee (q \wedge p)$	

EXAMPLE 4.4. Show that $\vDash (p \to r) \to ((\neg p \to \neg q) \to (q \to r))$.

$(\neg p \to \neg q) \wedge q$	[Mod Tol]
$\vDash\ \neg\neg p$	[Doub Neg, P]
$\vDash\ p \wedge (p \to r)$	[Mod Pon]
$\vDash\ r$	

Using the deduction theorem, we have shown that $p \to r, \neg p \to \neg q, q \vDash r$. In the following, we give a proof without using the deduction theorem.

$$\begin{array}{ll} (p \to r) \to ((\neg p \to \neg q) \to (q \to r)) & \text{[Contra]} \\ \equiv (p \to r) \to ((q \to p) \to (q \to r)) & \text{[Dist]} \\ \equiv (p \to r) \to (q \to (p \to r)) & \text{[Hyp Inv]} \\ \equiv \top & \end{array}$$

EXAMPLE 4.5. Show that $(\neg x \vee y) \wedge (x \vee z) \equiv (x \wedge y) \vee (\neg x \wedge z)$.

$$\begin{array}{l} (\neg x \vee y) \wedge (x \vee z) \\ \equiv (\neg x \wedge x) \vee (\neg x \wedge z) \vee (y \wedge x) \vee (y \wedge z) \\ \equiv (\neg x \wedge z) \vee (y \wedge x) \vee (y \wedge z) \\ \equiv (\neg x \wedge z) \vee (y \wedge x) \vee (y \wedge z \wedge (x \vee \neg x)) \\ \equiv (\neg x \wedge z) \vee (y \wedge x) \vee (y \wedge z \wedge x) \vee (y \wedge z \wedge \neg x) \\ \equiv ((\neg x \wedge z) \vee (y \wedge z \wedge \neg x)) \vee ((y \wedge x) \vee (y \wedge z \wedge x)) \\ \equiv (\neg x \wedge z) \vee (y \wedge x) \\ \equiv (x \wedge y) \vee (\neg x \wedge z) \end{array}$$

Document the above calculation.

Strong adequacy of calculations follows from the compactness theorem and the normal form theorem.

Exercises for § 4.1

Construct calculations for the valid ones among the following propositions and consequences. For others, construct a falsifying interpretation.

1. $(q \to p) \to p$
2. $p \to (q \to p)$
3. $\neg p \to (p \to q)$
4. $\neg p \to (p \to \bot)$
5. $p \to (q \to p \wedge q)$
6. $(((p \wedge q) \leftrightarrow p) \to q)$
7. $(\neg p \to \neg q) \to (q \to p)$
8. $(p \vee q) \to (\neg p \wedge q \to q)$
9. $(p \to q) \to (q \wedge r \to (p \to r))$
10. $((p \vee (p \wedge q)) \to (p \wedge (p \vee q)))$
11. $(((p \vee q) \wedge (\neg q \vee r)) \to (p \vee r))$
12. $(((p \wedge q) \wedge (\neg q \vee r)) \to (p \wedge r))$
13. $((p \leftrightarrow q) \leftrightarrow r) \leftrightarrow ((p \leftrightarrow q) \wedge (q \leftrightarrow r))$
14. $(p \to (q \to r)) \to ((p \to q) \to (q \to r))$
15. $\neg(p \to (q \to r)) \vee ((p \to q) \to (p \to r))$
16. $(p \to q) \to ((q \to r) \to ((r \to s) \to (p \to s)))$
17. $((p \wedge q \to r) \wedge (p \wedge \neg q \to r)) \leftrightarrow (p \to (q \leftrightarrow r))$
18. $\neg(r \wedge \neg\neg q) \,!\!\vdash (\neg q \vee \neg r)$
19. $p \vee \neg q,\ p \to \neg r \,!\!\vdash q \to \neg r$
20. $p \vee q \to r \wedge s,\ t \wedge s \to u \,!\!\vdash p \to u$
21. $p \vee q \to r \wedge s,\ s \vee t \to u,\ p \vee \neg u \,!\!\vdash p \to (q \to r)$
22. $p \to q \wedge r,\ q \to s,\ d \to t \wedge u,\ q \to p \wedge \neg t \,!\!\vdash q \to t$
23. $p \vee q \to r \wedge s,\ r \vee u \to \neg v \wedge w,\ v \vee x \to p \wedge y \,!\!\vdash \neg v$
24. $(r \to r \wedge s) \to t,\ t \to (\neg u \vee u \to p \wedge u),\ p \vee q \to (r \to r) \,!\!\vdash p \leftrightarrow t$
25. $p,\ \neg r \to \neg p,\ (p \to q) \wedge (r \to s),\ (s \to u) \wedge (q \to t),\ s \to \neg t \,!\!\vdash \bot$
26. $p \to \neg q,\ r \to s,\ \neg t \to q,\ s \to \neg u,\ t \to \neg v,\ \neg u \to w,\ p \wedge r \,!\!\vdash \neg v \wedge w$

4.2 NATURAL DEDUCTION

In PC, substitutions in axiom schemes were tricky. In quasi-proofs and calculations, an appropriate law is required to be chosen at each stage. To minimize such choices, we plan to have two kinds of inference rules for each connective. The proof system differs slightly from the one advocated by G. Gentzen. It is customary to call such a system a **natural deduction system**.

In the system **PND** (Propositional Natural Deduction system), the propositions are all PL-propositions. This system has only one axiom, which is $\top$; however, this is now written as an inference rule. PND has the following inference rules (read 'i' for introduction and 'e' for elimination):

$$(\top i)\quad \frac{\cdot}{\top} \qquad\qquad (\top e)\quad \frac{\boxed{\top \cdots p}}{p} \qquad \frac{\top}{p\vee\neg p}$$

$$(\bot i)\quad \frac{p,\ \neg p}{\bot} \qquad\qquad (\bot e)\quad \frac{\bot}{p}$$

$$(\neg i)\quad \frac{\boxed{p \cdots \bot}}{\neg p} \qquad \frac{p\wedge\neg q}{\neg(p\to q)} \qquad\qquad (\neg e)\quad \frac{\neg\bot}{\top} \qquad \frac{\neg(p\to q)}{p\wedge\neg q} \qquad \frac{p\vee\neg q,\ q}{p}$$

$$(\neg\neg i)\quad \frac{p}{\neg\neg p} \qquad\qquad (\neg\neg e)\quad \frac{\neg\neg p}{p}$$

$$(\wedge i)\quad \frac{p,\ q}{p\wedge q} \qquad\qquad (\wedge e)\quad \frac{p\wedge q}{p} \qquad \frac{p\wedge q}{q}$$

$$(\vee i)\quad \frac{p}{p\vee q} \qquad \frac{q}{p\vee q} \qquad\qquad (\vee e)\quad \frac{\boxed{p\cdots r}\ \boxed{q\cdots r},\ p\vee q}{r}$$

$$(\to i)\quad \frac{\boxed{p\cdots q}}{p\to q} \qquad\qquad (\to e)\quad \frac{p,\ p\to q}{q} \qquad \frac{\neg q,\ p\to q}{\neg p}$$

$$(\leftrightarrow i)\quad \frac{p\to q,\ q\to p}{p\leftrightarrow q} \qquad\qquad (\leftrightarrow e)\quad \frac{p\leftrightarrow q}{(p\to q)\wedge(q\to p)}$$

Propositions separated by a comma on the numerators of rules will appear vertically in separate lines, in a proof. A box written horizontally in the above rules will also appear vertical in a proof. A box indicates the conditionality of the premises.

For example, in the rule $(\to i)$, the proposition p is introduced from nowhere, an extra assumption. The extra assumption p is, of course, introduced in an actual proof by targeting towards a particular conclusion such as q. But then, all those propositions that are derived with this extra assumption p do depend upon it, and thus must be written inside the box.

Once you close the box, and write $p\to q$, all it says is that the propositions outside the box, in particular, $p\to q$ does not depend upon the extra assumption p.

Notice that a proposition that does not depend upon p (e.g., a premise) may also be written inside this box.

The rule $(\rightarrow i)$ is simply another form of the deduction theorem better suited to be used inside a proof. In this form, the deduction theorem applies on a block of propositions, those contained in the box. The box corresponds to the block within the DTB-DTE in a quasi-proof. (See § 2.7).

Similarly, the rule $(\vee e)$ is the law of the cases expressed differently. The rule $(\top i)$ says that $\top$ may be derived without any specific requirement, i.e., $\top$ can be derived from any proposition; even in the absence of any proposition $\top$ can be introduced. This puts forth the convention that axioms can be written as fractions with empty numerators.

A **PND-deduction** is a sequence of propositions (may be, in boxes), where each one is obtained by applying one of the rules of PND. A **PND-proof of the consequence** $\Sigma \,!\!\vdash A$ is a PND-deduction, where each proposition, except the first proposition inside a box, is a premise in Σ or is obtained by an application of an inference rule of PND on earlier propositions, and the proposition A is the last proposition of the sequence not inside a box.

A consequence $\Sigma \,!\!\vdash A$ is said to be **PND-provable**, written, $\Sigma \vdash_{PND} A$ iff there exists a proof of the consequence $\Sigma \,!\!\vdash A$ in PND. In this section, we write $\Sigma \vdash_{PND} A$ as $\Sigma \vdash A$; and abbreviate 'PND-deduction' to 'deduction'.

Any box contains a full fledged deduction, except that propositions outside the box but occurring prior to it can also be used for deductions inside the box. That is, a rule can be applied on propositions occurring before the box and the result can be written as a proposition inside a box. A proposition inside the box may not be a premise; typically, the first proposition inside a box is not a premise. We have a constraint on the boxes:

A box can never cross another box; only nesting of boxes is allowed.

A proposition p is a **theorem** of PND iff $\varnothing \vdash p$; the deduction is then called a **PND-proof** of the theorem. We write $\vdash_{PND} p$, and abbreviate it to $\vdash p$, to say that p is a theorem. A set Σ of propositions is called **inconsistent** iff $\Sigma \vdash \bot$ else, it is **consistent**.

Σ is consistent means that there cannot be any deduction showing $\Sigma \vdash \bot$. We follow the same three-columns style of writing a deduction as in PC, writing 'P' for premises and 'CP' for an extra or *conditional premise.* The 'CP' is justified by the deduction theorem. See the following examples.

EXAMPLE 4.6. A proof for $\vdash p \rightarrow (q \rightarrow p)$ is as follows:

1.	p	CP
2.	q	CP
3.	p	1
4.	$q \rightarrow p$	$\rightarrow i$
5.	$p \rightarrow (q \rightarrow p)$	$\rightarrow i$

To write the proofs with ease, we will dispense with the boxes. We will rather use the pair CPB and CPE with or without a number. CPB1 will close with CPE1, CPB2 will close with CPE2, etc. When we mention CPE on the line numbered $n+1$, it would mean that the conditionality of the premise introduced by the corresponding CPB has ended by the line numbered n. Take care of the nesting of the boxes. The proof in Example 4.6 is rewritten in the following, using this four-columns style.

1.	p		CPB1
2.	q		CPB2
3.	p	1	
4.	$q \to p$	$\to i$	CPE2
5.	$p \to (q \to p)$	$\to i$	CPE1

EXAMPLE 4.7. Show that $\vdash (p \to (q \to r)) \to ((p \to q) \to (p \to r))$.

1.	$p \to (q \to r)$		CPB1
2.	$p \to q$		CPB2
3.	p		CPB3
4.	q	$2, 3, \to e$	
5.	$q \to r$	$1, 3, \to e$	
6.	r	$4, 5, \to e$	
7.	$p \to r$	$2, 6, \to e$	CPE3
8.	$(p \to q) \to (p \to r)$	$1, 7, \to e$	CPE2
9.	$(p \to (q \to r)) \to (p \to q) \to (p \to r))$	$1, 8, \to i$	CPE1

EXAMPLE 4.8. Show that $\vdash (\neg q \to \neg p) \to ((\neg q \to p) \to q)$.

1.	$\neg q \to \neg p$		CPB1
2.	$\neg q \to p$		CPB2
3.	$\neg q$		CPB3
4.	$\neg p$	$1, 3, \to e$	
5.	p	$2, 3, \to e$	
6.	$\bot$	$4, 5, \bot i$	
7.	$\neg\neg q$	$3, 6, \neg i$	CPE3
8.	q	$7, \neg\neg e$	
9.	$(\neg q \to p) \to q$	$2, 8, \to i$	CPE2
10.	$(\neg q \to \neg p) \to ((\neg q \to p) \to q)$	$1, 9, \to i$	CPE1

EXAMPLE 4.9. Show that $\vdash (\neg q \to \neg p) \to (p \to q)$.

1.	$\neg q \to \neg p$		CPB1
2.	p		CPB2
3.	$\neg\neg p$	$\neg\neg i$	
4.	$\neg\neg q$	$1, 3, \to e$	
5.	q	$\neg\neg e$	
6.	$p \to q$	$1, 5, \to i$	CPE2
7.	$(\neg q \to \neg p) \to (p \to q)$	$1, 6, \to i$	CPE1

Sometimes, in a deduction, we number only those lines which may be mentioned latter in the documentation column. See the following example.

EXAMPLE 4.10. $p \to \neg q, r \to s, \neg t \to q, s \to \neg u, t \to \neg v, \neg u \to w \vdash p \wedge r \to \neg v \wedge w.$

1.	$p \wedge r$		CPB
	p	$\wedge e$	
	$p \to \neg q$	P	
	$\neg q$	$\to e$	
	$\neg t \to q$	P	
	$\neg\neg t$	$\to e$	
	t	$\neg\neg e$	
	$t \to \neg v$	P	
2.	$\neg v$	$\to e$	
	r	$1, \wedge e$	
	$r \to s$	P	
	s	$\to e$	
	$s \to \neg u$	P	
	$\neg u$	$\to e$	
	$\neg u \to w$	P	
3.	w	$\to e$	
4.	$\neg v \wedge w$	$2, 3, \wedge i$	
	$p \wedge r \to \neg v \wedge w$	$1, 4, \to i$	CPE

EXAMPLE 4.11. $p \vee (\neg q \wedge r) \to s,\ (t \wedge \neg u) \to \neg s,\ v \vee \neg u,\ \neg(v \vee \neg r),\ t,\ p \vdash \bot.$

	p	P	
	$p \vee (\neg q \wedge r)$	$\vee i$	
	$p \vee (\neg q \wedge r) \to s$	P	
1.	s	$\to e$	
	t	P	
	$\neg u$		CPB
	$t \wedge \neg u$	$\wedge i$	
	$t \wedge \neg u \to \neg s$	P	
2.	$\neg s$	$\to e$	
	$\bot$	$1, 2, \bot i$	
	$\neg\neg u$	$\neg i$	CPE
	u	$\neg\neg e$	
	$v \vee \neg u$	P	
	v	$\neg e$	
	$v \vee \neg r$	$\vee i$	
	$\neg(v \vee \neg r)$	P	
	$\bot$	$\bot i$	

As you see, PND proofs are very much similar to the quasi-proofs. The quasi-proofs use any of the laws and also earlier proved consequences, whereas a PND proof uses strictly the prescribed rules.

Examples 4.6-4.8 show that the axioms of PC are, indeed, theorems of PND. Moreover, the inference rule MP of PC is simply the rule $(\to e)$ of PND. Hence PND is complete. But not yet, because PND works with all the five connectives and PC has only two. The other connectives and the constants $\top$ and $\bot$ have been introduced through definitions into PC. To prove completeness, show the following using PND:

$$
\begin{aligned}
\top \vdash p \to p, &\quad p \to p \vdash \top,\\
\bot \vdash \neg(p \to p), &\quad \neg(p \to p) \vdash \bot,\\
p \vee q \vdash \neg p \to q, &\quad \neg p \to q \vdash p \vee q,\\
p \wedge q \vdash \neg(p \to \neg q), &\quad \neg(p \to \neg q) \vdash p \wedge q,\\
p \leftrightarrow q \vdash (p \to q) \wedge (q \to p), &\quad (p \to q) \wedge (q \to p) \vdash p \leftrightarrow q.
\end{aligned}
$$

Alternatively, you may prove completeness of PND by constructing a maximally consistent set, etc. You can also show that all the rules of PND are sound; that is, the rules represent valid consequences of PL. Since the proofs in PND are finite in length, strong adequacy of PND to PL follows naturally.

Theorem 4.1 (Strong Adequacy of PND). *Let Σ be a set of propositions, and let w be any proposition. $\Sigma \vDash w$ iff $\Sigma \vdash_{PND} w$.*

Exercises for § 4.2

1. For all the tautologies among the following propositions give a natural deduction proof.

   (a) $p \to (q \to p)$
   (b) $(q \to p) \to p$
   (c) $(((p \wedge q) \leftrightarrow p) \to q)$
   (d) $(\neg p \to \neg q) \to (q \to p)$
   (e) $((p \vee (p \wedge q)) \to (p \wedge (p \vee q)))$
   (f) $(((p \vee q) \wedge (\neg q \vee r)) \to (p \vee r))$
   (g) $(((p \wedge q) \wedge (\neg q \vee r)) \to (p \wedge r))$
   (h) $((p \leftrightarrow q) \leftrightarrow r) \leftrightarrow ((p \leftrightarrow q) \wedge (q \leftrightarrow r))$
   (i) $((p \wedge q \to r) \wedge (p \wedge \neg q \to r)) \leftrightarrow (p \to (q \leftrightarrow r))$

2. Are the following consequences valid? Justify with a PND-deduction or give a non-model.

   (a) $\neg(r \wedge \neg\neg q)\ !\vdash (\neg q \vee \neg r)$
   (b) $p \vee \neg q,\ p \to \neg r\ !\vdash q \to \neg r$
   (c) $p \vee q \to r \wedge s,\ t \wedge s \to u\ !\vdash p \to u$
   (d) $p \vee q \to r \wedge s,\ s \vee t \to u,\ p \vee \neg u\ !\vdash p \to (q \to r)$
   (e) $p \to q \wedge r,\ q \to s,\ d \to t \wedge u,\ q \to p \wedge \neg t\ !\vdash q \to t$
   (f) $p,\ \neg r \to \neg p,\ (p \to q) \wedge (r \to s),\ (s \to u) \wedge (q \to t),\ s \to \neg t\ !\vdash \bot$

3. Construct another PND-derivation for the consequence in Example 4.11.

4.3 GENTZEN SEQUENT CALCULUS

Our treatment of natural deduction system follows closely the style of quasi-proofs. Instead of supplying a proof we may shift our attention to provability. For example, the deduction theorem in PC implies that if $x \vdash y$ then $\vdash x \to y$. Reading $\vdash$ as provability of a consequence, we may think of deduction theorem as

if $x\ !\vdash y$ is provable, then $!\vdash x \to y$ is provable.

Thus instead of constructing proofs, we will be interested in proving that certain consequences are provable. This idea gives rise to the notion of a *sequent* and the formal system is then called a *sequent calculus*. Due to its mechanical nature, it is often used in automated theorem proving.

In a sequent calculus, one starts from a given sequent (consequence) and goes on applying *sequent rules* to get newer sequents. If all the new sequents can be considered to be correct, then the initial one is also considered correct. Thus Gentzen system identifies some of the sequents as correct or self-evident and tries to reduce everything to the self-evident ones, which terminate a proof.

Gentzen's original sequent calculus is almost a translation of PND rules into sequents. We will present a modified version of it, which is sometimes called *Gentzen's symmetric sequents*.

A **sequent** is of the form $\Sigma \vdash \Gamma$, where Σ and Γ are sets of propositions. We assume, for technical reasons, that $\top$ is also a sequent, though the symbol $\vdash$ does not appear in it. When $\top$ occurs in other sequents, it is taken as a proposition, as usual. We omit the curly brackets around the propositions in Σ and Γ while writing the sequents. For example, the following are all sequents:

$$\top \qquad p,r \vdash q,s,t \qquad p,r \vdash q \qquad p \vdash q \qquad p \vdash \qquad \vdash q \qquad \vdash$$

Informally, a sequent "$\Sigma \vdash \Gamma$ is provable" means that "for any interpretation i, if i satisfies all propositions in Σ, then i satisfies some proposition in Γ". An inference rule of the form

$$\frac{\Sigma \vdash \Gamma}{\Delta_1 \vdash \Omega_1 \qquad \Delta_2 \vdash \Omega_2}$$

means that the sequent $\Sigma \vdash \Gamma$ is provable if both the sequents $\Delta_1 \vdash \Omega_1$ and $\Delta_2 \vdash \Omega_2$ are provable. Mark the direction of implication here:

if the denominator, then the numerator.

The *empty sequent* '$\vdash$' represents a consequence which never holds; and the *universal sequent* $\top$ represents a valid consequence, which is used to terminate a proof. We name our system as **GPC**, Gentzen's Propositional Calculus.

Let $\Sigma, \Gamma, \Delta, \Omega$ be generic sets of propositions, and let x, y be generic propositions. The **inference rules** or the **sequent rules** of GPC, along with their mnemonics, are as follows:

$$(\top) \quad \frac{\Sigma, x, \Gamma \vdash \Delta, x, \Omega}{\top} \qquad\qquad \frac{x \vdash x}{\top}$$

$$(\top L) \quad \frac{\Sigma, \top, \Gamma \vdash \Delta}{\Sigma, \Gamma \vdash \Delta} \qquad\qquad \frac{\top \vdash}{\cdot}$$

$$(\top R) \quad \frac{\Sigma \vdash \Gamma, \top, \Delta}{\top} \qquad\qquad \frac{\vdash \top}{\top}$$

$$(\bot L) \quad \frac{\Sigma, \bot, \Gamma \vdash \Delta}{\top} \qquad\qquad \frac{\bot \vdash}{\top}$$

$$(\bot R) \qquad \frac{\Sigma \vdash \Gamma, \bot, \Delta}{\Sigma \vdash \Gamma, \Delta} \qquad\qquad \frac{\vdash \bot}{\cdot}$$

$$(\neg L) \qquad \frac{\Sigma, \neg x, \Gamma \vdash \Delta}{\Sigma, \Gamma \vdash x, \Delta} \qquad\qquad \frac{\neg x \vdash}{\vdash x}$$

$$(\neg R) \qquad \frac{\Sigma \vdash \Gamma, \neg x, \Delta}{x, \Sigma \vdash \Gamma, \Delta} \qquad\qquad \frac{\vdash \neg x}{x \vdash}$$

$$(\vee L) \qquad \frac{\Sigma, x \vee y, \Gamma \vdash \Delta}{\Sigma, x, \Gamma \vdash \Delta \qquad \Sigma, y, \Gamma \vdash \Delta} \qquad\qquad \frac{x \vee y \vdash}{x \vdash \quad y \vdash}$$

$$(\vee R) \qquad \frac{\Sigma \vdash \Gamma, x \vee y, \Delta}{\Sigma \vdash \Gamma, x, y, \Delta} \qquad\qquad \frac{\vdash x \vee y}{\vdash x, y}$$

$$(\wedge L) \qquad \frac{\Sigma, x \wedge y, \Gamma \vdash \Delta}{\Sigma, x, y, \Gamma \vdash \Delta} \qquad\qquad \frac{x \wedge y \vdash}{x, y \vdash}$$

$$(\wedge R) \qquad \frac{\Sigma \vdash \Gamma, x \wedge y, \Delta}{\Sigma \vdash \Gamma, x, \Delta \qquad \Sigma \vdash \Gamma, y, \Delta} \qquad\qquad \frac{\vdash x \wedge y}{\vdash x \qquad \vdash y}$$

$$(\to L) \qquad \frac{\Sigma, x \to y, \Gamma \vdash \Delta}{\Sigma, \Gamma \vdash x, \Delta \qquad \Sigma, y, \Gamma \vdash \Delta} \qquad\qquad \frac{x \to y \vdash}{\vdash x \qquad y \vdash}$$

$$(\to R) \qquad \frac{\Sigma \vdash \Gamma, x \to y, \Delta}{\Sigma, x \vdash \Gamma, y, \Delta} \qquad\qquad \frac{\vdash x \to y}{x \vdash y}$$

$$(\leftrightarrow L) \qquad \frac{\Sigma, x \leftrightarrow y, \Gamma \vdash \Delta}{\Sigma, x, y, \Gamma \vdash \Delta \qquad \Sigma, \Gamma \vdash x, y, \Delta} \qquad\qquad \frac{x \leftrightarrow y \vdash}{x, y \vdash \qquad \vdash x, y}$$

$$(\leftrightarrow R) \qquad \frac{\Sigma \vdash \Gamma, x \leftrightarrow y, \Delta}{\Sigma, x \vdash \Gamma, y, \Delta \qquad \Sigma, y \vdash \Gamma, x, \Delta} \qquad\qquad \frac{\vdash x \leftrightarrow y}{x \vdash y \qquad y \vdash x}$$

The rules look numerous. But once you go through the mnemonics of the rules written on the right-hand side, you find that there is nothing to remember. The rules $(\top L)$ and $(\bot R)$ say that $\top$ on the left and $\bot$ on the right of $\vdash$ can be omitted. Thus the empty sequent $\vdash$ may be seen as the sequent $\top \vdash \bot$. Similarly, the universal sequent $\top$ may be thought of as any of the following sequents:

$$\bot \vdash \top, \qquad \top \vdash \top, \qquad \bot \vdash \bot, \qquad \vdash \top, \qquad \bot \vdash.$$

The rules for $\neg$ say that you can flip the sides and while so doing, drop or add a $\neg$. The rules for $\vee$ and $\wedge$ say that whenever $\vee$ is on the right of the sequent symbol $\vdash$, just replace it by a comma; a similar thing happens when $\wedge$ is on the left of $\vdash$. This suggests that we interpret a comma on the left of $\vdash$ as $\wedge$, and one on the right as

$\vee$. Whenever $\vee$ is on the left or $\wedge$ is on the right of $\vdash$, the sequent gives rise to two sequents. The other rules are obtained by employing the equivalences:

$$x \to y \equiv \neg x \vee y, \quad x \leftrightarrow y \equiv (\neg x \vee y) \wedge (\neg y \vee x).$$

A **derivation** (GPC-derivation) is a tree whose root is a sequent, and it is generated by applications of sequent rules on the leaves recursively. The new sequents are added as children of the original (leaf) node.

Rules that have a single denominator are called *stacking rules*, and the ones with two denominators are called *branching rules*. Sequents arising out of an application of a stacking rule are written one after another from top to bottom, while those arising out of branching rules are written with the help of slanted lines.

EXAMPLE 4.12. In the following derivation, we use the rules ($\to$R), ($\to$R), ($\neg$R), ($\neg$L), ($\to$L), ($\top$), ($\top$) in that order.

$$\vdash p \to (\neg q \to \neg(p \to q))$$
$$p \vdash \neg q \to \neg(p \to q)$$
$$p, \neg q \vdash \neg(p \to q)$$
$$p, \neg q, p \to q \vdash$$
$$p, p \to q \vdash q$$

$$p \vdash p, q \qquad\qquad p, q \vdash q$$
$$\top \qquad\qquad\qquad\qquad \top$$

A **proof of a sequent** (GPC-proof) is a derivation with the sequent at its root and $\top$ at all its leaves. We say that the sequent $\Sigma \vdash \Gamma$ is **provable** iff there exists a proof of the sequent, and in such a case, we write $\Sigma \Vdash \Gamma$. A proposition x is a **theorem**, written $\Vdash x$, (GPC-theorem) if the sequent $\vdash x$ is provable. A set of propositions Σ is **inconsistent** in GPC iff $\Sigma \Vdash \bot$.

Since it is customary to write sequents with the symbol $\vdash$, we use $\Vdash$ for provable (GPC-provable) sequents. Example 4.12 shows that $\Vdash p \to (\neg q \to \neg(p \to q))$.

Construction of proofs in GPC is straightforward; just use the rules and go on taking symbols from one side to the other till you reach at $\top$, or that when you cannot possibly apply any rule.

However, following a simple heuristic will shorten the proofs. For instance, consider the two proofs of the sequent $p \wedge \neg p \vdash p \wedge \neg p$ given below.

$$p \wedge \neg p \vdash p \wedge \neg p$$

$$p \wedge \neg p \vdash p \qquad p \wedge \neg p \vdash \neg p$$
$$p, \neg p \vdash p \qquad p, \neg p \vdash \neg p$$
$$\top \qquad\qquad\qquad \top$$

$$p \wedge \neg p \vdash p \wedge \neg p$$
$$p, \neg p \vdash p \wedge \neg p$$

$$p, \neg p \vdash p \qquad p, \neg p \vdash \neg p$$
$$\top \qquad\qquad\qquad \top$$

Both the rules ($\wedge$L), ($\wedge$R) are applicable on the sequent $p \wedge \neg p \vdash p \wedge \neg p$. The rule ($\wedge$R) is a branching rule. By choosing to apply this first, we have generated the proof on the left, above. On the other hand, the proof on the right is generated by choosing the stacking rule ($\wedge$L) first. Clearly, there is less writing when we apply a stacking rule before applying a branching rule. We follow the heuristic:

Postpone applying a branching rule if a stacking rule can be applied.

EXAMPLE 4.13. We show that $\Vdash p \to (q \to p))$.

$$\vdash p \to (q \to p)$$
$$p \vdash q \to p$$
$$p, q \vdash p$$
$$\top$$

EXAMPLE 4.14. A proof of $\Vdash (p \to (q \to r)) \to ((p \to q) \to (p \to r))$ follows.

$$\vdash (p \to (q \to r)) \to ((p \to q) \to (p \to r))$$
$$p \to (q \to r) \vdash (p \to q) \to (p \to r)$$
$$p \to (q \to r), p \to q \vdash p \to r$$
$$p \to (q \to r), p \to q, p \vdash r$$

Left branch: $p \to (q \to r), p \vdash p, r$ — $\top$

Right branch: $p \to (q \to r), q, p \vdash r$

- Left: $q, p \vdash p, r$ — $\top$
- Right: $q \to r, q, p \vdash r$
  - Left: $r, q, p \vdash q, r$ — $\top$
  - Right: $r, q, p \vdash r$ — $\top$

EXAMPLE 4.15. We construct a GPC proof of $\vdash (\neg q \to \neg p) \to ((\neg q \to p) \to q)$.

$$\vdash (\neg q \to \neg p) \to ((\neg q \to p) \to q)$$
$$\neg q \to \neg p \vdash (\neg q \to p) \to q$$
$$\neg q \to \neg p, \neg q \to p \vdash q$$

Left branch: $\neg q \to p \vdash \neg q, q$; $\neg q \to p, q \vdash q$ — $\top$

Right branch: $\neg p, \neg q \to p \vdash q$

- Left: $\neg p \vdash \neg q, q$; $\neg p, q \vdash q$ — $\top$
- Right: $\neg p, p \vdash q$; $p \vdash p, q$ — $\top$

EXAMPLE 4.16. A GPC proof of $\Vdash (\neg p \to \neg q) \to (q \to p)$ is as follows.

$$\begin{array}{c} \vdash (\neg p \to \neg q) \to (q \to p) \\ \neg p \to \neg q \vdash q \to p \\ \neg p \to \neg q,\, q \vdash p \end{array}$$

$$\begin{array}{cc} q \vdash \neg p,\, p & \neg q,\, q \vdash p \\ p,\, q \vdash p & q \vdash q,\, p \\ \top & \top \end{array}$$

EXAMPLE 4.17. The following proof shows that $\Vdash (p \vee q) \leftrightarrow (\neg p \to q)$.

$$\vdash p \vee q \leftrightarrow (\neg p \to q)$$

$$\begin{array}{cc} \begin{array}{c} p \vee q \vdash \neg p \to q \\ p \vee q,\, \neg p \vdash q \\ p \vee q \vdash p,\, q \end{array} & \neg p \to q \vdash p \vee q \end{array}$$

$$\begin{array}{cccc} p \vdash p,\, q & q \vdash p,\, q & \vdash \neg p,\, p \vee q & q \vdash p \vee q \\ \top & \top & p \vdash p \vee q & q \vdash p,\, q \\ & & p \vdash p,\, q & \top \\ & & \top & \end{array}$$

Notice that $\Sigma \vdash \Gamma$ is a sequent for sets of propositions Σ and Γ. However, $\Sigma \vDash \Gamma$ is not a valid consequence in PL, in general. $\Sigma \vDash \Gamma$ may become a valid consequence when Γ is a singleton. To bring both the symbols $\vdash$ and $\vDash$ on par, we generalize the meaning of $\vDash$ a bit.

> We say that $\Sigma \vDash \Gamma$, that is, the consequence $\Sigma\, !\!\vdash \Gamma$ is valid, iff any model of all the propositions in Σ is a model of some proposition in Γ.

If $\Gamma = \varnothing$, then a model of Σ cannot be a model of 'some proposition in Γ', for there is none in Γ. We thus interpret $\Sigma \vDash \varnothing$ as $\Sigma \vDash \bot$. This extension of the notion of consequence is called **generalized consequence.** Notice that this generalization means that in a sequent, the propositions on the left side of $\vdash$ are $\wedge$-ed whereas those on the right are $\vee$-ed. You can now confirm adequacy of GPC to PL in this generalized sense of a consequence.

Observe that GPC proofs are trees, where the theorem that is proved, is at the root, and the leaves are all $\top$. Thus a proof is also called a *proof tree*.

Soundness here means that, if every leaf of a proof tree is the universal sequent $\top$, then the consequence obtained from the root sequent by replacing $\vdash$ by $\vDash$ must be a valid consequence. This asks you to verify that for each rule of the form

$$\frac{\Sigma \vdash \Gamma}{\Delta \vdash \Omega}$$

the metastatement: "If $\Delta \vDash \Omega$, then $\Sigma \vDash \Gamma$" holds. Then apply induction on the height of a proof tree to complete the soundness proof. In the basis case, however, you have to check whether the universal sequent $\top$ corresponds to a valid consequence, which is the case due to our assumption.

Similarly, completeness may first be proved when Σ and Γ are finite. Using König's lemma one can prove that each proof tree is necessarily finite. Then finiteness of proofs will imply compactness. Finally, using compactness, the completeness results can be lifted to infinite sets Σ and Γ. This would imply the following result.

Theorem 4.2 (Strong Adequacy of GPC). *Let Σ be a set of propositions, and let w be a proposition. Then, $\Sigma \Vdash w$ iff $\Sigma \vDash w$.*

Due to the adequacy of GPC to PL, we informally say that a proof tree of the sequent $\Sigma \vdash w$ is a GPC-proof of the consequence $\Sigma \,!\!\vdash w$; and with a misuse of language, we also say that the proof tree is a proof of, or, proves that $\Sigma \vDash w$. For instance, the proof tree in Example 4.17 is a GPC-proof of the consequence $!\!\vdash (p \vee q) \leftrightarrow (\neg p \to q)$; and also is a GPC-proof of $\vDash (p \vee q) \leftrightarrow (\neg p \to q)$.

Exercises for § 4.3

Construct GPC-proofs of the following consequences:

(a) $p, p \to q \,!\!\vdash q$
(b) $p, p \to q \,!\!\vdash q$
(c) $!\!\vdash \top \leftrightarrow p \vee \neg p$
(d) $!\!\vdash \bot \leftrightarrow p \wedge \neg p$
(e) $!\!\vdash ((\neg p \to p) \to p)$
(f) $!\!\vdash p \wedge q \leftrightarrow \neg(p \to \neg q)$
(g) $!\!\vdash (((p \to q) \to p) \to p)$
(h) $(p \wedge (q \vee r)) \,!\!\vdash ((p \wedge q) \vee (p \wedge r))$
(i) $(p \to q) \,!\!\vdash (\neg(q \vee r) \to \neg(p \vee r))$
(j) $!\!\vdash (p \leftrightarrow q) \leftrightarrow ((p \to q) \wedge (q \to p))$

4.4 ANALYTIC TABLEAUX

In this section we present the proof system advocated by R. M. Smullyan improving E. W. Beth's *semantic trees*. This will be our last proof method for PL.

Consider the proposition $p \wedge q$; it is true when both p and q are true. Similarly, for $p \vee q$ to be true, you consider two cases: one, when p is true; and two, when q is true. We reach at the following diagram:

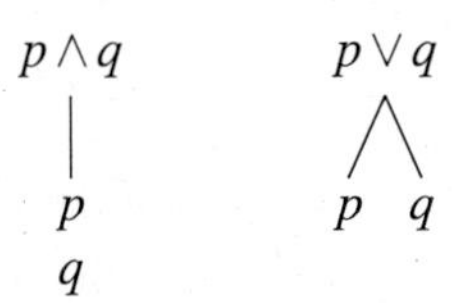

In the first case, the parent proposition has two children in the same branch; they are stacked. In the second case, the children are in different branches. When stacked, the parent proposition is true if both its children are true; and when branched out, the parent proposition is true provided that at least one of its children is true. This type of *semantic trees* remind you of the sets of models semantics. If $\mathbb{M}(A)$ denotes the sets of all models of A, then

$$\mathbb{M}(p \vee q) = \mathbb{M}(p) \cup \mathbb{M}(q) \text{ and } \mathbb{M}(p \wedge q) = \mathbb{M}(p) \cap \mathbb{M}(q).$$

What would happen if you take a more complicated proposition, say, $(p \vee q) \wedge r$? Well, $(p \vee q) \wedge r$ is true when both $p \vee q$ and r are true. Next, go for $p \vee q$. Continuing this way, we obtain the following semantic trees for $(p \vee q) \wedge r$ and $(p \vee q) \wedge \neg p \wedge \neg q$.

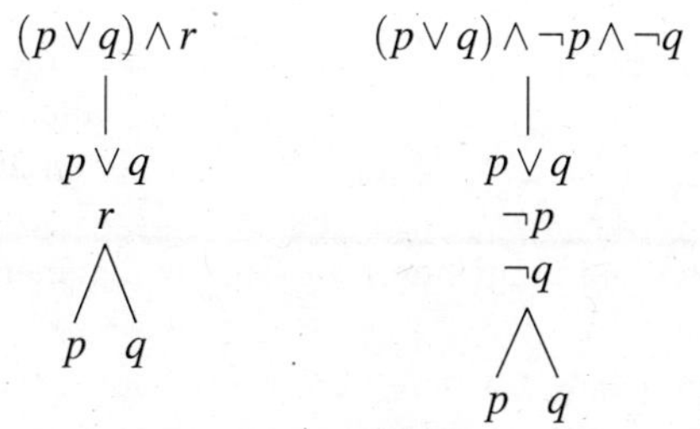

A model of $(p \vee q) \wedge r$ is obtained by looking at both the paths, one from the root $(p \vee q) \wedge r$ to the leaf p, which contains the literals r and p, and the other from the root to the leaf q containing the literals r and q. The two models thus obtained are i, j, where $i(r) = i(p) = 1$, and $j(r) = j(q) = 1$. Moreover, the tree gives a dnf representation of the root proposition, i.e., $(p \vee q) \wedge r \equiv (r \wedge p) \vee (r \wedge q)$.

Consider the second tree. In the leftmost path, we have the literals $p, \neg q, \neg p$, and the other path contains the literals $q, \neg q, \neg p$. This means that if you have a model of the root proposition, then it must satisfy (at least) one of the sets $\{p, \neg q, \neg p\}$ or $\{q, \neg q, \neg p\}$. But none of these sets is satisfiable since they contain complementary literals. Hence the root proposition is unsatisfiable. That means, if a path contains an atomic proposition and its negation, then the proposition at the root must be unsatisfiable We want to formalize this heuristic of semantic trees by formulating rules to tackle the connectives.

The resulting system is named as **PT**, the **propositional analytic tableau**. The stacked propositions in a path are simply written one below the other. The branching propositions are joined to the parent proposition by slanted lines, or separated by some blank spaces as in the rule $(\vee)$ below. The rules of inference of the system PT are, in fact, the tableau expansion rules, and are given as follows (x, y are generic propositions).

$$(\neg\neg) \quad \frac{\neg\neg x}{x} \qquad\qquad (\neg\top) \quad \frac{\neg\top}{\bot}$$

$$(\vee) \quad \frac{x \vee y}{x \quad\quad y} \qquad\qquad (\neg\vee) \quad \frac{\neg(x \vee y)}{\begin{array}{c}\neg x \\ \neg y\end{array}}$$

$$(\wedge)\quad \frac{x\wedge y}{\begin{array}{c}x\\ y\end{array}} \qquad\qquad (\neg\wedge)\quad \frac{\neg(x\wedge y)}{\neg x \qquad \neg y}$$

$$(\rightarrow)\quad \frac{x\rightarrow y}{\neg x \qquad y} \qquad\qquad (\neg\rightarrow)\quad \frac{\neg(x\rightarrow y)}{\begin{array}{c}x\\ \neg y\end{array}}$$

$$(\leftrightarrow)\quad \frac{x\leftrightarrow y}{\begin{array}{cc}x & \neg x\\ y & \neg y\end{array}} \qquad\qquad (\neg\leftrightarrow)\quad \frac{\neg(x\leftrightarrow y)}{\begin{array}{cc}x & \neg x\\ \neg y & y\end{array}}$$

Rules $(\neg\neg)$, $(\neg\top)$, $(\neg\vee)$, $(\wedge)$, $(\neg\rightarrow)$ are the **stacking rules** and propositions in the forms $\neg\neg x$, $\neg\top$, $\neg(x\vee y)$, $(x\wedge y)$, $\neg(x\rightarrow y)$ are called **stacking propositions**. Whereas the rules $(\vee)$, $(\neg\wedge)$, $(\rightarrow)$, $(\leftrightarrow)$, $(\neg\leftrightarrow)$ are **branching rules** and propositions in the forms $(x\vee y)$, $\neg(x\wedge y)$, $(x\rightarrow y)$, $(x\leftrightarrow y)$, $\neg(x\leftrightarrow y)$ are the **branching propositions**. Stacking and branching propositions together are called **compound propositions**.

A **tableau for** a proposition w is a tree whose root is w, and it is generated by applying PT-rules. A tableau is generated by first determining in which form the proposition is, and then applying the corresponding rule. The children of the node considered are the denominators of the corresponding rule.

Similarly, a **tableau for** a set of propositions Σ is a tableau whose root node contains all propositions from Σ, and which is generated by applying the PT-rules. We often write the propositions in Σ one below the other.

A **path in a tableau** is the sequence of propositions at the nodes which one encounters while travelling from the root to any leaf. If on a path, a rule has been applied on each compound proposition, then the path is called **complete**.

A path in a tableau is called a **closed path** if it contains $\bot$, or it contains p and $\neg p$ for some proposition p. In a tableau, we put a cross ($\times$) below a closed path. A path which is not closed is called an **open path**. Consequently, a complete path is closed if it contains a pair of complementary literals or it contains $\bot$. A **completed path** is a path which is either closed, or complete, or both closed and complete.

A tableau is called a **closed tableau** if each path in the tableau is a closed path. A tableau is called an **open tableau** if at least one of its paths is an open path. A **completed tableau** is a tableau in which each path is a completed path.

A set of propositions Σ is **inconsistent** (in fact, PT-inconsistent) iff there exists a closed tableau for Σ; otherwise, Σ is called **consistent**. That is, Σ is consistent iff each tableau for Σ contains an open path. By default, we take $\varnothing$ as a consistent set.

Let Σ be a set of propositions, and let w be a proposition. Then, $\Sigma\vdash_{PT} w$ iff $\Sigma\cup\{\neg w\}$ is inconsistent. We read $\Sigma\vdash_{PT} w$ as "w follows from Σ", or as "Σ **entails** w **in PT**", or even as "the consequence $\Sigma\,!\!\vdash w$ is PT-provable". We also abbreviate $\Sigma\vdash_{PT} w$ to $\Sigma\vdash w$, in this section. Thus a proposition w is a **theorem in PT** iff $\{\neg w\}$ is inconsistent iff there exists a closed tableau for $\neg w$. In what follows, when a tableau is constructed for a set Σ, we refer to the elements of Σ as **premises** with respect to that tableau.

You may generate a tableau either in depth-first or in breadth-first way. While generating it breadth-first, you must remember to add children of a proposition to each of the leaves on the (open) paths where the proposition occurs. Further, when a branching rule is applied on a proposition, we have to add its children to all those leaves of which the proposition is an ancestor. Look at the following tableaux for $\{p \vee q,\ q \wedge r\}$.

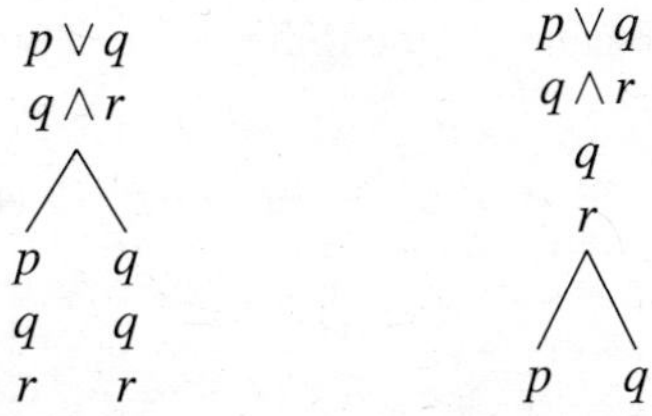

In the tableau on the left, we have used the rule $(\vee)$ on $p \vee q$ to get the tableau up to the third line. The path from the root to the leaf p contains $q \wedge r$, the same is true for the path ending in leaf q. So, in the next stage, the tableau is extended by adding the children q and r of $q \wedge r$ to both these leaves.

In the tableau on the right, we first use the proposition $q \wedge r$, and then use $p \vee q$. This requires less writing than the other. Similar to GPC, we use the heuristic:

If possible, apply all stacking rules before applying a branching rule.

EXAMPLE 4.18. For $\Sigma = \{p \to (\neg q \to r),\ p \to \neg q,\ \neg(p \to r)\}$, we have the following tableau.

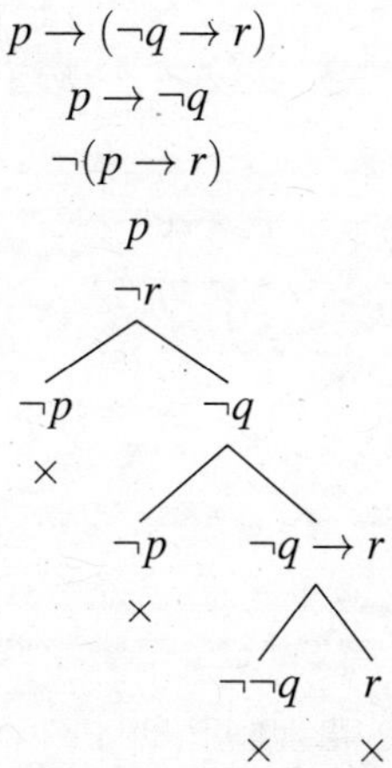

The root of the tableau contains all the three propositions from Σ, written one below the other. The fourth and fifth propositions come from the third proposition $\neg(p \to r)$. The first branching comes from the second proposition $p \to \neg q$; the second branching from the first proposition $p \to (\neg q \to r)$, and the third comes from the proposition $\neg q \to r$. We then check for complementary literals in each path.

The first (leftmost) path comprises all the premises and the propositions $\neg p, \neg r, p$. Since both p and $\neg p$ are on this path, it is a closed path and is thus crossed. Similarly, the second path contains the propositions $\neg p, \neg q, \neg r, p$, the third contains $\neg\neg q, \neg q \to r, \neg q, \neg r, p$, and the the last contains the propositions $r, \neg q \to r, \neg q, \neg r, p$, along with the premises. All of them are closed paths. Therefore, the tableau is a closed tableau, showing that Σ is inconsistent.

EXAMPLE 4.19. The tableaux for the following sets are shown as under.

(a) $\{p, p \to q\} \vdash q$

(b) $\vdash p \to (q \to p)$

(c) $\vdash (p \to (q \to r)) \to ((p \to q) \to (p \to r))$

(d) $\vdash (\neg q \to \neg p) \to ((\neg q \to p) \to q)$

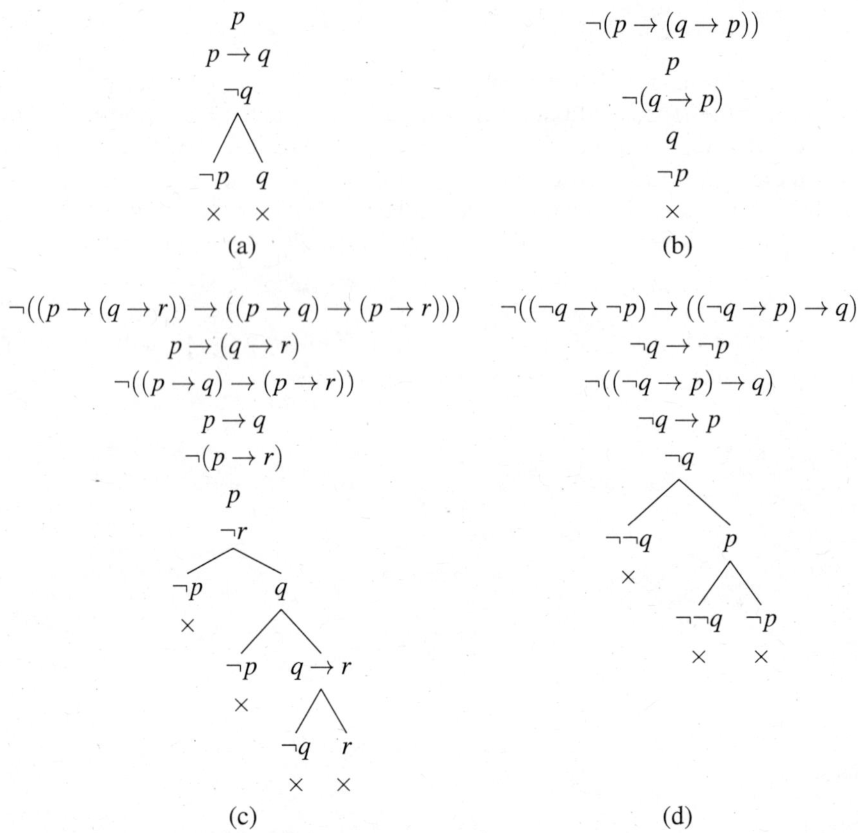

Example 4.19 says something about completeness of PT via PC. Before discussing completeness of PT, we look at completed tableaux.

EXAMPLE 4.20. The completed tableaux for the following sets are given below.

(a) $\Sigma = \{(p \to q) \wedge (r \to s), s \wedge (q \to t), \neg t, \neg(\neg p \vee \neg r)\}$

(b) $\Gamma = \{p \to q \wedge r, \neg p \vee s, r \to s \wedge t, \neg u\}$

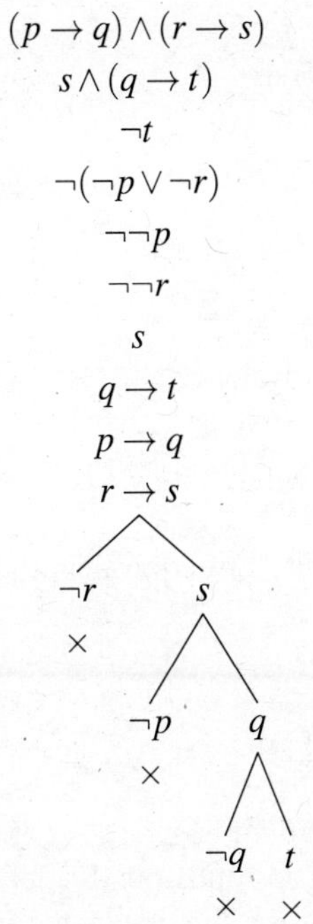

(a)

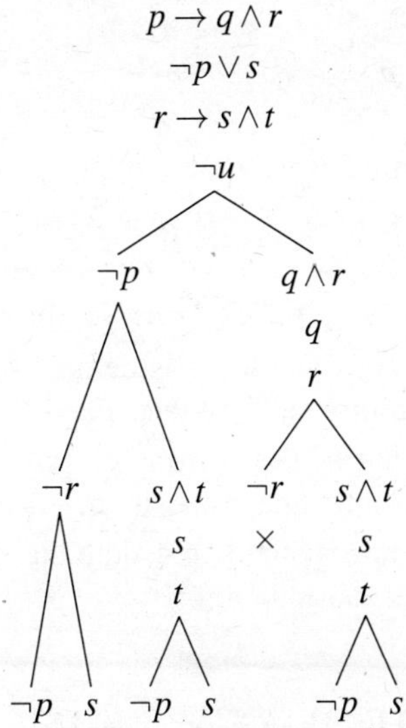

(b)

We find that the completed tableau for Σ is closed. Thus Σ is inconsistent. Whereas the completed tableau for Γ remains open. Is Γ consistent?

If some tableau for a proposition closes, then the proposition is a contradiction. Similarly, if some tableau for a set of propositions closes, then the set is inconsistent. Hence, in order to be consistent, all tableau for a set must remain open. However, copies of all tableau are found in a completed tableau. Also, a completed tableau cannot be expanded further (essentially). Thus, we observe the following:

Observation 4.1.
A set of propositions is inconsistent iff some *(completed) tableau for it is closed.*
A set of propositions is consistent iff some *completed tableau for it is open.*

Hence the set Γ in Example 4.20 is consistent. For showing consistency, we must construct a completed tableau, though a completed tableau is not required for showing inconsistency!

Exercises for § 4.4

1. Try to construct tableau proofs for the following:

(a) $\vdash p \to (\neg q \to \neg\neg p)$
(b) $\vdash \neg(p \to q) \to (r \to \neg q)$
(c) $\vdash (p \to q) \to (\neg q \to \neg p)$
(d) $\vdash \neg(\neg q \to \neg(p \to q)) \to \neg p$
(e) $\vdash (p \to q) \to ((\neg p \to q) \to q)$
(f) $\vdash (\neg p \to q) \to ((\neg p \to \neg q) \to p)$
(g) $\vdash p \to ((q \to (p \to r)) \to (q \to r))$
(h) $\vdash (p \to (q \to r)) \to (q \to (p \to r))$

(i) $\vdash (p \to \neg q) \to ((q \to \neg p) \to (p \to \neg q))$
(j) $\vdash ((\neg p \to \neg q) \to q) \to ((\neg p \to \neg q) \to p)$
(k) $\vdash p \to (\neg q \to \neg(p \to \neg(q \to (\neg p \to p))))$
(l) $(\neg p \to q) \to ((q \to \neg p) \to p) \vdash ((\neg p \to q) \to (q \to \neg p)) \to ((\neg p \to q) \to p)$

2. Determine whether the following sets of propositions are PT-consistent.

   (a) $\{p \vee q, p \vee (q \wedge t), p \to \neg r\}$
   (b) $\{p \wedge q \to r, \neg p \to t, q \wedge \neg r \wedge \neg t\}$
   (c) $\{p \to q, (p \wedge q) \vee \neg r, q \to \neg p, r \to s, q \leftrightarrow \neg s, p \vee \neg t\}$

3. The truth function $\oplus$ is defined by the equivalence $x \oplus y \equiv \neg(x \leftrightarrow y)$. Give tableau proofs of the facts that $\oplus$ is commutative and associative.
4. From the tableau for the proposition in Example 4.20(b), construct the dnf equivalent to the proposition.
5. Describe a general procedure that constructs a dnf equivalent to a proposition from its tableau.

4.5 ADEQUACY OF PT TO PL

A completed tableau can be generated systematically. Let Σ be a set of propositions. Since the set of all propositions is countable, Σ is also countable. So, let $X_1, X_2, X_3, \ldots$ be an enumeration of Σ. The **systematic tableau** for Σ is generated in stages. An inductive construction follows.

Stage 1: Start the tableau with X_1 as the root.

Stage $n+1$: Suppose a tableau has already been generated up to Stage n. If any path of the tableau contains $\bot$ or a pair of complementary literals, then close the path. If all paths are closed, stop; else, expand each open path ρ as follows:

1. Add X_{n+1} to ρ provided Σ has more than n propositions.
2. Scan ρ from root to leaf for a compound proposition on which a tableau rule has not yet been applied. If no such compound proposition is found, then stop expanding ρ. Else, call the first compound proposition found as A.
3. Apply the suitable tableau rule on A and add the necessary proposition(s) to the path as new leaf (leaves).

Generation of the systematic tableau stops when for some n both Stage n and Stage $n+1$ produce the same result; that is, when a rule has already been applied on each compound proposition in each path. Thus the systematic tableau is necessarily a completed tableau. In the systematic tableau, we sacrifice the short-cut of closing a branch when a proposition and its negation is found; we go up to the level of literals. If Σ is a finite set, then the systematic tableau for Σ is a finite binary tree. If Σ is infinite, then either the tableau is closed after a finite number of propositions from Σ are used, or it continues to grow to an infinite completed tableau.

EXAMPLE 4.21. Let $\Sigma = \{p \to q \wedge r, \neg p \vee s, r \to s \wedge t, \neg u\}$. We consider the ordering on Σ as its elements are written. Using this ordering, we construct the systematic tableau for Σ as follows.

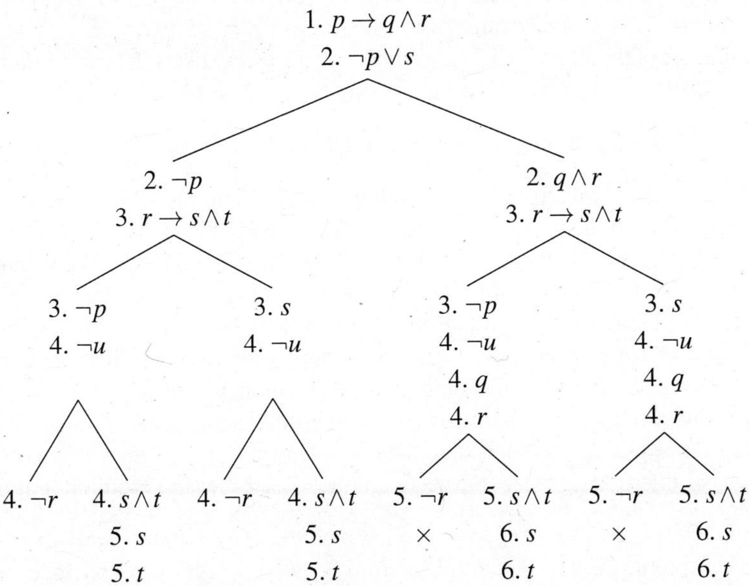

The numbers in front of the propositions in the tableau are the stage numbers. In the first stage, we just introduce the first proposition. In the second stage, we introduce the second proposition and then expand each path in the tableau. Compare the systematic tableau with the tableau in Example 4.20(b).

In an ordered set, we follow the ordering to enumerate its elements. Thus, there is a unique systematic tableau for an ordered set.

Lemma 4.1. *Let Σ be an ordered nonempty set of propositions. Let τ be the systematic tableau for Σ, and let ρ be a path in τ.*

(1) *If ρ is closed, then it is finite.*
(2) *If ρ is open, then it contains all propositions from Σ.*
(3) *If Σ is infinite and ρ is open, then ρ is infinite.*

Proof. (1) Once ρ is found closed at Stage n, it is no more expanded. Thus, it is finite.

(2) The first proposition X_1 of Σ occurs in ρ. If some proposition in Σ does not occur in ρ, then there exist propositions X_m and X_{m+1} of Σ such that X_m occurs in ρ but X_{m+1} does not. Then X_{m+1} has not been added to this path while generating τ systematically. This is possible only when ρ has been found to be closed in Stage m. But ρ is open. Therefore, ρ contains all propositions from Σ.

(3) By (2), ρ contains all propositions of Σ. Since Σ is infinite, so is ρ. ♦

Suppose the systematic tableau for an ordered infinite set Σ of propositions is closed. Obviously, each path in the tableau is finite. Is the tableau finite or infinite?

We say that a tree is **finitely generated**, if each node in it has a finite number of children. Recall that König's lemma asserts that a finitely generated tree in which each path has only a finite number of nodes must have only a finite number of nodes. We had derived König's lemma from the compactness of PL. Here, we intend to prove finiteness theorem for PT, and then compactness, using König's lemma. We give a proof of König's lemma without using compactness of PL.

Lemma 4.2 (König). *Each finitely generated infinite tree has an infinite path.*

Proof. Let τ_0 be a finitely generated infinite tree. There are finitely many, say, k_0 children of the root of τ_0. Deleting the root, we end up with k_0 different trees; these are the subtrees of τ_0 whose roots are the children of τ_0. If all these subtrees are finite, then as a finite union of finite sets is finite, τ_0 is also finite. But this is not the case. Thus, there exists at least one subtree of τ_0 which is infinite. Choose one such subtree and call it τ_1. Repeat the same procedure with τ_1 as you had done with τ_0. There exists at least one infinite subtree τ_2 of τ_1, and hence of τ_0.

By induction it follows that there exists an infinite sequence of finitely generated infinite trees $\tau_0, \tau_1, \tau_2, \ldots$ such that each is a subtree of all preceding trees. The sequence of the roots of these trees taken in the same order is a required infinite path in τ_0. ♦

At this point, do Exercise 6 taken from Smullyan (1968) to convince yourself that König's lemma is not so trivial.

Theorem 4.3 (Finiteness in PT). *Let Σ be any set of propositions, and let w be any proposition.*

(1) *If Σ is infinite and inconsistent, then it has a finite inconsistent subset.*

(2) *If $\Sigma \vdash_{PT} w$, then Σ has a finite subset Γ such that $\Gamma \vdash_{PT} w$.*

Proof. (1) Let Σ be infinite and inconsistent. Let τ be a closed systematic tableau for Σ. Each path in τ is closed, and therefore, finite. Let Γ be the set of all propositions from Σ occurring in τ. Since a tableau is finitely generated (binary), due to König's Lemma, τ has a finite number of nodes. Then Γ is a finite set. Moreover, τ is a closed tableau for Γ. Thus Γ is inconsistent.

(2) By the definition of $\Sigma \vdash_{PT} w$, $\Sigma \cup \{\neg w\}$ is inconsistent. By (1), we have a finite subset Σ_0 of $\Sigma \cup \{\neg w\}$ which is inconsistent. Let τ be a closed tableau for Σ_0. If $\neg w \notin \Sigma_0$, then add $\neg w$ to the root of τ, else leave τ as it is. The new tableau is a closed tableau for $\Sigma_0 \cup \{\neg w\}$. This shows that $\Sigma_0 \cup \{\neg w\}$ is inconsistent. Take $\Gamma = \Sigma_0 \setminus \{\neg w\}$. Γ is finite. Since $\neg w \notin \Gamma$, $\Gamma \subseteq \Sigma$. Also, $\Gamma \cup \{\neg w\} = \Sigma_0 \cup \{\neg w\}$ is inconsistent. Therefore, $\Gamma \vdash_{PT} w$. ♦

We know that Σ in Example 4.21 is consistent. Is it also satisfiable? It is, since you can construct a model of Σ from an open path in its systematic tableau. For instance, take the leftmost path. The literals in this path are: $\neg p, \neg r$. The set $\{\neg p, \neg r\}$ is a model of Σ. Explicitly, define an interpretation $i : \{p,q,r,s,t\} \to \{0,1\}$ by taking $i(p) = 0 = i(r)$ and $i(q) = i(s) = i(t) = 1$. You can verify that $i \vDash \Sigma$. It does not matter what you assign to the variables q,s,t here. Take different interpretations by assigning different values to these variables but keep both of p,r assigned to 0; and verify that they are indeed models of Σ.

Further, the left most path in the tableau of Example 4.21 contains the propositions $p \to q \wedge r$, $\neg p \vee s$, $\neg p$, $r \to s \wedge t$, $\neg p$, $\neg u$, $\neg r$. The first proposition in this path is $p \to q \wedge r$, from which came the second proposition $\neg p$. This means that $p \to q \wedge r$ is true (assigned to 1 under an interpretation) whenever $\neg p$ is true. From the second element $\neg p \vee s$ of Σ comes the next proposition $\neg p$ in the path. Here also, whenever $\neg p$ is true, $\neg p \vee s$ is true. From the third element $r \to s \wedge t$ of Σ comes the next literal $\neg r$. Here again, if an interpretation assigns $\neg r$ to 1, then it must assign 1 to $r \to s \wedge t$. Finally, $\neg u$, the fourth element of Σ, is itself a literal, and it would be assigned to 1.

As you have rightly observed, the propositions in a path of a tableau are implicitly $\wedge$-ed together. In addition, we observe the following.

Observation 4.2. *Let i be any interpretation. Any tableau rule with parent proposition x and children y, z (or only y), satisfies the following properties:*

(S) *If it is a stacking rule, then $i(x) = 1$ iff $i(y) = i(z) = 1$.*

(B) *If it is a branching rule, then $i(x) = 1$ iff $i(y) = 1$ or $i(z) = 1$.*

EXAMPLE 4.22. Consider the tableau rule $(\neg\wedge)$. It says that a node with $\neg(x \wedge y)$ when expanded gives rise to the propositions $\neg x$ and $\neg y$ as children. Now, suppose $i(\neg(x \wedge y)) = 1$. Then, $i(x \wedge y) = 0$ which implies that $i(x) = 0$ or $i(y) = 0$. Clearly, $i(\neg x) = 1$ or $i(\neg y) = 1$. Conversely, if $i(\neg x) = 1$ holds or $i(\neg y) = 1$ holds, then $i(\neg(x \wedge y)) = 1$ also holds. That means, the tableau rule $(\neg\wedge)$ satisfies the property (B). Since $\neg(x \wedge y)$ is a branching proposition, (S) is satisfied vacuously.

In fact, all tableau rules satisfy both the properties (S) and (B); one of these correctly holds whereas the other is vacuously true.

Lemma 4.3. *Let τ be the systematic tableau for a nonempty finite set Γ of propositions. Then, any model of Γ is also a model of some path in τ.*

Proof. Note that a model of a path ρ is simply a model of the set of propositions occurring in ρ.

Consider a simpler case first: when $\Sigma = \{w\}$, a singleton. We prove the lemma in this case by induction on the length of a longest path in the systematic tableau τ for w. In the basis step, suppose a longest path in τ has length one. This means that in τ, the root containing w is a stacking proposition having only one child (the rules $(\neg\neg)$ or $(\neg\bot)$) or w is a branching proposition having two children. By the properties (S) and (B), any model i of w is also a model of at least one of its children, say, of x. Now, i is a model of $\{w, x\}$, proving the result.

Lay out the induction hypothesis that if the systematic tableau for any proposition w has a longest path with length less than n, then any model of w is also a model of at least one path in the tableau. Suppose x is a proposition of which τ is the systematic tableau having a longest path with length n. Let i be a model of x. Suppose the children of the root x in τ are y and z (or only y). Now, by the properties (S) and (B), as in the basis step, i is a model of at least one of y or z. Without loss of generality, suppose i is a model of y.

Let τ' be the subtree of τ with y as the root. Now, a longest path in τ' has length less than n, since such a path is obtained from one longest path in τ by removing x. By the induction hypothesis, i is a model of at least one path in τ'. Call such a path as ρ'. Consider the path ρ in τ with x, followed by y, and then other nodes in ρ'. Since i is a model of x, y and also of ρ', we see that i is a model of ρ. This proves the induction step.

When Γ is finite, write $\Gamma = \{w_1, w_2, \ldots, w_k\}$. Take $x = w_1 \wedge w_2 \wedge \cdots \wedge w_k$. The systematic tableau for Γ coincides with that of x with the additional proposition x at the root. Then the statement in the lemma follows for Γ from that for x. ♦

Lemma 4.3 is, essentially, the completeness of the tableau method. Can you argue the same way even if Σ is infinite? Note that an open path in the tableau for Σ is now infinite.

Theorem 4.4 (Strong Adequacy of PT to PL). *Let Σ be a set of propositions, and let w be any proposition.*

(1) *Σ is PT-consistent iff Σ is satisfiable.*

(2) *$\Sigma \vdash_{PT} w$ iff $\Sigma \vDash w$.*

Proof. (1) The empty set is both consistent and satisfiable. So, suppose that Σ is a nonempty consistent set. Let τ be the systematic tableau for Σ. Let ρ be an open path in τ. Let L be the set of all literals occurring in ρ. Define a function i mapping each literal in L to 1. Since ρ is not closed, L does not have a pair of complementary literals; also $\bot$ does not occur in ρ. Thus, i is a boolean valuation.

Now, if w is a proposition occurring in ρ, then w occurs in ρ at level n, for some n; i.e., along the path ρ, if the root node is the first node, then w is the $(n+1)$th node. By induction on n and due to the properties (S) and (B), it follows that $i(w) = 1$. Therefore, i is a model of each proposition occurring in ρ. By Lemma 4.1, ρ contains all propositions of Σ. Therefore, Σ is satisfiable.

Conversely, assume that Σ is satisfiable. Let Γ be any finite subset of Σ. Then Γ is also satisfiable. Let i be a model of Γ. Let τ be the systematic tableau for Γ. By Lemma 4.3, i is a model of at least one path of τ. Then, such a path in τ contains neither $\bot$ nor a pair of complementary literals. That is, such a path is necessarily open, and hence, Γ is consistent. Since every finite subset Γ of Σ is consistent, by the finiteness theorem, Σ is consistent.

(2) We observe that $\Sigma \vdash_{PT} w$ iff $\Sigma \cup \{\neg w\}$ is inconsistent iff $\Sigma \cup \{\neg w\}$ is unsatisfiable (by (1)) iff $\Sigma \vDash w$ (by RA in PL). ♦

Notice that compactness of PL now follows from the finiteness of tableaux.

Exercises for § 4.5

1. Construct two systematic tableaux for the following consequence by choosing different ordering of the premises:

$$\{(\neg p \to q) \to ((q \to \neg p) \to p), (p \to r) \to (q \to \neg p), p \to r, \neg p \to q\} \vdash p.$$

2. Verify that each tableau rule satisfies the properties (S) and (B).
3. Give an example of a proposition which is not a theorem, but every path in every completed tableau for it is open.

4. Let Σ be any set of propositions. Show the following in PT.
   (a) Σ is inconsistent if some completed tableau for it is closed.
   (b) Σ is inconsistent if every completed tableau for it is closed.
   (c) Σ is consistent if every completed tableau for it is open.
   (d) Σ is consistent if some completed tableau for it is open.
5. In a tree, if each node has at most m children, and each path consists of at most n nodes, then show that the total number of nodes is at most $\sum_{i=0}^{n} m^i$. Does it prove König's lemma for binary trees?
6. Assume that corresponding to each positive integer we have infinite supply of balls labelled with that positive integer. There is a box having a finite number of labelled balls. We remove a ball from the box, read its label. Suppose the label is m. Then we choose two numbers ℓ and n, where $\ell < m$. Next, we put into the box n number of balls all labelled with ℓ. Obviously, if the removed ball has label 1, then nothing can be put into the box. Using König's lemma, prove that eventually all balls will be removed from the box. [Hint: Create a tree with the box as the root, and the balls it contains as its children; next, children of a ball are the ones that replace the ball.]

4.6 SUMMARY AND PROBLEMS

In this chapter, you have come across four types of proof techniques. The method of calculations were used mainly for showing equivalences. It was formally used in Gries & Schneider (1993) as a proof procedure. We have extended the formalism to include one-sided entailments in calculations.

As another alternative, you have learnt the natural deduction system, which is more like quasi-proofs. Almost all texts on logic include this proof technique. For instance, You may see Huth & Ryan (2000). Though there are more rules of inference in PND, construction of a proof is easier. For a history of natural deduction, see Pelletier (1999).

As another variation to the proof methods, you have learnt how a proof may be seen as a tree by way of Gentzen systems. A Gentzen system uses a different strategy than the earlier methods. It takes a consequence as its basic block in a proof rather than taking the propositions. The consequences are named as sequents in the system. This renaming is used to demarcate the line between syntactic manipulation from the semantic overload. A Gentzen system then goes on arguing with sequents by transforming them into simpler sequents. If the universal sequent is eventually generated, then the original sequent is proved, otherwise not.

The Gentzen systems were invented by G. Gentzen in 1935, though in a very different form. The original form of the sequents was rather close to the natural deduction system PND. The system GPC was formulated by H. Wang in the form of an algorithm while trying to write a theorem prover for PL using FORTRAN. Since then, the system has been recognized as Gentzen's sequent calculus. The texts Gallier (1987) and Manaster (1978) provide you with complete references on Gentzen systems.

Finally, you came across another tree method of proof, the analytic tableaux. It employs *reductio ad absurdum* by starting from the negation of the conclusion as a new premise and later confirming that it leads to inconsistency. Here, inconsistency is defined by closing of a tableau. We also proved adequacy of the tableau method without using that of PC. The analytic tableaux had their origin in E. W. Beth's semantic trees. Three good texts on Tableaux are Fitting (1996), Smullyan (1968), and Smullyan (2014).

Problems for Chapter 4

1. Formalize the stories and your answers in Problem 44 of Chapter 1 as consequences. You may use the following abbreviations:

   G: The portrait is in the gold casket.
   g: The inscription on the gold casket is true.

   Similarly, use the abbreviations S, s, L, ℓ. Justify the consequences using a quasi-proof, a calculation, PND, GPC, and Tableau. [Hint: See that $G \leftrightarrow g$, $S \leftrightarrow s$, $\neg \ell \to g \wedge s$, $\neg(G \wedge S)$, $\neg G \wedge \neg S \to L$ are premises in (a).]

2. For each of the following arguments, either construct a quasi-proof, a calculation, a PND-proof, a GPC-proof, and an Analytic tableau; or, construct an interpretation to show that the argument is invalid.

   (a) If Sam was at the fair, then his father was negligent or his mother was not at home. If his mother was not at home, then his father was not negligent. His mother was at home. Therefore, Sam was at the fair.

   (b) Either Logic is elegant or many students like it. If Computer Science is a difficult discipline, then Logic has to be elegant. Therefore, if many students like Computer Science, then Logic is elegant.

   (c) If tomorrow morning, it is chilly and not so clear a sky, then we go swimming unless you do not have any special liking for boating. It isn't always the case that if the sky is not clear, then you don't go boating. Therefore, if the weather is not chilly tomorrow morning, then we go swimming.

   (d) Yanka would have been at home, had he been to the club or not to the theatre while his friend was waiting for him at the college. He had been to the club premises while it was dusk only if he didn't come home. Unless the watchman saw him at the club premises, it is certain that it was dusk, since the watchman is night-blind. Therefore, Yanka did not go to the theatre.

   (e) If anyone is in a guest house, which is located in a city, then he is in that city. None can be in two different cities at the same time. One who snatched the necklace away must have been in the guest house at Chennai. Since Chennai and Mumbai are two different cities and Yanka was in the Mumbai guest house, he did not snatch the necklace.

   (f) If all the politicians praise a bandit, then the bandit must be none other than Robin Hood. A politician praises a person if the person has indeed helped him in his career. There is a bandit who has not helped any politician. Therefore, there is a bandit other than Robin Hood.

(g) If Shaktiman were able and wiling to eradicate evil, he would do so. If Shaktiman were not able to eradicate evil, he would be transformed into a donkey. If Shaktiman were unwilling to eradicate evil, he would be joining the evil. As a matter of fact, Shaktiman does not eradicate evil. Therefore, if Shaktiman exists, then he is neither transformed into a donkey nor does he join the evil.

3. Formulate and prove monotonicity, deduction theorem, and reductio ad absurdum for PND.

4. Show that if two boxes are allowed to overlap, then the soundness of PND may not be retained.

5. Formulate and prove the deduction theorem and monotonicity for PT without using those for PL.

6. Let Σ be any set of propositions, and let p, q be any propositions. Show the following in GPC and in PT:

   (a) $\Sigma \vdash p$ and $\Sigma \vdash q$ iff $\Sigma \vdash p \wedge q$.
   (b) If at least one of $\Sigma \vdash p$ or $\Sigma \vdash q$, then $\Sigma \vdash p \vee q$.

7. Try to construct proofs in PND, GPC, and PT, for the following:

   (a) $\vDash \neg p \to (p \to q)$
   (b) $\vDash \neg p \to (p \to \bot)$
   (c) $\vDash p \to (q \to p \wedge q)$
   (d) $\vDash (p \vee q) \to (\neg p \wedge q \to q)$
   (e) $\vDash (p \to q) \to (q \wedge r \to (p \to r))$
   (f) $\vDash \neg(p \to (q \to r)) \vee \neg(p \to q) \vee \neg p \vee r$
   (g) $\vDash (p \to q) \to ((q \to r) \to ((r \to s) \to (p \to s)))$
   (h) $\{p \vee q \to r \wedge s, r \vee u \to \neg v \wedge w, v \vee x \to p \wedge y\} \vDash \neg v$
   (i) $\{(r \to r \wedge s) \to t, t \to (\neg u \vee u \to p \wedge u), p \vee q \to (r \to r)\} \vDash p \leftrightarrow t$
   (j) $\{p \to \neg q, r \to s, \neg t \to q, s \to \neg u, t \to \neg v, \neg u \to w, p \wedge r\} \vDash \neg v \wedge w$

8. Solve the following by using Calculation, PND, GPC, and PT.

   (a) For each $i \in \mathbb{N}$, let x_i be a proposition; and let $\Sigma = \{x_i \to x_{i+1} : i \in \mathbb{N}\}$. Show that $\Sigma \vdash x_0 \to x_n$ for each $n \in \mathbb{N}$.
   (b) Let Σ be a set of propositions, and let w be a proposition. Show that if $\Sigma \cup \{w\} \vdash \bot$ and $\Sigma \cup \{\neg w\} \vdash \bot$, then $\Sigma \vdash \bot$.
   (c) Let Σ and Γ be sets of propositions, and let w be a proposition. Show that if $\Sigma \cup \{w\} \vdash \bot$ and $\Gamma \cup \{\neg w\} \vdash \bot$, then $\Sigma \cup \Gamma \vdash \bot$.

9. For finite sets of propositions Σ and Γ, prove that $\Sigma \Vdash \Gamma$ iff $\Sigma \vDash \Gamma$.

10. Formulate finiteness theorem for GPC and use König's lemma to prove it.

11. Using finiteness theorem prove strong adequacy of GPC to PL.

12. Let $\Sigma = \{w_1, w_2, w_3, \ldots\}$ be a denumerable set of propositions. Show that for each $n \geq 1$, $\{w_1, \ldots, w_n\}$ is PT-consistent iff Σ is PT-consistent.

13. Formulate tableau rules for the connectives $\uparrow$ and $\downarrow$.

14. In PC, the metatheorems are used outside a proof. The metatheorems can be used inside a proof provided a proof can use the (meta)symbol $\vdash$ in its body, as in GPC. A proof would then be a finite sequence of consequences of the form $\Sigma \vdash w$, where each consequence is either a meta-axiom or is derived from earlier consequences by an application of a rule. One such meta-system for PC, called **MPC** goes as follows.

    Let Σ, Γ be any generic sets of PC-propositions; A, B generic propositions. The meta-system MPC has the following inference rules (meta-rules):

    (P) $\dfrac{\cdot}{\Sigma \cup \{A\} \vdash A}$ **(M)** $\dfrac{\Sigma \vdash A}{\Sigma \cup \Gamma \vdash A}$

    (MP) $\dfrac{\Sigma \vdash A \qquad \Sigma \vdash A \to B}{\Sigma \vdash B}$ **(DT)** $\dfrac{\Sigma \cup \{A\} \vdash B}{\Sigma \vdash A \to B}$

    (RA) $\dfrac{\Sigma \cup \{\neg A\} \vdash B \quad \Sigma \cup \{\neg A\} \vdash \neg B}{\Sigma \vdash A}$ $\dfrac{\Sigma \cup \{A\} \vdash B \quad \Sigma \cup \{A\} \vdash \neg B}{\Sigma \vdash \neg A}$

    An *MPC-proof* is a finite sequence of consequences of the form $\Sigma \vdash X$, where each of them is obtained by an application of the rules of P, M, DT, MP, RA on consequence(s) occurring somewhere prior to it. Notice that an application of P does not require an earlier consequence; all others need one or two.The last consequence of a proof is considered *proved* by the proof. Here is an example of an MPC-proof:

1.	$p, q \vdash p$	P
2.	$p \vdash q \to p$	DT
3.	$\vdash p \to (q \to p)$	DT

    Show the following in MPC:

    (a) $\vdash p \to (\neg q \to \neg(p \to q))$
    (b) If $p \vdash q$, then $\neg q \vdash \neg p$
    (c) $\Sigma \cup \{\neg\neg p\} \vdash p$, for any set Σ of propositions.
    (d) $\neg p \to q,\ p \to q \vdash q$
    (e) $\vdash \neg(p \wedge q) \to (\neg p \vee \neg q)$
    (f) For any set of propositions Σ, and propositions p and q, if $\Sigma \vdash p$ and $\Sigma \vdash q$, then $\Sigma \vdash p \wedge q$.
    (g) Formulate an inference rule from (e), call it Rule (A). Using Rule (A), formulate an inference rule for the biconditional and call it Rule (B).
    (h) Using Rule (B), construct an MPC-proof for $\vdash \neg(p \wedge q) \leftrightarrow (\neg p \vee \neg q)$.
    (i) Formulate an inference rule for the connective $\wedge$.

15. What about Lemma 2.1 for MPC? Prove that MPC is adequate to PL.

Chapter 5

First Order Logic

5.1 SYNTAX OF FL

Propositional logic is not enough for carrying out simple mathematical reasoning. The argument "Each natural number is rational; and each rational number is real. Therefore, each natural number is real." cannot be justified in PL. The three sentences will be symbolized with three distinct propositional variables, showing no connection between them. Why justifying an argument, even a simple mathematical sentence cannot be truly translated to PL. Consider the sentence

> If a positive integer is a perfect square and less than four, then it must be equal to one.

We may rewrite it as

> For each x, if x is a positive integer less than four, and if there exists a positive integer y such that x is equal to the square of y, then x is equal to one.

For symbolizing this sentence we require *quantifiers* 'for each', and 'there exists'; *predicates* '$\cdots$ is a positive integer', '$\cdots$ is less than $\cdots$', and '$\cdots$ is equal to $\cdots$'; *function symbol* 'square of $\cdots$'; *constants* 'four' and 'one', and the variables x, y. The logic obtained by extending PL and including these types of symbols is called first order logic.

Notice that the variables range over some objects but they are not objects. Variables are different from the propositional variables; the latter can be either true or false, whereas the former are simply named gaps. To make them distinct, variables are also termed as *individual variables*. They behave like English pronouns. For instance, the following two sentences mean the same thing:

> All natural numbers are integers.
> For whatever an object may be, if *it* is a natural number, then *it* is an integer.

Individual variables give an infinite supply of *it* in the form $it_1, it_2, \ldots$. In this sense, they are named gaps.

The **alphabet of FL**, *first order logic*, is the union of the following sets:

$\{\top, \bot\}$, the set of **propositional constants**,

$\{f_i^j : i, j \in \mathbb{N}\}$, the set of **function symbols**,

$\{P_i^j : i, j \in \mathbb{N}\} \cup \{\approx\}$, the set of **predicates**,

$\{x_0, x_1, x_2, \ldots\}$, the set of **variables**,

$\{\neg, \wedge, \vee, \rightarrow, \leftrightarrow\}$, the set of **connectives**,

$\{\forall, \exists\}$, the set of **quantifiers**, and

$\{), (, , \}$, the set of **punctuation marks**.

Look at the subscripts and superscripts in the function symbols and predicates. The symbol f_i^j is a function symbol which could have been written as f_i ; the superscript j says that the function symbol f_i^j has j arguments.

The superscript j in the function symbol f_i^j is referred to as its **arity**. The 0-ary function symbols do not require any variable or names to give us definite descriptions, that is, they themselves are definite descriptions. Thus the 0-ary function symbols are also termed as the **names**, or **individual constants**, or just **constants**.

The intention is to translate the definite descriptions that depend on j parameters. For example, the definite description 'author of Anna Karenina' will be written as $f_0^1(f_0^0)$, where f_0^0, a constant, stands for Anna Karenina; and f_1^1 stands for 'author of'. The superscript 1 in f_0^1 cannot be any other number, whereas the subscript could be different from 0.

Similarly, the superscripts in the predicates also refer to the arity of those. The relation 'brother of' is a binary predicate and is denoted by a predicate P_i^2; the subscript i may be one of $0, 1, 2, 3, 4, \ldots$. The 0-ary predicates do not have any gaps to be filled in so that they would become sentences; they are sentences already. Thus, 0-ary predicates P_i^0 s are simply the *propositional variables* which, in some contexts, may not be analysed any deeper. This way, we really extend the syntax of PL to FL. The symbol $\approx$ denotes the **equality** or **identity** predicate, assumed to be binary.

The symbol $\forall$ is called the **universal quantifier** and the symbol $\exists$ is called the **existential quantifier**.

Any string over the alphabet of FL is an **expression** (an FL-expression). The function symbols allow you to express very complex definite descriptions such as 'the left leg of mother of the eldest brother of father of the youngest sister of Gargi', by using composition of functions. All these definite descriptions, along with some others arising out of the use of variables are taken as *terms*. These are special types of expressions. The following is an inductive definition of terms.

Write t for a generic term. The grammar for **terms** is

$$t ::= x_i \mid f_i^0 \mid f_i^j(t, \ldots, t)$$

In the expression $f_i^j(t, \ldots, t)$, the symbol t occurs j times. The grammar says that the variables, and the constants or 0-ary function symbols are terms, and if $t_1, \ldots, t_j$ are terms with f_i^j, a j-ary function symbol, then the expression $f_i^j(t_1, \ldots, t_j)$ is a term.

Moreover, terms are obtained only this way. A term is called **closed** iff no variable occurs in it.

EXAMPLE 5.1. f_5^0 is a term; it requires no arguments as its superscript is 0. Similarly, $f_0^1(f_0^0)$ and $f_5^1(f_3^2(f_0^0, f_1^0))$ are terms. Both of them are closed terms. f_5^1 is not a term; there is a vacant place as its superscript 1 shows. $f_5^1(f_1^0)$ is a closed term. Similarly, $f_5^1(f_3^2(x_7, f_1^0))$ is also a term; it is not a closed term since a variable, namely, x_7 occurs in it.

The **level of a term** is defined as follows. The variables and the constants are called as terms of level 0. For $n \geq 1$, terms of level n are of the form $f(t_1, \ldots, t_m)$, where each of $t_1, \ldots, t_m$ are terms of level less than n, out of which at least one is of level $n-1$. For instance, the term $f_5^1(f_3^2(f_0^0, f_1^0))$ is of level 2.

In our formal language, the names such as 'Bapuji' and 'Tolstoy' are constants and as such they should be symbolized as 0-ary function symbols. Similarly, other definite descriptions are symbolized via function symbols of suitable arity. For example, 'Bapuji' may be symbolized as f_0^0 and 'father of' as f_0^1, then the definite description 'father of Bapuji' is symbolized as $f_0^1(f_0^0)$. The use of variables as arguments of function symbols will be clarified shortly. We will use terms for defining the (well-formed) formulas, which would represent sentences or rather sentence-like phrases.

Writing X for a generic formula, x for a generic variable, and t for a generic term, the grammar for **formulas** is:

$$X ::= \top \mid \bot \mid P_i^0 \mid (t \approx t) \mid P_i^m(t, \ldots, t) \mid \neg X \mid (X \wedge X) \mid (X \vee X) \mid$$
$$(X \to X) \mid (X \leftrightarrow X) \mid \forall x X \mid \exists x X$$

In the expression $P_i^m(t, \ldots, t)$, the symbol t occurs m times. The grammar says that the special symbols $\top, \bot$, and the 0-ary predicates are (FL-) formulas. If P is any m-ary predicate, then for m terms $t_1, \ldots, t_m$, the expression $P(t_1, \ldots, t_m)$ is a formula. The equality predicate is written in infix notation; it allows $(s \approx t)$ as a formula for terms s and t. The formulas might be obtained by using connectives as in PL or by prefixing a quantifier followed by a variable, to any other formula. Notice that all propositions of PL (generated from P_i^0 s and connectives) are now treated as formulas (in FL).

The formulas in the forms $\top$, $\bot$, P_i^0, $(s \approx t)$, and $P_i^m(t_1, t_2, \ldots, t_m)$ are called **atomic formulas**; and other formulas are called **compound formulas**.

EXAMPLE 5.2. The following expressions are formulas:

$$\top, \quad (\bot \to \top), \quad (f_1^0 \approx f_5^0), \quad (f_1^2(f_1^0, f_2^1(f_1^0)) \approx f_{11}^0), \quad P_2^1(f_1^1(x_5)),$$
$$\neg \forall x_3 (P_5^2(f_1^1(x_5), f_1^0) \to P_3^0), \quad \forall x_2 \exists x_5 (P_5^2(x_0, f_1^1(x_1)) \leftrightarrow P_1^3(x_1, x_5, x_6)).$$

Whereas the following expressions are not formulas:

$$\top(x_0), \quad P_1^1(f_1^0(f_0^0)), \quad f_1^0 \approx f_5^0, \quad (f_1^2(f_1^0, f_2^0(f_1^0)) \approx f_{11}^2(f_{12}^1, f_1^0)),$$
$$P_2^1(f_4^1(x_7), f_1^0), \quad \neg \forall x_1 (P_5^2(f_1^0(x_2), x_3)), \quad \forall x_2 \exists x_5 (P_5^2(x_0, f_1^0(x_1)),$$
$$\forall x_2 \exists x_5 (P_5^1(f_1^0(x_1)) \leftrightarrow P_1^1(x_6)).$$

The first expression is not a formula since after $\top$, a variable is not allowed to occur in parentheses. The second expression is not a formula since $f_1^0(f_0^0)$ is not a term, as f_1^0 is a 0-ary function symbol and as such it cannot take an argument. The third expression is not a formula since $\approx$ needs a pair of parentheses. In the fourth expression, f_{12}^1 needs a term as an argument. Similarly, in the fifth expression the predicate P_2^1 can have only one argument, and in the sixth and seventh, f_1^0 cannot take any term as an argument.

Can we retrieve the rules that have been applied for obtaining a formula? If a formula X starts with $\neg$, then it is the rule $X ::= \neg X$ that has been applied last. Similarly, if it starts with (, then it is one of the binary connective rules or the equality predicate rule that had been applied last. If it starts with a P_i^0, then the last rule applied was $X ::= P_i^0$, etc. These observations (and some more) will show that formulas are uniquely parsed. Of course, for the proof of unique parsing of formulas, you need to first show that every term is uniquely parsed.

Theorem 5.1 (Unique Parsing). *Any formula X is in exactly one of the following forms:*

(1) $X = \top$.

(2) $X = \bot$.

(3) $X = P_i^0$ *for a unique predicate* P_i^0.

(4) $X = (s \approx t)$ *for unique terms* s, t.

(5) $X = P_i^j(t_1, \ldots, t_j)$ *for unique predicate* P_i^j *and unique terms* $t_1, \ldots, t_j$.

(6) $X = \neg Y$ *for a unique formula* Y.

(7) $X = (Y \circ Z)$ *for a unique connective* $\circ \in \{\wedge, \vee, \rightarrow, \leftrightarrow\}$, *and unique formulas* Y *and* Z.

(8) $X = \forall x Y$ *for a unique variable* x *and a unique formula* Y.

(9) $X = \exists x Y$ *for a unique variable* x *and a unique formula* Y.

Exercises for § 5.1

Categorize each of the following as a term, a formula, or neither. Draw the corresponding parse trees.

1. $f_5^4(x_1, x_3, f_6^2(x_1, x_3), f_4^2(f_5^2(x_3, x_6), x_4))$
2. $(\neg\forall x((P_4^1(x_5) \rightarrow \neg P^1(c_4)) \wedge P_3^2(x_3, f_1^1(c_3))))$
3. $f_1^4(x_2, x_4, f_1^2(x_4, x_5), f_5^2(f_1^2(x_4, x_6), c_3))$
4. $f((x,y), g(x,y,z), h(f(x,y,z), w))$
5. $\exists x_1 \forall x_2 (P_2^2(f_3^1(x_2, x_6, f_5^2(f_3^1((x_4, x_3), c_4)), x_3) \rightarrow P_2^1(x_7)))$
6. $\forall x_1 \forall x_2 (P_1^2(x_1, f_2^1(x_1)) \rightarrow P_2^3(f_6^1(x_1), x_2, f_1^3(x_1, x_2, c_6)))$
7. $\forall x_1 \forall x_2 (P_1^3(x_1, x_2, x_3) \leftrightarrow \exists x_2 P_1^3(x_1, x_2, x_3))$
8. $\exists x_1 \forall x_2 (P_1^2(f_1^3(x_1, x_2, f_1^2(x_3, c_1)), x_2) \rightarrow P_2^1(f_1^2(x_2, x_4)))$
9. $\forall x_1 ((\forall x_2 P_0^3(x_1, x_2, x_3) \wedge \forall x_4 P_1^1(x_3)) \leftrightarrow \exists x_1 \forall x_2 P_0^3(x_2, x_2, x_2))$
10. $\forall x_1 (\exists x_2 \forall x_3 (\forall x_2 P_0^3(x_1, x_2, x_3) \wedge \forall x_3 P_1^1(x_3)) \rightarrow \exists x_1 \forall x_2 P_2^2(x_1, x_2))$

5.2 SCOPE AND BINDING

There are differences between any arbitrary formula and a sentence. Intuitively, a formula such as $(\forall x_1 P_1^1(x_1) \to P_2^1(x_2))$ would tell:

If P_1^1 holds for every object, then P_2^1 holds for x_2.

Since x_2 is a variable, a named gap, it does not refer to a definite object, unlike constants, names, or closed terms. Thus $(\forall x_1 P_1^1(x) \to P_2^1(y))$ is not a (first order) sentence. We must filter out sentences from all formulas.

We consider another example. Suppose, x_1 and x_2 are viewed as variables over positive integers. The formula $(x_2 \approx 2 \times x_1)$ may be true, or may not; it depends on what the values of x_1 and x_2 are. (You may think $2 \times (\cdot)$ as a unary function, and $\approx$ as 'equal to'.) Whereas the formula $\exists x_1 (x_2 \approx 2 \times x_1)$ is true when x_2 is even; it does not depend on the value of x_1. In the first case, we say that both x_1 and x_2 are free variables, whereas in the second case, we say that x_1 is a bound variable, and x_2 is a free variable. In the formula $(\exists x_1 (x_2 \approx 2 \times x_1) \wedge \forall x_2 \exists x_1 \neg (x_2 \approx 2 \times x_1))$ there is a confusion; there are both free and bound occurrences of the variable x_2. We introduce some more concepts so that things will be clearer and easier.

Let Y be a formula. A sub-string Z of Y is called a **subformula** of Y iff Z is a formula on its own. The **scope** of an *occurrence of a quantifier* occurring in Y is the subformula of Y starting with that occurrence. (From that place to the right.)

EXAMPLE 5.3. The subformulas of $\forall x_1 \exists x_2 ((P_1^1(x_3) \wedge P_1^1(x_1)) \to P_1^1(x_2))$ are

$$P_1^1(x_3), \quad P_1^1(x_1), \quad P_1^1(x_2), \quad (P_1^1(x_3) \wedge P_1^1(x_1)),$$
$$((P_1^1(x_3) \wedge P_1^1(x_1)) \to P_1^1(x_2)), \quad \exists x_2((P_1^1(x_3) \wedge P_1^1(x_1)) \to P_1^1(x_2)),$$
$$\forall x_1 \exists x_2((P_1^1(x_3) \wedge P_1^1(x_1)) \to P_1^1(x_2)).$$

The original formula has a single occurrence of $\forall$ and a single occurrence of $\exists$. The scope of the occurrence of $\forall$ is the whole formula; and the scope of the occurrence of $\exists$ is $\exists x_2((P_1^1(x_3) \wedge P_1^1(x_1)) \to P_1^1(x_2))$.

An occurrence of a variable x in Y is a **bound occurrence** iff this occurrence is within the scope of an occurrence of $\forall x$ or $\exists x$ (a quantifier that uses it). If a variable occurs within the scopes of more than one occurrence of quantifiers using that variable, then this *occurrence of the variable* is said to be **bound by** the rightmost among all these occurrences of quantifiers.

An occurrence of a variable in a formula is called a **free occurrence** iff it is not bound. If there is a free occurrence of a variable x in a formula Y, we say that x **occurs free in** Y, and also, we say that x is a **free variable** of Y. A variable x is a **bound variable** of Y iff there is at least one bound occurrence of x in Y.

EXAMPLE 5.4. In the formula $\exists x_2(P_1^2(x_2, x_1) \wedge \forall x_1 P_3^1(x_1))$, the scope of $\exists$ is the whole formula; the scope of $\forall$ is the formula $\forall x_1 P_3^1(x_1)$. Here, all the occurrences of the variable x_2 are bound; the first occurrence of x_1 is free while the last two occurrences of x_1 are bound occurrences. The variable x_2 is a bound variable of the formula while x_1 is both a free and a bound variable.

A formula having no free variables is called a **closed formula** or a **sentence**. Thus, in a sentence, each occurrence of each variable is a bound occurrence. A formula that is not closed is called an **open formula**.

EXAMPLE 5.5. In $\forall x_1(\forall x_2(P_1^3(x_1,x_2,f_1^0) \land \forall x_1 P_2^1(x_1)) \to \exists x_3 P_1^3(x_3,x_1,x_3))$, all occurrences of x_1 are bound. All occurrences of x_1 are within the scope of the first $\forall$. The third and the fourth occurrences are also within the scope of the third $\forall$. However, these occurrences of x_1 are bound by the third occurrence of $\forall$, and not by the first $\forall$. The fifth occurrence of x_1 is bound by the first $\forall$. In binding a variable, the scope of the innermost quantifier that uses the variable becomes relevant. The second occurrence of $\forall$ uses the variable x_2. All occurrences of variables x_1,x_2,x_3 are bound occurrences. The formula is a sentence.

EXAMPLE 5.6. In each of the following formulas, find out the scopes of each occurrence of each quantifier, free and bound variables, and mark which quantifier binds which occurrences of variables. Also, determine which of these are sentences.

(a) $\exists x_1((P_1^1(x_1) \land P_2^1(x_1)) \to (\neg P_1^1(x_1) \lor P_2^1(x_2)))$
(b) $\forall x_1(\exists x_2 P_1^2(x_1,x_2) \land \forall x_2(\neg P_2^2(x_1,x_2) \lor P_1^2(x_2,x_1)))$
(c) $(\neg\exists x_1(\forall x_2 P_1^3(x_1,x_2,x_3) \land \exists x_1 P_2^3(x_1,x_2,x_3)) \to \top)$
(d) $(\forall x_1 \exists x_2(P_1^1(x_1) \leftrightarrow P_2^1(x_2)) \land \forall x_3 \exists x_2(P_1^1(x_1) \to (P_1^1(x_3) \lor P_2^1(x_2))))$

We will use underlines to show the scope. The scopes also show the bound occurrences of a variable by the quantifier that uses it.

(a) The scope of the only quantifier in this formula is the whole formula:

$$\underline{\exists x_1((P_1^1(x_1) \land P_2^1(x_1)) \to (\neg P_1^1(x_1) \lor P_2^1(x_2)))}$$

All occurrences of x_1 are bound by this $\exists x_1$, while the only occurrence of x_2 is free. Here, x_1 is a bound variable and x_2 is a free variable. The formula is not a sentence; it is an open formula.

(b) The scopes of the quantifiers are as follows:

$$\forall x_1(\,\underline{\exists x_2 P_1^2(x_1,x_2)}\, \land \forall x_2(\neg P_2^2(x_1,x_2) \lor P_1^2(x_2,x_1)))$$
$$\forall x_1(\exists x_2 P_1^2(x_1,x_2) \land\, \underline{\forall x_2(\neg P_2^2(x_1,x_2) \lor P_1^2(x_2,x_1))}\,)$$
$$\underline{\forall x_1(\exists x_2 P_1^2(x_1,x_2) \land \forall x_2(\neg P_2^2(x_1,x_2) \lor P_1^2(x_2,x_1)))}$$

First two occurrences of x_2 are bound by $\exists x_2$; third, fourth, and fifth occurrences of x_2 are bound by $\forall x_2$. All occurrences of x_1 are bound by $\forall x_1$. All occurrences of all variables are bound. The formula is a sentence.

(c) The scopes of the quantifiers are as follows:

$$(\neg\exists x_1(\,\underline{\forall x_2 P_1^3(x_1,x_2,x_3)}\, \land \exists x_1 P_2^3(x_1,x_2,x_3)) \to \top)$$
$$(\neg\exists x_1(\forall x_2 P_1^3(x_1,x_2,x_3) \land\, \underline{\exists x_1 P_2^3(x_1,x_2,x_3)}\,) \to \top)$$
$$(\neg\, \underline{\exists x_1(\forall x_2 P_1^3(x_1,x_2,x_3) \land \exists x_1 P_2^3(x_1,x_2,x_3))}\, \to \top)$$

All occurrences of x_1 are bound; first and second occurrences are bound by the first $\exists x_1$; while the third and fourth occurrences of x_1 are bound by the second $\exists x_1$. First occurrence of x_2 is bound but the second occurrence of x_2 is free. Both the occurrences of x_3 are free occurrences. So, x_1 is a bound variable and not a free variable, x_2 is both a bound and a free variable, and x_3 is a free variable, but not a bound variable. The formula is not a sentence.

(d) The scopes of the quantifiers are as follows:

$$(\forall x_1\, \underline{\exists x_2 (P_1^1(x_1) \leftrightarrow P_2^1(x_2))} \wedge \forall x_3 \exists x_2 (P_1^1(x_1) \to (P_1^1(x_3) \vee P_2^1(x_2))))$$

$$(\, \underline{\forall x_1 \exists x_2 (P_1^1(x_1) \leftrightarrow P_2^1(x_2))} \wedge \forall x_3 \exists x_2 (P_1^1(x_1) \to (P_1^1(x_3) \vee P_2^1(x_2))))$$

$$(\forall x_1 \exists x_2 (P_1^1(x_1) \leftrightarrow P_2^1(x_2)) \wedge \forall x_3\, \underline{\exists x_2 (P_1^1(x_1) \to (P_1^1(x_3) \vee P_2^1(x_2)))}\,)$$

$$(\forall x_1 \exists x_2 (P_1^1(x_1) \leftrightarrow P_2^1(x_2)) \wedge\, \underline{\forall x_3 \exists x_2 (P_1^1(x_1) \to (P_1^1(x_3) \vee P_2^1(x_2)))}\,)$$

All occurrences of variables except the third occurrence of x_1 are bound. The formula is not a sentence.

Once you are sure that unique parsing holds, and you are confident of scope and binding, we will follow some conventions for using less number of parentheses and commas. If in occasions where exact sequence of symbols become important, we must revert back to our original expanded version of formulas.

Convention 5.1. We will drop the outer parentheses from formulas.

Convention 5.2. We will drop the superscripts from the predicates and function symbols; the arguments will show their arity. However, we must not use the same symbol with different number of arguments in any particular context.

For example, in the same formula, we must not use $P_5(x,y)$ and $P_5(f_2)$ since the first one says that P_5 is a binary predicate, and the second would require P_5 to be unary. In the formula

$$\forall x_2 \exists x_5 (P_4(x_0, f_1(x_1)) \leftrightarrow P_1(x_2, x_5, x_1)),$$

P_4 is a binary predicate, f_1 is a unary function symbol; and P_1 is a ternary predicate. The following expression would not be considered a formula:

$$\forall x_2 \exists x_5 (P_4(x_0, f_1(x_1)) \leftrightarrow P_4(x_2, x_5, x_1)).$$

Reason: P_4 has been used once as a binary and once as a ternary predicate.

Convention 5.3. We will drop writing subscripts with variables, function symbols and predicates, whenever possible. Instead, we will use $x, y, z, \ldots$ for variables, $f, g, h, \ldots$ for function symbols, and $P, Q, R, \ldots$ for predicates. The 0-ary predicates or the propositional variables will be denoted by $A, B, C, \ldots$. Whenever we feel short of symbols, we may go back to writing them with subscripts. Moreover, the 0-ary function symbols (which stand for names) will be written as $a, b, c, \ldots$, from the first few small letters of the Roman alphabet.

Following this convention, the formula $\forall x_2 \exists x_5 (P_4(x_0, f_1(x_1)) \leftrightarrow P_1(x_2, x_5, x_1))$ may be rewritten as $\forall x \exists y (P(z, f(u)) \leftrightarrow Q(x, y, u))$.

Take care to see that each occurrence of x_2 has been replaced by x, each occurrence of P_4 has been replaced by P, etc.

Convention 5.4. We will omit the parentheses and commas in writing the arguments of function symbols and predicates provided no confusion arises. If, however, some formula written this way is not easily readable, we will retain some of them.

For example, the formula $\forall x \exists y (P(z, f(u)) \leftrightarrow Q(x, y, u))$ may be rewritten as $\forall x \exists y (Pzf(u) \leftrightarrow Qxyu)$.

Similarly, the term $f(t_1, \ldots, t_n)$ will sometimes be written as $f(t_1 \ldots t_n)$ or as $ft_1 \ldots t_n$. And, $\forall x \exists y (Pzf(u) \leftrightarrow Qxyu)$ may be rewritten as $\forall x \exists y (Pzfu \leftrightarrow Qxyu)$.

Convention 5.5. We will have precedence rules for the connectives and quantifiers to reduce parentheses. We will preserve the precedence of connectives as in PL and give the same precedence to the quantifiers and the connective $\neg$. That is,

$\neg, \forall x, \exists x$ will have the highest precedence.
$\wedge, \vee$ will have the next precedence.
$\rightarrow, \leftrightarrow$ will have the lowest precedence.

For example, the formula

$$\forall x_1 \neg (\exists x_2 ((P_1^1(f_1^2(f_0^0, f_1^0)) \wedge P_1^0) \rightarrow P_2^2(x_2, f_1^0) \leftrightarrow \forall x_3 ((P_1^1(f_5^0) \wedge P_2^1(x_1)) \rightarrow P_3^0))$$

is rewritten as $\forall x \neg (\exists y (Pf(a,b) \wedge A \rightarrow Qyb) \leftrightarrow \forall z (Pc \wedge Rx \rightarrow B))$, where the variables x_1, x_2, x_3 are rewritten as x, y, z; the function symbols $f_0^0, f_1^0, f_5^0, f_1^2$ are rewritten as a, b, c, f; and the predicates $P_1^1, P_1^0, P_2^2, P_2^1, P_3^0$ are rewritten as P, A, Q, R, B, respectively.

Caution: When considering the subformulas, scopes, and binding in a formula, we must take the formula in its original form, not in its abbreviated form. For instance, $Px \rightarrow Py$ is not a subformula of $\forall x \exists y (Pz \wedge Px \rightarrow Py)$. The given formula with adequate parentheses looks like $\forall x \exists y ((Pz \wedge Px) \rightarrow Py)$, of which $Px \rightarrow Py$ is not a subformula.

The rewritten forms of formulas are, strictly speaking, not formulas. They are called *abbreviated formulas*. But we will regard them as formulas since they can be written back as formulas by following our conventions.

Exercises for § 5.2

1. For all formulas in the exercise of § 5.1, find the scopes of each occurrence of a quantifier. Also, mark the free and bound occurrences of variables.
2. Mark the free and bound occurrences of variables in the following formulas:
   (a) $(P_4^3(x_3, x_2, x_1) \leftrightarrow P_1^3(x_1, c_3, c_2))$
   (b) $\forall x_1 (P_4^3(x_3, x_2, x_1) \leftrightarrow P_1^3(x_1, c_3, c_2))$
   (c) $\exists x_3 ((P_4^3(x_3, x_2, x_1) \leftrightarrow P_1^3(x_1, c_3, c_2)) \wedge P_5^1(x_3))$
   (d) $\forall x_1 ((P_4^4(x_3, x_2, x_1, a) \leftrightarrow P_1^3(x_1, c_3, c_2)) \rightarrow \exists x_3 P_3^4(x_1, x_2, x_3, x_4))$
3. Define the notions of subformula, free variable, and bound variable inductively.

5.3 SUBSTITUTIONS

In what follows, we will require to substitute free variables by constants, other variables, or terms, in general. We fix a notation for such substitutions and discuss what kind of substitutions are allowed.

We write $[x/t]$ for the **substitution of the variable x by the term t**, and then $(X)[x/t]$ for the formula obtained by replacing all *free occurrences* of the variable x with the term t in the formula X. For example,

$$\begin{aligned}(Px \to Qx)[x/t] &= Pt \to Qt \\ (\forall xPxy)[x/t] &= \forall xPxy \\ \forall x(Pxy[x/t]) &= \forall xPty \\ \forall x\exists y((Px \land Qyx) \to Rzy[y/t]) &= \forall x\exists y(Px \land Qyx) \to Rzt \\ (\forall x\exists y(Px \land Qyx) \to Rxy)[x/t] &= \forall x\exists y(Px \land Qyx) \to Rty\end{aligned}$$

We may abbreviate $(X)[x/t]$ to $X[x/t]$ if no confusion arises. Note that in effecting a substitution, all and only *free* occurrences of a variable are replaced, and not every occurrence.

Consider the formula: $\forall x\exists y(Hx \to Fxy)$, which you might have obtained by symbolizing the English sentence, "Each human being has a father". To verify its truth, you are going to see whether for every object x, the formula $\exists y(Hx \to Fxy)$ is satisfied or not. Now this 'every object x' can also stand for terms (definite descriptions, etc). For example, $f(a)$, the mother of a, is an object anyway. After replacement, the formula

$$(\exists y(Hx \to Fxy))[x/f(a)] = \exists y(Hf(a) \to Ff(a)y)$$

says that "if the mother of a is a human being, then s/he has a father". Instead of $f(a)$, suppose you substitute $f(y)$, then you would obtain

$$(\exists y(Hx \to Fxy))[x/f(y)] = \exists y(Hf(y) \to Ff(y)y).$$

This formula says that "there exists a human being such that if s/he has a mother then the mother is her own father". This is absurd, whereas the original sentence with our common understanding sounds plausible. So, what went wrong?

Before the substitution, the occurrences of x were free in $\exists y(Hx \to Fxy)$. By substituting x as $f(y)$, all these new occurrences of y become bound. This is not a faithful substitution. Such a substitution is said to *capture the variable*. Our substitution should not capture a variable; it should not make a free occurrence bound. We formalize this notion.

Let Z be a formula; and x, y variables. The variable y is **free for** x in Z iff x does not occur free within the scope of any $\forall y$ or $\exists y$ in Z. We observe that y is free for x in the formula Z is equivalent to the following condition:

> After replacing each free occurrence of x by y in Z, the new occurrences of y remain free in the new formula.

We say that a term t is **free for** the variable x in the formula Z iff each variable that occurs in t is free for x in the formula Z.

Informally, it means that no variable of t is captured by replacing all free occurrences of x with t in Z. Thus t is free for x means that t is allowed to be substituted in place of a free x, in some sense.

The formula $Z[x/t]$ is obtained from Z by replacing each free occurrence of the variable x by t, provided t is free for x in Z. The term $f[x/t]$ is obtained from $f(\cdot)$ by replacing *each occurrence* of x by t, in $f(\cdot)$.

Unless otherwise stated, whenever we use $Z[x/t]$, we assume that the term t is free for variable x in the formula Z. Such substitutions are sometimes called *admissible substitutions.* In our notation, all substitutions are assumed to be admissible.

EXAMPLE 5.7. In the formula $\exists y(Hx \to Fxy)$, y is not free for x since x occurs free within the scope of $\exists y$. This is the reason that after replacing this occurrence of x by $f(y)$, the new occurrence of y becomes bound; y is getting captured by the substitution.

The variable x is free for x in $\exists y(Hx \to Fxy)$. Similarly, z is free for x in the formula $\exists y(Hx \to Fxy)$ as z does not at all occur in this formula. If t is a closed term, that is, no variable occurs in it, then vacuously, each variable of t is free for each variable in each formula; t is free for each variable in each formula.

If no variable of t is bound in a formula Y, then t is free for each variable occurring in Y. In the formula $\exists z(Pxy \leftrightarrow Qyz)$, the term $t = f(x,y,f(a,b,c))$ is free for each of the variables x,y,z. However, z is neither free for x nor free for y in this formula.

Only free occurrences of a variable can be substituted by a term, and that to, when the substitution is admissible: $(\forall xPx)[x/t] = \forall xPx$. For replacing a variable by a term in a term, there is no such restriction: $f(x)[x/t] = f(t)$, and $f(x,y,z,g(a))[x/f(x)] = f(f(x),y,z,g(a))$.

Exercises for § 5.3

1. Let X be a formula; x,y distinct variables; and a,b constants. Show that $X[x/a][y/b] = X[y/b][x/a]$. What happens if x,y are not distinct?
2. Suppose, X is a formula, x,y are distinct variables, c is a constant, and t is a term free for x in X. Show that if y does not occur in t, then $X[x/t][y/c] = X[y/c][x/t]$. What happens if y occurs in t?
3. Decide whether the terms $x,y,f(x),g(y,z)$ are free for y in each of the following formulas:
   (a) $P(z,y,x) \leftrightarrow P(x,a,b)$
   (b) $\forall z(P(x,y,z) \leftrightarrow Q(x,a,b))$
   (c) $\exists z((P(z,y,x) \leftrightarrow Q(x,a,b)) \wedge R(z))$
   (d) $\forall x((P(x,y,z) \leftrightarrow Q(x,a,b)) \to \exists zR(x,y,z,u))$
4. Let X be a formula. Suppose x is a free variable of X, y is a variable different from x, z is a variable not occurring in X, and t is a term free for x in X. Show the following:
   (a) $X[x/t][y/z] = X[y/z][x/t[y/z]]$
   (b) The term $t[x/y]$ is free for x in the formula $X[x/y]$.

5.4 SEMANTICS OF FL

Interpretation of first order formulas starts with fixing a nonempty set as the domain or universe of that interpretation. All constants are interpreted as certain elements in the domain. All function symbols are interpreted as partial functions on the domain. All predicates are interpreted as relations over the domain. This is how first order sentences are interpreted as sentences that talk about relations, functions, and elements of a domain. Here are three different interpretations of the sentence $\forall xPxf(x)$:

> Everyone is younger than his father.
> Every number is less than its square.
> Every integer is divisible by half of it.

Proceeding similarly, we would interpret the formula $Pxf(x)$ as follows.

> x is younger than his father.
> The number x is less than its square.
> The integer x is divisible by half of it.

All these are unfinished sentences because variables are just gaps. Only after substitution of a constant or a name there, you can get a sentence from it; or else, you may use a quantifier. You cannot possibly assume this sentence to be read as $\forall xPxf(x)$ nor as $\exists xPxf(x)$. Moreover, which one is to be taken and why?

One way is to think of a *state* where x is assigned to an object. Then the formula becomes a sentence, which speaks about that object in that state. If in a state, x has been assigned to a, then in that state, $Pxf(x)$ can be read as

> a and $f(a)$ are related by P.

When we interpret $Pxf(x)$ in the set of human beings, with f as 'father of', P as 'younger than', and if x is assigned to Soumya, then in this state, the formula $Pxf(x)$ would be interpreted as the sentence:

> Soumya is younger than her father.

Such an assignment ℓ, which associates variables to elements of the universe or domain of an interpretation is called a *valuation* (or a *variable assignment function*). Do not confuse this with the boolean valuation of propositions.

While assigning x to 'Soumya', you had taken

$$\ell(x) = \text{Soumya}, \quad \ell(f(x)) = \text{Soumya's father}.$$

In so doing, you have taken ℓ as a function that associates not only variables but also terms, to elements of the domain. If ℓ is extended to terms, we must see that it agrees with the function that associates predicates to relations and function symbols to actual functions over the domain.

Writing as ϕ, the function that associates predicates and function symbols to relations and functions over the domain, we have here

$$\phi(f) = \text{'father of'}, \quad \ell(f(x)) = \phi(f)(\ell(x)).$$

That is how a valuation must agree with the function ϕ of the interpretation.

Suppose in a state, we fix $\ell(x) = a$ and $\ell(y) = b$. Now, the reading of $\forall xPxy$ uses b instead of y. But also it requires x to take each element in the domain of our interpretation as a value, and not only this a. While varying the values of x over the domain, we must keep the value b assigned to y as it is. One way is to use the notation $\ell[x \mapsto a]$; it denotes a valuation that is equal to the valuation ℓ in all respects, except fixing x to a. Then we would require the following for any arbitrary object a in the domain:

> $\forall xPxy$ is true in a state with the valuation ℓ if Pxy is true in each state with the valuation $\ell[x \mapsto a]$.

Suppose we interpret a binary predicate P as 'less than or equal to' in $\mathbb{N}$, and a constant c as 0. Then the formula $\forall xPcx$ is interpreted as the sentence

> 0 is less than or equal to every natural number.

To know whether $\forall xPcx$ is satisfied by this interpretation, we must ascertain whether the interpreted sentence is true in $\mathbb{N}$ or not. So, we *assume* the following:

> Every interpretation has an inbuilt mechanism of *truth* that determines whether objects in the domain are related in a certain way or not.

Along with the usual interpretation of the connectives, our formalism must capture the following ideas:

> Interpret the predicate P as the property or relation $\phi(P)$ on a domain.
> Interpret the predicate $\approx$ as $=$.
> For the open formula Px, first assign x to an element of the domain via a valuation. If the assigned element has the property $\phi(P)$, then Px is satisfied.
> If at least one object in the domain has the property $\phi(P)$, then the formula $\exists xPx$ is satisfied.
> If every object in the domain has the property $\phi(P)$, then the formula $\forall xPx$ is satisfied.

We implement these ideas and present the formal semantics of FL.

An **interpretation** is a pair $I = (D, \phi)$, where D is a nonempty set, called the **domain** or **universe** of I, and ϕ is a function associating function symbols with partial functions on D and predicates with relations on D. Further, ϕ preserves arity, that is,

(a) If P is a 0-ary predicate (a propositional variable), then $\phi(P)$ is a sentence in D, which is either true or false.

(b) If P is $\approx$, then $\phi(P)$ is the equality relation on D, expressing "same as", that is, $\phi(P) = \{(d,d) : d \in D\}$.

(c) If P is an n-ary predicate for $n \geq 1$, other than $\approx$, then $\phi(P)$ is an n-ary relation on D, a subset of D^n.

(d) If f is a 0-ary function symbol (a constant, a name), then $\phi(f)$ is an object in D; that is, $\phi(f) \in D$.

(e) If f is an n-ary function symbol, $n \geq 1$, then $\phi(f) : D^n \to D$ is a partial function of n arguments on D.

Sometimes, the domain of an interpretation $I = (D, \phi)$ is written as D^I and the map ϕ as ϕ^I.

A **valuation** under the interpretation $I = (D, \phi)$ is a function ℓ that assigns terms to elements of D, which is first defined for variables, with $\ell(x) \in D$ for any variable x, and then extended to terms satisfying:

(i) If f is a 0-ary function symbol, then $\ell(f) = \phi(f)$.

(ii) If f is an n-ary function symbol, $n \geq 1$, and $t_1, \ldots, t_n$ are terms, then $\ell(f(t_1, \ldots, t_n)) = \phi(f)(\ell(t_1), \ldots, \ell(t_n))$.

For a valuation ℓ, a variable x, and an object $a \in D$, we write $\ell[x \mapsto a]$ (also ℓ_a^x) as a new valuation obtained from ℓ which fixes x to a, but assigns every other variable to what ℓ assigns. That is,

$$\ell[x \mapsto a](x) = a, \quad \ell[x \mapsto a](y) = \ell(y) \text{ for } y \neq x.$$

A **state** I_ℓ is a triple (D, ϕ, ℓ), where $I = (D, \phi)$ is an interpretation and ℓ is a valuation under I.

Let X, Y, Z be formulas and let $I_\ell = (D, \phi, \ell)$ be a state. Satisfaction of a formula in the state I_ℓ is defined inductively by the following. We read $I_\ell \vDash X$ as I_ℓ **satisfies** X or as I_ℓ **verifies** X or as I_ℓ is a **state-model** of X. Similarly, $I_\ell \nvDash X$ is read as I_ℓ does not satisfy X, or I_ℓ does not verify X, or I_ℓ is not a state-model of X, or I_ℓ **falsifies** X.

1. $I_\ell \vDash \top$.
2. $I_\ell \nvDash \bot$.
3. For a 0-ary predicate P, $I_\ell \vDash P$ iff $\phi(P)$ is a true sentence in D.
4. For terms s, t, $I_\ell \vDash (s \approx t)$ iff $\ell(s) = \ell(t)$ as elements of D.
5. For an n-ary predicate P other than $\approx$, $n \geq 1$, and terms $t_1, \ldots, t_n$, $I_\ell \vDash P(t_1, \ldots, t_n)$ iff $(\ell(t_1), \ldots, \ell(t_n)) \in \phi(P)$. (when the objects $\ell(t_1), \ldots, \ell(t_n)$ are related by the relation $\phi(P)$.)
6. $I_\ell \vDash \neg X$ iff $I_\ell \nvDash X$.
7. $I_\ell \vDash X \wedge Y$ iff both $I_\ell \vDash X$ and $I_\ell \vDash Y$ hold.
8. $I_\ell \vDash X \vee Y$ iff at least one of $I_\ell \vDash X$ or $I_\ell \vDash Y$ holds.
9. $I_\ell \vDash X \to Y$ iff at least one of $I_\ell \nvDash X$ or $I_\ell \vDash Y$ holds.
10. $I_\ell \vDash X \leftrightarrow Y$ iff either $I_\ell \vDash X$ and $I_\ell \vDash Y$ hold, or $I_\ell \nvDash X$ and $I_\ell \nvDash Y$ hold.
11. $I_\ell \vDash \forall x Y$ iff for each $d \in D$, $I_{\ell[x \mapsto d]} \vDash Y$.
12. $I_\ell \vDash \exists x Y$ iff for at least one (some) $d \in D$, $I_{\ell[x \mapsto d]} \vDash Y$.

If the domain of a state-model has m elements, we say that the state-model has m elements. **Finite** or **infinite state-models** are the state-models whose domains are finite or infinite nonempty sets, respectively. We say that a *formula has a finite (infinite) state-model* iff there exists a state whose domain is a nonempty finite (infinite) set and the state is a state-model of the formula.

Observe that we have not yet defined when an interpretation satisfies a formula. We have only defined when a state under a given interpretation would satisfy a formula.

EXAMPLE 5.8. Consider the formulas Pxy and $Pcf(c)$ along with the following interpretations I, J and valuations ℓ, m:

$I = (\mathbb{N}, \phi)$, where	$J = (H, \psi)$, where
$\mathbb{N}$ is the set of all natural numbers,	H is the set of all human beings,
$\phi(P) =$ 'is less than',	$\psi(P) =$ 'is a brother of',
$\phi(c) = 0$,	$\psi(c) =$ Rajiv,
$\phi(f) =$ 'successor function',	$\psi(f) =$ 'mother of',
$\ell(x) = 0,\ \ell(y) = 1.$	$m(x) =$ Rajiv, $m(y) =$ Sanjay.

As we know, Rajiv and Sanjay are the grand sons of Pandit Jawaharlal Nehru. Determine whether

(a) $I_\ell \vDash Pxy$ (b) $I_\ell \vDash Pcf(c)$ (c) $J_m \vDash Pxy$ (d) $J_m \vDash Pcf(c)$.

Observe that f is a unary function symbol, and it is associated with the functions 'successor of' and 'mother of', which take only one argument. Similarly, P is a binary predicate, and it is associated with binary relations 'less than' and 'is a brother of'.

(a) To check whether the state $I_\ell = (\mathbb{N}, \phi, \ell)$ is a state-model of Pxy, we see that $I_\ell \vDash Pxy$ iff $(\ell(x), \ell(y)) \in \phi(P)$ iff $(0, 1)$ is a member of the relation 'less than' iff $0 < 1$. This is true in $\mathbb{N}$. Therefore, $I_\ell \vDash Pxy$.

(b) $I_\ell \vDash Pcf(c)$ iff $(\ell(c), \ell(f(c))) \in \phi(P)$ iff $(\phi(c), \phi(f)(\phi(c))) \in \phi(P)$ iff (0, successor of 0) $\in \phi(P)$ iff $0 < 1$. Since this is true in $\mathbb{N}$, $I_\ell \vDash Pcf(c)$.

(c) $J_m \vDash Pxy$ iff $(m(x), m(y)) \in \psi(P)$ iff (Rajiv, Sanjay) $\in$ 'is a brother of' iff Rajiv is a brother of Sanjay. This latter sentence is true. Hence $J_m \vDash Pxy$.

(d) $J_m \vDash Pcf(c)$ iff $(m(c), m(f(c))) \in \psi(P)$ iff $(\psi(c), \psi(f)(\psi(c))) \in \psi(P)$ iff (Rajiv, mother of Rajiv) $\in$ 'is a brother of' iff Rajiv is a brother of his own mother, which is not true. Thus, $J_m \nvDash Pcf(c)$.

We end this section with an important technical result, which will be used at many places without mention. Roughly, it says that substitution of a free variable by a term can be done either at the formula, or at the valuation; so that when interpreted, they have the same effect.

Lemma 5.1 (Substitution Lemma). *Let t be a term free for a variable x in a formula Y. Let s be any term. Let $I_\ell = (D, \phi, \ell)$ be a state. Then*

(1) $\ell[x \mapsto \ell(t)](s) = \ell(s[x/t])$;

(2) $I_{\ell[x \mapsto \ell(t)]} \vDash X$ *iff* $I_\ell \vDash X[x/t]$.

Proof. Let us write the valuation $\ell[x \mapsto \ell(t)]$ as m. Then $m(x) = \ell(t)$; and $m(y) = \ell(y)$ for all variables $y \neq x$.

(1) We use induction on the level of a term s. If $s = c$, a constant, then $m(c) = \phi(c) = \ell(c[x/t])$. If $s = x$, the given variable, then $m(x) = \ell(t) = \ell(x[x/t])$. If $s = y \neq x$, then $m(y) = \ell(y) = \ell(y[x/t])$. So, suppose $s = f(t_1, \ldots, t_n)$, where

$$m(t_i) = \ell(t_i[x/t]) \quad \text{for } 1 \leq i \leq n.$$

Then we have

$$
\begin{aligned}
m(s) &= m(f(t_1,\ldots,t_n)) = \phi(f)(m(t_1),\ldots,m(t_n)) \\
&= \phi(f)(\ell(t_1[x/t]),\ldots,\ell(t_n[x/t])) = \ell(f(t_1[x/t],\ldots,t_n[x/t])) \\
&= \ell(f(t_1,\ldots,t_n)[x/t]) = \ell(s[x/t]).
\end{aligned}
$$

(2) We use induction on the number of connectives and quantifiers occurring in X. If X is $\top$, then both I_ℓ and I_m satisfy X. If X is $\bot$, then both I_ℓ and I_m falsify it. If $X = P(t_1,\ldots,t_n)$, then using (1), we have

$$
\begin{aligned}
I_m \vDash X \text{ iff } & I_m \vDash P(t_1,\ldots,t_n) \text{ iff } (m(t_1),\ldots,m(t_n)) \in \phi(P) \\
\text{iff } & (\ell(t_1[x/t]),\ldots,\ell(t_n[x/t])) \in \phi(P) \text{ iff } I_\ell \vDash P(t_1,\ldots,t_n)[x/t] \\
\text{iff } & I_\ell \vDash X[x/t].
\end{aligned}
$$

In the inductive step, suppose $X = \neg Y$, or $X = (Y \circ Z)$ for $\circ \in \{\wedge, \vee, \rightarrow, \leftrightarrow\}$, or $X = \forall y Z$, or $X = \exists y Z$. Lay out the induction hypothesis that

$$I_m \vDash Y \text{ iff } I_\ell \vDash Y[x/t], \quad I_m \vDash Z \text{ iff } I_\ell \vDash Z[x/t].$$

When $X = \neg Y$, we see that $I_m \vDash X$ iff $I_m \nvDash Y$ iff $I_\ell \nvDash Y[x/t]$ iff $I_\ell \vDash X[x/t]$. The cases of other connective are similar. When $X = \forall y Z$, there are two cases,

(i) x does not occur free in Z.

(ii) x occurs free in Z.

(i) In this case, the valuations ℓ and m agree on all variables that are free in Z; and also $Z[x/t] = Z$. Thus the conclusion follows.
(ii) Here, $X = \forall y Z$ and x occurs free in Z. Since t is free for x in X, we know that y does not occur in t. Also, t is free for x in Z. Hence for each $d \in D$, we obtain

$$\ell[y \mapsto d](t) = \ell(t), \quad \ell[y \mapsto d][x \mapsto \ell(t)] = \ell[x \mapsto \ell(t)][y \mapsto d] = m[y \mapsto d].$$

Since x occurs free in X, $x \neq y$; consequently, $X[x/t] = \forall y(Z[x/t])$. Now,

$$I_\ell \vDash X[x/t] \text{ iff } I_\ell \vDash \forall y(Z[x/t]) \text{ iff for each } d \in D,\ I_{\ell[y \mapsto d]} \vDash Z[x/t]. \tag{5.1}$$

To apply the induction hypothesis, we must know what is the corresponding m for the valuation $\ell[y \mapsto d]$. Let us write that as μ. Then

$$\mu = \ell[y \mapsto d][x \mapsto (\ell[y \mapsto d])(t)] = \ell[y \mapsto d][x \mapsto \ell(t)] = m[y \mapsto d].$$

Using the induction hypothesis on the last statement of (5.1), we have

$$
\begin{aligned}
I_\ell \vDash X[x/t] & \text{ iff for each } d \in D,\ I_\mu \vDash Z \\
& \text{ iff for each } d \in D,\ I_{m[y \mapsto d]} \vDash Z \text{ iff } I_m \vDash \forall y Z \text{ iff } I_m \vDash X.
\end{aligned}
$$

The other quantifier case is similar to this. ♦

Exercises for § 5.4

1. Let B be a formula, c a constant, x, y distinct variables, D a domain, and let $d, e \in D$. Show the following:

   (a) $\ell[x \mapsto d][x \mapsto e] = \ell[x \mapsto e]$
   (b) $\ell[x \mapsto d][y \mapsto e] = \ell[y \mapsto e][x \mapsto d]$
   (c) $\forall y(B[x/c]) = (\forall yB)[x/c]$
   (d) $\exists y(B[x/c]) = (\exists yB)[x/c]$

2. Let $I = (D, \phi, \ell)$ be a state, and let the variable y be free for x in a formula X. Show that $I_{\ell[x \mapsto y][y \mapsto d]} \vDash X$ iff $I_{\ell[y \mapsto d][x \mapsto d]} \vDash X$.

3. Suppose that $I_\ell = (D, \phi, \ell)$ is a state; $x_1, \ldots, x_n$ are variables; $t_1, \ldots, t_n$ are terms; f ia an n-ary function symbol; and Y is a formula. Then show the following:

   (a) $\phi(f(x_1, \ldots, x_n)[x_1/t_1, \ldots, x_n/t_n]) = \phi(f)(\phi(t_1), \ldots, \phi(t_n))$
   (b) $I_\ell \vDash Y[x_1/t_1, \ldots, x_n/t_n]$ iff $I_{\ell[x_1 \mapsto t_1, \ldots, x_n \mapsto t_n]} \vDash Y$

4. Let f be a binary function symbol, and let P be a unary predicate. For each of the following formulas, find a state-model, and a falsifying state.

   (a) $\forall x(f(x,y) \approx y)$ (b) $\exists y \forall x(f(x,y) \approx y)$ (c) $\exists x(Px \wedge \forall y P f(x,y))$

5. Determine whether the state $I_\ell = (D, \phi, \ell)$ satisfies the following formulas, where $D = \{1, 2\}$, $\phi(c) = 1$, $\phi(P) = \{1\}$, $\phi(Q) = \{(1,1), (1,2)\}$, and ℓ is some valuation.

   (a) $\forall x(Pc \vee Qxx) \to Pc \vee \forall xQxx$ (b) $\forall x(Pc \wedge Qxx) \to Pc \vee \forall xQxx$
   (c) $\forall x(Pc \vee Qxx) \to Pc \wedge \forall xQxx$ (d) $\forall x(Pc \wedge Qxx) \to Pc \wedge \forall xQxx$

6. Let I_ℓ be a state, and let X be a formula. If $I_\ell \nvDash X$, is it necessary that $I_\ell \vDash \neg X$? Conversely, if $I_\ell \vDash \neg X$, does it imply that $I_\ell \nvDash X$?

5.5 Translating into FL

We will consider some examples of symbolizing English sentences into FL.

EXAMPLE 5.9. With the vocabulary Hx: x is a human being, Mx: x is mortal, the Aristotelian sentences are translated as follows:

All human beings are mortal :	$\forall x(Hx \to Mx)$
Some human beings are mortal :	$\exists x(Hx \wedge Mx)$
No human being is mortal :	$\forall x(Hx \to \neg Mx)$
Some human beings are not mortal :	$\exists x(Hx \wedge \neg Mx)$
All human beings are not mortal :	$\neg \forall x(Hx \to Mx)$

The last two sentences mean the same thing. Though the last sentence starts with an 'all', the quantifier is really 'some'. This usually (not always) happens in the presence of a 'not'.

Notice that the quantifier $\exists$ goes with the connective $\wedge$, and $\forall$ goes with $\to$. This is again usual for sentences in natural languages.

EXAMPLE 5.10. Each one is older than his younger sisters.

We start with identifying the names, definite descriptions, and predicates. We do not have any names here. We cannot take 'his younger sister' as a definite description. The sentence says that

For each x, x is older than y if y is a younger sister of x.

In 'y is a younger sister of x' the article 'a' refers to 'any' as per the original sentence. Our semi-formal sentence looks as follows:

For each x, for each y, if y is a younger sister of x, then x is older than y.

With the vocabulary as

$$Oxy: \ x \text{ is older than } y, \qquad Sxy: \ y \text{ is a younger sister of } x.$$

we have the symbolization: $\forall x \forall y(Sxy \to Oxy)$.

EXAMPLE 5.11. Translate: If there is a man on Mars, then he has fifteen fingers.

In this sentence there is an ambiguity in the scope of the quantifier 'there is'. The sentence means the following:

Suppose there exists a man on Mars. Call that man x. Then x has fifteen fingers.

Take any man on Mars; he has fifteen fingers.

With suitable vocabulary, the sentence is translated as $\forall x(M(x) \to F(x))$

EXAMPLE 5.12. To translate the sentence "If two persons fight over third one's property, then the third one gains", we use the vocabulary:

$$Fxyz: \ x \text{ and } y \text{ fight over } z, \qquad Gx: \ x \text{ gains}, \qquad h(x): \ \text{property of } x.$$

The sentence may be symbolized as $\forall x \forall y \forall z(Fxyh(z) \to Gz)$.

Notice that this symbolization allows a person to fight with himself and also gain his own property. To convey the fact that there are exactly three distinct persons involved here, you can use the equality predicate and symbolize the sentence as $\forall x \forall y \forall z(\neg(x \approx y) \land \neg(y \approx z) \land \neg(z \approx x) \land Fxyh(z) \to Gz)$.

EXAMPLE 5.13. For each pair of primes differing by 2, there exists a pair of greater primes differing by 2.

$$\forall x \forall y(Px \land Py \land Dxy \to \exists z \exists w(Gzx \land Gwy \land Pz \land Pw \land Dzw)).$$

What do the predicates P, G, D stand for?

EXAMPLE 5.14. Translate the following argument into an FL-consequence:

A politician praises a person if the person has helped him. Some bandit helped no politicians. If all politicians praise a bandit, then the bandit must be none other than Robin Hood. Therefore, there exists a bandit other than Robin Hood.

We use the following vocabulary:

Px: x is a politician,	Qx: x is a person,	Bx: x is a bandit,
Rxy: x praises y,	Hxy: x has helped y,	r: Robin Hood.

As in PL, the symbol $!\vdash$ stands for 'therefore'. And we have the consequence as

$$\{\forall x \forall y(Px \land Qy \to (Hyx \to Rxy)),\ \exists x(Bx \land \forall y(Py \to \neg Hxy)),$$
$$\forall x(Bx \land \forall y(Py \land Ryx \to (x \approx r))\} \ !\vdash \exists x(Bx \land \neg(x \approx r)).$$

Exercises for § 5.5

1. Translate the following into FL using suggested vocabulary:
   - (a) All men are women. $[Mx,\ Wx]$
   - (b) No man is a woman. $[Mx,\ Wx]$
   - (c) Some men are women. $[Mx,\ Wx]$
   - (d) Some men are not women. $[Mx,\ Wx]$
   - (e) All men are sons of some woman. $[Mx,\ Wx,\ Sxy]$
   - (f) Some man is not a son of any woman. $[Mx,\ Wx,\ Sxy]$
   - (g) Any man is not a husband of any woman. $[Mx,\ Wx,\ Hxy]$
   - (h) Some man is not a husband of any woman. $[Mx,\ Wx,\ Hxy]$
   - (i) Some man is not a husband of some woman. $[Mx,\ Wx,\ Hxy]$
   - (j) Anybody's brother's sister is that person's sister. $[Bxy,\ Sxy,\ Px]$
   - (k) Ali and Susy have the same maternal grand-father. $[f(x),\ a,\ s]$
   - (l) If anyone is Susy's son, then someone is a daughter of Susy's father's nephew. $[s,\ Sxy,\ Dxy,\ f(x)]$
   - (m) No student attends every lecture and no lecture is attended by all students. $[Sx,\ Ax]$
   - (n) If there are no jobs, then nobody would study in an IIT. $[Jx,\ Ix,\ Sxy]$
   - (o) Successor of a prime number need not be a prime number. $[Px,\ s(x)]$
   - (p) A number is prime or not can be decided in polynomial time. $[Px,\ Dx]$
   - (q) A number is composite or not can be decided in polynomial time. $[Cx,\ Dx]$
   - (r) There always are triples of numbers such that one's fifth power is the sum of the fifth powers of the other two. $[f(x),\ Sxy]$
   - (s) The binary relation R is reflexive. [Use Rxy when x is related to y by R. From this question onwards, you require a different type of translation.]
   - (t) The binary relation R is an equivalence relation. $[Rxy]$
   - (u) The function f is bijective. [Use the notation $y \approx f(x)$]
   - (v) The function f is continuous at a point a. $[y \approx f(x),\ a]$
   - (w) The function is not continuous on a set A. $[y \approx f(x),\ \in,\ A]$
   - (x) The sequence $\{x_n\}$ does not converge. $[|\cdot|,\ <]$
   - (y) The series $\sum_{n=1}^{\infty} x_n$ is not absolutely convergent. $[|\cdot|,\ <,\ \sum_{n=1}^{\infty} x_n]$
   - (z) Every even number bigger than four can be expressed as a sum of two prime numbers. $[\times,\ >,\ +, 4]$

2. Let Mxy stand for the phrase 'x is a member of y', and let Sxy stand for x is a subset of y'. Express the following as formulas.
   - (a) Each set has a complement.
   - (b) For any two sets, there exists a set which is their union.
   - (c) Any member of a subset is a member of the original set.
   - (d) For any two sets there exists a set which is their intersection.
   - (e) There is a set which is a subset of every set, and this set has no member.
   - (f) For any set there corresponds another set whose members are the subsets of the first.

3. Symbolize: There is a unique person who authored the book named *Logics for Computer Science*. [Hint: Use the equality predicate $\approx$.]

4. Taking 'France' as a name, symbolize the sentence: The present king of France is bald.
5. Translate the following into FL:
   (a) There are more Muslims in India than Pakistan.
   (b) There is more water in milk than beans.
   (c) There is more water in milk than fat.
   (d) There are more Muslims in India than Christians.
6. Explain whether the following sentences mean the same thing or not.
   (a) If a mathematician finds a mistake in a proof, then it must be discarded.
   (b) If some mathematician finds some mistake in some proof, then it must be discarded.
   (c) For all mathematicians, if one of them finds a mistake in a proof, then it must be discarded.
7. Translate $\forall x(Px \wedge Qx)$ and $\exists x(Px \to Qx)$ into English by reading P, Q suitably.

5.6 SATISFIABILITY AND VALIDITY

Let A be a formula. We say that A is **satisfiable** iff some state satisfies it; A is **unsatisfiable** iff each state falsifies it; A is **valid** iff each state satisfies it; and A is **invalid** iff some state falsifies it.

EXAMPLE 5.15. Revisit Example 5.8. The formula Pxy is satisfiable since it has a state-model I_ℓ. The formula $Pcf(c)$ is satisfiable since it too has a state-model I_ℓ. The formula Pxy is invalid as the state I_m falsifies Pxy. Similarly, since $J_m \nvDash Pcf(c)$, the formula $Pcf(c)$ is also invalid.

For a predicate P, its corresponding relation $\phi(P)$ is informally written as P'. For example, to interpret the formula $Pxf(yz)$, we write the interpretation $I = (\mathbb{N}, \phi)$, with $\phi(P) =$ '$<$', $\phi(f) =$ 'sum of so and so', as $I = (\mathbb{N}, P', f')$, where P' is '$<$' and f' is 'sum of so and so'. We follow this convention of writing interpretations in the next example.

EXAMPLE 5.16. Is the formula $A = \forall xPxf(x)$ satisfiable? Is it valid?

Take an interpretation $I = (\mathbb{N}, P', f')$, where P' is the 'less than' relation and f' is the function 'plus 5', i.e., $f'(n) = n + 5$. Let ℓ be a valuation with $\ell(x) = 2$.

The state $I_\ell \vDash \forall xPxf(x)$ iff for each $n \in \mathbb{N}$, $I_{\ell[x \mapsto n]} \vDash Pxf(x)$. Suppose we want to verify for $n = 3$. Now, $\ell[x \mapsto n] = \ell[x \mapsto 3]$ maps x to 3, and every other variable y to $\ell(y)$. However, it does not matter what this $\ell(y)$ is since y does not occur in the formula. We see that $I_{\ell[x \mapsto 3]} \vDash Pxf(x)$ iff $3 < f'(3)$ iff $3 < 3 + 5$. Since $3 < 3 + 5$ is true in $\mathbb{N}$, $I_{\ell[x \mapsto 3]} \vDash Pxf(x)$.

Thus the formula $\forall xPxf(x)$ is satisfiable as it has a state-model such as I_ℓ. Moreover, where have you used the information $\ell(x) = 2$? It seems that had you taken any other ℓ (e.g., $\ell(x) = 10$), then also I_ℓ would have satisfied the formula. In fact, for each $n \in \mathbb{N}$, $I_{\ell[x \mapsto n]} \vDash Pxf(x)$ iff $n < f'(n)$ iff $n < n + 5$. That is, $I_\ell \vDash \forall xPxf(x)$ for each ℓ under I. Informally, each state I_ℓ interprets the formula as the sentence:

Each natural number n is less than $n+5$.

Since $\mathbb{N}$ is an infinite set, we have infinite state-models for the formula.

Is the formula also valid? It does not seem likely since there is too much of arbitrariness in this formula. To see that it is invalid, you must find a state that may falsify it. For instance, consider the interpretation $J = (\mathbb{N}, \bar{P}, f')$, where $\bar{P}$ is the 'greater than' relation. Take f' as the same 'plus 5' as above.

Now, $J_\ell \vDash Pxf(x)$ iff for each $n \in \mathbb{N}$, $\ell[x \mapsto n] \vDash Pxf(x)$. For $n = 3$, we see that $\ell[x \mapsto 3] \vDash Pxf(x)$ iff $3 > 3+5$. As $3 \not> 3+5$, $J_\ell \nvDash Pxf(x)$. That is, the formula $\forall x Pxf(x)$ is invalid. Notice that J interprets the formula as the sentence:

Each natural number n is greater than $n+5$.

We define the notions of consequence and equivalence in FL as follows.

Let Σ be a set of formulas, I an interpretation, and ℓ a valuation under I. The state I_ℓ **is a state-model of** (or satisfies, or verifies) the set Σ, written as $I_\ell \vDash \Sigma$, iff for each $X \in \Sigma$, $I_\ell \vDash X$.

The set Σ is called **satisfiable** iff Σ has a state-model, i.e., iff for some interpretation I and for some valuation ℓ under I, the state I_ℓ is a state-model of Σ.

For a formula B, Σ **semantically entails** B, written as $\Sigma \vDash B$, iff each state-model of Σ is a state-model of B. For $\Sigma = \{X_1, \ldots, X_n\}$, we also write $\Sigma \vDash B$ as $X_1, \ldots, X_n \vDash B$. We read $\Sigma \vDash B$ as "Σ entails B", "B is a semantic consequence of Σ", and also as "the consequence $\Sigma \,!\!\vdash B$ is valid".

Two formulas A, B are called **equivalent**, written as $A \equiv B$, iff each state-model of A is a state-model of B, and also each state-model of B is a state-model of A. That is, $A \equiv B$ if and only if "for each interpretation I and for each valuation ℓ under I, we have $I_\ell \vDash A$ iff $I_\ell \vDash B$."

EXAMPLE 5.17. Show that $\exists y \forall x Pxy \vDash \forall x \exists y Pxy$.

Informally, the first sentence says that the same y works for each x in such a way that Pxy holds, while the second sentence asks for existence of a y corresponding to each given x so that Pxy may hold. Clearly, the first sentence implies the second.

To see it formally, let $I = (D, \phi)$ be an interpretation and ℓ a valuation under I. Assume that $I_\ell \vDash \exists y \forall x Pxy$. This means $\phi(P)$ is some subset of $D \times D$, and for some $d \in D$, for each $d' \in D$, we have $(d', d) \in \phi(P)$. It demands that

$$(d'_1, d) \in \phi(P),\ (d'_2, d) \in \phi(P),\ (d'_3, d) \in \phi(P), \ldots$$

Then for each $d' \in D$, we have a corresponding element of D, here it is $d \in D$, such that $(d', d) \in \phi(P)$. Thus, $I_\ell \vDash \forall x \exists y Pxy$.

EXAMPLE 5.18. Show that $\forall x \exists y Pxy \nvDash \exists y \forall x Pxy$.

We try with an interpretation. Let $I = (D, P')$, where $D = \{2, 3\}$ and $P' = \{(2,3), (3,2)\}$. Suppose $\ell(x) = 2$, $\ell(y) = 3$. To check $I_\ell \vDash \forall x \exists y Pxy$, we must check whether both of

$$I_{\ell[x \mapsto 2]} \vDash \exists y Pxy \text{ and } I_{\ell[x \mapsto 3]} \vDash \exists y Pxy \tag{5.2}$$

hold. The first entailment in (5.2) holds when at least one of

$$I_{\ell[x \mapsto 2][y \mapsto 2]} \vDash Pxy \text{ or } I_{\ell[x \mapsto 2][y \mapsto 3]} \vDash Pxy \tag{5.3}$$

holds. The first entailment in (5.3) does not hold since $(2,2) \notin P'$. The second one in (5.3) holds since $(2,3) \in P'$. Therefore, $I_{\ell[x \mapsto 2]} \vDash \exists y Pxy$ in (5.2) holds.

We must check whether the second entailment $I_{\ell[x \mapsto 3]} \vDash \exists y Pxy$ in (5.2) holds. For this, at least one of the following must hold:

$$I_{\ell[x \mapsto 3][y \mapsto 2]} \vDash Pxy \text{ or } I_{\ell[x \mapsto 3][y \mapsto 3]} \vDash Pxy. \tag{5.4}$$

The first entailment in (5.4) holds since $(3,2) \in P'$. Consequently, $I_{\ell[x \mapsto 3]} \vDash \exists y Pxy$ holds. The conditions in (5.2) are satisfied; thus $I_\ell \vDash \forall x \exists y Pxy$.

For $I_\ell \vDash \exists y \forall x Pxy$, we must have

$$I_{\ell[y \mapsto 2]} \vDash \forall x Pxy \text{ or } I_{\ell[y \mapsto 3]} \vDash \forall x Pxy. \tag{5.5}$$

The first entailment in (5.5) demands

$$I_{\ell[y \mapsto 2][x \mapsto 2]} \vDash Pxy \text{ and } I_{\ell[y \mapsto 2][x \mapsto 3]} \vDash Pxy. \tag{5.6}$$

As $(2,2) \notin P'$, the first one in (5.6) does not hold. Consequently, the first one in (5.5) does not hold. But the second one might. The second entailment in (5.5) demands

$$I_{\ell[y \mapsto 3][x \mapsto 2]} \vDash Pxy \text{ and } I_{\ell[y \mapsto 3][x \mapsto 3]} \vDash Pxy. \tag{5.7}$$

As $(3,3) \notin P'$, the second one in (5.7) does not hold. Consequently, the second one in (5.6) does not hold.

That is, the demands of (5.5) are not met. Thus, $I_\ell \nvDash \exists y \forall x Pxy$.

Since $I_\ell \vDash \forall x \exists y Pxy$ but $I_\ell \nvDash \exists y \forall x Pxy$, we conclude that $\forall x \exists y Pxy \nvDash \exists y \forall x Pxy$.

Again, to see that $\forall x \exists y Pxy \nvDash \exists y \forall x Pxy$ informally, take the domain as $\mathbb{N}$ and P as the relation of 'less than'. Then, $\forall x \exists y Pxy$ says that

For each natural number, there is a larger natural number.

The sentence $\exists y \forall x Pxy$ says that

There is a largest natural number.

We see that the first one is true, whereas the second is false, in $\mathbb{N}$. Therefore, the consequence $\forall x \exists y Pxy \,!\!\vdash \exists y \forall x Pxy$ is not valid.

EXAMPLE 5.19. Let t be a term free for a variable x in a formula X. We show that $\forall x X \to X[x/t]$.

Let $I_\ell = (D, \phi, \ell)$ be a state. If $I_\ell \nvDash \forall x X$, then $I_\ell \vDash \forall x X \to X[x/t]$. So, suppose that $I_\ell \vDash \forall x X$. Then for each $d \in D$, $I_{\ell[x \mapsto d]} \vDash X$. In particular, $I_{\ell[x \mapsto \ell(t)]} \vDash X$. However, this is same as $I_\ell \vDash X[x/t]$. Therefore, $I_\ell \vDash \forall x X \to X[x/t]$.

EXAMPLE 5.20. We show that $\exists x \neg X \equiv \neg \forall x X$.

Let $I_\ell = (D, \phi, \ell)$ be a state. Now, $I_\ell \vDash \exists x \neg X$ iff for some $d \in D$, $I_{\ell[x \mapsto d]} \vDash \neg X$ iff for some $d \in D$, $I_{\ell[x \mapsto d]} \nvDash X$ iff it is not the case that for each $d \in D$, $I_{\ell[x \mapsto d]} \vDash X$ iff $I_\ell \vDash \neg \forall x X$.

Exercises for § 5.6

1. Let P be a unary predicate, Q a binary predicate, f a binary function symbol, and let x,y,z be variables. Let $I = (\mathbb{N}, P', Q', f')$ be an interpretation where $P' = \{m \in \mathbb{N} : m \text{ is odd}\}$, Q' be the 'less than' relation, and $f'(m,n) = m+n$. Let $\ell(x) = 3, \ell(y) = 4, \ell(z) = 0$. Decide whether the state I_ℓ satisfies the following formulas:
   (a) $Pfxfxfxfxy$
   (b) $\forall x \forall y Qxf(xy) \to \forall z Qzf(xz)$
   (c) $\forall x \forall y (Px \wedge Py \to Pf(xy)) \leftrightarrow \forall z (Px \wedge Py \to Pf(xy))$
   (d) $\forall y (\neg Pf(xy) \leftrightarrow Pf(yz)) \vee \forall x (Qxy \to \exists y (Qzy \wedge Qyz))$
2. Try to construct state-models for each of the following (sets of) formulas, and determine their satisfiability and validity:
   (a) $\forall x \forall y \forall z (Pxyz \to \neg Qyz)$
   (b) $\forall x \forall y (Pxy \to (\neg Pxy \to Qxyf(y)))$
   (c) $\forall x \exists y (Px \to Qy) \to \exists y \forall x (Px \to Qy)$
   (d) $\forall x \exists y \exists z Pxyz \wedge \forall x \forall y (Pxyy \to \neg Pxxy)$
   (e) $\forall x \exists y \forall z ((Pxy \leftrightarrow Pyz) \vee (pxy \leftrightarrow \neg Pyx))$
   (f) $\exists y \forall x (Pxy \to Pyx) \wedge (Pxf(x) \leftrightarrow Pcf(c))$
   (g) $\exists x Pxf(x) \leftrightarrow Pf(x)x \wedge Qxc \wedge (Pcc \to \neg Qc)$
   (h) $\forall x \forall y (Pxy \to Pyx) \wedge \exists x \exists y (Qxyz \leftrightarrow Qyxz \wedge Qyzx)$
   (i) $\forall x \forall y \forall z ((Pxyz \to \neg Qyz) \wedge (Qyz \vee Qxy) \wedge (Qyz \to \neg Pxyz))$
   (j) $\{\forall x \neg Pxx, \exists x Qx, \forall x \exists y Pxy, \forall x (Qx \to \exists y Pyx)\}$
   (k) $\{\forall x (Px \to Qx), \forall x (Qx \to Rx), \neg \exists x (Px \wedge Qx)\}$
   (l) $\{\forall x \neg Pxx, \forall x \exists y Pxy, \forall x \forall y \forall z (Pxy \wedge Pzy \to Pzx)\}$
   (m) $\{\forall x (Px \vee Qx) \to \exists x Rx, \forall x (Rx \to Qx), \exists y (\neg (Py \to Qy))\}$
3. Determine whether the following consequences are valid.
   (a) $\{P(f(c), g(c)), P(f(c), c)\} \mathrel{!\vdash} Q(c, f(c))$
   (b) $\forall x \forall y (Pxy \wedge Pyx) \mathrel{!\vdash} \exists x \exists y (\neg Pxy \wedge Pxy)$
   (c) $\{\exists x Pxx, \forall x \forall y Pxy\} \mathrel{!\vdash} (x \approx y)\}$
   (d) $\{\exists x Px, \exists x Qx\} \mathrel{!\vdash} \exists x (Px \wedge Qx)$
   (e) $\forall x Px \to S \mathrel{!\vdash} \forall x (Px \to S)$, where S is a sentence.
   (f) $((\forall x (\neg Px \leftrightarrow Pf(x)) \vee (\neg Qx \leftrightarrow Qf(f(x)))) \wedge \exists y (Py \to Qy)) \mathrel{!\vdash} \bot$
4. Let X be a formula. Prove that $\varnothing \vDash X$ iff $\Sigma \vDash X$ for each set of formulas Σ.

5.7 SOME METATHEOREMS

In Examples 5.8-5.17, we only considered how the predicates and function symbols appearing in the formulas were interpreted. There was no need of considering how the other predicates or function symbols of FL would be interpreted for checking the satisfiability or validity of the formulas concerned.

Theorem 5.2 (Relevance Lemma). *Let X be a formula, and let $I_\ell = (D, \phi, \ell)$ and $J_m = (D, \psi, m)$ be states. Assume that for each predicate P occurring in X, $\phi(P) = \psi(P)$; for each function symbol occurring in X, $\phi(f) = \psi(f)$; and for each variable x occurring free in X, $\ell(x) = m(x)$. Then $I_\ell \vDash X$ iff $J_m \vDash X$.*

Proof. We use induction on the total number of occurrences of connectives and quantifiers in X. In the basis step, we observe that X is in one of the following forms:

(i) $\top$ (ii) $\bot$ (iii) a 0-ary predicate A (iv) $(s \approx t)$ for terms s, t
(v) $P(t_1, \ldots, t_n)$, for an n-ary predicate $P \neq \approx$ and terms $t_1, \ldots, t_n$.

We consider these cases separately.

(i) Both $I_\ell \vDash \top$ and $J_m \vDash \top$.

(ii) Both $I_\ell \nvDash \bot$ and $J_m \nvDash \bot$.

(iii) $I_\ell \vDash B$ iff $\phi(A)$ is true in D iff $\psi(Y)$ is true in D iff $J_m \vDash A$.

(iv) Since all variables appearing in $(s \approx t)$ are free variables, we have $\ell(x) = m(x)$ for each variable occurring in $(s \approx t)$. It follows that $\ell(s) = m(s)$ and $\ell(t) = m(t)$. Hence, $I_\ell \vDash (s \approx t)$ iff $\ell(s) = \ell(t)$ iff $m(s) = m(t)$ iff $J_m \vDash (s \approx t)$.

(v) Under the given conditions, $\ell(t) = m(t)$ for any term t. Now,

$$\begin{aligned} &I_\ell \vDash P(t_1, \ldots, t_n) \text{ iff } (\ell(t_1), \ldots, \ell(t_n)) \in \phi(P) \\ &\text{iff } (m(t_1), \ldots, m(t_n)) \in \phi(P) \text{ since } \ell(t_i) = m(t_i) \\ &\text{iff } (m(t_1), \ldots, m(t_n)) \in \psi(P) \text{ iff } J_m \vDash P(t_1, \ldots, t_n). \end{aligned}$$

Lay out the induction hypothesis that for any formula having total number of occurrences of connectives and quantifiers less than k, the statement holds. Let A be a formula having this number as k. Then we have the following cases:

(a) $A = \neg B$ for some formula B.
(b) $A = (B * C)$ for some formulas B, C and $* \in \{\wedge, \vee, \rightarrow, \leftrightarrow\}$.
(c) $A = \exists x B$ for some formula B and some variable x.
(d) $A = \forall x B$ for some formula B and some variable x.

The cases (b) and (d) are similar to the cases (a) and (c), respectively.

(a) $I_\ell \vDash \neg B$ iff $I_\ell \nvDash B$ iff $J_m \nvDash B$ (induction hypothesis) iff $J_m \vDash \neg B$.

(c) Suppose that $I_\ell \vDash \exists x B$. Then for some $d \in D$, $I_{\ell[x \mapsto d]} \vDash B$. Now, $V_B \subseteq V_A \cup \{x\}$. For each $y \in V_A$, $y \neq x$, we have $\ell[x \mapsto d](y) = \ell(y) = m(y) = m[x \mapsto d](y)$, and $\ell[x \mapsto d](x) = d = m[x \mapsto d](x)$. That is,

$$\ell[x \mapsto d](z) = m[x \mapsto d](z) \quad \text{for each } z \in V_B.$$

By the induction hypothesis, $J_{m[x \mapsto d]} \vDash B$. It follows that $J_m \vDash \exists x B$. Similarly, $J_m \vDash \exists x B$ implies $I_\ell \vDash \exists x B$. ♦

If for each element x in the domain of the definition D of two functions f and g, we have $f(x) = g(x)$, we say that the functions *agree on D*. Informally speaking, the Relevance lemma asserts that if two states agree on all free variables, predicates, and function symbols occurring in a formula, then either both satisfy the formula, or both falsify the formula.

A sentence A does not have any free variables. Let ℓ and m be two valuations under an interpretation I. Vacuously, ℓ and m agree on all free variables of A. By the

Relevance Lemma, $I_\ell \vDash A$ iff $I_m \vDash A$. Thus satisfiability of sentences is independent of the valuations; an interpretation interprets a sentence. We may generalize a bit by specifying how an interpretation may satisfy a formula.

An interpretation I **satisfies** a formula A, written as $I \vDash A$, iff for each valuation ℓ under I, the state $I_\ell \vDash A$. We also read $I \vDash A$ as I verifies A or as I is a **model** of A. Analogously, we read $I \nvDash A$ as I does not satisfy A, or I does not verify A, or I is not a model of A, or as I **falsifies** A. The interpretation I is a **model** of a set of formulas Σ (also read as I satisfies Σ or as I verifies Σ), written as $I \vDash \Sigma$, iff $I \vDash A$ for each $A \in \Sigma$. A model is called **finite** or **infinite** according as its domain is finite or infinite.

EXAMPLE 5.21. Let $A = \forall x \forall y (Pxa \wedge Pyx \to \neg Pya)$. Take $I = (D, P', a')$, where $D = \{a', b', c'\}$ and $P' = \{(a', a'), (b', a'), (c', a')\}$. Here, we are implicitly writing $\phi(P) = P'$, and $\phi(a) = a'$. Now, does the interpretation I satisfy A?

We start with a valuation ℓ mapping the relevant variables to D. Let $\ell(x) = a'$ and $\ell(y) = b'$. We must first decide whether the state I_ℓ satisfies A or not.

$$
\begin{aligned}
I_\ell \vDash A \text{ iff for each } d \in D,\ & I_{\ell[x \mapsto d]} \vDash \forall y (Pxa \wedge Pyx \to \neg Pya) \\
\text{iff } & I_{\ell[x \mapsto a']} \vDash \forall y (Pxa \wedge Pyx \to \neg Pya),\ I_{\ell[x \mapsto b']} \vDash \forall y (Pxa \wedge Pyx \to \neg Pya), \\
\text{and } & I_{\ell[x \mapsto c']} \vDash \forall y (Pxa \wedge Pyx \to \neg Pya).
\end{aligned}
$$

For the first out of the three above, we see that

$$
\begin{aligned}
& I_{\ell[x \mapsto a']} \vDash \forall y (Pxa \wedge Pyx \to \neg Pya) \\
& \text{iff } I_{\ell[x \mapsto a'][y \mapsto a']} \vDash (Pxa \wedge Pyx \to \neg Pya),\ I_{\ell[x \mapsto a'][y \mapsto b']} \vDash (Pxa \wedge Pyx \to \neg Pya), \\
& \quad \text{and } I_{\ell[x \mapsto a'][y \mapsto c']} \vDash (Pxa \wedge Pyx \to \neg Pya).
\end{aligned}
$$

As $\phi(a) = a'$, the first of the above holds iff whenever both $(a', a') \in P'$ and $(a', a') \in P'$, we have $(a', a') \notin P'$. This is false since $(a', a') \in P'$. Hence,

$$I_{\ell[x \mapsto a'][y \mapsto a']} \nvDash (Pxa \wedge Pyx \to \neg Pya).$$

Then, $I_{\ell[x \mapsto a']} \nvDash \forall y (Pxa \wedge Pyx \to \neg Pya)$, $I_\ell \nvDash \forall x \forall y (Pxa \wedge Pyx \to \neg Pya)$; and consequently,

$$I \nvDash \forall x \forall y (Pxa \wedge Pyx \to \neg Pya).$$

It would be easier to see informally how the interpretation works. The sentence $\forall x \forall y (Pxa \wedge Pyx \to \neg Pya)$ would be satisfied under the interpretation I provided that for each possibility for x and y as elements of the domain D, the sentence holds. Since $D = \{a', b', c'\}$ has three elements, and there are two variables x, y to be instantiated to these elements, we would have to consider the following nine sentences:

1. If $(a', a') \in P'$ and $(a', a') \in P'$, then $(a', a') \notin P'$.
2. If $(a', a') \in P'$ and $(b', a') \in P'$, then $(b', a') \notin P'$.

$\vdots$

9. If $(c', a') \in P'$ and $(c', c') \in P'$, then $(c', a') \notin P'$.

All these sentences must hold on D. But the very first sentence does not hold. Therefore, $I \nvDash A$.

Theorem 5.3 (Relevance Lemma for Sentences). *Let A be a sentence, and let I be an interpretation.*

(1) *$I \vDash A$ iff $I_\ell \vDash A$ for some valuation ℓ under I.*

(2) *Either $I \vDash A$ or $I \vDash \neg A$.*

Proof. Since sentences have no free variables, Theorem 5.2 implies that if some state satisfies a sentence, then every state under the same interpretation satisfies the sentence. This proves (1). Since any state is either a state-model of A or of $\neg A$, (2) follows from (1). ♦

An interpretation may neither satisfy an open formula nor satisfy its negation.

EXAMPLE 5.22. Let $I = (\mathbb{N}, P')$ be an interpretation of the formula Px, where $P' \subseteq \mathbb{N}$ is the set of all prime numbers. Let ℓ and m be valuations under I such that $\ell(x) = 4$ and $m(x) = 5$. Now, $I_\ell \vDash Px$ iff 4 is a prime number; and $I_m \vDash \neg Px$ iff 5 is not a prime number. We see that $I_\ell \nvDash Px$ and $I_m \nvDash \neg Px$. Therefore, $I \nvDash Px$ and $I \nvDash \neg Px$.

In fact, one may start with defining satisfiability and validity of sentences; and then using these, define satisfiability and validity of formulas. To see this, we require to define two sentences corresponding to each open formula. Let X be a formula with the only (and all) free variables $x_1, \ldots, x_n$. Write X as $X[x_1, \ldots, x_n]$. The **existential closure** of X, denoted by $\exists^* X$, is the formula obtained from X by existentially quantifying over all free variables in it, that is,

$$\exists^* X = \exists x_1 \exists x_2 \cdots \exists x_n X[x_1, x_2, \ldots, x_n].$$

The **universal closure** of X, denoted by $\forall^* X$, is the formula obtained from X by universally quantifying over all free variables in it, that is,

$$\forall^* X = \forall x_1 \forall x_2 \cdots \forall x_n X[x_1, x_2, \ldots, x_n].$$

If $n = 0$, then the formula X is a sentence; consequently, $X = \exists^* X = \forall^* X$.

Theorem 5.4. *Let X be any formula. Let $\exists^* X$ and $\forall^* X$ be the existential and universal closures of X, respectively.*

(1) *X is satisfiable iff $\exists^* X$ is satisfiable.*

(2) *X is valid iff $\forall^* X$ is valid.*

Proof. (1) Use induction on $n(X)$, the number of free variables of X. In the basis step, when $n(X) = 0$, we have $X = \exists^* X$ and the statement follows. Assume that for $n(X) < k$, the statement in (1) holds. Let X be a formula having k free variables; write X as $X[x_1, \ldots, x_k]$. Take $X_e = \exists x_k X[x_1, \ldots, x_k]$. Then X_e has $k-1$ free variables; and the induction hypothesis applies to X_e. Further, $\exists^* X = \exists^* X_e$.

Suppose X is satisfiable. Let $I_\ell \vDash X$, where $I = (D, \phi)$ is an interpretation and ℓ is a valuation under I. Suppose $\ell(x_k) = d \in D$. Then $\ell = \ell[x_k \mapsto d]$. And, for this

$d \in D$, $I_{\ell[x_k \mapsto d]} \vDash X$. That is, $I_\ell \vDash X_e$, and therefore, X_e is satisfiable. By the induction hypothesis, $\exists^* X_e$ is satisfiable. As $\exists^* X = \exists^* X_e$, $\exists^* X$ is satisfiable.

Conversely, suppose $\exists^* X$ is satisfiable. Since $\exists^* X = \exists^* X_e$, the formula $\exists^* X_e$ is satisfiable. By the induction hypothesis, X_e is satisfiable. Suppose $I_\ell \vDash X_e$, where $I = (D, \phi)$ is an interpretation and ℓ is a valuation under I. Now, $I_\ell \vDash X_e$ iff for some $d \in D$, the state $I_{\ell[x_k \mapsto d]} \vDash X$. Thus, X is satisfiable.

Proof of (2) is similar to that of (1). ♦

A state in FL works the same way on a formula as an interpretation (of PL) on a proposition. Proofs of the following results can be constructed using this analogy.

Theorem 5.5. *Let X and Y be formulas.*

(1) $X \equiv Y$ *iff* $\vDash X \leftrightarrow Y$ *iff* ($X \vDash Y$ *and* $Y \vDash X$).

(2) $\vDash X$ *iff* $X \equiv \top$ *iff* $\top \vDash X$ *iff* $\varnothing \vDash X$ *iff* $\neg X \equiv \bot$ *iff* $\neg X \vDash \bot$.

(3) *X is unsatisfiable iff* $X \equiv \bot$ *iff* $X \vDash \bot$ *iff* $\neg X \equiv \top$ *iff* $\vDash \neg X$.

Theorem 5.6 (Paradox of Material Implication). *A set of formulas Σ is unsatisfiable iff $\Sigma \vDash X$ for each formula X.*

Theorem 5.7 (M: Monotonicity). *Let $\Sigma \subseteq \Gamma$ be sets of formulas, and let X be a formula.*

(1) *If Γ is satisfiable, then Σ is satisfiable.*

(2) *If $\Sigma \vDash X$, then $\Gamma \vDash X$.*

Theorem 5.8 (RA: Reductio ad absurdum). *Let Σ be a set of formulas, and let X be a formula.*

(1) $\Sigma \vDash X$ *iff* $\Sigma \cup \{\neg X\}$ *is unsatisfiable.*

(2) $\Sigma \vDash \neg X$ *iff* $\Sigma \cup \{X\}$ *is unsatisfiable.*

Theorem 5.9 (DT: Deduction Theorem). *Let Σ be a set of formulas. Let X and Y be formulas.* $\Sigma \vDash X \to Y$ *iff* $\Sigma \cup \{X\} \vDash Y$.

Exercises for § 5.7

1. Which of the following interpretations $I = (D, P')$ are models of the formula $\exists x \exists y \exists z (Pxy \wedge Pyz \wedge Pzx \wedge \neg Pxz)$?
   (a) $D = \mathbb{N}$, $P' = \{(m,n) : m > n\}$
   (b) $D = \mathbb{N}$, $P' = \{(m, m+1) : m \geq 4\}$
   (c) $D = 2^{\mathbb{N}}$, $P' = \{(A,B) : A \subseteq B\}$
   (d) $D =$ the set of all strings over $\{0,1\}$, $P' = \{(a,b) : a$ is a substring of $b\}$
   (e) $D =$ the set of all strings over $\{0,1\}$, $P' = \{(m,n) : m < n$ as binary integers$\}$
2. Let t be a term, and let (D, ϕ, ℓ), (D, ψ, m) be states. Suppose that for each function symbol occurring in t, $\phi(f) = \psi(f)$, and for each variable x occurring in t, $\ell(x) = m(x)$. Show by induction on the number of occurrences of constants and variables that $\ell(t) = m(t)$.

3. Let $D = \{0,1,2,3,4,5,6,7,8,9\}$. Consider the closed formulas

$$W = \exists x(Px \to \exists xQx) \qquad X = \forall x(Px \lor Qx \lor Rx \lor Sx)$$
$$Y = \exists x(Px \land Qx \land Rx \land Sx) \qquad Z = \forall x(Px \lor \forall x(Qx \lor \forall x(Rx \lor \forall xSx)))$$

   (a) Construct ϕ so that (D, ϕ) satisfies all the four formulas.
   (b) Construct ψ so that (D, ψ) falsifies all the four formulas.
   (c) Does there exist an interpretation (D, ξ) that satisfies $Y \land Z$ but falsifies $X \land W$? If yes, construct ξ, else give reasons why it is not possible.

4. Let X be any formula, and let Y be a formula where the variable x is not free. Then prove or give counter examples for the following:

   (a) $Y \to \forall xX \equiv \forall x(Y \to X)$
   (b) $Y \to \exists xX \equiv \exists x(Y \to X)$
   (c) $\forall xX \to Y \equiv \forall x(X \to Y)$
   (d) $\exists xX \to Y \equiv \exists x(X \to Y)$
   (e) If $\vDash Y \to X$, then $\vDash Y \to \forall xX$.
   (f) If $\vDash X \to Y$, then $\vDash \exists xX \to Y$.
   (g) If $\vDash Y \to \forall xX$, then $\vDash Y \to X$.
   (h) If $\vDash \exists xX \to Y$, then $\vDash X \to Y$.

   What happens if x is allowed to occur free in Y?

5. Show the following equivalences:

   (a) $\forall x \exists y(Px \to Qy) \equiv \exists y \forall x(Px \to Qy)$
   (b) $\forall x \exists y(Px \to Qy) \equiv \exists xPx \to \exists yQy$
   (c) $\exists xPx \land \exists x\neg Px \to \exists x(Px \land \neg Px) \equiv \forall x(Px \lor \neg Px) \to \forall xPx \lor \forall x\neg Px$

5.8 EQUALITY SENTENCES

We have interpreted the special predicate $\approx$ as the particular relation $=$ on any domain. For instance, consider the formula $a \approx b$, where a and b are constants. The only way this formula can be satisfied by an interpretation is that both a and b must be mapped to the same element in the domain. Instead of $\approx$, suppose it is a different predicate, say E. Now, the formula is Eab. There are many ways this formula can be satisfied. Is it possible to add some restrictions and interpret E as any other predicate, and essentially achieve what $=$ achieves on the domain? Can we capture the essential properties of the equality predicate and use them as additional premises?

The equality relation is an equivalence relation having the substitutive property. That is, for any function g, any relation R, and elements a, b, c in the domain of interpretation, $=$ satisfies the following properties:

$a = a$.
If $a = b$, then $b = a$.
If $a = b$ and $b = c$, then $a = c$.
If $a = b$, then $g(\ldots, a, \ldots) = g(\ldots, b, \ldots)$.
If $a = b$, then $(\ldots, a, \ldots) \in R$ implies $(\ldots, b, \ldots) \in R$.

The first three properties above say that $=$ is an equivalence relation and the next two properties assert that $=$ has the substitutive property. We want to interpret $\approx$ as any other predicate and enforce these properties.

With this understanding, let X be a given formula. Let E be a binary predicate, which does not occur in X. We replace each occurrence of $\approx$ with E in X; and call the resulting formula $\bar{X}$. Let D be a nonempty set. Let ϕ be a function that associates all function symbols to partial functions on D, and all predicates to relations on D, preserving arity. We take $\phi(E) = \bar{E}$, which is a binary relation on D satisfying the following properties:

(a) $\bar{E}$ is an equivalence relation.

(b) If $(s,t) \in \bar{E}$, then for all $d_1, \ldots, d_{i-1}, d_{i+1}, \ldots d_n \in D$ and for each n-ary function $g : D^n \to D$, $(g(d_1, \ldots, d_{i-1}, s, d_{i+1}, \ldots d_n), g(d_1, \ldots, d_{i-1}, t, d_{i+1}, \ldots d_n)) \in \bar{E}$.

(c) If $(s,t) \in \bar{E}$ then for all $d_1, \ldots, d_{i-1}, d_{i+1}, \ldots, d_n \in D$, for each n-ary relation $R \subseteq D^n$, $(d_1, \ldots, d_{i-1}, s, d_{i+1}, \ldots t_n) \in R$ implies $(d_1, \ldots, d_{i-1}, t, d_{i+1}, \ldots d_n) \in R$.

Due to the relevance lemma, we need only to prescribe the properties that $\bar{E}$ must satisfy with regard to the function symbols and the predicates occurring in X.

Our aim is to characterize these special properties of $\bar{E}$ by some first order formulas. For example, the reflexivity property of $\bar{E}$ can be captured by requiring that $\forall x Exx$ is always satisfied. The symmetry requirement may be satisfied by imposing the truth of the sentence $\forall x \forall y (Exy \to Eyx)$. Notice that the corresponding sentence $\forall x (x \approx x)$ and $\forall x \forall y ((x \approx y) \to (y \approx x))$ are valid in FL since $\approx$ is interpreted as $=$. We thus formulate the **equality axioms** as follows.

E1. $\forall x Exx$

E2. $\forall x \forall y (Exy \to Eyx)$

E3. $\forall x \forall y \forall z (Exy \wedge Eyz \to Exz)$

E4. For any n-ary function symbol f,
$\forall x_1 \cdots \forall x_n \forall y_1 \cdots \forall y_n (Ex_1y_1 \wedge \cdots \wedge Ex_ny_n \to Ef(x_1, \ldots, x_n)f(y_1, \ldots, y_n))$.

E5. For any n-ary predicate P,
$\forall x_1 \cdots \forall x_n \forall y_1 \cdots \forall y_n (Ex_1y_1 \wedge \cdots \wedge Ex_ny_n \to (Px_1, \ldots, x_n \to Py_1, \ldots, y_n))$.

The sentences E1-E3 say that E is an equivalence relation; E4-E5 say that all function symbols and all predicates respect the equivalence classes of E. Instead of terms we have used variables in E4-E5. This is enough since from $\forall x X$, we can obtain $X[x/t]$ for any term t. These are called equality axioms because when E is replaced by $\approx$, all of them are valid sentences.

Our plan is to replace $\approx$ by E, adjoin E1-E3, instances of E4-E5 for all function symbols and all predicates used in the context; and then interpret E as an ordinary binary predicate. Of course, one of the interpretations of E can be the equality relation $=$. But E can also be interpreted as any other binary relation. Will satisfiability or validity remain intact?

EXAMPLE 5.23. Consider the set of formulas $A = \{\forall x(Pxa \to Qx),\ f(a) \approx b\}$. Following our proposal, we form the set

$$\begin{aligned} A' = \{ & \forall x(Pxa \to Qx), Ef(a)b,\ \forall x Exx, \forall x \forall y (Exy \to Eyx), \\ & \forall x \forall y \forall z (Exy \wedge Eyz \to Exz),\ \forall x \forall y (Exy \to Ef(x)f(y)), \\ & \forall x \forall y \forall u \forall v (Exu \wedge Eyz \to (Pxy \to Puz)),\ \forall x \forall u (Exu \to (Qx \to Qu))\}. \end{aligned}$$

If A has a model, extend this model (since E is new to A) by interpreting the predicate E as $=$. The extended model is a model of A'. Similarly, if A is valid, so is the conjunction of all sentences in A'. The reason is that the equality axioms are valid when E is replaced by $\approx$.

Conversely, suppose A' has a model. Here, E is interpreted as any binary predicate and not as the equality relation $=$. Thus, the elements of the domain related by E are not necessarily equal. Since E is an equivalence relation, we take its equivalence classes and then all elements related by this E become a single element, so to say. In the new domain of the equivalence classes, E behaves as '$=$'.

Example 5.23 gives an idea for generating models if we replace $\approx$ with E so that satisfiability and/or validity may be preserved.

Let Σ be a set of formulas in at least one of which $\approx$ occurs. Assume that E is never used in any formula. Construct the sets Σ' and Σ_E as follows:

$$\begin{aligned}\Sigma' =& \{Y : Y \text{ is obtained by replacing each occurrence of } (s \approx t) \text{ by } Est \text{ in } X, \text{ for} \\ & X \in \Sigma \text{ and for terms } s,t\}.\\ \Sigma_E =& \{\forall x Exx,\ \forall x \forall y (Exy \to Eyx),\ \forall x \forall y \forall z (Exy \land Eyz \to Exz)\}\\ & \cup \{\forall x_1 \cdots \forall x_n \forall y_1 \cdots \forall y_n (Ex_1y_1 \land \cdots \land Ex_ny_n \to Ef(x_1,\ldots,x_n)f(y_1,\ldots,y_n)) :\\ & \quad f \text{ is an } n\text{-ary function symbol occurring in } \Sigma\}\\ & \cup \{\forall x_1 \cdots \forall x_n \forall y_1 \cdots \forall y_n (Ex_1y_1 \land \cdots \land Ex_ny_n \to (Px_1,\ldots,x_n \to Py_1,\ldots,y_n)) :\\ & \quad P \text{ is an } n\text{-ary predicate occurring in } \Sigma\}.\end{aligned}$$

When $\Sigma = \{X\}$, we write Σ' as X', and Σ_E as X_E. We call the sentences in Σ_E as the **equality sentences appropriate to Σ.**

Let ℓ be a valuation under an interpretation $I = (D, \phi)$ of the set $\Sigma' \cup \Sigma_E$. Notice that E is interpreted as $\phi(E)$. Suppose $I_\ell \vDash \Sigma' \cup \Sigma_E$. Since the first three sentences in Σ_E are true in I_ℓ, E is an equivalence relation on D. For each $d \in D$, write the equivalence class to which d belongs, as $[d]$. Let $[D]$ be the set of all equivalence classes of E. That is,

$$[d] = \{s \in D : (d,s) \in \phi(E)\} \quad \text{and} \quad [D] = \{[d] : d \in D\}.$$

The equivalence classes in $[D]$ satisfy the following properties:

$$(d,d') \in \phi(E) \text{ iff } [d] = [d'], \quad (d,d') \notin \phi(E) \text{ iff } [d] \cap [d'] = \varnothing.$$

Define the interpretation $J = ([D], \psi)$, where the map ψ assigns function symbols and predicates to functions and relations over $[D]$ as in the following:

1. For any n-ary function symbol f, $\psi(f)$ is a partial function from $[D]^n$ to $[D]$ with $\psi(f)([d_1],\ldots,[d_n]) = [\phi(f)(d_1,\ldots,d_n)]$
2. For any n-ary predicate P, $\psi(P) \subseteq [D]^n$ with $([d_1],\ldots,[d_n]) \in \psi(P)$ iff $(d_1,\ldots,d_n) \in \phi(P)$.

For 0-ary predicates, i.e., propositions P, we declare it as a convention that $I \vDash P$ iff $J \vDash P$. This is possible since they are not affected by the equivalence class construction. We define a valuation ℓ' under J corresponding to the valuation ℓ under I as in the following:

(a) $\ell'(x) = [\ell(x)]$, for any variable x;
(b) $\ell'(c) = [\ell(c)]$, for any constant c; and
(c) $\ell'(f(t_1,\ldots,t_n)) = \psi(f)(\ell'(t_1),\ldots,\ell'(t_n))$, for any n-ary function symbol f and terms $t_1,\ldots,t_n$.

The following lemma shows the relation between the states I_ℓ and $J_{\ell'}$.

Lemma 5.2. *Let X be a formula. Let $d \in D$, x a variable, and let t be a term. Construct X' and X_E corresponding to the formula X, as explained earlier. Then*

(1) $\ell'[x \to [d]] = (\ell[x \to d])'$;
(2) $\ell'(t) = [\ell(t)]$;
(3) *if* $I_\ell \vDash \{X'\} \cup X_E$, *then* $J_{\ell'} \vDash X$.

Proof. (1) Now, $\ell'[x \to [d]](x) = [d] = [\ell[x \to d](x)] = (\ell[x \to d])'(x)$. And, for $y \neq x$, $\ell'[x \to [d]](y) = \ell'(y) = [\ell(y)] = [\ell[x \to d](y)] = (\ell[x \to d])'(y)$.

(2) The proof is by induction on the level of the term t. In the basis step, when t is a constant c or a variable x, we have $\ell'(c) = [\ell(c)]$, and $\ell'(x) = [\ell(x)]$, by construction.

Assume the induction hypothesis that for all terms s of level less than m, (2) holds. Let t be a term of level m. That is, $t = f(t_1,\ldots,t_n)$, where all of $t_1,\ldots,t_n$ are terms of level less than m. Now,

$$\begin{aligned}\ell'(t) &= \psi(f)(\ell'(t_1),\ldots,\ell'(t_n))\\ &= \psi(f)([\ell(t_1)],\ldots,[\ell(t_n)]), \text{ by the induction hypothesis}\\ &= [\phi(f)(\ell(t_1),\ldots,\ell(t_n))], \text{ by construction}\\ &= [\ell(f(t_1,\ldots,t_n))] \;=\; [\ell(t)].\end{aligned}$$

(3) The proof employs induction on $n(X)$, the number of occurrences of connectives and quantifiers in X. If $n(X) = 0$, then X is a proposition or $Pt_1\ldots t_n$, or $s \approx t$. When X is a proposition, by our convention, $J_{\ell'} \vDash X$ iff $I_\ell \vDash X$.
If X is $Pt_1\ldots t_n$, then $X' = X$ and $X_E = \varnothing$. In this case,

$$\begin{aligned}J_{\ell'} \vDash X \;&\text{iff } J_{\ell'} \vDash Pt_1\ldots t_n \text{ iff } (\ell'(t_1),\ldots,\ell'(t_n)) \in \psi(P)\\ &\text{iff } ([\ell(t_1)],\ldots,[\ell(t_n)]) \in \psi(P) \text{ (by (2)) iff } (\ell(t_1),\ldots,\ell(t_n)) \in \phi(P)\\ &\text{iff } I_\ell \vDash Pt_1\ldots t_n \text{ iff } I_\ell \vDash X \text{ iff } I_\ell \vDash \{X'\} \cup X_E.\end{aligned}$$

If X is $(s \approx t)$, then

$$\begin{aligned}J_{\ell'} \vDash X \text{ iff } J_{\ell'} \vDash (s \approx t) \text{ iff } \ell'(s) = \ell'(t) \text{ iff } [\ell(s)] = [\ell(t)] \text{ (by (2))}\\ \text{iff } (\ell(s),\ell(t)) \in E \text{ iff } I_\ell \vDash Est \text{ iff } I_\ell \vDash \{X'\} \cup X_E.\end{aligned}$$

Assume the induction hypothesis that whenever the number of occurrences of connectives and quantifiers is less than m, the statement (3) holds. Let $n(X) = m$. Then X is in one of the following forms:

$$\neg Y, \quad (Y \wedge Z), \quad (Y \vee Z), \quad (Y \to Z), \quad (Y \leftrightarrow Z), \quad \forall x Y, \quad \exists x Y.$$

When $X = \neg Y$, $J_{\ell'} \models X$ iff $J_{\ell'} \not\models Y$ iff $I_\ell \not\models Y' \cup Y_E$ (due to induction hypothesis) iff $I_\ell \models \neg Y' \cup Y_E$ iff $I_\ell \models \{X'\} \cup X_E$, since $\neg Y' = (\neg Y)'$ and $Y_E = X_E$. Similarly other connectives are tackled.

When $X = \forall xY$, $J_{\ell'} \models \forall xY$ iff for each $d \in D$, $J_{\ell'[x \to [d]]} \models Y$ iff for each $d \in D$, $J_{(\ell[x \to d])'} \models Y$ (due to (1)) iff for each $d \in D$, $I_{\ell[x \to d]} \models Y$ iff $I_\ell \models X$ if $I_\ell \models \{X'\} \cup X_E$. The case of $X = \exists xY$ is tackled similarly. ♦

Theorem 5.10 (Equality Theorem). *Let Σ be a set of formulas. Let Σ' be the set of all formulas obtained from those of Σ by replacing $\approx$ with E. Let Σ_E be the set of equality sentences appropriate to Σ. Then Σ is satisfiable iff $\Sigma' \cup \Sigma_E$ is satisfiable.*

Proof. Let $I_\ell \models \Sigma$. The predicate E is new to Σ. For interpreting Σ', we extend I_ℓ by interpreting E as the equality relation $=$. The equality sentences in Σ_E are satisfied by the extended I_ℓ. Moreover, I_ℓ also satisfies all the formulas in Σ'. Hence the extended I_ℓ is a model of $\Sigma' \cup \Sigma_E$.

Conversely, suppose $I_\ell \models \Sigma' \cup \Sigma_E$. Construct the equivalence classes and the interpretation $J_{\ell'}$ as is done for Lemma 5.2 by adding the equality sentences appropriate to Σ. Since $I_\ell \models X$ for each $X \in \Sigma$, by Lemma 5.2, $J_{\ell'} \models \{X'\} \cup X_E$ for each $X \in \Sigma$. Since $\Sigma' \cup \Sigma_E = \{X' : X \in \Sigma\} \cup \{X_E : X \in \Sigma\}$, we have $J_{\ell'} \models \Sigma' \cup \Sigma_E$. ♦

The following corollary shows that even validity of formulas and of consequences can be tackled by interpreting $\approx$ as E.

Theorem 5.11. *Let Σ be a set of formulas, and let X be a formula. Let Σ' be the set of all formulas obtained from those of Σ by replacing $\approx$ with E. Let $\Delta = (\Sigma \cup \{X\})_E$ be the set of all equality sentences appropriate to $\Sigma \cup \{X\}$. Then, $\Sigma \models X$ iff $\Sigma' \cup \Delta \models X'$.*

Proof. $\Sigma \models X$ iff $\Sigma \cup \{\neg X\}$ is unsatisfiable (by RA) iff $(\Sigma \cup \{\neg X\})' \cup \Delta$ is unsatisfiable, by Theorem 5.10. However, $(\Sigma \cup \{\neg X\})' \cup \Delta = \Sigma' \cup \Delta \cup \{\neg X'\}$. Another application of RA completes the proof. ♦

Theorems 5.10-5.11 provide a way to eliminate the equality predicate without derailing satisfiability and validity. However, the predicate E along with the appropriate equality sentences (in Σ_E) do not quite account for the equality relation $=$. The reason is that the equivalence classes identify a bunch of elements as the same element but do not make them the same element. The semantic equality is thus never captured in its entirety by a set of first order sentences without equality. Look at the following examples.

EXAMPLE 5.24. Does there exist a sentence all of whose models have exactly m elements?

For $k = 1$, the sentence $A_1 = \forall x \forall y (x \approx y)$ does the job.

For $k = 2$, the sentence A_2 is $\forall x_1 \forall x_2 \forall x_3 (((x_3 \approx x_1) \vee (x_3 \approx x_2)) \wedge \neg(x_1 \approx x_2))$.

In general, take A_m as follows:

$$\forall x_1 \forall x_2 \cdots \forall x_{m+1} (((x_{m+1} \approx x_1) \vee \cdots (x_{m+1} \approx x_m)) \wedge \neg(x_1 \approx x_2) \wedge \cdots$$
$$\wedge \neg(x_1 \approx x_m) \wedge \neg(x_2 \approx x_3) \wedge \cdots \wedge \neg(x_2 \approx x_m) \wedge \cdots \wedge \neg(x_{m-1} \approx x_m)).$$

EXAMPLE 5.25. Let $\Sigma = \{\forall x \forall y (x \approx y)\}$. All models of Σ are singleton sets. Now,

$$\Sigma' \cup \Sigma_E = \{\forall x Exx,\ \forall x \forall y Exy,\ \forall x \forall y (Exy \to Eyx),\ \forall x \forall y \forall z (Exy \wedge Eyz \to Exz)\}.$$

Consider any nonempty set D and the interpretation $I = (D, \phi)$, with $\phi(E) = D \times D$. We see that I is a model of $\Sigma' \cup \Sigma_E$. This shows that $\Sigma' \cup \Sigma_E$ has models of every cardinality.

EXAMPLE 5.26. Consider the sentence $\forall x Px$. It has models of all cardinalities. For instance, with $D = \{1\}$ and $\phi(P) = \{(1,1)\}$ we have $I = (D, \phi) \vDash \forall x Px$. Also, $J = (\mathbb{N}, \psi)$ with $\psi(P) = \mathbb{N} \times \mathbb{N}$ is a model of $\forall x Px$. In fact, this happens for all satisfiable sentences where $\approx$ does not occur.

Let X be a satisfiable sentence, where $\approx$ does not occur. Let $I = (D, \phi)$ be its model, and let $d \in D$. Write

$$\bar{D} = D \cup \{d_i : i \in \mathbb{N}\}, \quad \text{where } d_i \notin D \text{ for any } i.$$

The d_is are simply some symbols. For each function symbol f occurring in X, let $\psi(f)$ treat each of these d_i along with d the same way as $\phi(f)$ treats d. Similarly, each relation $\psi(P)$ treats each d_i along with d the same way as $\phi(P)$ does to d. Then, $(\bar{D}, \psi)$ is also a model of X.

This shows that in the absence of $\approx$, a satisfiable sentence can have models of arbitrary cardinalities.

Example 5.25 shows that every model of $\Sigma = \{\forall x \forall y (x \approx y)\}$ has only one element, whereas $\Sigma' \cup \Sigma_E = \{\forall x \forall y Exy\} \cup \Sigma_E$ has models of arbitrary cardinalities. The technique of *inflating* a point as is done in Example 5.26 in a model can always be done in the absence of the equality predicate $\approx$. This cannot be done if $\approx$ is present as Example 5.24 shows. However, if we are concerned with the issues of satisfiability, validity, and consequences, then the equality predicate can be replaced with E by adding the appropriate equality sentences.

Elimination of the equality predicate will come of help at many places later. It has two note worthy applications; one in proving completeness of an axiomatic system for FL, and two, in constructing a model in an abstract fashion. We will come back to these issues at appropriate places.

Exercises for § 5.8

1. The quantifier 'there exists exactly one', written as $\exists!$ may be defined by $\exists! xY \equiv \exists x(Y \wedge \forall z(Y[x/z] \to (x \approx z))$. For $n > 1$, give similar definitions of the following new quantifiers:
   (a) there exists at most n number of
   (b) there exists at least n number of
   (c) there exists exactly n number of
2. Let $x_1, \ldots, x_n$ be variables not occurring in the terms $t_1, \ldots, t_n$. Show that for any formula Y, $Y[x_1/t_1, \ldots, x_n/t_n] \equiv \forall x_1 \cdots \forall x_n((x_1 \approx t_1) \cdots (x_n \approx t_n) \to Y)$.
3. Complete the proof of Lemma 5.2 by proving the left out cases.

5.9 SUMMARY AND PROBLEMS

Since PL is not expressive enough, we took up breaking a sentence into parts. Using the token such as constants, variables, function symbols, predicates, and quantifiers, the first order logic (FL) has been constructed. The function symbols along with constants and variables express the definite descriptions by way of terms, and the predicates express the relations between terms. The two quantifiers (for all, there exists) quantify over the variables so that propositions or sentences could be formed.

Meanings to the syntactic entities are supplied by taking a nonempty set, called the domain (or universe of discourse) and then by assigning constants to objects in the domain, function symbols to concrete partial functions on the domain, and predicates to relations over the domain. The variables are assigned to elements in the domain by valuations or assignment functions. The quantifier 'for all' and 'there exists' are given meaning through these valuations. Finally, the semantics enables you to categorize formulas and sentences into four classes such as valid, invalid, satisfiable or unsatisfiable. The consequences are tackled in a similar manner.

The metaresults such as Monotonicity, reductio ad absurdum, and Deduction hold FL. We have seen that an open formula is valid iff its universal closure is valid; and it is satisfiable iff its existential closure is satisfiable. Though the meaning of the equality predicate is fixed, we tried to replace it with another usual binary predicate. This could be done by enforcing the equality sentences to be true along with existing premises.

The modern form of FL is recent compared to the study of PL. After Aristotle formalized a part of FL in the form of syllogisms, there was a gap of almost two centuries. The next big leap was taken by Frege (1934, 1984). Later, others followed the work to give us the first order logic as we know of it today. For an account of such contributions towards the development of the subject, see Gabbay & Guenthner (2002). For discussions on theoretical connection of FL to topics such as type theory, logic programming, algebraic specifications and term rewriting, see the works such as van Dalen (1989), Gallier (1987), and Sperchneider & Antoniou (1991). The formal semantics was developed by Tarski in 1933 in a Polish journal. It was later exposed in Tarski (1944). You may refer Ebbinghaus et al. (1994), Manaster (1978), Manin (1977), Rautenberg (2010), Shoenfield (1967), and Smullyan (1968) for the material covered in this chapter.

Problems for Chapter 5

1. Give formal proofs of unique parsing for terms.
2. Prove the unique parsing theorem by first proving a prefix theorem that if a substring of a formula is also a formula, then it must be equal to the formula.
3. Show that given any expression of FL, it can be determined whether the expression is a formula or not. Write procedures for determining and parsing formulas.
4. Prove that each occurrence of a quantifier has a unique scope and hence the notion of scope is well defined.

5. Show that free occurrences of a variable in a formula can be defined inductively the following way:

    (a) In an atomic formula, each occurrence of a variable is free.
    (b) The free occurrences of a variable x in $\neg X$ are the same as those in X.
    (c) The free occurrences of a variable x in $X \circ Y$, for $\circ \in \{\wedge, \vee, \rightarrow, \leftrightarrow\}$, are the free occurrences of x in X and also the free occurrences of x in Y.
    (d) All occurrences of the variable x in $\forall x X$ and also in $\exists x X$ are bound (non-free) occurrences. If y is a variable different from x, then all free occurrences of x in X are the free occurrences of x in $\forall y X$ and in $\exists y X$.

6. Suppose X is a formula having at least one free occurrence of the variable x, and t is a term free for x in X. Define $X[x/t]$ inductively.

7. Present the syntax of FL in a prefix (Polish) notation and then prove unique parsing for that language. Define also the notion of scope in that language.

8. If 'existence' is a predicate, then so is 'non-existence'. Can the predicate of 'non-existence' be truthfully interpreted?

9. Show that a formula which does not involve the connectives $\neg, \rightarrow, \leftrightarrow$ is satisfiable.

10. Let X be a formula having at least one free occurrence of x in it. Let t be a term free for x in X. Let $I = (D, \phi)$ be an interpretation. Suppose ℓ is a valuation under I such that $\ell(t) = d \in D$. Prove by induction on the number of occurrences of function symbols in t that $I_{\ell[x \mapsto d]} \vDash X$ iff $I_\ell \vDash X[x/t]$.

11. Let Σ be a satisfiable set of formulas, and let X be a formula. Show:

    (a) If X is valid, then $\Sigma \cup \{X\}$ is satisfiable.
    (b) If $\Sigma \cup \{X\}$ is unsatisfiable, then for any sentence Y, the set $\Sigma \cup \{X \rightarrow Y\}$ is satisfiable.

12. Let X and Y be formulas. Which of the following hold(s) for a state I_ℓ?

    (a) If $I_\ell \vDash X \rightarrow Y$, then ($I_\ell \vDash X$ implies $I_\ell \vDash Y$).
    (b) If ($I_\ell \vDash X$ implies $I_\ell \vDash Y$), then $I_\ell \vDash X \rightarrow Y$.
    (c) If $X \vDash Y$, then ($\vDash X$ implies $\vDash Y$).
    (d) If ($\vDash X$ implies $\vDash Y$), then $X \vDash Y$.

13. Let X, Y and Z be three sentences. Answer the following:

    (a) If $X \vDash Y$, does it follow that $\neg X \nvDash Y$?
    (b) If $X \wedge Y \vDash Z$, then does it follow that $X \vDash Y$ and $X \vDash Z$?
    (c) If $X \wedge Y \vDash Z$, then does it follow that $X \vDash Y$ or $X \vDash Z$?
    (d) If $X \vDash Y \vee Z$, then does it follow that $X \vDash Y$ and $X \vDash Z$?
    (e) If one of $X \vDash Y$ or $Z \vDash Y$ holds, then does $X \vee Z \vDash Y$ hold?
    (f) If $X \vDash (Y \rightarrow Z)$, then do $X \vDash Y$ and/or $X \vDash Z$ hold?

14. Let X be a formula with free variables $x_1, \ldots, x_m$. Show that there exists a state-model of X iff there exists a model of $\exists x_1 \cdots \exists x_m X$.

15. Let $y_1, \ldots, y_n$ be all the free variables of a formula X. Let ℓ be any state under an interpretation $I = (D, \phi)$. Show that $I \vDash \forall y_1 \cdots \forall y_n X$ iff for each $(d_1, \ldots, d_n) \in D^n$, $I_{\ell[y_1 \mapsto d_1] \cdots [y_n \mapsto d_n]} \vDash X$.

16. Let $\forall^* X$ be the universal closure of a formula X. For a set of formulas Σ, let $\Sigma^* = \{\forall^* X : X \in \Sigma\}$. Let Y be any formula. Show that if $\Sigma \vDash Y$, then $\Sigma^* \vDash Y$. Show also that $\Sigma^* \vDash Y$ does not guarantee that $\Sigma \vDash Y$.
17. Show that $\exists x Px \nvDash Pc$ and $\exists x Q(x,c) \nvDash Q(c,c)$, in general.
18. Consider the domains $\mathbb{N}, \mathbb{Q}, \mathbb{R}$ of natural numbers, rational numbers, and real numbers, respectively.
    (a) For each of these domains, construct a sentence which is true in it but false in the other two.
    (b) For each pair of these domains, construct a sentence that is true in both of them, but false in the other.
    (c) Construct an invalid sentence that is true in all the three domains.
    (d) Construct a satisfiable sentence that is false in all the three domains.
19. Show that the sentence $\forall x \exists y Pxy \wedge \forall x \neg Pxx \wedge \forall x \forall y \forall z (Pxy \wedge Pyz \to Pxz)$ is true in some infinite domain and is false in some finite domain.
20. Show that the sentence $\forall x Pxx \wedge \forall x \forall y \forall z (Pxz \to Pxy \vee Pyz) \to \exists x \forall y Pxy$ is true in any finite domain but is false in some infinite domain.
21. Construct a sentence which is true in a domain with no more than m elements, but false in some domain with more than m elements where m equals 1, 2, or 3. Can you have a general formula for generating such a sentence?
22. Suppose that a domain of an interpretation is allowed to be empty. What will be the change in satisfiability and validity of formulas? Will there be formulas which are valid, but now they become invalid, or the converse?
23. For a set Σ of formulas and a formula X, we say Σ *weakly entails* X, and write $\Sigma \vDash^w X$ if and only if for each interpretation I, if $I \vDash \Sigma$, then $I \vDash X$. Show the following:
    (a) If $\Sigma \vDash X$, then $\Sigma \vDash^w X$.
    (b) It is not true, in general, that if $\Sigma \vDash^w X$, then $\Sigma \vDash X$.
    (c) Suppose no free variable of X occurs free in any formula of Σ. Then, $\Sigma \vDash^w X$ implies $\Sigma \vDash X$.
    (d) If Σ is a set of sentences, then $\Sigma \vDash^w X$ implies $\Sigma \vDash X$.
    (e) If $\Sigma = \varnothing$, then $\Sigma \vDash^w X$ implies $\Sigma \vDash X$.
    (f) The deduction theorem fails for the weak entailment.
24. Translate the following arguments to FL and then check whether they are valid consequences.
    (a) Every computer scientist is a logician and also a programmer. Some computer scientists are old fashioned. Therefore, there are old fashioned programmers.
    (b) Some computer scientists like all logicians. No computer scientist likes any old fashioned programmer. Therefore, no logician is an old fashioned programmer.
    (c) All doctors take Hippocratic oath. All spouses of the persons who take Hippocratic oath cannot be relied upon. Therefore, no spouse of any doctor can be relied upon.

(d) Everyone who commits a crime receives a jail term. Anyone who receives a jail term goes to jail. Therefore, if there are no jails, then nobody commits a crime.

(e) Every businessman likes all his children to study abroad. Therefore, the eldest child of any businessman is the child of a person who likes all his children to study abroad.

(f) All children of surgeons are children of doctors. Therefore, if there exists a child of a surgeon, then there exists a doctor.

25. Two valuations ℓ and ℓ' are said to be *equivalent along the variable* x iff $\ell(y) = \ell'(y)$ for all variables $y \neq x$. Also, two states I_ℓ and $I_{\ell'}$ are said to be *equivalent along the variable* x iff the valuations ℓ and ℓ' are equivalent along the variable x. Prove that satisfaction of formulas can be defined alternatively by modifying only the quantifier cases as in the following:

    $I_\ell \vDash \forall x B$ iff for each valuation ℓ' equivalent to ℓ along x, $I_{\ell'} \vDash B$.
    $I_\ell \vDash \exists x B$ iff for some valuation ℓ' equivalent to ℓ along x, $I_{\ell'} \vDash B$.

26. Let I be an interpretation of a formula X, and ℓ, m be valuations under I such that m is equivalent to ℓ along x and that $m(x) = \ell(x)$. Is it true that I_ℓ satisfies X iff I_m satisfies X?

27. Let t be a term which contains at least one occurrence of the variable x. Let s be another term, and ℓ, m be valuations under an interpretation I equivalent along the variable x such that $m(x) = \ell(s)$. Let t' be a term obtained from t by substituting each occurrence of x in t by the term s. Show that $m(t) = \ell(t')$.

28. Let $X(x)$ be a formula having at least one free occurrence of the variable x. Let t be free for x in $X(x)$. Let ℓ and m be two valuations under an interpretation I such that m is equivalent to ℓ along x and that $m(x) = \ell(t)$. Let $X(t)$ be a formula obtained from $X(x)$ by substituting each free occurrence of x in $X(x)$ by t. Then show that I_m satisfies $X(x)$ iff I_ℓ satisfies $X(t)$.

29. Let x be a variable, t a closed term, X a formula, $I = (D, \phi, \ell)$ a state, and let m be a valuation equivalent to ℓ along x. Prove that $I_m \vDash X[x/t]$ iff $I_\ell \vDash X$.

30. Given a formula and an interpretation $I = (D, \phi)$, the alphabet is extended by adding new (individual) constants as the symbols in the set $NC = \{\bar{d} : d \in D\}$. The function ϕ is extended to include in its domain the new constants by $\phi(\bar{d}) = d$. Any valuation ℓ under I is similarly extended by being faithful to ϕ, i.e., by defining $\ell(\bar{d}) = \phi(\bar{d}) = d$ for each $\bar{d} \in NC$. The quantifier cases are tackled in the following manner:

    $I_\ell \vDash \forall x B$ iff for each $d \in D$, $I_\ell \vDash B[x/\bar{d}]$.
    $I_\ell \vDash \exists x B$ iff for some $d \in D$, $I_\ell \vDash B[x/\bar{d}]$.

    Let x be a variable, t a term, A a formula, ℓ a valuation under an interpretation $I = (D, \phi)$, and let d be an element of D. Show the following.

    (a) $\ell[x \mapsto d](t) = \ell(t[x/\bar{d}])$ (b) $I_{\ell[x \mapsto d]} \vDash A$ iff $I_\ell \vDash A[x/\bar{d}]$

    Conclude that this provides another alternative definition of a formula being true in a state.

31. Let $X = \forall x \exists y Pxy \to \exists y \forall x Pxy$, $Y = \forall x \forall y (Pxy \land Pyx \to (x \approx y))$, and $Z = \forall x \forall y \forall z (Pxy \land Pyz \to Pxz)$. Show that $\{X, Y\} \nvDash Z$, $\{Y, Z\} \nvDash X$, and $\{Z, X\} \nvDash Y$.

32. Let P be a binary predicate. Let $I = (D, \phi)$ be an interpretation with $\phi(P) = R$, a binary relation on D. Construct formulas X, Y, Z involving P so that

    (a) $I \vDash X$ iff R is reflexive.
    (b) $I \vDash Y$ iff R is symmetric.
    (c) $I \vDash Z$ iff R is transitive.

    Further, show that $\{X, Y\} \nvDash Z$, $\{X, Z\} \nvDash Y$, and $\{Y, Z\} \nvDash X$. [This would show reflexivity, symmetry and transitivity are independent properties.]

33. Recall Smullyan's island, where an islander is either a knight, who always tells the truth, or is a knave, who always lies. You asked a person, whether he has seen the moon yesterday evening. He answered "All knights here have seen the moon yesterday evening." In fact, everyone on the island answers the same. What do you conclude about the islanders sighting the moon yesterday evening?

34. Determine which of the following consequences is/are valid:

    (a) $\forall x \exists y(Pxy \wedge Qz) \vDash \exists y \forall x(Pxy \wedge Qz)$
    (b) $\forall x \exists y(Px \wedge Qy) \vDash \exists y \forall x(Px \wedge Qy)$

    What do you observe about the consequence $\forall x \exists y Z \vDash \exists y \forall x Z$?

35. Explain the following situations:

    (a) Let $\varepsilon > 0$ be fixed but arbitrary. We see that $P(\varepsilon)$ is true. Therefore, $\forall x((x > 0) \to P(x))$ is true. However, $(x > 0) \to P(x)$ does not entail $\forall x((x > 0) \to P(x))$.
    (b) We know that there exists a point x between 1 and 2 such that $x^2 - 2 = 0$. Call that point α. Now, $\alpha^2 - 2 = 0$. However, $\exists x P(x)$ does not entail $P(\alpha)$ for any constant α.

Chapter 6

A First Order Calculus

6.1 AXIOMATIC SYSTEM FC

First order logic is an extension of propositional logic. The inherent circularity present in PL extends to FL also. For proving an argument, we translate it to a consequence in FL. Next, for justifying the consequence, we consider all possible interpretations, and require that in all these interpretations, the consequence must be true. Notice that one of the interpretations is the argument we began with!

We wish to break this circularity by modelling FL as an axiomatic system, where there would be no concern for truth or falsity. It should be a mere rule following activity like PC. In fact, we extend PC to an adequate axiomatic system for first order logic. We call this system for FL as First Order Calculus (**FC**).

The axiom schemes of FC are A1, A2, A3 of PC, two for the quantifier $\forall$, and two for the equality predicate $\approx$. The propositional constants $\top$ and $\bot$, the connectives $\wedge, \vee$ and $\leftrightarrow$, and the quantifier $\exists$ will be defined in terms of $\neg, \rightarrow$ and $\forall$. Besides MP, we also include one more inference rule to tackle the quantifier $\forall$. The details are as follows.

The **Axiom schemes** of FC:

For formulas X, Y, Z, variable x, and terms s, t,

(A1) $X \rightarrow (Y \rightarrow X)$

(A2) $(X \rightarrow (Y \rightarrow Z)) \rightarrow ((X \rightarrow Y) \rightarrow (X \rightarrow Z))$

(A3) $(\neg X \rightarrow \neg Y) \rightarrow ((\neg X \rightarrow Y) \rightarrow X)$

(A4) $\forall x Y \rightarrow Y[x/t]$, provided t is free for x in Y.

(A5) $\forall x(Y \rightarrow Z) \rightarrow (Y \rightarrow \forall x Z)$, provided x does not occur free in Y.

(A6) $(t \approx t)$

(A7) $(s \approx t) \rightarrow (X[x/s] \rightarrow X[x/t])$, provided s, t are free for x in X.

The **Rules of Inference** of FC:

(MP) $\dfrac{X \qquad X \to Y}{Y}$

(UG) $\dfrac{X}{\forall x X}$ provided x is not free in any premise used thus far.

The rule UG is the rule of *universal generalization.* The phrase "premise used thus far" will be made clear in a short while. To compensate for the missing connectives and quantifiers, we include the definitions (D1)-(D6) and the rule (RD) as in the following.

(D1) $p \wedge q \mathrel{\hat{=}} \neg(p \to \neg q)$

(D2) $p \vee q \mathrel{\hat{=}} \neg p \to q$

(D3) $p \leftrightarrow q \mathrel{\hat{=}} \neg((p \to q) \to \neg(q \to p))$

(D4) $\top \mathrel{\hat{=}} p \to p$

(D5) $\bot \mathrel{\hat{=}} \neg(p \to p)$

(D6) $\exists x X \mathrel{\hat{=}} \neg \forall x \neg X$

(RD) $\dfrac{X \mathrel{\hat{=}} Y \quad Z}{Z[X := Y]} \qquad \dfrac{X \mathrel{\hat{=}} Y \quad Z}{Z[Y := X]}$

As in PC, a **proof** is a finite sequence of formulas, each of which is either an axiom (an instance of an axiom scheme), or is obtained (derived) by an application of some inference rule on earlier formulas. Note that MP is applied on two formulas while UG is applied on a single formula. The condition in UG means that

> *in order to apply UG on a formula, say $X(x)$ in Line n, we must make sure that the variable x is not free in any premise used in the proof up to and including Line n.*

The last formula of a proof is a **theorem**; the proof is said to *prove* the theorem. The fact that a formula X is a theorem of FC is written as $\vdash_{FC} X$; in that case, we also say that the formula X is **provable**. We read $\vdash_{FC} X$ as X is an FC-theorem, and also as X is FC-provable. If there is no confusion about the axiomatic systems in a context, we write $\vdash_{FC} X$ as $\vdash X$.

For a set of formulas Σ and a formula Y, a **proof of the consequence** $\Sigma \mathrel{!\vdash} Y$ is again a finite sequence of formulas, each of which is an axiom, or a premise (a formula) in Σ, or is derived from earlier formulas by an application of an inference rule; the last formula of the sequence is Y. The fact that there is a proof of the consequence $\Sigma \mathrel{!\vdash} Y$ is written simply as $\Sigma \vdash_{FC} Y$; $\Sigma \vdash Y$. In this case, we also say that the consequence $\Sigma \mathrel{!\vdash} Y$ is **provable**, or FC-provable.

We also write $\{X_1, \ldots, X_n\} \vdash Y$ as $X_1, \ldots, X_n \vdash Y$. Notice that $\varnothing \vdash Y$ expresses the same fact as $\vdash Y$.

Axiom schemes A1 to A3 are the same as in PC; A4 is taken from its semantic counterpart: $\vDash \forall xX \to X[x/t]$. The axiom scheme A5 comes with a condition. To see the reason behind it, take $X = Y = Px$ in A5. The formula in A5 now reads

$$\forall x(Px \to Px) \to (Px \to \forall xPx).$$

Since $\forall x(Px \to Px)$ is valid, it follows that $Px \to \forall xPx$ is valid. But this formula is invalid. And we would not like to have an invalid formula as an axiom!

The condition in UG warns us to first check that the variable on which we generalize does not occur free in any premise used up to that point in a proof. In a proof of a theorem, this warning becomes vacuous as there would not be any premise. If the restriction on UG is removed, then we will be able to derive $\forall xPx$ from Px; and this will be wrong! In fact, we want the relation $\vdash$ to match with $\vDash$ somehow. In this sense, the axiom schemes A6 and A7 are self-evident.

In documenting a proof, when MP is applied on the preceding two lines, we will not mention those line numbers. Similarly, when MP is applied on the preceding line and a remote line, we will mention only the remote line number.

EXAMPLE 6.1. If x does not occur in Z, then show that $\forall yZ \vdash \forall xZ[y/x]$.

$\forall yZ$	P
$\forall yZ \to Z[y/x]$	A4, since x is free for y in Z.
$Z[y/x]$	MP
$\forall xZ[y/x]$	UG, since x is not free in $\forall yZ$.

EXAMPLE 6.2. The following is a proof of $\forall x\forall yZ \vdash \forall y\forall xZ$

$\forall x\forall yZ$	P
$\forall x\forall yZ \to \forall yZ$	A4
$\forall yZ$	MP
$\forall yZ \to Z$	A4
Z	MP
$\forall xZ$	UG
$\forall y\forall xZ$	UG

EXAMPLE 6.3. In proving $\vdash \forall xY \to \forall xY$, you can imitate the proof of $p \to p$ in PC. However, the same can be proved using the quantifier axioms.

$\forall xY \to Y$	A4
$\forall x(\forall xY \to Y)$	UG
$\forall x(\forall xY \to Y) \to (\forall xY \to \forall xY)$	A5
$\forall xY \to \forall xY$	MP

Since $\forall xY$ has no free occurrence of the variable x, the third line is indeed A5.

In the following example, we use the PC-theorem $\vdash (p \to q) \to (\neg q \to \neg p)$ after a suitable uniform replacement of the propositional variables by formulas of FC. In fact, we do not formulate any such principle of replacement; it is implicitly assumed due to the nature of axiom schemes, rule schemes, theorem schemes, and the fact that PC is a subsystem of FC. It means that a proof of $\vdash (p \to q) \to (\neg q \to \neg p)$ can simply be duplicated with p, q substituted with suitable formulas from FC.

EXAMPLE 6.4. The following is a proof of $\forall x \neg Y \vdash \neg \forall x Y$:

	$\forall x \neg y$	P
	$\forall x \neg y \to \neg Y$	A4
1.	$\neg Y$	MP
	$\forall x Y \to Y$	A4
	$(\forall x Y \to Y) \to (\neg Y \to \neg \forall x Y)$	Th
	$\neg Y \to \neg \forall x Y$	MP
	$\neg \forall x Y$	1, MP

EXAMPLE 6.5. The following proof shows that $(s \approx t) \vdash (t \approx s)$.

$(s \approx t)$	P
$(s \approx t) \to ((s \approx s) \to (t \approx s))$	A7, $X = (x \approx s)$
$(s \approx s) \to (t \approx s)$	MP
$(s \approx s)$	A6
$(t \approx s)$	MP

Exercises for § 6.1

1. Try proving $\vdash (s \approx t) \to (t \approx s)$ in FC.
2. Suppose x does not occur free in X, y does not occur free in Y, and z does not occur free in Z. Try to construct FC-proofs for the following:
   (a) $\vdash (X \to \forall x Z) \to \forall x(X \to Z)$
   (b) $\vdash (X \to \exists x Z) \to \exists x(X \to Z)$
   (c) $\vdash (\exists y Z \to Y) \to \forall y(Z \to Y)$
   (d) $\vdash (\forall y Z \to Y) \to \exists y(Z \to Y)$
   (e) $\vdash \exists x Z \leftrightarrow \exists z Z[x/z]$
   (f) $\vdash \forall x(Z \to \forall z((x \approx z) \to Z[x/z]))$
   (g) $\vdash \forall x(\forall z((x \approx z) \to Z[x/z]) \to Z)$
3. Give FC-proofs of the following using PC-theorems as theorems in FC.
   (a) $\vdash Z \to \neg \forall x \neg Z$
   (b) $\vdash \forall x Z \to \forall y Z[x/y]$ if y does not occur in Z.
   (c) $\vdash \neg \forall y \neg Z \to Z$ if y does not occur free in Z.
   (d) If $\vdash (Y \to Z)$, then $\vdash (\forall x Y \to \forall x Z)$.
   (e) $\vdash \forall x Y \to \neg \forall x \neg Y$
   (f) $\vdash \neg \forall x \neg Y \to \forall x Y$ if x does not occur free in Y.

6.2 SIX THEOREMS ABOUT FC

Along with the monotonicity, deduction, RA, and Finiteness, we have strong generalization, peculiar to FC. The proofs of monotonicity, RA, and Finiteness are similar to those in PC. We will prove the new cases in the deduction theorem that come up due to the universal quantifier, while quickly mentioning the cases similar to PC. Then, we will discuss some applications of these metatheorems in proving some more formulas and consequences.

A set of formulas Σ is said to be **inconsistent** (in FC) iff there exists a formula Y such that $\Sigma \vdash Y$ and $\Sigma \vdash \neg Y$, else Σ is said to be **consistent** (in FC). We also say that a formula X is inconsistent or consistent according as the set $\{X\}$ is inconsistent or consistent.

Theorem 6.1 (M: Monotonicity). *Let $\Sigma \subseteq \Gamma$ be sets of formulas, and let w be any formula.*

(1) *If $\Sigma \vdash w$, then $\Gamma \vdash w$.*

(2) *If Σ is inconsistent, then Γ is inconsistent.*

Theorem 6.2 (DT: Deduction Theorem). *Let Σ be a set of formulas. Let X and Y be any formulas. Then*

$$\Sigma \vdash X \to Y \text{ iff } \Sigma \cup \{X\} \vdash Y.$$

Proof. The proof, quite naturally, resembles that for PC. If $\Sigma \vdash X \to Y$, then there is a proof P whose last formula is $X \to Y$. We add to P, the premise X from $\Sigma \cup \{X\}$, and then use MP to conclude Y.

Conversely, suppose that P is a proof of $\Sigma \cup \{X\} \vdash Y$. We prove $\Sigma \vdash X \to Y$ by induction on the length of P, i.e., the number of formulas (lines) in P. In the basis step, if P has only one formula, then it is Y; and Y is an axiom, a premise in Σ, or the formula X itself. If Y is an axiom, then as in PC, we have the following proof of $\Sigma \vdash X \to Y$:

$Y \to (X \to Y)$	A1
Y	An axiom
$X \to Y$	MP

If Y is a premise in Σ, then also the above proof works; only that we mention Y to be a premise in Σ instead of an axiom.

If Y is X itself, then we use the PC-theorem: $\vdash X \to X$ and monotonicity to conclude $\Sigma \vdash X \to X$. This completes the basis step.

Lay out the induction hypothesis that if the number of formulas in P is less than n, then there is a proof of $\Sigma \vdash X \to Y$. Suppose that $\Sigma \cup \{X\} \vdash Y$ has a proof P1 of n formulas. Then the nth formula is necessarily Y; and Y can be

(a) an axiom, a premise in Σ, or X itself,

(b) derived from two earlier formulas by MP, or

(c) derived from an earlier formula by UG.

In each case, we construct a proof P5 for $\Sigma \vdash X \to Y$.

(a) These cases are covered in the basis step.

(b) This case is similar to that in PC. In the proof P1, we have formulas Z, $Z \to Y$, Y in lines numbered, n_1, n_2, n_3, respectively, where $1 \le n_1, n_2 < n_3 < n$, and Z is some formula. By the induction hypothesis, $\Sigma \vdash X \to Z$, $\Sigma \vdash X \to (Z \to Y)$ have proofs, say, P2, P3, respectively. We use these proofs to construct a proof P5 for $\Sigma \vdash X \to Y$. To obtain P5, we adjoin P3 to P2, and use A2 in the form

$$(X \to (Z \to Y)) \to ((X \to Z) \to (X \to Y)).$$

We then apply MP to conclude $(X \to Z) \to (X \to Y)$. This formula along with $X \to Z$ give, by MP, the required conclusion.

(c) Here, $Y = \forall xA$ for a variable x and a formula A. The proof P1 of $\Sigma \cup \{X\} \vdash Y$ looks like:

P1:	1.	$\cdots$	
		$\vdots$	
	$m.$	A	for some formula A
		$\vdots$	
	$n.$	$\forall xA$	m, UG

If the premise X has not been used in P1, then P1 itself is a proof of $\Sigma \vdash Y$. Using A1 as in the basis step, we get a proof of $\Sigma \vdash X \to Y$. (Do it.) More realistically, suppose that X has been used somewhere in P1. Due to the restriction on the applicability of UG, the variable x does not occur in any premise (from Σ) used in P1. In particular, x is not free in X. (It is used in two crucial situations in the proof below while using UG and A5.) By the induction hypothesis, since $m < n$, there is a proof P4 of length j for $\Sigma \vdash X \to A$. We use P4 to construct the proof P5 for $\Sigma \vdash X \to \forall xA$ as follows:

P5:	1.	$\cdots$	P4 begins
		$\vdots$	
	$j.$	$X \to A$	P4 ends
	$j+1.$	$\forall x(X \to A)$	UG
	$j+2.$	$\forall x(X \to A) \to (X \to \forall xA)$	A5
	$j+3.$	$X \to \forall xA$	$j+1, j+2$, MP

As $Y = \forall xA$, P5 is a proof of $\Sigma \vdash X \to Y$. ♦

The following theorems are proved the same way as in PC.

Theorem 6.3 (RA: Reductio ad Absurdum). *Let Σ be a set of formulas, and let Y be any formula.*

(1) $\Sigma \vdash Y$ *iff* $\Sigma \cup \{\neg Y\}$ *is inconsistent.*

(2) $\Sigma \vdash \neg Y$ *iff* $\Sigma \cup \{Y\}$ *is inconsistent.*

Theorem 6.4 (Finiteness). *Let Σ be a set of formulas, and let w be any formula.*

(1) *If $\Sigma \vdash w$, then there exists a finite subset Γ of Σ such that $\Gamma \vdash w$.*

(2) *If Σ is inconsistent, then there exists a finite inconsistent subset of Σ.*

Theorem 6.5 (Paradox of material Implication). *Let Σ be an inconsistent set of formulas, and let X be any formula. Then $\Sigma \vdash X$.*

Using the paradox of material implication, we can have an alternate proof of RA. If $\Sigma \cup \{\neg Y\}$ is inconsistent, then by Theorem 6.5, $\Sigma \cup \{\neg Y\} \vdash Y$. By DT, $\Sigma \vdash \neg Y \to Y$. However, $\neg Y \to Y \vdash Y$. Therefore, $\Sigma \vdash Y$.

Below are some examples of theorems, consequences and proofs that use the metatheorems RA and DT.

EXAMPLE 6.6. Show that $\vdash \forall x(X \to Y) \to (\forall x \neg Y \to \forall x \neg X)$.

Due to DT, we only show that $\{\forall x(X \to Y),\ \forall x \neg Y\} \vdash \forall x \neg X$.

	$\forall x(X \to Y)$	P
	$\forall x(X \to Y) \to (X \to Y)$	A4
	$X \to Y$	MP
	$(X \to Y) \to (\neg Y \to \neg X)$	Th
1.	$\neg Y \to \neg X$	MP
	$\forall x \neg Y$	P
	$\forall x \neg Y \to \neg Y$	A4
	$\neg Y$	MP
	$\neg X$	1, MP
	$\forall x \neg X$	UG

EXAMPLE 6.7. Show that $\vdash \forall x(X \to Y) \to (\neg \forall x \neg X \to \neg \forall x \neg Y)$.

$\vdash \forall x(X \to Y) \to (\neg \forall x \neg X \to \neg \forall x \neg Y)$
iff $\forall x(X \to Y), \neg \forall x \neg X \vdash \neg \forall x \neg Y$, by DT
iff $\{\forall x(X \to Y), \neg \forall x \neg X, \forall x \neg Y\}$ is inconsistent, by RA
iff $\forall x(X \to Y), \forall x \neg Y \vdash \forall x \neg X$, again by RA.

The proof of the last consequence is in Example 6.6.

EXAMPLE 6.8. If x is not free in Y, then $\vdash \neg(\forall x X \to Y) \to \forall x \neg(X \to Y)$.

Using DT and RA, we first transfer the theorem to a convenient consequence in the following manner:

$\vdash \neg(\forall x X \to Y) \to \forall x \neg(X \to Y)$
iff $\neg(\forall x X \to Y) \vdash \forall x \neg(X \to Y)$
iff $\{\neg(\forall x X \to Y), \neg \forall x \neg(X \to Y)\}$ is inconsistent.
iff $\neg \forall x \neg(X \to Y) \vdash \forall x X \to Y$
iff $\neg \forall x \neg(X \to Y), \forall x X \vdash Y$
iff $\{\neg \forall x \neg(X \to Y), \forall x X, \neg Y\}$ is inconsistent.
iff $\forall x X, \neg Y \vdash \forall x \neg(X \to Y)$.

The last consequence has the following proof:

$\forall x X$	P
$\forall x X \to X$	A4
X	MP
$X \to (\neg Y \to \neg(X \to Y))$	Th
$\neg Y \to \neg(X \to Y)$	MP
$\neg Y$	P
$\neg(X \to Y)$	MP
$\forall x \neg(X \to Y)$	UG

EXAMPLE 6.9. Show that $\vdash \forall x((x \approx f(y)) \to Qx) \to Qf(y)$.

Due to DT, we give a proof of $\forall x((x \approx f(y)) \to Qx) \vdash Qf(y)$.

$\forall x((x \approx f(y)) \to Qx)$	P
$\forall x((x \approx f(y)) \to Qx) \to ((f(y) \approx f(y)) \to Qf(y))$	A4
$((f(y) \approx f(y)) \to Qf(y)$	MP
$f(y) \approx f(y)$	A6
$Qf(y)$	MP

EXAMPLE 6.10. $\{Pa, \forall x(Px \to Qx), \forall x(Rx \to \neg Qx), Rb\} \vdash \neg(a \approx b)$.

	$\forall x(Px \to Qx)$	P
	$\forall x(Px \to Qx) \to (Pa \to Qa)$	A4
	$Pa \to Qa$	MP
	Pa	P
1.	Qa	MP
	$a \approx b$	P
	$(a \approx b) \to (Qa \to Qb)$	A7
	$Qa \to Qb$	MP
2.	Qb	1, MP
	$\forall x(Rx \to \neg Qx)$	P
	$\forall x(Rx \to \neg Qx) \to (Rb \to \neg Qb)$	A4
	$Rb \to \neg Qb$	MP
	Rb	P
3.	$\neg Qb$	MP

The set $\{Pa, \forall x(Px \to Qx), \forall x(Rx \to \neg Qx), Rb, a \approx b\}$ is inconsistent due to formulas numbered 2 and 3. Then RA takes care.

EXAMPLE 6.11. $\forall x \forall y(f(x,y) \approx f(y,x)), \forall x \forall y(f(x,y) \approx y) \vdash \neg \forall x \neg \forall y(x \approx y)$

Read the following proof and rewrite it without omission of any step. Look at the lines 9 and 12. They show that Σ is inconsistent; what is Σ here?

1.	$\forall x \forall y(f(x,y) \approx y)$	P
	$\forall x \forall y(f(x,y) \approx y) \to \forall y \forall x(f(y,x) \approx x)$	Th
2.	$\forall y \forall x(f(y,x) \approx x)$	MP
3.	$f(x,y) \approx y$	1, A4, MP
4.	$f(y,x) \approx x$	2, A4, MP
	$\forall x \forall y(f(x,y) \approx f(y,x))$	P
5.	$f(x,y) \approx f(y,x)$	A4, MP
	$x \approx y$	3, 4, 5, A7, MP
6.	$\forall y(x \approx y)$	UG
	$\forall x \neg \forall y(x \approx y)$	P
	$\forall x \neg \forall y(x \approx y) \to \neg \forall y(x \approx y)$	A4
7.	$\neg \forall y(x \approx y)$	MP

Remark 6.1. If you drop the restriction on UG, then you can have a proof of $Px \vdash \forall x Px$. It will not be correct if $\vdash$ is to be kept on par with $\vDash$. In that case, the metastatement $Px \vdash \forall x Px$ will be on par with the metastatement "If $\vDash Px$, then $\vDash \forall x Px$", and not with "$Px \vDash \forall x Px$". Such an unrestricted use of UG will force the deduction theorem to take a different shape, such as

> If there is a proof of $\Sigma \cup \{X\} \vdash Y$, where UG has not been applied on a free variable of X, then $\Sigma \vdash X \to Y$.

And, the metastatement "$\Sigma \cup \{X\} \vdash Y$ iff $\Sigma \vdash X \to Y$" would hold only for sentences. Of course, this is sufficient for proving theorems in mathematics. But in computer science, we require to argue with open formulas, formulas with free variables! And for this purpose, our version of UG with a restriction is more appropriate.

You should be able to read other texts where UG comes with no restrictions. In that case, you must also look for a restriction on the deduction theorem. Note that the restriction as mentioned above does not require every proof of $\Sigma \cup \{X\} \vdash Y$ to satisfy the free-variable condition. It only requires one such proof.

If you restrict UG too much, e.g., by allowing UG to be applicable only when the variable x is not free in *any* premise, then probably, monotonicity will hold no longer. Try to construct an example to see this.

Another result related to UG says that FC allows generalizing on a constant. In the scenario of a consequence, the constant must be a new constant, not occurring in any premise. If a constant does not occur in premises but it occurs in the proof of the consequence, then it must have been introduced by a universal specification. Now, instead of instantiating with a constant, one could have instantiated with a new variable. And then universal generalization could be applied on that variable. Therefore, it is reasonable to expect that on such a constant, we will be able to apply universal generalization.

Theorem 6.6 (Strong Generalization). *Let Σ be a set of formulas, X a formula, x a variable, and let c be a constant. Suppose, in any formula of $\Sigma \cup \{X\}$, x does not occur free, and c does not occur at all. If $\Sigma \vdash X[y/c]$, then $\Sigma \vdash \forall x X[y/x]$. Moreover, there exists a proof of $\Sigma \vdash \forall x X[y/x]$ in which c does not occur at all.*

Proof. Write $X(c)$ for $X[y/c]$ and $\forall x X(x)$ for $\forall x X[y/x]$. Assume that there is an FC-proof of $\Sigma \vdash X(c)$. We show, by induction on the length of a proof of $\Sigma \vdash X(c)$, i.e., on the number of formulas occurring in a proof of $\Sigma \vdash X(c)$, that $\Sigma \vdash \forall x X(x)$.

In the basis step, if $\Sigma \vdash X(c)$ has a proof consisting of just one formula, then $X(c)$ must be an axiom. We observe that if $X(c)$ is an axiom, then so is $X(x)$. For instance, if $X(c)$ is A4, then $X(c) = \forall y A(y) \to A(c)$. Now, $\forall y A(y) \to A(x)$ is also A4, where x is not free in any formula of $\Sigma \cup \{\forall y A(y)\}$. Now that $X(x)$ is an axiom, by UG we obtain $\forall x X(x)$. Observe that in this two-lines proof, the constant c does not occur.

Lay out the induction hypothesis that for any proof of length less than n of the consequence $\Sigma \vdash X(c)$, there is a proof of $\Sigma \vdash \forall x X(x)$ in which c does not occur. Suppose P is a proof of $\Sigma \vdash X(c)$ having length n. In P the nth formula is $X(c)$. If $X(c)$ is an axiom, then we get a proof of $\forall x X(x)$ as in the basis step. So, assume that $X(c)$ has been obtained, in P, by an application of either (a) MP, or (b) UG.

(a) The formula $X(c)$ has been obtained by an application of MP. Thus, earlier to $X(c)$ occur the formulas $Y(c)$ and $Y(c) \to X(c)$. Here $Y(c)$ is some formula where the constant c may or may not occur. By the induction hypothesis, proofs `P1` for $\Sigma \vdash Y(x)$ and `P2` for $\Sigma \vdash Y(x) \to X(x)$ exist. Moreover, c neither occurs in `P1` nor in `P2`. Then construct the proof `P3` by taking first `P1`, then `P2`, and then the formulas $X(x)$, $\forall x X(x)$ in that order. The formula $X(x)$ follows by an application of MP on the last lines of P1 and of P2, and then by using UG on $X(x)$, the last formula $\forall xX(x)$ is obtained. Then P3 is a proof of $\Sigma \vdash \forall xX(x)$ in which c does not occur. Notice that if c does not occur in Y, then instead of $Y(x)$ we work with Y, and the above argument is still justified.

(b) The formula $X(c)$ has been obtained by an application of UG. Then $X(c)$ occurs on the nth line, and $X(c)$ is in the form $X(c) = \forall yA(c)$, where $A(c)$ is some formula occurring in P earlier to the nth line. Due to the occurrence of $A(c)$, by the induction hypothesis, $\forall xA(x)$ has a proof, say, P4, where c does not occur. Extend P4 adding the formula $\forall y\forall xA(x)$ using UG. Next, write the formula $\forall x\forall yA(x)$, using an already proved theorem in Example 6.2. Now, $\forall xX(x) = \forall x\forall yA(x)$. Therefore, the extended proof is a proof of $\Sigma \vdash \forall xX(x)$, where c does not occur. ♦

Our proof of strong generalization indirectly shows that in a proof of $X[y/c]$ if we replace each occurrence of c by x; then the result is a proof of $X[y/x]$. Next, using the inference rule UG the formula $\forall xX[y/x]$ is derived.

Exercises for § 6.2

1. Write all axiom schemes as rules of inference by using the deduction theorem.
2. Should we use the deduction theorem to prove A5 and $\vdash A \to A$?
3. Show the following:
   (a) $\{Px,\ \forall xQx\} \vdash \forall x(Px \to \forall xQx)$
   (b) If S any sentence, then $S \to \forall xPx \vdash \forall x(S \to Px)$.
   (c) If x is not free in X, then $X \to \forall xPx \vdash \forall x(X \to Px)$.
4. Prove the consequences in Exercise 2 of § 6.1, using the metatheorems.

6.3 ADEQUACY OF FC TO FL

Recall that a proof system is called sound with respect to a logic if each provable formula in the system is also valid in the logic. The proof system is called complete with respect to the logic if each valid formula in the logic is provable in the proof system. And, the adjective *strong* is used for similar notions with regard to consequences.

We start with strong soundness. The symbol $\vdash$ stands for '$\vdash$ in FC' for formulas and consequences. Similarly, the symbol $\vDash$ will denote '$\vDash$ in FL'. Moreover, we consider only the fragment of FC and FL, where the symbols $\wedge, \vee, \leftrightarrow, \exists$ are not used; the definitions of these symbols take care of the rest.

Theorem 6.7 (Strong Soundness of FC). *Let Σ be a set of formulas, and let A be a formula.*

(1) *If $\Sigma \vdash A$, then $\Sigma \vDash A$.*

(2) *If Σ is satisfiable, then Σ is consistent.*

Proof. We check that the axioms are valid; the rules of inference are valid consequences; and then apply induction on the lengths of proofs.

Let P be a proof of $\Sigma \vdash A$. In the proof P, all the premises in Σ might not have been used. Let Σ_{P} be the set of premises that have been actually used in P. Then Σ_{P} is a finite subset of Σ and $\Sigma_{\mathsf{P}} \vdash A$. We use induction on n, the number of (occurrences of) formulas in P that proves $\Sigma_{\mathsf{P}} \vDash A$. By monotonicity in FL, it will follow that $\Sigma \vDash A$.

In the basis step, $n = 1$; A is either an axiom or a premise in Σ_{P}. Clearly, $\Sigma_{\mathsf{P}} \vDash A$. Lay out the induction hypothesis that if $\Sigma_{\mathsf{P}} \vdash A$ has a proof of less than m formulas, then $\Sigma_{\mathsf{P}} \vDash A$. Let P1 be a proof of $\Sigma_{\mathsf{P}} \vdash A$ having m formulas. If A is again an axiom or a premise in Σ_{P}, then clearly $\Sigma_{\mathsf{P}} \vDash A$ holds. Otherwise, A has been obtained in P1 by an application of (a) MP or (b) UG.

(a) There are formulas B and $B \to A$ occurring earlier to A in P1. By the induction hypothesis, $\Sigma_{\mathsf{P}} \vDash B$ and $\Sigma_{\mathsf{P}} \vDash B \to A$. Since $\{B, B \to A\} \vDash A$, we have $\Sigma_{\mathsf{P}} \vDash A$.

(b) There is a formula C occurring prior to A in P1 such that $A = \forall x C$, for some variable x. Further, let Σ_{C} be the subset of Σ_{P} containing exactly those formulas which have been used in P1 in deriving C. Then the variable x does not occur free in any formula of Σ_{C} due to the restriction on applicability of UG. By the induction hypothesis, $\Sigma_{\mathsf{C}} \vDash C$. By Theorem 6.20, $\Sigma_{\mathsf{C}} \vDash \forall x C$ i.e., $\Sigma_{\mathsf{C}} \vDash A$. Since $\Sigma_{\mathsf{C}} \subseteq \Sigma$, by monotonicity, $\Sigma \vDash A$.

For (2), let i be a model of Σ. If Σ is inconsistent, then $\Sigma \vdash B$ and $\Sigma \vdash \neg B$ for some formula B. By (1), $\Sigma \vDash B$ and $\Sigma \vDash \neg B$. Then i is a model of B as well as of $\neg B$. This is impossible. Therefore, Σ is consistent. ♦

For the completeness of FC with respect to FL, we prove that every consistent set of formulas is satisfiable. Though similar to PC, construction of a maximally consistent set in FC is a bit involved.

Let Σ be a consistent set of formulas. First we wish to make an infinite list of new constants available. We also require a spare binary predicate. To do this, we rewrite the formulas in Σ. For each formula $X \in \Sigma$, denote by $\bar{X}$, the formula obtained from X by replacing each constant c_i by c_{2i} for $i \in \mathbb{N}$; and replacing each binary predicate P_n^2 by P_{n+1}^2 for each $n \in \mathbb{N}$. Construct the set

$$\Sigma_1 = \{\bar{X} : X \in \Sigma\}.$$

Observe that the constants c_{2n+1} for $n \in \mathbb{N}$, and the binary predicate P_0^2 do not occur in any formula of Σ_1. We show that this construction does not affect consistency.

Lemma 6.1. *The set Σ is consistent iff Σ_1 is consistent.*

Proof. Assume that Σ_1 is inconsistent. Then we have a formula A and proofs P1 proving $\Sigma_1 \vdash A$, and P2 proving $\Sigma_1 \vdash \neg A$. Construct proofs P3 and P4 by replacing each occurrence of each constant c_{2i} with c_i; and each binary predicate P_{i+1}^2 with P_i^2. Now, $A = \bar{B}$ and $\neg A = \neg \bar{B}$ for some formula B. Then P3 and P4 prove $\Sigma \vdash B$ and $\Sigma \vdash \neg B$, respectively. That is, Σ is inconsistent.

Similarly, if Σ is inconsistent, it follows that Σ_1 is inconsistent. ♦

Next, we wish to eliminate the equality predicate in the lines of § 5.8. To simplify notation, let us write P_0^2 as E. Now, the binary predicate E (that is, P_0^2) is never used in any formula of Σ_1. For each formula $X \in \Sigma_1$, let $\tilde{X}$ be the formula obtained from X by replacing each occurrence of the subformula $(s \approx t)$ of X with Est, for terms s and t. Construct the set Σ_2 as follows:

$$\begin{aligned}\Sigma_2 = &\{\tilde{X} : X \in \Sigma_1, \text{ and } s,t \text{ are terms}\}\\ &\cup \{\forall x Exx,\ \forall x\forall y(Exy \to Eyx),\ \forall x\forall y\forall z(Exy \land Eyz \to Exz)\}\\ &\cup \{\forall x_1 \cdots \forall x_n \forall y_1 \cdots \forall y_n (Ex_1y_1 \land \cdots \land Ex_ny_n \to Ef(x_1,\ldots,x_n)f(y_1,\ldots,y_n)) :\\ &\quad f \text{ is an } n\text{-ary function symbol occurring in } \Sigma_1\}\\ &\cup \{\forall x_1 \cdots \forall x_n \forall y_1 \cdots \forall y_n (Ex_1y_1 \land \cdots \land Ex_ny_n \to (Px_1,\ldots,x_n \to Py_1,\ldots,y_n)) :\\ &\quad P \text{ is an } n\text{-ary predicate occurring in } \Sigma_1\}.\end{aligned}$$

The equality theorem (Theorem 5.10) says that the above construction preserves satisfiability. We now show that consistency is also not affected by this construction.

Lemma 6.2. *The set Σ_1 is consistent iff Σ_2 is consistent.*

Proof. Let Σ_1 be inconsistent. There exists a formula A such that $\Sigma_1 \vdash A$ and $\Sigma_1 \vdash \neg A$. Let P be a proof of $\Sigma_1 \vdash A$. In P, replace an axiom (A6) of the form

$$(t \approx t) \quad \text{by} \quad \forall x Exx, \quad \forall x Exx \to Ett, \quad Ett;$$

and replace an axiom (A7) of the form

$$(s \approx t) \to (X[x/s] \to X[x/t]) \quad \text{by} \quad Est \to (\bar{X}[x/s] \to \bar{X}[x/t]).$$

Finally, replace all formulas of the form $(s \approx t)$ by Est in the updated P. Let P1 be the sequence of formula obtained from P after all these replacements have taken place. Let B be obtained from A by replacing all subformulas of the form $(s \approx t)$ with Est. We claim that P1 is a proof of $\Sigma_2 \vdash B$.

Observe that the replacements do not affect applications of inference rules. Also, the replacements do not affect axioms (A1) - (A5). The replacement for (A6) is provable:

$$\forall x Exx, \quad \forall x Exx \to Ett, \quad Ett.$$

Here, the formula $\forall x Exx \in \Sigma_2$; the formula $\forall x Exx \to Ett$ is (A5); and Ett is obtained from these two formulas by MP. To show that the replacement of (A7) is provable, we use the deduction theorem and prove that for terms s,t and any formula X,

$$\Sigma_2 \cup \{Est\} \vdash \bar{X}[x/s] \to \bar{X}[x/t]$$

where $\bar{X}$ is obtained from X by replacing each occurrence of a subformula of the form $(t_1 \approx t_2)$ by Et_1t_2. Notice that $\approx$ does not occur in $\bar{X}$. For instance if $X = Px$, then a proof is given as follows:

$Est \to \forall x\forall y(Px \to Py)$	Premise in Σ_2
Est	Premise

$\forall x \forall y(Px \to Py)$	MP
$\forall x \forall y(Px \to Py) \to \forall y(Ps \to Py)$	A4
$\forall y(Ps \to Py)$	MP
$\forall y(Ps \to Py) \to (Ps \to Pt)$	A4
$Ps \to Pt$	MP

The proof of $\Sigma_2 \cup \{Est\} \vdash \bar{X}[x/s] \to \bar{X}[x/t]$ uses induction on the total number of occurrences of connectives and quantifiers appearing in $\bar{X}$. (Work it out.)

So, we have shown that P1 is a proof of $\Sigma_2 \vdash B$. Similarly, it follows that $\Sigma_2 \vdash \neg B$. Therefore, Σ_2 is inconsistent.

On the other hand, if Σ_2 is inconsistent then there exist proofs of $\Sigma_2 \vdash C$ and $\Sigma_2 \vdash \neg C$ for some formula C. Replace all occurrences of formulas of the form Est by $(s \approx t)$ in the proofs of $\Sigma_2 \vdash C$ and $\Sigma_2 \vdash \neg C$ to obtain proofs of $\Sigma_1 \vdash \hat{C}$ and $\Sigma_2 \vdash \neg \hat{C}$, where $\hat{C}$ is obtained from C after the replacement has been effected. This shows that Σ_1 is inconsistent. ♦

We will extend Σ_2 further so that generalization on the constants would not produce a formula outside this extension. For this purpose, we use an enumeration of formulas and variables. Since the set of all formulas and the set of all variables are countable, their Cartesian product

$$S = \{(X, x) : X \text{ is a formula, and } x \text{ is a variable}\}$$

is countable. So, fix an enumeration of S. In this enumeration, the first n formulas possibly have occurrences of a finite number of constants of the form c_{2i+1}. Suppose that $c_{k(n)}$ is the constant of minimum odd index which does not occur in the first n pairs in this enumeration, and which is different from earlier chosen constants $c_{k(1)}, \ldots, c_{k(n-1)}$. (We write $k(n)$ instead of k_n for avoiding subscripts of subscripts.) Corresponding to the nth pair (Y, z), we construct the formula X_n as follows:

$$X_n = Y[z/c_{k(n)}] \to \forall z Y \quad \text{for } n \geq 1.$$

Then we extend the set Σ_2 to

$$\Sigma_3 = \Sigma_2 \cup \{X_1, \ldots, X_n, \ldots\}.$$

Observe that the constant symbol $c_{k(n)}$ occurs exactly in one formula of Σ_3, which is X_n. We show that consistency is still preserved.

Lemma 6.3. *The set Σ_2 is consistent iff Σ_3 is consistent.*

Proof. If Σ_3 is consistent, by monotonicity it follows that its subset Σ_2 is consistent. For the converse, suppose that Σ_2 is consistent. If Σ_3 is inconsistent, then there exists a formula B such that $\Sigma_3 \vdash B$ and $\Sigma_3 \vdash \neg B$. Since proofs are finite sequences of formulas, there are only finite number of such formulas used in the proofs of $\Sigma_3 \vdash B$ and $\Sigma_3 \vdash \neg B$. Let m be the maximum index of such finite number of formulas. Using monotonicity, we see that

$$\Sigma_2 \cup \{X_1, \ldots, X_m\} \vdash B, \quad \Sigma_2 \cup \{X_1, \ldots, X_m\} \vdash \neg B.$$

So, $\Sigma_2 \cup \{X_1, \ldots, X_m\}$ is inconsistent. We wish to eliminate X_m. By RA,

$$\Sigma_2 \cup \{X_1, \ldots, X_{m-1}\} \vdash \neg X_m.$$

Here, for $m = 1$ we take $\{X_1, \ldots, X_{m-1}\} = \varnothing$. Now, $\neg X_m = \neg(Z[x/c_{k(m)}] \to \forall x Z)$, for some formula Z and some variable x. By Example 2.24,

$$\Sigma_2 \cup \{X_1, \ldots, X_{m-1}\} \vdash Z[x/c_{k(m)}], \quad \Sigma_2 \cup \{X_1, \ldots, X_{m-1}\} \vdash \neg \forall x Z.$$

Form the first formula, using Strong generalization (Theorem 6.6), we obtain

$$\Sigma_2 \cup \{X_1, \ldots, X_{m-1}\} \vdash \forall x Z.$$

Hence $\Sigma_2 \cup \{X_1, \ldots, X_{m-1}\}$ is inconsistent.

Continuing this way, we eliminate $X_{m-1}, \ldots, X_1$ to conclude that Σ_2 is inconsistent. This is not possible. Therefore, Σ_3 is consistent. ♦

Our construction is not yet over. We have used a very special kind of formulas in defining Σ_3. We now extend this set in a manner analogous to PC. To this end, we use the countability of formulas of FC.

Let $Y_0, Y_1, Y_2, \ldots$ be an enumeration of all formulas of FC. Define the sequence of sets of formulas $\Gamma_0, \Gamma_1, \Gamma_2, \ldots$ inductively by

$$\Gamma_0 = \Sigma_3, \quad \Gamma_{n+1} = \begin{cases} \Gamma_n & \text{if } \Gamma_n \cup \{Y_n\} \text{ is inconsistent} \\ \Gamma_n \cup \{Y_n\} & \text{if } \Gamma_n \cup \{Y_n\} \text{ is consistent} \end{cases}$$

Finally, take $\Sigma' = \cup_{n \in \mathbb{N}} \Gamma_n$. This is the required **Hintikka set** for the set Σ. Unlike PC, this Hintikka set is not a superset of Σ.

Lemma 6.4. *The Hintikka set Σ' is a maximally consistent extension of Σ_3.*

Proof. Clearly, $\Sigma_3 \subseteq \Sigma'$. If Σ' is inconsistent, then $\Sigma' \vdash Z$ and $\Sigma' \vdash \neg Z$ for some formula Z. There exist $i, j \in \mathbb{N}$ such that $\Gamma_i \vdash Z$ and $\Gamma_j \vdash \neg Z$. Take $k = \max\{i, j\}$. Then, $\Gamma_i \subseteq \Gamma_k$ and $\Gamma_j \subseteq \Gamma_k$. By monotonicity, $\Gamma_k \vdash Z$ and $\Gamma_k \vdash \neg Z$. This contradicts the fact that each Γ_k is consistent. Hence Σ' is consistent.

We next show that $\Sigma' \cup \{Z\}$ is inconsistent for any formula $Z \notin \Sigma'$. Assume, on the contrary, that $\Sigma' \cup \{Z\}$ is consistent for some formula $Z \notin \Sigma'$. Due to the enumeration $Y_0, Y_1, Y_2, \ldots$ of all formulas, $Z = Y_m$ for some $m \in \mathbb{N}$. Since $\Sigma' \cup \{Z\}$ is consistent, by monotonicity, $\Gamma_m \cup \{Z\}$ is consistent. It then follows that $Z = Y_m \in \Gamma_{m+1} \subseteq \Sigma'$, contradicting the fact that $Z \notin \Sigma'$.

Therefore, $\Sigma' \cup \{Z\}$ is inconsistent for any formula $Z \notin \Sigma'$. ♦

Lemma 6.5. *Let Σ be a consistent set of formulas. Let Σ' be the Hintikka set for Σ, and let X, Y be any formulas.*

(1) *$\Sigma' \vdash X$ iff $X \in \Sigma'$.*
(2) *Either $X \in \Sigma'$ or $\neg X \in \Sigma'$.*
(3) *If $Y \in \Sigma'$, then $X \to Y \in \Sigma'$.*
(4) *If $X \notin \Sigma'$, then $X \to Y \in \Sigma'$.*

(5) *If* $X \in \Sigma'$ *and* $Y \notin \Sigma'$, *then* $X \to Y \notin \Sigma'$.

(6) *For each term* t, $X[x/t] \in \Sigma'$ *iff* $\forall x X \in \Sigma'$.

Proof. (1) If $X \in \Sigma'$, then clearly $\Sigma' \vdash X$. Conversely, if $X \notin \Sigma'$, then $\Sigma' \cup \{X\}$ is inconsistent. By RA, $\Sigma' \vdash \neg X$. Since Σ' is consistent, $\Sigma' \nvdash X$.

(2) Since Σ' is consistent, if $X \in \Sigma'$, then $\neg X \notin \Sigma'$. On the other hand, if $X \notin \Sigma'$, then $\Sigma' \cup \{X\}$ is inconsistent. By RA, $\Sigma' \vdash \neg X$. By (1), $\neg X \in \Sigma'$.

(3) Let $Y \in \Sigma'$. By monotonicity, $\Sigma' \cup \{X\} \vdash Y$. Then $\Sigma' \vdash X \to Y$, by the deduction theorem. Due to (1), $X \to Y \in \Sigma'$.

(4) Let $X \notin \Sigma'$. Then $\Sigma' \cup \{X\}$ is inconsistent. By monotonicity, $\Sigma' \cup \{X, \neg Y\}$ is inconsistent. By RA, $\Sigma' \cup \{X\} \vdash Y$. By the deduction theorem, $\Sigma' \vdash X \to Y$. Due to (1), $X \to Y \in \Sigma'$.

(5) Let $X \in \Sigma'$ and let $Y \notin \Sigma'$. If $X \to Y \in \Sigma'$, then by MP, $\Sigma' \vdash Y$. By (1), $Y \in \Sigma'$, a contradiction. Hence, $X \to Y \notin \Sigma'$.

(6) Suppose $\forall x X \in \Sigma'$. Due to A4 and MP, $\Sigma' \vdash X[x/t]$ for any term t. Then by (1), $X[x/t] \in \Sigma'$. Conversely, suppose that $X[x/t] \in \Sigma'$ for all terms t. Suppose that the pair (X, x) is the nth pair in the enumeration used in the construction of Σ_3. Since $\Sigma_3 \subseteq \Sigma'$ we have $(X[x/c_{k(n)}] \to \forall x X) \in \Sigma'$. Also $X[x/c_{k(n)}] \in \Sigma'$. So, by MP, $\Sigma' \vdash \forall x X$. Then by (1), $\forall x X \in \Sigma'$. ♦

Theorem 6.8 (Model Existence). *Each consistent set of formulas has a state-model.*

Proof. Let Σ be a consistent set of formulas. Let Σ' be the Hintikka set as constructed earlier. We first show that Σ' has a model. Observe that the equality predicate $\approx$ does not occur in any formula of Σ'. Let D be the set of all terms generated from the constants, variables, and function symbols occurring in the formulas of Σ'. Define $\phi(c) = c$ for any constant, $\phi(f) = f$ for each function symbol, and $\ell(x) = x$ for each variable x. Extend ℓ to all terms, using ϕ as usual. For any proposition P_i^0, define

$$\phi(P_i^0) = 1 \text{ if } P_i^0 \in \Sigma'; \text{ else } \phi(P_i^0) = 0.$$

For any n-ary relation P, $n \geq 1$, define $\phi(P) \subseteq D^n$ as follows:

$$(t_1, \ldots, t_n) \in \phi(P) \text{ iff } P(t_1, t_2, \ldots, t_n) \in \Sigma'.$$

We show that the state I_ℓ, with $I = (D, \phi)$, is a state-model of Σ'. That is, for each formula $X \in \Sigma'$, we must show that $I_\ell \vDash X$.

For this, we use induction on $n(X)$, the total number of occurrences of $\neg, \to$ and $\forall$ in X. In the basis step, when $\nu(X) = 0$, X is either a proposition, or in the form $P(s_1, s_2, \ldots, s_n)$ for terms $s_1, s_2, \ldots, s_n$.

If X is a proposition then by the very definition of ϕ in the state I_ℓ, we have $I_\ell(X) = 1$ iff $X \in \Sigma'$.

If $X = P(s_1, s_2, \ldots, s_n)$, where $s_1, \ldots, s_n$ are terms, then $I_\ell \vDash X$ iff $(s_1, \ldots, s_n) \in \phi(P)$ iff $X \in \Sigma'$, which holds.

In the induction step, assume that for any formula Y with $\nu(Y) < k$, $I_\ell \vDash Y$ iff $Y \in \Sigma'$. Let $X \in \Sigma'$ be a formula with $\nu(X) = k$. Then X is in one of the forms:

(a) $\neg A$ (b) $A \to B$ (c) $\forall xA$

(a) $X = \neg A,\ \nu(A) < k$. Now, $X \in \Sigma'$ iff $\neg A \in \Sigma'$ iff $A \notin \Sigma'$ (by Lemma 6.4(2)) iff $I_\ell \nvDash A$ (induction hypothesis) iff $I_\ell \vDash X$.

(b) $X = A \to B,\ \nu(A) < k,\ \nu(B) < k$. Here, $X \in \Sigma'$ iff $A \to B \in \Sigma'$ iff $A \notin \Sigma'$ or $B \in \Sigma'$ (Lemma 6.4(3)-(5)) iff $I_\ell \nvDash A$ or $I_\ell \vDash B$ (induction hypothesis) iff $I_\ell \vDash X$.

(c) $X = \forall xA,\ \nu(A) < k$. We have $X \in \Sigma'$ iff $\forall xA \in \Sigma'$ iff for each $t \in D$, $A[x/t] \in \Sigma'$ (Lemma 6.4(6)) iff for each $t \in D$, $I_\ell \vDash A[x/t]$ (by induction hypothesis) iff for each $t \in D$, $I_{\ell[x \mapsto t]} \vDash A$ iff $I_\ell \vDash \forall xA$ iff $I_\ell \vDash X$.

Now that Σ' is satisfiable, by monotonicity in FL, its subsets Σ_3 and Σ_2 are also satisfiable. The set Σ_2 has been obtained from Σ_1 by replacing $\approx$ with the binary predicate E and adjoining to the updated set the equality axioms. By the equality theorem, we conclude that Σ_1 is satisfiable.

Recall that the formulas in Σ_1 are obtained from those of Σ by replacing each predicate P_i^j with P_{i+1}^j, and replacing each constant c_i with c_{2i}. Thus the constants c_{2i+1} and the predicate P_0^2 do not occur in any formula of Σ_1. Let $J_m = (S, \psi, m)$ be a state-model of Σ_1. Due to the relevance lemma, we assume that ψ is left undefined for constants c_{2i+1} and for the predicate P_0^2. Construct another state $J_m' = (S, \psi', m)$ with $\psi'(P_i^j) = \psi(P_i^j)$ for $j \neq 2$, $\psi'(f) = \psi(f)$ for all non-constant function symbols; and

$$\psi'(P_i^2) = \psi(P_{i+1}^2), \quad \psi'(c_i) = \psi(c_{2i}) \quad \text{for } i \in \mathbb{N}.$$

Then, clearly J_m' is a state-model of Σ. ♦

The model existence theorem implies that every consistent set of formulas is satisfiable. Due to RA in both FL and FC, we conclude the *completeness* of FC to FL. It states that for any formula X, if $\vDash X$, then $\vdash_{FC} X$. Combining the strong soundness and the model existence theorems, we obtain the following stronger version.

Theorem 6.9 (Strong Adequacy of FC to FL). *Let Σ be a set of formulas, and let X be any formula.*

(1) $\Sigma \vDash A$ *iff* $\Sigma \vdash_{FC} A$.

(2) Σ *is satisfiable iff* Σ *is consistent.*

If the restriction on UG had not been imposed, as is done in many texts, we would have obtained soundness and completeness for sentences only.

Since the formula $Px \to \forall xPx$ is invalid (in FL), the adequacy of FC implies that $Px \to \forall xPx$ is not a theorem of FC. Then an application of the paradox of material implication shows that the set of all axioms of FC is consistent.

Exercises for § 6.3

1. Let Σ be a consistent set. Assume that $\Sigma \nvdash X$ for some formula X. Prove that $\Sigma \cup \{\neg X\}$ is consistent.
2. Prove that a set Σ of formulas is inconsistent iff $\Sigma \vdash \neg(X \to X)$ for some formula X iff $\Sigma \vdash \neg(X \to X)$ for each formula X.

3. Let Σ be a set of formulas, and let X be a formula. Show that if $\Sigma \cup \{X\}$ and $\Sigma \cup \{\neg X\}$ are inconsistent, then Σ is inconsistent.
4. Let Σ and Γ be sets of formulas, and let X be a formula. Show that if $\Sigma \cup \{X\}$ and $\Gamma \cup \{\neg X\}$ are inconsistent, then $\Sigma \cup \Gamma$ is inconsistent.
5. Recall that the *deductive closure* of a set of formulas Γ is the set of all formulas X such that $\Gamma \vdash X$. Let Σ be a set of formulas.
   (a) Does a Hintikka set for Σ coincide with its deductive closure?
   (b) Does the deductive closure of Σ coincide with a Hintikka set for it?

6.4 COMPACTNESS OF FL

Analogous to PL, consequences with infinite number of premises can be reduced to those with finite number of premises. Our technique is also similar to that in PL; we use a proof system and its completeness.

Theorem 6.10 (Compactness of FL). *Let Σ be any nonempty set of formulas, and let X be any formula.*

(1) *If $\Sigma \vDash X$, then Σ has a finite subset Γ such that $\Gamma \vDash X$.*

(2) *If Σ is unsatisfiable, then Σ has a finite subset Γ which is unsatisfiable.*

(3) *If all finite nonempty subsets of Σ are satisfiable, then Σ is satisfiable.*

The proof of compactness of FL is similar to that of Theorem 2.9; where we use FC, FL in place of PC, PL. A purely semantic proof can be given via Herbrand's expansions and the compactness of PL. However, tracking the premises that really contribute to the consequences may be difficult due to the equality predicate E.

A noteworthy application of the compactness theorem of FL is the existence of Ramsey numbers. In a simple graph, a clique is a subgraph where each vertex is joined to every other vertex; and an independent set is a subset of vertices, where no vertex is joined to any other. Ramsey's theorem implies that

> For each $n \geq 1$, there exists an $R_n \geq 1$ such that any simple graph with at least R_n vertices has a clique with n vertices or an independent set with n vertices.

Trivially, $R_1 = 1$ and $R_2 = 2$. It may be proved that if G is any simple graph with six vertices, then it has a clique with three vertices or an independent set of three vertices. Further, a simple graph with five vertices can be constructed where neither any subgraph with three vertices is a clique, nor any three vertices form an independent set. Thus, $R_3 = 6$. Ramsey number R_n grows very rapidly as a function of n.

Ramsey's theorem as stated above is really hard to prove. However, its infinite version is relatively straight forward. It looks as follows.

> In any simple infinite graph, there exists an infinite clique or an infinite independent set of vertices.

Then an application of the compactness theorem proves Ramsey's theorem. We execute this plan using the notion of colouring.

Let $n,k \in \mathbb{N}$. Let X be any nonempty set. Denote by $X^{(n)}$ the set of all subsets of X of size n. That is,

$$X^{(n)} = \{Y \subseteq X : |Y| = n\}.$$

A **colouring** of $X^{(n)}$ with k colours is a function $f : X^{(n)} \to \{1,\ldots,k\}$. A subset A of X is called **monochromatic for** f if there exists a $j \in \{1,\ldots,k\}$ such that for all $S \in A^{(n)}$, $f(S) = j$. For a subset $A \in X^{(n)}$ if $f(A) = j$ for some $j \in \{1,\ldots,k\}$, we say that the subset A **has colour** j.

EXAMPLE 6.12. Let $X = \{1,2,3,4,5,6\}$. Using $k = 2$ colours, a particular colouring of $X^{(2)}$ is as follows:

$$f(\{1,2\}) = f(\{1,3\}) = f(\{2,5\}) = f(\{3,6\}) = f(\{4,5\}) = f(\{4,6\}) = 1;$$
$$f \text{ of any other 2 elements-subset of } X \text{ is } 2.$$

In this colouring, the subset $\{4,5,6\}$ is monochromatic.

In fact, $R_3 = 6$ asserts that if X is any set of size 6 or greater and the collection of all unordered pairs of X are coloured with two colours, then there is a subset A of X of size 3 such that all unordered pairs of A are having the same colour.

The question is what happens if we take n-elements subsets of X instead of unordered pairs? And, what happens if we require that A should have k elements? That is, does there exist a natural number b so that if X is a set of size at least r and $X^{(n)}$ is coloured with k colours, then it is guaranteed that there exists a subset A of X of size a having the same colour?

Consider $X = \mathbb{N}$. If $\mathbb{N}^{(n)}$ is coloured with k colours, does there exist a monochromatic infinite subset of $\mathbb{N}$? We first answer a particular case; $n = 2$. It may be stated as follows:

In any colouring of $\mathbb{N}^{(2)}$, there is an infinite monochromatic subset of $\mathbb{N}$.

To see why this is the case, suppose $\mathbb{N}^{(2)}$ is coloured with k colours. Pick $m_1 \in \mathbb{N}$. There are infinitely many two-elements subsets from $\mathbb{N}^{(2)}$ of which m_1 is an element. So, there is an infinite set $A_1 \subseteq \mathbb{N} \setminus \{m_1\}$ such that the two-elements subsets from $\mathbb{N}^{(2)}$ of the form $\{m_1, \ell\}$ with $\ell \in A_1$ have the same colour. Let the colour of all these two-elements subsets be C_1.

Choose $m_2 \in A_1$. There are infinitely many two-elements subsets in $\mathbb{N}^{(2)}$ of the form $\{m_2, \ell\}$, where $\ell \in A_1 \setminus \{m_2\}$. So, there is an infinite set $A_2 \subseteq A_1 \setminus \{m_1\}$ such that the two-elements subsets of the form $\{m_2, \ell\}$ with $\ell \in A_2$ have the same colour, say C_2.

Continue inductively to obtain a sequence of distinct numbers $m_1, m_2, \ldots$ and a sequence of colours $C_1, C_2, \ldots$. Notice that if $i < j$, then the two-elements set $\{m_i, m_j\}$ is coloured C_i. By the Pigeon Hole Principle, there are indices $r_1 < r_2 < \cdots$ such that $C_{r_1} = C_{r_2} = \cdots$. Then $\{m_{r_1}, m_{r_2}, \ldots\}$ is an infinite monochromatic set.

The same scheme of construction proves the general case.

Theorem 6.11 (Infinite Ramsey). *Let $n,k \in \mathbb{N}$. If $\mathbb{N}^{(n)}$ is coloured with k colours, then there exists an infinite monochromatic subset of $\mathbb{N}$.*

Proof. We use induction on n. For $n = 1$, $\mathbb{N}^{(1)} = \mathbb{N}$. If $\mathbb{N}$ is coloured with k colours, then by the Pigeon Hole Principle, it has an infinite monochromatic subset. Lay out the induction hypothesis that if $\mathbb{N}^{(n)}$ is coloured with k colours, then there exists an infinite monochromatic subset of $\mathbb{N}$. Let $f : \mathbb{N}^{(n+1)} \to \{1,2,\ldots,k\}$ be any function. We define a sequence of infinite subsets (X_n) as follows.

Write $X_{-1} = \mathbb{N}$. Suppose X_{j-1} has already been defined. Then pick $x_j \in X_{j-1}$. Let $Y_{j-1} = X_{j-1} \setminus \{x_j\}$. Construct $f_j : Y_{j-1}^{(n)} \to \{1,2,\ldots,k\}$ by

$$f_j(\{y_1,\ldots,y_n\}) = f(\{x_j,y_1,\ldots,y_n\}) \quad \text{for } \{y_1,\ldots,y_n\} \in Y_{j-1}^{(n)}.$$

Using the induction hypothesis, let X_j be an infinite monochromatic subset of Y_{j-1} for the colouring f_j. Suppose the colour of X_j is $c(x_j)$.

It means that X_j is an infinite subset of X_{j-1} all n-element subset of which join with x_j to form $(n+1)$-elements subsets of colour $c(x_j)$. Then $\mathbb{N} = X_{-1} \supseteq X_0 \supseteq X_1 \supseteq \cdots$ and for $j < \ell$, we have $x_\ell \in X_j \supseteq X_{\ell-1}$. Suppose $\{x_j, x_{r(1)}, \ldots, x_{r(n)}\}$ is an $(n+1)$-element subset of X_{j-1} ordered so that $j < r(1) < \cdots < r(n)$. Since $\{x_j, x_{r(1)}, \ldots, x_{r(n)}\} \subseteq X_j$, by our choice of x_j, we have

$$f(\{x_j, x_{r(1)}, \ldots, x_{r(n)}\}) = c(x_j).$$

That is, if A is any n-elements subset of X_{j-1}, then $f(A) = c(x_j)$. Since X_{j-1} is infinite, by the Pigeon Hole Principle, there exists a colour $i \in \{1,\ldots,k\}$ such that the set $B = \{x_j \in X_{j-1} : c(x_j) = i\}$ is an infinite set. Any n-elements subset D of B where j is the smallest index such that $x_j \in D$ satisfies $f(D) = i$. That is, B is the required infinite monochromatic subset of $\mathbb{N}$. ♦

Theorem 6.12 (Ramsey). *For all positive integers n,k,a, there exists a positive integer b such that if X is any set of size at least b, then for every colouring of $X^{(n)}$ with k colours, there exists a monochromatic subset $Y \subseteq X$ of size a.*

Proof. On the contrary, assume that there exist positive integers n,k,a such that for all positive integers b, there is a set X of size b and there is a colouring of $X^{(n)}$ in k colours so that no subset $Y \subseteq X$ of size a is monochromatic. Define the n-ary predicates $P_1,\ldots,P_k$ by

$P_i(x_1,\ldots,x_n)$ to mean "the set $\{x_1,\ldots,x_n\}$ has colour i."

Let $A_i = \forall x_1 \cdots \forall x_n \big(P_i(x_1,\ldots,x_n) \to \bigwedge_{1\le i<j\le n} (x_i \not\approx x_j)\big) \wedge$

$$\bigwedge_{\sigma\in S_n} \big(P_i(x_1,\ldots,x_n) \leftrightarrow P_i(x_{\sigma(1)},\ldots,x_{\sigma(n)})\big).$$

where S_n is the set of all permutations of $\{1,\ldots,n\}$ leaving out the identity permutation. The sentence A_i means that

the truth of $P_i(x_1,\ldots,x_n)$ does not depend on the ordering of $x_1,\ldots,x_n$.

For $1 \le i \le n$, let

$$B_i = \forall x_1 \cdots \forall x_n \Big(P_i(x_1,\ldots,x_n) \to \bigwedge_{1\le j\le n, i\ne j} (\neg P_j(x_1,\ldots,x_n))\Big).$$

Thus, B_i means that if a set is coloured i then it cannot be coloured with a colour other than i. Next, let

$$C = \forall x_1 \cdots \forall x_n \Big(\bigwedge_{1 \le \ell < j \le n} (x_\ell \not\approx x_j) \to \bigvee_{1 \le i \le k} P_i(x_1, \ldots, x_n) \Big).$$

It means that each n-elements subset is coloured with some colour.

It follows that the conjunction of these sentences, that is,

$$D = \bigwedge_{1 \le i \le n} (A_i \wedge B_i) \wedge C.$$

means that P_is define the colouring of an n-elements subset. In any model of D, the colouring is determined by the unique colour of the subset $\{m_1, \ldots, m_n\}$, where the model satisfies the formula $P_i(x_1, \ldots, x_n)$ by assigning the variable x_j to m_j.

Next, for $1 \le i \le k$, let define the formula

$$Q_i(x_1, \ldots, x_a) = \bigvee_{1 \le \sigma(1) < \sigma(2) < \cdots < \sigma(n) \le a} P_i(x_{\sigma(1)}, \ldots, x_{\sigma(n)}).$$

For instance, if $n = 2$ and $a = 3$, then

$$Q_i(x_1, x_2, x_3) = P_i(x_1, x_2) \vee P_i(x_1, x_3) \vee P_i(x_2, x_3).$$

The formula $Q_i(x_1, \ldots, x_a)$ says that at least one n-elements subset of $\{x_1, \ldots, x_a\}$ has the colour i. Using these formulas, we define the sentence E as follows:

$$E = \forall x_1 \cdots \forall x_a \Big(\bigwedge_{1 \le \ell < j \le a} (x_\ell \ne x_j) \to \bigvee_{1 \le r < i \le k} (Q_r(x_1, \ldots, x_a) \wedge Q_i(x_1, \ldots, x_k)) \Big).$$

It means each a-elements subset has at least two subsets having different colours. That is, E asserts that there exists no monochromatic a-elements subset. Therefore, a model of both D and E is a set whose n-elements subsets are coloured with k colours and no a-elements subset is monochromatic.

Finally, for each integer $b \ge 2$, let

$$R_b = \exists x_1 \cdots \exists x_b \bigwedge_{1 \le i < j \le b} (x_i \not\approx x_j).$$

Clearly, any model of R_b has at least b elements. Therefore, any model of all sentences R_b is an infinite set.

Putting these sentences together, we see that any model of the set

$$S_b = \{D,\ E,\ R_2,\ R_3,\ \ldots,\ R_b\}.$$

has at least b elements, such that the set of each n-elements subset of the model is coloured with k colours, and no a-elements subset is monochromatic. Our assumption says that each S_b is satisfiable. By the compactness theorem, the infinite set

$$S = S_2 \cup S_3 \cup \cdots$$

is satisfiable. It means that S has a model, which is an infinite set X with $X^{(n)}$ coloured using k colours and having no monochromatic subset of size a. This contradicts Theorem 6.11. ♦

Another application of compactness is the creation of non-standard analysis. It shows an infinitesimal can be added to the system of real numbers so that the resulting system is still consistent. Using such infinitesimals analysis can be done following the schemes of Leibniz and Newton. In fact, most of the arguments involving δ and ε in analysis can now be omitted altogether. We illustrate the creation of nonstandard large and small numbers by way of some examples.

Recall that a first order language starts with a set of symbols that include constants, function symbols, and predicates, along with all connectives and quantifiers. A first order language is like a consequence, where we require only some function symbols and some predicates out of the infinite supply of them. Next, we may have some sentences which are assumed to hold so that a particular theory is defined in a given first order language.

EXAMPLE 6.13. Consider a first order language L which has two constants a and b, two binary function symbols f and g, and a binary predicate P. Interpret the language L in the system of natural numbers $\mathbb{N}$ with a as 0, b as 1, f as addition, g as multiplication, and P as the relation of 'less than'. Let c be a new constant. Let Σ be the set of all true sentences of $\mathbb{N}$. Define a set of formula Γ by

$$\Gamma = \{P(n,c) : n \in \mathbb{N}\} = \{P(0,c),\ P(1,c),\ P(2,c),\ \ldots\}.$$

If $S \subseteq \Sigma \cup \Gamma$ is a finite set, then it contains a finite number of sentences from Γ. Clearly, the same interpretation with domain as $\mathbb{N}$ is a model of S.

That is, every finite subset of $\Sigma \cup \Gamma$ is satisfiable. By the compactness theorem, the set $\Sigma \cup \Gamma$ is also satisfiable. In such a model all true sentences of $\mathbb{N}$ are true; and also there exists an element which is bigger than all natural numbers. We may think of such an element in this model as an *infinity.*

It follows that if $\mathbb{N}$ is characterized by a set of axioms (See § 10.3.), then the same set of axioms have a *nonstandard model,* where there exists an element which is bigger than every natural number.

EXAMPLE 6.14. Consider a first order language with constants a, b; binary function symbols f, g; and a binary predicate P. Interpret the language in the system of real numbers $\mathbb{R}$ with a as 0, b as 1, f as addition, g as multiplication, and P as the relation of 'less than'. Let c be a new constant. Let Σ be the set of all true sentences of $\mathbb{R}$. Define the set Γ of sentences as follows:

$$\Gamma = \{P(0,c) \wedge P(g(n,c),1) : n \in \mathbb{N}\}.$$

Now, each finite subset of $\Sigma \cup \Gamma$ has the same model $\mathbb{R}$. By the compactness theorem, the set $\Sigma \cup \Gamma$ is satisfiable. In this new model of axioms of $\mathbb{R}$ there exists an element (that corresponds to c) which is smaller than all positive real numbers and is also greater than 0. We do not say that such a number is positive, for, 'positive' is applicable only to real numbers, and this number is not a real number. Such an element in this *nonstandard model* of the axioms of $\mathbb{R}$ is called an *infinitesimal.*

We say that a formula X has **arbitrarily large models** iff for each $n \in \mathbb{N}$, there exists a model of X having at least n elements in its domain. A typical application of compactness is to extend a property from arbitrarily large to infinite.

Theorem 6.13 (Skolem). *If a set of first order sentences has arbitrarily large models, then it has an infinite model.*

Proof. Let Σ be a set of sentences. Assume that Σ has arbitrarily large models. For each positive integer n, let

$$Y_n = \exists x_0 \cdots \exists x_n \big(\bigwedge_{0 \le i < j \le n} \neg(x_i \approx x_j) \big).$$

For instance, $Y_2 = \exists x_0 \exists x_1 \exists x_2 (\neg(x_0 \approx x_1) \wedge \neg(x_0 \approx x_2) \wedge \neg(x_1 \approx x_2))$. Next, let

$$S = \{Y_n : n \text{ is a positive integer}\}.$$

If A is any finite subset of $\Sigma \cup S$, then it contains a finite number of Y_ns. If m is the maximum of all those n, then A has a model whose domain has at least m elements. The fact that A has a model is enough for us. By the compactness theorem, $\Sigma \cup S$ has a model, say, $I = (D, \phi)$. If D is a finite set, say, with r elements, then it does not satisfy Y_{r+1}. As $Y_{r+1} \in S$, it contradicts the fact that I is a model of $\Sigma \cup S$. Therefore, I must be an infinite model of $\Sigma \cup S$. ♦

This trick of extending a model gives rise to the *Skolem-Löwenheim upward theorem* which states that if a set of sentences having cardinality α has a model with a domain of an infinite cardinality β, and $\gamma \ge \max\{\alpha, \beta\}$, then the set of sentences also has a model with domain of cardinality γ. The proof of this remarkable theorem requires first order languages allowing the set of constants to have cardinality γ.

Suppose Σ is a set of cardinality α which has a model with a domain of cardinality β. We start with a set S of cardinality γ; and introduce γ number of constants c_a to our language for each $a \in S$. Next, we define the set of sentences

$$\Gamma = \Sigma \cup \{\neg(c_a \leftrightarrow c_b) : a, b \in S, \ a \ne b\}.$$

Then using compactness we show that Γ has a model.

In a similar vein, we obtain fascinating results in other branches of mathematics; for example, see Ebbinghaus et al. (1994), Hodges (1993) and Rautenberg (2010).

Exercises for § 6.4

1. Show that $\neg(\forall x(Px \vee Qx) \to \forall x Px \vee \forall x Qx)$ is satisfiable in a domain with two elements.
2. Write a sentence X involving a binary predicate P so that if $I = (D, \phi)$ is any interpretation, then $I \vDash X$ iff D has at least two elements.
3. Write a sentence which is true in any domain with two elements, but is false in any domain with a single element.
4. Given an integer $n \ge 1$, write a sentence X involving a binary predicate P so that if $I = (D, \phi)$ is any interpretation, then $I \vDash X$ iff D has at least n elements.
5. Write a formula X involving a binary predicate P so that if $I = (D, \phi)$ is any interpretation, then $I \vDash X$ iff D is an infinite set.

6. Show that a first order sentence X cannot be found so that for any interpretation (D, ϕ), we have $I \vDash X$ iff D is a finite set.
7. Find a sentence which is true in a denumerable domain, but false in each finite domain.

6.5 LAWS IN FL

Now that FC is found to be adequate to FC, we may prove any law about either of them using the machinery of the other. We start with the law that pertains to equivalence replacement.

Theorem 6.14 (Equivalence Replacement). *Let A, B, X and Y be formulas with $A \equiv B$. For any formula W, let $W[A :=_e B]$ denote a formula obtained from W by replacing some or no or all occurrences of A by B. Then the following are true:*

(1) $X \equiv X[A :=_e B]$.

(2) *If* $X \equiv Y$, *then* $X[A :=_e B] \equiv Y[A :=_e B]$.

(3) *If* $X \vDash Y$, *then* $X[A :=_e B] \vDash Y[A :=_e B]$.

Proof. (1) A formal proof requires induction on the number of occurrences of connectives and quantifiers in X. Here, we give an outline. If A has not been replaced by B at all, then $X = X[A :=_e B]$, and there is nothing to prove. Otherwise, let I_ℓ be a state. Now, to check whether $I_\ell \vDash X[A :=_e B]$, we proceed as follows.

Depending upon the form of $X[A :=_e B]$, we may write down expressions after expressions involving predicates explicitly:

$$I_\ell \vDash X[A :=_e B] \text{ iff } \cdots S \cdots .$$

Proceeding step by step, the expression S will involve somewhere $I_\ell \vDash B$ or $I_\ell \nvDash B$, as the case demands. And these satisfaction relations will be coming exactly where A has been replaced by B in X. Due to equivalence of A and B, we have $I_\ell \vDash B$ iff $I_\ell \vDash A$. And then, some of these satisfactions can be replaced by $I_\ell \vDash A$ or $I_\ell \nvDash A$. Replace only those occurrences of $I_\ell \vDash B$ or of $I_\ell \nvDash B$ which correspond to the replacements of A while you obtained $X[A :=_e B]$. Retracing the steps in S, you reach at $I_\ell \vDash X$.

Proofs of (2)-(3) are similar to that of (1). ♦

In the proposition $\neg q \wedge p \leftrightarrow \neg(p \to q)$, replace p with Qz, and q with Pxy. You obtain the formula $\neg Pxy \wedge Qz \leftrightarrow \neg(Qz \to Pxy)$. Now that the proposition $\neg q \wedge p \leftrightarrow \neg(p \to q)$ is valid, we argue that the formula $\neg Pxy \wedge Qz \leftrightarrow \neg(Qz \to Pxy)$ must also be valid. We generalize this observation.

To avoid conflict in terminology, each PL-valid proposition is called a **tautology**, while considering PL as a fragment of FL. That is, a tautology is a valid formula where the only symbols used are atomic propositions ($\top, \bot$ and/or 0-ary predicates), connectives and, possibly, the left and right parentheses. For example, $\neg q \wedge p \leftrightarrow \neg(p \to q)$ is a tautology.

If X is a formula, p is a propositional variable, and A is a proposition (in PL), then write $A[p := X]$ for the formula obtained from A by substituting all occurrences of p

in A by X. This is **uniform replacement** of propositional variables by formulas. We require here to replace every occurrence of p by X. Contrast this with the equivalence replacement $A[p :=_e X]$ introduced in Theorem 6.14.

It is easy to see that $A[p := X][q := Y] = A[q := Y][p := X]$, provided p does not occur in Y and q does not occur in X. In fact, more than one or two propositional variables can be substituted in A simultaneously. We will write such a simultaneous uniform replacement as $A[p_1 := X_1, \ldots, p_n := X_n]$ or as $A[p := X_p]$. Notice that the notation $A[p := X_p]$ says that all occurrences of each propositional variable p in A has been substituted by the corresponding formula X_p.

Theorem 6.15 (Tautological Replacement). *Let A be a proposition. For each propositional variable p occurring in A, identify a formula X_p. Let $A[p := X_p]$ denote the formula obtained from A by substituting all occurrences of each such p by the corresponding X_p. If A is a tautology, then $A[p := X_p]$ is valid.*

Proof. Assume that A is a tautology. Then it has a proof in FC using only the axioms A1, A2, A3, and the inference rule MP. In such a proof, replace all occurrences of p with the corresponding X_p; and do this for all propositional variables occurring in A. The result is an FC-proof of $A[p := X_p]$. By the adequacy of FC, $A[p := X_p]$ is valid. ♦

Notice that tautological replacement is uniform replacement in a tautology. Moreover, you can formulate and prove statements analogous to those in Theorems 2.10(2)-(3). The tautological replacement allows you to get valid formulas from the laws in Theorem 2.12. This can be generalized to replacements in valid formulas (in FL), but with a proviso.

Theorem 6.16 (Uniform Replacement). *Let Z be a formula. For each propositional variable p occurring in Z, identify a formula X_p. Let $Z[p := X_p]$ denote the formula obtained by replacing all occurrences of each such p by the corresponding X_p in the formula Z. Assume that no free variable of X_p becomes bound in $Z[p := X_p]$. If $\vDash Z$, then $\vDash Z[p := X_p]$.*

Proof. In a proof of Z, replace all occurrences of each propositional variable p by the corresponding X_p. The result is a proof of $Z[p := X_p]$. The restriction of 'no variable capture' allows any application of UG in Z to be a correct application after the replacement. A formal proof is readily constructed by using induction on the length of a proof of Z, as usual. ♦

The restriction of 'no variable capture' cannot be ignored. For instance $p \to \forall x p$ is valid for a propositional variable p. Replacing p by Px yields an invalid formula $Px \to \forall x Px$ due to variable capturing.

Since $X_1, X_2, \ldots, X_n \vDash X$ iff $\vDash X_1 \wedge X_2 \wedge \cdots \wedge X_n \to X$, and since $X \equiv Y$ iff $\vDash X \leftrightarrow Y$, uniform replacement can be used on equivalences and consequences. The laws in Theorem 2.12 can be used as they are, but being valid for formulas, instead of just propositions. For instance, the distributive law

$$x \wedge (y \vee z) \equiv (x \wedge y) \vee (x \wedge z)$$

in Theorem 2.12 now reads as

$$X \wedge (Y \vee Z) \equiv (X \wedge Y) \vee (X \wedge Z).$$

Here, X, Y and Z are any formulas in FL. In addition to the laws obtained from PL, we have some more laws involving quantifiers as given in the following theorem; check their correctness. Note the same names in some cases. Further, remember that whenever $X[x/t]$ appears, it is assumed that t is free for x in X.

Theorem 6.17 (Laws). *The following laws hold for any formulas X, Y, Z, variables x, y, and terms r, s, t.*

(1) COMMUTATIVITY $\forall x\forall yX \equiv \forall y\forall xX$, $\exists x\exists yX \equiv \exists y\exists xX$, $\exists x\forall yX \vDash \forall y\exists xX$.
If both x and y do not occur in any atomic subformula of Z, then $\forall y\exists xZ \vDash \exists x\forall yZ$.

(2) CONSTANTS $\forall x(\bot \to X) \equiv \top$, $\exists x(\bot \wedge X) \equiv \bot$.

(3) DE MORGAN $\neg\forall xX \equiv \exists x\neg X$, $\neg\exists xX \equiv \forall x\neg X$, $\forall xX \equiv \neg\exists x\neg X$, $\exists xX \equiv \neg\forall x\neg X$.

(4) DISTRIBUTIVITY $\forall x(X \wedge Y) \equiv \forall xX \wedge \forall xY$, $\exists x(X \vee Y) \equiv \exists xX \vee \exists xY$,
$\forall xX \vee \forall xY \vDash \forall x(X \vee Y)$, $\exists x(X \wedge Y) \vDash \exists xX \wedge \exists xY$.
If x does not occur free in Z, then
$\forall x(Z \vee Y) \equiv Z \vee \forall xY$, $\exists x(Z \wedge Y) \equiv Z \wedge \exists xY$,
$\forall x(Z \to Y) \equiv Z \to \forall xY$, $\exists x(Z \to Y) \equiv Z \to \exists xY$,
$\forall x(Y \to Z) \equiv \exists xY \to Z$, $\exists x(Y \to Z) \equiv \forall xY \to Z$.

(5) EMPTY QUANTIFICATION *If x does not occur free in Z, then*
$\forall xZ \equiv Z$ *and* $\exists xZ \equiv Z$.

(6) EQUALITY $(t \approx t) \equiv \top$, $(s \approx t) \equiv (t \approx s)$,
$\{r \approx s, s \approx t\} \vDash (r \approx t)$, $\{s \approx t, X[x/s]\} \vDash X[x/t]$.

(7) ONE-POINT RULE *If x does not occur in t, then*
$\forall x((x \approx t) \to X) \equiv X[x/t]$, $\exists x((x \approx t) \wedge X) \equiv X[x/t]$.

(8) RENAMING *If x does not occur free in Z, then*
$\forall yZ \equiv \forall x(Z[y/x])$, $\exists yZ \equiv \exists x(Z[y/x])$.

What happens to the One-Point Rule if x occurs in t? With $t = x$ and $X = Px$, the rule is reduced to $\forall xPx \equiv Px$ and $\exists xPx \equiv Px$, which are not correct. Contrast this with the law of empty quantification.

In the law of commutativity, $\forall y\exists xX \nvDash \exists x\forall yX$, in general; see Example 5.18. Similarly, in the law of distributivity the following happens in general:

$$\forall x(X \vee Y) \nvDash \forall xX \vee \forall xY \quad \exists xX \wedge \exists xY \nvDash \exists x(X \wedge Y)$$

For example, with $X = Px$ and $Y = \neg Px$, you have $\forall x(X \vee Y) \equiv \top$. Whereas the formula $\forall xX \vee \forall xY = \forall xPx \vee \forall x\neg Px$ is invalid. To see this, take an interpretation $I = (\{2,3\}, P')$ with $P' = \{2\}$. Then,

$$I \vDash \forall xPx \vee \forall x\neg Px \text{ iff } (2 \in P' \text{ and } 3 \in P') \text{ or } (2 \notin P' \text{ and } 3 \notin P')$$

which clearly does not hold. Similarly, you can show that

$$\exists xX \wedge \exists xY \nvDash \exists x(X \wedge Y).$$

See why the condition 'x does not occur free in X' is imposed on the other laws of distributivity and on the law of renaming.

In FL, you may assert that from $\forall xPx$ follows Pc for each constant c. This is so because each constant c is interpreted as an element of the domain of the interpretation. Similarly, from Pc follows $\exists xPx$. Also, the rule UG of FC specifies conditions on deriving $\forall xPx$ from Px. We formulate these three laws as follows, whose proofs are easily obtained using FC.

Theorem 6.18 (US: Universal Specification). *Let t be a term free for a variable x in a formula X. Then $\forall xX \vDash X[x/t]$.*

Theorem 6.19 (EG: Existential Generalization). *Let t be a term free for a variable x in a formula X. Then $X[x/t] \vDash \exists xX$.*

Theorem 6.20 (UG: Universal Generalization). *Let Σ be a set of formulas. Let x be a variable that is not free in any formula of Σ. If $\Sigma \vDash X$, then $\Sigma \vDash \forall xX$.*

In particular, when $\Sigma = \varnothing$, UG says that "if $\vDash X$, then $\vDash \forall xX$". It states that

> if each state I_ℓ satisfies X, then each state I_ℓ satisfies $\forall xX$.

It is different from $X \vDash \forall xX$, which means that

> for each state I_ℓ, if I_ℓ satisfies X, then I_ℓ satisfies $\forall xX$.

The former can be vacuously true whereas the latter may be false. For instance, with $X = Px$, "if $\vDash Px$ then $\vDash \forall xPx$" holds since $\forall xPx$ is the universal closure of Px. For that matter, since Px is not valid, the statement "if $\vDash Px$, then $\vDash Qx$" also holds whatever Qx may be. But, $Px \vDash \forall xPx$ does not hold.

Similar is the case for the existential quantifier. In mathematical proofs we *deduce* Pc from $\exists xPx$, using an ambiguous name c. For example, the intermediate value theorem implies the following:

> Let $f : [\alpha, \beta] \to \mathbb{R}$ be a continuous function. If $f(\alpha) = -1$ and $f(\beta) = 1$, then there exists $\gamma \in (\alpha, \beta)$ such that $f(\gamma) = 0$.

To see how this result is applied, suppose $g : [-1, 1] \to \mathbb{R}$ is a continuous function with $g(-1) = -1$ and $g(1) = 1$. Using the intermediate value theorem, we take such a γ as c. We have $g(c) = 0$. Later, we use this c in our argument freely and conclude something finally where this c does not appear. And we take for granted such a conclusion. It is important that c must not occur in our final conclusion. Though $g(c) = 0$ does not follow from "there exists γ with $g(\gamma) = 0$", our final conclusion where this c does not occur is considered a valid conclusion.

A formulation of the existential specification is given in the following.

Theorem 6.21 (ES: Existential Specification). *Let Σ be a set of formulas, and let X, Y be formulas. Let α be a constant or a variable that does not occur in any formula of $\Sigma \cup \{X, Y\}$. If $\Sigma \cup \{X[x/\alpha]\} \vDash Y$, then $\Sigma \cup \{\exists xX\} \vDash Y$.*

Proof. We use RA serially. $\Sigma \cup \{X[x/\alpha]\} \vDash Y$ implies $\Sigma \cup \{X[x/\alpha], \neg Y\}$ is unsatisfiable. Then $\Sigma \cup \{\neg Y\} \vDash \neg X[x/\alpha]$. By Strong generalization (Theorem 6.6) and the adequacy of FC to FL, $\Sigma \cup \{\neg Y\} \vDash \forall x \neg X$. As $\forall x \neg X \equiv \neg \exists x X$, we have $\Sigma \cup \{\neg Y, \exists x X\}$ is unsatisfiable. Then $\Sigma \cup \{\exists x X\} \vDash Y$. ♦

The conclusion of Existential Specification is written equivalently as follows:

If $\Sigma \vDash \exists x X$ and $\Sigma \cup \{X[x/\alpha]\} \vDash Y$, then $\Sigma \vDash Y$.

In this scenario, the constant or variable α is called a **new constant**. In a quasi-proof or a calculation (to be discussed soon), due to the presence of $\exists x X$, we introduce an extra premise $X[x/\alpha]$ provisionally. Once a formula Y having no occurrence of this new constant α is derived, we consider that Y has been derived from Σ in the presence of $\exists x X$, thereby ending the provisionality of the extra premise $X[x/\alpha]$. It appears that a new constant α is introduced to conclude $X[x/\alpha]$ from $\exists x X$; thus the name *existential specification*. However, the new constant must never figure out in the final conclusion.

EXAMPLE 6.15. Use the quantifier laws to conclude $\exists x \forall y Pxy \vDash \forall y \exists x Pxy$.

Take $\Sigma = \{\exists x \forall y Pxy\}$, $X = \forall y Pxy$. Let c be a new constant that does not occur in $\Sigma \cup \{X\}$. Here, $X[x/c] = \forall y Pcy$. By universal specification, $\forall y Pcy \vDash Pcy$. By existential generalization, $Pcy \vDash \exists x Pxy$. That is, $\Sigma \cup \{X[x/c]\} \vDash \exists x Pxy$. Since c does not occur in $Y = \exists x Pxy$, we conclude with existential specification that $\Sigma \vDash \exists x Pxy$, i.e., $\exists x \forall y Pxy \vDash \exists x Pxy$. Use of universal generalization yields $\exists x \forall y Pxy \vDash \forall y \exists x Pxy$.

A wrong use of other quantifier laws along with existential specification can lead to paradoxical situations; see the following example.

EXAMPLE 6.16. (*An Incorrect Argument*) Take $\Sigma = \{\forall x \exists y Pxy\}$. By universal specification, we have $\Sigma \vDash \exists y Pxy$. For applying existential specification, we consider $X = Pxc$ for a new constant c. Next, we universally generalize on x to obtain $\forall x Pxc$. By existential generalization, we have $\exists y \forall x Pxy$. Since c does not occur in the last formula, we conclude that $\Sigma \vDash \exists y \forall x Pxy$. Therefore, $\forall y \exists x Pxy \vDash \exists x \forall y Pxy$. What is wrong?

Consider $\Sigma = \{\forall x \exists y Pxy\}$. Now, $\Sigma \vDash \exists y Pxy$. If we introduce Pxc due to Existential specification, then the next step of deducing $\forall x Pxc$ is not allowed since in the premise (new) Pxc, the variable x is free. On the other hand, if this Pxc is not a premise, then it must have been inferred from an existing premise, which is not so, since $\exists y Pxy$ does not entail Pxc.

Exercises for § 6.5

Prove the following.

1. Theorem 6.14 by using FC.
2. Theorems 6.15-6.16 by using FL.
3. All laws in Theorem 6.17.
4. Theorems 6.18-6.20.
5. For a set of formulas Σ, and formulas A, B write $\Sigma[A :=_e B] = \{Y[A :=_e B] : Y \in \Sigma\}$. If $\Sigma \vDash X$ for a formula X, then $\Sigma[A :=_e B] \vDash X[A :=_e B]$.

6. Let Σ be a set of formulas, and let Y be any formula. For each propositional variable p occurring in $\Sigma \cup \{Y\}$, identify a formula X_p. Write $\Sigma[p := X_p] = \{A[p := X_p] : A \in \Sigma\}$. If $\Sigma \vDash Y$, then $\Sigma[p := X_p] \vDash Y[p := X_p]$.
7. Let Σ be a set of formulas, X, Y formulas, and let α be a constant or a variable that does not occur in any formula of $\Sigma \cup \{X, Y\}$. If $\Sigma \vDash \exists x X$ and $\Sigma \cup \{X[x/\alpha]\} \vDash Y$, then $\Sigma \vDash Y$.

6.6 QUASI-PROOFS IN FL

Analogous to PL, quasi-proofs can be adopted to FL. However, you have to be a bit careful in tackling closed and open formulas. When open formulas are introduced as conditional hypotheses, we must remember the free variables introduced by them. On these free variables, we cannot apply Universal Generalization before the application of the deduction theorem is over. This amounts to asserting that all those formulas inside this block of DTB-DTE possibly depend on these free variables; we record it by writing the pair as DTBx-DTEx. The restriction on the use of Universal Generalization is at work!

Similarly, for applications of the law of existential specification we use blocks ESB-ESE. We also document the line number of the existential premise used to start and close this block. Also, remember that the formula introduced at the line documented ESB is an extra premise; its conditionality remains until its corresponding ESE is met. We cannot thus use the rule UG inside this block of ESB-ESE on all those variables (including the new constant) that occur free in the formula introduced by ESB. If the new constant is α and the variables occurring free in the formula introduced by BSB are $x, y, z, \ldots$, then we write the pair ESB-ESE as ESB$\alpha, x, y, z, \ldots$-ESE$\alpha, x, y, z, \ldots$.

EXAMPLE 6.17. We use the idea explained in Example 6.15 to develop a quasi-proof of $\exists x \forall y Pxy \vDash \forall y \exists x Pxy$.

1.	$\exists x \forall y Pxy$	P
2.	$\forall y Pcy$	1, ESBc
3.	Pcy	2,US
4.	$\exists x Pxy$	3, EG
5.	$\exists x Pxy$	2, 4, ESEc
6.	$\forall x \exists y Pxy$	5, UG

The following incorrect quasi-proof tries to justify $\forall x \exists y Pxy \vDash \exists y \forall x Pxy$.

1.	$\forall x \exists y Pxy$	P
2.	$\exists y Pxy$	1, US
3.	Pxc	2, ESBc, x
4.	$\forall x Pxc$	3, UG
5.	$\exists y \forall x Pxy$	4, EG
6.	$\exists x \forall y Pxy$	3, 5, ESEc, x

This is a faulty quasi-proof since in Line 4, we cannot generalize on x that occurs free in the (extra) premise of Line 3.

EXAMPLE 6.18. Construct a quasi-proof of $\forall x \forall y Pxy \vDash \forall y Pyy$.

1.	$\forall x \forall y Pxy$	P
2.	$\forall y Pyy$	1, US$[x/y]$

The variable y is not free for x in the formula $\forall y Pxy$. Thus the substitution $[x/y]$ is not admissible; therefore, the attempted quasi-proof is a faulty one. A correct quasi-proof for $\forall x \forall y Pxy \vDash \forall y Pyy$ first instantiates and then generalizes.

1.	$\forall x \forall y Pxy$	P
2.	$\forall y Pxy$	1, US
3.	Pxx	2, US
4.	$\forall x Pxx$	3, UG
5.	$\forall y Pyy$	4, Renaming

EXAMPLE 6.19. Construct a quasi-proof for showing that the following argument is correct:

> Some mathematicians like all logicians. No mathematician likes any fashion designer. Therefore, no logician is a fashion designer.

Use the vocabulary – Mx: x is a mathematician, Lx,: x is a logician, Fx: x is a fashion designer, and Pxy: x likes y. The argument is translated to the following FL-consequence:

$$\exists x(Mx \wedge \forall y(Ly \to Pxy)),\ \forall x(Mx \to \forall y(Fy \to \neg Pxy))\ !\vdash\ \forall x(Lx \to \neg Fx).$$

A quasi-proof of validity of the consequence goes as follows:

1.	$\exists x(Mx \wedge \forall y(Ly \to Pxy))$	P
2.	$Mc \wedge \forall y(Ly \to Pcy)$	1, ESBc
3.	$\forall y(Ly \to Pcy)$	2, T
4.	$Lx \to Pcx$	3, US ($[y/x]$)
5.	$\forall x(Mx \to \forall y(Fy \to \neg Pxy))$	P
6.	$Mc \to \forall y(Fy \to \neg Pcy)$	5, US ($[x/c]$)
7.	Mc	2, T
8.	$\forall y(Fy \to \neg Pcy)$	6, 7, T
9.	$Fx \to \neg Pcx$	8, US ($[y/x]$)
10.	Lx	DTBx
11.	Pcx	4, 10, T
12.	$\neg Fx$	9, 11, T
13.	$Lx \to \neg Fx$	10, 12, DTEx
14.	$Lx \to \neg Fx$	1, 13, ESEc
15.	$\forall x(Lx \to \neg Fx)$	13, UG

In the quasi-proof, the conditional hypothesis Lx is introduced in Line 10 while marking the free variable x on the right of DTB on the documentation column. It says that we are not allowed to universally quantify on this *flagged variable* x until the conditionality of Lx is over. In Lines 10 to 12, we are not allowed to generalize on the variable x, since, possibly those formulas use a premise (namely, that on Line 10) where x is a free variable. Since on Line 13, the block of DTB-DTE is over; we mark x on the right of DTE. Then after, We are allowed to use UG with the variable x.

Since the formula on Line 13 has no occurrence of the *new constant* c introduced in Line 2, we repeat it in Line 14 and document it by $1, 13, \text{ESE}c$. Here, the formula on Line 1 is the existential premise used outside the block. Finally, universal generalization is applied to obtain the required conclusion.

Form a quasi-proof, an actual FC-proof can always be constructed. Compared to an FC-proof a quasi-proof is intuitive.

EXAMPLE 6.20. Justify the following argument (Stoll (1963)) by a quasi-proof:

> Everyone who buys a ticket receives a prize. Therefore, if there are no prizes, then nobody buys a ticket.

Notice that the phrase 'buys a ticket' is used as it is, whereas 'receives a prize' needs to be broken down since in the conclusion we require to symbolize 'there are no prizes'. With Bx: x buys a ticket, Px: x is a prize, Rxy: x receives y, we have the FL-consequence:

$$\forall x(Bx \to \exists y(Py \wedge Rxy)) \,!\!\vdash \neg\exists yPy \to \neg\exists xBx.$$

The following quasi-proof shows that the consequence is valid.

1.	$\forall x(Bx \to \exists y(Py \wedge Rxy))$	P
2.	$\exists xBx$	DTB
3.	Bc	$2, \text{ESB}c$
4.	$Bc \to \exists y(Py \wedge Rcy)$	$1, \text{US}$
5.	$\exists y(Py \wedge Rcy)$	$3, 4, \text{MP}$
6.	$Pd \wedge Rcd$	$5, \text{ESB}d$
7.	Pd	6, Elimination
8.	$\exists yPy$	$7, \text{EG}$
9.	$\exists yPy$	$5, 8, \text{ESE}d$
10.	$\exists yPy$	$3, 9, \text{ESE}c$
11.	$\exists xBx \to \exists yPy$	$2, 10, \text{DTE}$
12.	$\neg\exists yPy \to \neg\exists xBx$	11, Contraposition

If we decide to break down the phrase 'buys a ticket' as we treated the phrase 'receives a prize', then instead of the unary predicate B we use Tx: x is a ticket, Bxy: x buys y. The corresponding consequence is

$$\forall x(\exists z(Tz \wedge Bxz) \to \exists y(Py \wedge Rxy)) \,!\!\vdash \neg\exists yPy \to \neg\exists xBx.$$

A quasi-proof can be constructed to show that this consequence is valid.

EXAMPLE 6.21. We show that $\vDash \neg\exists y\forall x(Pxy \leftrightarrow \neg Pxx)$.

1.	$\exists y\forall x(Pxy \leftrightarrow \neg Pxx)$	RAB
2.	$\forall x(Pxc \leftrightarrow \neg Pxx)$	$\text{ESB}c$
3.	$Pcc \leftrightarrow \neg Pcc$	US
4.	$\bot$	PL
5.	$\bot$	$\text{ESE}c$
6.	$\neg\exists y\forall x(Pxy \leftrightarrow \neg Pxx)$	RAE

In Example 6.21, interpreting Pxy as $x \in y$ for sets x, y, it follows that there exists no set of all sets.

The same restriction using flagged variables in DTB-DTE applies to RAB-RAE pair. You can formulate them and use in solving the exercises given below. In addition, you must also restrict the nesting of these pairs as in PC; that is, the nestings should not overlap, though one completely lying inside another is allowed.

Exercises for § 6.6

1. For each of the following consequences, construct a quasi-proof, or a falsifying interpretation.

   (a) $\forall x P(x) \,!\!\vdash \forall y P(y)$ (b) $Pc \,!\!\vdash \forall x(x \approx c \to Px)$

   (c) $\forall x \forall y Pxy \,!\!\vdash \forall x \forall y Pyx$ (d) $\varnothing \,!\!\vdash \exists x(Px \to \forall x Px)$

   (e) $\exists x \exists y P(x,y) \,!\!\vdash \exists z \exists u P(z,u)$ (f) $\exists x \forall y P(x,y) \,!\!\vdash \forall y \exists x P(x,y)$

   (g) $\exists x Px \vee \exists x Qx \,!\!\vdash \exists x(Px \vee Qx)$ (h) $\forall x \forall y P(x,y) \,!\!\vdash \forall z \forall u P(z,u)$

   (i) $\forall x Px \vee \forall x Qx \,!\!\vdash \forall x(Px \vee Qx)$ (j) $\exists x(Px \wedge Qx) \,!\!\vdash \exists x Px \wedge \exists x Qx$

   (k) $\forall x(Px \wedge Qx) \,!\!\vdash \forall x Px \to \forall x Qx$ (l) $\forall x(Px \wedge Qx) \,!\!\vdash \forall x Px \wedge \forall x Qx$

   (m) $\forall x \forall y(Py \to Qx) \,!\!\vdash \exists y Py \to \forall x Qx$ (n) $\forall x(Px \to Qx) \,!\!\vdash \forall x \neg Qx \to \forall x \neg Px$

   (o) $\forall x(Px \to \neg Qx) \,!\!\vdash \neg(\exists x(Px \wedge Qx))$

   (p) $\{\exists x \exists y(Pxy \vee Pyx), \neg \exists x Pxx\} \,!\!\vdash \exists x \exists y \neg(x \approx y)$

   (q) $S \to \forall x Px \,!\!\vdash \forall x(S \to Px)$, for any sentence S.

   (r) $X \to \forall x Px \,!\!\vdash \forall x(X \to Px)$, if x is not free in X

   (s) $\{\forall x Paxx, \forall x \forall y \forall z(Pxyz \to Pf(x)yf(z))\} \,!\!\vdash Pf(a)af(a)$

   (t) $\{\forall x Paxx, \forall x \forall y \forall z(Pxyz \to Pf(x)yf(z))\} \,!\!\vdash \exists z Pf(a)zf(f(a))$

   (u) $\{\forall x Pcx, \forall x \forall y(Pxy \to Pf(x)f(y))\} \,!\!\vdash \exists z(Pcz \wedge Pzf(f(c)))$

2. Let X and Y be formulas. Construct quasi-proofs for the following:

   (a) $\vdash \forall x(X \wedge Y) \leftrightarrow \forall x X \wedge \forall Y$ (b) $\vdash \exists x(X \vee Y) \leftrightarrow \exists x X \vee \exists x Y$

   (c) $\vdash \forall x X \vee \forall x Y \to \forall x(X \vee Y)$ (d) $\vdash \exists x(X \wedge Y) \to \exists x X \wedge \exists x Y$

3. Symbolize and try to construct a quasi-proof of the following argument given by Lewis Carroll:

   Babies are illogical. Nobody is despised who can manage a crocodile. Illogical persons are despised. Therefore, babies cannot manage crocodiles.

6.7 SUMMARY AND PROBLEMS

To avoid circularity in the semantical method, we have tried to model reasoning axiomatically. For first order logic, we have constructed the axiomatic system FC as an extension of PC. All tautologies of PC could be imported to FC as theorems via tautological replacements. In addition to other replacement laws, we have also proved monotonicity, deduction theorem, and reductio ad absurdum. FC has been shown to be adequate to FL; that is, the set of valid FL-consequences coincide with the set of FC-provable consequences.

The finiteness of a proof in FC is translated to compactness of FL, as in PC and PL. Though compactness is straight forward, its applications to construction of non-standard models is surprising. We have shown that nonstandard models of arithmetic implies the existence of infinite numbers. Similarly, existence of infinitesimals could be shown by way of constructing nonstandard models of the real number system.

You can find the axiomatic systems PC and FC in almost all texts in logic, though in different incarnations; see for example, Barwise & Etchemendy (1999), Ebbinghaus et al. (1994), Enderton (1972), Ershov & Palyutin (1984), Mates (1972), Mendelson (1979), Rautenberg (2010), Shoenfield (1967), Singh & Goswami (1998), Smullyan (2014), and Srivastava (2013). The one presented here is made up from the axiomatic systems considered in Bilaniuk (1999), and Singh & Goswami (1998). The completeness proof for the systems follows the ideas of many logicians such as L. Henkin, J. Hintikka, G. Hasenjaeger, A. Lindenbaum, and K. Gödel; their relevant works can be found in van Heijenoort (1967). For nonstandard analysis, see Robinson (1996), a book by its creator. The quasi-proofs, which are in fact pre-proofs or abbreviated proofs, follow the ideas presented in Copi (1979), Mates (1972), Stoll (1963), and Suppes (1957).

Problems for Chapter 6

1. Let X and Y be formulas. Show the following:
   (a) If $\vdash X \to Y$, then $\vdash \forall x X \to \forall x Y$.
   (b) In general, it is not true that $X \to Y \vdash \forall x X \to \forall x Y$.

   Do (a)-(b) contradict the Deduction theorem? Why or why not?
2. Show that there does not exist a formula X such that $\vdash X$ and $\vdash \neg X$.
3. Show that $\Sigma \cup \{A\}$ is consistent iff $\Sigma \cup \{\neg\neg A\}$ is consistent, without using RA and DT.
4. Let Σ be a consistent set of formulas, and let X be a formula such that $\Sigma \nvdash X$. Show that $\Sigma \cup \{\forall^* X\}$ is consistent. [$\forall^*$ denotes the universal closure.]
5. Uniform replacement can be introduced structurally. Let σ be a function from the set of all atomic propositions to the set of all formulas, FORM. Extend σ to a function from the set of all propositions PROP to FORM by:
   $$\sigma(\top) = \top,\ \sigma(\bot) = \bot,\ \sigma(\neg A) = \neg\sigma(A), \text{ and}$$
   $$\sigma(A \star B) = (\sigma(A) \star \sigma(B)) \text{ for } \star \in \{\wedge, \vee, \to, \leftrightarrow\}.$$

   Let X be any formula. Show that $\sigma(X) = X[p := \sigma(p)]$, for each propositional variable p occurring in X.
6. A set Σ of sentences is called *finitely satisfiable* iff every finite subset of Σ is satisfiable. Show that if S is any set of sentences and X is any sentence, then at least one of the sets $S \cup \{X\}$ or $S \cup \{\neg X\}$ is finitely satisfiable.
7. Show that a set Σ of formulas is maximally consistent iff for each formula Y, either $Y \in \Sigma$ or $\neg Y \in \Sigma$. Conclude that a maximally consistent set Γ contains all consequences of Γ.
8. A set Σ of formulas is called *negation complete* iff for each formula w, either $\Sigma \vdash w$ or $\Sigma \vdash \neg w$. Show that each consistent set of formulas is a subset of a negation complete set.

9. For an interpretation I, the *theory of an interpretation* is defined as the set of all sentences true in I, i.e., $Th(I) = \{S : I \vDash S \text{ and } S \text{ is a sentence}\}$. Show that for any interpretation I, $Th(I)$ is maximally consistent.
10. Assume compactness of FL and that the set of all FC-theorems coincide with the set of all valid formulas. Let Σ be any set of formulas, and let X be any formula. Prove that if $\Sigma \vDash X$ then $\Sigma \vdash X$.
11. Can you find a formula which is true in some non-denumerable domain but not satisfiable in any denumerable domain?
12. Prove that if $\Sigma \vdash X$, then there exists a proof of $\Sigma \vdash X$ in which if a predicate occurs, then it must have occurred in $\Sigma \cup \{X\}$.
13. Let P be a unary predicate. Is the set $\{\exists x_0 \neg P x_0,\ P x_1,\ P x_2, \ldots\}$ consistent?
14. Prove *Skolem-Löwenheim Theorem*: If a first order formula has a model, then it has a countable model.
15. Let e be a constant, and let $\circ$ be a 2-place function symbol, which is written in infix notation. Let G be the set of sentences

$$\forall x(x \circ e \approx x),\ \forall x \exists y(x \circ y \approx e),\ \forall x \forall y(x \circ y \approx y \circ x),\ \forall x \forall y \forall z((x \circ y) \circ z \approx x \circ (y \circ z)),$$

$$\forall x(x \circ x \approx e),\ \exists x_1 \cdots \exists x_n \Big(\bigwedge_{1 \le i < j \le n} \neg(x_i \approx x_j)\Big) \quad \text{for each } n \ge 2.$$

Any model of G is an abelian group with at least n elements, where each element is of order 2. In fact abelian groups with 2^k elements exist where each element is of order 2. Deduce that there exists an infinite abelian group where each element is of order 2.
16. Can you give an infinite abelian group where each element is of order 2?
17. Show that there exists an infinite bipartite graph.
18. Show that if the nesting of DT and/or RA are allowed to overlap, then an invalid consequence can have a quasi-proof of validity.
19. Construct a quasi-proof to show that $\{\forall x(Px \wedge Qx \to Rx) \to \exists x(Px \wedge \neg Qx),$ $\forall x(Px \to Qx) \vee \forall x(Px \to Rx)\} \vDash \forall x(Px \wedge Rx \to Qx) \to \exists x(Px \wedge Qx \wedge \neg Rx)$.
20. Analogous to MPC, you can construct a proof system **MFC** adding the following axiom and rules to MPC [See Problem 14 in Chapter 4]:

(US) $\dfrac{\Sigma \vdash \forall x X}{\Sigma \vdash X[x/t]}$ provided t is free for x in X.

(UG) $\dfrac{\Sigma \vdash X}{\Sigma \vdash \forall x X}$ provided x is not free in Σ.

(EA) $\Sigma \vdash (t \approx t)$ for each term t.

(EQ) $\dfrac{\Sigma \vdash s \approx t \qquad \Sigma \vdash X[x/s]}{\Sigma \vdash X[x/t]}$ provided s, t are free for x in X.

(a) In MFC, show that $\vdash \neg(\forall x X \to Y) \to \forall x \neg(X \to Y)$ if x is not free in Y.
(b) Give MFC-proofs of all consequences in Examples 6.1-6.11.
(c) Prove adequacy of the proof system MFC to FL.

Chapter 7

Clausal Forms and Resolution

7.1 PRENEX FORM

Theorem 5.4 asserts that if we require only satisfiability of a formula, then it is enough to consider its existential closure. Similarly, validity of a formula can be decided by the validity of its universal closure. Looking from a different perspective, if a formula has all its quantifiers in the beginning, and all of them are universal quantifiers, then we may omit all those quantifiers to obtain another formula. Now, both these formulas are either valid together or invalid together. Similarly, if all quantifiers are existential, and if all of them occur in the beginning, then their omission preserves satisfiability.

It is quite possible that we may not be able to express every sentence in the form where all quantifiers are in the beginning, and all of those are of the same type. For instance, $\forall x \exists y Pxy$ is not equivalent to either $\forall x \forall y Pxy$ or $\exists x \exists y Pxy$. But can we express each formula in a form where all quantifiers are in the beginning?

Can we bring all the quantifiers of $\forall xPx \to \forall xQx$ to the beginning, preserving equivalence? We may not write $\forall xPx \to \forall xQx \equiv \forall x(Px \to Qx)$ as x occurs in $\forall xQx$. The law of distributivity says that $\forall xX \to Y \equiv \exists x(X \to Y)$ if x does not occur in Y. Renaming the variable x in the subformula $\forall xQx$ as y, we can write the formula as $\forall xPx \to \forall yQy$. Consequently, distributivity will give us $\exists x(Px \to \forall yQy)$, and then, $\forall y \exists x(Px \to Qy)$, or $\exists x \forall y(Px \to Qy)$. The renaming of bound variables here is called **rectification**.

A formula is called **rectified** if no variable in it is both free and bound, and each occurrence of a quantifier uses a different variable. A formula is said to be in **prenex form** if all occurrences of quantifiers in it are in the beginning, i.e., if it is in the form $Q_1x_1Q_2x_2 \cdots Q_nx_nX$ with $Q_i \in \{\forall, \exists\}$, for each i, and X contains neither $\forall$ nor $\exists$. The string of quantifiers $Q_1x_1Q_2x_2 \cdots Q_nx_n$ is called the **prefix** and the quantifier-free sub-formula X is called the **matrix** of the prenex form $Q_1x_1Q_2x_2 \cdots Q_nx_nX$.

Observe that a formula can always be rectified by using the law of renaming. In fact, it becomes a prerequisite for bringing a formula to its prenex form in certain cases.

EXAMPLE 7.1. The formula $\forall x(Px \to Qy \wedge \exists xQx)$ is not a rectified formula as there are two occurrences of quantifiers using the same variable x.

In the formula $\forall x(Px \to Qy \wedge \exists yQy)$, different occurrences of quantifiers use different variables; but y is both free and bound. So, this is not a rectified formula. Note that free variables cannot be renamed if you want to preserve equivalence.

The formula $\forall x(Px \to Qy \wedge \exists zQz)$ is rectified, but there are occurrences of other symbols to the left of an occurrence of a quantifier. So, it is not in prenex form.

The formula $\forall x\exists z(Px \to Qy \wedge Qz)$ is in prenex form, where the prefix is $\forall x\exists z$ and the matrix is $(Px \to Qy \wedge Qz)$.

EXAMPLE 7.2. Consider the formula $\forall xPx \leftrightarrow \forall xQx$. Renaming the x in $\forall xQx$ as y, we have $\forall xPx \leftrightarrow \forall yQy$. For using distributivity, we eliminate $\leftrightarrow$ to obtain $(\forall xPx \to \forall yQy) \wedge (\forall yQy \to \forall xPx)$. But the formula is not rectified; we need renaming once more. Renaming y to u, and x to v in $(\forall yQy \to \forall xPx)$, we get

$$(\forall xPx \to \forall yQy) \wedge (\forall uQu \to \forall vPv).$$

Notice that had we chosen to eliminate $\leftrightarrow$ before renaming the bound variables, then the second use of renaming could have been avoided. In this case, from $\forall xPx \leftrightarrow \forall xQx$ we obtain $(\forall xPx \to \forall xQx) \wedge (\forall xQx \to \forall xPx)$. Then renaming would give $(\forall xPx \to \forall yQy) \wedge (\forall uQu \to \forall vPv)$ as earlier. Next, we use the laws of distributivity to obtain the prenex form

$$\exists x\forall y\exists u\forall v((Px \to Qy) \wedge (Qu \to Pv)).$$

It has the prefix $\exists x\forall y\exists u\forall v$ and matrix $((Px \to Qy) \wedge (Qu \to Pv))$.

The following result shows that every formula has a prenex form.

Theorem 7.1 (Prenex Form). *For each formula X, a formula Y in prenex form can be constructed so that the set of free variables of X is sme as that of Y, and $X \equiv Y$.*

Proof. We describe a procedure for converting a formula to prenex form. The procedure first eliminates $\leftrightarrow$. Next, it rectifies the formula using renaming of bound variables. Finally, the quantifiers are pulled to the beginning by using various laws. (We use the symbol $:=$ in procedures for assigning a new value to a variable, as in programming languages.)

PROCEDURE ***PrenForm***

Input: A formula X

Output: A prenex form formula equivalent to X

1. Eliminate $\leftrightarrow$ using $A \leftrightarrow B \equiv (A \to B) \wedge (B \to A)$ on all subformulas of X.
2. Rename the bound variables to rectify X (After this step, X is assumed to be a rectified formula).
3. Move $\neg$ to precede the predicates by using the laws of implication, double negation, and De Morgan, that is, the equivalences:

$$\neg(A \to B) \equiv A \wedge \neg B, \qquad \neg(A \vee B) \equiv \neg A \wedge \neg B, \qquad \neg(A \wedge B) \equiv \neg A \vee \neg B,$$
$$\neg\neg A \equiv A, \qquad \neg\exists xA \equiv \forall x\neg A, \qquad \neg\forall xA \equiv \exists x\neg A.$$

4. Pull out the quantifiers using the laws of distributivity, that is, the equivalences (x does not occur in B as the formula is rectified):

$$\begin{array}{lll} \forall xA \to B \equiv \exists x(A \to B), & \exists xA \to B \equiv \forall x(A \to B), \\ B \to \forall xA \equiv \forall x(B \to A), & B \to \exists xA \equiv \exists x(B \to A), \\ \forall xA \wedge B \equiv \forall x(A \wedge B), & \exists xA \wedge B \equiv \exists x(A \wedge B), \\ \forall xA \vee B \equiv \forall x(A \vee B), & \exists x(A \vee B) \equiv \exists xA \vee B. \end{array}$$

Use induction on the number of occurrences of connectives and quantifiers in X to show that the procedure *PrenForm* converts a formula into a prenex form, preserving equivalence. Clearly, prenex form conversion does not change the set of free variables. ◆

EXAMPLE 7.3. Construct a prenex form formula equivalent to

$$A = \exists z(Pxy \to \neg\forall y(Qy \wedge Ryz)) \wedge (Qx \to \forall xSx).$$

The connective $\leftrightarrow$ does not occur in A; so, we rectify A by renaming the bound variables if needed. Both y and x occur free and also bound in A. Rename the bound variables: y as v, and x as u. The formula so obtained is

$$B = \exists z(Pxy \to \neg\forall v(Qv \wedge Rvz)) \wedge (Qx \to \forall uSu).$$

Now, B is rectified. Start moving $\neg$ closer to the predicates, by using the equivalences in Step 3 in *PrenForm*. You obtain an equivalent formula

$$C = \exists z(Pxy \to \exists v(\neg Qv \vee \neg Rvz)) \wedge (Qx \to \forall uSu)$$

Next, pull the quantifiers to the left using the equivalences in Step 4. You get the formula

$$G = \forall u\exists z\exists v((Pxy \to \neg Qv \vee \neg Rvz) \wedge (Qx \to Su)).$$

This is in prenex form with prefix $\forall u\exists z\exists v$ and matrix

$$(Pxy \to \neg Qv \vee \neg Rvz) \wedge (Qx \to Su).$$

Note that you could also have brought C to the formula

$$H = \exists z\exists v\forall u((Qx \to Su) \wedge (Pxy \to \neg Qv \vee \neg Rvz)).$$

Are the formulas G and H really equivalent?

EXAMPLE 7.4. Find a prenex form for the formula

$$\exists x(Px \to \neg\exists y(Py \to (Qx \to Qy)) \wedge \forall x(Px \leftrightarrow \forall yQz)).$$

We use equivalences to obtain:

$$\begin{aligned} &\exists x(Px \to \neg\exists y(Py \to (Qx \to Qy)) \wedge \forall x(Px \leftrightarrow \forall yQz)) \\ &\equiv \exists x(Px \to \neg\exists y(Py \to (Qx \to Qy))) \wedge \forall x((Px \to \forall yQz) \wedge (\forall yQz \to Px)) \\ &\equiv \exists x(Px \to \forall y(Py \wedge Qx \wedge \neg Qy)) \wedge \forall u(\forall v(Pu \to Qz) \wedge \exists w(Qz \to Pu)) \\ &\equiv \exists x(\forall y(Px \to (Py \wedge Qx \wedge \neg Qy)) \wedge \forall u\forall v\exists w((Pu \to Qz) \wedge (Qz \to Pu))) \\ &\equiv \exists x\forall y\forall u\forall v\exists w((Px \to Py \wedge Qx \wedge \neg Qy) \wedge (Pu \to Qz) \wedge (Qz \to Pu)). \end{aligned}$$

It is in prenex form with prefix $\exists x \forall y \forall u \forall v \exists w$ and matrix

$$((Px \to Py \wedge Qx \wedge \neg Qy) \wedge (Pu \to Qz) \wedge (Qz \to Pu)).$$

Point out the suitable law applied at each line, and identify the appropriate step of the procedure *PrenForm* in the above equivalences.

Exercises for § 7.1

1. Try other ways of bringing to prenex form the formula in Example 7.4, where the prefix may be having a different order of occurrences of $\exists$ and $\forall$, proceeding in a different way after the third line in the solution. Give semantic arguments as to why your answer is equivalent to the one obtained in the text.
2. Complete the proof of Theorem 7.1.
3. Convert the following formulas into prenex form:
   (a) $\forall Px \leftrightarrow \exists xQx$
   (b) $\exists xPx \wedge \exists xQx \to Rx$
   (c) $\forall x \forall y(Pxyz \wedge (\forall x \forall y Qyu \to Rx))$
   (d) $\forall xPxf \wedge (\forall xQx \to \exists y \neg Qx) \vee \forall x \exists y Pxy$
   (e) $\forall x(\exists yPxy \wedge Qy) \to (\exists y(Ry \wedge Uxy) \to Qy)$
   (f) $(\neg \forall x \neg \forall y \neg \forall z Pxy \to \exists x \exists y(\neg \exists z Qxyz \leftrightarrow Rxy))$
   (g) $\exists x(Px \wedge \forall y(Qy \leftrightarrow Rxy)) \wedge \forall x(Px \to \forall y(Uy \to \neg Rxy))$
   (h) $\forall x(Px \leftrightarrow \forall y(Py \to \exists x(Qx \to Qy)) \wedge \exists zPz) \vee \forall x(Px \to \exists yQz)$

7.2 QUANTIFIER-FREE FORMS

Next, we wish to get rid of the quantifiers. Write $X(x)$ for recording the fact that the variable x occurs free in the formula X. From $\forall xX(x)$, we can simply drop $\forall x$ resulting in $X(x)$ only. Of course, dropping the universal quantifier here means that $\forall xX(x)$ is valid iff $X(x)$ is valid. Alternatively, we may drop $\exists x$ from $\exists xX(x)$, since $\exists xX(x)$ is satisfiable iff $X(x)$ is satisfiable. Look at the following example.

EXAMPLE 7.5. Let c be a constant that does not occur in the formula $X(x)$. Write $X(c)$ for the formula $X(x)[x/c]$. Show the following:

(1) $X(x)$ is valid iff $X(c)$ is valid.
(2) $X(x)$ is satisfiable iff $X(c)$ is satisfiable.
(3) $\exists xX(x)$ is satisfiable iff $X(x)$ is satisfiable iff $X(c)$ is satisfiable.
(4) $\forall xX(x)$ is valid iff $X(x)$ is valid iff $X(c)$ is valid.
(5) If $\forall xX(x)$ is satisfiable, then both $X(x)$ and $X(c)$ are satisfiable.
(6) If one of $X(x)$ or $X(c)$ is satisfiable, then $\exists xX(x)$ is satisfiable.
(7) $X(c)$ is satisfiable does not imply that $\forall xX(x)$ is satisfiable.
(8) $X(x)$ is satisfiable does not imply that $\forall xX(x)$ is satisfiable.
(9) $\exists xX(x)$ is valid does not imply that $X(c)$ is valid.
(10) $\exists xX(x)$ is valid does not imply that $X(x)$ is valid.

We use the substitution lemma without mentioning explicitly.

(1) Suppose $X(x)$ is valid. Let $I_\ell = (D, \phi, \ell)$ be a state. Let $\ell(c) = d \in D$. Then $I_\ell \vDash X(c)$ iff $I_{\ell[x \mapsto d]} \vDash X(x)$. Since $X(x)$ is valid, $I_{\ell[x \mapsto d]} \vDash X(x)$. So, $I_\ell \vDash X(c)$. Since any such $I_\ell \vDash X(c)$, $X(c)$ is valid.

Conversely, let $X(c)$ be valid. Let $I_\ell = (D, \phi, \ell)$ be a state. Let $\ell(x) = d \in D$. Consider an assignment function ℓ' that agrees with ℓ except at c and $\ell'(c) = d$. Since $X(c)$ is valid, the state (D, ϕ, ℓ') satisfies $X(c)$. As $\ell(x) = \ell'(c) = d$, the state I_ℓ satisfies $X(x)$. That is, each state satisfies $X(x)$. Therefore, $X(x)$ is valid.

(2) Similar to the proof of (1).

(3)-(4) The proofs of the first 'iff' are shown in the proof of Theorem 5.4. The second 'iff' parts follow from (1)-(2).

(5) $\forall x X(x) \vDash X(c)$. Therefore, satisfiability of $\forall x X(x)$ implies that of $X(c)$. Similar is the case for $X(x)$.

(6) Similar to the proof of (5).

(7) Take $X(x) = Px \wedge \neg \forall y Py$, $I_\ell = (\mathbb{N}, \phi, \ell)$, where $\phi(P)$ is the set of all prime numbers, and $\ell(c) = \phi(c) = 2$. Since $2 \in \phi(P)$, and all natural numbers are not prime, $I_\ell \vDash X(c)$. However, $\forall x X(x) \equiv \forall x Px \wedge \neg \forall y Py$, which is unsatisfiable.

(8) Similar to the proof of (7). Also, it follows from (1) and (7).

(9) Let $X(x) = Qx \vee \neg \exists y Qy$. Then $\exists x X(x) \equiv \exists x Qx \vee \neg \exists y Qy$, which is valid. Take $J_\ell = (\mathbb{N}, \psi, \ell')$, with $\psi(Q)$ as the set of all composite numbers. Let $\ell'(c) = \psi(c) = 2$. Since 2 is not a composite number and there are composite numbers, $J_\ell \nvDash X(x)$. That is, $X(x)$ is invalid.

(10) It follows from (2) and (9).

Example 7.5(3) says that for preserving satisfiability, we may eliminate all existential quantifiers from the beginning of the formula by replacing the occurrences of those variables with suitable constants (or terms, in general). Similarly, Part (4) implies that to preserve validity, we may eliminate the universal quantifiers. We discuss both the cases, in turn.

Suppose we want satisfiability to be preserved. Due to Theorem 5.4, we consider the existential closure of the given formula to reach at a sentence X, which we assume to be in prenex form.

We find out the first occurrence of $\exists$ in the prefix of the prenex form sentence X. Suppose this $\exists$ uses the variable x. We determine the dependence of x on other variables by considering all those variables used by the universal quantifiers to the left of it. From among those we choose a variable only when it is used along with x in some predicate occurring in the formula. If there are k such variables, say, $x_{i1}, \ldots, x_{ik}$ on which x depends, then we introduce a new k-ary function symbol g and replace every occurrence of x in the matrix of the formula by the term $g(x_{i1}, \ldots, x_{ik})$. We then remove the occurrence $\exists x$ from the prefix.

This step is repeated until all occurrences of $\exists$ are eliminated from X. Finally, all occurrences of the universal quantifiers are simply ignored to output the quantifier-free formula X_s. Note that all variables in X_s are now universally quantified. Since the free variables are first existentially quantified, no universal quantifier precedes these existential quantifiers. Therefore, in the process of elimination of existential quantifiers, these variables will be replaced by new constants. The procedure *QuaEli* takes care of this observation by replacing the free variables directly by new constants and then proceeds to eliminate other existential quantifiers.

In *QuaEli* given below, we use $X[x/a,y/b]$ for abbreviating $X[x/a][y/b]$; and use the symbol := for updating the value of a variable as in programming languages.

PROCEDURE ***QuaEli***

Input: A prenex form formula X.
Output: A quantifier-free formula X_s

Let the set of free variables of X be $\{y_1, y_2 \ldots, y_m\}$.
Create 0-ary function symbols $f_1, f_2, \ldots, f_m$ that do not occur in X.
$Y := X[y_1/f_1, y_2/f_2, \ldots, y_m/f_m]$
Let $Y = Q_1x_1Q_2x_2 \cdots Q_nx_nZ$, where Z is quantifier-free.
while $1 \leq i \leq n$ do:
  if $Q_1 = Q_2 = \cdots = Q_{i-1} = \forall$ and $Q_i = \exists$ then let $S_i = \{x_1, \ldots, x_{i-1}\}$
  while $1 \leq j \leq i-1$ do:
    if no atomic subformula of Y contains both x_i, and $x_j \in S_i$, then
      $S_i := S_i \setminus \{x_j\}$
  Let $S_i := \{x_{i1}, \ldots, x_{ik}\}$.
  Create a new k-ary function symbol g_i.
  $Y := Q_1x_1 \cdots Q_{i-1}x_{i-1}Q_{i+1}x_{i+1} \cdots Q_nx_nZ[x_i/g_i(x_{i1}, \ldots, x_{ik})]$
$X_s :=$ matrix of Y

The process of elimination of the existential quantifiers in the procedure *QuaEli* is called **Skolemization**. The quantifier-free form $\bar{X}$ of the formula X computed by *QuaEli* is referred to as the **Skolem form** of the formula X, after the logician T. Skolem, The new function symbols g_i are called **indical functions** or **Skolem functions**, and the terms $g_i(x_{k1}, x_{k2}, \ldots, x_{kj})$ are called **Skolem terms**.

When a machine creates a Skolem term, it simply chooses a function symbol looking at the indices of other function symbols used in the context. For example, if f_1, f_2, f_5 are all the function symbols used in a context, a machine would use f_6 for a Skolem term. In this sense, sometimes, we speak of *the* Skolem term.

We must remember that in arriving at the Skolem form, the free variables in the given formula are treated as if existentially quantified, and finally the free variables that remain in the Skolem form are assumed to be universally quantified.

EXAMPLE 7.6. Find the Skolem form of the prenex form formula

$$X = \forall y \exists z \exists v \forall u((Qx \to Su) \wedge (Pxy \to \neg Qv \vee \neg Rvz)).$$

QuaEli creates a 0-ary function symbol f_1 for replacing the only free variable x. The formula obtained after the replacement is

$$X_1 = \forall y \exists z \exists v \forall u((Qf_1 \to Su) \wedge (Pf_1y \to \neg Qv \vee \neg Rvz)).$$

Next, it finds the first existential quantifier $\exists z$. The set of variables preceding it, which are universally quantified is $S_z = \{y\}$. However, no atomic subformula of X

has both z and y. Hence, $S_z := S_z \setminus \{y\} = \varnothing$. That is, z does not depend upon any other variable; so, z is to be replaced by a new 0-ary function symbol, say, f_2. We update the formula to:

$$X_2 = \forall y \exists v \forall u ((Qf_1 \to Su) \land (Pf_1 y \to \neg Qv \lor \neg Rvf_2)).$$

The above procedure is repeated for $\exists v$. You see that v may depend upon the variable y preceding it; but no atomic subformula contains both v and y. Hence, again, a new constant, say, f_3, is introduced to replace v. The updated formula is

$$X_3 = \forall y \forall u ((Qf_1 \to Su) \land (Pf_1 y \to \neg Qf_3 \lor \neg Rvf_2)).$$

No existential quantifier occurs in the updated formula; we thus drop all $\forall$'s to obtain the (quantifier-free) Skolem form formula

$$X_s = (Qf_1 \to Su) \land (Pf_1 y \to \neg Qf_3 \lor \neg Rf_3 f_2).$$

EXAMPLE 7.7. Use *QuaEli* to get a quantifier-free formula for

$$Y = \exists x \forall y \forall u \forall v \exists w ((Px \to Py \land Qx \land \neg Qy) \land (Pu \to Qz) \land (Qz \to Pu)).$$

For the free variable z, we choose c; and for the existentially quantified variables x, w, we choose the constants a, b, respectively, since there is no predicate having occurrences of w along with any one of y, u, v. Then,

$$Y_s = (Pa \to Py \land Qa \land \neg Qy) \land (Pu \to Qc) \land (Qc \to Pu).$$

Notice that b does not occur in Y_s, since $\exists w$ is a vacuous quantification.

EXAMPLE 7.8. Find Skolem forms of the following sentences:

(a) $\exists z \exists v \forall u \forall x \forall y ((Qxv \to Szu) \land (Pxy \to \neg Qzv \lor \neg Rvz))$

(b) $\forall x \forall y \forall u \exists v \exists z ((Qxv \to Szu) \land (Pxy \to \neg Qzv \lor \neg Rvz))$

(a) No $\forall$ precedes any $\exists$. Thus, existentially quantified variables z, v are replaced by constants b, c, respectively. The Skolem form of the sentence is

$$(Qxc \to Sbu) \land (Pxy \to \neg Qbc \lor \neg Rcb).$$

(b) Out of x, y, u, only x occurs along with v in a predicate. Thus, v is replaced by the Skolem term $f(x)$. Similarly, z is replaced by $g(u)$. The Skolem form is

$$(Qxf(x) \to Sg(u)u) \land (Pxy \to \neg Qg(u)f(x) \lor \neg Rf(x)g(u)).$$

We show that satisfiability is preserved by Skolemization.

Theorem 7.2 (Skolem Form). *A formula is satisfiable if and only if its Skolem form is satisfiable.*

Proof. Given a formula X, use Theorem 7.1 to construct a prenex form formula X_p equivalent to X. Let X_e be the existential closure of X_p. Now, X_p is satisfiable iff X_e is satisfiable. Use Skolemization on X_e to construct the formula X_s. Our aim is to show that X_e is satisfiable iff X_s is satisfiable. Let $I_\ell = (D, \phi, \ell)$ be a state. We use induction on $\nu(X_e)$, the number of occurrences of $\exists$ in X_e, to show the following:

(a) If $I_\ell \models X_s$ then $I_\ell \models X_e$.

(b) If $I_\ell \models X_e$, then there exist extensions ψ of ϕ, and m of ℓ such that the state $J_m = (D, \psi, m)$ satisfies X_s.

In the basis case, $\nu(X_e) = 0$ gives $X_e = X_s$; thus, both (a) and (b) hold trivially. Assume that (induction hypothesis) (a)-(b) hold for any formula A in prenex form whenever $\nu(A) < n$. Let X_e be a formula with $\nu(X_e) = n$. Scan X_e from left to right; find out the first occurrence of $\exists$. Then $X_e = \forall x_1 \ldots \forall x_k \exists x B$ for suitable variables $x_1, \ldots, x_k$, and x. It is possible that $x_1, \ldots, x_k$ are absent altogether; this corresponds to the case $k = 0$. Now, B is a formula in prenex form with $\nu(B) = n - 1$. And $X_s = \forall x_1 \ldots \forall x_k (B[x/t])_s$, where t is a Skolem term. We use the subscript s for denoting Skolemization.

Assume, for simplicity in notation, that each of the variables $x_1, \ldots, x_k$, occurs along with x in some predicate in B. This implies that $t = f(x_1, \ldots, x_k)$ and $(B[x/t])_s = B_s[x/t]$. Assume also that the variable x occurs free in B, ignoring the otherwise trivial case of the vacuous quantifier $\exists x$.

(a) Let $I_\ell \models X_s$. Then for each $d_1, \ldots, d_k \in D$, $I_m \models (B[x/t])_s$, where the valuation $m = \ell[x_1 \mapsto d_1] \cdots [x_k \mapsto d_k]$. Write $m(t) = d$. Since $(B[x/t])_s = B_s[x/t]$ for each $d_1, \ldots, d_k \in D$, $I_{m[x \mapsto d]} \models B_s$. By the induction hypothesis, $I_{m[x \mapsto d]} \models B$ for each $d_1, \ldots, d_k \in D$. Then, $I_\ell \models \forall x_1 \ldots \forall x_k \exists x B$, i.e., $I_\ell \models X_e$.

(b) Suppose $I_\ell \models X_e$. Then, for each $d_1, \ldots, d_k \in D$, there exists $d \in D$ such that $I_{\ell[x_1 \mapsto d_1] \cdots [x_k \mapsto d_k][x \mapsto d]} \models B$. By the induction hypothesis, there are extensions ψ of ϕ, and m of ℓ such that $J_{m[x_1 \mapsto d_1] \cdots [x_k \mapsto d_k][x \mapsto d]} \models B_s$. For interpreting the new function symbol f, extend ψ to ψ', and m to m' by defining

$$\psi'(f)(m(x_1), \ldots, m(x_k)) = d = m'(t).$$

Write $J'_{m'} = (D, \psi', m')$. Then, for each $d_1, \ldots, d_k \in D$, $J'_{m'[x_1 \mapsto d_1] \cdots [x_k \mapsto d_k]} \models B_s[x/t]$. Therefore, $J'_{m'} \models B_s$. The required extension of I_ℓ is $J'_{m'}$. ♦

Notice that we started with a prenex form formula which is already rectified. Had it not been rectified, then the proof of Theorem 7.2 would not have worked. See where exactly it goes wrong. We also assumed, during the proof, that the variables $x_1, \ldots, x_k$ occur along with x in some predicate in B. See that no generality is lost due to this assumption.

The procedure *QuaEli* eliminates all those variables y from the list of universally quantified ones preceding the existentially quantified variable x which do not occur along with x in any predicate in the formula. This brings in a canonical Skolem form. See the following example.

EXAMPLE 7.9. Construct a Skolem form for the sentence $\forall x Px \wedge \exists y Qy$.

$$\forall x Px \wedge \exists y Qy \equiv \exists y Qy \wedge \forall x Px \equiv \exists y (Qy \wedge \forall x Px) \equiv \exists y \forall x (Qy \wedge Px).$$

There is no universal quantifier preceding the $\exists y$ in $\exists y \forall x (Qy \wedge Px)$. Hence y is replaced by a constant, say, c. The Skolem form of the sentence is $Qc \wedge Px$.

Alternatively,

$$\forall x Px \wedge \exists y Qy \equiv \forall x (Px \wedge \exists y Qy) \equiv \forall x \exists y (Px \wedge Qy).$$

In this formula, the variable y possibly depends on x; but there is no predicate having the occurrences of both x and y. Thus, a constant c is chosen as the Skolem term for y and the Skolem formula is $Px \wedge Qc$.

Had this condition of 'occurrence of both the variables in a predicate' not been used in *QuaEli*, the Skolem form of $\forall x \exists y(Px \wedge Qy)$ would have been taken as $Px \wedge Qf(x)$. Notice that satisfiability would still have been preserved but unnecessary dependence of y on x would also have been proclaimed. This is unnecessary since in the process of prenex form conversion, ordering of quantifiers is not canonical. We will see later that absence of an extra function symbol will ease the process of model construction.

For conversion of a formula to a quantifier-free formula preserving validity a similar procedure may be adopted. Look at Example 7.5 once again. In view of *QuaEli*, it suggests the following:

> Let A be a rectified formula in prenex form. Take the universal closure of the resulting formula. Change all occurrences of $\forall$ to $\exists$ and of $\exists$ to $\forall$ simultaneously. Apply *QuaEli*.

Alternatively, you can modify *QuaEli* by treating all $\exists$ as $\forall$ and all $\forall$ as $\exists$. Call the new procedure as ***QuaEli*-$\forall$**. Like *QuaEli*, the free variables are replaced by constants also. Notice that for the validity form, the free variables are universally quantified in the beginning and after the procedure *QuaEli*-$\forall$ has been performed, the remaining free variables are existentially quantified.

The quantifier-free form of a formula X thus obtained is called the **functional form** of X. The functional form is unique, just like the Skolem form, up to the choice of the function symbols. The function symbols are created in a machine sequentially with unique subscripts; so we talk of *the* functional form of a formula.

EXAMPLE 7.10. Let $A = \exists z \exists v \forall u((Qx \to Su) \wedge (Pxy \to \neg Qv \vee \neg Rvz))$. Find the functional form of A, and the Skolem form of $\neg A$.

QuaEli$-\forall$ replaces the free variables x, y by constants a, b, respectively, to obtain

$$\exists z \exists v \forall u((Qa \to Su) \wedge (Pab \to \neg Qv \vee \neg Rvz)).$$

Next, $\exists z$ and $\exists v$ precede $\forall u$, but there is no atomic subformula containing both z, u or both v, u. Hence, we use a new constant c to eliminate $\forall u$, giving

$$\exists z \exists v((Qa \to Sc) \wedge (Pab \to \neg Qv \vee \neg Rvz)).$$

Finally, we simply drop the existential quantifiers to get the functional form

$$A_f = (Qa \to Sc) \wedge (Pab \to \neg Qv \vee \neg Rvz).$$

For the Skolem form of $\neg A$, we first use the law of De Morgan. It gives

$$\neg A \equiv \forall z \forall v \exists u \neg((Qx \to Su) \wedge (Pxy \to \neg Qv \vee \neg Rvz)).$$

We then choose new constants a, b for replacing the free variables x, y. Since there is no predicate in this formula having occurrences either of u, z or of u, v, we choose a new constant c for replacing the existentially quantified variable u. Finally, we drop all the universal quantifiers to obtain the Skolem form

$$(\neg A)_s = \neg((Qa \to Sc) \wedge (Pab \to \neg Qv \vee \neg Rvz)).$$

Compare the functional form A_f of A and the Skolem form $(\neg A)_s$ of $\neg A$ in Example 7.10. It suggests the following result.

Theorem 7.3 (Functional Form). *A formula is valid if and only if its functional form is valid.*

Proof. Let X be a formula, X_p its prenex form, X_m the matrix of X_p, and let X_f be the functional form of X. Denote by $(\neg X)_p$ the prenex form of $\neg X$, by $(\neg X)_m$ the matrix of $(\neg X)_p$, and by $(\neg X)_s$ the Skolem form of $\neg X$.

Due to the law of De Morgan, $(\neg X)_m \equiv \neg X_m$. Comparing the prefix of $(\neg X)_p$ with that of X_p, we see that each quantifier has been changed: each $\forall$ is now $\exists$ and each $\exists$ is now $\forall$, appearing in the same order as per the variables they use. Thus, use of *QuaEli* on $(\neg X)_p$ results in the same formula as using *QuaEli*-$\forall$ on X_p except that an extra $\neg$ is in the beginning. That is, $(\neg X)_s = \neg X_f$.

Now, X is valid iff $\neg X$ is unsatisfiable iff $(\neg X)_s$ is unsatisfiable (by Theorem 7.2) iff $\neg X_f$ is unsatisfiable iff X_f is valid. ♦

We write the universal closure of the Skolem form as X_S; it is called the **satisfiability form** of X. Similarly, the existential closure of the functional form is written as X_V; and it is called the **validity form** of X. The formulas X_S and X_V are computed by *QuaEli* and *QuaEli*-$\forall$, respectively, before finally ignoring the block of quantifiers. Both the forms are commonly referred to as the **sentential forms** of the given formula.

We summarize our results as in the following.

Theorem 7.4 (Sentential Form). *Let X be any formula. Then quantifier-free formulas Y, Z, and sentences $X_S = \forall^* Y$, $X_V = \exists^* Z$ can be constructed so that*

(1) *X is satisfiable iff X_S is satisfiable;*

(2) *X is valid iff X_V is valid.*

Exercises for § 7.2

1. Show that $\forall y \exists x(Px \to Qy) \vDash \exists x \forall y(Px \to Qy)$. Contrast this consequence with $\forall y \exists x(Ax \to Bxy) \nvDash \exists x \forall y(Ax \to Bxy)$.
2. Obtain Skolem form and functional form of the following formulas:
   (a) $\forall x \forall y(Pxyz \wedge (\forall x \forall y Qyu \to Rx))$
   (b) $\forall x Pxf \wedge (\forall x Qx \to \exists y \neg Qx) \vee \forall x \exists y Pxy$
   (c) $\forall x(\exists y Pxy \wedge Qy) \to (\exists y(Ry \wedge Uxy) \to Qy)$
   (d) $\neg \forall x \neg \forall y \neg \forall z Pxy \to \exists x \exists y(\neg \exists z Qxyz \leftrightarrow Rxy)$
   (e) $\exists x(Px \wedge \forall y(Qy \leftrightarrow Rxy)) \wedge \forall x(Px \to \forall y(Uy \to \neg Rxy))$
   (f) $\forall x(Px \leftrightarrow \forall y(Py \to \exists x(Qx \to Qy)) \wedge \exists z Pz) \vee \forall x(Px \to \exists y Qz)$
3. Let the formula X have a prenex form with matrix as Y. When is Y a subformula of X?

4. Show that, in Example 7.6, X is satisfiable iff $\bar{X}$ is satisfiable.
5. Find the Skolem form and the functional form of the formula $\exists y \forall x(Px \to Py)$, and then decide whether it is valid. [Hint: $\exists z(Pf(z) \to Pz)$ is valid or not?]

7.3 CLAUSES

Look at the matrix of a prenex form. You can further use the replacement in tautologies to convert it into either a conjunction of disjunctions or a disjunction of conjunctions, just like the conversion of propositions into cnf or dnf. For this purpose, you have to redefine (or extend to FL) the notions of literals and clauses. Recall that in FL, you have the atomic formulas as $\top$, $\bot$, and $P(t_1, \ldots, t_n)$ for n-ary predicates P and terms $t_1, \ldots, t_n$.

A **literal** is either an atomic formula or negation of an atomic formula. A **conjunctive clause** is a conjunction of literals, and a **disjunctive clause** is a disjunction of literals. A **cnf** is a conjunction of disjunctive clauses, and a **dnf** is a disjunction of conjunctive clauses. A formula in prenex form with its matrix as a cnf is said to be in **pcnf** or in prenex conjunctive normal form, and one whose matrix is in dnf is in **pdnf** or in prenex disjunctive normal form. Both pcnf and pdnf are commonly called **prenex normal forms** or **pnf**.

Your experience with prenex forms and the propositional normal forms will enable you to prove the following theorem easily.

Theorem 7.5 (Prenex Normal Form). *For each formula X, a pcnf formula Y and a pdnf formula Z can be constructed so that $X \equiv Y$ and $X \equiv Z$.*

Let X be a formula. An **scnf** or *Skolem conjunctive normal form* of X is a cnf equivalent to the Skolem form of X. An **sdnf** or *Skolem disjunctive normal form* of X is a dnf equivalent to the Skolem form of X. Both scnf and sdnf of X are called **Skolem normal forms** or **Skolem standard forms** of X. An **fcnf** or *functional conjunctive normal form* of X is a cnf equivalent to the functional form of X. An **fdnf** or *functional disjunctive normal form* of X is a dnf equivalent to the functional form of X. Both fcnf and fdnf of X are called **functional normal forms** or **functional standard forms** of X. It is now obvious that any formula can be converted to a standard form preserving satisfiability or validity as appropriate.

Theorem 7.6 (Standard Form). *For each formula X, formulas X_1 in scnf, X_2 in sdnf, X_3 in fcnf, and X_4 in fdnf can be constructed so that the following are true:*

(1) *X is satisfiable iff X_1 is satisfiable iff X_2 is satisfiable.*

(2) *X is valid iff X_3 is valid iff X_4 is valid.*

EXAMPLE 7.11. Convert the following formula to scnf, sdnf, fcnf, and fdnf:

$$X = \exists x \forall y \forall u \forall v \exists w \forall z((Rux \to Py \wedge Qx \wedge \neg Qy) \wedge (Pu \to Qz) \wedge (Qz \to Pu)).$$

It is a sentence in prenex form. No universal quantifier occurs to the left of $\exists x$. To the left of $\exists w$, the universally quantified variables are y, u and v. But none of these variables occurs in a predicate along with w. Moreover, w does not occur in the matrix at all. Thus, we replace x by constants, say, a, and we need not replace w by anything. The satisfiability form of X is

$$X_S = \forall y \forall u \forall v \forall z((Rua \to Py \wedge Qa \wedge \neg Qy) \wedge (Pu \to Qz) \wedge (Qz \to Pu)).$$

The Skolem form of the formula is the matrix of X_S, that is,

$$X_s = (Rua \to Py \wedge Qa \wedge \neg Qy) \wedge (Pu \to Qz) \wedge (Qz \to Pu)).$$

Converting the Skolem form to cnf and dnf, we have the following scnf and sdnf:

$$\begin{aligned} X_1 = &\ (\neg Rua \vee Py) \wedge (\neg Rua \vee Qa) \wedge (\neg Rua \vee \neg Qy) \wedge (\neg Pu \vee Qz) \wedge (\neg Qz \vee Pa). \\ X_2 = &\ (\neg Rua \wedge \neg Pu \wedge \neg Qz) \vee (\neg Rua \wedge \neg Qz \wedge Pu) \vee (Py \wedge Qa \wedge \neg Qy \wedge \neg Pu \wedge \neg Qz) \\ &\ \vee (Py \wedge Qa \wedge \neg Qy \wedge Qz \wedge Pu). \end{aligned}$$

For the validity form, we similarly eliminate the universal quantifiers. The first $\forall$ from the left is $\forall y$, which occurs after $\exists x$. But x, y do not occur in any predicate simultaneously. Hence y is replaced by a constant, say, c. Next, $\forall u$ occurs after $\exists x$, and both u, x occur in Rux. Thus, a new indical function, say, f of arity 1, is introduced and $f(x)$ replaces u. Similarly, v is replaced by a constant, say, d, and z is replaced by a constant e. Thus, we have the validity form

$$X_V = \exists x \exists w((Rf(x)x \to Pc \wedge Qx \wedge \neg Qc) \wedge (Pf(x) \to Qe) \wedge (Qe \to Pf(x))).$$

The functional form is the matrix of X_V:

$$X_f = (Rf(x)x \to Pc \wedge Qx \wedge \neg Qc) \wedge (Pf(x) \to Qe) \wedge (Qe \to Pf(x)).$$

We eliminate $\to$ and use distributivity to obtain the required fcnf and fdnf:

$$\begin{aligned} X_3 = &\ (\neg Rf(x)x \vee Pc) \wedge (\neg Rf(x)x \vee Qx) \wedge (\neg Rf(x)x \vee \neg Qc) \\ &\ \wedge (\neg Pf(x) \vee Qe) \wedge (\neg Qe \vee Pf(x)). \\ X_4 = &\ (\neg Rf(x)x \wedge \neg Pf(x) \wedge \neg Qe) \vee (\neg Rf(x)x \wedge \neg Qe \wedge Pf(x)) \\ &\ \vee (Pc \wedge Qx \wedge \neg Qc \wedge \neg Pf(x) \wedge \neg Qe) \vee (Pc \wedge Qx \wedge \neg Qc \wedge Qe \wedge Pf(x)). \end{aligned}$$

We must stress that in scnf and sdnf, all free variables are universally quantified, while in fcnf and fdnf, all free variables are existentially quantified. In an scnf, since $\forall$ distributes over $\wedge$, you may regard the scnf as a conjunction of sentences obtained by universally quantifying over the free variables of individual clauses. But in an sdnf, $\forall$ do not distribute over $\vee$; the conjunctive clauses do share their variables. Similarly, in an fdnf, each clause may be regarded as a sentence where the free variables are existentially quantified; but the free variables in an fcnf are shared by individual clauses. This is why conversion of a formula to scnf and fdnf is more natural than conversion to sdnf or fcnf.

Exercises for § 7.3

Construct clause sets corresponding to the following formulas and consequences. [The clause sets for a consequence $\Sigma \,!\!\vdash X$ are the clause sets for the set $\Sigma \cup \{\neg X\}$.]

1. $\exists xX \leftrightarrow \neg\forall x\neg X$
2. $\forall xPx \rightarrow \exists x\exists y(Qx \vee Rxy)$
3. $\exists x\exists y(Pxy \rightarrow \forall x(Qx \wedge Rxy))$
4. $\forall x(\exists y(Pxy \rightarrow Qxy) \wedge \exists y(Qxy \rightarrow Pxy))$
5. $\forall x(\exists yPxy \wedge \neg Qxy) \vee \forall y\exists z(Qyz \wedge \neg Rxyz)$
6. $\neg(\exists x\forall yPxy \rightarrow (\forall x\exists z\neg Qzx \wedge \forall y\neg\forall zRzy))$
7. $\forall x\forall y(\forall zPxyz \vee (\forall yRxy \rightarrow \exists u(Rxu \wedge Quz)))$
8. $\exists x\forall y\forall z\exists x(\exists u(Pxz \vee Qxy) \leftrightarrow \neg\exists u\neg\exists w(Qxw \wedge \neg Rxu))$
9. $\{\forall x(\exists y(Pxy \wedge Qy) \rightarrow \exists y(Ry \wedge Bxy)), \forall x\neg Rx\} \,!\!\vdash (Qy \rightarrow Pxy)$
10. $\{\forall x(Px \rightarrow \forall y(Qxy \rightarrow Ry)), \exists y(Py \wedge \forall x(Bx \rightarrow Qyx))\} \,!\!\vdash \forall zBz$

7.4 UNIFICATION OF CLAUSES

You have seen how resolution works for deciding satisfiability of a cnf, or a finite set of clauses in PL. Since scnf conversion preserves satisfiability, resolution is a viable option for FL. But, can we apply resolution straightforward on an scnf? For example, consider the scnf $A = (\neg Px \vee Qxy) \wedge Px \wedge \neg Qxy$, or in set notation,

$$A = \{\{\neg Px, Qxy\}, \{Px\}, \{\neg Qxy\}\}.$$

A resolution refutation may proceed as follows.

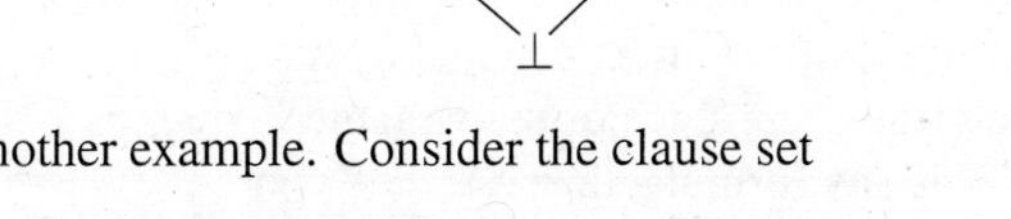

Let us take another example. Consider the clause set

$$B = \{\{\neg Hx, Mx\}, \{Ha\}, \{\neg Ma\}\}.$$

The scnf B corresponds to the consequence $\{\forall x(Hx \rightarrow Mx), Ha\} \vDash Ma$. We know that B is a valid consequence. But how do we proceed in resolution? It should be possible to resolve $\{\neg Hx, Mx\}$ and $\{Ha\}$ to get $\{Ma\}$; and then $\bot$ may be derived as in Figure 7.1.

Since free variables in an scnf are universally quantified, the clause $\{\neg Hx, Mx\}$, is indeed the formula $\forall x(\neg Hx \vee Mx)$. By universal specification, we have $\neg Ha \vee Ma$.

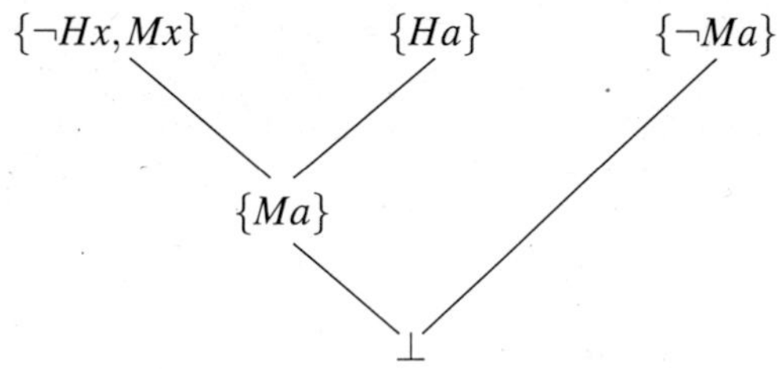

Figure 7.1: Suggested refutation of B

Hence we should be able to extend our definition of resolvents in such a way that the substitution $[x/a]$ can be used to effect the specification. But how do we choose this particular substitution among many others? Moreover, if more than one variable are involved (as x above), then we may require a substitution such as $[x/a, y/b, z/c, \ldots]$ for simultaneously substituting the constants in place of the variables.

A **substitution** is an expression of the form $[x_1/t_1, x_2/t_2, \ldots x_n/t_n]$, where x_i is a variable, t_i is a term, $x_i \neq t_i$, and $x_i \neq x_j$, for $1 \leq i \neq j \leq n$. We consider such a substitution as an ordered set, a list of individual elements $x_1/t_1,\ x_2/t_2,\ \ldots,\ x_n/t_n$. We also allow the empty substitution $[\,]$, which when applied on a term yields the same term; and applied on a formula returns the same formula.

Both $[x_1/t_1]$ and $[x_{19}/t_5, x_5/t_{21}]$ are substitutions, but neither $[x/c, x/f(a)]$ nor $[x/c, y/y]$ is a substitution.

If $\sigma = [x_1/t_1, \ldots, x_n/t_n]$ is a substitution and t is a term, then the **result of applying the substitution** σ on the term t, denoted by $t\sigma$, is the term obtained from t by replacing each occurrence of x_i by the corresponding term t_i simultaneously for all i. For instance,

$$
\begin{aligned}
f(a)[x/b] &= f(a)\\
g(f(a),x)[x/f(b)] &= g(f(a),f(b))\\
g(f(x),y)[x/f(y),y/a] &= g(f(f(y)),a)\\
g(f(x),y)[x/f(y)][y/a] &= g(f(f(y)),y)[y/a] = g(f(f(a)),a)
\end{aligned}
$$

Clearly, $t[\,] = t$ for any term t. You can also define $t\sigma$ recursively using the grammar of terms.

If X is a formula and $\sigma = [x_1/t_1, x_2/t_2, \ldots, x_n/t_n]$ is a substitution, then the **result of applying the substitution σ on X**, denoted by $X\sigma$, is the formula obtained from X by replacing each free occurrence of the variable x_i by t_i in X simultaneously for all i. Obviously, if X is any formula, then $X[\,] = X$. For

$$X = \forall x(Pxy \to Qx) \wedge Rxy, \quad \sigma = [x/a], \quad \theta = [x/a, y/b, z/c],$$

$$
\begin{aligned}
X\sigma &= \forall x(Pxy \to Qx) \wedge Ray;\\
X\theta &= \forall x(Pxb \to Qx) \wedge Rab;\\
(X\theta)\sigma &= (\forall x(Pxb \to Qx) \wedge Rab)\sigma = \forall x(Pxb \to Qx) \wedge Rab;\\
(X\sigma)\theta &= (\forall x(Pxy \to Qx) \wedge Ray)\theta = \forall x(Pxb \to Qx) \wedge Rab.
\end{aligned}
$$

The union of two lists $L_1 = [x_1/s_1, \ldots, x_m/s_m]$ and $L_2 = [y_1/t_1, \ldots, y_n/t_n]$ is taken as the list $L_1 \cup L_2 = [x_1/s_1, \ldots, x_m/s_m, y_1/t_1, \ldots, y_n/t_n]$. In computing the union, we list out all elements of the first, and then list out all the elements of the second, preserving their order. For instance, if $L_1 = [x_1/s_1, x_2/s_2]$ and $L_2 = [x_4/t_4, x_3/t_3]$, then $L_1 \cup L_2 = [x_1/s_1, x_2/s_2, x_4/t_4, x_3/t_3]$, and $L_2 \cup L_1 = [x_4/t_4, x_3/t_3, x_1/s_1, x_2/s_2]$.

The **composition** of two substitutions σ and θ, denoted by $\sigma \circ \theta$, is the substitution computed by using the following procedure.

PROCEDURE ***CompSub***

Input: Substitutions $\sigma = [x_1/s_1, x_2/s_2, \ldots, x_m/s_m]$, $\theta = [y_1/t_1, y_2/t_2, \ldots, y_n/t_n]$.
Output: The substitution $\sigma \circ \theta$.

1. Compute $L_1 := [x_1/s_1\theta, x_2/s_2\theta, \ldots, x_m/s_m\theta]$.
2. Compute the list L_2 by deleting all expressions y_i/t_i from θ if $y_i \in \{x_1, \ldots, x_m\}$.
3. Compute L_3 by deleting from L_1 all elements of the form $x_j/s_j\theta$ if $x_j = s_j\theta$.
4. Compute $\sigma \circ \theta := L_3 \cup L_2$.

EXAMPLE 7.12. To compute $[x/f(y)] \circ [z/y]$, we take $\sigma = [x/f(y)]$ and $\theta = [z/y]$. Next, we begin with the list $L_1 = [x/f(y)\theta] = [x/f(y)[z/y]] = [x/f(y)]$. In θ the numerator of the only expressions z/y is z, which is assumed to be different from the numerator x of the only expression $x/f(y)$ in L_1. So, $L_2 = [z/y]$. Next, $L_3 = L_1$ as $x \neq f(y)$. Thus, $[x/f(y)] \circ [z/y] = L_3 \cup L_2 = [x/f(y), z/y]$.

EXAMPLE 7.13. Let $\sigma = [x/f(y), y/z]$ and $\theta = [x/a, y/b, z/c]$.

To compute $\sigma \circ \theta$, we start with the list $[x/f(y)\theta, y/z\theta]$. Since $f(y)\theta = f(b)$ and $z\theta = c$, we have $L_1 = [x/f(b), y/c]$. We look at θ. Since the variables x, y already appear as numerators of elements in L_1, we have $L_2 = [z/c]$. Notice that no numerator equals its denominator in L_1. So, $L_3 = L_1$. Then

$$\sigma \circ \theta = L_3 \cup L_2 = [x/f(b), y/c, z/c].$$

For $\theta \circ \sigma$, we start with the list $L_1 = [x/a\sigma, y/b\sigma, z/c\sigma] = [x/a, y/b, z/c]$. The variables x, y in the numerators of the elements of σ already occur as numerators in L_1. Thus $L_2 = [\,]$. All elements in L_1 have numerators different from the respective denominators; so $L_3 = L_1$.

$$\theta \circ \sigma = L_3 \cup L_2 = L_3 = L_1 = [x/a, y/b, z/c].$$

You see that $\sigma \circ \theta \neq \theta \circ \sigma$; order does matter in compositions.

EXAMPLE 7.14. Let $X = Pxyz$, $\sigma = [x/f(y), y/z]$, and let $\theta = [y/b, z/y]$. Check whether $X(\sigma \circ \theta) = (X\sigma)\theta$.

For computing the composition $\sigma \circ \theta$, we start with the list

$$L_1 = [x/f(y)\theta, y/z\theta] = [x/f(b), y/y].$$

From θ the element y/b is deleted to obtain $L_2 = [z/y]$. Next, from L_1, the element y/y is deleted to get $L_3 = [x/f(b)]$. Then

$$\sigma \circ \theta = L_3 \cup L_2 = [x/f(b), z/y].$$

Applying the substitutions on the formula X, we obtain

$$(X\sigma)\theta = (Pxyz[x/f(y),y/z])\theta = (Pf(y)zz)\theta = Pf(b)yy;$$
$$X(\sigma\circ\theta) = Pxyz[x/f(b),z/y] = Pf(b)yy.$$

That is, $X(\sigma\circ\theta) = (X\sigma)\theta$.

To see why composition of substitutions is defined in such a way, consider a term $t = f(x)$, and substitutions $\sigma = [x/y]$ and $\theta = [y/z]$. Now,

$$(t\sigma)\theta = f(y)\theta = f(z).$$

The net effect is the application of the substitution $[x/y\theta]$ on t. This justifies our starting point of the list as

$$[x_1/s_1\theta, x_2/s_2\theta, \ldots, x_m/s_m\theta].$$

Consider the same σ, θ but the term $s = f(y)$. Here,

$$(s\sigma)\theta = s\theta = f(y)\theta = f(z).$$

This justifies adding to the previous list the elements from θ whose numerators are not appearing as numerators of elements in our list. Finally the updated list is not a substitution since there can be *vacuous substitutions* of the form z/z in it; these are deleted to form the composition. Is it not obvious that a composition results in a repeated application of the individual substitutions?

Lemma 7.1. *Let σ and θ be two substitutions. Let t be any term, and let X be any formula. Then, $t(\sigma\circ\theta) = (t\sigma)\theta$ and $X(\sigma\circ\theta) = (X\sigma)\theta$.*

Proof. We plan to use induction on the *level* of terms for proving the result for terms. In the basis step, the term t is equal to a constant c or a variable x. When $t = c$, we see that $t(\sigma\circ\theta) = c = (t\sigma)\theta$. When $t = x$, the following cases are possible: (Write s, u, v for generic terms, and x, y for variables.)

(a) x/s does not occur in σ but x/u occurs in θ.
(b) x/s does not occur in σ and x/u does not occur in θ.
(c) x/s occurs in σ and y/u does not occur in θ for any y occurring in s.
(d) x/s occurs in σ and y/u occurs in θ for some y occurring in s.

We tackle each of the cases as follows.

(a) In this case, x/u occurs in $\sigma\circ\theta$. Thus

$$t(\sigma\circ\theta) = x(\sigma\circ\theta) = x[x/u] = u = x\theta = (x\sigma)\theta = (t\sigma)\theta.$$

(b) In this case, x/v never occurs in $\sigma\circ\theta$ for any term v. Hence

$$t(\sigma\circ\theta) = x(\sigma\circ\theta) = x = x\sigma = (x\sigma)\theta = (t\sigma)\theta.$$

(c) In this case, $s\theta = s$; and consequently, x/s is in L_1. Then x/u is not an element of L_2 for any term u. Since x/s occurs in σ, $x \neq s$. Thus, x/s is an element of L_3. That is, x/s is an element of $\sigma\circ\theta$. Therefore,

$$t(\sigma \circ \theta) = x(\sigma \circ \theta) = x[x/s] = s = x\sigma = (x\sigma)\theta = (t\sigma)\theta.$$

(d) A special subcase is $s = y$. Here, $s\theta = u$; and x/u is in L_2. Thus x/u occurs in $\sigma \circ \theta$. Whether $u = x$ or not, we have

$$t(\sigma \circ \theta) = x(\sigma \circ \theta) = x[x/u] = u = s\theta = (x\sigma)\theta = (t\sigma)\theta.$$

The other subcase is $s \neq y$. Write $s = f(\cdots y \cdots)$, schematically. Notice that there can be more than one occurrence of y in s; it is only a suggestive way of showing that y occurs in s. Here, $s\theta = f(\cdots u \cdots) \neq x$. Hence, $x/f(\cdots u \cdots)$ is an element of $\sigma \circ \theta$. (If $y = x$, then $y/u = x/u$ is deleted from the list.) Therefore,

$$t(\sigma \circ \theta) = x[x/f(\cdots u \cdots)] = f(\cdots u \cdots) = f(\cdots y \cdots)\theta = s\theta = (x\sigma)\theta = (t\sigma)\theta.$$

For formulas, we use induction on the number of free variables; it is similar to the proof for terms. ♦

Observe that the composition of substitutions is associative, but not commutative, in general. We write the composition $\sigma \circ \theta$ of substitutions σ and θ as $\sigma\theta$.

Substitutions are applied on sets of formulas as well. For a set Σ of formulas, and a substitution θ, we define

$$\Sigma\theta = \{X\theta : X \in \Sigma\}.$$

That is, the substitution θ is applied on every formula in Σ, and then the formulas are collected together to have $\Sigma\theta$.

Renaming of variables in a formula can be seen as an application of a substitution. These special substitutions are called variants. A **variant** is a substitution of the form $[x_1/y_1, x_2/y_2, \ldots, x_m/y_m]$, where x_i's are distinct variables, y_i's are distinct variables, and no y_j is an x_i.

We need to use variants in such a way that two clauses will have different variables after renaming. If B and C are two clauses, then two variants σ and θ are called **a pair of separating variants** iff $B\sigma$ and $C\theta$ have no common variables.

We plan to choose substitutions in resolving clauses mechanically. For instance, we should choose the substitution $[x/a]$ while resolving the clauses $\{\neg Hx, Mx\}$ and $\{Ha\}$. The substitution $[x/a]$ is that one which makes both the literals $\neg Hx$ and $\neg Ha$ equal. So to say, it unifies the literals $\neg Hx$ and $\neg Ha$.

Let $A = \{A_1, A_2, \ldots, A_m\}$ be a set of literals. A substitution σ is a **unifier** of A iff $A_1\sigma = A_2\sigma = \cdots = A_m\sigma$. That is, the set $A\sigma$ is a singleton. We say that A is **unifiable** iff there is a unifier of it.

For example, $\{\neg Hx, \neg Ha\}$ has a unifier $[x/a]$ as $\{\neg Hx, \neg Ha\}\sigma = \{\neg Ha\}$, a singleton. Thus $\{\neg Hx, \neg Ha\}$ is unifiable whereas $\{\neg Hx, Ha\}$ is not unifiable.

As in PL, a set of literals will be referred to as a clause.

EXAMPLE 7.15. Is $A = \{Pxyf(g(z)), Puf(u)f(v)\}$ unifiable?

With $\sigma = [x/a, y/f(a), u/a, z/a, v/g(a)]$, $A\sigma = \{Paf(a)f(g(a))\}$. Hence σ is a unifier of A; and A is unifiable.

Moreover, with $\delta = [x/u, y/f(u), v/g(z)]$ and $\theta = [x/u, y/f(u), z/a, v/g(a)]$, we find that $A\delta = \{Puf(u)f(g(z))\}$ and $A\theta = \{Puf(u)f(g(a))\}$. That is, δ and θ are also unifiers of A. A unifier need not be unique.

In Example 7.15, $\sigma = \delta[u/a, z/a]$ and $\theta = \delta[z/a]$. If you choose δ as *the unifier*, then later, you can still choose other substitutions to get back the effect of σ or of θ using composition. A unifier such as δ here is called a most general unifier. We are interested in a most general unifier since we do not want to restrict our universal specification in such a way that we lose information.

A unifier δ of a set of literals A is called a **most general unifier** of A if for each (other) unifier θ of A, there exists a substitution σ such that $\theta = \delta\sigma$. Similarly, a most general unifier of a set of terms is also defined.

Like a unifier, a most general unifier of a set of literals (or terms) need not be unique. In Example 7.15, for $A = \{Pxyf(g(z)), Puf(u)f(v)\}$, two most general unifiers are

$$\delta = [x/a, y/f(a), v/g(z)], \quad \lambda = [u/x, y/f(x), v/g(z)].$$

Here, $\delta = \lambda[x/u]$, and $\lambda = \delta[u/x]$. Of course, any most general unifier can be obtained from another by applying a suitable variant.

EXAMPLE 7.16. Unify $A = \{Pxyf(g(z)), Puf(u)f(v)\}$.

Our target is to finally match all the literals by applying a suitable substitution. Naturally, we scan the literals symbol by symbol, say, from left to right. The first symbol P matches. A discrepancy occurs at the second symbol: one is x and the other is u. So, we start with a substitution $[x/u]$. Then,

$$A[x/u] = \{Puyf(g(z)), Puf(u)f(v)\}.$$

Matching the literals in this new set, we find a discrepancy at the third symbol. One is y, a variable, and the other is a term $f(u)$. So, we construct the substitution $[y/f(u)]$. Applying this, we obtain

$$(A[x/u])[y/f(u)] = \{Puf(u)f(g(z)), Puf(u)f(v)\}.$$

Next discrepancy suggests the substitution $[v/g(z)]$; its application yields the clause

$$((A[x/u])[y/f(u)])[v/g(z)] = \{Puf(u)f(g(z))\}.$$

Therefore, by Lemma 7.1, we have the unifier

$$\sigma = ([x/u] \circ [y/f(u)]) \circ [v/g(z)] = [x/u, y/f(u), v/g(z)].$$

The unification procedure given below mimics this manual construction.

PROCEDURE ***Unify***

Input: A set A of literals.

Output: A most general unifier of A if one exists; else, 'A is not unifiable'

1. If some literal in A starts with $\neg$ and another does not, then output 'A is not unifiable'.
2. If two elements of A use different predicates, then output 'A is not unifiable'.
3. Set $A_0 := A$; $\sigma_0 := [\,]$, the empty substitution; $\theta_0 := \sigma_0$, $k := 0$.
4. If A_k has only one element, then output θ_k.

5. Else, scan the first two elements of A_k to find a mismatch.
6. If the mismatch is due to different function symbols, then output 'A is not unifiable'.
7. If the mismatch is due to a variable x in one and a term t in the other, then
(a) if x occurs in t, output 'A is not unifiable',
(b) else, set $\sigma_{k+1} := [x/t]$; $\theta_{k+1} := \theta_k \sigma_{k+1}$.
8. Set $A_{k+1} := A_k \sigma_{k+1}$; $k := k+1$; go to Step 4.

In Step 7, if t is also a variable, then the variable of the first literal is taken as x and the variable in the second is taken as t. In general, the unified clause is $A\theta_{k+1}$, where the most general unifier is $\theta_{k+1} = \sigma_1 \sigma_2 \cdots \sigma_{k+1}$. Unification can also be applied on a set of terms the same way.

EXAMPLE 7.17. Use *Unify* on $A = \{Pxf(y), Pf(y)f(x)\}$.
The first mismatch is at x in the first literal and $f(y)$ in the second. Thus,

$$\theta_1 = \sigma_1 = [x/f(y)]; \text{ and } A_1 = A\sigma_1 = \{Pf(y)f(y), Pf(y)f(f(y))\}.$$

The next mismatch is at y in the first literal and $f(y)$ in the second. Since y occurs in $f(y)$, the clause is not unifiable (Step 7).

EXAMPLE 7.18. Unify $A = \{P(x,y,g(x,z,f(y))), P(z,f(x),u)\}$.

$$\begin{aligned}
\sigma_1 &= [x/z],\ \theta_1 = \sigma_1, \\
A_1 &= A\sigma_1 = \{P(z,y,g(z,z,f(y))), P(z,f(z),u)\}; \\
\sigma_2 &= [y/f(z)],\ \theta_2 = \sigma_1\sigma_2, \\
A_2 &= A_1\sigma_2 = \{P(z,f(z),g(z,z,f(f(z)))), P(z,f(z),u)\}; \\
\sigma_3 &= [u/g(z,z,f(f(z))],\ \theta_3 = \theta_2\sigma_3, \\
A_3 &= A_2\sigma_3 = \{P(z,f(z),g(z,z,f(f(z))))\}, \text{ a singleton.}
\end{aligned}$$

Thus, $\theta_3 = \theta_2\sigma_3 = [x/z][y/f(z)][u/g(z,z,f(f(z))] = [x/z, y/f(z), u/g(z,z,f(f(z))]$ is the most general unifier.

Convention 7.1. Henceforth, we will use the term *the most general unifier* or the acronym **mgu** for the one computed by the procedure *Unify*. If the set of literals $\{A, B\}$ is (not) unifiable, we say that "A and B are (not) unifiable".

Exercises for § 7.4

1. Find a pair of separating variants for each of the following pairs of clauses:

(a) $\{Pxyf(z)\}$, $\{Pzyf(y)\}$ (b) $\{Pxy, Pyz\}$, $\{Qzy, Rf(y)z\}$
(c) $\{Pxg(x)y\}$, $\{Pyg(x)x\}$ (d) $\{Pxg(x)y\}$, $\{Pxg(x)y\}$

2. Show that the composition of substitutions is associative, i.e., for any substitutions σ, θ, τ, we have $(\sigma \circ \theta) \circ \tau = \sigma \circ (\theta \circ \tau)$.
3. Find clauses A, B and a substitution σ such that $(A \setminus B)\sigma$ is not a subset of $A\sigma \setminus B\sigma$.

4. Compute the compositions $\sigma \circ \tau$ and $\tau \circ \sigma$ in each of the following cases:

   (a) $\sigma = [x/a, y/c, z/x]$, $\theta = [y/z, x/a]$
   (b) $\sigma = [y/x, z/f(y)]$, $\theta = [x/a, y/x, z/f(a)]$
   (c) $\sigma = [x/a, y/a, z/g(x)]$, $\theta = [x/a, y/f(z,a), z/y]$

5. See that $\lambda = [u/x, y/f(x), v/g(z)]$ is a most general unifier of the set of literals $\{Pxyf(g(z)),\ Puf(u)f(v)\}$. Does this set of literals have any other most general unifier?
6. Show that $\theta = [x/a, y/g(f(a)), z/f(a), u/f(f(a))]$ is a unifier of the clause $A = \{Pxyf(z), Pag(z)u\}$. Find a most general unifier σ of A and also a nonempty substitution δ such that $\theta = \sigma\delta$.
7. Use *Unify* to find the mgu, if it exists, for each of the following clauses:

   (a) $\{Pxy, Pf(x)y\}$
   (b) $\{Pxayf(y), Pzyg(c)u\}$
   (c) $\{Pf(x)y, Pzz, Pxf(u)\}$
   (d) $\{Pxf(y)z, Pcg(u)w, Puvg(w)\}$
   (e) $\{Pxf(x)g(f(y)),\ Pcf(g(z))g(y)\}$
   (f) $\{Pxug(f(y)),\ Pcf(g(z))g(u)\}$
   (g) $\{P(f(c),x,y),\ P(z,f(c),y),\ P(z,x,f(c))\}$
   (h) $\{P(x, f(x,g(x),y), f(x,y,z)),\ P(c,g(y),g(z))\}$

8. How many occurrences of the variable x_1 are there in the mgu of the terms $f(x_2, x_3, \ldots, x_n)$ and $f(g(x_1,x_1), g(x_2,x_2), \ldots, g(x_{n-1}, x_{n-1}))$?

7.5 EXTENDING RESOLUTION

Recall that in PL, we considered resolution of disjunctive clauses. As a prelude to resolution in FL, we consider the scnf of a formula. Then, the scnf is expressed as a set of clauses; each clause being disjunctive. Further, each such clause may be viewed as a set of literals, as earlier. Thus, we use both disjunction notation and set notation for clauses. For example, we may write the clause $Pxy \vee Qz$ as $\{Pxy, Qz\}$ also. Due to the set notation, that mgu of a clause is meaningful.

To see how mgu is helpful in taking resolution, consider the set of clauses $\{C_1, C_2\}$, where $C_1 = \{\neg Hx, Mx\}$ and $C_2 = \{Ha\}$. The mgu of $\neg Hx$ and $\neg Ha$ (note the extra $\neg$ with Ha) is $[x/a]$. Now, $C_1[x/a] = \{\neg Ha, Ma\}, C_2[x/a] = \{Ha\}$. Taking the resolvent, we get $\{Ma\}$. Intentionally, we had taken $C_2[x/a]$ to keep generality.

Consider another clause set, say, $A = \{\neg Hxy \vee Mxy, Hya\}$. The mgu of the clause $\{\neg Hxy, \neg Hya\}$ is $\sigma = [x/y][y/a] = [x/a, y/a]$. Then $A\sigma = \{\neg Haa \vee Maa, Haa\}$, from which resolution gives Maa.

Notice that during Skolemization, the universal quantifiers are simply dropped. Thus the clause $\neg Hxy \vee Mxy$ represents the formula $\forall x \forall y(Hxy \to Mxy)$. Similarly, the clause Hya represents the formula $\forall y Hya$. Hence A represents the formula

$$B = \forall x \forall y(Hxy \to Mxy) \wedge \forall y Hya.$$

Obviously, $B \vDash \forall y Mya$. By resolution, we have obtained the weaker sentence Maa. Why did we lose information?

When the substitution $[y/a]$ was applied after $[x/y]$, the variable x got replaced by a. In general, this is not required. In the formula $\forall x \forall y(Hxy \to Mxy) \wedge \forall y Hya$, the variable y that occurs in $\forall y Hya$ could have been renamed. Renaming y as z, we have

$$B \equiv \forall x \forall y(Hxy \to Mxy) \wedge \forall z Hza.$$

The clause set representation of this formula is $C = \{\neg Hxy \vee Mxy, Hza\}$. Now, the mgu of $\{\neg Hxy, \neg Hza\}$ is $[x/z]$. Thus $C[x/z] = \{\neg Hza \vee Mza, Hza\}$. And the resolvent of the clauses in $C[x/z]$ is Mza. It keeps the generality intact. We observe:

For resolution to work, clauses should not have common variables.

So, you find the usefulness of separating variants! If the clauses in a clause set have common variables, then we use separating variants to have distinct variables in different clauses.

Let C_1 and C_2 be two clauses with no common variables, and let $\ell_1 \in C_1$, $\ell_2 \in C_2$ be two literals such that σ is the most general unifier of $\{\ell_1, \neg\ell_2\}$. Then the clause

$$((C_1 \setminus \{\ell_1\}) \cup (C_2 \setminus \{\ell_2\}))\sigma$$

is the **resolvent** of the clauses C_1 and C_2 with respect to the literal ℓ_1 (or ℓ_2). We denote the resolvent of C_1 and C_2 with respect to ℓ_1 as $res(C_1, C_2; \ell_1, \sigma)$. Clauses C_1 and C_2 are called the **parent clauses** of the resolvent clause $res(C_1, C_2; \ell_1, \sigma)$.

We may write $res(C_1, C_2; \ell_1, \sigma)$ as $res(C_1, C_2; \ell_1)$ and also as $res(C_1, C_2)$ provided no confusion arises.

EXAMPLE 7.19. Find all resolvents of the clauses $A = \{Pxf(y), Qg(y), Rxzb\}$ and $B = \{\neg Pxf(b), \neg Qz, Rxab\}$.

Notice that A and B have common variables. We first use separating variants. When implemented in a machine, the separating variants will be something like

$$\delta_1 = [x/x_1, y/x_2, z/x_3], \quad \delta_2 = [x/x_4, z/x_5]$$

so that instead of A, B, the clauses considered are $A\delta_1, B\delta_2$, respectively. While doing manually, we keep one of the clauses as it is and rename the common variables in the second clause. With $\delta = [x/u, z/v]$ we rename B to have

$$B_1 = B\delta = \{\neg Puf(b), \neg Qv, Ruab\}.$$

Now, with A and B_1, we have a literal $Pxf(y)$ in A and $\neg Puf(b)$ in B. The mgu of first and $\neg$ of the other is to be computed. Since the literal $\neg\neg Puf(b)$ is taken as $Puf(b)$, we compute the mgu of $\{Pxf(y), Puf(b)\}$. It is $\sigma = [x/a, y/b]$. Then

$$\begin{aligned} res(A, B_1; Pxf(y)) &= ((A \setminus \{Pxf(y)\}) \cup (B_1 \setminus \{Puf(b)\}))[x/u, y/b] \\ &= \{Qg(b), Ruzb, \neg Qv, Ruab\}. \end{aligned}$$

Similarly, choosing the literals $Qg(y)$ from A and $\neg Qv$ from B_1, we have the mgu $[v/g(u)]$ for the set $\{Qg(y), Qv\}$. This gives

$$res(A, B_1, Qg(y)) = \{Pxf(y), Rxzb, \neg Puf(b), Ruab\}.$$

For the literal $Rxzb$ from A, the corresponding literal from B_1 is $Ruab$. But the set $\{Rxzb, \neg Ruab\}$ is not unifiable; it gives no resolvent.

As in PL, we would expect the resolvent to be a logical consequence of its parent clauses. In Example 7.19, we would have $\{A, B_1\} \vDash C$, where

$$C = \{Qg(b), Ruzb, \neg Qv, Ruab\}.$$

Is it really so? Let $I = (D, \phi)$ be an interpretation and m be a valuation under I. Suppose the state I_m satisfies both A and B_1. That is,

$$I_m \vDash Pxf(y) \vee Qg(y) \vee Rxzb, \quad I_m \vDash \neg Puf(b) \vee \neg Qv \vee Ruab.$$

If $I_m \nvDash \neg Puf(b)$, then $I_m \vDash \neg Qv \vee Ruab$. In this case, $I_m \vDash C$. On the other hand, if $I_m \vDash \neg Puf(b)$, then $I_m \nvDash Pxf(y)$, since u is universally quantified in $\neg Puf(b)$. Thus, $I_m \vDash Qg(y) \vee Rxzb$. Since x and y are universally quantified, $I_m \vDash Qg(b) \vee Ruzb$. Consequently, $I_m \vDash C$. In any case, $I_m \vDash C$.

If we repeat the same argument in general, we obtain the following result.

Theorem 7.7 (Resolution Principle). *Let A and B be two first order clauses. Let C be a resolvent of A and B with respect to some literal. Then,* $\{A, B\} \vDash C$.

As in PL, we proceed towards taking resolvents, resolvents of resolvents with the goal of generating $\bot$. If at all $\bot$ is generated, then the set of clauses is unsatisfiable.

EXAMPLE 7.20. Let $A = \{\{\neg Px, Qx\}, \{Pa\}, \{Rba\}, \{\neg Qy, \neg Rby\}\}$. We apply the resolution principle to construct the refutation DAG as follows:

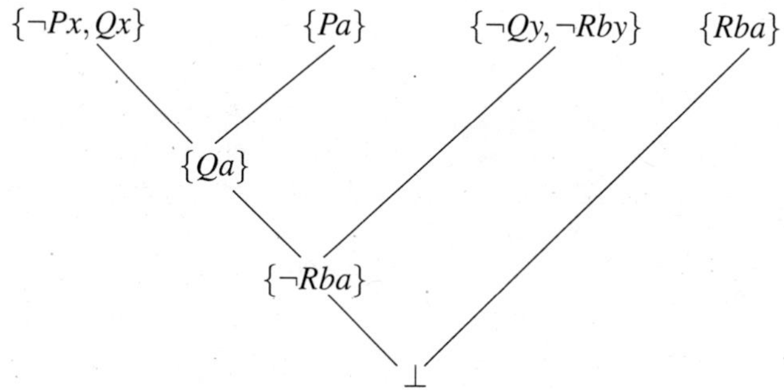

We may write the refutation in three column style. It shows that A is unsatisfiable.

1. $\{\neg Px, Qx\}$ P
2. $\{Pa\}$ P
3. $\{Qa\}$ $res(1, 2; \neg Px, [x/a])$
4. $\{\neg Qy, \neg Rby\}$ P
5. $\{\neg Rba\}$ $res(3, 4; Qa, [y/a])$
6. $\{Rba\}$ P
7. $\bot$ $res(5, 6; \neg Rba, [\,])$

Exercises for § 7.5

1. Prove Theorem 7.7.
2. Determine whether the following sets of clauses entail $\bot$ by resolution.
   (a) $\{\{Px, Qx\}, \{Pa\}, \{\neg Py\}, \{\neg Qz\}\}$
   (b) $\{\{Pxy, Qxa\}, \{Pax, \neg Qyx\}, \{\neg Pyy\}\}$
   (c) $\{\{\neg Px, Qx\}, \{Pc\}, \{Rac\}, \{\neg Qz, \neg Raz\}\}$
   (d) $\{\{Px, Qx, Rxf(x)\}, \{\neg Px, Qx, Sf(x)\}, \{Ac\}, \{Pa\}, \{\neg Ray, Ay\}, \{\neg Ax, \neg Qx\}, \{\neg Az, \neg Sz\}\}$

7.6 FACTORS AND PARAMODULANTS

Consider the formula $A = \forall x \forall y(Px \vee Py) \wedge \forall u \forall z(\neg Pu \vee \neg Pz)$. Simplifying the conjuncts, we see that $\forall x \forall y(Px \vee Py) \equiv \forall x Px$ and $\forall u \forall z(\neg Pu \vee \neg Pz) \equiv \forall y \neg Py$. Therefore, $A \equiv \forall x Px \wedge \forall y \neg Py \equiv \bot$.

The formula A is represented by the clause set $\{\{Px, Py\}, \{\neg Pu, \neg Pz\}\}$. We wish to apply resolution on this clause set towards deriving $\bot$. Here is a trial:

1.	$\{Px, Py\}$	P
2.	$\{\neg Pu, \neg Pz\}$	P
3.	$\{Py, \neg Pz\}$	$res(1, 2; Px, [x/u])$
4.	$\{\neg Pz, \neg Pv\}$	$res(2, 3; \neg Pu, [u/y])$

Why does $\{\neg Pz, \neg Pv\}$ come as the resolvent of clauses 2 and 3; why not $\{\neg Pz\}$? Because, resolution is taken only after it is guaranteed that the clauses have no common variables. Thus, (2) is kept as it is, whereas (3) is first rewritten as $\{Py, \neg Pv\}$ by using a renaming substitution $[z/v]$ (in fact, the pair of variants $[\,]$ and $[z/v]$). In a machine implementation, lines (2) and (3) will appear as

2′. $\{\neg Px_3, \neg Px_4\}$
3′. $\{Px_5, \neg Px_6\}$

The resolvent of (2′) and (3′) is $\{\neg Px_4, \neg Px_6\}$. It is again rewritten as

4′. $\{\neg Px_7, \neg Px_8\}$

In this case, resolution will bring forth a clause in one of the following forms:

$$\{Px_i, Px_j\}, \{\neg Px_i, Px_j\}, \{\neg Px_i, \neg Px_j\}.$$

And this will never give us $\bot$. The resolution principle says that a derived clause is a consequence of the given clauses. It does not say that every unsatisfiable set will eventually yield $\bot$. Perhaps, resolution, as formulated till now, is not a complete method in FL!

We require an extra rule to capture the equivalence $\forall x \forall y(Px \vee Py) \equiv \forall x Px$. That is, we must be able to deduce $\{Pz\}$ from $\{Px, Py\}$.

Let C be a clause. Let $D \subseteq C$ have at least two literals. Let σ be a (the) most general unifier of D. Then $C\sigma$ is called a **factor** of C. A factor of C with respect to the clause D and the mgu σ is written as $fac(C; D, \sigma)$ or as $fac(C, \sigma)$ if D is obvious from the context. We will use the factor as we use a resolvent.

EXAMPLE 7.21. Using resolvents and factors show that $\{\{Px, Py\}, \{\neg Pu, \neg Pz\}\}$ is unsatisfiable.

1. $\{Px, Py\}$	P
2. $\{Py\}$	$fac(1, [x/y])$
3. $\{\neg Pu, \neg Pz\}$	P
4. $\{\neg Pz\}$	$fac(3, [u/z])$
5. $\bot$	$res(2, 4; Py, [y/z])$

EXAMPLE 7.22. Using resolvents and factors show that $C = \{\{a \approx b\}, \{Pa\}, \{\neg Pb\}\}$ is unsatisfiable.
A Trial Solution: C is clearly unsatisfiable. But how to deduce $\bot$? There is no variables at all. So, taking factors is useless since $\{a \approx b\}$ and $\{Pa\}$ would not give $\{Pb\}$. We are stuck. Reason? We do not know yet how to handle the special predicate $\approx$. We must be able to deduce Pb given the literals $a \approx b$ and Pa.

In general, if we have $X[x/s]$ and $s \approx t$, then we must be able to deduce $X[x/t]$. More generally, from $t \approx u$ and $X[x/s]$, with σ being the mgu of s and t, we must deduce $X[x/u\sigma]$. Here we need unification of terms also.

Convention 7.2. We write $X(s)$ for a formula X, where there are occurrences of a term s. When we substitute some or all occurrences of s in $X(s)$ by t, we obtain another formula. All those formulas are written generically as $X(t)$.

Let X be a formula, and let s, t, u be terms with s, t having no common variables. Let A and B be two clauses such that $(t \approx u) \in A$, $X(s) \in B$, and that A, B have no common variables. Let σ be a most general unifier of the terms s and t. Then the **paramodulant** of A and B is the clause

$$\big((A \setminus \{t \approx u\}) \cup (B \setminus \{X(s)\}) \cup \{X(u)\}\big)\sigma.$$

Adding a paramodulant is often referred to as *paramodulation*.

EXAMPLE 7.23. What is the paramodulant of $\{a \approx b\}$ and $\{Pa\}$?

With $A = \{a \approx b\}$, $B = \{Pa\}$, $s = a$, $t = a$, we have $\sigma = [\,]$, the empty substitution, and $u = b$. Since $X(s) = Pa$, the paramodulant is $X(u)\sigma = Pb$.

EXAMPLE 7.24. What is the paramodulant of $\{f(f(a,c),h(c)) \approx f(f(b,c),h(c))\}$ and $\{f(x, f(y,z)) \approx f(f(x,y),z)\}$?

Since two equalities are involved, you can choose one of them as $(t \approx u)$ and the other as $X(s)$. Let us take the first as $(t \approx u)$. Then $t = f(f(a,c),h(c))$, and $u = f(f(b,c),h(c))$.

With $s = f(x, f(y,z))$, we find that s and t are not unifiable. However, with $s = f(f(x,y),z)$, s and t are unifiable and the mgu is $\sigma = [x/a, y/c, z/h(c)]$. Then,

$$X(s) = (f(x, f(y,z)) \approx s), \quad X(u) = (f(x, f(y,z)) \approx f(f(b,c),h(c))).$$

The paramodulant is

$$X(u)\sigma = (f(a, f(c,h(c))) \approx f(f(b,c),h(c))).$$

There is one more way of computing a paramodulant here; that is, by taking the second clause as $t \approx u$. In that case, you have

$$t = f(f(x,y),z), u = f(x, f(y,z)), s = f(f(a,c),h(c)), X(s) = (s \approx f(f(b,c),h(c))).$$

And then, $\sigma = [x/a, y/c, z/h(c)]$, and the paramodulant is

$$X(u)\sigma = (u \approx f(f(b,c),h(c)))\sigma = (f(a, f(c,h(c))) \approx f(f(b,c),h(c)))$$

which, incidentally, is the same as earlier.

EXAMPLE 7.25. We redo Example 7.22 using paramodulants.

For $C = \{\{a \approx b\}, \{Pa\}, \{\neg Pb\}\}$, let $A = \{a \approx b\}$, and $B = \{Pa\}$. We have

$$t = a,\ u = b,\ s = x,\ X(s) = Px,\ A \setminus \{t \approx u\} = B \setminus \{X(s)\} = \varnothing.$$

The mgu of s and t (in fact of $\{s,t\}$) is $\sigma = [x/a]$. Hence the paramodulant is

$$(\varnothing \cup \varnothing \cup X(u))\sigma = (Pb)[x/a] = Pb.$$

Then C is unsatisfiable as $\perp$ is a resolvent of Pb and $\neg Pb$.

Each of the three rules, such as resolution, factor, and paramodulant, requires more than one clause. Thus we cannot justify that $\{\neg(t \approx t)\}$ is unsatisfiable. To accommodate this, we take an extra rule for equality, namely,

For any term t, derive $(t \approx t)$ even when there is no premise.

Like an axiom, the literal $(t \approx t)$ is added anywhere in a deduction. This simple looking rule supplements the factors also. For instance, consider the accepted clause $\{a \approx a\}$; then compute the paramodulant of this and $\{Px\}$. You obtain $t = a$, $u = a$, $s = x$, $X(s) = Px$, and the mgu of s and t as $\sigma = [x/a]$. The paramodulant is

$$((\{a \approx a\} \setminus \{a \approx a\}) \cup (\{Px\} \setminus \{Px\}) \cup \{X(s)\})\sigma = \{(Px)[x/a]\} = \{Pa\}.$$

This shows how Px may entail Pa using paramodulation.

Exercises for § 7.6

1. Show that if a clause is satisfiable, each of its factors is also satisfiable.
2. In each of the following cases, explain how C is a paramodulant of A and B.
   (a) $A = f(x,h(x)) \approx a,\ B = c \approx c,\ C = f(c,h(c)) \approx a$
   (b) $A = f(c,h(c)) \approx a,\ B = f(b, f(c,h(c))) \approx f(d, f(c,h(c)))$,
   $C = f(b,a) \approx f(d, f(c,h(c)))$
   (c) $A = f(b,c) \approx f(d,c),\ B = f(f(b,c),h(c)) \approx f(f(b,c),h(c))$,
   $C = f(f(b,c),h(c)) \approx f(f(d,c),h(c))$
   (d) $A = f(f(b,c),h(c)) \approx f(f(d,c),h(c)),\ B = f(f(x,y),z) \approx f(x, f(y,z))$,
   $C = f(f(d,c),h(c)) \approx f(b, f(c,h(c)))$
   (e) $A = f(f(d,c),h(c)) \approx f(b, f(c,h(c))),\ B = f(f(x,y),z) \approx f(x, f(y,z))$,
   $C = f(b, f(c,h(c))) \approx f(d, f(c,h(c)))$
3. Let C be a paramodulant of two clauses A and B. Show that if $\{A,B\}$ is satisfiable, then so is $\{A,B,C\}$.

7.7 RESOLUTION FOR FL

We rewrite the operations of taking resolution, factor, paramodulant and adding the equality clauses of the form $t \approx t$ as rules. All the rules taken together form the **method of resolution**. Summing up, we have the following four rules for working out a resolution refutation or a resolution deduction:

(R) From two clauses, deduce their resolvents:

$$\frac{C_1 \vee \ell_1 \qquad C_2 \vee \ell_2}{(C_1 \vee C_2)\sigma} \quad (\sigma \text{ is the mgu of the literals } \ell_1 \text{ and } \neg\ell_2.)$$

(F) From a clause derive its factor(s):

$$\frac{C \vee \ell_1 \vee \cdots \vee \ell_k}{(C \vee \ell_1)\sigma} \quad (\sigma \text{ is the mgu of the literals } \ell_1, \ell_2, \cdots \ell_k.)$$

(M) From two clauses, one of them being in the form $t \approx u$ or $u \approx t$, derive their paramodulant:

$$\frac{C(s) \qquad (t \approx u) \vee D}{(C(u) \vee D)\sigma} \qquad\qquad \frac{C(s) \qquad (u \approx t) \vee D}{(C(u) \vee D)\sigma}$$

Here, σ is the mgu of terms s, t; and at least one s is replaced by u in $C(s)$.

(E) For any term t, derive $(t \approx t)$ from any clause:

$$\frac{\cdot}{(t \approx t)}$$

To show that a set of clauses is unsatisfiable, we only derive $\bot$ from it; and call the derivation as a **resolution refutation.** Using RA, we define a **resolution proof** of a consequence $\Sigma \vDash w$ as a (resolution) refutation of a clause set equivalent of $\Sigma \cup \{\neg w\}$. Let us work out some examples.

EXAMPLE 7.26. Use resolution to show that the following argument is valid:

> No student reads a boring book seriously. This book is read seriously by at least one student (you). Therefore, this book is not boring.

Let us fix our vocabulary – *Sx*: *x* is a student, *b*: this book, *Rxy*: *x* reads *y* seriously, and *Bx*: *x* is a boring book. The consequence is

$$\{\neg\exists x\exists y(Sx \wedge By \wedge Rxy),\ \exists x(Sx \wedge Rxb)\} \mathrel{!\vdash} \neg Bb.$$

By RA, the consequence is valid iff the set of formulas

$$\{\neg\exists x\exists y(Sx \wedge By \wedge Rxy),\ \exists x(Sx \wedge Rxb),\ Bb\}$$

is unsatisfiable. We first rewrite this set as a set of clauses. Now,

$$\neg\exists x\exists y(Sx \wedge By \wedge Rxy) \equiv \forall x\forall y(\neg Sx \vee \neg By \vee \neg Rxy).$$

It gives the clause $\neg Sx \vee \neg By \vee \neg Rxy$. The second formula $\exists x(Sx \wedge Rxb)$ gives $Sa \wedge Rab$ after Skolemization. Hence the clause set is

$$\{\neg Sx \vee \neg By \vee \neg Rxy,\ Sa,\ Rab,\ Bb\}.$$

We try a resolution refutation by using the rules R, F, M and E.

1.	$\neg Sx \vee \neg By \vee \neg Rxy$	P
2.	Sa	P
3.	$\neg By \vee \neg Ray$	1, 2, R
4.	Bb	P
5.	$\neg Rab$	3, 4, R
6.	Rab	P
7.	$\bot$	R

EXAMPLE 7.27. Show that $\exists x \forall y(Py \vee Px \vee \neg Qyx) \vDash \exists z(Pz \vee \neg Qzz)$.

We must show that $\{\exists x \forall y(Px \vee Py \vee \neg Qyx),\ \neg\exists z(Pz \vee \neg Qzz)\}$ is unsatisfiable. The corresponding clause set is $\{\{Pa, Py, \neg Qya\},\ \{\neg Pz\},\ \{Qzz\}\}$. The following is a resolution refutation:

1.	$\{Pa, Py, \neg Qya\}$	P
2.	$\{Pa, \neg Qaa\}$	F:$[y/a]$
3.	$\{\neg Pz\}$	P
4.	$\{\neg Qaa\}$	2, 3, R
5.	$\{Qzz\}$	P
6.	$\bot$	4, 5, R

EXAMPLE 7.28. Show by resolution that

$$\{\forall x(f(x,a) \approx x),\ \forall x \forall y \forall z(f(f(x,y),z) \approx f(x, f(y,z))),\ \forall x(f(x,h(x)) \approx a)\}$$
$$\vDash \forall x \forall y \forall z((f(y,x) \approx f(z,x)) \to (y \approx z)).$$

Adding the negation of the conclusion to the set of premises, and changing into scnf, we have the clause set

$$A = \{\{f(x,a) \approx x\},\ \{f(x,h(x)) \approx a\},\ \{f(f(x,y),z) \approx f(x, f(y,z))\},$$
$$\{f(b,c) \approx f(d,c)\},\ \{\neg(b \approx d)\}\}$$

where b, c, d are Skolem constants. A resolution refutation of A is as follows.

1.	$f(b,c) \approx f(d,c)$	P
2.	$f(f(b,c),h(c)) \approx f(f(b,c),h(c))$	E
3.	$f(f(b,c),h(c)) \approx f(f(d,c),h(c))$	1, 2, M:[ ]
4.	$f(f(x,y),z) \approx f(x, f(y,z))$	P
5.	$f(f(d,c),h(c)) \approx f(b, f(c,h(c)))$	3, 4, M:$[x/b, y/c, z/h(c)]$
6.	$f(b, f(c,h(c))) \approx f(d, f(c,h(c)))$	5, 4, M:$[x/d, y/c, z/h(c)]$
7.	$f(x,h(x)) \approx a$	P
8.	$c \approx c$	E
9.	$f(c,h(c)) \approx a$	7, 8, M:$[x/c]$

10.	$f(b,a) \approx f(d, f(c,h(c)))$	9, 6, M:[ ]
11.	$f(b,a) \approx f(d,a)$	9, 10, M:[ ]
12.	$f(x,a) \approx x$	P
13.	$f(d,a) \approx b$	11, 12, M:$[x/b]$
14.	$b \approx d$	13, 12, M:$[x/d]$
15.	$\neg(b \approx d)$	P
16.	$\bot$	14, 15, R:[ ]

If you interpret $f(x,y)$ as $x+y$, then the first premise says that a is the identity of addition, the second premise asserts the associativity of addition, and the third one says that $h(x)$ is the additive inverse of x. Thus, we have proved the cancellation law in a group, by resolution.

The soundness and completeness of resolution for FL can be proved as earlier. Soundness is accomplished by showing that for each rule having a numerator Σ and denominator w, the corresponding consequence $\Sigma \,!\!\vdash w$ is valid.

Though soundness is straightforward, completeness is quite involved. The central idea is the observation that due to Rules F, E and P, if $X(x)$ is in A, then for any closed term t, the formula $X(t)$ can be derived. Then by induction you will show that every finite subset of the Herbrand expansion (See Chapter 10.) of A can be derived by resolution.

Next, you will use the compactness theorem for PL, which guarantees that if a set of propositions is unsatisfiable, then there exists a finite subset of it, which is also unsatisfiable. Since every finite set of the Herbrand expansion is derived from A by resolution, so is this particular finite subset. Moreover, this finite subset of the Herbrand expansion is propositionally unsatisfiable. Due to the completeness of resolution (Rule R is used here) for PL, we conclude that $\bot$ is derivable from this finite subset. This would prove the completeness of resolution for FL.

With compactness of FL, we see that $\Sigma \cup \{\neg W\}$ is unsatisfiable iff for some finite subset Σ_0 of Σ, $\Sigma_0 \cup \{\neg W\}$ is unsatisfiable. Writing $\Sigma_0 = \{X_1, \cdots, X_m\}$, we obtain $X_1 \wedge \cdots \wedge X_m \wedge \neg W$ is unsatisfiable. By using completeness of resolution for FL, we then conclude that $\bot$ is derived from $\Sigma_0 \cup \{\neg W\}$. Then it will follow that $\bot$ is derived from $\Sigma \cup \{\neg W\}$. This will prove the strong completeness of resolution.

Another alternative to extending resolution to FL is to use Herbrand expansions directly. For a given set of formulas, we can have its Herbrand expansion, which is countable. Then, we can use propositional resolution in trying to see whether the Herbrand expansion is satisfiable or not. When, the Herbrand expansion is unsatisfiable, eventually the propositional resolution will determine it by deducing $\bot$. But, when the Herbrand expansion is satisfiable and also infinite, resolution will run for ever. This phenomenon is the so-called semi-decidability of FL. We will discuss this issue in Chapter 10.

Exercises for § 7.7

1. Attempt resolution proofs of the following consequences. Also construct the resolution DAGs.

   (a) $\exists x X \leftrightarrow \neg \forall x \neg X$

(b) $\forall x(Px \vee Qx) \rightarrow \exists xPx \vee \forall xQx$
(c) $\forall xX \rightarrow X[x/t]$, if t is a free for x in X.
(d) $\forall x(X \rightarrow Y) \rightarrow (X \rightarrow \forall xY)$, if x does not occur free in X.
(e) $\{Pc, \forall x(Px \rightarrow Qx), \forall x(Rx \rightarrow \neg Qx), Ra\} \vDash \neg(c \approx a)$
(f) $\forall x\forall y(fxy \approx fyx), \forall x\forall y(fxy \approx y)\forall x\exists y\neg(x \approx y) \vDash \forall x\exists yQxy \wedge \exists y\forall x\neg Qyx$
(g) $\forall x\forall y\forall z(Pxy \wedge Pyz \rightarrow \neg Qxz) \wedge \forall x\forall y(Pxy \leftrightarrow (Qyx \vee Rxy)) \wedge \forall x\exists yPxy \vDash \forall xPxx$

2. Use resolution to determine whether the following formulas are satisfiable:
   (a) $\forall y\exists x(Pyx \wedge (Qy \leftrightarrow \neg Qx)) \wedge \forall x\forall y\forall z((Pxy \wedge Pyz) \rightarrow Pxz)$ $\wedge \forall x\neg\exists z(Qx \wedge Qz \wedge Pxz)$
   (b) $\forall x\forall y\forall z((Px \wedge Qy \wedge Rzy \wedge Syx) \rightarrow Rzx) \wedge Qa \wedge Rba \wedge Sac \wedge Pc \wedge Pd \wedge Rsd$ $\wedge \neg(c \approx d) \wedge (s \approx b) \wedge \neg\exists x\exists y\exists z(Px \wedge Py \wedge \neg(x \approx y) \wedge Rzx \wedge Rzy)$

7.8 HORN CLAUSES IN FL

The Rules E and P of equality and paramodulant take care of the equality predicate. The fragment of FL without equality is handled by the other two Rules R and F of resolution and factor. In Rule R, recall that, from $A \vee C$ and $B \vee \neg D$, you derive $(A \vee B)\sigma$, where σ is the most general unifier of the literals C and D. Instead of just two literals (such as C and D), if you take an arbitrary number of literals, the resulting rule is the *full resolution*. In this context, the Rule R, as stated in Section 7.7, is often referred to as the rule of *binary resolution*. The full resolution rule says that

> From $A \vee C_1 \vee \cdots \vee C_m$ and $B \vee \neg D_1 \vee \cdots \vee \neg D_n$, derive $(A \vee B)\sigma$, where σ is the mgu of $\{C_1, \cdots, C_m, D_1, \cdots D_n\}$ for literals C_i, D_j, and clauses A, B.

This is written schematically as the following rule:

$$\textbf{(FR)} \qquad \frac{\{A_1,\ldots,A_l,C_1,\ldots,C_m\} \quad \{B_1,\ldots,B_k,\neg D_1,\ldots,\neg D_n\}}{\{A_1\sigma,\ldots,A_l\sigma,B_1\sigma,\ldots,B_k\sigma\}}$$

where σ is the mgu of the literals $C_1,\ldots,C_m,D_1,\ldots,D_n$.

The two rules of (binary) resolution and factor together are equivalent to the single rule of 'full resolution'. We will rewrite the clauses in a different form and see how resolution may possibly be implemented. A clause of the form

$$\{C_1,\ C_2,\ \ldots,\ C_m,\ \neg D_1,\ \neg D_2,\ \ldots,\ \neg D_n\}$$

where C_i, D_j are atomic formulas can be rewritten as

$$D_1 \wedge D_2 \wedge \cdots \wedge D_n \rightarrow C_1 \vee C_2 \vee \cdots \vee C_m$$

due to the equivalences $X \rightarrow Y \equiv \neg X \vee Y$ and $\neg X \vee \neg Y \equiv \neg(X \wedge Y)$. Traditionally, the clause is written with the arrow in reverse direction, that is, as

$$C_1 \vee C_2 \vee \cdots \vee C_m \leftarrow D_1 \wedge D_2 \wedge \cdots \wedge D_n$$

the reverse arrow being read as 'if'. Since the connective on the left of $\leftarrow$ is only $\vee$ and on the right is only $\wedge$, both of them are replaced by commas to rewrite the formula as

$$C_1, C_2, \cdots, C_m \leftarrow D_1, D_2, \cdots, D_n.$$

A clause in this form is said to be in **Kowalski form**. When $m = 1$, such a clause is called a **Horn clause** as in PL.

A clause is written this way due to its associated procedural meaning, while searching for a model. Let us see the case of a Horn clause

$$C \leftarrow D_1, \ldots, D_n.$$

For example, we may express the *grandfather* relation as

$$grandfather(x,y) \leftarrow father(x,z), father(z,y).$$

To check whether a is a grand father of b, you would first find out whether there is some c such that a is father of c and also that c is a father of b. Quantification of the variables in such a clause is seen as

$$\forall x \forall y (grandfather(x,y) \leftarrow \exists z (father(x,z), father(z,y))).$$

That is, the extra variables to the right of *if* are all existentially quantified whose scope begins just after the symbol $\leftarrow$, and universal quantification of all the other variables is taken with the whole formula in their scopes.

Suppose that you have already built up a database of *facts* describing the relation of *father* as follows:

$$father(rajiv, rahul)$$
$$father(firoz, rajiv)$$
$$father(firoz, sanjay)$$
$$father(jehangir, firoz)$$
$$father(jehangir, banu)$$

Along with this, you also have the *rule*

$$grandfather(x,y) \leftarrow father(x,z), father(z,y).$$

Then you can query such a database, and the resolution is applied for concluding whether $grandfather(jehangir, rahul)$ holds or not. As you see, It is enough to instantiate x, y, z with the constants

rajiv, rahul, firoz, sanjay, jehangir, banu

one after another and then try to see whether they hold by matching with the facts. Let us see how the procedural meaning is given to the clauses (and quantifiers) here. Suppose you have the query

$$? - grandfather(firoz, rahul).$$

Since *grandfather*(.,.) is not a fact, but a rule of the database, it is applied first. While doing this, x becomes bound to (is instantiated to) *firoz* and y becomes bound to *rahul*, so that the goal would be satisfied provided both $father(firoz, z)$ and $father(z, rahul)$ become true for some z.

In our database, the first fact to match with $father(firoz, z)$ is $father(firoz, rajiv)$. Thus, z becomes bound to *rajiv* as a trial solution. This would be a solution provided that $father(rajiv, rahul)$ is true. Since it is a fact, $grandfather(firoz, rahul)$ holds.

This is how the logic programming language PROLOG works for satisfying a goal. It looks fine for a Horn clause. But Horn clauses do not cover the whole of FL. Nonetheless, the method can be extended to a bigger fragment such as Kowalski forms; these form the subclass of formulas that can be written as a conjunction of Horn clauses. This is practically enough for many problem solving tasks.

In fact, it works with a slightly bigger fragment. This extension comes from augmenting *negation as failure* to it. For example, to define a subset relationship between two sets x and y, the usual way is to write $x \subseteq y \leftarrow \forall z(z \in x \to z \in y)$. As it is, in a Horn clause, we cannot allow $\forall$ on the right side of $\leftarrow$.

We must look for alternate ways of writing this formula. We may express $x \subseteq y$ as "no z in x fails to belong to y". That is,

$$x \subseteq y \leftarrow not\ \exists z(z \in x \wedge not\ (z \in y)).$$

Here, the connective *not* is not quite the same as $\neg$. The interpretation of *not* is procedural, in the sense that *not* X holds if X cannot be falsified, basing our reasoning on the given database. You can interpret this *not* in defining subsets, as

> x is a subset of y if it cannot be shown on the basis of the database of facts that x is not a subset of y.

Since we have data only in terms of "a subset of", the definition of "not a subset of" looks like

> x is not a subset of y if there is some z in x which fails to be in y.

This is all right as long as we are concerned with "not a subset of", but it is not quite all right to capture the abstract concept of "subset of". However, this procedural meaning of $\neg$ as *not* adds more power to the Horn clauses. Sometimes, "negation as failure" is referred to as the *closed world assumption*. That is, if something does not hold in the given database (now all of our world), then it is false.

Again, negation as failure with Horn clauses still do not have the full expressive power of FL. Let us see an example. The sentence $\neg p \to p$ semantically entails p. Writing it as a rule, you have

$$p \leftarrow q, \text{ where } q \text{ is } \neg p \to p.$$

Taking $\neg$ as *not*, the rule is rewritten as

$$p \leftarrow q, \text{ where } q \text{ is } not\ p \to p.$$

Now, to satisfy the goal p, we have to first satisfy the condition $not\ p \to p$. We have the new goal $p \leftarrow not\ p$. But this goes on a loop if *not* is interpreted as a failure since it says that *p succeeds if p fails.*

To see it another way, suppose that p is $P(x)$ for a unary predicate P. Now $P(x)$ succeeds if *not* $P(x)$ fails. In other words, for deciding satisfaction of $P(x)$, a call is made for the 'falsification of *not* $P(x)$'. Again this happens if "$P(x)$ is falsified" is falsified, calling falsification of 'falsification of $P(x)$'. This goes on *ad infinitum.* Thus, PROLOG fails in proving $P(x)$ given that $P(x) \leftarrow \neg P(x)$.

This shows that the procedural interpretation along with the Horn clauses would not be sufficient to capture the whole of FL.

You should not look down upon PROLOG due to its inability in recognizing a situation where a goal is unsolvable. In fact, every theorem prover will have this inability; it cannot handle all the situations of solving a goal expressed in FL. This is essentially the undecidability of first order logic, which we will discuss later.

Exercises for § 7.8

1. Apply full resolution, in all possible ways, on the following pairs of clauses: (In three ways you can apply FR on the last pair.)
   (a) $\{P(x), Q(f(x))\}$, $\{\neg R(y), \neg P(f(y))\}$
   (b) $\{P(x), \neg P(f(c))\}$, $\{P(x), \neg P(f(c))\}$
   (c) $\{P(x), \neg P(f(c)), Q(x)\}$, $\{P(x), \neg P(f(c)), Q(x)\}$
   (d) $\{P(x,c), P(f(c),y), Q(x,y)\}$, $\{\neg P(f(z),z), R(z)\}$
2. Use resolution to prove correctness of the following argument:

   Everyone who gets admission into an IIT gets a job.
   Therefore, if there are no jobs, then nobody gets admission into an IIT.
3. Transform the formula $\forall x Px \to \exists y \forall z (Pu \vee Qxy \to \forall u Rxu)$ to Kowalski form.
4. Explain how a sentence can be converted to Kowalski form.

7.9 SUMMARY AND PROBLEMS

We wanted to explore whether there exists some sort of normal form analogous to PL. This has taken us to prenex form, and then quantifier-free forms. We have discussed two kinds of quantifier-free forms, one preserves validity and the other preserves satisfiability. We pursued the satisfiability preserving form leading to extension of the resolution method.

The resolution method required binary resolution and factors for equality-free fragment of FL. In the presence of equality, we have discussed the use of paramodulants in addition to the reflexive property of the equality predicate. We have given some hints as to how the completeness of resolution method could be proved. In the lines of Horn clauses, we have introduced Kowalski form.

The extension of resolution method to first order logic through paramodulation has first appeared in Robinson & Wos (1969). For completeness of the resolution method for first order logic (using the rules R,F,E,P) refer Loveland (1979). The resolution method has been extended to higher order logics also; see for example, Andrews (1970).

Problems for Chapter 7

1. Show that there exists an algorithm to transform any formula X to a formula Z with a prefix of the form $\forall x_1 \cdots \forall x_m \exists y_1 \cdots \exists y_n$ such that X is satisfiable iff Z is satisfiable. Can you construct a formula W similar to Z so that X is valid iff W is valid?
2. Write *QuaEli* in steps.
3. Give a proof of Theorem 7.3 without using Theorem 7.2.
4. Let X be a formula in the form: $\forall x_1 \cdots \forall x_m \exists xY$, and let P be an $(m+1)$-ary predicate not occurring in Y. Let

$$Z = \forall x_1 \cdots \forall x_m \exists x P x_1 \ldots x_m x \wedge \forall x_1 \cdots \forall x_m \forall x (P x_1 \ldots x_m x \to Y).$$

Show that X is satisfiable iff Z is satisfiable.
5. Let X be a prenex form formula such that each atomic subformula contains an existentially quantified variable whose quantifier is in the scope of each quantifier that uses some other variable occurring in that atomic subformula. Show that X is satisfiable iff its matrix is satisfiable.
6. Existential specification as given in Theorem 6.21 does not capture the idea in its totality. The naming of y in $\forall x \exists y Pxy$ by a constant c hides the dependence of y on the universally quantified variable x. The remedy is to use a Skolem term instead of the constant. However, in the scenario of a quasi-proof, you may have derived the formula $\exists y Pxy$ from $\forall x \exists y Pxy$ and now the Skolem term must treat the free variable x as a universally quantified variable. It suggests the following procedure to name the entities introduced by an existential quantifier:

> Let Σ be a set of formulas, X a formula, and let x be a variable not occurring free in any formula of Σ. Let $\{x_1, x_2, \ldots, x_n\}$ be the set of all variables occurring free in the formulas of $\Sigma \cup \{\exists xX\}$. If there is no predicate in $\Sigma \cup \{X\}$ with the occurrence of both x_i and x, then delete x_i from the set $\{x_1, x_2, \ldots, x_n\}$. Do this for each x_i. Suppose the updated set of variables is $\{x_{k1}, x_{k2}, \ldots, x_{kj}\}$. Let f be a j-ary function symbol not occurring in any formula of $\Sigma \cup \{\exists xX\}$. Then construct the *Skolem term* $t = f(x_{k1}, x_{k2}, \ldots, x_{kj})$. We say that t is a Skolem term for x in the consequence $\Sigma \,!\!\vdash \exists xX$.

Prove the following:

(a) Let Σ be a set of formulas having no free occurrence of the variable x, and let $I_\ell = (D, \phi, \ell)$ be a state-model of Σ. Suppose $\Sigma \vDash \exists xX$, and that $t = f(x_{k1}, x_{k2}, \ldots, x_{kj})$ is a Skolem term for x in the consequence $\Sigma \,!\!\vdash \exists xX$. Then there exist extensions ϕ' of ϕ and ℓ' of ℓ such that the state $J_{\ell'} = (D, \phi', \ell')$ satisfies $X[x/t]$.

(b) Let Σ be a set of formulas, X, Y formulas, x a variable having no free occurrence in any formula of Σ, and let $t = f(x_{k1}, x_{k2}, \ldots, x_{kj})$ be a Skolem term for x in the consequence $\Sigma \,!\!\vdash \exists xX$. If $\Sigma \vDash \exists xX$ and $\Sigma \cup \{X[x/t]\} \vDash Y$ for a formula Y having no occurrence of f, then $\Sigma \vDash Y$.

7. *Skolem form Theorem*: Let X be a formula with the set of free variables as F. Prove that there exits a formula Z in the form $Z = \forall x_1 \cdots \forall x_n Y$ such that the set of free variables of Y is F, no quantifier occurs in Y, $Z \vDash X$, and Z is satisfiable iff X is satisfiable. Here, Y may have more functions symbols than X.
8. Show that each formula is equivalent to one in which none of $\forall, \exists, \neg$ occurs within the scope of any $\neg$.
9. A *negation normal form* formula or an **nnf** is defined as follows.
   (i) For any atomic formula X, both X and $\neg X$ are in nnf.
   (ii) If X, Y are in nnf, then both $(X \wedge Y)$ and $(X \vee Y)$ are in nnf.
   (iii) If X is in nnf, then both $\forall x X$ and $\exists x X$ are in nnf.
   (iv) These are the only way an nnf is generated.

   Show that each formula is equivalent to one in nnf.
10. The unification procedure is written for a set of literals. Write a procedure for a set of terms. Also, prove by induction on the number of loops *Unify* executes on an input, that it correctly unifies a set of literals or terms.
11. Is it true that if σ and θ are two most general unifiers of a clause A, then $\theta = \sigma\delta$ for a variant δ? If you think 'no', give a counter example. If 'yes', give a proof.
12. Let A be a unifiable clause. Let δ be a substitution computed by the procedure *Unify*. Show that $A\delta$ is unifiable.
13. By using Problem 12, or in some other way, prove the correctness of the procedure *Unify*.
14. Show that if a clause A is unifiable, then there exists a most general unifier. Can you prove this without using the correctness of the procedure *Unify*?
15. A trivial example to show that an mgu is not unique is to use a variant. Give a nontrivial example.
16. Show that the factor rule can be restricted to clauses consisting of a pair of literals only; and still we do not loose generality.
17. If C is a factor of a clause A, then does $A \vDash C$? Justify your answer either with a proof or with a counter example.
18. If C is a paramodulant of two clauses A and B, then does $\{A, B\} \vDash C$? Justify your answer either with a proof or with a counter example.
19. Use resolution to determine the validity of the following arguments.
   (a) Some students read logic books seriously. No student ever reads a boring logic book. All logic books in your library, including this one, is read by all students seriously. Therefore, none of the logic books in your library is boring.
   (b) Some people love anyone who likes the leader. Everyone loves someone who likes the leader. None, who loves someone who likes the leader, likes the leader. Therefore, the leader does not like himself.
   (c) No teacher who likes to write logic books or who devotes himself to his students will be in the good books of the administration. No one who is not in the good books of the administration will be promoted. Therefore, no teacher who likes to write logic books will be promoted.

(d) Arjun loves all and only those who love Urvasi. Urvasi loves all and only those who love Arjun. Arjun loves himself. Therefore, Urvasi loves herself.

(e) (Lewis Carroll) The only animals in this house are cats. Every animal that loves to gaze at the moon is suitable for a pet. When I detest an animal, I avoid it. No animals are carnivorous unless they prowl at night. No cat fails to kill mice. No animals ever like me, except those that are in this house. Kangaroos are not suitable for pets. None but carnivorous animals kill mice. I detest animals that do not like me. Animals that prowl at night always love to gaze at the moon. Therefore, I always avoid a kangaroo.

20. Let D be a nonempty set of constants. The *ground terms* over D are terms that use variables, and the elements of D as constants. The ground literals and ground clauses are defined using the ground terms instead of any arbitrary term. For any clause, its *ground instances* are obtained by replacing a variable in the clause by a ground term. Show the following:

    (a) For ground clauses, whatever that can be derived by full resolution, can also be derived by binary resolution.

    (b) For any two clauses A, B, each resolvent of a ground instance of A and a ground instance of B is a ground instance of some resolvent of A and B.

    (c) Let A and B be clauses. Then each ground instance of a resolvent of A and B contains some resolvent of a ground instance of A and a ground instance of B.

21. (*Adequacy of Resolution*) Use Problem 20 to show that a clause set is unsatisfiable iff $\bot$ can be derived from it by resolution.

22. Prove strong adequacy of resolution assuming compactness for both PL and FL. That is, show that for any set Σ of formulas and any formula W, $\Sigma \vDash W$ iff $\bot$ is derivable from $\Sigma \cup \{\neg W\}$ by resolution. [Here you are using all the Rules R, F, E, and P.]

23. Construct a resolution proof of

$$\{\forall x(Px \wedge Qx \to Rx) \to \exists x(Px \wedge \neg Qx),\ \forall x(Px \to Qx) \vee \forall x(Px \to Rx)\}$$
$$\vDash \forall x(Px \wedge Rx \to Qx) \to \exists x(Px \wedge Qx \wedge \neg Rx).$$

24. How can we apply binary resolution on two clauses in Kowalski form?

25. Determine, if possible, from the Kowalski form of the following knowledge base whether (a) the unicorn is mythical, (b) the unicorn has a horn:

    If the unicorn is mythical, then it is immortal. If it is not mythical, then it is a mortal mammal. If the unicorn is immortal or a mammal, then it has a horn. The unicorn is mythical if it has a horn.

Chapter 8

Other Proof Systems for FL

8.1 CALCULATION

Calculations can be extended to first order logic with the help of the laws listed in Theorem 6.17 and also the laws that result from PL as listed in Theorem 2.12. In addition to these, we have the four quantifier laws. To have a feel, see the following calculation:

$\forall x(Px \to Qx)$	[Hyp, Universal Specification]
$\vDash Px \to Qx$	[Tautology]
$\equiv \neg Px \vee Qx$	[Universal Generalization]
$\Rightarrow \forall x(\neg Px \vee Qx)$	

The symbol $\Rightarrow$ (Read it as *implies*.) in the above calculation does not connect the last line with the previous one quite the same way as the symbols $\equiv$ and $\vDash$. In a calculation if $X \Rightarrow Y$ appears, it does not mean that Y follows from X; it says that if from all the premises used thus far the formula X follows, then from all those premises the formula Y also follows. See Theorem 6.20. The symbol $\Rightarrow$ thus connects Y with all the premises used till the derivation of X. It is used as a shorthand for the meta-statement "if $\Sigma \vDash X$, then $\Sigma \vDash Y$," where Σ is the set of formulas used in the calculation (so far).

In existential specification, once we have $\exists xX$, we introduce $X[x/c]$ and then go onto deriving Y, where c does not occur. See Theorem 6.21. This can be tackled by writing $\exists xX \Rightarrow X[x/c]$ documenting the line as "ESBc", a shortcut for

Existential specification begins with the new constant c.

When we obtain a formula Y having no occurrence of the constant c, we will document it by writing "ESEc" signalling the fact that

Existential specification ends with the new constant c.

The block of the calculation with the pair of ESBc and ESEc is a sub-calculation, proof of a lemma with the extra assumption $X[x/c]$. Thus the symbol $\Rightarrow$ used here has a slightly different meaning than that in the context of Universal Generalization.

Existential specification needs a block, which we show up in a calculation by proper indentation, in addition to using the symbol $\Rightarrow$. The blocks are nested as usual; one block may lie inside another, but they are prohibited to intersect. For instance, we cannot have ESBc, ESBd, ESBc, and ESEd in that order. But we can have ESBc, ESBd, ESEd, and ESEc.

We continue using the deduction theorem and RA outside a calculation for better readability. Though the corresponding sub-calculations for these theorems can be made just like existential specification, we refrain from doing so.

A **calculation** in FL looks like $C_0 \star C_1 \star \cdots \star C_m$, where an instance of $\star$ is one of the symbols $\equiv$, $\vDash$, or $\Rightarrow$; each step $C_{i-1} \star C_i$ must be an instance of a law $E_1 \star E_2$ when $\star$ is $\equiv$ or $\vDash$. The case $\star$ as $\Rightarrow$ is used for the laws of universal generalization and of existential specification, as explained earlier. The calculation is taken as a **proof** of the metastatement $C_0 \odot C_m$, where

$$\odot \text{ equals } \begin{cases} \equiv & \text{if each } \star \text{ equals } \equiv \\ \vDash & \text{if at least one instance of } \star \text{ equals } \vDash, \text{ or } \Rightarrow \end{cases}$$

In fact, we can have $\odot$ as $\vDash$ even if each instance of $\star$ equals $\equiv$. Similarly, a law such as $X \equiv Y$ can be used both the ways: $X \vDash Y$ and $Y \vDash X$. A calculational proof of $\Sigma \vDash X$ typically begins with one premise from Σ and uses other premises as and when necessary. If Σ is empty, we may begin a calculation with $\top$.

We continue using the abbreviated names of the laws such as Const, Mod Pon, De Mor, Dist, etc. in calculations. Sometimes we just mention PL when the law is obtained by taking formulas in place of propositions in Theorem 2.12. We write 'Hyp' when a premise is introduced in the succeeding step. In addition, we use the following abbreviations:

UG: Universal Generalization
US: Universal Specification
EG: Existential Generalization
ES: Existential Specification, with the new constant and block marking
Eq: Equality; See Theorem 6.17.

Whenever the symbol $\Rightarrow$ is used, the provisos in the laws of universal generalization and existential specification are in vogue. We also use a little indentation with the use of $\Rightarrow$ with existential specification since we enter a sub-calculation. The conclusion in such a sub-calculation is not our main conclusion. In the case of universal generalization, a conclusion of such a sub-calculation is a conclusion of the main calculation, and we do not use any indentation. Thus, the last line must be without any indentation.

EXAMPLE 8.1. Show by calculation that $\vDash \forall x((\neg Px \to \neg Qx) \to (Qx \to Px))$.

$\top$ [PL]
$\equiv (\neg Px \to \neg Qx) \to (Qx \to Px)$ [UG]
$\Rightarrow \forall x((\neg Px \to \neg Qx) \to (Qx \to Px))$

Since x is not free in the premise $\top$, use of universal generalization is allowed.

EXAMPLE 8.2. Show that $\vDash \forall x(Px \to Qx) \to (\exists xPx \to \exists xQx)$.

Due to DT, we show that $\forall x(Px \to Qx) \wedge \exists xPx \vDash \exists xQx$.

$$
\begin{array}{ll}
\forall x(Px \to Qx) \wedge \exists xPx & \text{[ESB}c\text{]} \\
\quad \Rightarrow \forall x(Px \to Qx) \wedge Pc & \text{[US]} \\
\quad \vDash (Pc \to Qc) \wedge Pc & \text{[Mod Pon]} \\
\quad \vDash Qc & \text{[EG]} \\
\quad \vDash \exists xQx & \text{[ESE}c\text{]} \\
\vDash \exists xQx &
\end{array}
$$

The repetition of the formula $\exists xQx$ at the end of the calculation signals the fact that the use of the new constant c is over and the formula thus obtained is independent of this c. It also shows clearly the preceding sub-calculation.

EXAMPLE 8.3. Show that $\exists xPx, \forall x\forall y(Px \to Qy) \vDash \forall yQy$.

$$
\begin{array}{ll}
\exists xPx & \text{[ESB}c\text{, Hyp]} \\
\quad \Rightarrow Pc \wedge \forall x\forall y(Px \to Qy) & \text{[US } [x/c]\text{]} \\
\quad \vDash Pc \wedge \forall y(Pc \to Qy) & \text{[Dist]} \\
\quad \vDash Pc \wedge (Pc \to \forall yQy) & \text{[Mod Pon]} \\
\quad \vDash \forall yQy & \text{[ESE}c\text{]} \\
\vDash \forall yQy &
\end{array}
$$

Sometimes, we mention the substitution used in an application of US.

EXAMPLE 8.4. Show the validity of the argument:

All horses are animals. Therefore, all legs of horses are legs of animals.

To translate the argument into FL, we use the following vocabulary:

$Hx : x$ is a horse, $Ax : x$ is an animal, $Lxy : x$ is a leg of y.

Then, "x is a leg of a horse" is symbolized as $\exists y(Hy \wedge Lxy)$, etc. You get the consequence

$$\forall x(Hx \to Ax) \, !\vdash \forall x(\exists y(Hy \wedge Lxy) \to \exists y(Ay \wedge Lxy)).$$

Here, it seems easier to use RA, since the conclusion has the predicate L which is absent in the premise. So, we show that

$$\forall x(Hx \to Ax), \neg\forall x(\exists y(Hy \wedge Lxy) \to \exists y(Ay \wedge Lxy)) \vDash \bot.$$

We start with one of the premises, introduce the other when needed, and intend to end with $\bot$.

$$
\begin{array}{ll}
\neg\forall x(\exists y(Hy \wedge Lxy) \to \exists y(Ay \wedge Lxy)) & \text{[De Mor, PL]} \\
\vDash \exists x(\exists y(Hy \wedge Lxy) \wedge \neg\exists y(Ay \wedge Lxy)) & \text{[ESB}c\text{]} \\
\quad \Rightarrow \exists y(Hy \wedge Lcy) \wedge \neg\exists y(Ay \wedge Lcy) & \text{[ESB}b\text{]} \\
\qquad \Rightarrow Hb \wedge Lcb \wedge \neg\exists y(Ay \wedge Lcy) & \text{[De Mor]}
\end{array}
$$

$\vDash Hb \wedge Lcb \wedge \forall y(\neg(Ay \wedge Lcy))$ [US $[y/b]$]

$\vDash Hb \wedge Lcb \wedge \neg(Ab \wedge Lcb)$ [PL]

$\vDash Hb \wedge Lcb \wedge (Lcb \to \neg Ab)$ [Mod Pon, Hyp]

$\vDash Hb \wedge \neg Ab \wedge \forall x(Hx \to Ax)$ [US $[x/b]$]

$\vDash Hb \wedge \neg Ab \wedge (Hb \to Ab)$ [Mod Pon]

$\vDash Ab \wedge \neg Ab$ [PL]

$\vDash \bot$ [ESEb]

$\vDash \bot$ [ESEc]

$\vDash \bot$

Example 8.4 was the one given by De Morgan (with heads instead of legs) to point out that Aristotle's syllogisms lack expressive power. In our terminology, Aristotle's syllogisms are captured by the first order logic restricted to unary (monadic) predicates, and without function symbols. This example requires a binary predicate.

EXAMPLE 8.5. Show the validity of the argument

Since all horses are animals, all heads of horses are heads of animals.

Writing Hx : x is a horse; Ax : x is an animal; and $f(x)$: the head of x, the argument is translated to the consequence

$$\forall x(Hx \to Ax) \,!\!\vdash \forall x(\exists y(Hy \wedge (x \approx f(y))) \to \exists y(Ay \wedge (x \approx f(y)))).$$

Comparing this consequence with that is Example 8.4, we replace Lxy with $(x \approx f(y))$ everywhere to obtain a calculation showing the validity of the consequence. Verify that this is indeed the case.

EXAMPLE 8.6. Show by calculation that the following set is unsatisfiable:

$$\{\forall x\forall y\forall z((Px \wedge Qy \wedge Rzy \wedge Syx) \to Rzx), \neg\exists x\exists y\exists z(Px \wedge Py \wedge \neg(x \approx y) \wedge Rzx \wedge Rzy),$$
$$Qa \wedge Rba \wedge Sac \wedge Pc \wedge Pd \wedge \neg(c \approx d), Red \wedge (e \approx b)\}.$$

$\forall x\forall y\forall z((Px \wedge Qy \wedge Rzy \wedge Syx) \to Rzx)$ [US $[x/c,y/a,z/b]$]

$\vDash (Pc \wedge Qa \wedge Rba \wedge Sac \to Rbc)$ [Hyp]

$\vDash (Pc \wedge Qa \wedge Rba \wedge Sac \to Rbc) \wedge$
$\neg\exists x\exists y\exists z(Px \wedge Py \wedge \neg(x \approx y) \wedge Rzx \wedge Rzy)$ [De Mor, PL]

$\vDash (Pc \wedge Qa \wedge Rba \wedge Sac \to Rbc) \wedge$
$\forall x\forall y\forall z(Px \wedge Py \wedge Rzx \wedge Rzy \to (x \approx y))$ [US $[x/d,y/c,z/e]$]

$\vDash (Pc \wedge Qa \wedge Rba \wedge Sac \to Rbc) \wedge (Pd \wedge Pc \wedge Red \wedge Rec \to (d \approx c))$ [Hyp]

$\vDash (Pc \wedge Qa \wedge Rba \wedge Sac \to Rbc) \wedge (Pd \wedge Pc \wedge Red \wedge Rec \to (d \approx c))$
$\wedge Qa \wedge Rba \wedge Sac \wedge Pc \wedge Pd \wedge \neg(c \approx d) \wedge Red \wedge (e \approx b)$ [Mod Pon]

$\vDash Rbc \wedge (Pd \wedge Pc \wedge Red \wedge Rec \to (d \approx c))$
$\wedge Qa \wedge Rba \wedge Sac \wedge Pc \wedge Pd \wedge \neg(c \approx d) \wedge Red \wedge (e \approx b)$ [Eq]

$\vDash Rbc \wedge (Pd \wedge Pc \wedge Rbd \wedge Rbc \to (d \approx c)) \wedge Qa \wedge Rba \wedge Sac$
$\quad \wedge Pc \wedge Pd \wedge \neg(c \approx d) \wedge Rbd \wedge (e \approx b)$ [Mod Pon, PL]

$\vDash (d \approx c) \wedge \neg(c \approx d)$ [Eq]

$\vDash (d \approx c) \wedge \neg(d \approx c)$ [PL]

$\vDash \bot$

In the last example, the specification choices were very important. Had you chosen something else instead of the chosen ones, you would not have ended at $\bot$ (but of course, you could use them later). The choices were motivated by the occurrences of the constants in the predicates. Experience only guides you to make the right choice!

Exercises for § 8.1

Check the following consequences for validity. Check also whether the set of premises in each case is satisfiable. For valid consequences, supply a calculational proof.

1. $\forall x((\exists y Pxy \wedge Qy) \to \exists y(Ry \wedge Uxy))\ !\vdash \exists x \exists y(Pxy \wedge Qy) \to \exists x Rx$
2. $\{\exists x(Px \wedge Qx) \to \forall y(Ry \wedge Hy), \exists x(Rx \wedge \neg Hx)\}\ !\vdash \forall y(Py \to \neg Qy)$
3. $\{\forall x(Px \to Qx), \exists x Px, \forall x \neg Qx\}\ !\vdash \forall x(Px \to Qx) \leftrightarrow \exists x(Px \to Qx)$
4. $\{\exists x(Px \wedge \forall y(Qy \to Rxy)) \wedge \forall x(Px \to \forall y(Uy \to \neg Rxy))\}\ !\vdash \forall x(Qx \to \neg Ux)$
5. $\{\exists x Px \wedge \exists x Qx \to \exists x(Px \wedge Qx), \forall x \exists y Rxy \to \exists y \forall x Rxy\}$
   $!\vdash \forall x(Px \vee Qx) \to \forall x Px \vee \forall x Qx$
6. Spouses of surgeons are teachers. Surgeons are doctors. Therefore, spouses of doctors are teachers.
7. Everyone who gets admission into an IIT gets a job. If there are no jobs, then nobody gets admission into IIT Madras. [Hint: There is a hidden premise.]

8.2 NATURAL DEDUCTION

Basing on PND, we construct a natural deduction system for FL. Let us call the system **FND**, first order natural deduction system. FND has all the inference rules of PND, (See § 4.2.) where p, q, r are taken as formulas. In addition, it has the following inference rules for the the quantifiers and the equality predicate. Recall that in an inference rule, we read e as elimination and i as introduction.

For formulas X, Y, variables x, y, terms s, t, and constant c,

$(\forall e)\quad \dfrac{\forall x X}{X[x/t]}$

$(\forall i)\quad$

y
$\vdots$
$X[x/y]$

$\forall x X$

where y is a new variable.

$$(\exists e)\quad \begin{array}{c} \exists x X \\ \boxed{\begin{array}{cr} & c \\ X[x/c] & \\ \vdots & \\ Y & \end{array}} \\ Y \end{array} \qquad\qquad (\exists i)\quad \frac{X[x/t]}{\exists x X}$$

where c is a new constant not occurring in Y.

$$(\approx e)\quad \frac{s \approx t, \quad X[x/s]}{X[x/t]} \qquad\qquad (\approx i)\quad \frac{\cdot}{t \approx t}$$

In the above rules, whenever $X[x/u]$ occurs, we assume that the term u is free for x in X. The 'new constant c' means that c should not have been used in the proof up to that stage where it is introduced. As earlier, we follow the restriction on boxes that no box will intersect another, though one box can completely lie inside another. We will explain the use of boxes taking the appropriate rules in turn. In case of $(\forall i)$, the "for all introduction", the box means the following:

> If starting with a new variable y, a formula $X[x/y]$ is proved, then the formula $\forall x X$ is considered proved.

The box is only a check for an important phrase used in mathematics: "Let x be a fixed but arbitrary number such that ... ". This is a formal expression of the informal statement that if you can prove $X(y)$ for an arbitrary y, then you can prove $\forall x X(x)$. The restriction allows you to draw the conclusion $\forall x X$ only when you have arrived at X in such a way that none of the assumptions you have used contains x as a free variable. It is exactly the restriction on the rule (UG) in FC. It now takes the form:

> The new variable y must not occur anywhere outside the box; and it cannot occur free in any premise.

In case of $(\exists e)$, we notice that $\exists x X \nvDash X[x/c]$ for any constant c. In mathematics, we say "Suppose that the element for which X holds is c." This constant c is an ambiguous name with the property $X(\cdot)$. We thus take this c as a new constant. In this case, the box means the following:

> If starting with a new constant c, a formula Y having no occurrence of c is proved, then Y is considered proved.

Thus the formula Y is repeated twice; first time, inside the box, just to show that this last formula inside the box follows from the earlier formulas, possibly depending on the extra assumption $X[x/c]$. It is mentioned second time outside the box to say that this last formula does not have any occurrence of c; and therefore, it does not depend on the special assumption $X[x/c]$ but possibly on the existential formula $\exists x X$, which is outside and on the top of the box. The restriction thus looks like:

> The new constant c cannot occur anywhere in the proof outside the box; and it cannot occur in any premise.

The box controls the scope of the fresh constant c which is also documented at the rightmost corner of the box. Note that the earlier boxes for conditional premises and the current boxes for quantifiers together obey the nesting rules:

> Only a complete box can be inside another; no intersection of boxes is allowed.

In this section, we use the symbol $\vdash$ for "$\vdash$ in FND". See the following examples.

EXAMPLE 8.7. $\vdash \forall xX \to X[x/t]$ if t is free for x in X.

1.	$\forall xX$		CPB
2.	$X[x/t]$	$\forall e$	
3.	$\forall xX \to X[x/t]$	$\to i$	CPE

Here, we use the nesting due to a conditional premise.

EXAMPLE 8.8. Construct an FND-proof of $\{\forall x(Pxy \to Qx), \forall zPzy\} \vdash \forall xQx$.

1.	$\forall x(Pxy \to Qx)$	P
2.	$\forall zPzy$	P

	u
3. $Puy \to Qu$	$\forall e$, $[x/u]$
4. Puy	2, $\forall e$
5. Qu	e

6. $\forall xQx$ $\forall i$

We can dispense with drawing the boxes by writing the scopes of the newly introduced variable or constant. For example, in the above proof, the new variable is u and we mention it by writing "u new var". When the scope ends, we write "Sc of u ends" as an acronym for "scope of u ends here". See the following rewriting of the above proof.

Proof in Example 8.8 rewritten:

1.	$\forall x(Pxy \to Qx)$	P	
2.	$\forall zPzy$	P	
3.	$Puy \to Qu$	$\forall e$, $[x/u]$	u new var
4.	Puy	2, $\forall e$	
5.	Qu	$\to e$	Sc of u ends
6.	$\forall xQx$	$\forall i$	

Similarly, we dispense with boxes for $\exists e$ rule, by mentioning when the new constant is introduced and what is its scope. We write "c new con" to say that c is a new constant and its scope, the box, starts here. Similarly, when its scope ends, we again mention the rule $\exists e$ and "Sc of c ends". See the following example.

EXAMPLE 8.9. Construct an FND-proof of $\forall x(Pxy \to Qx), \exists zPzy \vdash \exists xQx$.

1.	$\forall x(Pxy \to Qx)$	P	
2.	$\exists z Pzy$	P	
3.	Pcy	2, $\exists e$	c new con
4.	$Pcy \to Qc$	1, $\forall e$	
5.	Qc	$\to e$	
6.	$\exists x Qx$	$\exists i$	Sc of c ends
7.	$\exists x Qx$	$\exists e$	

EXAMPLE 8.10. $\vdash \forall x(X \to Y) \to (X \to \forall x Y)$ if x does not occur free in X.

1.	$\forall x(X \to Y)$		CPB1
2.	X		CPB2
3.	$X \to Y[x/y]$	1, $\forall e$	y new var
4.	$Y[x/y]$	$\to e$	Sc of y ends
5.	$\forall x Y$	$\forall i$	
6.	$X \to \forall x Y$	$\to i$	CPE2
7.	$\forall x(X \to Y) \to (X \to \forall x Y)$	$\to i$	CPE1

Since x does not occur free in X, we see that $(X \to Y)[x/y] = X \to Y[x/y]$. This has been used in the above proof.

EXAMPLE 8.11. Show that $\vdash (s \approx t) \to (X[x/s] \to X[x/t])$.

1.	$s \approx t$		CPB1
2.	$X[x/s]$		CPB2
3.	$X[x/t]$	$\approx e$	
4.	$X[x/s] \to X[x/t]$	$\to i$	CPE2
5.	$(s \approx t) \to (X[x/s] \to X[x/t])$	$\to i$	CPE1

Axiom A6 of FC is simply the rule ($\approx i$). Therefore, the above examples, completeness of PND to PL, and completeness of FC to FL yield the following result.

Theorem 8.1 (Strong Adequacy of FND). *Let Σ be a set of formulas, and let X be a formula. Then, $\Sigma \vDash X$ iff $\Sigma \vdash X$ in FND.*

The following examples will make you better acquainted with FND.

EXAMPLE 8.12. $Pa, \forall x(Px \to Qx), \forall x(Rx \to \neg Qx), Rb \vDash \neg(a \approx b)$

Due to RA in FL, and strong adequacy of FND, it is enough to show that

$$\{Pa, \forall x(Px \to Qx), \forall x(Rx \to \neg Qx), Rb, \neg\neg(a \approx b)\} \vdash \bot.$$

However, the system FND (as an extension of PND) has already a form of RA built in it. See the following proof:

1.	Pa	P
2.	Rb	P
3.	$\forall x(Px \to Qx)$	P
4.	$\forall x(Rx \to \neg Qx)$	P
5.	$Pa \to Qa$	3, $\forall e$
6.	Qa	1, 5, $\to e$

7.	$Rb \to \neg Qb$	4, $\forall e$	
8.	$\neg Qb$	2, 7, $\to e$	
9.	$a \approx b$		CPB
10.	$\neg Qa$	8, 9, $\approx a$	
11.	$\bot$	6, 10, $\bot i$	
12.	$\neg(a \approx b)$	$\neg i$	CPE

EXAMPLE 8.13. All logicians are wise persons. Therefore, all students of logicians are students of wise persons.

Using the vocabulary: Lx : x is a logician, Fx : x is a wise person, and Pxy : x is a student of y, we prove the consequence:

$$\forall x(Lx \to Fx) \mathrel{!\vdash} \forall x(\exists y(Ly \wedge Pxy) \to \exists y(Fy \wedge Pxy)).$$

1.	$\forall x(Lx \to Fx)$	P	
2.	$\exists y(Ly \wedge Pzy)$		z new var, CPB
3.	$Lc \wedge Pzc$	$\exists e$	c new con
4.	Lc	$\wedge e$	
5.	$Lc \to Fc$	1, $\forall e$	
6.	Fc	$\to e$	
7.	Pzc	3, $\wedge e$	
8.	$Fc \wedge Pzc$	$\wedge i$	
9.	$\exists y(Fy \wedge Pzy)$	$\exists i$	Sc of c ends
10.	$\exists y(Fy \wedge Pzy)$	$\exists e$	
11.	$\exists y(Ly \wedge Pzy) \to \exists y(Fy \wedge Pzy)$	$\to i$	CPE, Sc of z ends
12.	$\forall x(\exists y(Ly \wedge Pxy) \to \exists y(Fy \wedge Pxy))$	$\forall i$	

Exercises for § 8.2

1. Try to construct FND-proofs in place of FC-proofs in Exercise 2 of § 6.1 and Exercise 3 of § 6.2.
2. Are the following arguments valid? Formalize into FL-consequences. Try proving each of them using FND.
   (a) Either Logic is elegant or many students like it. If Computer Science is a difficult discipline, then Logic has to be elegant. Therefore, if many students like Computer Science, then Logic is elegant.
   (b) If tomorrow morning it is chilly and not so clear a sky, then we go swimming unless you do not have any special liking for boating. It isn't always the case that if the sky is not clear, then you don't go boating. Therefore, if the weather is not chilly tomorrow morning, then we go swimming.
   (c) Yanka would have been at home, had he been to the club or not to the theatre while his friend was waiting for him at the college. He had been to the club premises while it was dusk only if he didn't come home. Unless the watchman saw him at the club premises, it is certain that it was dusk, since the watchman is night blind. Therefore, Yanka did not go to the theatre.

(d) If anyone is in a guest house, which is located in a city, then he is in that city. None can be in two different cities at the same time. One who snatched the necklace away must have been in the guest house at Chennai. Since Chennai and Mumbai are two different cities and Yanka was in the Mumbai guest house, he did not snatch the necklace.

(e) If all the politicians praise a bandit, then the bandit must be none other than Robin Hood. A politician praises a person if the person has indeed helped him in his career. There is a bandit who has not helped any politician. Therefore, there is a bandit other than Robin Hood.

8.3 GENTZEN SEQUENT CALCULUS

We turn towards a Gentzen system for FL. We call our system **GFC**, Gentzen's First Order Calculus. In GFC, we take all the rules of GPC as they are, remembering that the sets $\Sigma, \Gamma, \Delta, \Omega$ are sets of formulas, and p, q are arbitrary formulas instead of propositions. In this section, we use the symbol $\vdash$ as an abbreviation for "$\vdash$ in GFC". In addition to the rules of GPC (See § 4.3.), we have the following rules to tackle the quantifiers and the equality predicate:

$(\forall L)$ $\quad \dfrac{\Sigma, \forall x X, \Gamma \vdash \Delta}{\Sigma, X[x/t], \forall x X, \Gamma \vdash \Delta} \qquad \dfrac{\forall x X \vdash}{X[x/t], \forall x X \vdash}$

$(\forall R)$ $\quad \dfrac{\Sigma \vdash \Gamma, \forall x X, \Delta}{\Sigma \vdash \Gamma, X[x/y], \Delta} \qquad \dfrac{\forall R x X}{\vdash X[x/y]}$

provided that y is a new variable.

$(\exists L)$ $\quad \dfrac{\Sigma, \exists x X, \Gamma \vdash \Delta}{\Sigma, X[x/y], \Gamma \vdash \Delta} \qquad \dfrac{\exists x X \vdash}{X[x/y] \vdash}$

provided that y is a new variable.

$(\exists R)$ $\quad \dfrac{\Sigma \vdash \Gamma, \exists x X, \Delta}{\Sigma \vdash \Gamma, X[x/t], \exists x X, \Delta} \qquad \dfrac{\exists R x X}{\vdash X[x/t], \exists x X}$

$(\approx r)$ $\quad \dfrac{\Sigma \vdash \Gamma}{\Sigma, (t \approx t) \vdash \Gamma} \qquad \dfrac{\vdash}{(t \approx t) \vdash}$

$(\approx c)$ $\quad \dfrac{\Sigma, (s \approx t), \Gamma \vdash \Delta}{\Sigma, (t \approx s), \Gamma \vdash \Delta} \qquad \dfrac{(s \approx t) \vdash}{(t \approx s) \vdash}$

$(\approx s)$ $\quad \dfrac{\Sigma, (s \approx t), X[x/s], \Gamma \vdash \Delta}{\Sigma, (s \approx t), X[x/t], \Gamma \vdash \Delta} \qquad \dfrac{(s \approx t), X[x/s] \vdash}{(s \approx t), X[x/t] \vdash}$

Here, y is a **new variable** means that the variable y does not occur free in the numerator. This restriction in the rules $(\forall R)$ and $(\exists L)$ on the variable y is called the **eigenvariable condition**. It is the same condition used in the FND-rules $(\forall i)$ and

$(\exists e)$. Compare the rule $(\forall R)$ with the universal generalization (Theorem 6.20) and the strong generalization (Theorem 6.6).

The rule $(\approx r)$ is the reflexivity, $(\approx c)$ is the commutativity, and $(\approx s)$ is the substitutivity property of $\approx$. Notice that $t \approx t$ is equivalent to $\top$ semantically. Moreover, $\top$ behaves as the identity on the left side of $\vdash$; that is, $p, q \vdash r$ and $p, \top, q \vdash r$ represent the same sequent. Thus $t \approx t$ is added on the left side of $\vdash$, in the rule $(\approx r)$. We cannot add $t \approx t$ on the right hand side of $\vdash$ since $p \vdash q, \top, r$ is not the same sequent as $p \vdash q, r$. Similarly, in $(\approx s)$, we cannot have a rule with $s \approx t$ on the right of $\vdash$. But we can have a commutativity rule for $\approx$, where $s \approx t$ and $t \approx s$ can both be on the right of $\vdash$.

The derivations and proofs are defined as for GPC. Recall that in a proof (tree), a sequent at the root is considered proved when each branch of it ends with $\top$. Further, $\top$ is derived when some formula occurs on both the sides of $\vdash$. We write $\Sigma \Vdash \Gamma$ when the sequent $\Sigma \vdash \Gamma$ is provable in GFC.

EXAMPLE 8.14. The following proof shows that the sequent $\vdash \forall RxX \rightarrow X[x/t]$ is GFC-provable. The rules applied in the derivation are $(\vdash\rightarrow)$, $(\forall L)$, and $(\top)$.

$$\vdash \forall xX \rightarrow X[x/t]$$
$$\forall xX \vdash X[x/t]$$
$$X[x/t], \forall xX \vdash X[x/t]$$
$$\top$$

EXAMPLE 8.15. If x does not occur free in X, then $\vdash \forall x(X \rightarrow Y) \rightarrow (X \rightarrow \forall xY)$ is GFC-provable

$$\vdash \forall x(X \rightarrow Y) \rightarrow (X \rightarrow \forall xY)$$
$$\forall x(X \rightarrow Y) \vdash X \rightarrow \forall xY$$
$$\forall x(X \rightarrow Y), X \forall RxY$$
$$\forall x(X \rightarrow Y), X \vdash Y$$
$$X \rightarrow Y, X \vdash Y$$

$$X \vdash X, Y \qquad Y, X \vdash Y$$
$$\top \qquad\qquad \top$$

Find out the rules that have been applied at each stage in the derivation. Where exactly the condition "x does not occur free in X" is used?

EXAMPLE 8.16. The following proof shows that $\Vdash (t \approx t)$.

$$\vdash (t \approx t)$$
$$(t \approx t) \vdash (t \approx t)$$
$$\top$$

EXAMPLE 8.17. The following proof shows that $\Vdash (s \approx t) \to (X[x/s] \to X[x/t])$.

$$\begin{array}{c} \vdash (s \approx t) \to (X[x/s] \to X[x/t]) \\ s \approx t \vdash X[x/s] \to X[x/t] \\ s \approx t, X[x/s] \vdash X[x/t] \\ s \approx t, X[x/t] \vdash X[x/t] \\ \top \end{array}$$

So, you see that all the axioms and inference rules of FC are theorems or provable sequents of GFC except one that we have not yet attempted. It is the rule of universal generalization or

$$\text{(UG)}: \quad \frac{X}{\forall x X} \quad \text{provided } x \text{ is not free in any premise used thus far.}$$

We must fix the correct meaning of the phrase "a premise used thus far". Suppose you have got a proof in FC of X by using some (or all) of the premises, and then you are applying UG. For convenience, let us take the premises as $X_1, \ldots, X_n$ which have been used in this proof for deriving X. Since UG is applied next for deriving $\forall x X$, we see that x is not free in any of the formulas $X_1, \ldots, X_n$.

Before the application of UG, we assume that the consequence $X_1, \ldots, X_n \vDash X$ is valid in FC. After the application of UG, we have proved that $X_1, \ldots, X_n \vDash \forall x X$. Thus, the formulation of UG in GFC must be the metastatement:

If $X_1, \ldots, X_n \Vdash X$, then derive $X_1, \ldots, X_n \Vdash \forall x X$ provided x does not occur free in any of $X_1, \ldots, X_n$.

This corresponds to the inference rule (in GFC style):

$$\textbf{(GUG):} \quad \frac{\Sigma \vdash \Gamma, \forall x X, \Delta}{\Sigma \vdash \Gamma, X, \Delta} \quad \text{if } x \text{ is not free in } \Sigma \cup \Gamma \cup \Delta.$$

You can easily see that GUG is a derived rule of GFC as a single application of $(\forall R)$ completes the derivation. With this, you have proved the completeness of GFC. At this point you must write a formal proof of the following theorem.

Theorem 8.2 (Strong Adequacy of GFC). *Let Σ be a set of formulas. Let X be a formula. Then, $\Sigma \Vdash X$ iff $\Sigma \vDash X$.*

Notice that a set of formulas Σ is inconsistent iff the sequent $\Sigma \vdash$ is provable. We discuss some more examples before closing this section.

EXAMPLE 8.18. Show that the following set Σ of formulas is unsatisfiable:

$$\Sigma = \{\forall x \forall y (f(x,y) \approx f(y,x)), \forall x \forall y (f(x,y) \approx y), \forall x \exists y \neg (x \approx y)\}.$$

Due to strong adequacy, it is enough to show that Σ is inconsistent in GFC. We construct a proof of the sequent $\Sigma \vdash$. For ease in writing let

$$P = \forall x \forall y (f(x,y) \approx f(y,x)) \text{ and } Q = \forall x \forall y (f(x,y) \approx y).$$

In the following proof, we use the rules $(\forall L)$, $(\exists L)$, $(\neg \vdash)$, $(\forall L)$ four times, the rules $(\forall L)$, $(\approx s)$ twice, and $(\approx c)$, $(\top)$ once each. Find out the substitutions used in the applications of the quantifier rules.

$$\begin{gathered}
\forall x \forall y(f(x,y) \approx f(y,x)), \forall x \forall y(f(x,y) \approx y), \forall x \exists y \neg(x \approx y) \vdash \\
\forall x \forall y(f(x,y) \approx f(y,x)), \forall x \forall y(f(x,y) \approx y), \exists y \neg(x \approx y) \vdash \\
\forall x \forall y(f(x,y) \approx f(y,x)), \forall x \forall y(f(x,y) \approx y), \neg(x \approx z) \vdash \\
\forall x \forall y(f(x,y) \approx f(y,x)), \forall x \forall y(f(x,y) \approx y) \vdash x \approx z \\
\forall x \forall y(f(x,y) \approx f(y,x)), Q, f(x,z) \approx z, f(z,x) \approx x \vdash x \approx z \\
P, Q, f(x,z) \approx z, f(z,x) \approx x, f(x,z) \approx f(z,x) \vdash x \approx z \\
P, Q, f(x,z) \approx z, f(z,x) \approx x, z \approx x \vdash x \approx z \\
P, Q, f(x,z) \approx z, f(z,x) \approx x, x \approx z \vdash x \approx z \\
\top
\end{gathered}$$

EXAMPLE 8.19. Construct a GFC proof to show that

$$\exists x \exists y \exists z(\neg Qx \wedge \neg Qy \wedge \neg Qz \wedge Qf(f(x,y),z)) \vDash \exists x \exists y(\neg Qx \wedge \neg Qy \wedge Qf(x,y)).$$

We apply $(\exists L)$ thrice, $(\wedge \vdash)$ thrice, $(\exists R)$ twice, and $(\vdash \wedge)$ twice, in succession, to obtain the following GFC proof:

$$\begin{gathered}
\exists x \exists y \exists z(\neg Qx \wedge \neg Qy \wedge \neg Qz \wedge Qf(f(x,y),z)) \vdash \exists x \exists y(\neg Qx \wedge \neg Qy \wedge Qf(x,y)) \\
\neg Qu \wedge \neg Qv \wedge \neg Qw \wedge Qf(f(u,v),w) \vdash \exists x \exists y(\neg Qx \wedge \neg Qy \wedge Qf(x,y)) \\
\neg Qu, \neg Qv, \neg Qw, Qf(f(u,v),w) \vdash \exists x \exists y(\neg Qx \wedge \neg Qy \wedge Qf(x,y)) \\
\neg Qu, \neg Qv, \neg Qw, Qf(f(u,v),w) \\
\vdash \exists x \exists y(\neg Qx \wedge \neg Qy \wedge Qf(x,y)), \neg Qu \wedge \neg Qv \wedge Qf(u,v)
\end{gathered}$$

On the right hand side of the $\vdash$ on the last sequent, we have

$$\neg Qu \wedge \neg Qv \wedge Qf(u,v).$$

It gives rise to three branches. The first branch is as follows:

$$\begin{gathered}
\neg Qu, \neg Qv, \neg Qw, Qf(f(u,v),w) \vdash \exists x \exists y(\neg Qx \wedge \neg Qy \wedge Qf(x,y)), \neg Qu \\
\top
\end{gathered}$$

The second branch is:

$$\begin{gathered}
\neg Qu, \neg Qv, \neg Qw, Qf(f(u,v),w) \vdash \exists x \exists y(\neg Qx \wedge \neg Qy \wedge Qf(x,y)), \neg Qv \\
\top
\end{gathered}$$

Applying rule $(\exists R)$ twice, with the substitutions $[x/f(u,v)]$ and $[y/w]$, the third branch is expanded as follows:

$$\begin{gathered}
\neg Qu, \neg Qv, \neg Qw, Qf(f(u,v),w) \vdash \exists x \exists y(\neg Qx \wedge \neg Qy \wedge Qf(x,y)), Qf(u,v) \\
\neg Qu, \neg Qv, \neg Qw, Qf(f(u,v),w) \vdash \neg Qf(u,v) \wedge \neg Qw \wedge Qf(f(u,v),w), Qf(u,v)
\end{gathered}$$

As earlier, this gives rise to three branches again. We suppress repeating the existential formula $\exists x \exists y(\neg Qx \wedge \neg Qy \wedge Qf(x,y))$, which you should write when rewriting this proof. The first branch here is:

$$\neg Qu, \neg Qv, \neg Qw, Qf(f(u,v),w) \vdash \neg Qf(u,v), Qf(u,v)$$
$$\neg Qu, \neg Qv, \neg Qw, Qf(f(u,v),w), Qf(u,v) \vdash Qf(u,v)$$
$$\top$$

The second branch is:

$$\neg Qu, \neg Qv, \neg Qw, Qf(f(u,v),w) \vdash \neg Qw, Qf(u,v)$$
$$\top$$

And the third branch is:

$$\neg Qu, \neg Qv, \neg Qw, Qf(f(u,v),w) \vdash Qf(f(u,v),w), Qf(u,v)$$
$$\top$$

Write the derivation on a large sheet of paper.

Here is a nice interpretation of the consequence you have just proved. In the set of real numbers, interpret Qx as x is a rational number, and $f(x,y)$ as x^y. Then the consequence says that "If there are irrational numbers a,b,c such that $(a^b)^c$ is rational, then there are irrational numbers s,t such that s^t is rational". The antecedent clearly holds since, with $a = b = c = \sqrt{2}$, you see that $\sqrt{2}$ is irrational and $(\sqrt{2}^{\sqrt{2}})^{\sqrt{2}} = (\sqrt{2})^2 = 2$ is rational. So, you conclude that there are irrational numbers s,t such that s^t is rational.

Further, if you interpret Qx as x is rational or not algebraic, then your conclusion would be: "there are irrational algebraic numbers s,t such that s^t is rational". Look at the above proof. Essentially, the proof shows that either $\sqrt{2}^{\sqrt{2}}$ is rational, in which case, you have $s = \sqrt{2}$, $t = \sqrt{2}$; or else, $(\sqrt{2}^{\sqrt{2}})^{\sqrt{2}}$ is rational, in which case, $s = \sqrt{2}^{\sqrt{2}}$, $t = \sqrt{2}$. However, it does not determine whether $\sqrt{2}^{\sqrt{2}}$ is rational or not.

Observe that provability of $\Sigma \vdash \Delta$ implies the provability of $\Sigma, \Gamma \vdash \Delta$. This proves monotonicity. Since provability of $\Sigma \vdash \Gamma, X \to Y$ implies the provability of $\Sigma, X \vdash \Gamma, Y$ for formulas X,Y, the deduction theorem is proved. Similarly, $\Sigma \cup \{\neg X\}$ is inconsistent iff $\Sigma, \neg X \vdash$ is provable iff $\Sigma \Vdash X$. Hence reductio ad absurdum holds in GFC. The metatheorems are easy to prove. No wonder many logicians prefer Gentzen systems.

Exercises for § 8.3

1. Try to construct GFC-proofs in place of FC-proofs in Exercise 2 of § 6.1 and Exercise 3 of § 6.2.
2. Decide validity of consequences in Exercise 2 of § 8.2 using GFC.
3. Give GFC-proofs of all the laws listed in Theorem 6.17.
4. Let X and Y be formulas. Construct GFC proofs for the following:

   (a) $\vDash \forall x(X \wedge Y) \leftrightarrow \forall xX \wedge \forall Y$ (b) $\vDash \exists x(X \vee Y) \leftrightarrow \exists xX \vee \exists xY$

   (c) $\vDash \forall xX \vee \forall xY \to \forall x(X \vee Y)$ (d) $\vDash \exists x(X \wedge Y) \to \exists xX \wedge \exists xY$

8.4 ANALYTIC TABLEAUX

In this section, we extend the analytic tableau to FL. We name the tableau system for FL as **FT**, the **first order analytic tableau**. As earlier, in a tableau for a set of formulas Σ, each formula of Σ is called a **premise.** In FT, all the earlier rules for PT are taken *in toto* by considering the symbols p, q as formulas; see § 4.4. We add more rules for the quantifiers and the equality predicate. The additional rules of inference are as follows.

Let t be a term free for a variable x in a formula X.

$(\forall)\quad \dfrac{\forall xX}{\begin{array}{c}X[x/t]\\ \forall xX\end{array}}\qquad\qquad (\neg\forall)\quad \dfrac{\neg\forall xX}{\neg X[x/t]}$ where t is a new term

$(\exists)\quad \dfrac{\exists xX}{X[x/t]}$ where t is a new term $\qquad\qquad (\neg\exists)\quad \dfrac{\neg\exists xX}{\begin{array}{c}\neg X[x/t]\\ \neg\exists xX\end{array}}$

$$(\approx r)\quad \frac{\cdot}{t \approx t}\qquad\qquad (\approx c)\quad \frac{s \approx t}{t \approx s}\qquad\qquad (\approx s)\quad \frac{\begin{array}{c}s \approx t\\ X[x/s]\end{array}}{X[x/t]}$$

The last three rules such as $(\approx r)$, $(\approx c)$ and $(\approx s)$ are the **equality rules** of reflexivity, commutativity, and substitutivity. Notice that in the rules $(\forall)$ and $(\neg\exists)$, the formula itself is also repeated. This means that we can use these formulas again if need arises, possibly, instantiating them with terms other than t. In practice, we do not repeat the formulas, but remember that we can reuse these formulas. Formulas of these two types are called **universal formulas** which can be instantiated again and again. The corresponding rules are the **universal rules**.

In contrast, the other two types of formulas in the rules of $(\neg\forall)$ and $(\exists)$ are called **existential formulas**, and the rules are called **existential rules**. An existential formula can be used only once in a path and with a new term. The restriction of 't is a new term' is in consonance with the restriction on (UG) in FC, the 'new variable' in FND, and the eigenvariable condition in GFC. We use the phrase 't is a **new term**' to mean the following:

If s is any term that occurs in t or in which t occurs, then

1. s does not occur in the current formula,
2. s does not occur in any premise used so far in the path, and
3. s has not been introduced to the path by an existential rule.

Notice that t must also satisfy all the above conditions, in particular. Moreover, if we take a constant c as a new term, then any term where c occurs is such an s. In that case, the conditions above mean that

> the constant c neither occurs in the current formula, nor in any premise used so far in the path, nor in any term that has been introduced to the path by an existential rule.

Further, if c is a constant that never occurs in the path prior to the current formula, then all the conditions are met vacuously. Thus we have the *simplified version of the new term* as follows. We refer to it by 'c is a new constant', or even abbreviate it to

new cons c : a constant that has not occurred earlier in the path.

Recall that in PT we have used the heuristic of applying all stacking rules before applying any branching rule if possible. Along with that, we use the following *heuristic* in FT :

If possible, apply existential rules before applying universal rules.

That is, whenever possible, use the $(\exists)$ and $(\neg\forall)$ rules before applying the $(\forall)$ and $(\neg\exists)$ rules. This is because any constant (in the simplified version) can be used for instantiating a universal formula, while a constant introduced by a universal rule cannot be used by an existential rule.

The notions of theorems, consequences, consistency, etc. are the same as in PT. In this section, we use the symbol $\vdash$ as an abbreviation to "a theorem in FT". See the following examples.

EXAMPLE 8.20. $\vdash \forall xX \to X[x/t]$, where t is a term free for x in X.

We take the negation of the given formula as the root and generate a tableau.

$$\begin{array}{ll} \neg(\forall xX \to X[x/t]) & \\ 1.\ \forall xX & \\ \neg X[x/t] & \\ X[x/t] & 1,\ (\forall) \\ \times & \end{array}$$

EXAMPLE 8.21. $\vdash \forall x(X \to Y) \to (X \to \forall xY)$, where x is not free in X.

$$\begin{array}{ll} \neg(\forall x(X \to Y) \to (X \to \forall xY)) & \\ 1.\ \forall x(X \to Y) & \\ \neg(X \to \forall xY) & \\ X & \\ \neg\forall xY & \\ \neg Y[x/c] & \text{new cons } c \\ X \to Y[x/c] & 1,\ x \text{ not free in } X \\ \neg X \qquad Y[x/c] & \\ \times \qquad\quad \times & \end{array}$$

EXAMPLE 8.22. The following tableau shows that $\vdash (t \approx t)$.

$$\begin{array}{ll} \neg(t \approx t) & \\ t \approx t & (\approx r) \\ \times & \end{array}$$

EXAMPLE 8.23. Show that $\vdash (s \approx t) \to (X[x/s] \to X[x/t])$, where s and t are terms free for x in X.

$$\neg((s \approx t) \to (X[x/s] \to X[x/t]))$$
$$1.\ s \approx t$$
$$\neg(X[x/s] \to X[x/t])$$
$$2.\ X[x/s]$$
$$\neg X[x/t]$$
$$X[x/t] \qquad 1, 2, (\approx s)$$
$$\times$$

EXAMPLE 8.24. The following is a tableau proof of $\vDash \exists x(\exists y Py \to Px)$:

$$1.\ \neg\exists x(\exists y Py \to Px)$$
$$2.\ \neg(\exists y Py \to Pa)$$
$$3.\ \exists y Py$$
$$\neg Pa$$
$$Pb \qquad \text{3, new cons } b$$
$$4.\ \neg(\exists y Py \to Pb) \qquad \text{reusing (1)}$$
$$\exists y Py$$
$$\neg Pb$$
$$\times$$

The repeated use of Formula 1 is required due to the simplified version of the new term; it is a constant that should not have occurred in the path. Look at the following alternative solution.

$$\neg\exists x(\exists y Py \to Px)$$
$$\neg(\exists y Py \to Pa)$$
$$1.\ \exists y Py$$
$$\neg Pa$$
$$2.\ Pa \qquad \text{1, new term } a$$
$$\times$$

Here, we are using the *new term* in its generality while introducing Formula 2 after Formula 1. First, a does not occur in the current formula $\exists y Py$. Second, a does not occur in the premise $\exists x(\exists y Py \to Px)$. Third, a has not been introduced by an existential rule in the path earlier to the current formula. Thus the constant a is indeed a new term and the second tableau is a proof.

EXAMPLE 8.25. Determine the correctness of the following argument:

> If all logicians are mathematicians and if there is a logician who is a computer scientist, then there must be a mathematician who is also a computer scientist.

We check whether $\{\forall x(Lx \to Mx), \exists x(Lx \wedge Cx)\} \vdash \exists x(Mx \wedge Cx)$.

$$
\begin{array}{c}
\forall x(Lx \to Mx) \\
\exists x(Lx \wedge Cx) \\
\neg\exists x(Mx \wedge Cx) \\
La \wedge Ca \qquad \text{new cons } a \\
La \\
Ca \\
La \to Ma
\end{array}
$$

$$
\begin{array}{cc}
\neg La & Ma \\
\times & \neg(Ma \wedge Ca) \\
 & \begin{array}{cc} \neg Ma & \neg Ca \\ \times & \times \end{array}
\end{array}
$$

EXAMPLE 8.26. The tableau proof of the consequence

$$\exists x \exists y \exists z(\neg Qx \wedge \neg Qy \wedge \neg Qz \wedge Qf(f(x,y),z)) \,!\!\vdash \exists x \exists y(\neg Qx \wedge \neg Qy \wedge Qf(x,y))$$

of Example 8.19 is as follows.

$$
\begin{array}{c}
\exists x \exists y \exists z(\neg Qx \wedge \neg Qy \wedge \neg Qz \wedge Qf(f(x,y),z)) \\
1.\ \neg\exists x \exists y(\neg Qx \wedge \neg Qy \wedge Qf(x,y)) \\
\neg Qa \wedge \neg Qb \wedge \neg Qc \wedge Qf(f(a,b),c) \\
\neg Qa \\
\neg Qb \\
\neg Qc \\
Qf(f(a,b),c) \\
2.\ \neg(\neg Qa \wedge \neg Qb \wedge Qf(a,b))
\end{array}
$$

$$
\begin{array}{cc}
\neg\neg Qa & \neg(\neg Qb \wedge \neg Qf(a,b)) \\
\times & \begin{array}{cc}
\neg\neg Qb & \neg Qf(a,b) \\
\times & 3.\ \neg(\neg Qf(a,b) \wedge \neg Qc \wedge Qf(f(a,b),c)) \\
 & \begin{array}{cc}
 \neg\neg Qf(a,b) & \neg(\neg Qc \wedge Qf(f(a,b),c)) \\
 \times & \begin{array}{cc} \neg\neg Qc & \neg Qf(f(a,b),c)) \\ \times & \times \end{array}
 \end{array}
\end{array}
\end{array}
$$

EXAMPLE 8.27. Let x be a variable not free in any of the formulas $X_1,\ldots,X_n$. If $\{X_1,\ldots,X_n\} \vdash X$ then show that $\{X_1,\ldots,X_n\} \vdash \forall xX$.

We show that if a tableau for $\{X_1,\ldots,X_n,\neg X\}$ is closed, then there is a tableau for $\Sigma = \{X_1,\ldots,X_n,\neg\forall xX\}$ which is also closed. We have a closed tableau τ for $\{X_1,\ldots,X_n,\neg X\}$. In τ, either $\neg X$ occurs or it does not. If $\neg X$ does not occur in it, then τ itself is a closed tableau for Σ.

On the other hand, suppose that $\neg X$ occurs in τ. Construct the tableau τ' from τ by replacing all occurrences of $\neg X$ with $\neg\forall xX$ followed by $\neg X$ as the sole child of $\neg\forall xX$. Now, τ' is a tableau for Σ since x is not free in any of $X_1,\ldots,X_n,\neg\forall xX$, and since $\neg X[x/x] = \neg X$. Notice that in τ' we have an extra entry corresponding to each occurrence of the formula $\neg\forall xX$; but each formula of τ occurs in τ'. Since τ was closed, so is τ'.

Example 8.27 shows that the rule (UG) of FC is a derived rule of FT. We have already seen that all the axioms of FC are also theorems in FT. Since FT is sound, this completes the proof of adequacy of analytic tableau. We will give a direct proof of completeness of FT shortly.

Exercises for § 8.4

1. Using tableau rules, determine satisfiability of the following sets of formulas:
   (a) $\{\exists xPx, \neg Pc\}$
   (b) $\{\exists xPx \wedge \exists xQx, \neg\exists x(Px \wedge Qx), \forall xPx \to Ps\}$
   (c) $\{\forall x(Px \to Qx), \exists xPx, \forall x\neg Qx, \exists xPx \vee \neg Pc\}$
2. Let X and Y be formulas. Construct tableau proofs for the following:
   (a) $\vDash \forall x(X \wedge Y) \leftrightarrow \forall xX \wedge \forall Y$ (b) $\vDash \exists x(X \vee Y) \leftrightarrow \exists xX \vee \exists xY$
   (c) $\vDash \forall xX \vee \forall xY \to \forall x(X \vee Y)$ (d) $\vDash \exists x(X \wedge Y) \to \exists xX \wedge \exists xY$
3. Construct tableau proofs of the following:
   (a) $\forall x\exists y(Px \to Qy) \vDash \exists y\forall x(Px \to Qy)$ (b) $\exists y\forall xPxy \vDash \forall x\exists yPxy$
4. Using FT, show the correctness of the following arguments:
   (a) Everyone who buys a ticket receives a prize. Therefore, if there are no prizes, then nobody buys a ticket.
   (b) Horses are animals; therefore, heads of horses are heads of animals.
   (c) None of Aristotle's followers like any materialist. Any of Aristotle's followers likes at least one of Kant's followers. Moreover, Aristotle does have followers. Therefore, some of Kant's followers are not materialists.
   (d) For every x, y if x succeeds y then it is not the case that y succeeds x. For every x, y, z, if x succeeds y and y succeeds z then x succeeds z. For every x, y, if x succeeds y then x is not equal to y. For every x, y, z, if y is between x and z, then either x succeeds y and y succeeds z, or z succeeds y and y succeeds x. For every x, z, if x is not equal to z, then there is a y such that y is between x and z. Therefore, for every x, z, if x succeeds z then there is a y such that x succeeds y and y succeeds z.
5. Give FT-proofs of all the laws listed in Theorem 6.17, and the replacement laws discussed in § 6.5.

8.5 ADEQUACY OF FT TO FL

There is nondeterminism in generating a tableau. We are free to choose a formula from a given set for expanding the currently generated tableau. To minimize nondeterminism, we may fix an ordering of the formulas in a given set and generate a tableau systematically.

Let Σ be a set of formulas. We will require terms for instantiating formulas and thus choose the so called **free universe** for this purpose. The free universe $D(\Sigma)$ for a given set of formulas Σ is the set of all terms generated from the constants and free variables occurring in (the formulas of) Σ. If there is no constant or free variable in Σ, then we start with an extra symbol, say, η.

For instance, if there are no constants, no variables, and no function symbols appearing in Σ, then the free universe is $\{\eta\}$. If a unary function symbol f occurs in Σ, but neither constants nor free variables occur in it, then the free universe is $\{\eta, f(\eta), f(f(\eta)), \ldots\}$.

We generate all possible terms starting with the set of all constants and free variables (else, η) and using all function symbols occurring in Σ. The set of all terms so generated is the free universe for Σ.

Since the free universe $D(\Sigma) = \{t_1, t_2, \ldots, t_n \ldots\}$ is enumerable, we take it as an ordered set. We also consider $\Sigma = \{X_1, X_2, \ldots, X_m \ldots\}$ as an ordered set. In FT, a **systematic tableau** for Σ is constructed inductively as follows.

In Stage 1, start the tableau with X_1 as the root. Suppose a tableau has already been generated up to Stage n. In Stage $n+1$, check whether any path of the tableau gets closed. If open paths exist, extend each open path ρ as follows:

1. Add X_{n+1} to ρ, if Σ has more than n propositions.
2. Scan the path ρ from root to leaf for a compound formula (not a literal) on which a tableau rule has not yet been applied; call the first compound formula as X.
3. Apply the suitable tableau rule on X to add the necessary formulas to the path:
   (a) If X is a stacking or a branching formula, then extend ρ by adding its children, as in PT. (See § 4.4.)
   (b) If $X = \exists xY$, then take the first 'new term' t_k from $D(\Sigma)$, and extend ρ by adding $Y[x/t_k]$.
   (c) If $X = \neg\forall xY$, then take the first 'new term' t_k from $D(\Sigma)$, and extend ρ by adding $\neg Y[x/t_k]$.
   (d) If $X = \forall xY$, and t_k is the first term in $D(\Sigma)$ such that $Y[x/t_k]$ does not occur in ρ, then add $Y[x/t_k]$ and also X to ρ.
   (e) If $X = \neg\exists xY$, and t_k is the first term in $D(\Sigma)$ such that $\neg Y[x/t_k]$ does not occur in ρ, then add $\neg Y[x/t_k]$ and also X to ρ.

The systematic tableau is finite when the tableau in Stage $n+1$ coincides with that in Stage n. This includes the case of the tableau getting closed at Stage n. Look at the following example for a systematic tableau.

EXAMPLE 8.28. Let $X_1 = \exists x(Lx \wedge Cx)$, $X_2 = \forall x(Lx \to Mx)$, $X_3 = \neg\exists x(Mx \wedge Cx)$; and let $\Sigma = \{X_1, X_2, X_3\}$. Since there is no constant, no free variable and no function symbol in the formulas, $D(\Sigma) = \{\eta\}$. Here is the systematic tableau:

1.	$\exists x(Lx \wedge Cx)$	X_1	(Stage 1)
2.	$\forall x(Lx \to Mx)$	X_2	(Stage 2)
3.	$L\eta \wedge C\eta$	$1, (\exists)$	(Stage 2)
4.	$\neg\exists x(Mx \wedge Cx)$	X_3	(Stage 3)
5.	$L\eta \to M\eta$	$2, (\forall)$	(Stage 3)
6.	$\forall x(Lx \to Mx)$	$2, (\forall)$	(Stage 3)
7.	$L\eta$	$3, (\wedge)$	(Stage 4)
8.	$C\eta$	$3, (\wedge)$	(Stage 4)
9.	$\neg(M\eta \wedge C\eta)$	$4, (\neg\exists)$	(Stage 5)
10.	$\neg\exists x(Mx \wedge Cx)$	$4, (\neg\exists)$	(Stage 5)
11.	$\neg L\eta$ $M\eta$	$5, (\to)$	(Stage 6)
12.	$\times$ $\neg M\eta$ $\neg C\eta$	$9, (\neg\wedge)$	(Stage 7)
13.	$\times$ $\times$		(Stage 8)

Notice that in Stage 7, the formula in Line 6 is not used since the instantiation produces an already generated formula (i.e., in Line 5). Compare this tableau with that in Example 8.25. A systematic tableau may run very lengthy, but the method guarantees that all the premises that can be used in a tableau will eventually be used. Obviously, the systematic procedure is not a good way of generating a tableau, but it is a mechanical way with book-keeping.

This is in sharp contrast to the more creative way of generating tableaux which may sometimes fail. That is, even if there is a closed tableau for a set of formulas, you may not get it easily by arbitrarily instantiating the quantified formulas, not to mention repeated trials. In contrast, the systematic tableau will close on a single trial. On the other hand, when the systematic tableau is unmanageably large, you may be able to construct a short tableau with ingenuous instantiations.

Once an ordering of a set of formulas is chosen, there exists a unique systematic tableau for the set. In this sense, we speak of *the* systematic tableau for a given (ordered) set of formulas. The systematic tableau is finite after each step, but it can eventually be an infinite tree. If the systematic tableau is infinite, then it remains open; and if it is finite, then it may be either closed or open. However, all possible instantiations of variables to terms are eventually taken in an open path of the systematic tableau. Therefore, we observe the following.

Observation 8.1. *Let Σ be any set of formulas. Then the following are true:*

(1) *There exists a closed tableau for Σ iff the systematic tableau for Σ is closed.*

(2) *Each tableau for Σ contains an open path iff there exists an open path in the systematic tableau for Σ.*

We say that a set of formulas Σ is **inconsistent** (in fact, FT-inconsistent) iff there exists a closed tableau for Σ. A set of formulas is called **consistent** if it is not inconsistent. That is, a set of formulas Σ is called consistent iff each tableau for Σ contains an open path. Our observations above amount to the following.

Lemma 8.1. *Let Σ be an ordered set of formulas. Then*

(1) *Σ is consistent iff the systematic tableau for Σ has an open path.*
(2) *Σ is inconsistent iff the systematic tableau for Σ is closed.*

Our aim is to connect the proof theoretic notion of consistency to the semantic notion of satisfiability. Let ρ be a path in a tableau for a set of formulas Σ. We visualize the path ρ as a set of formulas. Call ρ a **satisfiable path** if the set of all formulas in ρ is satisfiable. Notice that a closed path is necessarily unsatisfiable; thus, a satisfiable path must be open. Along with this, we have the following result for systematic tableaux.

Lemma 8.2. *Let Σ be an ordered set of formulas. Let τ_n be the systematic tableau for Σ generated in Stage n. If Σ is satisfiable, then for each $n \geq 1$, τ_n contains a satisfiable path.*

Proof. Assume that Σ is satisfiable. Since τ_1 contains only the first premise from Σ, τ_1 is satisfiable. This proves the basis step of our inductive proof.

For the induction step, assume that τ_m contains a satisfiable path. We will show that τ_{m+1} has a satisfiable path. If $\tau_{m+1} = \tau_m$, then there is nothing to prove. Otherwise, Let $Z \in \tau_m$ be the formula in such a satisfiable path ρ, which has been used in Stage m for extending τ_m to τ_{m+1}. All possible extensions of ρ are tackled by considering the following cases:

(a) If Z is a stacking formula with Z_1, Z_2 as its children (Z_2 may be absent.) then the extended path ρ, Z_1, Z_2 is satisfiable.
(b) If Z is a branching formula with Z_1, Z_2 as its children, then at least one of the extended paths ρ, Z_1 or ρ, Z_2 is satisfiable.
(c) If Z is an existential formula with its child as $Z'[x/t]$, then the path $\rho, Z'[x/t]$ is satisfiable. [*Notation*: If $Z = \exists x U$, then $Z' = U$. If $Z = \neg\forall x U$, then $Z' = \neg U$.]
(d) If Z is a universal formula with its children as $Z'[x/t], Z$, then the path $\rho, Z'[x/t], Z$ is satisfiable. [*Notation*: If $Z = \forall x U$, then $Z' = U$. If $Z = \neg\exists x U$, then $Z' = \neg U$.]
(e) If Z' has been obtained by using the equality rules ($\approx r$), ($\approx c$), or ($\approx s$), then the path ρ, Z' is satisfiable.
(f) An addition of a premise from Σ to ρ keeps the extended path satisfiable.

Proofs of (a)-(b) are propositional. In (a), $Z \equiv Z_1 \wedge Z_2$; thus satisfiability of ρ, which contains Z, implies the satisfiability of ρ, Z_1, Z_2. In (b), $Z \equiv Z_1 \vee Z_2$. If both ρ, Z_1 and ρ, Z_2 are unsatisfiable, then ρ itself becomes unsatisfiable. Therefore, at least one of the paths ρ, Z_1 or ρ, Z_2 is satisfiable.

For (c), suppose that $I_\ell = (D, \phi, \ell)$ is a state such that $I_\ell \vDash \rho$. (This D need not be the free universe.) The new term t either does not occur in ρ at all or it has occurred in ρ already satisfying the constraints of a new term.

In the former case, extend ℓ to ℓ' by defining $\ell'(t) = \alpha$, where $\alpha \notin D$, a new symbol, and keeping the values of ℓ' as those of ℓ for all other terms. Let $D' = D \cup \{\alpha\}$. Extend the function ϕ to ϕ' by redefining $\phi(Z')$. Note that $\phi(Z')$ might have been already defined in the state I_ℓ. However, we now view $\phi(Z')$ as a relation on D' instead of D. The redefinition of this relation $\phi(Z')$ is an extension of the old $\phi(Z')$ as existing on D plus the assertion that $\phi(Z'[x/t])$ holds.

For instance, if $Z' = Pxa$ and we have already $\phi(P) = \{(a,b),(b,c)\}$, then $Z'[x/t] = Pta$; and the redefinition of $\phi(P)$ is $\phi'(P) = \{(a,b),(b,c),(\alpha,a)\}$, since t is assigned to α by ℓ'.

In the latter case, when the new term t has already occurred in ρ, the existential formula, say $\exists xU$, is satisfied by I_ℓ. So, we have an element $d \in D$ such that $I_{\ell[x\mapsto d]} \vDash U(x)$. Now, modify ℓ to ℓ' by reassigning t to this d but keeping all other assignments as in ℓ. The reassignment does not affect satisfiability due to constraints on the new term t. Notice that had t been brought forth by an existential rule, it would not have been possible to reassign it.

Now it is clear that the new state $I'_\ell = (D', \phi', \ell')$ is still a state-model of all the formulas in ρ and, in addition, it is a state-model of the new formula $Z'[x/t]$. Thus, the extension of ρ, i.e., the set $\rho \cup \{Z'[x/t]\}$, is satisfiable.

The case (d) is similar to (c); and (e) follows due to the Laws of Equality. The statement in (f) follows from the satisfiability of Σ, and (a)-(e). ♦

Theorem 8.3 (Strong Soundness of FT). *If a set of formulas Σ is satisfiable, then it is consistent.*

Proof. Use some ordering in Σ, and let τ be the systematic tableau for Σ. If Σ is inconsistent, then by Lemma 8.1, τ is a closed tableau. Each path in τ is closed and finite. By König's Lemma (Theorem 4.2), τ is finite. Therefore, τ has been generated in Stage n, for some n. Moreover, τ does not contain any satisfiable path. By Lemma 8.2, Σ is unsatisfiable. ♦

Theorem 8.4 (Strong Completeness of FT). *If a set of formulas Σ is consistent, then it is satisfiable.*

Proof. Let Σ be consistent. We then have an open path ρ in the systematic tableau for Σ. Further, ρ satisfies the following properties:

1. No atomic formula and its negation are both in ρ.
2. If $Z \in \rho$ is a stacking formula with children Z_1, Z_2, then $Z_1 \in \rho$ and $Z_2 \in \rho$. Note that Z_2 may not exist for some formulas.
3. If $Z \in \rho$ is a branching formula with children Z_1, Z_2, then $Z_1 \in \rho$ or $Z_2 \in \rho$.
4. If $Z \in \rho$ is a universal formula, then $Z'[x/t] \in \rho$ for each term $t \in D$, where either $Z = \forall xZ'$, or $Z = \neg\exists xY$ and $Z' = \neg Y$.
5. If $Z \in \rho$ is an existential formula, then $Z'[x/t] \in \rho$ for at least one term $t \in D$, where either $Z = \exists xZ'$, or $Z = \neg\forall xY$ and $Z' = \neg Y$.

To see that ρ is satisfiable, we start with a domain. An obvious choice is the free universe $D := D(\Sigma)$. Choose the assignment function ℓ as the identity function. We then need to declare suitable atomic formulas as true and others as false. For this, we define the function ϕ from the set of all predicates occurring in Σ except the equality predicate $\approx$, to the set of all relations over D the following way:

If $Q(t_1,t_2,\ldots,t_m) \in \rho$, then $(t_1,t_2,\ldots,t_m) \in \phi(Q)$.
If $\neg Q(t_1,t_2,\ldots,t_m) \in \rho$, then $(t_1,t_2,\ldots,t_m) \notin \phi(Q)$.
If neither of the above two happens, then $(t_1,t_2,\ldots,t_m) \in \phi(Q)$.

For the equality predicate, define the equality relation E on the domain D, as was done in § 5.8. Now, the function ϕ satisfies the condition "$(s \approx t)$ is satisfied by this interpretation iff $(s,t) \in E$". Formally, one formulates and proves a statement like Lemma 6.2 using FT. Due to (a)-(e), $(D,\phi,\ell) \vDash \rho$. Thus, ρ is satisfiable. Since $\Sigma \subseteq \rho$, Σ is also satisfiable. ♦

We have thus proved the following result.

Theorem 8.5 (Strong Adequacy of FT). *Let Σ be a set of formulas, and let X be a formula. Then the following are true:*

(1) *$\Sigma \vDash X$ iff there is a closed tableau for $\Sigma \cup \{\neg X\}$.*
(2) *Σ is unsatisfiable iff Σ is FT-inconsistent.*

Notice that whenever a systematic tableau for a set Σ of formulas is closed, the free universe restricted to those terms occurring in the tableau is finite. Hence, Σ is unsatisfiable on a finite domain. On the other hand, if a systematic tableau for Σ is finite and open, then any open path in it will give rise to a finite model of Σ.

What if a set is neither satisfiable nor unsatisfiable on any finite domain, but is satisfiable on an infinite domain? The systematic tableau will then have an infinite open path. But then, how to obtain such an infinite open path by the tableau method? Obviously, the tableau method will not be able to give it; but some meta-argument might prove its existence. Look at the following example.

EXAMPLE 8.29. Is $\Sigma = \{\forall x \exists y Pxy,\ \neg \exists x Pxx,\ \forall x \forall y \forall z (Pxy \wedge Pyz \to Pxz)\}$ a satisfiable set of formulas?

$$\forall x \exists y Pxy$$
$$\neg \exists x Pxx$$
$$\forall x \forall y \forall z (Pxy \wedge Pyz \to Pxz)$$
$$\exists y Pby$$
$$\neg Pbb$$
$$Pbd$$
$$Pbc \wedge Pcd \to Pbd$$

$$\neg(Pbc \wedge Pcd) \qquad Pbd$$
$$\neg Pcc \qquad\qquad \neg Pcc$$

This is not a systematic tableau; you can construct one anyway. Look at the tableau carefully. It will go on for ever by reusing the universal formulas; and it will never close. This set Σ is neither satisfiable nor unsatisfiable in any finite domain, but is satisfiable in an infinite domain. For instance, you can interpret P as 'less than' in $\mathbb{N}$ and see that Σ has a model there.

As a procedure, analytic tableau fails to determine satisfiability of any arbitrary set of formulas. However, analytic tableau is a complete proof procedure, so nothing better can be achieved. At this point, you may try with other proof procedures to determine satisfiability of Σ in Example 8.29. A somewhat convincing argument is that an algorithm is a finite procedure, and it cannot find out an answer to such an infinite construction of a model. That is exactly the undecidability of FL, which we plan to tackle later.

Exercises for § 8.5

1. Use König's Lemma to show that a closed tableau contains only a finite number of formulas.
2. Using the construction of a systematic tableau, prove that if every finite subset of a set of formulas is FT-consistent, then the set itself is FT-consistent.
3. Construct an infinite tree where for each $n \geq 1$, there exists a path of length n, but there exists no infinite path.
4. Construct a tableau for $X = A \wedge B \wedge C$, where $A = \forall x \exists y Pxy$, $B = \forall x \neg Pxx$, and $C = \forall x \forall y \forall z(Pxy \wedge Pyz \rightarrow Pxz)$. Show that X is satisfiable but it is not satisfiable in any finite domain.

8.6 SUMMARY AND PROBLEMS

The four types of proof procedures such as calculation, natural deduction, Gentzen sequents, and analytic tableaux for PL could be extended successfully to FL. In each extension, some axioms or rules of inference have been added to tackle the quantifiers and the equality predicate.

Calculation is used in every text book on logic informally. It has been popularized by Gries & Schneider (1993) as a proof procedure, where calculations have been taken as sequences of FL-sentences chained together by the relation of equivalence ($\equiv$). In this system, each implication is converted to an equivalence by using the Golden rule. We have extended the calculations to tackle implications directly by allowing entailment along with equivalence. Also, we have allowed formulas in a calculation instead of restricting to sentences.

For an exposition of natural deductions, see Huth & Ryan (2000) and Rautenberg (2010). The latter text deals with Gentzen style natural deduction. Our treatment is closer to the former text. It is also closer to quasi-proofs and the informal deductions treated in Copi et al. (2010), Lewis & Langford (1938), Mates (1972), Suppes (1957), and Stoll (1963).

The Gentzen sequents for FL has been extensively used in Ebbinghaus et al. (1994), Fitting (1996), Gallier (1987), and Rautenberg (2010). The present symmetric system has been considered by Manaster (1978) and Smullyan (2014). Some logicians advocate Gentzen systems for automated theorem proving due to its mechanical nature.

The method of analytic tableau has been made popular by Smullyan (1968). It may be found in almost all modern texts on logic. We have also proved its adequacy to FL independent of FC. See Fitting (1996) for its implementation using Prolog language. Many computer scientists advocate analytic tableau due to its transparency in model constructions.

Problems for Chapter 8

1. Show that each of the following consequences is valid by using Calculation, FND, GFC, and FT:

   (a) $\forall x \forall y(Pxy \to Pyx),\ \forall x \forall y \forall z(Pxy \wedge Pyz \to Pxz),\ \forall x \exists y Pxy \,!\!\vdash \forall x Pxx$
   (b) $\{\forall x Pxx,\ \forall x \forall y(Pxy \to Pyx),\ \forall x \forall y \forall z(Pxy \wedge Pyz \to Pxz)\}$
   $!\!\vdash \forall x \forall y(\exists z(Pxz \wedge Pyz) \to \forall z(Pxz \leftrightarrow Pyz))$
   (c) $\forall x(Px \wedge Qx \to Rx) \to \exists x(Px \wedge \neg Qx),\ \forall x(Px \to Qx) \vee \forall x(Px \to Rx)$
   $!\!\vdash \forall x(Px \wedge Rx \to Qx) \to \exists x(Px \wedge Qx \wedge \neg Rx)$

   In (b), the premises say that P is an equivalence relation. Then, what does the conclusion say?

2. Are the following arguments valid? Formalize each into FL; and try a proof using calculation, FND, GFC, and FT.

   (a) Either Logic is elegant or many students like it. If Computer Science is a difficult discipline, then Logic has to be elegant. Therefore, if many students like Computer Science, then Logic is elegant.
   (b) If tomorrow morning it is chilly and not so clear a sky, then we go swimming unless you do not have any special liking for boating. It isn't always the case that if the sky is not clear, then you don't go boating. Therefore, if the weather is not chilly tomorrow morning, then we go swimming.
   (c) Yanka would have been at home, had he been to the club or not to the theatre while his friend was waiting for him at the college. He had been to the club premises while it was dusk only if he didn't come home. Unless the watchman saw him at the club premises, it is certain that it was dusk, since the watchman is night blind. Therefore, Yanka did not go to the theatre.
   (d) If anyone is in a guest house, which is located in a city, then he is in that city. None can be in two different cities at the same time. One who snatched the necklace away must have been in the guest house at Chennai. Since Chennai and Mumbai are two different cities and Yanka was in the Mumbai guest house, he did not snatch the necklace.
   (e) If all the politicians praise a bandit, then the bandit must be none other than Robin Hood. A politician praises a person if the person has indeed helped him in his career. There is a bandit who has not helped any politician. Therefore, there is a bandit other than Robin Hood.

3. Show by constructing an example that if two boxes are allowed to overlap, then the soundness of FND may not be retained.
4. Prove monotonicity, RA, and the deduction theorem for FND.
5. Are the rules of FND independent? If yes, show that no rule can be derived from others taken together. If no, then pick the rule(s) which can be derived from others.

6. Show that the following inference rules (in GFC) are not sound:

Rule 1: $\dfrac{\Sigma \vdash \Gamma, \Delta}{\Sigma \vdash \Gamma, (t \approx t), \Delta}$ Rule 2: $\dfrac{\Sigma \vdash \Gamma, (s \approx t), X[x/s], \Delta}{\Sigma \vdash \Gamma, (s \approx t), X[x/t], \Delta}$

[Hint: A rule with numerator $\Sigma \vdash \Gamma$ and denominator $\Delta \vdash \Omega$ is sound if the metastatement "if $\Delta \vDash \Omega$ then $\Sigma \vDash \Gamma$" holds.]

7. Are the rules of GFC independent? If yes, show that no rule can be derived from others taken together. If no, then pick the rule(s) which can be derived from others.
8. Formulate and prove a statement like Lemma 6.2 using FT.
9. Assume compactness of FL and that each valid formula has an FT-proof. Prove that if $\Sigma \vDash X$, then it has an FT-proof, where Σ is a set of formulas, and X is a formula.
10. Let Σ be a set of formulas, and let X be a formula. Show that if $\Sigma \cup \{X\} \vDash \bot$ and $\Sigma \cup \{\neg X\} \vDash \bot$ have proofs by calculation, then $\Sigma \vDash \bot$ also has a proof by calculation.
11. Let Σ and Γ be sets of formulas, and let X be a formula. Show that if $\Sigma \cup \{w\}$ and $\Gamma \cup \{\neg w\}$ have proofs by calculation, then $\Sigma \cup \Gamma$ has a proof by calculation.
12. Repeat the previous two problems with FND, GFC, and FT instead of calculation.

Chapter 9

Program Verification

9.1 DEBUGGING OF A PROGRAM

Before you start writing a program, you must know the job at hand, and the computer language you would be using to write it. Typically, you would have an idea as to what are the inputs to your program and what are the expected outputs. You must also know how the program would transform the inputs to the outputs.

For example, you are asked to write a program for checking whether two strings are equal. Immediately you think of a shortcut. If the given strings are of different lengths, then they are not equal. So, a subclass of the problems is solved. Once the strings are found to be of the same length, you are going to check them character by character. So, this describes *how* the job is done. Now, how to write this procedure as a program?

Well, you imagine a Boolean variable, say, *matched*, which is assigned a value *true* when the given strings s_1 and s_2 are equal, and *false* when they are not equal. Assume that you had already a ready-made program to compute the length of a string s, denoted by $length(s)$. Suppose that the language in which you are writing your program uses '=' for comparing two natural numbers. That is, the expression '$5 = 5$' is evaluated *true* and '$5 = 6$' is evaluated *false*. Then you would like to write a line:

$$matched := (length(s_1) = length(s_2))$$

It says that the variable *matched* is assigned the value of the expression $length(s_1) = length(s_2)$ which is either true or false depending upon whether the length of the string s_1 is equal to the length of s_2 or not.

Convention 9.1. In this chapter, the symbol $:=$ is used for assigning a value to a variable; it is not the same as the substitution used earlier. We also use the equality symbol $=$ instead of $\approx$, for ease in reading.

If $length(s_1)$ is not equal to $length(s_2)$, then the variable *matched* is assigned *false*, and you have the required result. Otherwise, you conclude that the strings s_1 and s_2 require further treatment. In that case, the variable *matched* is assigned the value *true* and $length(s_1) = length(s_2) = m$, say. Now to match the strings s_1 and s_2 character by character, assume that you already have a function $ch(i,s)$ which, given a string s, and a positive integer i, outputs the ith character of s. You can call this function if required.

Suppose that you can compare the characters by the same relation '='. That is, the expression $ch(i,s_1) = ch(j,s_2)$ is evaluated *true* if the ith character of the string s_1 is same as the jth character of the string s_2; else, it is evaluated *false*. Then you would like to write:

$$matched := (ch(i,s_1) = ch(i,s_2)) \text{ for each } i \text{ from 1 to } m$$

And finally, you have the program:

PROGRAM : *StringMatching*

```
matched := (length(s1) = length(s2))
if matched then for i = 1 to length(s1)
   do matched := (ch(i,s1) = ch(i,s2)) od
```

If there is a stake on writing this program correctly, you would not just leave it here. You would like to test the program on some inputs. As a student of logic, you start testing the program on strings

(a) which are identical,

(b) which have unequal lengths, and

(c) which are of equal lengths but unequal.

This phase of program development is usually called **debugging**. As test inputs you run the program on the following strings:

(a) $s_1 = pen, s_2 = pen$; $s_1 = chalk, s_2 = chalk$; $s_1 = pencil, s_2 = pencil$; etc.

(b) $s_1 = pen, s_2 = chalk$; $s_1 = pen, s_2 = pencil$; $s_1 = chalk, s_2 = pen$; $s_1 = pencil, s_2 = paper$, etc.

(c) $s_1 = pen, s_2 = ink$; $s_1 = chalk, s_2 = paper$; $s_1 = pencil, s_2 = redink$; $s_1 = blackboard, s_2 = bluepencil$, etc.

Now, in all runs, your program was a success and you have submitted your program to your instructor on Friday. The following Monday your instructor announces in the class that you have been awarded with zero marks as the program is incorrect. To justify himself, he says that your program evaluates *matched* to *true* for the inputs $s_1 := pen, s_2 := ten$. You then verify and see that he is correct. You have lost your quiz marks.

Imagine what would happen to a company where they would have invested in millions on a problem for which you have supplied the software; and that too, the software uses the string matching program you have written. Once this happened to the Intel Pentium chips having a flaw in multiplication of floating point numbers, and they had to bear the loss. The moral:

Debugging is not a foolproof method of program development.

Debugging cannot prove a correct program correct. It is not a reliable method to prove an incorrect program incorrect. If it finds, mostly by chance, a mistake in a program, then of course, the program is incorrect. To encapsulate, E. W. Dijkstra said,

> Program testing can be used to show the presence of bugs, but never to show their absence.

Programmers use a face saving word 'bug', instead of 'mistake'. However, they are afraid of bugs as is evident in the principle they follow:

> A program must not deliver what it is not supposed to even though it fails in delivering what it is supposed to.

This chapter addresses the issue of how to prove that a program does its intended job. This is referred to as proving correctness of a program or verifying a program. You will see how logic comes of help in achieving this.

Exercises for § 9.1

1. In debugging the *StringMatching* program, were the cases not exhaustive? Then why did it fail?
2. Modify *StringMatching* so that the intended job is correctly done.
3. If the output of *StringMatching* is $true$, then what could be the input?
4. If the output of *StringMatching* is $false$, then what could be the input?

9.2 ISSUE OF CORRECTNESS

What happens if a program goes on an infinite loop? You can instruct a person in a treasure hunt to move to a place where he finds the instruction for moving back to the original place again. You would not write such a program unless you want to make a Sisyphus out of a computer. However, in some circumstances you may want the computer not to come to a halt stage unless it is switched off manually; for example, a surveillance system, or an operating system. Otherwise, for most jobs, you may need your program to come to a finishing stage. It is worthwhile to examine termination of a program.

The next important issue is, whether it gives the expected output after termination. For example, *StringMatching* of § 9.1 does not give the expected result; it finally assigns $true$ to the variable $matched$ when two strings s_1 and s_2 are of equal length, and having the same last character.

The issues with a program P are the following:

Termination: Does P terminate for all specified inputs?

Partial Correctness: Given that P terminates for all specified inputs, does P end up in delivering the required output, corresponding to each input?

Total Correctness: For each specified input whether P terminates and delivers the corresponding output?

For proving termination, partial correctness, or total correctness of a program, we have to take care of the "specified inputs" and the "corresponding outputs". For example, an input to *StringMatching* is a pair of strings (s_1, s_2); and an expected output is the value *true* or *false* assigned to the program variable *matched*. One string such as *mat* is assigned to the **program variable** s_1, and another string, say *cat*, is assigned to the program variable s_2. In this case, an expected output is *false*. This particular input may be described as $(s_1 = mat) \wedge (s_2 = cat)$, and its output, as you know, is $matched = true$.

In abstract terms, the program variables satisfy some property before the execution of the program. This property, called the **precondition** of the program, is described in this particular case by the (first order) formula

$$(s_1 = mat) \wedge (s_2 = cat)$$

Similarly, some property holds for the program variables after the execution of the program. Of course, we are interested in a specified or required property to be satisfied after the program is executed. Such a property is called a **postcondition** of the program. The property

$$matched = false$$

is the required postcondition when we have the input strings as *mat* and *cat*. Here, as you see the required postcondition is not satisfied by the program; hence, the program is not correct.

In fact, the precondition of *StringMatching* is not completely expressed by the above formula. It only expresses a particular input. Soon, we will discuss how to correctly express the precondition and postcondition.

In developing a program, our main intention is to meet the required postcondition by manipulating the program variables.

A **state** of a program is described by what values are assigned to the program variables, at some instant of time. A typical state of our program *StringMatching* is

$$s_1 = mat,\ s_2 = cat,\ matched = false$$

Then a precondition of a program is a property satisfied by the program states; it may just describe the inputs. Here the precondition $(s_1 = mat) \wedge (s_2 = cat)$ is such a property. Note that all program variables need not be assigned values in a precondition. An unassigned variable can be assigned each possible value in turn and then $\vee$-ed together. For example, our particular precondition for *StringMatching* can be rewritten using the equivalence (Hear, read $(s_1 = mat) \wedge (s_2 = cat)$ etc, with brackets.):

$$s_1 = mat \wedge s_2 = cat \equiv s_1 = mat \wedge s_2 = cat \wedge matched = false \vee matched = true$$

Thus, instead of talking of inputs and outputs, we may speak of preconditions and postconditions, which are first order properties satisfied by program states.

Suppose the predicate Q is the precondition, and the predicate R is the postcondition of the program S. Then the triple

$$\langle Q \rangle\ S\ \langle R \rangle$$

is called a **specification** of the program S. A specification is also called a **Hoare triple** after the computer scientist C. A. R. Hoare. The predicates Q and R are properties of the program variables. The semantics of the Hoare triple is as follows:

> $\langle Q \rangle S \langle R \rangle$ is partially correct (also called conditionally correct) iff "if initially any state of the program variables satisfies the predicate Q and the program S is executed, then on termination of S, any resulting final state of the program variables will satisfy the predicate R."

The Hoare triple expresses partial correctness of the program S. To argue about partial correctness of a program we need some abstraction. For instance, consider the *StringMatching* program. Will you try proving that all of the following Hoare triples hold?

$$\langle s_1 = mat \wedge s_2 = cat \rangle \; StringMatching \; \langle matched = false \rangle$$
$$\langle s_1 = chalk \wedge s_2 = duster \rangle \; StringMatching \; \langle matched = false \rangle$$
$$\langle s_1 = pen \wedge s_2 = pen \rangle \; StringMatching \; \langle matched = true \rangle \text{ and so on.}$$

There are certainly an infinite number of such Hoare triples which must be verified. We would rather like to introduce some new variables for the strings. Suppose we write all possible strings to be assigned to s_1 as $st1$, and those to s_2 as $st2$. Then a typical precondition is "$s_1 = st1$ and $s_2 = st2$," where the required postcondition is "$st1 = st2$ if and only if $matched = true$." Thus the infinite number of Hoare triples would be represented by the specification

$$\langle s_1 = st1 \wedge s_2 = st2 \rangle \; StringMatching \; \langle st1 = st2 \leftrightarrow matched = true \rangle$$

The new variables $st1$ and $st2$ are called the **logical variables** or **ghost variables** with respect to the program. The logical variables do not occur in the program; they only occur in the logical representations of the precondition and the postcondition. They relate the final values of the program variables to their initial values.

The correctness of the *StringMatching* program means that the afore-mentioned specification holds. That is,

> If *StringMatching* terminates, and if initially, the variables s_1, s_2 are assigned the values (strings) $st1, st2$, respectively, then finally no matter what is assigned to $matched$, the formula $(st1 = st2 \leftrightarrow matched = true)$ will hold.

Notice that the notation of a Hoare triple captures the concept of partial correctness only. We will address the issue of total correctness a bit later.

Exercises for § 9.2

1. Given a program and its supposed input, is it possible to find all required properties of the output?
2. Given a program and its supposed output, is it possible to compute the necessary input?
3. Find out all possible inputs corresponding to output as $true$ or $false$, for *StringMatching*.

4. Repeat the previous exercise for your corrected program for matching two strings.
5. Suppose a program does not terminate on all inputs. Then what is the use of partial correctness?

9.3 THE CORE LANGUAGE CL

To argue about a program, we must also describe what a program is. You have already written programs in many languages. As you know, syntax and semantics of commands vary from one language to another. To argue about them all, we develop a methodology independent of any particular language. Further, we would like to consider procedural languages only, thus excluding languages like PROLOG and LISP.

For procedural languages the core may be thought of as comprising three types of commands. They are the assignment statements, the conditional statements, and the loop statements. These statements are enough to simulate a Turing machine, which is an accepted definition of an algorithm. Notice that these three types of statements correspond to the three basic types of operations a Turing machine uses, such as symbol writing, conditional movement of the read-write head, and repeating certain required sequence of moves. Moreover, we assume the capability of sequential execution, so that statements in a program are executed one after another. The sequential execution corresponds to building complex Turing machines from simple ones using compositionality. We describe the syntax and semantics of our core language CL. All our programs will be assumed to be written in this language.

In **CL**, *variables* are some names, such as $x, y, z, \ldots, x_0, x_1, x_2, \ldots,$ or even as *string*, *book*, *string*1,... just like identifiers in procedural programming languages. You may also think of variables as names for memory locations.

CL has two types of expressions: integer expressions and Boolean expressions. An **integer expression** is any integer from the set $\mathbb{Z} = \{\ldots, -2, -1, 0, 1, 2, \ldots\}$, or any variable, or is in any of the forms: $-E1$, $(E1 + E2)$, $(E1 - E2)$, $(E1 \times E2)$, or $(E1/E2)$, where $E1, E2$ are any integer expressions. This recursive definition will let us generate integer expressions such as $(5 \times (-3 + (x \times x)))$, $((2 \times 3) \times 4), \ldots$. These are the arithmetic expressions in many procedural languages.

The symbol '$-$' represents both the unary 'minus' and the binary 'subtraction' as in -3 and $(5 - 3)$, respectively; $+, \times$ represent the operations of addition, and multiplication of integers as usual. The symbol '/' represents integer division; for instance, $8/3 = 2$. Similarly, $=$ and $<$ mean the usual equality and 'less than' relations of integers. Note that there is some redundancy in keeping $(E1 = E2)$ since it could be defined by using the connective $\neg$ and the predicate $<$. However, allowing '$=$' will simplify long expressions, and we decide to keep it. Recall that for ease in reading, we are using $=$ instead of the formal $\approx$ in this chapter.

For doing logical checks, we also keep Boolean expressions. These are simply the propositions of PL, but now have a syntax including the integer expressions. To be definite, a **Boolean expression** is in one of the following forms:

$$\top,\ \bot,\ \neg B1,\ (B1 \wedge B2),\ (B1 \vee B2),\ (E1 < E2),\ \text{or}\ (E1 = E2)$$

where $B1, B2$ are some Boolean expressions and $E1, E2$ are integer expressions. The value of a Boolean expression can be either 0 or 1, i.e., *false* or *true*.

Of the four types of *statements* in CL, we first describe the assignment statement. If x is a variable and E is an integer expression, then an **assignment statement** looks like

$$x := E$$

Execution of the assignment statement proceeds as follows:

> the expression E is evaluated and the computed value is stored in the name (memory location) x. Thus, we say that after the execution of the assignment statement, the variable x becomes **bound** to this computed value of E.

Boolean expressions are used to describe conditional statements just as integer expressions are used in an assignment statement. A **conditional statement** looks like

$$\texttt{if } C \texttt{ then } \{S1\} \texttt{ else } \{S2\}$$

where C is a condition, a Boolean expression, and $S1, S2$ are some statements. The curly brackets are used as punctuation marks.

For instance, `if` $(m < n)$ `then` $\{m := n\}$ `else` $\{n := m\}$ is a conditional statement. The execution of the conditional statement

$$S : \texttt{if } C \texttt{ then } \{S1\} \texttt{ else } \{S2\}$$

proceeds as follows:

> The Boolean expression C is evaluated. If its value turns out to be 1, i.e., *true*, then the statement $S1$ is executed; and after this execution, the whole statement S is considered executed. On the other hand, if the value of C turns out to be 0, i.e., *false*, then the statement $S2$ is executed instead of $S1$; and after this execution, execution of S is considered over.

For example, consider the statement S as

$$\texttt{if } (m < n) \texttt{ then } \{m := n\} \texttt{ else } \{n := m\}$$

Suppose that before S is executed the variables m and n have been bound to 2 and 3, respectively. Then the condition $(m < n)$ is evaluated to 1, and consequently, execution of S proceeds in executing the statement $m := n$. After the execution of S, m becomes bound to 3, the value of n, and also n is bound to 3 as before.

Before the execution of S if m, n have been bound to 10, 5, respectively, then the condition $(m < n)$ is evaluated to 0. Thus, execution of S forces execution of $n := m$, the statement that comes after `else`. Consequently, after S is executed, both m and n become bound to 10, the value of m.

The **sequential control statement** or the **composition** has the following syntax:

$$S1 ; S2$$

where $S1$ and $S2$ are any statements or programs (program fragments). Its semantics is described as follows.

> First, $S1$ is executed. After this execution is over, $S2$ is executed. After the execution of $S2$, the execution of $S1\,;S2$ is considered over. If $S1$ does not terminate, then $S2$ is never executed, and in that case, the composition program $S1\,;S2$ does not terminate. Similarly, if $S2$ does not terminate, then also $S1\,;S2$ does not terminate.

Thus, termination of $S1\,;S2$ is guaranteed only when both $S1$ and $S2$ terminate, and in that order. The sequential composition is assumed to be *left associative*; we do not need parentheses. The program $S1\,;S2;S3$ is interpreted as $(S1\,;S2)\,;S3$, i.e., first $S1$ is executed, next $S2$, and then $S3$.

Finally, we describe the looping statement. Among many alternatives, we choose the 'while loop format'. A while statement looks like

$$\texttt{while}\ C\,\{S\}$$

where C is a condition, a Boolean expression, and S is a statement (a program or a program fragment). In a while statement, the condition C is called the **guard**, and the statement S is called the **body** of the while loop. Its execution means the following:

> The Boolean expression C is first evaluated. If its value is 1 (*true*), then the statement S is executed. Upon termination of this execution, the Boolean expression C is again evaluated. If its value is 1 this time, then S is once again executed. The loop of 'evaluation of C' followed by 'execution of S' is repeated. This repeated execution stops when the value of C becomes 0 (*false*).

It is often the case that execution of S changes values of some program variables occurring in C so that after a finite number of repeated executions (evaluation of C and then execution of S), C would eventually become bound to 0. If this does not happen, then the while statement would never terminate. Thus, vacuously, if C and S do not share any program variables and C is initially bound to 1, then the while statement will not terminate. We emphasize,

> at the termination of the while statement, the condition C must be bound to 0.

The while statement is a looping statement meant for repeated execution of its body until its guard is falsified. It is like a 'for command' found in procedural languages. The difference is that in a for command, you know beforehand how many times S would be repeatedly executed, whereas in a while statement, this is not known beforehand.

A while statement is more suitable for recursion, whereas a for command is more suitable for iteration. The while statement has more direct connection to a machine scheme representation of Turing machines. However, it comes with the potential danger of non-termination.

EXAMPLE 9.1. Trace the execution of S: $\texttt{while}\ m \neq n\ \{m := m+1\,;s := s+m\}$.

Suppose that before execution of S, the variable m has been bound to 0, n has been bound to 5, and s has been bound to 0. With this initial state, execution of S begins.

Now, the guard $m \neq n$ is satisfied (evaluated to 1) as $0 \neq 5$; consequently, the body $m := m+1\,;s := s+m$ is executed. After this first execution of the body, m is bound to 1, s is bound to $s+m$, i.e., to 1. As S is to be executed repeatedly until the guard $m \neq n$ becomes false, execution of S is initiated once more. Again, the guard $m \neq n$ is satisfied and consequently, the body is executed. This makes m bound to 2, and s bound to 3.

After five executions of the body, it turns out that m is bound to 5 and s is bound to 15. On the sixth execution, the guard $m \neq n$ is found to be false, as m becomes equal to 5, the value of n. Then execution of S is stopped; S terminates with the resulting state satisfying $m = 5 \wedge n = 5 \wedge s = 15$.

If, initially, m is bound to 5 and n is bound to 0, then the guard $m \neq n$ is satisfied; the body is executed once increasing the value of m to 6, and of s to the earlier value of s plus 6. Again, the guard is satisfied and execution of the body is initiated. You realize that the guard will always be satisfied in each such successive execution, and consequently, the loop never terminates.

In the detailed trace of execution of S in Example 9.1, there are some variables whose values have not changed while the values of some other variables have changed. The ones whose values have changed are m, s, and the value of n has not changed. In case, the program is terminated, the (changed) value of s stores the sum of numbers $0, 1, \ldots, n$.

Though s changes, it is unlike the change in m. The variable m goes successively through the natural numbers. The change in s can be captured by a formula by looking at its pattern of change at each successive execution of the body of S. When the body of S is executed once, s contains the value 1. At the end of the second execution, it contains the value $1+2$. In general, at the end of the ith execution, s contains the value $1+2+\ldots+i$. Now you see that though the value of s is changing through the repeated execution of the body of the loop, the statement

after the ith execution of the body of S, $s = 0+1+2+\ldots+i$

does not change. This statement holds before the execution of S, it holds after S terminates, and it even holds throughout the execution of the loop S. Such a property which holds throughout the execution of a loop is called an *invariant* of the loop. It is often the invariant of a loop that signals towards the real job undertaken by the loop. Getting the invariant(s) of a loop is not mechanical; it needs some experience, but often it comes from the requirements or the postcondition. We will see in the following section, how an invariant is used for proving correctness of programs.

Exercises for § 9.3

1. The language CL does not have arrays. But arrays can be manipulated in CL by restricting operations to array elements directly. Using this, write programs in CL to perform the following operations on arrays of numbers A and B each of length n. We write the ith entry of an array A as $A[i]$.

   (a) Add A and B to get an array C where $C[i] = A[i] + B[i]$.

   (b) Reverse the entries of A. For instance the program working on $[1, 2, \ldots, 9]$ will output $[9, 8, \ldots, 1]$.

   (c) Determine whether more than half of the corresponding entries of A and B match.

2. When does `if` C `then` $\{S1\}$ `else` $\{S2\}$ fail to terminate?
3. In an urn there are a certain number of black marbles and a certain number of white marbles. Outside the urn we have unlimited supply of black and white marbles. We take out two marbles randomly out of the urn; read their colours and keep them outside. If both are of the same colour, then we put one white marble back into the urn; else, we put a black marble back into the urn. After certain finite number of such moves, only one marble will remain in the urn. This game executes a while loop. What is the invariant of this while loop? Use the invariant to find out the colour of the marble remaining in the urn.
4. Can you describe how to implement a Turing machine in CL? [If you have not yet worked with Turing machines, ignore this exercise.]

9.4 PARTIAL CORRECTNESS

All our programs will be written in the language CL. Whenever some new constructs like arrays or lists are required, we will introduce them informally, without making any hassle and without sacrificing on the precise notions of syntax and semantics. You will be able to formalize the constructs with your rich experience in the syntax and semantics of logical languages like PL and FL.

To recollect, the language CL has two types of expressions: integer and Boolean. These expressions are used in defining statements, which are of four types. The syntax of CL is summarized by the following BNF:

$$E ::= n \mid x \mid -E \mid (E+E) \mid (E-E) \mid (E \times E) \mid (E/E)$$
$$B ::= \top \mid \bot \mid \neg B \mid (B \wedge B) \mid (B \vee B) \mid (E = E) \mid (E < E)$$
$$S ::= x := E \mid S;S \mid \texttt{if } B \texttt{ then } \{S\} \texttt{ else } \{S\} \mid \texttt{while } B\,\{S\}$$

We write $x \neq y$ as a shorthand for $\neg(x = y)$. We assume the usual properties of the operations $+, \times, -, /$ and of the connectives $\neg, \wedge, \vee$, etc. Note that m/n is the greatest integer less than or equal to the rational number $\frac{m}{n}$, and it presumes that n is not equal to 0. For example, $5/3 = 1$ and $-5/3 = -2$. However, in the preconditions and postconditions, we (sometimes) use the symbol '$/$' for real number division instead of this integer division. You should be able to interpret it correctly from the given context. We also assume the usual precedence of operations and connectives.

To argue about programs, which are statements in CL, we have introduced the Hoare triple, which has the syntax:

$$\langle Q \rangle\, S\, \langle R \rangle$$

where Q and R are FL-formulas; the precondition and the postcondition of the statement (program) S, respectively. Recall that the specification $\langle Q \rangle\, S\, \langle R \rangle$ represents our job expectation from the program. It means:

> When the precondition Q is satisfied by the states of the program variables of S, upon termination of S, the resulting states are required to satisfy the postcondition R.

Next, we say that the specification $\langle Q\rangle S\langle R\rangle$ is **partially correct** iff

> for each state of the program S, which satisfies the precondition Q, the states resulting from the execution of S satisfy R, provided that S actually terminates.

Whenever $\langle Q\rangle S\langle R\rangle$ is partially correct, we write $\models \langle Q\rangle S\langle R\rangle$. In such a case, we also say that the (Hoare) triple $\langle Q\rangle S\langle R\rangle$ is **satisfied** under partial correctness. Intuitively, $\models \langle Q\rangle S\langle R\rangle$ means that our job expectation from S is actually met provided its execution is completed. The difference between $\langle Q\rangle S\langle R\rangle$ and $\models \langle Q\rangle S\langle R\rangle$ is analogous to the difference between $!\vdash$ and $\vDash$ in PL and FL.

EXAMPLE 9.2. Determine whether $\models \langle x=x_0\rangle\ y:=x\langle y=x_0\rangle$.

Here x and y are the program variables and x_0 is a logical variable. Let s be a state of program variables, which satisfies the precondition $x=x_0$. That is, in state s, we have $x=x_0$, and y can be bound to anything whatsoever. Being in state s, the statement $y:=x$ is executed. After its execution, y becomes bound to x_0. Thus, the resulting state $\bar{s}$ satisfies $x=x_0\wedge y=x_0$. we see that $\bar{s}$ satisfies the postcondition $y=x_0$. Hence the specification $\langle x=x_0\rangle\ y:=x\langle y=x_0\rangle$ is partially correct. That is, $\models \langle x=x_0\rangle\ y:=x\langle y=x_0\rangle$.

EXAMPLE 9.3. Is it true that $\models \langle x=y\rangle\ x:=x+1;y:=y+1\langle x=y\rangle$?

Let s be a state satisfying the precondition $x=y$. Here x and y may have been bound to any (integer) values. Once the state s satisfies $x=y$, we have in state s, $x=x_0$ and $y=x_0$ for some x_0. Now the statement $x:=x+1;y:=y+1$ is executed. After the execution of $x:=x+1$, the new state $\bar{s}$ satisfies $x=x_0+1\wedge y=x_0$. Then the statement $y:=y+1$ is executed. After this execution, the new state s' satisfies (with $\bar{s}$ as the initial state for $y:=y+1$) the formula $x=x_0+1\wedge y=x_0+1$.

Therefore, the postcondition $x=y$ is satisfied by the final state s'. We conclude that $\models \langle x=y\rangle\ x:=x+1;y:=y+1\langle x=y\rangle$.

EXAMPLE 9.4. Is the following specification partially correct?

$\langle (i=j\rightarrow k=j)\wedge(i\neq j\rightarrow k=m)\rangle$
$\texttt{if } i=j \texttt{ then } \{m:=k\} \texttt{ else } \{j:=k\}$
$\langle j=k\wedge j=m\rangle$

Let s be a state satisfying the precondition $(i=j\rightarrow k=j)\wedge(i\neq j\rightarrow k=m)$. The statement

$$S:\ \texttt{if } i=j \texttt{ then } \{m:=k\} \texttt{ else } \{j:=k\}$$

is executed. The condition $i=j$ may or may not be satisfied by s. Thus we have two cases to consider.

When s satisfies $i=j$, due to the precondition, s satisfies $k=j$. Execution of S then proceeds to execute the statement $m:=k$. Here ends the execution of S, resulting in a new state $\bar{s}$ satisfying $i=j\wedge k=j\wedge m=k$, i.e., $\bar{s}$ satisfies the postcondition $j=k\wedge j=m$.

On the other hand, when s satisfies $i\neq j$, we see that s satisfies $k=m$. Since the condition $i=j$ of S is evaluated to 0 (in the state s), execution of S initiates the execution of the statement $j := k$ (look after the punctuation 'else'). This brings in a new and final state $\bar{s}$ satisfying $k = m \wedge j = k$. That is, $\bar{s}$ satisfies the postcondition $j = k \wedge j = m$.

This proves the partial correctness of the specification.

EXAMPLE 9.5. Is $\models \langle i = 0 \wedge \sigma = 0 \wedge n \geq 0 \rangle$

$$\texttt{while } i \neq n \, \{i := i+1 \,;\, \sigma := \sigma + i\}$$

$$\langle \sigma = \textstyle\sum_{i=0}^{n} i \wedge i \leq n \rangle ?$$

Let s be any state where $i = 0, \sigma = 0$, and $n = n_0 \geq 0$. This is the only way s might satisfy the precondition. When execution of

$$S: \texttt{while } i \neq n \, \{i := i+1 \,;\, \sigma := \sigma + i\}$$

is initiated, the guard $i \neq n$ is first evaluated.

If $n_0 = 0$, then this guard is not satisfied, and consequently, execution of S is terminated. The new state, in this case, s itself, obviously satisfies the postcondition, as $\sigma = 0$ and $\sum_{i=0}^{n_0} i = \sum_{i=0}^{0} i = 0$.

If $n_0 = 1$, then the guard $i \neq n$ is satisfied and the body $i := i+1 \,;\, \sigma = \sigma + i$ is executed to have the resulting state $\bar{s}$, which satisfies

$$i = 1 = n, \; \sigma = 0 + 1 = \sum_{i=0}^{n_0} i = \sum_{i=0}^{n} i$$

That is, $\bar{s}$ satisfies the postcondition. You can repeat this argument for any n_0. But this will not prove the statement. What you require is that for each natural number n_0, the resulting state $\bar{s}$ will satisfy the postcondition. So, induction?

All right, for $n_0 = 0$, you have already shown the partial correctness. Now lay out the induction hypothesis that for $n_0 = m \in \mathbb{N}$, partial correctness holds. Let $n_0 = m + 1$. Let s be any state satisfying the precondition. Since $n_0 \geq 1$ and $i = 0$, the guard $i \neq n$ is satisfied, and the body is then executed. This yields a new state $\bar{s}$ which satisfies $i = 1 \wedge \sigma = \sum_{i=0}^{1} i$.

So, how to use the induction hypothesis? Leaving it here amounts to the hand waving remark: "proceed up to $n_0 + 1$ and similarly ... " – not a proof!

Exercises for § 9.4

1. Determine partial correctness of the following specifications:
   (a) $\langle m = n^k \rangle \, k := k+1 \,;\, m := m \times n \, \langle m = n^k \rangle$
   (b) $\langle j = m^n \wedge s = (m^{n+1} - 1)/(m-1) \rangle$
   $j := j \times m \,;\, s := s + j \,;\, n := n+1$
   $\langle j = m^n \wedge s = (m^{n+1} - 1)/(m-1) \rangle$
   (c) $\langle k^2 = k + 1 \wedge k^m = a \times k + b \rangle$
   $m := m+1 \,;\, t := a+b \,;\, b := a \,;\, a := t$
   $\langle k^m = a \times k + b \rangle$
2. In Example 9.5, first show that the number of times the body of the loop is executed is n_0. Then use induction on the number of times the body of the loop is executed to complete the proof of partial correctness.

3. Determine the preconditions Q and the postconditions R such that the following hold:
(a) $\models \langle Q \rangle$ `while` $\top \{i := 0\} \langle R \rangle$ (b) $\Vdash \langle Q \rangle$ `while` $\top \{i := 0\} \langle R \rangle$
(The symbol $\Vdash$ means 'totally correct', that is, along with partial correctness, the program also terminates.)

9.5 AXIOMS AND RULES

Our attempt in Example 9.5 may be compared to proving the validity of a very complicated first order formula using semantics directly. It is better to have some proof system. We take up the assignment statement first. Its specification looks like

$$\langle Q \rangle\, x := E\, \langle R \rangle$$

where x is a program variable, E is an arithmetic expression, and Q, R are FL-formulas. We may assert $\models \langle Q \rangle\, x := E\, \langle R \rangle$ in the following scenario:

> if a state s satisfies Q, then after x is assigned the value of E, s is expected to satisfy R.

In Example 9.2, you have seen such a specification. Since the value of x is changed to the value of E, you see that R is satisfied for a state $s[x \mapsto E]$. The state $s[x \mapsto E]$ is the same as that in FL; it is the state obtained from s by fixing the variable x to E. Now, the resulting state $\bar{s}$, which equals $s[x \mapsto E]$ satisfies R. That means $R[x/E]$ must have been satisfied by s, due to the substitution lemma. Thus, Q must be equal to $R[x/E]$ or at least that Q must imply $R[x/E]$.

We break the last two alternatives into two rules. The latter case will be taken care by a more general rule. The former rule will be taken as the rule of assignment, or the assignment axiom. The **Assignment Axiom** is then expressed as

$$\models \langle R[x/E] \rangle\, x := E\, \langle R \rangle$$

Notice that $\models \langle Q \rangle\, x := E\, \langle Q[x/E] \rangle$ is not correct, in general. For instance, take $Q \equiv x = 5$, and $E = 2$. Had it been correct, we would have obtained the partially correct specification $\langle x = 5 \rangle\, x := 2\, \langle (x = 5)[x/2] \rangle$. Or that $\models \langle x = 5 \rangle\, x := 2\, \langle 2 = 5 \rangle$. But this is not possible as no state can satisfy the postcondition $2 = 5$.

On the other hand, the assignment axiom allows partial correctness of the specification $\langle 2 = 2 \rangle\, x := 2\, \langle x = 2 \rangle$, which is true, since $(2 = 2) = (x = 2)[x/2]$.

The assignment axiom demands backward reasoning, from the postcondition to the precondition. We will see shortly how to use the axiom in proving partial correctness of programs. To see that it is all right, argue with the specification $\langle x = 5 \rangle\, x := 2\, \langle x = 2 \rangle$. This is partially correct since for any state s satisfying $x = 5$ before the execution of the statement $x := 2$, the resulting state after the execution will satisfy $x = 2$. It does not really matter whether the precondition is $x = 5$; it could have been any Q. The reason is: $Q \to (2 = 2)$ is a valid FL-formula.

This suggests the rule that "if $Q \models R[x/E]$, then $\models \langle Q \rangle\, x := E\, \langle R \rangle$ holds". Similarly, if P is any formula such that $R \models P$, then also $\models \langle R[x/E] \rangle\, x := E\, \langle P \rangle$. For example, $\models \langle 2=2 \rangle\, x := 2\, \langle x^2 = 2^2 \rangle$ since $(x=2) \vDash (x^2 = 2^2)$ is a valid consequence in FL. These observations are true for any type of statements, and not just for assignment. We may express it as

$$\text{If } P \vDash Q,\ \models \langle Q \rangle\, S\, \langle R \rangle, \text{ and } R \vDash U, \text{ then } \models \langle P \rangle\, S\, \langle U \rangle.$$

We call this rule as the **Rule of Implication**.

Next, we consider the composition or the sequential execution. When can we assert that $\langle Q \rangle\, S1\,;\, S2\, \langle R \rangle$ is partially correct? Note that we are reasoning backward, from the postcondition to the precondition. If after the execution of $S1\,;\, S2$, a state satisfies R, then what would have happened before the execution? Let us first think about the execution of $S2$. Before $S2$ has been executed, there must have been some state that satisfies its precondition so that R is satisfied by the resulting state after the execution of $S2$. Call the precondition P. That is, we hypothesize the partial correctness of the specification

$$\langle P \rangle\, S2\, \langle R \rangle$$

Then, obviously, P must have been satisfied by a resulting state after the execution of $S1$, which was initiated by the state s satisfying Q. That is, the partial correctness of the specification

$$\langle Q \rangle\, S1\, \langle P \rangle$$

should have been obtained earlier. This argument is encapsulated in the **Rule of Sequential Execution**, or the **Rule of Composition**, which says that

$$\text{If } \models \langle Q \rangle\, S1\, \langle P \rangle \text{ and } \models \langle P \rangle\, S2\, \langle R \rangle, \text{ then } \models \langle Q \rangle\, S1\,;\, S2\, \langle R \rangle.$$

Note that for proving $\models \langle Q \rangle\, S1\,;\, S2\, \langle R \rangle$ some such P will do provided that the other two specifications are partially correct. Look back at Example 9.3 now. There, you have obtained the following:

$$\models \langle x=y \rangle\, x := x+1\, \langle x = y+1 \rangle \text{ and } \models \langle x = y+1 \rangle\, y := y+1\, \langle x=y \rangle$$

From these two partially correct specifications, we derive, by the rule of sequential execution, that $\models \langle x=y \rangle\, x := x+1\,;\, y := y+1\, \langle x=y \rangle$.

Next, consider the conditional statement. When can we guarantee the partial correctness of

$$\langle Q \rangle \texttt{ if } B \texttt{ then } \{S1\} \texttt{ else } \{S2\}\, \langle R \rangle ?$$

Go back to Example 9.4. There, we had to break the proof into two cases depending on whether the Boolean expression B is evaluated to 1 or 0. If s is a state that satisfies Q, and B is evaluated to 1, then in this state $S1$ is executed. After such an execution the resulting state must satisfy R. This suggests the partial correctness of the specification $\langle Q \wedge B \rangle\, S1\, \langle R \rangle$. On the other hand, when B is evaluated to 0, i.e., when $\neg B$ holds, the initial state s satisfies $Q \wedge \neg B$. In this case, $S2$ is executed and the resulting state satisfies R. This suggests, similarly, the partial correctness of the specification $\langle Q \wedge \neg B \rangle\, S2\, \langle R \rangle$. Remember that we are going from the postcondition to the precondition. Summarizing, we have the **Rule of Conditional statement** as

$$\text{If } \models \langle Q \wedge B \rangle\, S1\, \langle R \rangle \text{ and } \models \langle Q \wedge \neg B \rangle\, S2\, \langle R \rangle,$$
$$\text{then } \models \langle Q \rangle \texttt{ if } B \texttt{ then } \{S1\} \texttt{ else } \{S2\}\, \langle R \rangle.$$

In Example 9.4, we had

$$\models \langle (i=j \to k=j) \wedge (i \neq j \to k=m) \wedge i=j \rangle\, m:=k \,\langle j=k \wedge j=m \rangle$$
$$\models \langle (i=j \to k=j) \wedge (i \neq j \to k=m) \wedge i \neq j \rangle\, j:=k \,\langle j=k \wedge j=m \rangle$$

By using the rule of conditional statement, we obtain

$$\models \langle (i=j \to k=j) \wedge (i \neq j \to k=m) \rangle$$
$$\texttt{if } i=j \texttt{ then } \{m=k\} \texttt{ else } \{j:=k\}$$
$$\langle j=k \wedge j=m \rangle$$

Finally, we consider the while statement. Here the task is to find out sufficient conditions (which should be reasonably weak) for determining the partial correctness of the specification

$$\langle Q \rangle \texttt{ while } B\,\{S\}\,\langle R \rangle$$

Look back at Example 9.5. We have seen that there are properties that change during repeated executions of the loop body, and there are some which do not change. The properties that do not change are called the **invariants** of the loop.

An invariant remains true (not false, for convenience) before, during, and after the execution of the loop. The invariant in Example 9.5 is the "current sum up to i", where i is the number of times the loop body has been executed (till that instant). That is, the invariant is the formula: $\sigma = \sum_{j=0}^{i} j$. Though the value of the variable i changes, and the value of the variable σ changes, the truth (value) of the statement $\sigma = \sum_{j=0}^{i} j$ does not change.

Suppose, the invariant of a while statement is already known. In order that $\langle Q \rangle$ `while` $B\,\{S\}\,\langle R \rangle$ is partially correct, we know that Q must contain the invariant, and R must also contain the invariant. Moreover, after the execution, assuming that the loop terminates, B must become false. Otherwise, the statement S is executed again contrary to the termination of the loop. That is, R must also contain $\neg B$. Denoting the loop invariant by I, we seek the conditions so that the specification

$$\langle I \rangle \texttt{ while } B\,\{S\}\,\langle I \wedge \neg B \rangle$$

is partially correct. Let us look at its execution once again. Here, s is a state of the program variables satisfying the invariant I. In such a state, execution of the while statement `while` $B\,\{S\}$ is initiated. Suppose that s satisfies the guard B. Then S is executed. After this execution, the invariant is satisfied by the resulting state. If B is also satisfied by the resulting state, then once again S is executed, and once again it results in a state that satisfies the invariant. Hence, in order that $\langle I \rangle$ `while` $B\,\{S\}\,\langle I \wedge \neg B \rangle$ is partially correct, we would have had the partial correctness of $\langle I \wedge B \rangle\, S\, \langle I \rangle$. Thus the **Rule of While** is

$$\text{If } \models \langle I \wedge B \rangle\, S\, \langle I \rangle, \text{ then } \models \langle I \rangle \texttt{ while } B\,\{S\}\,\langle I \wedge \neg B \rangle$$

Here I is an invariant of the while loop. In fact, an invariant may be defined as any formula I so that the above statement holds.

EXAMPLE 9.6. Look at the specification in Example 9.5. Our goal is to show that

$$\begin{aligned}&\models \langle i=0 \land \sigma=0 \land n \geq 0 \rangle\\ &\quad \texttt{while } i \neq n \,\{i:=i+1\,;\, \sigma:=\sigma+i\}\\ &\quad \langle \sigma=\textstyle\sum_{i=0}^{n} i \land i \leq n \rangle\end{aligned}$$

Pretend that we want to discover an invariant of the loop, i.e., a formula I which would make the rule of while true. We start with the postcondition.

The postcondition is $\sigma = \sum_{i=0}^{n} i \land i \leq n$. Since negation of the guard will be satisfied after termination, we will have $i = n$. This will of course imply the formula $i \leq n$. Then, matching with $I \land \neg B$, we may consider I to be something that would express $\sigma = \sum_{i=0}^{n} i = \sum_{m=0}^{n} m$, upon termination. Note that upon termination, we have $i = n$. Moreover, the running sum of the ith execution of the loop is $\sum_{m=0}^{i}$ and when $i = n$, we would get σ. So, let us start with $I \equiv \sigma = \sum_{m=0}^{i} m$ as an invariant. Due to the identity

$$\sigma = \sum_{m=0}^{i} m \land i = n \models \sigma = \sum_{i=0}^{n} i \land i \leq n$$

and the rule of implication, it is enough to show that

$$\begin{aligned}&\models \langle i=0 \land \sigma=0 \land n \geq 0 \rangle\\ &\quad \texttt{while } i \neq n \,\{i:=i+1\,;\, \sigma:=\sigma+i\}\\ &\quad \langle \sigma=\textstyle\sum_{m=0}^{i} m \land i = n \rangle\end{aligned}$$

Look at the postcondition again. It is $I \land \neg B$. Then to apply the while rule, we require $\models \langle I \land B \rangle\, i:=i+1\,;\, \sigma:=\sigma+i\, \langle I \rangle$. That is,

$$\models \langle \sigma = \sum_{m=0}^{i} m \land i \neq n \rangle\, i:=i+1\,;\, \sigma:=\sigma+i \langle \sigma = \sum_{m=0}^{i} m \rangle$$

To complete the proof, first show that

$$\models \langle \sigma = \sum_{m=0}^{i} m \land i \neq n \rangle\, i:=i+1; \sigma:=\sigma+i \langle \sigma = \sum_{m=0}^{i} m \rangle$$

Next, use the rule of implication, and the consequence

$$(i=0 \land \sigma=0 \land n>0) \models \left(\sigma = \sum_{m=0}^{i} m \land i \neq n\right)$$

These are left as exercises for you. In the following exercises, $\Vdash S$ means that the program S is totally correct, that is, S terminates and also it is partially correct.

Exercises for § 9.5

1. Which of the following are assignment axioms?

   (a) $\models \langle 5=5 \rangle\, m:=5 \,\langle m=5 \rangle$
   (b) $\Vdash \langle 5=6 \rangle\, m:=5 \,\langle m=6 \rangle$

(c) $\models \langle n=5 \rangle\, m := 5\, \langle m=n \rangle$
(d) $\not\models \langle 5>3 \rangle\, m := 5\, \langle m>3 \rangle$
(e) $\models \langle m+1=5 \rangle\, m := m+1\, \langle m=5 \rangle$
(f) $\not\models \langle m+1=n \rangle\, m := m+1\, \langle m=n \rangle$
(g) $\models \langle m+1>0 \wedge n>0 \rangle\, m := m+1\, \langle m>0 \wedge n>0 \rangle$

2. Using the assignment axiom and the rule of implication, show that the following specifications are partially correct:

(a) $\langle x=y \rangle\, x := x+1\, \langle x=y+1 \rangle$
(b) $\langle x-1=y \rangle\, y := y+1\, \langle x=y \rangle$
(c) $\langle (i=j \to k=j) \wedge (i \neq j \to k=m) \wedge i=j \rangle\, m := k\, \langle j=k \wedge j=m \rangle$
(d) $\langle (i=j \to k=j) \wedge (i \neq j \to k=m) \wedge i \neq j \rangle\, j := k\, \langle j=k \wedge j=m \rangle$

3. By using the assignment axiom and the rule of sequential composition show that $\models \langle \sigma = \Sigma_{m=0}^{i} m \wedge i \neq n \rangle\, i := i+1; \sigma := \sigma + i\, \langle \sigma = \Sigma_{m=0}^{i} m \rangle$

9.6 HOARE PROOF

A summary of the rules for arguing about programs in CL follows. The names of the rules are self-explanatory: 'A' stands for the assignment axiom, 'S' for the sequential execution, 'C' for the conditional statement, 'W' for the while statement, and 'I' for implication.

(RA) $$\frac{}{\langle R[x/E] \rangle\, x := E\, \langle R \rangle}$$

(RS) $$\frac{\models \langle Q \rangle\, S1\, \langle P \rangle \qquad \models \langle P \rangle\, S2\, \langle R \rangle}{\models \langle Q \rangle\, S1; S2\, \langle R \rangle}$$

(RC) $$\frac{\models \langle Q \wedge B \rangle\, S1\, \langle R \rangle \qquad \models \langle Q \wedge \neg B \rangle\, S2\, \langle R \rangle}{\models \langle Q \rangle\, \texttt{if}\ B\ \texttt{then}\ \{S1\}\ \texttt{else}\ \{S2\}\, \langle R \rangle}$$

(RW) $$\frac{\models \langle I \wedge B \rangle\, S\, \langle I \rangle}{\models \langle I \rangle\, \texttt{while}\ B\, \{S\}\, \langle I \wedge \neg B \rangle}$$

(RI) $$\frac{P \models Q \qquad \models \langle Q \rangle\, S\, \langle R \rangle \qquad R \models U}{\models \langle P \rangle\, S\, \langle U \rangle}$$

Remember that $R[x/E]$ is obtained from R by replacing all free occurrences of the variable x by the expression E. We assume that the symbols when used in a context are well defined. For example, $R[x/E]$ must be well defined, meaning that the types of x and E must match. Note that in FL, this discussion was unwarranted, since variables there could only be substituted by terms. Further, RA here is the rule of assignment, not reductio ad absurdum.

At this point go back to the rules as stated earlier and match them with rules written above as fractions. These rules say that if you have already proved the partial correctness of the specification in the numerator, then the denominator follows. The denominator of RA does not need the partial correctness of any other specification; it is an axiom.

You can use these rules to define and construct proofs. A **proof of partial correctness** of a specification is a finite sequence of specifications, and possibly some FL-formulas. The formulas must be valid (or provable in a proof system), each specification is either an axiom (RA), or follows from earlier specifications by an application of one of the other four rules. Further, RA terminates a path.

The logic defined by these rules is obviously an extension of FL. Occasionally we will have to prove the valid FL-formulas that may be used in a proof. But we will refrain from doing so here; rather we give more attention to the proofs of specifications. The proof system so obtained is known as the **Hoare Logic** for CL. If you take a different language, say, C, then the corresponding Hoare logic will be different. The proofs in any Hoare logic is called a **Hoare proof**.

We follow the three-column style of writing a proof; the first column keeps track of the entries by giving each a serial number, the second column is the actual proof, and the third column documents the proof by giving justification. As justifications we will mention the rules by their names RA, RS, RC, RW, or RI as appropriate, and 'FL' for the valid FL-formulas. Occasionally, we may add a separate proof of the valid formulas. If a rule is applied on the preceding line(s), then we will not mention the line numbers; we will mention the remote line numbers.

EXAMPLE 9.7. Give a Hoare proof of

$$\models \langle 1+a-a^2=0 \wedge a^n=b+c\times a\rangle$$
$$n:=n+1\,;\, m:=b+c\,;\, b:=c\,;\, c:=m$$
$$\langle a^n=b+c\times a\rangle$$

In this specification only assignment statements are sequentially composed. We may only require the rules RA, RS, and RI. We proceed from the postcondition to the precondition. The last statement is $c:=m$ with the postcondition $a^n=b+c\times a$. So, what should be the precondition?

By RA, it is $(a^n=b+c\times a)[c/m]$, which equals $a^n=b+m\times a$. This is taken as a postcondition for the statement $b:=c$, preceding the last statement. Again, by RA, the precondition would be $(a^n=b+m\times a)[b/c]$ which equals $a^n=c+m\times a$. This is, essentially, the rule RS. Read the following proof from lines 9 back to 1, from postcondition to precondition; and then from lines 1 through 9.

1.	$\langle a^n=b+m\times a\rangle\, c:=m\, \langle a^n=b+c\times a\rangle$	RA
2.	$\langle a^n=c+m\times a\rangle\, b:=c\, \langle a^n=b+m\times a\rangle$	RA
3.	$\langle a^n=c+(b+c)\times a\rangle\, m:=b+c\, \langle a^n=c+m\times a\rangle$	RA
4.	$\langle a^{n+1}=c+(b+c)\times a\rangle\, n:=n+1\, \langle a^n=c+(b+c)\times a\rangle$	RA
5.	$\langle a^{n+1}=c+(b+c)\times a\rangle$ $n:=n+1\,;\, m:=b+c\, \langle a^n=c+m\times a\rangle$	RS
6.	$\langle a^{n+1}=c+(b+c)\times a\rangle$ $n:=n+1\,;\, m:=b+c\,;\, b:=c\, \langle a^n=b+m\times a\rangle$	2, RS

7. $\langle a^{n+1} = c+(b+c)\times a \rangle$
$n := n+1; m := b+c; b := c; c := m \langle a^n = b+c\times a \rangle$ 1, RS

8. $1+a-a^2 = 0 \wedge a^n = b+c\times a \vDash a^{n+1} = c+(b+c)\times a$ FL

9. $\langle 1+a-a^2 = 0 \wedge a^n = b+c\times a \rangle$
$n := n+1; m := b+c; b := c; c := m \langle a^n = b+c\times a \rangle$ RI

A proof of validity of the consequence in line 8 goes as follows:

$$1+a-a^2 = 0 \wedge a^n = b+c\times a$$
$$\vDash a^{n+1} = a\times(b+c\times a) \wedge 1+a = a^2$$
$$\vDash a^{n+1} = a\times b+a^2\times c \wedge 1+a = a^2$$
$$\vDash a^{n+1} = a\times b+(1+a)\times c$$
$$\vDash a^{n+1} = a\times b+c+a\times c$$
$$\vDash a^{n+1} = c+(b+c)\times a$$

A **Hoare proof tree** can be defined by using the rules from denominators to the numerators using branching of the tree for the rules RS, RC, and RI, and stacking for the rules RA and RW. The leaves of a Hoare proof tree must be axioms of the Hoare logic for CL, i.e., instances of the assignment axiom or the valid formulas of FL. The root of the proof tree must be the specification for which a proof is sought. The Hoare proof tree for the specification of Example 9.7 is as follows.

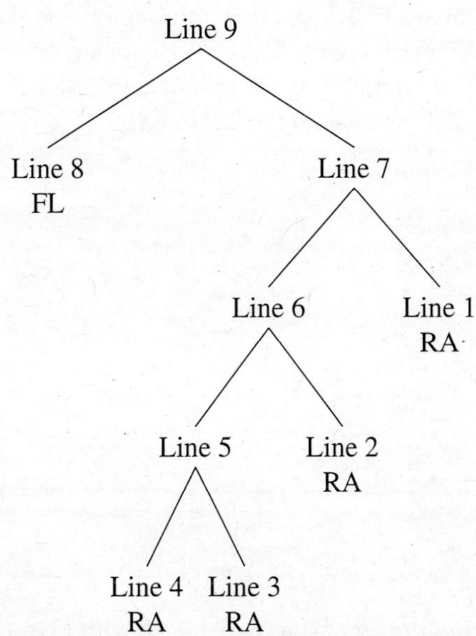

The line numbers in the Hoare tree refer to those in the Hoare proof given in the solution to Example 9.7. Look at the tree and try to understand the phrase: "from denominator to numerator".

Exercises for § 9.6

Check whether the following specifications are partially and/or totally correct. For partially correct specifications, construct a Hoare proof. What are the programs supposed to compute?

1. $\langle n = m^2 \wedge s = m \times (m+1) \times (2 \times m+1)/6 \rangle$
   $m := m+1; n = n+2 \times m-1; s := n+s$
   $\langle n = m^2 \wedge s = m \times (m+1) \times (2 \times m+1)/6 \rangle$
2. $\langle \top \rangle x := m+1;$ `if` $x = 1$ `then` $\{n := 1\}$ `else` $\{n := x\} \langle n := m+1 \rangle$
3. $\langle m \geq 0 \rangle n := 1; k := 0;$ `while` $k \neq m$ $\{k := k+1; n := n \times k\} \langle n := m! \rangle$
4. $\langle \top \rangle n := 1; k := 0;$ `while` $k \neq m$ $\{k := k+1; n := n \times k\} \langle n := m! \rangle$
5. $\langle m \geq 0 \rangle n := 1;$ `while` $m \neq 0$ $\{n := n \times m; m := m-1\} \langle n := m! \rangle$
6. $\langle m = m_0 \wedge m \geq 0 \rangle n := 1;$ `while` $m \neq 0$ $\{n := n \times m; m := m-1\} \langle n := m_0! \rangle$
7. $\langle m = m_0 \wedge m \geq 0 \rangle k := 0;$ `while` $m > 0$ $\{k := k+m; m := m-1\}$
   $\langle k = m \times (m+1)/2 \rangle$

9.7 PROOF SUMMARY

It is often desirable to omit the small details in a proof and only sketch the important steps so that a formal proof may be constructed out of the sketch. To develop such a sketch, called a **proof summary**, let us go through the Hoare proof given in Example 9.7. A proof summary is as follows. We number the lines below for further reference, though they are not part of the proof summary. Read the proof summary from bottom to top and compare with the original Hoare proof.

Proof summary for Example 9.7 with line numbers:

1. $\langle 1+a-a^2 = 0 \wedge a^n = b+c \times a \rangle$
2. $\langle a^{n+1} = c+(b+c) \times a \rangle$
3. $n := n+1;$
4. $\langle a^n = c+(b+c) \times a \rangle$
5. $m := b+c;$
6. $\langle a^n = c+m \times a \rangle$
7. $b := c;$
8. $\langle a^n = b+m \times a \rangle$
9. $c := m$
10. $\langle a^n = b+c \times a \rangle$

The last three lines of the proof summary match with Line 1 of the original Hoare proof. Lines 6, 7, 8 match with Line 2 of the original. Lines 4, 5, 6 correspond to Line 3, and Lines 2, 3, 4 correspond to Line 4 of the Hoare proof. The other lines in the original Hoare proof have been omitted, where the rule of sequential execution has worked implicitly in the proof summary.

In the proof summary, Lines 1 and 2 comprise a **verification condition** which corresponds to the FL-consequence in Line 8 of the detailed proof given in Example 9.7. Notice that a verification condition $\langle P \rangle\ \langle Q \rangle$ is written as

$$\langle P \rangle$$
$$\langle Q \rangle$$

one below the other. This is suggestive as it says that P is the precondition and Q is the postcondition of the "empty code"; a real fun! It means that the Hoare logic is an extension of FL, where $P \vDash Q$ is rewritten as $\langle P \rangle\ \langle Q \rangle$.

Specification for the sequential execution is written by repeating the condition Q as follows.

$$\langle P \rangle\, S1 \,\langle Q \rangle\ ;\ \langle Q \rangle\, S2 \,\langle R \rangle$$

In a proof summary, it is written easily mentioning Q only once:

$$\langle P \rangle\, S1;\ \langle Q \rangle\, S2 \,\langle R \rangle$$

How should we abbreviate the specification for the conditional execution? The rule of the conditional (RC) looks like

$$\text{From } \langle Q \wedge B \rangle\, S1 \,\langle R \rangle \text{ and } \langle Q \wedge \neg B \rangle\, S2 \,\langle R \rangle\text{, derive}$$
$$\langle Q \rangle\ \texttt{if}\ B\ \texttt{then}\ \{S1\}\ \texttt{else}\ \{S2\}\,\langle R \rangle.$$

All the notations of the three specifications occurring in the above must be true in the abbreviation, and we must be able to read it through. The proof summary for this fragment would look like

$$\langle Q \rangle\ \texttt{if}\ B\ \texttt{then}\ \{\langle Q \wedge B \rangle\, S1 \,\langle R \rangle\}\ \texttt{else}\ \{\langle Q \wedge \neg B \rangle\, S2 \,\langle R \rangle\}\,\langle R \rangle$$

Our next aim would be to prove partial correctness of both the specifications

$$\langle Q \wedge B \rangle\, S1 \,\langle R \rangle \text{ and } \langle Q \wedge \neg B \rangle\, S2 \,\langle R \rangle$$

Note that there are repetitions of the postcondition inside the braces following `then` and `else`. We also use indentation for improving readability, though unnecessary. See the following example.

EXAMPLE 9.8. Construct a proof summary for showing that

$$\begin{array}{l} \vDash \langle \top \rangle\ \texttt{if}\ i<j\ \texttt{then}\ \{\ \texttt{if}\ j<k\ \texttt{then}\ \{m:=k\}\ \texttt{else}\ \{m:=j\}\} \\ \quad \texttt{else}\ \{\ \texttt{if}\ i<k\ \texttt{then}\ \{m:=k\}\ \texttt{else}\ \{m:=i\}\} \\ \quad \langle m \geq i \wedge m \geq j \wedge m \geq k \rangle \end{array}$$

We start with expanding the specification towards constructing a proof summary.

$$\begin{array}{l} \langle \top \rangle\ \texttt{if}\ i<j\ \texttt{then} \\ \quad \{\langle \top \wedge i<j \rangle\ \texttt{if}\ j<k\ \texttt{then}\ \{m:=k\}\ \texttt{else}\ \{m:=j\} \\ \quad \langle m \geq i \wedge m \geq j \wedge m \geq k \rangle\} \\ \texttt{else}\ \{\langle \top \wedge i \nless j \rangle\ \texttt{if}\ i<k\ \texttt{then}\ \{m:=k\}\ \texttt{else}\ \{m:=i\} \end{array}$$

$\langle m \geq i \wedge m \geq j \wedge m \geq k \rangle \}$
$\langle m \geq i \wedge m \geq j \wedge m \geq k \rangle$

But this is not a proof summary because the two conditional statements themselves involve other statements. We supply the necessary preconditions and postconditions. We also use indentations to logically group the conditional statements together.

$\langle \top \rangle$ `if` $i < j$ `then`
  $\{\langle \top \wedge i < j \rangle$ `if` $j < k$ `then`
    $\{\langle \top \wedge i < j \wedge j < k \rangle m := k \langle m \geq i \wedge m \geq j \wedge m \geq k \rangle \}$
     `else` $\{\langle \top \wedge i < j \wedge j \not< k \rangle m := j \langle m \geq i \wedge m \geq j \wedge m \geq k \rangle \}$
  $\langle m \geq i \wedge m \geq j \wedge m \geq k \rangle \}$
 `else` $\{\langle \top \wedge i \not< j \rangle$ `if` $i < k$ `then`
    $\{\langle \top \wedge i \not< j \wedge i < k \rangle m := k \langle m \geq i \wedge m \geq j \wedge m \geq k \rangle \}$
     `else` $\{\langle \top \wedge i \not< j \wedge i \not< k \rangle m := i \langle m \geq i \wedge m \geq j \wedge m \geq k \rangle \}$
  $\langle m \geq i \wedge m \geq j \wedge m \geq k \rangle \}$
$\langle m \geq i \wedge m \geq j \wedge m \geq k \rangle$

The proof summary requires the Hoare proofs of the following specifications:

(a) $\langle \top \wedge i \not< j \wedge i \not< k \rangle m := i \langle m \geq i \wedge m \geq j \wedge m \geq k \rangle$
(b) $\langle \top \wedge i \not< j \wedge i < k \rangle m := k \langle m \geq i \wedge m \geq j \wedge m \geq k \rangle$
(c) $\langle \top \wedge i < j \wedge j \not< k \rangle m := j \langle m \geq i \wedge m \geq j \wedge m \geq k \rangle$
(d) $\langle \top \wedge i < j \wedge j < k \rangle m := k \langle m \geq i \wedge m \geq j \wedge m \geq k \rangle$

Read the proof summary from bottom to top and see how the rules are working, and how the abbreviations help us to read a Hoare proof.

A proof summary shows applications of all the rules except the assignment axiom and possibly, verification conditions. These are to be seen separately. Now, what about the while statement? The while rule looks like

From $\langle Q \wedge B \rangle S \langle Q \rangle$, derive $\langle Q \rangle$ `while` $B \, \{S\} \, \langle Q \wedge \neg B \rangle$

Notice that in this notation, Q is the invariant of the while loop. It is instructive to keep this special property and mark it as the invariant, for it requires a lot of ingenuity to discover this. Moreover, it improves readability. The fragment of the proof summary for the while statement thus looks like:

$\langle$Invariant: $Q \rangle$ `while` $B \, \{\langle Q \wedge B \rangle S \langle Q \rangle \} \langle Q \wedge \neg B \rangle$

Mark the movement of the curly brackets above from $\{S\}$ to $\{\langle Q \wedge B \rangle S \langle Q \rangle \}$. We take up this movement of the curly brackets in order that $\langle Q \rangle$ and $\langle Q \wedge \neg B \rangle$ would not come together; for, that would mean $Q \vDash Q \wedge \neg B$, which is completely unwarranted.

Recall that an invariant of the while statement `while` $B \, \{S\}$ having guard B and body S is an FL-formula I such that $\vDash \langle I \wedge B \rangle S \langle I \rangle$ holds, i.e., if I and B are both satisfied by any state of the program variables (occurring in S) and S is executed, then upon termination (assumed here) of S, the resulting state will satisfy the formula I.

The disturbing fact is that there are always many invariants of a while loop. This is simple to see since both $\top$ and $\bot$ are invariants of every while statement. (Prove it!) But then these might be the useless invariants, in general. The useful invariants express a relationship between the program variables that are manipulated in the body of the loop. If we have the specification

$$\langle P\rangle \texttt{ while } B\,\{S\}\,\langle R\rangle$$

then in order to be able to prove it (by RW and RI), we must look for an invariant Q such that all of

$$P \vDash Q,\ Q\wedge\neg B \vDash R, \text{ and } \vDash \langle Q\rangle \texttt{ while } B\,\{S\}\,\langle Q\wedge\neg B\rangle$$

hold. Discovering an invariant requires the knowledge of what job the while statement is supposed to perform, and some ingenuity.

EXAMPLE 9.9. Construct a proof summary for the following specification:

$$\langle 0\le n\wedge 0<x\rangle y:=1;\, z:=x;\, k:=n;\ \texttt{while } 0\ne k\,\{k:=k-1;\, y:=y\times z\}\,\langle y=x^n\rangle$$

Since the postcondition of the while statement will be in the form $Q\wedge\neg B$, we must look for an invariant Q so that $Q\wedge\neg B\equiv y=x^n$ or $Q\wedge\neg B \vDash y=x^n$, or even the weaker consequence $\forall^*(Q\wedge\neg B)\vDash\forall^*(y=x^n)$, where B is the guard $0\ne k$ of the loop. We must also have a formula P such that

$$\vDash \langle 0\le n\wedge 0<x\rangle y:=1;\, z:=x;\, k:=n\,\langle P\rangle,\ \text{and } P\vDash Q$$

Well, what does the loop do? Suppose that $k=2$. The guard $0\ne k$ is satisfied. Now, $k:=k-1$ is executed, so $k=1$. Next, $y:=y\times z$ is executed, thus in place of y, we now have the value of $y\times z$. Once again, the guard is satisfied, and then k becomes 0, and y becomes bound to $(y\times z)\times z$, i.e., to $y\times z^2$. Finally, y becomes bound to $y\times z^k$. The postcondition is $y=x^n$. Combining these two, we would obtain an invariant which looks like

$$y\times z^k=x^n$$

All these suggestions implicitly assume that $0\le k$. To make it explicit, we start with the invariant Q as

$$0\le k\wedge y\times z^k=x^n$$

Then our specification is pushed one step closer to a proof summary, which, at this stage, appears as

$\langle 0\le n\wedge 0<x\rangle$
$y:=1;\, z:=x;\, k:=n;$
$\langle P\rangle\,\langle Q\rangle$
$\texttt{while } 0\ne k\{k:=k-1;\, y:=y\times z\}$
$\langle 0=k\wedge Q\rangle\,\langle y=x^n\rangle$

We do not know yet what P is. Trying with $P=Q$ (instead of $P\vDash Q$), the specification would be simplified. Further, using the specification of a proof summary for the while statement, it would look like

$\langle 0 \leq n \wedge 0 < x \rangle$
$y := 1; z := x; k := n;$
$\langle$Invariant: $Q\rangle$
`while` $0 \neq k\{ \langle Q \wedge 0 \neq k \rangle k := k-1; y := y \times z \langle Q \rangle \}$
$\langle 0 = k \wedge Q \rangle \; \langle y = x^n \rangle$

We now focus our attention on the first part:

$$\langle 0 \leq n \wedge 0 < x \rangle y := 1; z := x; k := n \langle Q \rangle$$

Pushing the postcondition towards the precondition through the assignments, we see that a proof summary of this fragment starts with

$$\langle 0 \leq n \wedge 0 < x \rangle y := 1; z := x \langle Q[k/n] \rangle k := n \langle Q \rangle$$

And, finally, the fragment will be

$$\langle 0 \leq n \wedge 0 < x \rangle \; \langle Q[k/n][z/x][y/1] \rangle y := 1 \langle Q[k/n][z/x] \rangle z := x; \; \langle Q[k/n] \rangle k := n \langle Q \rangle$$

Taking Q as the formula $0 \leq k \wedge y \times z^k = x^n$, the substitutions above will be simplified. We then use the fragment for the while statement as done earlier to obtain the required proof summary as:

$\langle 0 \leq n \wedge 0 < x \rangle$
$\langle 0 \leq n \wedge 1 \times x^n = x^n \rangle$
$y := 1;$
$\langle 0 \leq n \wedge y \times x^n = x^n \rangle$
$z := x;$
$\langle 0 \leq n \wedge y \times z^n = x^n \rangle$
$k := n;$
$\langle$Invariant: $0 \leq k \wedge y \times z^k = x^n \rangle$
`while` $0 \neq k$
$\{ \langle 0 \leq k \wedge y \times z^k = x^n \wedge 0 \neq k \rangle$
$\langle 0 \leq k-1 \wedge (y \times z) \times z^{k-1} = x^n \rangle$
$k := k-1;$
$\langle 0 \leq k \wedge (y \times z) \times z^k = x^n \rangle$
$y := y \times z$
$\langle 0 \leq k \wedge y \times z^k = x^n \rangle \}$
$\langle 0 \leq k \wedge y \times z^k = x^n \wedge 0 = k \rangle$
$\langle y = x^n \rangle$

EXAMPLE 9.10. Let $odd(k) = \exists m (m \in \mathbb{N} \wedge k = 2 \times m + 1)$. We consider $odd(k)$ to be a predicate which expresses the fact that k is odd. Construct a proof summary with the necessary verification condition(s) for the following specification:

$\langle 0 \leq n \rangle k := n; y := 1; z := x;$ `while` $0 \neq k \{$
`if` $odd(k)$ `then` $\{k := k-1; y := y \times z\}$ `else` $\{y := y\}$;
$k := k/2; z := z \times z \} \langle y = x^n \rangle$

Convince yourself that $Q(y,z,k) \equiv y \times z^k = x^n \wedge 0 \le k$ is an invariant of the while statement. Notice that writing $Q(y,z,k)$ instead of Q will make further substitutions visible. We write $even(k)$ for $\neg odd(k)$. The proof summary now looks like

$\langle 0 \le n \rangle$
$\langle 1 \times x^n = x^n \wedge 0 \le n \rangle$
$k := n;\, y := 1;\, z := x;$
$\langle$ Invariant: $Q(y,z,k) \rangle$
`while` $0 \ne k$
  $\{ \langle 0 \ne k \wedge Q(y,z,k) \rangle$
`if` $odd(k)$ `then`
    $\{ \langle odd(k) \wedge 0 \ne k \wedge Q(y,z,k) \rangle$
    $\langle even(k-1) \wedge Q(y \times z, z, k-1) \rangle$
    $k := k-1;\, y := y \times z$
    $\langle even(k) \wedge Q(y,z,k) \rangle \}$
  `else` $\{ \langle \neg odd(k) \wedge 0 \ne k \wedge Q(y,z,k) \rangle$
    $\langle even(k) \wedge Q(y,z,k) \rangle$
    $\langle Q(y, z \times z, k/2) \rangle$
    $k := k/2;\, z := z \times z$
    $\langle Q(y,z,k) \rangle \}$
  $\langle Q(y,z,k) \rangle \}$
$\langle y = x^n \rangle$

Prove the verification conditions in the proof summary.

EXAMPLE 9.11. Let $k! = 1 \times 2 \times 3 \times \cdots \times k$, the "$k$ factorial", with $0! = 1$. For the partial correctness of the specification

$$\langle \top \rangle y := 1;\, z := 0;\ \texttt{while}\ z \ne x\, \{z := z+1;\, y := y \times z\}\, \langle y = x! \rangle$$

the proof summary is as follows:

$\langle \top \rangle$
$\langle 1 = 0! \rangle y := 1;\ \langle y := 0! \rangle z := 0;$
$\langle$ Invariant: $y = z! \rangle$
`while` $z \ne x$
  $\{ \langle y = z! \wedge z \ne x \rangle$
  $\langle y \times (z+1) = (z+1)! \rangle z := z+1;\ \langle y \times z = z! \rangle y := y \times z \langle y = z! \rangle \}$
$\langle y = z! \wedge z = x \rangle$
$\langle y = x! \rangle$

Exercises for § 9.7

1. Give Hoare proofs of partial correctness of the specifications (a)-(d) mentioned in the solution to Example 9.8.

2. Prove the following three verification conditions met in the proof summary in Example 9.9:

   (a) $0 \le n \wedge 0 < x \vDash 0 \le n \wedge 1 \times x^n = x^n$
   (b) $0 \le k \wedge y \times z^k = x^n \wedge 0 \ne k \vDash 0 \le k-1 \wedge (y \times z) \times z^{k-1} = x^n$
   (c) $0 \le k \wedge y \times z^k = x^n \wedge 0 = k \vDash y = x^n$

   Develop a complete Hoare proof from the proof summary.

3. Annotate the proof summaries in Examples 9.9-9.11 with the names of the rules where they have been applied.

4. Develop proof summaries and then the complete Hoare proofs of partial and total correctness (if possible) for the following specifications:

   (a) $\langle m > 0 \rangle n := m+1 \langle n > 1 \rangle$
   (b) $\langle \top \rangle n := m; n := 2 \times m + n \langle n = 3 \times m \rangle$
   (c) $\langle \top \rangle$ `if` $n < m$ `then` $\{k := n\}$ `else` $\{k := m\} \langle k = \min(m, n) \rangle$
   (d) $\langle m \ge 0 \rangle x := m; n := 0;$ `while` $x \ne 0 \{n := n+1; x := x-1\} \langle m := n \rangle$
   (e) $\langle \top \rangle x := m; n := 0;$ `while` $x \ne 0 \{n := n+1; x := x-1\} \langle m := n \rangle$
   (f) $\langle n \ge 0 \rangle x := 0; k := 0;$ `while` $x \ne n \{k := m+k; x := x+1\}$ $\langle k := m \times n \rangle$
   (g) $\langle n = n_0 \wedge n \ge 0 \rangle k := 0;$ `while` $n \ne 0 \{k := m+k; n := n-1\}$ $\langle k := m \times n_0 \rangle$
   (h) $\langle m \ge 0 \rangle n := 0;$ `while` $n \ne m \{n := n+1\} \langle m = n \rangle$
   (i) $\langle m \ge 0 \rangle x := m; n := 1;$ `while` $x \ge 0 \{n := x \times n; x := x-1\} \langle n = m! \rangle$
   (j) $\langle n \ne 0 \rangle r := m; d := 0;$ `while` $r \ge n \{r := r-n; d := d+1\}$ $\langle (m := d \times n + r) \wedge (r < n) \rangle$

9.8 TOTAL CORRECTNESS

Partial correctness of a program is conditional; it assumes that the (execution of the) program actually terminates. If the program does not terminate, then the Hoare proof of its partial correctness becomes vacuous. Total correctness requires partial correctness and that the program actually terminates.

> A specification $\langle Q \rangle S \langle R \rangle$ is **totally correct**, written as $\Vdash \langle Q \rangle S \langle R \rangle$, iff for any state s of the program variables of S, if s satisfies the precondition Q, then S terminates and the resulting state $\bar{s}$ satisfies the postcondition R.

Notice that non-termination of a program might result due to the presence of a while loop. A typical proof of termination of a while statement proceeds as follows. We identify an integer expression, related to the program variables, whose value decreases as the body of the while statement is repeatedly executed. Further, this expression must have a lower bound, typically 0, so that it cannot be decremented arbitrary number of times. Such an expression is called a **variant** of the loop. Once the variant achieves its lower bound, the loop terminates.

For instance, consider the loop in Example 9.11 The while statement starts with an initial value bound to the variable x, and z being bound to 0. When the loop body is executed once, the value of z is incremented to 1. The guard of the loop holds for all values of z from 0 to "the value of x minus 1". Once z becomes bound to the value of x, the loop terminates. We see that the value of the expression $x-z$ is decremented by 1 each time the loop is executed "once more". Therefore, a variant of the loop is $x-z$.

Suppose E is a variant for the while statement `while` $B\,\{S\}$, whose value decreases with each (repeated) execution of S. That is, if the value of E is E_0 before the loop is executed, then after the execution, the value of E is strictly less than E_0. Moreover, to note that E has a lower bound, we will put a restriction on the value of E such as $0 \le E_0$. We thus incorporate a variant with these properties into the while rule. The while rule for partial correctness was (Write Q in place of I.)

$$\frac{\models \langle Q \wedge B \rangle\, S\, \langle Q \rangle}{\models \langle Q \rangle \ \texttt{while}\ B\,\{S\}\, \langle Q \wedge \neg B \rangle}$$

where Q was the invariant of the while statement. Now, since the value of the variant is taken non-negative, we have an additional condition that $0 \le E$. Notice that a variant with a lower bound can always be modified to have the new lower bound as 0. The variant E satisfies $E = E_0$ before execution of S, for some E_0, and after execution $E < E_0$. Thus the required additional condition is the correctness of the specification

$$\langle Q \wedge B \wedge 0 \le E = E_0 \rangle\, S\, \langle Q \wedge 0 \le E < E_0 \rangle$$

That is, we add the new condition $0 \le E$ to the precondition of the while statement. Since the condition $0 \le E$ is not a part of the *goal* of the while statement, we need not add it to the postcondition. The goal or the postcondition is usually fixed even before the program is written, whereas we only invented the condition $0 \le E$ for the proof of correctness. Hence, the **rule of total while**, written as a fraction, is

(TW) $$\frac{\Vdash \langle Q \wedge B \wedge 0 \le E = E_0 \rangle\, S\, \langle Q \wedge 0 \le E < E_0 \rangle}{\Vdash \langle Q \wedge 0 \le E \rangle \ \texttt{while}\ B\,\{S\}\, \langle Q \wedge \neg B \rangle}$$

In all other rules of partial correctness, we simply replace the symbol $\models$ by $\Vdash$. However, we will refer to them with the same names, even after this replacement.

In a proof summary, along with the invariant, we will document the variant E also. The proof summary fragment for total correctness of a while statement, corresponding to the rule TW, will look like

$\langle$ Invariant: $Q \wedge$ Variant: $0 \le E \rangle$
`while` $B\{\, \langle Q \wedge B \wedge 0 \le E = E_0 \rangle S \langle Q \wedge 0 \le E < E_0 \rangle \,\}$
$\langle Q \wedge \neg B \rangle$

It is written in such a way that by omitting the strings "Invariant:" and "Variant:", you would get the clear-cut application of the total-while rule. Let us redo Example 9.11 for proving its total correctness.

EXAMPLE 9.12. Construct a proof summary to show that

$$\Vdash \langle x \ge 0 \rangle\, y := 1;\, z := 0;\ \texttt{while}\ z \ne x\, \{z := z+1;\, y := y \times z\}\, \langle y = x! \rangle$$

The variant is $E = z - x$. Compare the following proof summary for total correctness with the one for partial correctness given in Example 9.11.

$\langle x \geq 0 \rangle$
$\langle 1 = 0! \wedge 0 \leq x - 0 \rangle\, y := 1;\ \langle y = 0! \wedge 0 \leq x - 0 \rangle\, z := 0;$
$\langle$ Invariant: $y = z! \wedge$ Variant: $0 \leq x - z \rangle$
`while` $x \neq z$
  $\{ \langle y = z! \wedge x \neq z \wedge 0 \leq x - z = E_0 \rangle$
  $\langle y \times (z+1) = (z+1)! \wedge 0 \leq x - (z+1) < E_0 \rangle\, z := z+1;$
  $\langle y \times z = z! \wedge 0 \leq x - z < E_0 \rangle\, y := y \times z;$
  $\langle y = z! \wedge 0 \leq x - z < E_0 \rangle \}$
$\langle y = z! \wedge x = z \rangle$
$\langle y = x! \rangle$

The choice of a variant depends upon the nature of the statements in the while loop. Discovering an appropriate variant requires ingenuity just like the case of an invariant. As E. W. Dijkstra pointed out

> understanding a while loop is tantamount to discovering its variants and invariants.

EXAMPLE 9.13. *(Binary Search)* Let a denote an array of n integers in which the elements are already ordered, say, in ascending order. Using binary search, split the array into two parts such that all the elements in the first part and none of the numbers in the second part precede a given integer m.

In binary search, you choose the middle element of the array. Compare it with m. Decide whether the new array of focus is the left part or the right part of the original array. Continue the same way with the new array.

Here we follow another version of it. Throughout our operation on the array, we will maintain three decks (imagine the array elements written on cards). The left deck contains array elements that are known to (at a certain instant during execution) precede m, in an ordered fashion. The right deck contains array elements which are all known "not to precede" m, again in an ordered fashion, in ascending order, of course. The middle deck contains array elements, in ascending order, which are yet unknown whether to precede or not to precede m. Thus, initially, both the left and the right decks are empty, and the middle deck contains the full array.

In our representation, we use two integers ℓ and r to represent the three decks, as in the following:

> The left deck is the array segment $a[0], \cdots, a[\ell - 1]$,
> the middle deck is the segment $a[\ell], \cdots, a[r-1]$, and
> the right deck is the segment $a[r], \cdots, a[n-1]$.

Initially, $\ell = 0$ and $r = n$. This suggests the initial assignments $\ell := 0; r := n$. During execution, we may need to move the segment $a[\ell], \ldots, a[i]$ to the left deck. This is accomplished by executing the assignment $\ell := i + 1$. Similarly, movement of the segment $a[i+1], \ldots, a[r-1]$ to the right deck is effected by the assignment $r := i$.

Then comes the question, as to where from we make the split. Assume that after some steps, we have the left, middle and the right decks; the middle deck is the array segment $a[\ell], \cdots, a[r-1]$. We want to split the middle deck into two parts by finding the middle element in this segment, say, it is the ith. In binary search, this i would be equal to $\lfloor \ell+r-1)/2 \rfloor$ or $\lceil (\ell+r-1)/2 \rceil$. We choose the former. That is, we have the assignment $i := (\ell+r-1)/2$. Now, if $a[i] < m$, then all of $a[\ell], \cdots, a[i]$ will be moved to the left deck. And if $a[i] \geq m$, then all of $a[i], \cdots, a[r-1]$ will be moved to the right deck. The program of *Binary Search* then looks like

```
ℓ := 0; r := n;
while ℓ < r
   {i := (ℓ+r−1)/2;
   if a[i] < m then {ℓ := i+1} else {r := i}}
```

What is the precondition and what is the postcondition of this program? Since we do not want an empty array, we may have the condition $n > 0$. The array is in ascending order, which means that if $j \leq k$ then $a[j] \leq a[k]$. This constitutes the precondition

$$Q \equiv \forall j \forall k (0 \leq j \leq k < n \rightarrow a[j] \leq a[k])$$

Similarly, after the execution of the program, our requirement is that the left deck would contain all array elements that precede m and the remaining part of the array would contain all array elements which do not precede m. Also, both ℓ and r must be within the range 0 to n. Thus, the required postcondition is

$$R \equiv 0 \leq \ell \leq n \wedge \forall j (0 \leq j < \ell \rightarrow a[j] < m) \wedge \forall j (\ell \leq j < n \rightarrow a[j] \geq m)$$

For the partial correctness of *Binary Search,* we must find an invariant for the while loop. The invariant, in general, relates the program variables. Since the decks are completely determined by the ordered pair (ℓ, r), it would be enough to have such a relation between the variables ℓ and r. The important property of ℓ is that all the array elements $a[0], \cdots, a[\ell-1]$ precede m. Similarly, the property of r is that none of the array elements $a[r], \cdots, a[n-1]$ precedes m. Moreover, $\ell \leq r$. Thus, we try an invariant in the form

$$I(\ell, r) \equiv 0 \leq \ell \leq r \leq n \wedge \forall j (0 \leq j < \ell \rightarrow a[j] < m) \wedge \forall j (r \leq j < n \rightarrow a[j] \geq m)$$

For total correctness, we also need a variant, whose value may decrease as the body of the loop is executed "once more". In the beginning, the middle deck is the full array and after execution, we expect it to become empty. Since the number of array elements of the middle deck is $r-\ell$, this is a natural variant. With Q as the precondition, R as the postcondition, $I(\ell, r)$ as the invariant of the while loop, and $r-\ell$ as the variant of the loop, we have the following proof summary for total correctness:

```
⟨∀j∀k(0 ≤ j ≤ k < n → a[j] ≤ a[k])⟩
ℓ := 0; r := n;
⟨Invariant: I(ℓ,r) ∧ Variant: r − ℓ ≤ n⟩
while ℓ < r
```

$\{\langle I(\ell,r)\wedge\ell<r\rangle$
$i:=(\ell+r-1)/2;$
$\langle I(\ell,r)\wedge\ell\le i<r\rangle$
`if` $a[i]<m$ `then`
$\quad\{\langle I(\ell,r)\wedge\ell\le i<r\wedge a[i]<m\rangle$
$\quad\ell:=i+1\,\langle I(\ell,r)\rangle\}$
`else` $\{\langle I(\ell,r)\wedge\ell\le i<r\wedge a[i]\ge m\rangle\, r:=i\}\,\langle I(\ell,r)\rangle\}$
$\langle I(\ell,r)\wedge\ell\ge r\rangle$
$\langle 0\le\ell\le n\wedge\forall j(0\le j<\ell\to a[j]<m)\wedge\forall j(\ell\le j<n\to a[j]\ge m)\rangle$

Exercises for § 9.8

1. Both ℓ and r are not required for the formalization in the Binary search. Write the postcondition using only r, and then prove total correctness.
2. Show that the precondition $x\ge 0$ cannot be replaced in the proof summary of Example 9.12 by $\top$ if total correctness is required. Construct total correctness proofs for the specifications in Examples 9.9-9.11.
3. Write programs P so that the following specifications are totally correct; also prove total correctness.
   (a) $\langle\top\rangle P\langle n=m+6\rangle$
   (b) $\langle\top\rangle P\langle k<m+n+0.5\times k\rangle$
   (c) $\langle\top\rangle P\langle k=\max(\ell,m,n)\rangle$
   (d) $\langle\top\rangle P\langle((x=4)\to(y=3))\wedge((x=7)\to(y=5))\rangle$

9.9 A PREDICATE TRANSFORMER

The Hoare logics are not the only way a program may be verified for total correctness. In this section we will describe another way to go for correctness proofs; historically this came prior to Hoare logics.

As we know, programming is a goal-oriented activity. Given inputs, we want to develop a program which would give us the required output. However, when we prove a program correct, we go backward. We ask: if we require certain output, with the given program, what should have been the input?

For instance, consider the rule of implication in proving the correctness of the specification $\langle Q\rangle S\langle R\rangle$. We know Q, S, and R. The rule of implication states that $\langle Q\rangle S\langle R\rangle$ is correct provided that P is a precondition for the program S with the postcondition R; and $Q\vDash P$. The condition $Q\vDash P$ will be easier to satisfy provided P is the weakest of all preconditions of the program S with respect to the postcondition R. We thus define the weakest precondition as follows.

Let S be a program (a statement) and R be any FL-formula. Then the **weakest precondition** of S with respect to R, denoted by $wp(S,R)$, is an FL-formula which describes the set of all initial states such that the execution of S in any one (or more) of the states is guaranteed to terminate in a state satisfying R.

In this language of "a formula describing a set of states", the formula $\top$ describes the set of all states; and $\bot$ describes the empty set of states.

EXAMPLE 9.14. The statement $t := x$ assigns the value of x to t. It is required that after this execution, the formula $t = 2$ must be satisfied. This can only happen provided x has the value 2 before execution. Hence $wp\,(t := x, t = 2) \equiv (x = 2)$.

It is obvious that wp satisfies two properties. First, it is a precondition, which means that the specification $\langle wp\,(S,R)\rangle\, S\,\langle R\rangle$ is totally correct. Second, it must be the weakest of such preconditions; that is, if $\langle Q\rangle\, S\,\langle R\rangle$ is totally correct, then Q must entail $wp\,(S,R)$. Our requirements may be stated as follows:

$$\Vdash \langle wp\,(S,R)\rangle\, S\,\langle R\rangle \tag{9.1}$$

$$\text{If } \Vdash \langle Q\rangle\, S\,\langle R\rangle, \text{ then } Q \vDash wp\,(S,R). \tag{9.2}$$

These two properties together define what $wp\,(S,R)$ is.

From the assignment rule (see also Example 9.14), it follows that

$$wp\,(x := E, R) \equiv R[x/E] \tag{9.3}$$

for any expression E, matching types with x. The rule of implication takes the form

$$\text{If } P \vDash wp\,(S,R), \text{ then } \Vdash \langle P\rangle\, S\,\langle R\rangle. \tag{9.4}$$

Similarly, the rule of sequential execution appears as

$$wp\,(S1\,;\,S2, Q) \equiv wp\,(S1, wp\,(S2,Q)) \tag{9.5}$$

Imagine pushing the postcondition up through the program for obtaining the required weakest precondition.

For the conditional statement $\texttt{if}\ B\ \texttt{then}\ \{S1\}\ \texttt{else}\ \{S2\}$, let R be the postcondition. We identify two possibilities: (a) executing $S1$, and (b) executing $S2$.

The case (a) happens when B is satisfied. Further, R is the postcondition for $S1$. Then $wp\,(S1,R)$ must have been satisfied before the execution. But we know that B has been satisfied. That is, B is a precondition for $S1$ with postcondition R. Referring to (9.1)-(9.2), we conclude that $B \vDash wp\,(S1,R)$.

Similarly the case (b) happens when $\neg B$ is a precondition for $S2$ with postcondition R. It follows that $\neg B \vDash wp\,(S2,R)$.

Thus the rule of conditional (RC) and the equivalence in Example 4.5 imply:

$$\begin{aligned} wp\,(\texttt{if}\ B\ \texttt{then}\ \{S1\}\ \texttt{else}\ \{S2\}, R) &\equiv (B \to wp\,(S1,R)) \wedge (\neg B \to wp\,(S2,R)) \\ &\equiv (B \wedge wp\,(S1,R)) \vee (\neg B \wedge wp\,(S2,R)) \end{aligned} \tag{9.6}$$

From the properties (9.1)-(9.2) of wp and (9.6) we obtain the following result.

Theorem 9.1. *The formula* $P \equiv (B \to wp\,(S1,R)) \wedge (\neg B \to wp\,(S2,R))$ *satisfies*

(1) $\Vdash \langle P\rangle\ \texttt{if}\ B\ \texttt{then}\ \{S1\}\ \texttt{else}\ \{S2\}\,\langle R\rangle$

(2) *If* $\Vdash \langle Q\rangle\ \texttt{if}\ B\ \texttt{then}\ \{S1\}\ \texttt{else}\ \{S2\}\,\langle R\rangle$, *then* $Q \vDash P$.

In addition, we have some nice properties of the predicate transformer wp.

Theorem 9.2. *The predicate transformer wp satisfies the following properties:*

(1) *Excluded Miracle:* $wp(S,\bot) \equiv \bot$.

(2) *Termination:* $wp(S,\top) \equiv$ *"S terminates"*.

(3) $\wedge$ *distributivity:* $wp(S,Q\wedge R) \equiv wp(S,Q)\wedge wp(S,R)$.

(4) $\vee$ *distributivity:* $wp(S,Q\vee R) \equiv wp(S,Q)\vee wp(S,R)$ *for a deterministic program S.*

(5) $\neg$ *distributivity:* $wp(S,\neg Q) \vDash \neg wp(S,Q)$.

(6) $\vDash$ *distributivity:* *If* $Q \vDash R$, *then* $wp(S,Q) \vDash wp(S,R)$.

(7) $\rightarrow$ *distributivity:* $wp(S,Q\rightarrow R) \vDash wp(S,Q)\rightarrow wp(S,R)$.

Proof. (1) If s is a state that satisfies $wp(S,\bot)$, then the resulting state would satisfy $\bot$. However, no (resulting) state can satisfy $\bot$. Therefore, no such state s exists that satisfies $wp(S,\bot)$. That is, $wp(S,\bot)\equiv\bot$.

(2) $wp(S,\top)$ is a formula that describes all states s such that after termination of S, the resulting state $\bar{s}$ satisfies $\top$. Since all states $\bar{s}$ satisfy $\top$, provided S terminates, $wp(S,\top)$ is simply a formula that guarantees termination of S.

(3) $wp(S,Q\wedge R)$ describes the set of all states s that guarantee the termination of S in a state satisfying both Q and R. Any such state s guarantees termination of S in a state satisfying Q. Hence, $wp(S,Q\wedge R)\vDash wp(S,Q)$. Similarly, $wp(S,Q\wedge R)\vDash wp(S,R)$. Together they give

$$wp(S,Q\wedge R)\vDash wp(S,Q)\wedge wp(S,R).$$

Conversely, let s be a state satisfying $wp(S,Q)\wedge wp(S,R)$. Then s is a state that guarantees termination of S resulting in a state $\bar{s}$ that satisfies Q, and also R. So,

$$wp(S,Q)\wedge wp(S,R)\vDash wp(S,Q\wedge R).$$

(4) Let s be a state that satisfies at least one of $wp(S,Q)$ or $wp(S,R)$. Then, after S terminates, the resulting state satisfies at least one of Q or R. So,

$$wp(S,Q)\vee wp(S,R)\vDash wp(S,Q\vee R).$$

Conversely, suppose that S is a *deterministic program*. This means that if s is a state in which execution of S is initiated, then, upon termination of S, the resulting state s' is unique. In contrast, one execution of a non-deterministic program can lead to one state, and another execution may drive the same initial state to another state.

Suppose that s is a state that satisfies $wp(S,Q\vee R)$ before S is executed. After S terminates, let s' be the resulting state. Then, s' satisfies $Q\vee R$, i.e., s' satisfies Q or s' satisfies R. In the first case, if s' satisfies Q, then by the definition of wp, s satisfies $wp(S,Q)$. In the second case, if s' satisfies R, then s must satisfy $wp(S,R)$. In any case, s satisfies $wp(S,Q)\vee wp(S,R)$. This shows that

$$wp(S,Q\vee R)\vDash wp(S,Q)\vee wp(S,R).$$

(5) Due to (1) and (3), $wp(S,\neg Q) \wedge wp(S,Q) \equiv wp(S,\neg Q \wedge Q) \equiv wp(S,\bot) \equiv \bot$. Thus, $wp(S,\neg Q) \wedge wp(S,Q) \vDash \bot$. By RA, $wp(S,\neg Q) \vDash \neg wp(S,Q)$.

(6) Suppose $Q \vDash R$. Then, $Q \equiv Q \wedge R$. Using (3) we have

$$wp(S,Q) \equiv wp(S,Q \wedge R) \vDash wp(S,Q) \wedge wp(S,R) \vDash wp(S,R).$$

(7) Notice that $(Q \to R) \wedge Q \vDash R$. Using (3) and (6), we obtain

$$wp(S,Q \to R) \wedge wp(S,Q) \equiv wp(S,(Q \to R) \wedge Q) \vDash wp(S,R).$$

By the deduction theorem, $wp(S,Q \to R) \vDash wp(S,Q) \to wp(S,R)$. ♦

In Theorem 9.2, Property (1) is called the law of the excluded miracle, since it would be a miracle if there is a state which would be satisfied before S is executed, and after the execution, S would terminate in no states.

In Property (2), $wp(S,\top)$ need not be equivalent to $\top$; a counter example would be a program S which does not terminate.

The distributivity laws in Properties (3)-(4) hold for all deterministic programs. One part of the $\vee$–distributivity, namely, $wp(S,Q \vee R) \vDash wp(S,Q) \vee wp(S,R)$ is not satisfied for nondeterministic programs, in general.

The three laws mentioned in the Properties (5)-(7) are one sided distributivity laws, whose converse statements do not hold, in general; see the following example.

EXAMPLE 9.15. Let $Q \equiv \bot$, and let $R \equiv \top$. Suppose that S is a non-terminating program; for instance, take S as `while` $(n \geq 0)\{n := n+1\}$.

(a) Now, $\neg wp(S,Q) \equiv \neg wp(S,\bot) \equiv \neg\bot \equiv \top$. Next, since S does not terminate, we have $wp(S,\neg Q) \equiv wp(S,\top) \equiv$ "S terminates" $\equiv \bot$. Therefore, $\neg wp(S,Q) \nvDash wp(S,\neg Q)$.

(b) Here, $wp(S,Q) \to wp(S,R) \equiv wp(S,\bot) \to wp(S,\top) \equiv \bot \to$ "S terminates" $\equiv \top$. And, $wp(S,Q \to R) \equiv wp(S,\bot \to \top) \equiv wp(S,\top) \equiv$ "S terminates" $\equiv \bot$. Therefore, $wp(S,Q) \to wp(S,R) \nvDash wp(S,Q \to R)$.

(c) Now, $wp(S,Q) \equiv wp(S,\bot) \equiv \bot$; and $wp(S,R) \equiv wp(S,\top) \equiv$ "S terminates" $\equiv \bot$. As $\bot \vDash \bot$, we have $wp(S,R) \vDash wp(S,Q)$. On the other hand, $R \equiv \top$ and $Q \equiv \bot$ imply that $R \nvDash Q$.

To see how wp works on a while statement, consider

W : `while` $B\,\{S\}$

Let R be a postcondition for W. We want to compute $wp(W,R)$ with the guarantee that W terminates, that is, the loop is executed a finite number of times. Denote by P_m the weakest precondition of W with respect to the postcondition R, where the body S of W is executed exactly m times.

If the body S of the loop is never executed ($m = 0$) then, before the execution of W is initiated, we have a state s that satisfies $\neg B$. After this execution of W (by skipping its body), the postcondition R must be satisfied by the same state s. Thus the required precondition is $\neg B \wedge R$. That is,

$$P_0 \equiv \neg B \wedge R.$$

If S is executed exactly once, then after this execution the guard B is falsified, and the body S is skipped. That is, the postcondition for the first execution is P_0; so precondition is $wp(S, P_0)$. Moreover, B had been satisfied for initiating the first execution. Thus, the required weakest precondition is

$$P_1 \equiv B \wedge wp\,(S, P_0).$$

In general, suppose that the kth execution of S is over, and then the $(k+1)$th execution is initiated. Then B must have been satisfied by any resulting state of the kth execution. Further, such a state must also have satisfied the weakest precondition for the kth execution. Hence,

$$P_{k+1} \equiv B \wedge wp\,(S, P_k).$$

Since we require W to terminate, the repeated execution must stop somewhere. That is, there must exist a natural number k such that the body S of W is executed exactly k times. It means that for some k, P_k holds. Thus,

$$P_0 \equiv \neg B \wedge R, \;\; P_{m+1} \equiv B \wedge wp\,(S, P_m),$$
$$wp\,(\,\texttt{while}\ B\ \{S\}, R) \equiv \exists k (k \in \mathbb{N} \wedge P_k). \tag{9.7}$$

Though this is enough for capturing the weakest precondition of a while statement, we must also look at the invariants. Recall that I is an invariant of W means that if S is executed with the precondition I and S terminates, then I is also a guaranteed postcondition. Now, with I as a postcondition, we have $wp\,(S, I)$ as the weakest precondition. Thus, a state that satisfies I, B, and "termination of S", must also satisfy $wp\,(S, I)$. This means that an invariant I of a while statement `while` $B\ \{S\}$ satisfies the property

$$I \wedge B \wedge wp\,(S, \top) \vDash wp\,(S, I). \tag{9.8}$$

We use the properties in Equations (9.1)-(9.8) and those in Theorem 9.2 (1)-(7) of the predicate transformer wp for proving total correctness of programs in CL.

EXAMPLE 9.16. Using wp show that (compare with Example 9.7)

$$\Vdash \langle 1 + a + a^2 = 0 \wedge a^n = b + c \times a \rangle$$
$$n := n + 1;\, m := b + c;\, b := c;\, c := m$$
$$\langle a^n = b + c \times a \rangle$$

We simply compute wp from the postcondition and then see that the precondition actually entails the wp. Using Equations (2.5), (2.3), etc.,

$$
\begin{aligned}
& wp\,(n := n+1;\, m := b+c;\, b := c;\, c := m, a^n = b + c \times a) \\
\equiv\; & wp\,(n := n+1, wp\,(m := b+c, wp\,(b := c, wp\,(c := m, a^n + b + c \times a)))) \\
\equiv\; & wp\,(n := n+1, wp\,(m := b+c, wp\,(b := c, a^n = b + m \times a))) \\
\equiv\; & wp\,(n := n+1, wp\,(m := b+c, a^n = c + m \times a)) \\
\equiv\; & wp\,(n := n+1, a^n = c + (b+c) \times a) \\
\equiv\; & a^{n+1} = c + (b+c) \times a.
\end{aligned}
$$

As in Example 9.7, $1 + a - a^2 = 0 \wedge a^n = b + c \times a \vDash a^{n+1} = c + (b+c) \times a$. By (9.4), we get the required total correctness.

EXAMPLE 9.17. Show by computing the weakest precondition that

$\models \langle m = i \times j + k + 1 \rangle$
  $\texttt{if } j = k+1 \texttt{ then } \{i := i+1; k := 0\} \texttt{ else } \{k := k+1\}$
  $\langle m = i \times j + k \rangle$

Denote the required *wp* by Q. Then,

$$\begin{aligned}
Q &\equiv wp(\texttt{ if } j := k+1 \texttt{ then } \{i := i+1; k := 0\} \\
&\quad \texttt{else } \{k := k+1\},\ m = i \times j + k) \\
&\equiv ((j = k+1) \to wp(i := i+1; k := 0, m = i \times j + k)) \\
&\quad \wedge ((j \neq k+1) \to wp(k := k+1, m = i \times j + k)).
\end{aligned}$$

$$\begin{aligned}
& wp(i := i+1; k := 0, m = i \times j + k) \\
& \equiv wp(i := i+1, wp(k := 0, m = i \times j + k)) \\
& \equiv wp(i := i+1, m = i \times j) \\
& \equiv m = (i+1) \times j.
\end{aligned}$$

Also, $wp(k := k+1, m = i \times j + k) \equiv m = i \times j + k + 1$. Hence

$$\begin{aligned}
Q &\equiv ((j = k+1) \to (m = (i+1) \times j)) \wedge ((j \neq k+1) \to (m = i \times j + k + 1)) \\
&\equiv ((j = k+1) \wedge (m = (i+1) \times j)) \vee ((j \neq k+1) \wedge (m = i \times j + k + 1)) \\
&\equiv ((j = k+1) \wedge (m = i \times j + j)) \vee ((j \neq k+1) \wedge (m = i \times j + k + 1)) \\
&\equiv ((j = k+1) \wedge (m = i \times j + k + 1)) \vee ((j \neq k+1) \wedge (m = i \times j + k + 1)) \\
&\equiv ((j = k+1) \vee (j \neq k+1)) \wedge (m = i \times j + k + 1) \\
&\equiv \top \wedge (m = i \times j + k + 1) \\
&\equiv m = i \times j + k + 1.
\end{aligned}$$

The total correctness of the specification now follows.

EXAMPLE 9.18. By computing *wp* show that

$\models \langle \exists k(k \in \mathbb{N} \wedge i = n - 2 \times k \wedge s = 0) \vee \exists k(k \in \mathbb{N} \wedge i = n - 2 \times k - 1 \wedge s = k) \rangle$
  $\texttt{while } i \neq n\ \{k := -k; s := s + k; i := i+1\}$
  $\langle s = 0 \rangle$

Here the guard is $B \equiv i \neq n$; the postcondition is $R \equiv s = 0$, and the body of the while statement S is $k := -k; s := s+k; i := i+1$. Now,

$$P_0 \equiv \neg B \wedge R \equiv i = n \wedge s = 0.$$

$$\begin{aligned}
P_1 &\equiv B \wedge wp(S, P_0) \equiv i \neq n \wedge wp(S, i = n \wedge s = 0) \\
&\equiv i \neq n \wedge wp(S, i = n) \wedge wp(S, s = 0).
\end{aligned}$$

$$\begin{aligned}
& wp(S, i = n) \equiv wp(k := -k, wp(s := s+k, wp(i := i+1, i = n))) \\
& \equiv wp(k := -k, wp(s := s+k, i+1 = n)) \equiv wp(k := -k, i+1 = n) \equiv i+1 = n.
\end{aligned}$$

$$\begin{aligned}
& wp(S, s = 0) \\
& \equiv wp(k := -k, wp(s := s+k, wp(i := i+1, s = 0))) \\
& \equiv wp(k := -k, wp(s := s+k, s = 0)) \equiv wp(k := -k, s+k = 0) \equiv s - k = 0.
\end{aligned}$$

Therefore,

$$P_1 \equiv i \neq n \wedge i+1 = n \wedge s-k = 0 \equiv i+1 = n \wedge s-k = 0.$$
$$P_2 \equiv i \neq n \wedge wp\,(S, i+1 = n) \wedge wp\,(S, s-k = 0) \equiv i+2 = n \wedge s = 0.$$

These formulas suggest that

$$P_{2k} \equiv i = n - 2 \times k \wedge s = 0, \quad P_{2k+1} \equiv i = n - 2 \times k - 1 \wedge s = k. \tag{9.9}$$

With this P_k, we have

$$wp\,(\,\texttt{while}\ i \neq n\ \{k := -k;\, s := s+k;\, i := i+1\}, s = 0)$$
$$\equiv \exists k(k \in \mathbb{N} \wedge i = n - 2 \times k \wedge s = 0) \vee \exists k(k \in \mathbb{N} \wedge i = n - 2 \times k - 1 \wedge s = k).$$

Notice that discovering an invariant for the Hoare proof of a while statement amounts to discovering a formula for P_k. Moreover, you will have to show that your conjecture on the form of P_k is, indeed, correct. This involves ingenuity, whereas computation of *wp* for other statements is quite mechanical.

EXAMPLE 9.19. Compute $wp\,(\,\texttt{while}\ n \neq m\ \{S\}, R)$, where

S is $i := i+2;\, s := s + n \times i + k;\, k := k+i;\, n := n+1$
R is $s = m^3 \wedge i = 2 \times m \wedge k = m \times (m+1) + 1$

Fill in the missing steps in the following computation of *wp* :

$$P_0 \equiv n = m \wedge s = m^3 \wedge i = 2 \times m \wedge k = m \times (m+1) + 1$$
$$\equiv n = m \wedge s = n^3 \wedge i = 2 \times n \wedge k = n \times (n+1) + 1.$$

$$wp\,(S, s = n^3 \wedge i = 2 \times n \wedge k = n \times (n+1) + 1)$$
$$\equiv wp\,(i := i+2;\, s := s + n \times i + k;\, k := k+i,$$
$$s = (n+1)^3 \wedge i = 2 \times (n+1) \wedge k = (n+1) \times (n+2) + 1)$$
$$\equiv s = n^3 \wedge i+2 = 2 \times (n+1) \wedge k = n \times (n+1) + 1$$
$$\equiv s = n^3 \wedge i = 2 \times n \wedge k = n \times (n+1) + 1.$$

Can you see that it is an invariant of the while statement? Now,

$$P_1 \equiv n \neq m \wedge wp\,(S, P_0)$$
$$\equiv n \neq m \wedge n+1 = m \wedge s = n^3 \wedge i = 2 \times n \wedge k = n * (n+1) + 1.$$

By induction, we obtain

$$P_k \equiv n \neq m \wedge n+k = m \wedge s = n^3 \wedge i = 2 \times n \wedge k = n \times (n+1) + 1$$
$$\equiv n = m - k \wedge s = n^3 \wedge i = 2 \times n \wedge k = n \times (n+1) + 1.$$

Thus, $wp\,(\,\texttt{while}\ n \neq m\ \{S\}, R) \equiv n \leq m \wedge s = n^3 \wedge i = 2 \times n \wedge k = n \times (n+1) + 1.$

Remark 9.1. Our definitions of $\models$ and $\Vdash$ are semantic, in the sense that for a specification Σ we write $\models \Sigma$ or $\Vdash \Sigma$, according as something happens for the initial and final states. However, the proof rules of Hoare logic or of *wp* are syntactic, in the sense that once you accept to follow the rules, you have no need to go back to the states for constructing a proof of correctness of Σ. A proof then shows that the specification Σ is provable (with partial or total correctness). So, we must have encoded these provabilities by some different symbols, say, $\vdash_p$ or $\vdash_t$ accordingly.

Then, we must show adequacy, such as $\vdash_p$ iff $\models$ and $\vdash_t$ iff $\Vdash$. This has not been attempted here. Try it!

You are presented with an informal description D of a problem in an application domain. Your aim is to develop a program to solve the problem, and then verify that the program completes the job correctly. As a first step, you represent D into a formula X_D in some logic. We have chosen here the first order logic FL. For some problem domains, FL may not be that appropriate and you may have to use other logics for problem representation. You will learn some more logics later.

The next step is to write a program P which would realize the formula X_D, i.e., it should meet the specifications as declared by X_D. This is the phase we have not discussed at all. We have only given some hints as to how to program in the core language CL. "How to program" is an art, and it must be mastered thoroughly. It would be nice if certain principles are followed; see the summary to this chapter for some references.

Moreover, programs in CL may not be acceptable to your customers. So, you must be able to carry out similar "principle following" activity in any language, which might be offered in your company environment, or which might be required by your customer.

The last step is to *prove* that the program P meets the requirements; it satisfies the specification X_D. Ideally, total correctness of the specification must be shown. This last issue has only been dealt with in this chapter, and that too, only partly. You must see how the art of proving programs correct helps you to specify and develop programs.

Exercises for § 9.9

1. If $Q \models R$, then is it true that $wp\,(S,R) \models wp\,(S,Q)$?
2. If $wp\,(S,Q) \equiv wp\,(S,R)$, then is it true that $Q \equiv R$?
3. Show: $wp\,(S1\,;\,S2\,;\,S3,Q) \equiv wp\,(S1\,;\,S2, wp\,(S3,Q)) \equiv wp\,(S1, wp\,(S2\,;\,S3,Q))$.
4. Give a direct argument to show (9.6), instead of taking the intermediary step.
5. Following the lines of proof in Theorem 9.2.(5)-(7), try proofs for their converse statements. See where the proofs break down.
6. Using wp prove the total correctness of specifications in Exercise 3 of § 9.8.
7. Using wp, determine if the following specifications are totally correct:
   (a) $\langle m > 0 \rangle\, n := m+1\, \langle n > 1 \rangle$
   (b) $\langle \top \rangle\, n := m;\, n := 2 \times m + n\, \langle n = 3 \times m \rangle$
   (c) $\langle \top \rangle$ `if` $n < m$ `then` $\{k := n\}$ `else` $\{k := m\}\, \langle k = \min\,(m,n) \rangle$
   (d) $\langle m \geq 0 \rangle\, x := m;\, n := 0;$ `while` $x \neq 0 \{n := n+1;\, x := x-1\}\, \langle m := n \rangle$
   (e) $\langle \top \rangle\, x := m;\, n := 0;$ `while` $x \neq 0 \{n := n+1;\, x := x-1\}\, \langle m := n \rangle$
   (f) $\langle n \geq 0 \rangle\, x := 0;\, k := 0;$ `while` $x \neq n \{k := m+k;\, x := x+1\}$
   $\langle k := m \times n \rangle$
8. Show that $wp\,($ `while` $B\,\{S\}, \top) \equiv wp\,($ `while` $B\,\{S\}, \neg B)$.
   [Hint: W terminates in a state satisfying $\neg B$.]
9. Prove that P_k in Example 9.18 satisfies (9.9).

9.10 SUMMARY AND PROBLEMS

Computer programming as is taught today concerns only the 'what' part of the bigger activity of program development. It is essential to address the 'why' part, namely, why the program does the intended job correctly. In this chapter we have tried to use logic for developing a program giving hints to all the three aspects of what, how and why of a program development. We have not dealt with the 'how' part in detail, which concerns the art of programming. It also requires the knowledge of the concerned problem domain.

For an easy presentation, we have defined the core language CL. It has all the basic features of a programming language such as assignment statement, sequential execution, conditional statement, and the while statement. A specification of a program explicitly mentions 'what is required of a program' in terms of a precondition and a postcondition. The program itself is written in between them and it codes 'how the job is done'.

In order to show that the program, indeed, does the required job, the specification is to be proved correct. Assuming that the program terminates, when it does its intended job correctly, we say that its given specification is partially correct. You have learnt how to prove partial correctness of a program by developing the Hoare logic for CL. In addition, if the termination condition is also proved, we say that the specification is totally correct. You have also learnt how to extend the Hoare logic to prove total correctness.

The proof summary so developed combines all the three aspects of a program, where you do not need extra documentation. Finally, you have learnt how to use the weakest precondition of a program with respect to a given postcondition in proving the total correctness of programs.

This chapter is only a short note on program verification focusing rather on a useful application of logic in computer science. The presentation is largely influenced by Backhouse (1986), Hoare (1969), Dijkstra (1976, 1982), Gries (1981), and Gries (1982). The motivating example of the string matching problem is taken from Backhouse (1986). For more details on non-deterministic executions, see Dijkstra (1976).

The ideas developed here can be used for program constructions also; the details can be found in Backhouse (1986) and Gries (1981). These texts include a plethora of educative and entertaining examples and exercises.

Other recommended texts are Apt & Olderog (1991), Francez (1992), Hehner (1984), Jones (1980), and Reynolds (1981), where you would find a relatively complete exposition of program verification including extended features such as writing to arrays, array cell aliasing, procedure calls, and parallelism. For a systematic extension of the core language to include other advanced features and then their verification, consult Schmidt (1994) and Tennent (1991).

For verification of functional programming languages, you may start with Turner (1991). For the freely available functional programming language ML, Paulson (1991) is a good text. You can also explore the web resources for newer presentations of the subject. The journal *Science of Computer Programming* is a good source for interesting new problems and their algorithmic solutions.

Problems for Chapter 9

1. Give Hoare proofs and also *wp*-proofs of correctness for the following specifications, prefixing to them one of $\models$ or $\Vdash$ as appropriate:

   (a) $\langle m = n^k \rangle k := k+1; m := m \times n \langle m = n^k \rangle$

   (b) $\langle n = m^2 \wedge s = m \times (m+1) \times (2 \times m+1)/6 \rangle$
   $m := m+1; n = n+2 \times m - 1; s := n+s$
   $\langle n = m^2 \wedge s = m \times (m+1) \times (2 \times m+1)/6 \rangle$

   (c) $\langle j = m^n \wedge s = (m^{n+1} - 1)/(m-1) \rangle$
   $j := j \times m; s := s+j; n := n+1$
   $\langle j = m^n \wedge s = (m^{n+1} - 1)/(m-1) \rangle$

   (d) $\langle s = n^3 \wedge i = 2 \times n \wedge k = n \times (n+1)+1 \rangle$
   $i := i+2; s := s+n \times i+k; k := k+i; n := n+1$
   $\langle s = n^3 \wedge i = 2 \times n \wedge k = n \times (n+1)+1 \rangle$

   (e) $\langle k^2 = k+1 \wedge k^m = a \times k+b \rangle$
   $m := m+1; t := a+b; b := a; a := t$
   $\langle k^m = a \times k+b \rangle$

   (f) $\langle 0 \le s < n \rangle$
   $q := s/(n-1); p := q+1; t := s+1-q \times (n-1)$
   $\langle 1 \le t \le n \wedge q \ge 0 \wedge p = q+1 \wedge s = p \times (t-1)+q \times (n-t) \rangle$

   (g) Let $swap(x,y)$ be a procedure which interchanges the values of x and y. Then $wp(swap(x,y),R) \equiv R[x/y,y/x]$. Recall: the substitution $[x/y,y/x]$ is not equal to $[x/y][y/x]$. Develop a Hoare proof for
   $\langle ((y \ge z) \to (y \ge x)) \wedge ((y < z) \to (z \ge x)) \rangle$
   `if` $y \ge z$ `then` $\{swap(x,y)\}$ `else` $\{swap(x,z)\}$
   $\langle (x \ge y) \wedge (x \ge z) \rangle$

   (h) $\langle \top \rangle$
   `if` $i < j$ `then` $\{swap(i,j)\}$ `else` $\{i := i\}$;
   `if` $j < k$ `then` $\{swap(j,k)\}$ `else` $\{j := j\}$;
   `if` $i < j$ `then` $\{swap(i,j)\}$ `else` $\{i := i\}$
   $\langle i \ge j \ge k \rangle$

   (i) $\langle p = m \times n \rangle$
   `if` $odd(m)$ `then` $\{x := 1\}$ `else` $\{x := 0\}$;
   `if` $odd(n)$ `then` $\{y := 1\}$ `else` $\{y := 0\}$
   $\langle (odd(p) \to (x = y = 1)) \wedge (\neg odd(p) \to (x = 0 \vee y = 0)) \rangle$

   (j) $\langle (odd(p) \to (x = y = 1)) \wedge (\neg odd(p) \to (x = 0 \vee y = 0)) \rangle$
   `if` $odd(p)$ `then` $\{z := 1\}$ `else` $\{z := 0\}$
   $\langle z = x \times y \rangle$

   (k) $\langle p = m \times n \rangle$
   `if` $odd(m)$ `then` $\{x := 1\}$ `else` $\{x := 0\}$;
   `if` $odd(n)$ `then` $\{y := 1\}$ `else` $\{y := 0\}$;
   `if` $odd(p)$ `then` $\{z := 1\}$ `else` $\{z := 0\}$
   $\langle z = x \times y \rangle$ [Hint: Use (i)-(j).]

   (l) $\langle \exists k(k \ge 0 \wedge i = n - 2 \times k \wedge s = 0) \vee \exists k(k \ge 0 \wedge i = n - 2 \times k - 1 \wedge s = k) \rangle$
   `while` $i \ne n\{k := -k; s := s+k; i := i+1\}$
   $\langle s = 0 \rangle$

(m) $\langle c = x \times y \rangle$ `while` $\neg odd(x)\{y := 2 \times y; x := x/2\}\ \langle c = x \times y \rangle$

(n) $\langle x \geq 0 \wedge c = x \times y \rangle$
`while` $x \neq 0\{$ `while` $\neg odd(x)\{y := 2 \times y; x := x/2\};$
$c := c - y; x := x - 1\}\ \langle c = x * y \rangle$

2. Construct a proof summary for the following specification for evaluating the power x^m for given numbers x and m:
$\langle 0 \leq m \rangle\, k := m;\, y := 1;$
$\langle$ Invariant: $y \times x^k = x^m$, Variant: $k\rangle$
`while` $k \neq 0\{k := k - 1; y := y \times x\}$
$\langle y = x^m \rangle$

3. Construct a proof summary along with the necessary verification conditions for the following specifications:
$\langle 0 \leq n \rangle$
$k := n;\, y := 1;\, z := x;$
$\langle$ Invariant: $I(y,z,k) \equiv y \times z^k = x^n \wedge 0 \leq k\rangle$
`while` $0 \neq k\{$ `if` $odd(k)$ `then` $\{k := k - 1; y := y \times z\}$ `else` $\{k := k\}$
$\langle even(k) \wedge I(y,z,k)\rangle$
$k := k/2;\, z := z^2\}$
$\langle y = x^n \rangle$

4. Suppose that the binary representation of a natural number m is stored in an array a. Construct a proof summary for the following specification:
$\langle 0 \leq m = \sum_{i=0}^{n-1} a[i] \times 2^i \rangle$
$y := 1;\, z := x;\, j = 0;$
$\langle$ Invariant: $y \times z^k = x^m \wedge k = \sum_{j=i}^{n-1} a[i] \times 2^i$, Variant: $n - j\rangle$
`while` $j \neq n\{$ `if` $a[j] = 1$ `then` $\{y := y \times z\}$ `else` $\{y := y\}$
$j := j + 1;\, z = z \times z\}$
$\langle y = x^m \rangle$

5. Construct a proof summary for the following specification written for computing the remainder of dividing p by q in binary arithmetic:
$\langle 0 \leq p \wedge 0 < q \rangle$
$r := p;\, m := q;$
$\langle$ Invariant: $\exists i(i \geq 0 \wedge m = 2^i \times q)$, Variant: $r - m\rangle$
`while` $r \geq m\{m := 2 \times m\}$
$\langle$ Invariant: $0 \leq r < m \wedge \exists d(p := q \times d + r) \wedge \exists i(i \geq 0 \wedge m = 2^i \times q)$, Variant: $m\rangle$
`while` $m \neq q\{m := m/2;$ `if` $r \leq m$ `then` $\{r := r - m\}$ `else` $\{r := r\}\}$
$\langle 0 \leq r < q \wedge \exists d(p = q \times d + r)\rangle$

6. Let a be an array and you are to search for an occurrence of an item, say, x in the array. You define a predicate *is* by $is(l,p) \equiv \exists i(l \leq i < p \wedge a[i] = x)$. Then, you write the following algorithm to do the (linear) search:
$\langle 0 \leq n \rangle\, a[n] := x;\, k := 0;$
$\langle$ Invariant: $0 \leq k \leq n \wedge (is(0,n) \leftrightarrow is(k,n)) \wedge a[n] = x$, Variant: $n - k\rangle$
`while` $a[k] \neq x\{k := k + 1\}$
$\langle a[k] = x \wedge 0 \leq k \leq n \wedge (is(0,n) \leftrightarrow k < n)\rangle$
Explain what exactly the algorithm does and then develop a proof summary.

7. Let $a[i]$ denote the ith element of an integer array a. Construct proof summaries for the following programs that sum up the array elements.
   (a) $\langle 0 \leq n \rangle\, s := 0;\, m := 0;$
   $\langle$Invariant: $s := \sum_{i=0}^{m-1} a[i]$, Variant: $n - m\rangle$
   `while` $m \neq n\{s := s + a[m];\, m := m + 1\}$
   $\langle s = \sum_{i=0}^{n-1} a[i]\rangle$
   (b) $\langle 0 \leq n \rangle\, s := 0;\, m := n;$
   $\langle$Invariant: $s = \sum_{i=m}^{n-1} a[i]$, Variant: $m\rangle$
   `while` $m \neq 0\{m := m - 1;\, s := s + a[m]\}$
   $\langle s = \sum_{i=0}^{n-1} a[i]\rangle$
8. Construct a proof summary for the following algorithm that evaluates a polynomial with integer coefficients which are stored in an array a:
   $\langle 0 \leq n \rangle\, s := 0;\, k := n;$
   $\langle$Invariant: $s \times x^k = \sum_{i=k}^{n-1} a[i] \times x^i$, Variant: $k\rangle$
   `while` $k \neq 0\{k := k - 1;\, s + s \times x + a[k]\}$
   $\langle s = \sum_{i=0}^{n-1} a[i] * x^i\rangle$
9. *The minimal sum section*: Let $a[1], \ldots, a[n]$ be the elements of an integer array a. A section of a is a continuous piece $a[i], a[i+1], \ldots, a[j]$ for $1 \leq i \leq j \leq n$. A minimal sum section is a section $a[i], \ldots, a[j]$ such that the sum $S_{ij} = a[i] + a[i+1] + \cdots + a[j]$ is minimal over all sections. Note that the elements in the array a are not necessarily ordered. To write a program which computes the minimal sum section of a given array, we store two values: the minimal sum seen so far (s) and the minimal sum seen so far of *all* the sections which end at the current element of the array (t). We also assume that we know how to compute $\min(x, y)$. Prove that
   $\models \langle \top \rangle\, k := 2;\, t := a[1];\, s := a[1];$
   `while` $k \neq n + 1\{t := \min(t + a[k], a[k]);\, s := \min(s, t);\, k := k + 1\}$
   $\langle \forall i \forall j (i \leq j \leq n \rightarrow s \leq S_{ij})\rangle$
   [Hint: Use the invariant: $\forall i \forall j (i \leq j < k \rightarrow s \leq S_{ij}) \wedge \forall i (i < k \rightarrow t \leq S_{i(k-1)})$. See Huth & Ryan (2000).]
10. Let S be the statement `if` B `then` $\{S1\}$ `else` $\{S2\}$. Assume that
    $P \wedge B \wedge wp(S1, \top) \models wp(S1, Q)$ and $P \wedge \neg B \wedge wp(S2, \top) \models wp(S2, Q)$.
    Show that $P \wedge wp(S, \top) \models wp(S, Q)$.
11. Prove the *Fundamental Invariance Theorem*:

    Let I be an invariant of the while loop `while` $B\{S\}$. Then
    $I \wedge wp($ `while` $B\{S\}, \top) \models wp($ `while` $B\{S\}, I \wedge \neg B)$.

    Relate this result to the Hoare logic rule RW. This will tell you why the result is fundamental. [Hint: With $P_0(Q) \equiv Q \wedge \neg B$, $P_k(Q) \equiv B \wedge wp(S, P_{k-1}(Q))$, show that $I \wedge P_k(\top) \equiv P_k(I \wedge \neg B)$.]
12. In many languages a for-loop is used instead of a while loop. For example, to sum the elements of an array a, whose elements are denoted by $a[i]$, and having 100 elements, you may write the following program:

    $s := 0;$ `for`$(i = 0, i := i + 1, i \leq 100)\{s := s + a[i]\}$

It first initializes s to 0, then starts the for-loop. In executing the for-loop, it initializes i to 0, then executes its body $s := s + a[i]$, and then increments i to $i+1$. It continues doing this repeatedly till the guard $i \le 100$ holds, and stops doing it when i becomes greater than 100. How do you write a program in CL to implement the for-loop? Try for the more general for-loop: $\texttt{for}(S1, S2, S3)\{S4\}$.

13. A repeat until loop looks like: $\texttt{repeat}\{S1\}\texttt{until}\{S2\}$. Execution of such a loop means:

    (a) $S1$ is executed in the current state,

    (b) $S2$ is evaluated in the resulting state,

    (c) if $S2$ is false, the program resumes with (a) and continues, otherwise the program terminates.

    Define this loop in CL. Can you define this loop through for-loop?

Chapter 10

First Order Theories

10.1 STRUCTURES AND AXIOMS

An FL-consequence has a set of formulas as premises and another formula as its conclusion. Sometimes it becomes important to determine what could be possible conclusions of a set of premises. In such a case, the set of premises defines a theory, and models of the set of premises receive names. For instance, the dyadic group in group theory is a model of some FL-sentences.

When the set of premises is finite, the number of predicates and function symbols that occur in the formulas are also finite in number. We become concerned with the fragment of FL restricted to formulas built upon these symbols. We fix some terminology so that we may be able to talk about these theories with ease.

The individual variables, connectives, quantifiers, the propositional constants $\top$ and $\bot$, and the punctuation marks are called the **logical symbols**. The constants, function symbols, propositional variables, and predicates are called the **non-logical symbols**. A **first order language** has an alphabet that includes all logical symbols and some of the non-logical symbols. The set of non-logical symbols used in the alphabet is called the **signature** of the language. By following the grammar of FL, the formulas of the language are generated using the logical symbols and symbols from its signature.

For example, consider the set $S = \{f, P\}$ as a signature of a first order language L, where f is a unary function symbol, and P is a binary predicate. The non-logical symbols of L are f and P; and the alphabet of L is

$$\{f, P, \top, \bot, \neg, \wedge, \vee, \rightarrow, \leftrightarrow, \forall, \exists, x_0, x_1, \ldots\} \cup \{), (, ,\}.$$

Some of the formulas that can be generated using these symbols are

$$\top,\ \bot,\ P(x_0,x_1),\ P(f(x_5),x_3),\ \forall x_2 P(f(f(x_1)),x_2),\ P(x_1,x_2) \leftrightarrow P(x_3,x_3).$$

The first order language L cannot use symbols other than those in its alphabet. Since the logical symbols are used by each first order language, we often say that L depends upon its signature.

In fact, all mathematical theories are restricted to the set of sentences rather than general formulas. Sentences of a first order language are given meaning through interpretations. To bring in flexibility, we consider a **structure** as a nonempty set along with some relations and functions defined over the set. The nonempty set is called the **domain** of the structure. For instance,

$$M_1 = (D_1, R_1), \text{ where } D_1 = \{0,1,2\} \text{ and } R_1 = \{(0,0),(1,1),(2,2)\} \tag{10.1}$$

is a structure with domain as $\{0,1,2\}$. The only relation that comes with the structure is the binary relation of equality, written here as R_1. Similarly,

$$(\mathbb{N},+,<)$$

is a structure with the domain as the set $\mathbb{N}$ of all natural number, the binary function of addition, $+ : \mathbb{N}\times\mathbb{N} \to \mathbb{N}$, and the binary relation of *less than*, $<$.

An **interpretation** interprets sentences of a language in a structure, via variable assignment functions and states, by associating predicates to relations and function symbols to functions preserving arity. To simplify the matter we consider interpreting function symbols as functions rather than the more general partial functions. It may happen that a language has a function symbol of arity k but a given structure does not come with a function of arity k. In such a situation, the language cannot be interpreted; the structure is *inappropriate* to the language. To circumvent this, we assume that in the context of interpreting a language, we consider only appropriate structures without explicitly mentioning it. Sometimes we write a structure just like an interpretation (D,ϕ), where ϕ is a list of relations and functions over D.

A sentence of the language is interpreted as a sentence in the structure. It is assumed that a structure comes with a notion of truth and falsity. If the interpreted sentence is true in the structure, the interpretation is called a **model** of the sentence. We also say that the structure is a model of the sentence. The word *model* is used for the interpretation as well as for the structure.

Suppose a sentence A in a first order language L is interpreted as the sentence A_M in a structure M. If A_M is a true sentence in the structure M, we say that A **is true in** M, and write it as $M \vDash A$. In such a case, we also say that M is a model of A, M satisfies A, and that M verifies A. For instance, let $A = \forall x P(x,x)$. The structure M_1 in (10.1) is a model of A. In general, if D is any nonempty set, and R is any binary relation such that

$$\{(d,d) : d \in D\} \subseteq R \subseteq D \times D,$$

then the structure (D,R) is a model of A. As earlier, if Σ is a set of sentences, then we say that M is a model of Σ, and write $M \vDash \Sigma$, iff $M \vDash X$ for each $X \in \Sigma$.

Suppose that an interpretation of all non-logical symbols of L in the structure M has already been specified. The set of all sentences A in the first order language L that are true in the structure M is called the **theory of** M. That is,

$$Th(M,L) = \{A : A \text{ is a sentence of } L \text{ with } M \vDash A\}.$$

If no confusion is expected, we write $Th(M,L)$ as $Th(M)$.

For instance, suppose L is a first order language with the sole non-logical symbol as a binary predicate P, and that it is interpreted in the structure M_1 of (10.1) as the relation R_1. Then $M_1 \vDash \forall x P(x,x)$. If $M_1 \vDash B$ for a formula B using possibly the predicate P, then clearly $A \vDash B$. Therefore,

$$Th(M_1) = \{B : \forall x P(x,x) \vDash B\}.$$

In $\forall x P(x,x) \vDash B$, the symbol $\vDash$ stands for the entailment (consequence) relation, as used earlier. That is, for a set of formulas Γ and a formula X, $\Gamma \vDash X$ means that all models of Γ are also models of X.

Let Σ be a set of sentences from L. Let S be a set of structures. We say that Σ is a set of **Axioms** for the set of structures S iff

$$\text{for each structure } M,\ M \in S \text{ iff } M \vDash \Sigma.$$

This is how a set of structures is characterized by a set of sentences in L. If A is any sentence in L, then all structures in S satisfy A iff $\Sigma \vDash A$. Therefore, the set of all sentences in L that follow as conclusions from Σ constitutes the theory of the set of all structures in S.

In fact, the set S of structures is not chosen arbitrarily, but is found out looking at a suitable set of axioms Σ. In parallel to the semantic theories coming up from structures, axiomatic theories can be built. Given a first order language a **first order theory** is built over it by identifying certain sentences of the language as axioms or axiom schemes. In fact, the theory consists of the body of conclusions that follow from the axiom schemes by using the entailment relation. Since the entailment relation is fixed, we often identify the theory with its axiom schemes. Thus a first order theory is a pair (L,Σ), where L is a first order language, and Σ is a set of sentences from L, called **axioms** or **axiom schemes** of the theory.

Convention 10.1. We will write formulas and sentences in abbreviated form using the conventions laid out in Chapter 5. Unless otherwise stated, a language will mean a first order language; and a theory will mean a first order theory.

EXAMPLE 10.1. Let L be a language with one non-logical symbol as a binary predicate P. The models of the sentence

$$\forall x \neg Pxx$$

are the directed graphs without self-loops. The models of

$$\{\forall x \neg Pxx,\ \forall x \forall y (Pxy \leftrightarrow Pyx)\}$$

are the (undirected) graphs without self-loops.

EXAMPLE 10.2. Let L_1 be the language with no non-logical symbol. Let A be the sentence

$$\exists x \exists y((\forall z(z \approx x) \vee (z \approx y)) \wedge \neg(x \approx y)).$$

If a structure M with domain D is a model of A, then D has exactly two elements. Thus the set S of all structures having two elements in the domains has axiom A. And the theory of all two-elements sets is characterized by the axiom A. That is, this theory is the set $\{X : X \text{ is a sentence with } A \vDash X\}$.

EXAMPLE 10.3. Let L_1 be the language with empty signature (of Example 10.2). For each natural number $n \geq 2$, let A_n be the sentence

$$\exists x_1 \exists x_2 \cdots \exists x_n (\wedge_{1 \leq i < j \leq n} \neg (x_i \approx x_j)).$$

Let $\Sigma = \{A_n : n \geq 2\}$. If M with domain D is a model of A_n, then D must have at least n elements. Thus, any model of Σ must have an infinite number of elements. Conversely, if M is a structure with an infinite set as its domain, then $M \vDash A_n$ for each $n \geq 2$. That is, $M \vDash \Sigma$. Therefore, the theory of infinite sets has the set of axioms Σ.

EXAMPLE 10.4. Let L_2 be the language with non-logical symbols as a constant 0, and a binary function symbol $+$. Using infix notation we write $(x+y)$ instead of $+(x,y)$. Let Σ be the set of the following sentences from L_2:

1. $\forall x \forall y \forall z (((x+y)+z) \approx (x+(y+z)))$
2. $\forall x (((x+0) \approx x) \wedge ((0+x) \approx x))$
3. $\forall x \exists y (((x+y) \approx 0) \wedge ((y+x) \approx 0))$

Any structure M that satisfies Σ is called a *group*. The function $+$ is called the *group operation*. The theory of groups is the set of all structures that satisfy the above three sentences. That is, the theory of groups has the axioms as (1)-(3).

The theory of *Abelian groups* bases on the language L_2 and has the axioms as (1)-(4) where the fourth axiom is the commutativity property given by:

4. $\forall x \forall y ((x+y) \approx (y+x))$

Thus we say that a group is Abelian iff the group operation is commutative.

EXAMPLE 10.5. Let L_3 be the extension of L_2 with additional non-logical symbols as a constant 1 different from 0, and a binary function symbol $\cdot$ different from $+$. Again, we write $(x \cdot y)$ instead of $\cdot(x,y)$. Along with the axioms (1)-(4), consider the following:

5. $\forall x \forall y \forall z (((x \cdot y) \cdot z) \approx (x \cdot (y \cdot z)))$
6. $\forall x (((x \cdot 1) \approx x) \wedge ((1 \cdot x) \approx x))$
7. $\forall x \forall y \forall z ((x \cdot (y+z)) \approx ((x \cdot y) + (x \cdot z)))$
8. $\forall x \forall y \forall z (((x+y) \cdot z) \approx ((x \cdot z) + (y \cdot z)))$

Any structure that satisfies the axioms (1)-(8) is called a *ring with unity*. Thus the theory of rings with unity has the axioms (1)-(8). The theory of *commutative rings with unity* has the following additional axiom:

9. $\forall x \forall y ((x \cdot y) \approx (y \cdot x))$

A field is a commutative ring with unity where each nonzero element has also a multiplicative inverse. That is, the *theory of fields* is a theory over the language L_3 having the axioms (1)-(10), where the tenth axiom is

10. $\forall x (\neg (x \approx 0) \rightarrow \exists y ((x \cdot y) \approx 1))$

In the theory of fields, the field operations $+$ and $\cdot$ are called addition and multiplication, respectively.

EXAMPLE 10.6. Let L_4 be an extension of the language L_3 with the additional binary predicate $<$. Once again, we use the infix notation. That is, $<(x,y)$ is written as $x < y$. Over L_4 we build a theory with its axioms as (1)-(15), where the additional axioms are as follows:

11. $\forall x \neg(x < x)$
12. $\forall x \forall y((x < y) \vee (x \approx y) \vee (y < x))$
13. $\forall x \forall y \forall z((x < y) \wedge (y < z) \to (x < z))$
14. $\forall x \forall y((x < y) \to \forall z((x+z) < (y+z)))$
15. $\forall x \forall y((0 < x) \wedge (0 < y) \to (0 < (x \cdot y)))$

The resulting theory is called the theory of *ordered fields*.

Observe that any sentence that is true in every group, that is, which is satisfied by each such structure, called a group now, is a consequence of the axioms of group theory. Due to the adequacy of FC, such a sentence has a proof in FC which possibly uses the axioms (1)-(3) as additional premises. Similar comments go for all first order theories.

As a last example, we will consider the completeness property of real numbers. It says that every nonempty subset of the set of real numbers which is bounded above has a least upper bound. If $A \neq \varnothing$ is a subset of the set of real numbers, we say that it is bounded above iff there exists a real number x such that each element of A is less than or equal to x. Motivated by this, we abbreviate the following formula as $x \leq y$:

$$(x < y) \vee (x \approx y).$$

Then the (order) completeness axiom scheme is formulated as follows.

16. *Axiom Scheme of Completeness*: For any formula $Y[\cdot]$ having exactly one free variable, the following is an axiom:

$$\exists x Y(x) \wedge \exists y \forall z(Y(z) \to (z \leq y)) \to$$
$$\exists u(\forall v(Y(v) \to (v \leq u)) \wedge \forall w(\forall x(Y(x) \to (x \leq w)) \to (u \leq w))).$$

Notice that if $Y(\cdot)$ is a formula with a single free variable, then its interpretation is a subset of the domain. Any model of axioms (1)-(16) is a complete ordered field. Of course, the underlying first order language is L_4.

Exercises for § 10.1

1. Translate the following sentences to the language of real numbers using the symbolism developed in the text for complete ordered fields.

   (a) Every non-negative real number has a unique non-negative square root.
   (b) If a function f is uniformly continuous on an interval (a,b), then it is continuous on that interval.
   (c) If a function f is continuous on a closed and bounded interval $[a,b]$, then it is uniformly continuous on that interval.
   (d) If a function f on an interval (a,b) is differentiable at any point x, then it is continuous at x.

2. Let L be a language with a finite signature. Let D be a finite nonempty set. Show that there are only finitely many structures with domain as D.
3. Let S be a sentence such that any model of $\neg S$ is infinite. Does it follow that S is true in each finite structure?
4. Let L be a language with one non-logical symbol as a binary predicate P. Translate the following:
   (a) P is an equivalence relation with exactly two equivalence classes.
   (b) P is an equivalence relation with at least one equivalence class that contains more than one element.
5. Show that the following sentences are true in each finite structure.
   (a) $\exists x \exists y \exists z((Pxy \wedge Pyz \to Pxz) \to (Pxf(x) \to Pxx))$
   (b) $\exists x \forall y \exists z(Pxy \wedge (Pzx \to Pzy) \to Pxx)$

10.2 SET THEORY

This section is devoted to a single example of an axiomatic theory, called the set theory. As you see our very definition of semantics uses sets. Thus set theory has foundational importance. We wish to present the theory **ZFC**, the Zermelo-Fraenkel set theory. It has ten axioms given in detail in the following. We also say in words what the axioms mean.

ZFC has only one non-logical symbol, a binary predicate, called the *membership predicate*. We write this symbol as $\in$, read it as *belongs to*, and use it via infix notation: $(x \in y)$. The individual variables of the language vary over sets. The word 'set' is left undefined for informal use. In fact, the axiom schemes taken together define the notion of a set.

1. *Axiom of Extensionality* : $\forall x \forall y(\forall z((z \in x) \leftrightarrow (z \in y)) \to (x \approx y))$

It says that two sets x and y are equal iff they have exactly the same elements. Moreover, in the universe of ZFC, sets have elements as sets only; for, all variables range over sets. This is not a restriction, since every entity may be regarded as a set. Only inconvenience is that there is no stopping criterion as to when the elements of elements of elements of $\cdots$ of a set comes to an end. But that is not a problem since one can build a model of the theory by starting form the empty set, which exists due to some other axiom(s). We will discuss that in due course.

For the next axiom, we use the following notation. If a formula X has free variables from among the distinct symbols $z, x_1, \ldots, x_n$, we write the formula as $X(z, x_1, \ldots, x_n)$.

2. *Axiom Scheme of Separation* : For each formula $X(z, x_1, \ldots, x_n)$,

$$\forall x_1 \cdots \forall x_n \forall x(\exists y \forall z((z \in y) \leftrightarrow (z \in x) \wedge X(z, x_1, \ldots, x_n)))$$

This axiom scheme is also called the *axiom scheme of comprehension*, and the *axiom scheme of subsets*. It says that given a set x, any subset y of it can be defined by collecting all elements of x that satisfy certain property. The axiom of extensionality implies that such a subset y of x is unique. We, generally, write the subset y as

$$y = \{z \in x : X(z, x_1, \ldots, x_n)\}.$$

This allows defining a subset of a given set by specifying a property. In a way it puts restrictions on building sets. For instance, there is no way to create the set of all sets, which is known to lead to Russell's paradox.

With $x = x_1$, $n = 1$, and $X(z, x_1, \ldots, x_n) = \neg(z \in x)$, we have

$$\forall x \exists y \forall z((z \in y) \leftrightarrow (z \in x) \wedge \neg(z \in x)).$$

It says that every set x has a subset y which does not contain anything. Such a subset y can be shown to be unique, and we denote this set by $\varnothing$, the empty set. We may also define $\varnothing$ by

$$\forall x((x \approx \varnothing) \leftrightarrow \forall y \neg(y \in x)).$$

Notice that the symbol $\varnothing$ is a defined constant in the language of set theory.

Further, the axiom of subsets allows to define a binary predicate that represents the relation of 'subset'. We say that x is a subset of y, written $x \subseteq y$, iff for each z, if $z \in x$, then $z \in y$. Formally,

$$\forall x \forall y((x \subseteq y) \leftrightarrow \forall z(z \in x \to z \in y)).$$

The next axiom allows to take union of two sets.

3. *Axiom of Union*: $\forall x \exists y \forall z \forall u((u \in x) \wedge (z \in u) \to (z \in y))$

It says that given a set x (of sets) there exists a set y which contains all elements of all sets in x. That is, the union of all sets in x is also a set. As earlier, we may define a binary function symbol in the language of set theory that represents union of two sets. For two sets x and y their union $x \cup y$ is defined as follows:

$$\forall x \forall y \forall z((z \approx x \cup y) \leftrightarrow \forall u((u \in z) \leftrightarrow (u \in x) \vee (u \in y))).$$

Analogously, the binary function symbol of intersection is defined as follows:

$$\forall x \forall y \forall z((z \approx x \cap y) \leftrightarrow \forall u((u \in z) \leftrightarrow (u \in x) \wedge (u \in y))).$$

4. *Axiom of Pairing*: $\forall x \forall y \exists z((x \in z) \wedge (y \in z))$

This axiom allows to build sets of the form $\{a\}$, $\{a, b\}$, $\{a, b, c\}$, etc provided $a, b, c, \ldots$ are known to be sets. It helps in building sets from given elements, so to say. Using this we define a binary function symbol for pairing, and denote it by $\{\,,\}$. That is,

$$\forall x \forall y \forall z((z \approx \{x, y\}) \leftrightarrow \forall u((u \in z) \leftrightarrow ((u \approx x) \vee (u \approx y)))).$$

Thus given two sets, we may build the set of those two sets and write it as $\{x, y\}$. The set $\{x, x\}$ is abbreviated to $\{x\}$.

5. *Axiom of Power Set*: $\forall x \exists y \forall z((z \in y) \leftrightarrow \forall u((u \in z) \to (u \in x)))$

The formula $\forall u((u \in z) \to (u \in x))$ says that z is a subset of x. Therefore, the axiom asserts that corresponding to each set x there exists a set which contains exactly all the subsets of x. That is, the power set of a set exists.

Formally, we may introduce a unary function symbol $\mathbb{P}$ for taking the power set of a set. It is defined as follows:

$$\forall x \forall y((y \approx \mathbb{P}x) \leftrightarrow \forall z((z \in y) \leftrightarrow \forall u((u \in z) \to (u \in x)))).$$

Now that the $\varnothing$ can be constructed, we may also build $\{\varnothing\}$. Going a bit further, we can build the sets

$$\varnothing,\ \{\varnothing\},\ \{\varnothing,\{\varnothing\}\},\ \{\varnothing,\{\varnothing\},\{\varnothing,\{\varnothing\}\}\},\ \ldots$$

However, we need an axiom to construct the set of all these sets. We plan to use the defined constant $\varnothing$ and the binary function symbol $\cup$.

6. *Axiom of Infinity*: $\exists x((\varnothing \in x) \wedge \forall y((y \in x) \to (y \cup \{y\} \in x)))$

Notice that a finite set can be constructed using axiom of pairing and union, whereas building infinite sets requires the axiom of infinity.

7. *Axiom of Foundation*: $\forall x(\exists y(y \in x) \to \exists z((z \in x) \wedge \forall u((u \in z) \to \neg(u \in x))))$

It says that every nonempty set has an element which is not a subset of the set. It prevents constructing a set in the following forms:

$$\cdots\{\{\cdots\{\ \}\cdots\}\}\cdots \quad \text{OR} \quad \{\cdots\{\cdots\{\cdots \quad \cdots\}\cdots\}\cdots\}$$

It implies that a set cannot be a member of itself. Its name comes from the informal statement 'the membership predicate is well-founded'.

Let $Y[x]$ denote a formula having at least one free variable, namely, x. We write $\exists! xY[x]$ as an abbreviation for the formula

$$\exists xY[x] \wedge \forall u \forall z(Y[u] \wedge Y[z] \to (u \approx z))$$

We may read $\exists! xY$ as "there exists a unique x such that $Y[x]$". In our next axiom scheme, we use this defined *quantifier* for shortening the expression. We also use the notation $X(x_1,,\ldots,x_n,x,y,z,u)$ for a formula having free variables from among the variables $x_1,\ldots,x_n,x,y,z,u$, which are assumed to be distinct.

8. *Axiom of Replacement*: For each formula $Z(x_1,\ldots,x_n,x,y)$ and distinct variables u,v not occurring free in Z,

$$\forall x_1 \cdots \forall x_n(\forall x \exists! yZ \to \forall u \exists v \forall y((y \in v) \leftrightarrow \exists x((x \in u) \wedge Z)))$$

It asserts that if for the parameters $x_1,\ldots,x_n$, the formula $Z(x_1,\ldots,x_n,x,y)$ defines the function that maps x to y, then the range of such a function is a set.

9. *Axiom of Choice*: $\forall x((\neg(\varnothing \in x) \wedge \forall u \forall v((u \in x) \wedge (v \in x) \wedge \neg(u \approx v)) \to$
$((u \cap v) \approx \varnothing)) \to \exists y \forall w((w \in x) \to \exists! z(z \in (w \cap y))))$

It asserts that given a set x of pairwise disjoint nonempty sets there exists a set that contains exactly one element from each set in x. It is known to be equivalent to (in first order logic) many interesting statements. The most useful ones are the following:

(a) The Cartesian product of a nonempty collection of nonempty sets is nonempty.

(b) *Zorn's Lemma*: If a partially ordered (nonempty) set P has the property that every totally ordered (nonempty) subset of P has an upper bound in P, then P contains at least one maximal element.

(c) *Well Ordering Principle*: Every set can be well-ordered.

It is known that all mathematical objects can be constructed in ZFC. However, ZFC does not give rise to a unique set theory. That is, ZFC does not have a unique model. In fact, the results of K. Gödel and P. Cohen show that ZFC is consistent with Cantor's *continuum hypothesis* and also with its negation.

Exercises for § 10.2

1. Define the quantifier $\exists!x$ which is read as 'there exists exactly one x such that' in a different way than the one defined in the text.
2. Prove that the axiom of choice is equivalent to both Zorn's lemma and Well ordering principle.
3. Is $\forall x \neg(x \in x)$ a theorem of ZFC?
4. How do you justify defining intersection of sets in ZFC?
5. Given a set S of sets, how do you construct a set that does not intersect with any element of S?

10.3 ARITHMETIC

In this section we briefly present the theory of natural numbers. This theory bases on the set of natural numbers $\mathbb{N}$, with a successor function that maps a number to its next one, the operations of addition, multiplication and exponentiation, and their properties. There can be many structures satisfying these minimal requirements. Among these, the standard structure is the one with $\mathbb{N} = \{0, 1, 2, \ldots\}$, known as the system of natural numbers.

The axiomatic theory of natural number system is called as *arithmetic*. The first order language of arithmetic has a constant 0, a unary function symbol s, three binary function symbols $+$, $\cdot$, $\hat{}$ and a binary predicate $<$. We agree to use infix notation for the function symbols and the predicate. For instance, instead of $+(a, b)$, we write $(a+b)$. Here, $x\hat{}y$ stands for the exponentiation x^y. The theory $\mathbb{A}$, *Peano's Arithmetic*, also called *Arithmetic* for short, has the following axioms.

1. $\forall x(\neg(0 \approx s(x))$
2. $\forall x(\neg(x \approx 0) \to \exists y(x \approx s(y))$
3. $\forall x \forall y((x \approx y) \leftrightarrow (s(x) \approx s(y)))$
4. $\forall x((x+0) \approx x)$

5. $\forall x \forall y((x+s(y)) \approx s(x+y))$
6. $\forall x((x \cdot 0) \approx 0)$
7. $\forall x \forall y((x \cdot s(y)) \approx ((x \cdot y)+x))$
8. $\forall x \neg(x < 0)$
9. $\forall x \forall y((x < s(y)) \leftrightarrow (x < y) \vee (x \approx y))$
10. $\forall x \forall y((x < y) \vee (x \approx y) \vee (y < x))$
11. $\forall x((x \hat{} 0) \approx s(0))$
12. $\forall x \forall y((x \hat{} s(y)) \approx ((x \hat{} y) \cdot x))$
13. *Induction Scheme* : For each formula $Y(\cdot)$ having exactly one free variable, the sentence $Y(0) \wedge \forall x(Y(x) \rightarrow Y(s(x))) \rightarrow \forall x Y(x)$ is an axiom.

We have not tried to be economic in formulating the theory $\mathbb{A}$. In fact, it is enough just to have axioms (1)-(3) and the axiom scheme (13). It is known that the operations $+$, $\cdot$, $\hat{}$ and the predicate $<$ can be defined inductively so that they satisfy the other axioms. However, without the induction axiom, these operations and the less than relation cannot be defined. Thus, if need arises, one may create different theories of arithmetic by deleting the induction axiom and choosing some of the axioms out of the first twelve. For ease in use, we will stick to the above formulation.

The standard model of $\mathbb{A}$ will be denoted by $\mathbb{N}$. Its domain is the set of natural numbers $\{0,1,2,\ldots,\}$, successor function is that which maps each n to $n+1$, and $+,\cdot$, and $\hat{}$ are the the usual addition, multiplication, and exponentiation of natural numbers. The terms $0, s(0), s(s(0)), \ldots, s^n(0), \ldots$ in $\mathbb{A}$ are called *numerals*, and they are interpreted in $\mathbb{N}$ as the numbers $0,1,2,\ldots,n,\ldots$, respectively. To keep the notation simple, we will write the numeral $s^n(0)$ as n; so that the numeral n will refer to $s^n(0)$, whereas the number n will refer to the natural number n in $\mathbb{N}$.

We remark that $\mathbb{N}$ is not the only model of $\mathbb{A}$. Another model is the nonstandard model of Example 6.13. As an application of compactness, we had shown that there exists a number bigger than every natural number. If the order properties are extended to such a model, then there will be ordering among those numbers. The number ω comes after all the (standard) natural numbers. Next comes $\omega+1$, the successor of ω, next, $\omega+2$, etc. After the numbers $\omega+n$ are listed, for each $n \in \mathbb{N}$, comes 2ω. Next comes $2\omega+1$, $2\omega+2$, etc. The nonstandard model is completely different from the standard model $\mathbb{N}$ since the former contains infinitely large numbers, whereas the latter does not.

Non-uniqueness of models of a first order theory is not an exception. However, a theory for natural numbers can be constructed which has essentially a single model. This is done by replacing the induction axiom scheme by the following axiom:

Induction Axiom: $\forall P(P(0) \wedge \forall x(P(x) \rightarrow P(s(x))) \rightarrow \forall x P(x)$

Here, it is assumed that P is any unary predicate variable. Observe that this sentence quantifies over unary predicates, also called monadic predicates. Therefore, Induction axiom is not a sentence of first order logic. It is a sentence of *monadic second order logic*.

In first order logic, the quantifiers use variables which could only be assigned to elements in the domain by any state. In second order logic, quantification is allowed on the predicates (or relations) also. The induction axiom does that. It says the following:

> For each property P of natural numbers, if P is true for 0, and that P is true for any n implies that it is true for $n+1$, then P is true for each natural number.

There is a difference in using the induction axiom in second order logic and the first order axiom scheme. For example, consider translating the sentence

> Each nonempty set of natural numbers has a least element.

We cannot translate this sentence to the first order theory of arithmetic where we use the induction axiom scheme. The reason is, we do not have any way of expressing 'the set of $\cdots$'. However, in the second order induction axiom, each such set of natural numbers is a unary predicate, and we can quantify over them. Thus the sentence can be translated to the monadic second order theory of arithmetic.

Of course, we do not claim that no sentence involving expressions of the type 'the set of $\cdots$' cannot be translated to the first order theory of arithmetic. Statements about particular subsets of natural numbers can be translated. For instance, we can translate the sentence

> The set of primes has a least element.

We convert this sentence to

> There exists a smallest prime.

And then this equivalent statement can easily be translated to the first order theory of arithmetic.

Similarly, Graph Theory uses statements concerning all graphs with certain properties, where each graph is a binary relation over a domain. Thus theorems in Graph Theory truly belong to second order logic.

There are different semantics of second order logic, where one considers the predicates to denote any relation on the domain or one may restrict them to only first order definable relations. In the former case, as K. Gödel had shown, there cannot be an adequate proof theory, whereas the latter is equivalent to the first order set theory.

These concerns bring in many questions. Is there a way to construct a model for a first order theory? In first order theories, what can be proved, what can be expressed, what can be defined, and what can be solved by following step-by-step procedures? In the following section, we will consider answering these questions in an elementary manner.

Exercises for § 10.3

Let X, Y, Z be formulas of Peano's arithmetic $\mathbb{A}$, and let u be a variable. Suppose, y is a variable not occurring in X, Y, and the variable z does not occur in Z. Show that the following are theorems in $\mathbb{A}$.

1. $\forall x((\forall y(y < x) \to X[x/y]) \to X) \to \forall x X$
2. $\exists x Y \to (\exists x Y \wedge \forall y((y < x) \to \neg Y[x/y]))$
3. $\forall x(((x < u) \to \exists y Z) \to \exists z(\forall x((x < u) \to \exists y((y < z) \wedge Z))))$

10.4 HERBRAND INTERPRETATION

Once consistency of a theory is established, due to Model existence theorem, we know that there exists a model of the theory. Recall that such a model is constructed by extending the theory to a maximally consistent set. Here, we wish to have a more direct construction. Further, this approach will yield a bonus by connecting a first order theory to a propositional theory.

Due to Theorem 7.2 on Skolem form, satisfiability of a formula X can be tested by searching for closed terms $t_1,\ldots,t_n$ such that the sentence $X_s[x_1/t_1]\cdots[x_n/t_n]$ is true in a domain. Similarly, by duality, validity of X can be tested by confirming the validity of the sentence $X_f[x_1/t_1]\cdots[x_n/t_n]$; see Theorem 7.3. We take up the issue of satisfiability. To make the matter simple, we start with a single formula and later discuss how to tackle a set of formulas.

Let X be a formula in Skolem form; so, all free variables are assumed to be universally quantified. Let D_0 be the set of all constants occurring in X. If $D_0 = \varnothing$, then take $D_1 = \{\alpha\}$, else, take $D_1 = D_0$. Here, α is a new symbol. Define the domain D_X for the formula X recursively:

1. $D_1 \subseteq D_X$.
2. If f is an n-ary function symbol occurring in X, and $t_1,t_2,\ldots,t_n \in D_X$, then $f(t_1,t_2,\ldots,t_n) \in D_X$.
3. D_X is the minimal set satisfying both (1) and (2).

The *minimal* is in the sense of the subset relation. The domain D_X is called the **Herbrand universe** for the formula X, named after the logician J. Herbrand. Given a formula X, you are supposed to generate the set D_X step by step starting from D_0 as the set of all constants occurring in X, as shown below:

$$
\begin{aligned}
D_0 &= \{c : c \text{ is a constant occurring in } X\}.\\
D_1 &= D_0 \text{ if } D_0 \neq \varnothing, \text{ else, } D_1 = \{\alpha\} \text{ for a new symbol } \alpha.\\
&\ \vdots\\
D_{i+1} &= D_i \cup \{f(t_1,\ldots,t_n) : t_1,\ldots,t_n \in D_i \text{ and } f \text{ is an } n\text{-ary function}\\
&\qquad \text{symbol occurring in } X\} \text{ for } i \geq 1.\\
D = D_X &= D_0 \cup D_1 \cup D_2 \cup \cdots = \cup_{i\in\mathbb{N}} D_i.
\end{aligned}
$$

We write D_X as D, whenever the formula X is clear in a context.

EXAMPLE 10.7. Let $X = \neg Pxf(x) \wedge Pya$, where a is a constant. Then

$$D_0 = \{a\}; \quad D_1 = D_0 = \{a\}, \quad D_2 = \{a, f(a)\}, \ \ldots$$

Consequently, $D = D_X = \{a, f(a), f(f(a)), \ldots\}$ is the Herbrand universe of X.

The elements of the Herbrand universe are also called the **ground terms**. Note that ground terms are simply the closed terms obtained from the function symbols occurring in a formula used recursively on the constants, or on the special symbol α if no constant occurs in the formula.

To define the Herbrand interpretation with its domain as the Herbrand universe D, we require a function ϕ which would assign each function symbol occurring in X to functions over D, and each predicate occurring in X to relations over D, preserving arity. This is defined as follows:

(a) If f is an n-ary function symbol occurring in X, then $\phi(f) = f$, the latter f is taken as a function from D^n to D defined by: the functional value of the n-tuple of terms $t_1, t_2, \ldots, t_n$ under f is $f(t_1, t_2 \ldots, t_n)$ for objects $t_1, t_2, \ldots, t_n \in D$.

(b) If P is an m-ary predicate, then $\phi(P) = P$, where the latter P is an m-ary relation defined on D. (It is any m-ary relation; we are not fixing it.)

The **Herbrand interpretation** of X is the pair $(D_X, \phi) = (D, \phi)$. Notice that we do not require a valuation as all our formulas are now sentences. A **Herbrand model** of X is a Herbrand interpretation that satisfies X, i.e., which makes X true, which assigns X to 1.

Any map ϕ associated with a Herbrand interpretation that assigns predicates to relations and function symbols to functions over D, must satisfy the above properties. ϕ also assigns truth values 1 or 0 to the atomic formulas $P(t_1, \ldots, t_n)$. Such maps may only differ from each other in how they assign values of 0 or 1 to the atomic formulas $P(t_1, \ldots, t_n)$. Thus, for any particular Herbrand interpretation (D, ϕ), we need only specify how ϕ assigns the ground atomic formulas to 0 or 1. Such a map ϕ is called a **Herbrand map**.

EXAMPLE 10.8. Let $X = (Qyx \to Px) \wedge (Py \to Rc)$ be a Skolem form formula. The Herbrand universe is the singleton $D = \{c\}$. By substituting the variables x, y with c in X, we obtain the formula

$$Y = (Qcc \to Pc) \wedge (Pc \to Rc).$$

By assigning truth values to the atomic formulas Qcc, Pc, Rc we would like to see whether the Herbrand interpretation is a model of X or not.

The Herbrand map ϕ with $\phi(Qcc) = 0$, $\phi(Pc) = 1 = \phi(Rc)$ evaluates Y to 1. Hence (D, ϕ) is a Herbrand model of X.

On the other hand, ψ with $\psi(Qcc) = 1 = \psi(Pc)$, $\psi(Rc) = 0$ evaluates Y to 0. That is, the Herbrand interpretation (D, ψ) is not a (Herbrand) model of X.

Recall that a propositional interpretation could be specified as a set of literals. In Example 10.8, the Herbrand model (D, ϕ) can also be written as $\{\neg Qcc, Pc, Rc\}$. In this Herbrand model, we declare the atomic formulas Pc, Rc as true and Qcc as false. The Herbrand interpretation (D, ψ) can be written as $\{Qcc, Pc, \neg Rc\}$, which again means that we take, in this interpretation, the atomic formulas Qcc, Pc as true and Rc as false. In such a formalism of writing out the Herbrand interpretations, the atomic formulas Qcc, Pc, Rc are called **ground atomic formulas**, and the literals $Qcc, \neg Qcc, Pc, \neg Pc, Rc, \neg Rc$ are called **ground literals**. The set of ground atomic formulas is called a **Herbrand base**.

A Herbrand interpretation is, essentially, a set of ground literals such that for each Y in the Herbrand base, either Y or $\neg Y$ is an element of this set.

We will be using the ground literals as the domain of our interpretation of a formula. However, there is certain difficulty when the equality predicate is involved.

For instance, consider the formula $\forall x(Pf(x)a \wedge \neg(f(x) \approx x))$. You can, of course, take a and $f(a)$ to be distinct, $f(f(a)) = a$, and $\phi(P) = \{(f(a),a), (a,f(a))\}$. But this fails for the formula $\forall x(Pf(x)a \wedge \neg(f(x) \approx x) \wedge \neg(f(f(x)) \approx x))$.

In general, f is just a function symbol of arity 1; $f(a)$ and a are distinct. Starting from a, it potentially generates the infinite set

$$D = \{a, f(a), f(f(a)), \ldots\}.$$

If a model is required for $f(x) \approx x$ on this domain D, we need to identify $f^n(a)$ with a for any $n \geq 1$.

Since this is a problem of identification, naturally, equivalence relations play a role. If we can define some equivalence relation on this syntactic domain, where a and $f(a)$ may be equivalent, then the equivalence classes of that relation would form the domain instead of the set $\{a, f(a), f(f(a)), \ldots\}$. Essentially, our domain will consist of representatives of each of the equivalence classes.

In fact, we suggest to replace the equality predicate with E as in § 5.8, and then add the necessary equality sentences as premises. From Theorem 5.10 we know that a set will be satisfiable iff another set with $\approx$ replaced by E along with the appropriate equality sentence is satisfiable.

We thus assume that our formulas do not have occurrences of $\approx$. If originally, $\approx$ occurs in any formula, then it has been replaced by E and the equality sentences appropriate to the formulas have already been added. In general, We would have a set of formulas having possible occurrences of E. Our plan is to construct a model for this new set, where equality predicate is absent.

Exercises for § 10.4

Construct two Herbrand interpretations of each of the following formulas after doing Skolemization; one should satisfy the formula, and the other should falsify it.

1. $\forall x \exists y Pxy \to \exists y \forall x Pxy$
2. $\forall x \exists y Pxy \wedge \neg \exists x Pxx \wedge \forall x \forall y \forall z(Pxy \wedge Pyz \to Pxz)$
3. $\forall x \forall y(Pxy \to Pyx) \wedge \forall x \forall y \forall z(Pxy \wedge Pyz \to Pxz) \to \forall x Pxx$

10.5 HERBRAND EXPANSION

Let X be a formula in Skolem form, and let D be its Herbrand universe. The Herbrand interpretation of X is associated with the set of its instantiations obtained by taking the elements of the Herbrand universe one by one. We define the **Herbrand expansion** of a formula X as the set H given below.

$$H(X) = \{X[x_1/d_1 \cdots x_m/d_m] : x_1, \ldots, x_m \text{ are the free variables of } X, \text{ and } d_1, \ldots, d_m \in D\}.$$

Sometimes we write the Herbrand expansion $H(X)$ of X as H. The formulas in $H(X)$ are called the **ground instances** of X. The ground instances are obtained by substituting the variables with all possible ground terms.

In the following examples we assume that the given formula X is already in Skolem form; thus the free variables are universally quantified. Try to see how closely Herbrand expansions and Herbrand interpretations are related.

EXAMPLE 10.9. Let $X = \neg Pxa \wedge Pxb$. Its Herbrand universe is $D = \{a, b\}$. The instantiations of X, where the free variable x takes values from D are $\neg Paa \wedge Pab$ and $\neg Pba \wedge Pbb$. Therefore, the Herbrand expansion is

$$H(X) = \{\neg Paa \wedge Pab,\ \neg Pba \wedge Pbb\}.$$

Notice that to construct a Herbrand interpretation, we would assign truth values to the literals Paa, Pab, Pba and Pbb. For instance, the Herbrand interpretation i with

$$i(Paa) = 1 = i(Pab), \quad i(Pba) = 0 = i(Pbb)$$

evaluates the first clause $\neg Paa \wedge Pab$ to 0. Therefore, $i \nvDash H(X)$.

Herbrand interpretations have no variable assignments. They interpret only sentences. The formula in Example 10.9 as a sentence is $\forall^* X = \forall x(\neg Pxa \wedge Pxb)$. To see i as an FL-interpretation, take $\phi(P) = \{(a, a), (a, b)\}$; just find out which ones have been taken to 1 by i. This interpretation is not a model of $\forall^* X$.

EXAMPLE 10.10. Let $X = Pxf(x) \wedge \neg Pby$. Then, $D = \{b, f(b), f(f(b)), \ldots\}$. The Herbrand expansion is given by

$$\begin{aligned} H(X) = \{&Pbf(b) \wedge \neg Pbb,\ Pbf(b) \wedge \neg Pbf(b),\ \ldots, \\ &Pf(b)f(f(b)) \wedge \neg Pbb,\ Pf(b)f(f(b)) \wedge \neg Pbf(b),\ \ldots\}. \end{aligned}$$

This is not propositionally satisfiable since the ground instance $Pbf(b) \wedge \neg Pbf(b)$, a member of $H(X)$, is unsatisfiable.

EXAMPLE 10.11. Let $X = \neg Pxf(x) \wedge Pya$, where a is a constant. Then the Herbrand universe is $D = \{a, f(a), f(f(a)), \ldots\}$. The Herbrand expansion is

$$\begin{aligned} H(X) = \{&\neg Paf(a) \wedge Paa,\ \neg Paf(a) \wedge Pf(a)a,\ \neg Paf(a) \wedge Pf(f(a))a,\ \ldots, \\ &\neg Pf(a)f(f(a)) \wedge Paa,\ \neg Pf(f(a))f(f(f(a))) \wedge Pf(a)a,\ \ldots\}. \end{aligned}$$

Now, the Herbrand interpretation (D, ϕ) satisfies X iff ϕ is a propositional model of $H(X)$. For example, ϕ defined by

$$\phi(Pst) = \begin{cases} 1 & \text{if } \ t = a \\ 0 & \text{otherwise} \end{cases} \qquad \text{for } s, t \in D$$

is such a propositional model of $H(X)$. This Herbrand model of X written as a set of ground literals is

$$\{Psa : s \in D\} \cup \{\neg Pst : s, t \in D, t \neq a\}.$$

EXAMPLE 10.12. Let $X = Pxy \wedge (Pxy \to Qxy) \wedge \neg Qxz \wedge (y \approx z)$. Since $\approx$ occurs in X, we replace it with E, and add the equality sentences (in quantifier-free form) appropriate to it. That is, we have the set of formulas

$$\begin{aligned}&\{Pxy \wedge (Pxy \to Qxy) \wedge \neg Qxz \wedge Eyz,\\ &Eu_1u_1,\ Eu_2u_3 \to Eu_3u_2,\ Eu_4u_5 \wedge Eu_5u_6 \to Eu_4u_6,\\ &Ex_1y_1 \wedge Ex_2y_2 \wedge Px_1x_2 \to Py_1y_2,\ Ex_3y_3 \wedge Ex_4y_4 \wedge Qx_3x_4 \to Qy_3y_4\}.\end{aligned}$$

Then, $D = \{\alpha\}$ and

$$\begin{aligned}H(X) = \{&P\alpha\alpha \wedge (P\alpha\alpha \to Q\alpha\alpha) \wedge \neg Q\alpha\alpha \wedge E\alpha\alpha,\\ &E\alpha\alpha,\ E\alpha\alpha \to E\alpha\alpha,\ E\alpha\alpha \wedge E\alpha\alpha \to E\alpha\alpha,\\ &E\alpha\alpha \wedge E\alpha\alpha \wedge P\alpha\alpha \to P\alpha\alpha,\ E\alpha\alpha \wedge E\alpha\alpha \wedge Q\alpha\alpha \to Q\alpha\alpha\}.\end{aligned}$$

Truth of $P\alpha\alpha \wedge (P\alpha\alpha \to Q\alpha\alpha)$ implies the truth of $Q\alpha\alpha$, which contradicts the truth of $\neg Q\alpha\alpha$. Hence, the Herbrand expansion $H(X)$ is propositionally unsatisfiable. Is X also unsatisfiable?

EXAMPLE 10.13. In the formula $Pxf(x) \wedge \neg Pxx \wedge (x \approx f(x))$ no constant occurs. So, $D = \{\alpha, f(\alpha), f(f(\alpha)), \ldots\}$. The Herbrand expansion is

$$\begin{aligned}H = \{&P\alpha f(\alpha) \wedge \neg P\alpha\alpha \wedge E\alpha f(\alpha),\ Pf(\alpha)f(f(\alpha)) \wedge \neg Pf(\alpha)f(\alpha)\\ &\wedge Ef(\alpha)f(f(\alpha)), \ldots,\ E\alpha\alpha,\ Ef(\alpha)f(\alpha),\ Ef(f(\alpha))f(f(\alpha)), \ldots\\ &E\alpha\alpha \to E\alpha\alpha,\ E\alpha\alpha \wedge E\alpha\alpha \to E\alpha\alpha,\ Ef(\alpha)f(\alpha),\ E\alpha f(\alpha) \to E\alpha f(\alpha),\\ &E\alpha\alpha \wedge E\alpha f(\alpha) \to E\alpha f(\alpha), \ldots,\ E\alpha\alpha \to Ef(\alpha)f(\alpha),\\ &E\alpha f(\alpha) \wedge Ef(\alpha)f(f(\alpha)) \to E\alpha f(f(\alpha)), \ldots,\\ &E\alpha\alpha \wedge E\alpha\alpha \wedge P\alpha\alpha \to P\alpha\alpha,\ E\alpha\alpha \wedge E\alpha f(\alpha) \wedge P\alpha\alpha \to P\alpha f(\alpha), \ldots\}.\end{aligned}$$

It is not easy to see what are or are not in $H(X)$ as written here. Notice that in $H(X)$, we have $P\alpha f(\alpha), \neg P\alpha\alpha$, and $E\alpha f(\alpha)$. Due to the presence of $E\alpha f(\alpha)$, we have $P\alpha f(\alpha) \to Pf(\alpha)f(\alpha)$. Secondly, we also have $Pf(\alpha)f(\alpha) \to P\alpha\alpha$. Now, in order that $H(X)$ is satisfiable, all of $P\alpha f(\alpha), \neg P\alpha\alpha, P\alpha f(\alpha) \to Pf(\alpha)f(\alpha)$ and $Pf(\alpha)f(\alpha) \to P\alpha\alpha$ must be true. However, this compels both $P\alpha\alpha$ and $\neg P\alpha\alpha$ to be true simultaneously, which is impossible. Therefore, H is unsatisfiable.

In Examples 10.10 and 10.11, satisfiability of H is propositional, i.e., its satisfiability is determined by taking each atomic formula in H as a sentence of PL and then assigning them a truth value 0 or 1. It is still applicable in Example 10.12, though the equality predicate $\approx$ is involved. However, in Example 10.13, equality predicate has some nontrivial effect. In this case, satisfiability of H is determined by using a property of the relation E. We can use the equivalence classes of the equality predicate E instead, as is done in the proof of Lemma 5.2. Look at Example 10.13 redone as in the following.

EXAMPLE 10.14. For $X = Pxf(x) \wedge \neg Pxx \wedge (x \approx f(x))$ in Example 10.13, we see that one of the conjuncts is $(x \approx f(x))$. Corresponding to this, we have the formulas

$E\alpha f(\alpha), Ef(\alpha)f(f(\alpha)), \ldots$ occurring as conjuncts in the Herbrand expansion H. The equivalence classes induced by E on the Herbrand universe D will identify α with $f(\alpha)$, $f(\alpha)$ with $f(f(\alpha))$, etc. This means that all the elements in D are in the same equivalence class; D thus collapses into the singleton $\{\alpha\}$. Correspondingly, H collapses into $\{P\alpha\alpha \wedge \neg P\alpha\alpha \wedge E\alpha\alpha\}$, which is propositionally unsatisfiable.

The *propositional satisfiability* of H may be understood as the propositional satisfiability of the new collapsed Herbrand expansion. However, the collapsed expansion may not always be that simple as in Example 10.14. We rather choose to work with the Herbrand expansion H itself. We will see that existence of a Herbrand model is equivalent to the satisfiability of the Herbrand expansion.

Theorem 10.1 (Syntactic Interpretation). *Let X be a formula in Skolem form. Let H be the Herbrand expansion of X. Then X is satisfiable iff X has a Herbrand model iff H is propositionally satisfiable.*

Proof. Let X be a formula in Skolem form. Due to the equality theorem (Theorem 5.10), assume that the equality predicate $\approx$ does not occur in X. The variables in X are assumed to be universally quantified; X is a sentence. Let $J = (A, \psi)$ be an interpretation of X. Let D be the Herbrand universe for X. D contains all closed terms generated from the constants (from α if no constant occurs in X) and the function symbols appearing in X. Define the Herbrand interpretation (D, ϕ) by taking

$$\phi(Pt_1 \ldots t_n) = 1 \text{ iff } J \vDash Pt_1 \ldots t_n .$$

for each n-ary predicate P occurring in X, and for each term $t_1, \ldots, t_n$ occurring in D. Notice that $J \vDash Pt_1 \ldots t_n$ iff $(\psi(t_1), \ldots, \psi(t_n)) \in \psi(P)$. In fact, ψ maps D into A. In particular, if X has no occurrence of a constant, then $\psi(\alpha) \in A$. To see that if $J \vDash X$, then (D, ϕ) is a Herbrand model of X, we use induction on $\nu(X)$, the number of free variables of X.

In the basis step, if $\nu(X) = 0$, then X is a proposition, and there is nothing to prove. For the induction step, suppose $(D, \phi) \vDash W$ whenever $J \vDash W$ and W is a formula in Skolem form with $\nu(W) < k$. Let X be a Skolem form formula with $\nu(X) = k$. As all free variables in X are universally quantified, if $J \vDash X$ then for each $a \in A$, $J_{[x \mapsto a]} \vDash X$. For each $t \in D$, $\psi(t) \in A$. Thus for each $t \in D$, $J \vDash X[x/t]$. We see that $\nu(X[x/t]) < k$, and the Herbrand interpretation for the formula $X[x/t]$ is same as the Herbrand interpretation (D, ϕ) for the formula X. By the induction hypothesis, for each $t \in D$, the Herbrand interpretation (D, ϕ) is a Herbrand model of $X[x/t]$; and this happens for each $t \in D$. Then, (D, ϕ) is a model of $\forall x X$, i.e., of X.

We have thus proved that if X is satisfiable, then it has a Herbrand model. Conversely, each Herbrand model is a model; this proves the first 'iff' statement in the theorem. The second 'iff' statement is obvious since Herbrand expansion is simply another way of writing the Herbrand model. ♦

The Herbrand expansion $H(X)$ is a set of formulas obtained from X by replacing the free variables with ground terms, which are elements of the Herbrand universe. If $x_1, \ldots, x_n$ are all the free variables of X, we may write X as $X(x_1, \ldots, x_n)$. Further, writing $\bar{x}$ for the n-tuple $(x_1, \ldots, x_n)$ and $\bar{t}$ for the n-tuple of closed terms $(t_1, \ldots, t_n)$, we abbreviate the series of substitutions $[x_1/t_1][x_2/t_2]\cdots[x_n/t_n]$ to $[\bar{x}/\bar{t}]$. Then, the Herbrand expansion can be written schematically as

$$H = \{X[\bar{x}/\bar{t}] : \bar{t} \in D^n\}.$$

If X is in functional form, then after constructing its corresponding D, you find that X is valid iff the set $H = \{X[\bar{x}/\bar{t}] : \bar{t} \in D^n\}$ is valid. Note that validity of a set here means that the disjunction of some finite number of formulas in it is valid. (See compactness of FL, Theorem 6.10.) In view of Theorem 10.1, the discussion may be summarized as follows.

Theorem 10.2 (Herbrand). *Let X be a formula. Then, a formula Y with free variables $\bar{y}$, a formula Z with free variables $\bar{z}$, and possibly infinite sets of tuples of closed terms $\bar{S}$ and $\bar{T}$ can be constructed so that the following are true:*

(1) *X is satisfiable iff $\{Y[\bar{y}/\bar{s}] : \bar{s} \in \bar{S}\}$ is propositionally satisfiable.*
(2) *X is valid iff $\{Z[\bar{z}/\bar{t}] : \bar{t} \in \bar{T}\}$ is propositionally valid.*

Exercises for § 10.5

1. Construct the Herbrand expansions for the following formulas. Then decide their satisfiability.
   (a) $\forall x(Px \vee \neg\forall y\exists z(Qyxz \vee \neg\exists uQuxz))$
   (b) $\forall x(Px \vee \neg\forall y\exists z(Qyxz \vee \neg\exists uQuxz))$
   (c) $\forall x(\neg Pxx \wedge \exists yPxy \wedge \forall y\forall z((Pxy \wedge Pyz) \rightarrow Pxz))$
   (d) $\forall y\exists x(Pyx \wedge (Qy \leftrightarrow \neg Qx)) \wedge \forall x\forall y\forall z((Oxy \wedge Pyz) \rightarrow Pxz) \wedge$
   $\forall x\neg\exists y(Qx \wedge Qy \wedge Pxy)$
2. Using Herbrand expansions prove the completeness of FL-calculations; that is, if $\Sigma \vDash \bot$, then there is a calculation that proves it.
3. Show that the distributive laws used in the conversion of a formula to prenex form can be proved in FC. Then follow the construction of Herbrand interpretation and prove that FC is complete.
4. Repeat the approach outlined in the previous problem to prove completeness of FND, GFC, and FT.
5. Herbrand's theorem implies that if X is a valid formula, then there is a quasi-proof of it where first we go on applying quantifier laws, and then use only connective laws. What are those possible quantifier laws?

10.6 SKOLEM-LÖWENHEIM THEOREMS

Suppose that you have been given a valid formula. To show that it is indeed valid, you can always have a *derivation* which uses the quantifier laws first, and then only propositional laws to get $\top$. This is how you can interpret Herbrand's theorem. Theorem 10.2 raises another important question. When can $\bar{S}$ and $\bar{T}$ be chosen to be finite sets?

Suppose X is a satisfiable formula. Its Herbrand expansion is countable. The Herbrand interpretation with the Herbrand domain is a model of the formula. Hence, it has a countable model, namely, the Herbrand interpretation. This observation is easily generalized to a countable set of formulas since the Herbrand expansion of such a set is also countable. However, as a caution, you must choose different indical functions for (even same variables in) different formulas in this countable set, while Skolemization is applied. Due to the axiom of choice, this can be done. With these observations, you have the following remarkable result:

Theorem 10.3 (Skolem-Löwenheim). *Any satisfiable countable set of formulas has a countable model.*

This theorem is called the *Downward Skolem-Löwenheim Theorem.* Among other thongs, it implies that any first order theory, which is assumed to posses a model, has a countable model. For instance, the theory $\mathbb{A}$ has a countable model. Of course the standard model $\mathbb{N}$ is one such countable model. The theory of the real number system, which is a complete ordered field containing the natural numbers, also has a countable model. However, Cantor's theorem says that the set of real numbers $\mathbb{R}$ is uncountable. This is no contradiction since the theory can have an uncountable model also, such as $\mathbb{R}$. But Cantor's proof uses nothing more than the axioms of a complete ordered field. Which means, any model of the first order theory of complete ordered field containing $\mathbb{N}$ is uncountable. This has conflict with Theorem 10.3.

The conflict is usually resolved by allowing the possibility that the map that makes the countable model in one-one correspondence with $\mathbb{N}$ cannot be constructed inside the model. This is, essentially, Cantor's theorem about the uncountability of a model of the first order theory of complete ordered fields. However, looking from outside, we may have such a map. This explanation allows the notion of countability, or even cardinality of sets, to be system dependent.

It is also known that the second order theory of real number system does have essentially a unique model. Therefore, Skolem-Löwenheim Theorem shows that no first order axiomatization of $\mathbb{R}$ will be able to capture the real number system in it entirety. Indeed, the completeness axiom of the real number system truly belongs to the second order logic.

In second order logic, along with variables, we also have predicate variables; and thus we may quantify over the predicates. A second order valuation assigns variables to elements of the domain, and predicate variables to relations over the domain. The Peano arithmetic with second order sentence as the induction axiom is categorical; in the sense that any two (second order) models of this arithmetic are isomorphic (Dedekind's theorem).

In second order logic, neither compactness nor Skolem-Löwenheim theorems hold. Moreover, there does not exist an adequate axiomatic system for the second order logic. The set of valid sentences of first order logic can be enumerated, say, as output of an axiomatic system; but the valid sentences of second order logic is not enumerable. These drawbacks discourage mathematicians to work in second order logic even if it has immense expressive power.

There is also an upward Skolem-Löwenheim theorem. It asserts that if a first order theory has an infinite model, then it has models of every larger cardinalities. Thus theories admitting of infinite models cannot characterize any single semantic theory, categorically. We are not going into details of its ramifications.

Moreover, Lindström's theorems assert that there exists no logical system more expressive than first order logic where both compactness and Skolem-Löwenheim theorems hold; and there exists no logical system more expressive than first order logic, where Skolem-Löwenheim theorems hold, and for which the valid sentences are enumerable. This is another reason why mathematicians stick to first order logic. You may refer Ebbinghaus et al. (1994) for Lindström's theorems.

Exercises for § 10.6

In the following we state some refinements and improvements of Skolem-Löwenheim theorem. Try to prove them; see Enderton (1972).

1. Let Σ be a set of formulas in a language of cardinality β. Suppose Σ has an infinite model. If κ is an infinite cardinal no less than β, then Σ has a model of cardinality κ.
2. Prove *Skolem-Löwenheim upward theorem*: If a first order theory has a model of infinite cardinality, then it has models of each higher cardinality.
3. Suppose a sentences S is true in all infinite models of a first order theory T. Show that there exists $k \in \mathbb{N}$ such that S is true in all models of T having cardinality more than k.

10.7 DECIDABILITY

Given any proposition in PL we can be sure whether it is valid or not. To take such a decision, one constructs its truth table. Even if the method is lengthy, it is not impossible, because the truth table of any proposition has finite size. We thus raise the issue of decidability in FL. It is as follows.

> Does there exist an algorithm which, given any FL-formula, determines whether it is valid or not?

We apply the proof techniques since each valid formula has a proof. However, we are bound to fail; for instance, see Example 8.29. We could not do anything with such a set of formulas by using Analytic tableau. We thus think, perhaps this is an impossible task. But how do we show that there exists no algorithm to do a job?

Any attempt to answer this question will lead us to formally define an algorithm. Any formal definition, again, poses the question whether the formal definition of an algorithm captures our intuition regarding an algorithm. First of all, the formal definition must satisfy the properties of an intuitive description. Second, the formal definition must be so general that any object which may be called an algorithm intuitively can be shown to be so in the formal sense.

Many such formalizations have been invented. And till date, all these definitions have been found to be equivalent. This belief that we have reached at a correct formal definition of an algorithm is referred to as the **Church-Turing thesis**. The thesis specifically says that an algorithm is a total Turing machine.

The thesis thus entails that a generic question regarding the existence of an algorithm for a class of problems can be settled if we can construct a total Turing machine for answering all instances of the question correctly. It has been shown that there are certain problems which cannot be settled by Turing machines. For example, the Halting Problem of Turing machines cannot be solved by any algorithm. This means that there exists no Turing machine which, given any Turing machine and an input to it, can answer correctly whether the given Turing machine halts on the given input. This result is quoted as "Halting Problem is undecidable." Similarly, the **Post Correspondence Problem (PCP)**, which we formulate below, has been shown to be undecidable.

Let S be an alphabet having at least two symbols. A **PCS** (Post Correspondence System) P over S, is a finite ordered set of ordered pairs of nonempty strings $(u_1, v_1), \ldots, (u_n, v_n)$, where the strings u_i, v_i use only symbols from S. A **match** in P is a sequence of indices $i_1, i_2, \ldots, i_k$, not necessarily distinct, such that

$$u_{i_1} u_{i_2} \cdots u_{i_k} = v_{i_1} v_{i_2} \cdots v_{i_k}.$$

PCP is the problem of determining whether an arbitrary PCS has a match. An **instance of PCP** is a particular PCS where we seek a match. It can be shown that if there exists an algorithm to solve any given PCP, then the halting problem for Turing machines would be decidable. Therefore, PCP is not decidable.

We connect the validity problem to Post correspondence problem. Let

$$P = \{(u_1, v_1), (u_2, v_2), \ldots, (u_n, v_n)\}$$

be a PCS over $\{0, 1\}$. Then each u_i, and each v_i, is a binary string. We choose an individual constant c, two unary function symbols f_0, f_1, and a binary predicate R. We may think of c as the empty string, f_0 as the function that concatenates its argument with a 0, f_1 as the function that concatenates its argument with a 1. Then we can write any binary string as compositions of f_0, f_1 evaluated on c.

For example, the binary string 0 is thought of as the empty string concatenated with 0, which then is written as $f_0(c)$. Similarly, $f_1(f_0(c))$ represents the binary string (read the composition backward) 01. In general, the binary string $b_1 b_2 \cdots b_m$ is represented by the term $f_{b_m}(f_{b_{m-1}}(\cdots (f_{b_2}(f_{b_1}(c))) \cdots))$, which we again abbreviate to $f_{b_1 b_2 \cdots b_m}(c)$ for better readability.

This nomenclature is like translating a given argument in English to a first order language by building an appropriate vocabulary. Here, we are translating the PCS P into a first order language. The predicate R below represents intuitively the initially available ordered pairs, and how the game of concatenating the strings u_i and v_i is played, through successive moves.

We first express the fact that (u_i, v_i) are the available ordered pairs. Next, we say that if we have an ordered pair (x, y) and the ordered pair (u_i, v_i), then we can have an extended ordered pair (xu_i, yv_i). A match in this game is then an extended ordered pair with the same first and second components. We write these available ordered pairs along with the extended ordered pairs by using the binary predicate R. That is,

$R(x,y)$ would mean that the ordered pair (x,y) is available as it is, or it is obtained by extending available ordered pairs. Given a PCS P, we then construct the related sentence X as in the following:

$$X_1 = R(f_{u_1}(c), f_{v_1}(c)) \wedge \cdots \wedge R(f_{u_n}(c), f_{v_n}(c)).$$
$$X_2 = \forall x_1 \forall x_2 (R(x_1,x_2) \rightarrow R(f_{u_1}(x_1), f_{v_1}(x_2)) \wedge \cdots \wedge R(f_{u_n}(x_1), f_{v_n}(x_2))).$$
$$X = (X_1 \wedge X_2 \rightarrow \exists x_3 R(x_3,x_3)).$$

Our goal is to show that the sentence X is valid iff P has a match. We break up the proof into two parts.

Lemma 10.1. *If X is valid, then P has a match.*

Proof. This part is a bit trivial. If you have translated an English sentence to first order, and the first order sentence is valid, then in particular, the English sentence should be true. We give a similar argument.

Since X is valid, each of its interpretations is a model. We construct an interpretation $I = (D, \phi)$ using the intended meanings of the symbols. We take the domain $D = \{0,1\}^*$, and $\phi(c) = \varepsilon$; hereby interpreting c as the empty string. We define the functions

$$\phi(f_0) : \{0,1\}^* \rightarrow \{0,1\}^* \quad \text{by} \quad \phi(f_0)(x) = x0$$
$$\phi(f_1) : \{0,1\}^* \rightarrow \{0,1\}^* \quad \text{by} \quad \phi(f_1)(x) = x1$$

and take $\phi(R)$ as the binary relation on $\{0,1\}^*$ defined by

$$\phi(R) = \{(x,y) \in \{0,1\}^* \times \{0,1\}^* : \text{there is a sequence of indices } i_1,\ldots,i_k \text{ with } x = u_{i_1}u_{i_2}\cdots u_{i_k} \text{ and } y = v_{i_1}v_{i_2}\cdots v_{i_k}, \text{ where } (u_{i_j}, v_{i_j}) \in P\}.$$

In the interpretation I, the sentence X_1 corresponds to the sentence

The pair $(u_i, v_i) \in \phi(R)$ for each i with $1 \le i \le n$.

This is true since the sequence of indices here has only one term, namely, i.

In I, the sentence X_2 is read as follows:

If the pair $(x,y) \in \phi(R)$, then $(xu_i, yv_i) \in \phi(R)$ for each i with $1 \le i \le n$.

This sentence is also true in I as the sequence of indices $i_1,\ldots,i_k$ for the pair (x,y) can be extended to the sequence $i_1,\ldots,i_k,i$.

Thus, I is a model of $X_1 \wedge X_2$. Since X is valid, I is a model of $\exists x_3 R(x_3,x_3)$. This means, the corresponding sentence in the interpretation I is true. That is, there exists $(w,w) \in \phi(R)$ for some $w \in \{0,1\}^*$. By the very definition of $\phi(R)$, we have got a sequence $i_1,\ldots,i_k$ such that $w = u_{i_1}u_{i_2}\cdots u_{i_k} = v_{i_1}v_{i_2}\cdots v_{i_k}$. Therefore, P has a match. ♦

Lemma 10.2. *If P has a match, then any interpretation of X is a model of X.*

Proof. Assume that P has a match. We have a sequence of indices $i_1,\ldots,i_k$ such that $u_{i_1}\cdots u_{i_k} = v_{i_1}\cdots v_{i_k} = w$, say. Let $J = (D, \psi)$ be any interpretation of X. Then $\psi(c) \in D$, $\psi(f_0), \psi(f_1) : D \rightarrow D$, and $\psi(R) \subseteq D \times D$. Since P has only binary strings in its ordered pairs, we must assign these binary strings to elements of D. To this end, define a map $\phi : \{0,1\}^* \to D$ recursively by

$$\phi(\varepsilon) = \psi(c),\ \phi(x0) = \psi(f_0)(\phi(x)),\ \text{and}\ \phi(x1) = \psi(f_1)(\phi(x)).$$

Here, ε is the empty string, and x is any string from $\{0,1\}^*$.

It follows that if $b_1b_2\cdots b_j$ is a binary string with $b_i \in \{0,1\}$, then

$$\phi(b_1\cdots b_j) = \psi(f_{b_j})(\psi(f_{b_{j-1}})\ (\cdots\ \psi(f_{b_2})(\psi(f_{b_1})(\psi(c))\ \cdots))).$$

The last expression is again abbreviated to $f_{b_1b_2\cdots b_j}(\psi(c))$. Thus, with the abbreviation at work, we have $f_s(\psi(c)) = \phi(s)$ for any binary string s. For instance, $\phi(011) = \psi(f_1)(\psi(f_1)(\psi(f_0)(\psi(c))))$. We are simply coding backward the elements of D, so to speak.

To show that J is a model of X, we assume that J is a model of X_1, J is a model of X_2, and then prove that J is a model of $\exists x_3 R(x_3,x_3)$. Since J is a model of X_1, for each i, $1 \le i \le n$, $(\psi(f_{u_i})(\psi(c)), \psi(f_{v_i})(\psi(c))) \in \psi(R)$. That is,

$$(\phi(u_i), \phi(v_i)) \in \psi(R) \quad \text{for each } i,\ 1 \le i \le n.$$

Similarly, J is a model of X_2 implies that

$$\text{If } (\phi(s), \phi(t)) \in \psi(R), \text{ then } (\phi(su_i), \phi(tv_i)) \in \psi(R).$$

Starting with $(\phi(u_1), \phi(v_1)) \in \psi(R)$, and repeatedly using the above statement, we obtain:

$$(\phi(u_{i_1}u_{i_2}\cdots u_{i_k}), \phi(v_{i_1}v_{i_2}\cdots v_{i_k})) \in \psi(R).$$

That is, $\phi(w,w) \in \psi(R)$. Therefore, J is a model of $\exists x_3 R(x_3,x_3)$. ♦

Suppose we have an algorithm A such that given any sentence Y, A decides whether Y is valid or not. Let P be any given PCS over the alphabet $\{0,1\}$. Construct the sentence X as in Lemma 10.1. Due to Lemmas 10.1-10.2, A decides whether P has a match or not. However, PCP is not decidable. Therefore, there cannot exist such an algorithm A. You have thus proved the following statement:

Theorem 10.4 (Turing's Undecidability). *The validity problem for first order languages is not decidable.*

The proof of Theorem 10.4 says that in any first order language with at least one individual constant, two unary function symbols, and one binary predicate, the validity problem is undecidable. In fact, presence of a single binary predicate makes a first order language undecidable. We do not prove this stronger version of Theorem 10.4 here.

However, we note that validity of *monadic first order logic* is decidable; this is in correspondence with the fact that the PCP with a single alphabet letter is decidable. It says that if we have a first order language with only a finite number of unary predicates, and a finite number of individual constants only, the validity problem there would be solvable. This logic is the so-called Aristotelian logic, and Aristotle had already given us an algorithm to determine the validity of an arbitrary sentence in his logic. It is worthwhile to prove this fact without using Aristotle's method of syllogisms.

Theorem 10.4 asserts that there exists no algorithm which given any arbitrary formula (or sentence) of first order logic, can report truthfully whether the formula ia valid or not. Observe that this does not contradict the completeness of the proof systems we discussed earlier. For instance, the axioms and the rules of inference of FC can be implemented into a computer program so that it goes on printing theorems after theorems. If the given formula is valid, the program would eventually print it. This property of the set of valid formulas is expressed as follows:

The valid formulas of any first order language is enumerable.

On the other hand, if the given formula is not valid, then it will never be printed by the program. That is, we will never come to know whether it is invalid or not. In this sense, we say that the validity problem for first order logic is *semi-decidable.*

Exercises for § 10.7

1. Let Y be a formula in the form $\exists x_1 \cdots \exists x_m \forall y_1 \cdots \forall y_n X$, where X is quantifier-free, and it does not involve any function symbols. Show that there exists an algorithm to decide whether such a formula Y is satisfiable or not.
2. Let Y be a formula in the form $\forall x_1 \cdots \forall x_m \exists y_1 \cdots \exists y_n X$, where X is quantifier-free, and it does not involve any function symbols. Show that there exists an algorithm to decide whether such a formula Y is valid or not.
3. Let Σ be a set of sentences over a finite language. Suppose that for each $X \in \Sigma$, if X has a model, then X has a finite model. Show that there exists an algorithm that decides whether any given $X \in \Sigma$ is satisfiable or not. (Such a Σ is said to have *finite model property*.)

10.8 EXPRESSIBILITY

Recall that $\mathbb{A}$ denotes the first order theory of arithmetic with the non-logical symbols as 0, s, $+$, $\cdot$, $\hat{}$ and $<$, defined by the axioms (1)-(13) in §10.3. The standard interpretation of $\mathbb{A}$ is the intuitive (semantic) theory $\mathbb{N}$ of natural numbers. In this interpretation, the constant 0 is interpreted as the number 0, the unary function s is interpreted as the successor function mapping n to $n+1$, $+$ as addition, $\cdot$ as multiplication, $\hat{}$ as exponentiation, and $<$ as the relation of less than. We will use the following assumptions about $\mathbb{A}$ and $\mathbb{N}$.

Assumptions:

1. Each sentence of $\mathbb{N}$ can be written down as a sentence in $\mathbb{A}$; and it can be either true or false.
2. The theory $\mathbb{A}$ is sound with respect to $\mathbb{N}$. That is, each provable formula in $\mathbb{A}$ is true in $\mathbb{N}$.
3. The theory $\mathbb{A}$ is consistent. That is, for any formula X of $\mathbb{A}$, both X and $\neg X$ are not provable in $\mathbb{A}$.

The assumptions are reasonable since the theory $\mathbb{A}$ is believed to be an axiomatization of $\mathbb{N}$. Moreover, with so many years of work we have not succeeded in finding a contradiction in $\mathbb{A}$. We will see later whether such an assumption on the consistency of $\mathbb{A}$ can be eliminated or not.

Recall that the terms $0, s(0), s(s(0)), \ldots$ in $\mathbb{A}$ are called numerals, which we have agreed to write as $0, 1, 2, \ldots$, respectively. The symbols, strings of symbols, and strings of strings of symbols of $\mathbb{A}$ are commonly referred to as *expressions*. The set of all expressions of $\mathbb{A}$ are countable; thus they can be encoded as numerals. However, we wish to have an encoding where the numeral associated with an expression of $\mathbb{A}$ can be computed by an algorithm. Such an encoding is called **Gödel numbering** following K. Gödel. We will use a simplified numbering scheme.

We start with the symbols used in the theory $\mathbb{A}$. Since a comma is also a symbol, we use blank space to separate the symbols in the list below. The following are the symbols of $\mathbb{A}$:

$$, \quad) \quad (\quad x \quad | \quad \neg \quad \wedge \quad \vee \quad \to \quad \leftrightarrow \quad \forall \quad \exists \quad \approx \quad 0 \quad s \quad + \quad \cdot \quad \hat{} \quad <$$

Instead of using infinite number of variables, $x_0, x_1, x_2, \ldots$, we will use the symbols x and $|$ to generate them. That is, x followed by n number of $|$s will be abbreviated to x_n. We abbreviate β written n times to β^n, where β is any of the digits (numerals) 1 or 2. For instance 222222 will be written as 2^6; you should not confuse 2^6 here with 64. We write the encoding as $g(\cdot)$, and start with the symbols:

$$g(,) = 1,\ g()) = 11,\ g(() = 111,\ g(x) = 1^4,\ \ldots,\ g(\hat{}) = 1^{18},\ g(<) = 1^{19}.$$

Next, a string of symbols $\sigma_1 \cdots \sigma_k$ is encoded as

$$g(\sigma_1 \cdots \sigma_k) = 2\,g(\sigma_1)\,2 \cdots 2\,g(\sigma_k)\,2.$$

We keep the digit 2 as a separator; it will help us in decoding the symbols. Notice that each string of symbols begins with a 2 and also ends with a 2. Next, if $s_1, s_2, \ldots, s_m$ are strings of symbols from the language of $\mathbb{A}$, then we define

$$g(s_1, s_2, \ldots, s_m) = 2\,g(s_1)\,2\,g(s_2)\,2 \cdots 2\,g(s_m)\,2.$$

In fact, we will read $g(w)$ as a numeral. If $g(w)$ is $a_k a_{k-1} \cdots a_1 a_0$, where each a_i is either 1 or 2, we read $g(w)$ as the value of the following expression in $\mathbb{A}$:

$$g(w) = a_k 3^k + a_{k-1} 3^{k-1} + \cdots + a_1 3^1 + a_0.$$

Here ends our encoding. Of course, for a small formula, its Gödel number may become very large. But that is not a problem for us. We assume that we have a lot of paper and ink to write it out as a sequence of ones and twos; and then we have sufficient computing resources to evaluate it as a polynomial in powers of three.

Clearly two different expressions have different encodings. That is, g is a one-one function from the set of expressions of $\mathbb{A}$ to the set of numerals. We will call any numeral n a **Gödel number** iff there exists an expression w such that $n = g(w)$. Further, we see that there exists an algorithm specified in the language of $\mathbb{A}$ that computes the numeral $g(w)$ corresponding to each expression w of $\mathbb{A}$; and also there exists an algorithm specified in the language of $\mathbb{A}$ that computes the expression $g^{-1}(n)$ corresponding to each Gödel number n.

The encoding of expressions of $\mathbb{A}$ as numerals in $\mathbb{A}$ makes self-reference possible. This is reflected in the following result.

Theorem 10.5 (Diagonalization Lemma). *Corresponding to each formula $B(\cdot)$ of $\mathbb{A}$ with a single free variable, there exists a sentence S in $\mathbb{A}$ such that $S \leftrightarrow B(g(S))$ is provable in $\mathbb{A}$.*

Proof. Let x_1 be the Gödel number of a formula with a single free variable x. Then such a formula is given by $g^{-1}(x_1)$. The Gödel numbering provides an algorithm for computing $g^{-1}(x_1)$, and also an algorithm for computing $g(w)$ for any expression w of $\mathbb{A}$. These algorithms are specified by formulas of $\mathbb{A}$. Thus we have an algorithm specified by formulas of $\mathbb{A}$ that takes x_1 as its input and gives the numeral $g(g^{-1}(x_1))$ as its output.

The specification of the algorithm has occurrences of x corresponding to the free occurrences of x in $g^{-1}(x_1)$. By changing x to x_2 everywhere in the specification we obtain a new algorithm which takes x_2 as its input and gives an output, which we write as $g((g^{-1}(x_1))[x/x_2])$. Notice that x may not occur explicitly in the numeral $g((g^{-1}(x_1))$. However, the substitution in the expression $g((g^{-1}(x_1))[x/x_2])$ is meaningful in the above sense.

In particular, for $x_2 = x_1$, the expression $g((g^{-1}(x_1))[x/x_1])$ evaluates to a numeral. Let $B(x)$ be a formula of $\mathbb{A}$ with the only free variable x. Then the expression $B(g((g^{-1}(x_1))[x/x_1]))$ is a well defined formula of $\mathbb{A}$ with the only free variable x_1.

For each Gödel number x_1 of a formula with a single free variable x, we take $H(x_1)$ as the formula $B(g((g^{-1}(x_1))[x/x_1]))$; and for each x_2 which is not the Gödel number of a formula with the free variable x, we take $H(x_2)$ as *false*. We take here the truth value *false*, since $g^{-1}(x_2)$ for such a numeral x_2 may become meaningless. This is how we obtain a formula $H(x)$ in $\mathbb{A}$ such that for each Gödel number x_1 of a formula with the only free variable x,

$$H(x_1) \leftrightarrow B\big(g\big((g^{-1}(x_1))[x/x_1]\big)\big) \text{ is provable in } \mathbb{A}.$$

In particular, with x_1 as $k = g(H(x))$, we have

$$H(k) \leftrightarrow B\big(g\big((g^{-1}(k))[x/k]\big)\big) \text{ is provable in } \mathbb{A}.$$

Now, $k = g(H(x))$ implies that $H(k) = H(x)[x/k] = (g^{-1}(k))[x/k]$. Therefore,

$$H(k) \leftrightarrow B\big(g\big(H(k)\big)\big) \text{ is provable in } \mathbb{A}.$$

This sentence $H(k)$ serves the purpose of S as required. ♦

Given a formula $B(\cdot)$ with a single free variable, the sentence "My Gödel number satisfies the formula $B(\cdot)$" is such a sentence provided by the Diagonalization lemma. It shows that the Arithmetic is such a rich axiomatic theory that a self-referring sentence as this one could be written down as a formula in it; further, such a formula could also be proved in it.

Recall that a unary predicate of $\mathbb{A}$ is interpreted in the standard interpretation $\mathbb{N}$ as its subset. In general, a formula with a single free variable is also interpreted as a subset of $\mathbb{N}$. We formalize this intuitive connection between subsets of $\mathbb{N}$ and formulas of $\mathbb{A}$ with one free variable as follows.

Let $C \subseteq \mathbb{N}$. We say that C is **expressed by a formula** $F(x)$ **in** $\mathbb{A}$ iff $F(x)$ is a formula of $\mathbb{A}$ with the only free variable as x, and in the standard interpretation of $\mathbb{A}$ in $\mathbb{N}$, the following holds:

$$\text{for each } n \in \mathbb{N}, \quad n \in C \text{ iff } F(n) \text{ is true in } \mathbb{N}.$$

Also, we say that C is **expressible in** $\mathbb{A}$ iff C is expressed by some formula $F(x)$ in $\mathbb{A}$. For example, the set of perfect squares is expressed in $\mathbb{A}$ by the formula $\exists y(x = y \cdot y)$; the set of composite numbers is expressed by the formula

$$\exists y \exists z((s(0) < y) \wedge (s(0) < z)(x \approx y \cdot z)).$$

As we know, there exist an uncountable number of subsets of $\mathbb{N}$. On the other hand, the formulas of $\mathbb{A}$ with one free variable are countable in number. Thus there exist an uncountable number of subsets of $\mathbb{N}$ which are not expressible in $\mathbb{A}$. However, giving an example has certain difficulties. For, how to demonstrate (express) an object which is not expressible? We use the Diagonalization lemma to show that it is possible.

Theorem 10.6 (Tarski). *The set of Gödel numbers of all true sentences of* $\mathbb{N}$ *is not expressible in* $\mathbb{A}$.

Proof. By our assumptions, any sentence of $\mathbb{N}$ can be written down as a sentence in $\mathbb{A}$. Thus the Gödel number of a true sentence of $\mathbb{N}$ is well defined. So, let

$$\mathbb{T} = \{g(X) : X \text{ is a true sentence of } \mathbb{N}\}.$$

Suppose that $\mathbb{T}$ as a subset of $\mathbb{N}$ is expressed by the formula $B(x)$ of $\mathbb{A}$. Then the subset $\mathbb{N} \setminus \mathbb{T}$ of $\mathbb{N}$ is expressed by the formula $\neg B(x)$. By the Diagonalization lemma (Theorem 10.5), corresponding to the formula $\neg B(\cdot)$, there exists a sentence S in $\mathbb{A}$ such that $S \leftrightarrow \neg B(g(S))$ is provable in $\mathbb{A}$. Since $\mathbb{A}$ is assumed to be sound, the sentence $S \leftrightarrow \neg B(g(S))$ is true in $\mathbb{N}$. Thus, we have

$$S \text{ is true in } \mathbb{N} \text{ iff } \neg B(g(S)) \text{ is true in } \mathbb{N}.$$

Now that the set $\mathbb{N} \setminus \mathbb{T}$ is expressed by the formula $\neg B(x)$, we see that for each $n \in \mathbb{N}$, $\neg B(n)$ is true in $\mathbb{N}$ iff $n \in \mathbb{N} \setminus \mathbb{T}$. In particular,

$$\neg B(g(S)) \text{ is true in } \mathbb{N} \text{ iff } g(S) \in \mathbb{N} \setminus \mathbb{T}.$$

Since $\mathbb{T}$ is the set of Gödel numbers of true sentences, we have

$$S \text{ is true in } \mathbb{N} \text{ iff } g(S) \in \mathbb{T}.$$

We thus arrive at the contradiction that $g(S) \in \mathbb{N} \setminus \mathbb{T}$ iff $g(S) \in \mathbb{T}$. Therefore, $\mathbb{T}$ is not expressible in $\mathbb{A}$. ♦

Exercises for § 10.8

Let S be a structure with domain D. We write $S_{[x_1 \mapsto d_1,\ldots,x_n \mapsto d_n]}$ for the state in the structure S where the variable x_i is assigned to the element $d_i \in D$ for $1 \le i \le n$. We say that a formula X with free variables among $x_1, \ldots, x_n$ *defines* an n-ary relation R on D iff for all elements $d_1, \ldots, d_n \in D$,

$$(d_1, \ldots, d_n) \in R \text{ iff } S_{[x_1 \mapsto d_1,\ldots,x_n \mapsto d_n]} \vDash X.$$

Informally, this happens when the sentence obtained from X by interpreting x_1 as $d_1, \ldots,$ and x_n as d_n, is true in the structure S. An n-ary relation on D is said to be *definable* when some formula defines it. For example, in any structure, substitution is definable; in the sense that if X is a formula, and x is a variable free for a term t in X, then $X[x/t] \equiv \forall x((x \approx t) \to X)$. Alternatively, you can use $X[x/t] \equiv \exists x((x \approx t) \wedge X)$, by the one-point rule. Show the following:

1. Consider the structure $(\mathbb{R}, 0, 1, +, \cdot)$ of the field of real numbers. Since the square of a real number is non-negative, show that the ordering relation $<$ is definable in this structure.
2. For any natural number n, the singleton set $\{n\}$ is definable in $\mathbb{A}$.
3. The set of primes is definable in $\mathbb{A}$.
4. Exponentiation is definable in $\mathbb{A}$. That is, the relation $\{(m,n,k) : k \approx m^n\}$ is definable in $\mathbb{A}$. [Hint: See § 3.8 in Enderton (1972).]
5. The interval $[1, \infty)$ is definable in the structure $(\mathbb{R}, 0, 1, +, \cdot)$.
6. The singleton $\{5\}$ is definable in $(\mathbb{R}, 0, 1, +, \cdot)$.
7. A finite union of intervals whose end-points are algebraic numbers is definable in $(\mathbb{R}, 0, 1, +, \cdot)$. [Its converse is also true.]

10.9 PROVABILITY PREDICATE

Each expression of $\mathbb{A}$ has a Gödel number. In particular, each formula has a Gödel number, and each proof has a Gödel number. Further, a numeral is or is not the Gödel number of some expression of $\mathbb{A}$ can be written as a formula of $\mathbb{A}$. Also, from the Gödel number of a proof of a formula, the Gödel number of the formula can be computed. Therefore, the following formula with its meaning as given, is a formula of $\mathbb{A}$ with two free variables x and x_1 :

$Proof(x, x_1)$: x is the Gödel number of a formula of $\mathbb{A}$ and x_1 is the Gödel number of a proof of that formula.

That is, $Proof(x, x_1)$ is true if x_1 is the Gödel number of a proof of a formula F whose Gödel number is x. Such a formula F in the definition of $Proof(x, x_1)$ is $g^{-1}(x)$. Next, we construct the formula $Pr(x)$ as follows:

$Pr(x) : \exists x_1 Proof(x, x_1)$

As a formula of $\mathbb{A}$, we see that $Pr(x)$ is true in $\mathbb{N}$ iff there exits a numeral n which is the Gödel number of a proof of $g^{-1}(x)$ iff the formula $g^{-1}(x)$ is provable in $\mathbb{A}$. Therefore, the set

$$\mathbb{P} = \{g(X) : X \text{ is a provable sentence of } \mathbb{A}\}$$

is expressed by the formula $Pr(x)$ which has only one free variable, namely x. Since $\mathbb{A}$ is assumed to be sound, each provable sentence of $\mathbb{A}$ is true in $\mathbb{N}$. Therefore, $\mathbb{P} \subseteq \mathbb{T}$, where $\mathbb{T}$ is the set of all true sentences of $\mathbb{N}$. Due to Theorem 10.6, we conclude that $\mathbb{P}$ is a proper subset of $\mathbb{T}$. It follows that there exists a true sentence in $\mathbb{N}$ which is not provable in $\mathbb{A}$.

It is easier to guess that there exists gaps between truth and povability. Consider a universally quantified sentence such as $\forall x P(x)$, where P is a unary predicate. By definition this sentence is true when for each x, "$P(x)$ is true". Whereas if for each x, "$P(x)$ is provable", then it does not follow that $\forall x Px$ is provable. To see this, suppose the variable x here ranges over $\mathbb{N}$. In this case, for each x, "Px is provable" means, we have proofs for $P(0)$, for $P(1)$, for $P(2)$, and so on. Now, how do we combine all these to get a proof for $\forall x P(x)$?

The liar's sentence (in the Liar's paradox) may be formulated as "This sentence is not true". Replacing truth with provability we obtain the sentence "This sentence is not provable". Notice that the liar's sentence is not a proposition, since we cannot meaningfully assign a truth value to it. Whereas the other sentence about provability is a sentence which is true but cannot be proved. However, it looks ridiculous that such a self-referring sentence is a sentence of arithmetic. In fact, using the Diagonalization lemma, we can have an incarnation of this self-referring sentence in the theory $\mathbb{A}$; see the proof of the following theorem.

Theorem 10.7 (Gödel's First Incompleteness). *There exists a sentence S in $\mathbb{A}$ such that S is true in $\mathbb{N}$, but neither S nor $\neg S$ is provable in $\mathbb{A}$.*

Proof. The set $\mathbb{P}$ of all Gödel numbers of provable sentences of $\mathbb{A}$ is expressed by $Pr(x)$. So, its complement $\mathbb{N} \setminus \mathbb{P}$ is expressed by $\neg Pr(x)$. By the Diagonalization lemma, there exists a sentence S such that $S \leftrightarrow \neg Pr(g(S))$ is provable in $\mathbb{A}$. By the soundness of $\mathbb{A}$, it follows that $S \leftrightarrow \neg Pr(g(S))$ is true in $\mathbb{N}$. Thus, S is true in $\mathbb{N}$ iff $\neg Pr(g(S))$ is true in $\mathbb{N}$.

Since $\mathbb{N} \setminus \mathbb{P}$ is expressed by $\neg Pr(x)$, for each $n \in \mathbb{N}$, $\neg Pr(n)$ is true in $\mathbb{N}$ iff $n \in \mathbb{N} \setminus \mathbb{P}$. In particular, $\neg Pr(g(S))$ is true in $\mathbb{N}$ iff $g(S) \in \mathbb{N} \setminus \mathbb{P}$. The definition of $\mathbb{P}$ implies that $g(S) \in \mathbb{N} \setminus \mathbb{P}$ iff S is not provable in $\mathbb{A}$.

We thus conclude that S is true in $\mathbb{N}$ iff S is not provable in $\mathbb{A}$.

Now, if S is not provable in $\mathbb{A}$, then S is true in $\mathbb{N}$. Also, soundness of $\mathbb{A}$ implies that if S is provable in $\mathbb{A}$, then it is true in $\mathbb{N}$. In any case, S is true in $\mathbb{N}$. And then, S is not provable in $\mathbb{A}$.

Further, if $\neg S$ is provable in $\mathbb{A}$, then $\neg S$ is true in $\mathbb{N}$. This is not possible as S is true in $\mathbb{N}$. Therefore, S is true in $\mathbb{N}$, and neither S nor $\neg S$ is provable in $\mathbb{A}$. ♦

Abbreviate $Pr(g(X))$ to $P(X)$ for any sentence X of $\mathbb{A}$. Now, $P(X)$ is true in $\mathbb{N}$ iff $g(X) \in \mathbb{P}$ iff X is a provable sentence of $\mathbb{A}$. That is,

$$X \text{ is provable in } \mathbb{A} \text{ iff } P(X) \text{ is true in } \mathbb{N}.$$

Informally, $P(X)$ is a formula of the theory $\mathbb{A}$ which expresses the fact that 'the sentence X of $\mathbb{A}$ is provable in $\mathbb{A}$. Thus $P(\cdot)$ is called a **provability predicate**. Observe that $P(\cdot)$ is not a predicate. You should not read the notation as 'the formula X is an argument of the predicate P'. It is just an abbreviation. For all sentences X and Y, the provability predicate satisfies the following properties:

$$\text{If } X \text{ is provable in } \mathbb{A} \text{ then } P(X) \text{ is provable in } \mathbb{A}. \tag{10.2}$$

$$P(X \to Y) \to (P(X) \to P(Y)) \text{ is provable in } \mathbb{A}. \tag{10.3}$$

$$P(X) \to P(P(X)) \text{ is provable in } \mathbb{A}. \tag{10.4}$$

The sentence in (10.2) says that if X is provable, then 'X is provable' is provable; in fact, the proof of X demonstrates that. Next, (10.3) follows from Modus Ponens in $\mathbb{A}$; and (10.4) combines (10.2) and a form of Deduction Theorem in $\mathbb{A}$. These statements imply the following:

$$\text{If } X \to (P(X) \to Y) \text{ is provable in } \mathbb{A}, \text{ then } P(X) \to P(Y) \text{ is provable in } \mathbb{A}. \tag{10.5}$$

To see this, assume that $X \to (P(X) \to Y)$ is provable. We need to give a proof of $P(X) \to P(Y)$. Due to the deduction theorem, it is enough to assume $P(X)$ to be provable and derive that $P(Y)$ is provable. So, assume $P(X)$ to be provable. We use Modus Ponens repeatedly. By (10.2), $P(X \to (P(X) \to Y))$ is provable. By (10.3), $P(X) \to P(P(X) \to Y)$ is provable. Since $P(X)$ is provable, it follows that $P(P(X) \to Y)$ is provable. By (10.3), $P(P(X)) \to P(Y)$ is provable. Since $P(X)$ is provable, by (10.2), $P(P(X))$ is provable. Thus follows $P(Y)$. This very proof of $P(Y)$ shows that $P(Y)$ is provable.

We use (10.5) in the proof of the following theorem.

Theorem 10.8 (Gödel's Second Incompleteness). *If $\mathbb{A}$ is consistent then the formula $\neg P(0 \approx 1)$ is not provable in $\mathbb{A}$.*

Proof. Using the Diagonalization lemma on the formula $\neg Pr(x)$, we obtain a sentence S such that $S \leftrightarrow \neg Pr(g(S))$ is provable in $\mathbb{A}$. Since, $Pr(g(S))$ is abbreviated to $P(S)$, we have

$$S \leftrightarrow \neg P(S) \text{ is provable in } \mathbb{A}. \tag{10.6}$$

Thus, $S \to \neg P(S)$ is provable in $\mathbb{A}$. As $\neg P(S) \equiv P(S) \to (0 \approx 1)$, it follows that $S \to (P(S) \to (0 \approx 1))$ is provable in $\mathbb{A}$. Taking $X = S$ and $Y = (0 \approx 1)$ in (10.5), we obtain the following:

$$\text{If } S \to (P(S) \to (0 \approx 1)) \text{ is provable in } \mathbb{A}, \text{ then } P(S) \to P(0 \approx 1) \text{ is provable in } \mathbb{A}.$$

Hence $P(S) \to P(0 \approx 1)$ is provable in $\mathbb{A}$. By contraposition, $\neg P(0 \approx 1) \to \neg P(S)$ is provable in $\mathbb{A}$.

If $\neg P(0 \approx 1)$ is provable in $\mathbb{A}$, then $\neg P(S)$ is provable in $\mathbb{A}$. By (10.6), S is provable in $\mathbb{A}$. By (10.2), $P(S)$ is provable in $\mathbb{A}$. So, both $\neg P(S)$ and $P(S)$ are provable in $\mathbb{A}$. This is not possible since $\mathbb{A}$ is assumed to be consistent. Therefore, $\neg P(0 \approx 1)$ is not provable in $\mathbb{A}$. ♦

Since any contradiction in $\mathbb{A}$ is equivalent to $(0 \approx 1)$, the sentence $\neg P(0 \approx 1)$ says that no contradiction is provable in $\mathbb{A}$. This expresses consistency of $\mathbb{A}$. Theorem 10.8 thus asserts that if $\mathbb{A}$ is consistent, then its consistency cannot be proved by using the proof mechanism of $\mathbb{A}$. Indeed, what sort of a system it would be if it proclaims and proves its own consistency!

As the proof of Theorem 10.8 revealed the sentences $\neg P(S)$ and $\neg P(0 \approx 1)$ serve the purpose of the sentence S in Theorem 10.7; they are true in $\mathbb{N}$ but neither they nor their negations can be proved in $\mathbb{A}$.

The incompleteness theorems of Gödel shattered Hilbert's program for proving the consistency of Arithmetic using the mechanism of Arithmetic. Herman Wyel thus commented:

> God exists because mathematics is undoubtedly consistent,
> and the devil exists because we cannot prove the consistency.

We may like to add the consistency of $\mathbb{A}$ as an extra axiom to those of $\mathbb{A}$. Then Gödel goes further in showing that the resulting system, say $\mathbb{A}_1$ will be unable to prove its own consistency. Once more adding the consistency of $\mathbb{A}_1$ to itself we land at a system $\mathbb{A}_2$ which again will not be able to prove its consistency. This process is unending; and there exists no finitely axiomatizable system of arithmetic which can prove its own consistency.

Of course, G. Gentzen had proved the consistency of $\mathbb{A}$ by using a different proof mechanism such as transfinite induction.

Exercises for § 10.9

1. Let S be a sentence as stipulated in (10.6). Show that $\neg P(S)$ is true in $\mathbb{N}$, but neither $P(S)$ nor $\neg P(S)$ is provable in $\mathbb{A}$.
2. A printer prints strings using four symbols: N, P, A, O. A string of these symbols is called a sentence if it is in one of the following four forms:

   $POXO$, $NPOXO$, $PAOXO$, $NPAOXO$ for any string X

   We define true sentences as follows.

   $POXO$ is true iff X is printed sooner or later.
   $NPOXO$ is true iff X is not printed sooner or later.
   $PAOXO$ is true iff $XOXO$ is printed sooner or later.
   $NPAOXO$ is true iff $XOXO$ is not printed sooner or later.

   Assume that if the printer prints a sentence, then it is true. For instance, if the printer prints $POXO$, then $POXO$ is true; thus X is printed sooner or later. It implies that X is also true. Exhibit a true sentence that is never printed. [This is a Gödelian puzzle invented by R. M. Smullyan.]
3. Consider the sentence S in (10.6). Write the formula $\neg Proof(g(S), x_1)$ as $Q(x_1)$. Show the following:

   (a) $S \equiv \forall x_1 Q(x_1)$.
   (b) $\forall x_1 Q(x_1)$ is not provable in $\mathbb{A}$.
   (c) For each $n \in \mathbb{N}$, $Q(n)$ is provable in $\mathbb{A}$.

   It shows that $\mathbb{A}$ is an *ω-incomplete* theory.

4. Let $R(x)$ be the formula $Q(x) \to \forall x_1 Q(x_1)$, where $Q(x_1)$ is as given in the previous exercise. Show the following:

   (a) The formula $\exists x R(x)$ is provable in $\mathbb{A}$.
   (b) For each $n \in \mathbb{N}$, $R(n)$ is not provable in $\mathbb{A}$.

   [R. M. Smullyan thus says that $\mathbb{A}$ is $\exists$-incomplete. P. R. Halmos compares it with a mother telling the child that it is there; but it is not this, go on find out; again, she says, no, it is not this, go on find out, and so on.]

10.10 SUMMARY AND PROBLEMS

First order logic is considered as the foundation of mathematics. The whole edifice of mathematics can be built on the first order theory of sets. In this chapter we have discussed some of the foundational problems that involved the most talented mathematicians of the twentieth century.

In nutshell, we have shown that all mathematical problems cannot be solved by computers. There exists a gap between what is assumed to be true about the natural numbers, and what could be proved in the first order theory of natural numbers. If the theory of natural numbers is really consistent, then we cannot prove its consistency by using the proof mechanism of natural numbers.

Our proofs of these important foundational results are neither complete nor self-contained. We have only touched the tip of the iceberg. The presentation here is based upon similar approach found in Boolos et al. (2007), Ebbinghaus et al. (1994), Enderton (1972), Rautenberg (2010), Singh & Goswami (1998), Singh (2009), and Smullyan (2014). We have not discussed many important issues such as definability, categoricity, and arithmetical hierarchy. To have a feel of the problems and their solutions, you are most invited to the works of E. W. Beth, K. Gödel, A. M. Turing, A. Tarski, T. A. Skolem, L. Löwenheim, J. Herbrand, J. B. Rosser, and P. Lindström. You can start with van Heijenoort (1967) to have a comprehensive view of these works.

Problems for Chapter 10

1. For $n \in \mathbb{N}$, let L_n be a language with signature S_n where $S_0 \subseteq S_1 \subseteq S_2 \subseteq \cdots$. Let Σ_n be a consistent set of formulas of L_n with $\Sigma_0 \subseteq \Sigma_1 \subseteq \Sigma_2 \subseteq \cdots$. Take $S = \cup_{n\in\mathbb{N}} S_n$ and $\Sigma = \cup_{n\in\mathbb{N}} \Sigma_n$. Show that Σ is a consistent set of formulas of a language with signature S.
2. Let L be a language with signature S. Let T be the set of all terms from L. Let Σ be a consistent set of formulas of L. Define a relation $\sim$ on T by $s \sim t$ iff $\Sigma \vdash (s \approx t)$. Show the following:

   (a) $\sim$ is an equivalence relation.
   (b) $\sim$ is *compatible with* S. That is, if s_i, t_i are terms with $s_1 \sim t_1, \ldots, s_n \sim t_n$, then for any n-ary function symbol f in S, $f(s_1, \ldots, s_n) \sim f(t_1, \ldots, t_n)$, and for any n-ary predicate P, $\Sigma \vdash P(s_1, \ldots, s_n)$ iff $\Sigma \vdash P(t_1, \ldots, t_n)$.

3. A *substructure* of a structure (D, ϕ) is (A, ψ), where $A \subseteq D$, $\psi(P) = \phi(P) \cap A^n$ for each n-ary predicate P, $\psi(f)$ is the restriction of the function $\phi(f)$ to A for any function symbol f, and $\psi(c) = \phi(c)$ for every constant c. These conditions hold for the non-logical symbols of the underlying language L. Let I be a substructure of J. Prove the following:

   (a) For each quantifier-free formula X of L, $I \vDash X$ iff $J \vDash X$.
   (b) Let X be a *universal formula*; that is, $X = \forall x_1 \cdots \forall x_n Y$ for some quantifier-free formula Y. Then for each valuation ℓ under I, $J_\ell \vDash X$ implies that $I_\ell \vDash X$. [You should first show that J_ℓ is a state.]
   (c) If X is a universal sentence, then $J \vDash X$ implies $I \vDash X$.
   (d) Let X be an *existential formula*; that is, $X = \exists x_1 \cdots \exists x_n Y$ for some quantifier-free formula Y. Then for each valuation ℓ under I, $I_\ell \vDash X$ implies that $J_\ell \vDash X$.
   (e) If X is an existential sentence, then $I \vDash X$ implies $J \vDash X$.

4. Let $X = \exists x_1 \cdots \exists x_m \forall y_1 \cdots \forall y_n Y$, where Y is quantifier-free. Show that every model of X contains a substructure with a domain at most $n+1$ elements, which is also a model of X. Conclude from this that a sentence of the form $\forall y \exists x Pxy$ is never equivalent to one in the form X.

5. Let $I = (A, \phi)$ and $J = (B, \psi)$ be structures for a first order language L. Define the *product structure* $I \times J = (A \times B, \theta)$ by the following:

   (i) For an n-ary predicate P, $((a_1, b_1), \ldots, (a_n, b_n)) \in \theta(P)$ iff $(a_1, \ldots, a_n) \in \phi(P)$ and $(b_1, \ldots, b_n) \in \psi(P)$.
   (ii) For an n-ary function symbol f,
   $\theta(f)((a_1, b_1), \ldots, (a_n, b_n)) = (\phi(f)(a_1, \ldots, a_n), \psi(f)(b_1, \ldots, b_n))$.
   (iii) For a constant in L, $\theta(c) = (\phi(c), \psi(c))$.

   Show the following:

   (a) The product structure K is indeed a structure.
   (b) If L is such that both I and J are groups, then K is also a group.
   (c) If L is such that both I and J are fields, then K need not be a field.

6. Let X be a sentence in the form $\forall x_1 \cdots \forall x_n Y$, where the quantifier-free formula Y has no occurrence of any function symbol.

   (a) Give a procedure to determine whether X is valid.
   (b) Give a procedure to determine whether X is satisfiable.
   (c) What happens to your procedures if function symbols are allowed to occur in X?
   (d) Can you modify the procedures so that they would work in the presence of function symbols?

7. Given that a formula has a finite model, can you describe a procedure that constructs one such model?

8. Show that if a sentence has a model of m elements, then it has models of n elements for each $n > m$ and also it has an infinite model.

9. Let X be a closed formula having only unary (monadic) predicates and having no function symbols. (X is a sentence of the monadic first order logic.) Let I be a model of X. Define an equivalence relation on the domain of I by: a is equivalent to b iff for each predicate P occurring in X, $P'(a)$ holds whenever $P'(b)$ holds. Show that the set of equivalence classes also forms a model of X. Use this to show that if a sentence X of monadic first order logic is satisfiable, then it has a finite model. Can you have a procedure to decide whether such a sentence is satisfiable?
10. A sentence in monadic first order logic is said to be in **miniscope form** if whenever $\forall xY$ or $\exists xY$ is a subformula, the only free variable in Y is x. Show that each sentence of monadic first order logic is equivalent to one in miniscope form.
11. Formulate and prove the compactness theorem and the Skolem-Löwenheim theorem using systematic tableaux.
12. Consider the proof systems FC, FND, GFC, and FT. Assume adequacy of one of them and try proving adequacy of all the others to FL.
13. Assume compactness for PL. Using Herbrand's theorem, prove compactness of FL.
14. Let Σ be a set of formulas, where each predicate is monadic and where no function symbols are used. Prove that if Σ is satisfiable, then there exists a finite state-model of Σ. [Hint: What could be the Herbrand model of Σ?]
15. Prove that the satisfiability problem for FL is not decidable, but
16. Prove that the satisfiability problem for monadic first order logic is decidable.
17. *Craig's interpolation*: Let X, Y be formulas having at least one common atomic subformula. A formula Z having all its predicates among the common ones of X and Y is called an **interpolant** of $X \to Y$ iff $\models X \to Z$ and $\models Z \to Y$. Show that, if $\models X \to Y$, then either X is unsatisfiable or Y is valid or $X \to Y$ has an interpolant. Show also that whenever an interpolant of $X \to Y$ exists, there is, in fact, an interpolant in which all the constants are among the common constants of X and Y.
18. *Beth's Definability Theorem*: Let Σ be a set of sentences, and let P be an n-ary predicate. Let P' be an n-ary predicate different from P such that P' does not occur in any sentence of Σ. Let Σ' be the set of sentences obtained from those of Σ by replacing each occurrence of P by P'. Prove that if

$$\Sigma \cup \Sigma' \models \forall x_1 \cdots \forall x_n (P(x_1, \ldots, x_n) \leftrightarrow P'(x_1, \ldots, x_n)),$$

then there exists a formula $X(x_1, \ldots, x_n)$ with free variables from $x_1, \ldots, x_n$ such that

$$S \models \forall x_1 \cdots \forall x_n (P(x_1, \ldots, x_n) \leftrightarrow X(x_1, \ldots, x_n)).$$

Informally, we thus say: "if an n-ary predicate is defined implicitly by a set of sentences Σ, then it is also defined explicitly by Σ." [See Fitting (1996).]
19. Let I and J be two structures with domain as D and E, respectively for a first order language L. Let (D, ϕ) and (E, ψ) be the interpretations that interpret L in I and J, respectively. The structures I and J are called *isomorphic*, iff there exists a one-one onto function $F : D \to E$ that satisfies the following:

(i) $F(\phi(c)) = \psi(c)$ for each constant of L.
(ii) $F(\phi(g)(d_1,\ldots,d_n)) = \psi(g)(F(d_1),\ldots,F(d_n))$ for each n-ary function symbol g.
(iii) $(a_1,\ldots,a_m) \in \phi(P)$ iff $(F(a_1),\ldots,F(a_n)) \in \psi(P)$ for each m-ary predicate P of L.
(iv) $I \vDash S$ iff $J \vDash S$ for each sentence S of L.

The structures I and J are called *elementarily equivalent* iff "for each sentence S of L, S is true in I iff S is true in J". Show the following:

(a) Two isomorphic structures are necessarily elementarily equivalent.
(b) Two elementarily equivalent structures need not be isomorphic. [Hint: What about the nonstandard model of arithmetic?]

20. Let M be a model of arithmetic non-isomorphic to the standard model $\mathbb{N}$. prove the following:
   (a) M contains an isomorphic copy of $\mathbb{N}$.
   (b) M has an infinite number, i.e., an element which is larger than all numbers in $\mathbb{N}$.
   (c) M contains a decreasing infinite sequence.
21. Let L be a language, and let I be a structure for L. Prove that the theory of I, which is the set of all sentences of L true in I, is maximally consistent.
22. For a set of sentences S, let $\mathbb{M}(S)$ denote the set of all models of S. Let Σ and Γ be sets of sentences such that $\Sigma \cup \Gamma$ is inconsistent. Show that there exists a sentence X such that $\mathbb{M}(\Sigma) \subseteq \mathbb{M}(\{X\})$ and $\mathbb{M}(\Gamma) \subseteq \mathbb{M}(\{\neg X\})$. [Hint: Apply compactness.]
23. Does there exist an equation in Group theory which is true in all finite groups, and false in all infinite groups? Why or why not?
24. Let Σ be a set of sentences of a first order language L. The set Σ is called *negation complete* iff for each sentence S of L, either $\Sigma \vdash S$ or $\Sigma \vdash \neg S$. We also define the theory of Σ as $Th(\Sigma) = \{S : S \text{ is a sentence of } L \text{ and } \Sigma \vdash S\}$. Prove that a consistent set Σ of sentences is negation complete iff $Th(\Sigma)$ is maximally consistent.
25. Let Σ be a decidable set of sentences of a first order language L. Prove the following:
   (a) An algorithm exists, which outputs all sentences of $Th(\Sigma)$.
   (b) $Th(\Sigma)$ is decidable iff Σ is negation complete.
26. Let T_1 be a sub-theory of a theory T_2, over the same first order language L. Show that if T_1 is negation complete and T_2 is satisfiable, then $T_1 = T_2$.
27. A first order axiomatic theory with infinitely many constants $c_0, c_1, c_2, \ldots$, is called ω-inconsistent iff there exists a unary predicate P in the theory such that when interpreted in $\mathbb{N}$, all the sentences

$$\exists x \neg P(x),\ P(c_0),\ P(c_1),\ P(c_2),\ \ldots$$

are provable in the theory. When the constant c_i is interpreted as the natural number i, and P as a subset of $\mathbb{N}$, we see that at least one of the above sentences must be false. Does it mean that each ω-inconsistent system is inconsistent?

28. A first order axiomatic theory with infinitely many constants $c_0, c_1, c_2, \ldots$ is called ω-incomplete iff there exists a unary predicate P in the theory such that $P(c_0), P(c_1), P(c_2), \ldots$ are all provable but $\forall x P(x)$ is not provable. Is it possible to interpret an ω-incomplete theory in $\mathbb{N}$ where each c_i is interpreted as the natural number i?
29. (Rosser): Abbreviate the formula $\exists y(Proof(y,x) \wedge \forall z((z < y) \rightarrow \neg Proof(z,w))$ to $Prf(x)$, where w is the Gödel number of the negation of the formula whose Gödel number is x. Show that a formula $R(x)$ of $\mathbb{A}$ with a single free variable x is provable in $\mathbb{A}$ iff $Prf(g(R(x)))$ is provable in $\mathbb{A}$. [While Gödel's sentence says that "I am not provable", Rosser's sentence says that "For any witness that I am provable, there is a smaller number that is a witness that I am refutable."]
30. Formalize the sentence "If ZFC is consistent, then consistency of ZFC cannot be proved by using its own proof machinery". Try a proof of this statement mimicking the proof of unprovability of consistency of arithmetic.

Chapter 11

Modal Logic K

11.1 INTRODUCTION

Let p and q be two propositions. Consider the following argument:

p is valid. $p \to q$ is valid. Therefore, q is valid.

Now, how do you symbolize this argument in PL? Here we have three atomic sentences:

$A : p$ is valid. $\quad B : p \to q$ is valid. $\quad C : q$ is valid.

The argument is symbolized as

$$\{A, B\} \mathrel{!\vdash} C.$$

Though we know that the argument is correct, there is no way to prove it *in* PL.

What about FL? Here, we can go a bit deeper into analysing the argument. Suppose that we denote 'is valid' as a unary predicate $P(\cdot)$. The argument would be symbolized as

$$\{P(p),\, P(p \to q)\} \mathrel{!\vdash} P(q).$$

But a proposition cannot occur in the argument of a predicate, only a term is allowed over there. So, symbolization fails. But suppose we write "$\cdots$ is valid" as an operator, just like the unary connective $\neg$, and try to construct a new logic, then? We may take $\vDash x$ for "x is valid". But it will possibly confuse with the "entailment relation". Well, let us write "x is valid" as $\Box x$ (Read it as box x.). Then, the symbolization would lead to the consequence:

$$\{\Box p,\, \Box(p \to q)\} \mathrel{!\vdash} \Box q.$$

It looks feasible, but we have to do so many things afresh, if we accept this symbolization. We have to allow such constructions syntactically and then give formal meaning to these constructs.

EXAMPLE 11.1. Symbolize: Anyone whose parents are dead is an orphan. Yanka believes that his parents are dead. Therefore, Yanka believes that he is an orphan.

With $D(x)$ for "x is dead", $O(x)$ for "x is orphan", $B(x,z)$ for "x believes z" and a for the constant "Yanka", you would symbolize the argument as

$$\{\forall x(D(x) \to O(x)), B(a, D(a))\} \mathrel{!\vdash} B(a, O(a)).$$

But this is syntactically wrong since the predicates D and O cannot occur as arguments of another predicate B. Further, the symbols D and O cannot be taken as functions since $D(x) \to O(x)$ would then be syntactically wrong.

The argument seems to be all right, but we are not able to symbolize it into FL. When an old theory is inappropriate, we create new theories. Let us try writing "Yanka believes" as an operator, say, $\Box$. Then our symbolization would look like

$$\{\forall x(D(x) \to O(x)),\ \Box D(a)\} \mathrel{!\vdash} \Box O(a).$$

To take some more examples, consider the following:

Yanka is bold.
Yanka is possibly bold.
Yanka ought to be bold.
Yanka must not be bold.
Yanka appears to be bold.
Yanka is necessarily bold.
Yanka is known to be bold.
Yanka is believed to be bold.
Yanka is supposed to be bold.
Yanka is obliged to be bold.
Yanka is permitted to be bold.
Yanka is not free not to be bold.
Yanka cannot afford to to be bold.

Except the first sentence all the others are modal sentences; they modify the first sentence in some way or the other. This is why the name "modal logics", and we will see later why this name is in plural. Out of all the above modalities (and possibly many more not written above), we take up two catch words "necessarily" and "possibly" as our basics. Other modalities will be treated as different readings of these basic ones. Different readings of these modalities may give rise to altogether different logics. As you progress through this chapter, you will understand how this is done.

Exercises for § 11.1

Let $\Box X$ mean 'It is necessary that X' and let $\Diamond X$ mean 'It is possible that X. Which of $\Box X$ or $\Diamond X$ or their negations, is closer to the modality described below?

1. It is known that X.
2. It was the case that X.
3. It will be the case that X.
4. It is sometimes the case that X.
5. It is always the case that X.
6. It is irrelevant to the case at hand that X.

11.2 SYNTAX AND SEMANTICS OF K

The logic K is an extension of PL; it has two more connectives $\Box$ (read as box) for *necessity*, and $\Diamond$ (read as diamond) for *possibility*. The alphabet of the language of K consists of all propositional variables $p_0, p_1, \ldots$, unary connectives $\neg, \Box, \Diamond$, binary connectives $\wedge, \vee, \rightarrow, \leftrightarrow$, propositional constants $\top, \bot$, and), (as punctuation marks.

The propositional constants $\top, \bot$ and the propositional variables together are called **atomic modal propositions**, or *atomic modal formulas*.

As in PL, you may choose a shorter list of connectives and propositional constants or a longer list including all the binary truth functions such as $\uparrow, \downarrow$, etc. **Modal propositions** are defined recursively by the following formation rules:

1. Each atomic modal proposition is a modal proposition.
2. If x is a modal proposition, then $\neg x, \Box x, \Diamond x$ are modal propositions.
3. If x, y are modal propositions, then so are $(x \wedge y), (x \vee y), (x \rightarrow y), (x \leftrightarrow y)$.
4. Each modal proposition is generated by applying recursively one or more of the rules (1)-(3).

Using the symbol p as a variable ranging over $\{p_i : i \in \mathbb{N}\}$, the grammar of modal propositions (written generically as z below) in the Bacus-Naur form can be given as

$$z ::= \top \mid \bot \mid p \mid \neg z \mid \Box z \mid \Diamond z \mid (z \wedge z) \mid (z \vee z) \mid (z \rightarrow z) \mid (z \leftrightarrow z)$$

We use the abbreviation **mp** for a modal proposition. The parse tree of an mp is a binary tree with branch points (non-leaf nodes) as the connectives and leaves as atomic mps.

For instance, the parse tree for the mp $\Diamond(\Box(p \leftrightarrow \neg p) \wedge \Diamond(\Diamond(q \rightarrow p) \vee \neg q))$ is given in Figure 11.1. Analogous to PL, unique parsing holds in K.

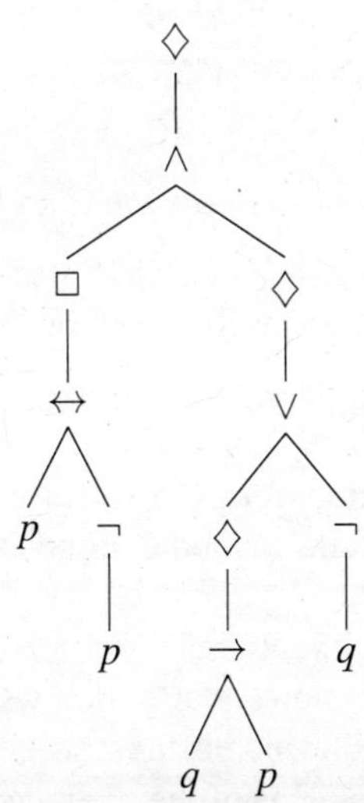

Figure 11.1: Parse tree for $\Diamond(\Box(p \leftrightarrow \neg p) \wedge \Diamond(\Diamond(q \rightarrow p) \vee \neg q))$

Theorem 11.1 (Unique Parsing in K). *If z is a modal proposition, then z is in exactly one of the following forms:*

$$\top,\ \bot,\ p,\ \neg x,\ \Box x,\ \Diamond x,\ (x\wedge y),\ (x\vee y),\ (x\to y),\ (x\leftrightarrow y)$$

for unique propositional variable p, and unique modal propositions x and y.

The expression $\Diamond(\Box(p\leftrightarrow\neg p)\Box(\Diamond(q\to p)\vee\neg q))$ is not an mp, because $\Diamond$ is a unary connective. $\Box(p\leftrightarrow\neg p)\wedge(\Diamond(q\to p)\vee\neg q)$ is not an mp, since outer brackets are missing. However, we now make it a convention to omit the outer parentheses. We also extend the precedence rules of PL, giving the unary connectives $\neg,\Box,\Diamond$ the same and the highest precedence. Next in the hierarchy are $\wedge$ and $\vee$. The connectives $\to,\leftrightarrow$ receive the least precedence.

Sometimes we override the precedence rules and use extra parentheses for easy reading. Further, we will not be rigid about writing the atomic mps as $p_0,p_1,\ldots$; we will rather use any other symbol, say $p,q,\ldots$, but mention that it is an atomic mp. You can define sub-mps just like sub-propositions in PL or subformulas in FL. They are well defined due to unique parsing.

Once the syntax is clear, we must discuss the semantics. The connectives $\neg,\wedge,\vee,\to,\leftrightarrow$ have the same meanings in K, as in PL, though the meanings of $\Box$ and $\Diamond$ complicate their use a bit. The symbols $\Box$ and $\Diamond$ may be interpreted in various ways as mentioned in § 11.1.

In the metalogic of PL, we may read the modalities as in the following:

$\Box$: it is valid that $\qquad$ $\Diamond$: it is satisfiable that

Recall that a proposition z in PL is valid iff it is evaluated to 1 (true) under each interpretation. We now consider each such interpretation as a **world**. A world is sometimes referred to as a *point*, a *situation*, a *place*, a *state*, etc.

Reading $\Box p$ as "p is valid", we see that

$\Box p$ is true iff p is valid iff p is true in each world.

What about the iterated modalities, say, the truth of $\Box\Box p$?

> $\Box\Box p$ is true iff $\Box p$ is true in each world iff it is true that p is true in each world iff p is true in each world iff $\Box p$ is true.

While considering other modalities, e.g., read $\Box$ as "Yanka knows that", we may have to define a world differently. Here, a world may be a set of all propositions that Yanka knows, etc. In abstract terms, a world would be taken as any object, a primary object. In giving meanings to modal propositions, we would start with a set of worlds.

When we read $\Box$ as "Yanka knows that", the iterated modality $\Box\Box p$ may be read more meaningfully as "Yanka knows that he knows p". Clearly, this sentence is different from "Yanka knows p", which is the translation of $\Box p$.

The point is that in some readings of the modal connectives the iterated modalities may not yield anything new, while other readings may still distinguish between the iterated modalities. We thus need to give meaning to "$\Box p$ is true" as well as to "$\Box p$ is true in a world".

We answer this problem with a relation defined over the set of worlds. This relation is, again, a primitive concept; it should *come* along with the set of worlds. This relation is called an *accessibility relation*, an agreed phrase taken for convenience. With this relation on the set of worlds, the worlds themselves become accessible from each other. The accessible relation on a particular set of worlds need not be symmetric; so we must distinguish between "x is accessible from y" and "y accessible from x". Notice that we require not only a set but a relational structure for giving meanings to the modal connectives.

Now $\Box p$ would be true in a world w if p is true in each world accessible from w. In the case of $\Box$ as validity, each world (an interpretation) is accessible from every other world, and also from itself. Thus, $\Box\Box p$ will be forcefully read as $\Box p$ hinting at self assertion of utterances in natural languages. (Do you see the hint?) If we do not agree that $\Box\Box p$ be read as $\Box p$, then, of course, the accessibility relation must be different. As a starting point for the semantics of K, we define a relational structure of worlds and the accessibility relation among them, as in the following.

A **frame** is an ordered pair (W,R), where W is a set, called the set of worlds, and R is a binary relation on W ($R \subseteq W \times W$), called the **accessibility relation**. For worlds $u, w \in W$, read wRu as u is accessible from w.

A frame is not sufficient to give meanings (of truth and falsity) to all modal propositions. We must specify when an mp is true at a world. Analogous to PL-interpretations, each world w may be considered as a mapping from the set of atomic propositions to the set $\{0,1\}$ of truth values. Then we would define **p is true at the world w** iff $w(p) = 1$. We write $w \Vdash p$ whenever p is true at w. We also read $w \Vdash p$ as w makes p true.

Recall that we had alternate semantics for PL, where an interpretation was taken as a set of literals, or of propositional variables. Similarly, we may regard each world w as a subset of the set of all atomic propositions which happen to be true at w. That is, we can associate the world w with the mapping $f_w : \{p_i : i \in \mathbb{N}\} \to \{0,1\}$, or with the set $S_w = \{p_i : i \in \mathbb{N} \text{ and } f_w(p_i) = 1\}$.

This association can be brought in by another mapping ϕ, which would take each world to f_w or to S_w, depending upon which way we want to go about. Nonetheless, they are equivalent. In the former case, we have $\phi(w) = f_w$, where

$$\phi : W \to \text{the set of all functions from } \{p_i : i \in \mathbb{N}\} \text{ to } \{0,1\}.$$

And in the latter case, we have $\phi(w) = S_w$, where

$$\phi : W \to \text{the power set of } \{p_i : i \in \mathbb{N}\}.$$

Alternatively, we can associate with each p_i, the set of worlds where p_i is true. One more alternative: ϕ can be defined as a map from $W \times \{p_i : i \in \mathbb{N}\}$ to $\{0,1\}$ so that $\phi(w, p_i) = 1$ means that p_i is true in the world w. All these approaches are, any way, equivalent. Why? We remember these alternatives and choose the second one for defining a model.

A model here, unlike PL, is simply an interpretation where a modal proposition may or may not hold. It would have been better to call these as interpretations rather than as models. But current practice uses the word "interpretation" for PL, and a "model" for modal logics. Also, a model in modal logics is defined for a logic (as the concept of an interpretation is defined for PL), and we do not say "model of an mp".

A **model** of K is a triple (W, R, ϕ), where the pair (W, R) is a frame, and ϕ is a mapping from W to the power set of $\{p_i : i \in \mathbb{N}\}$ associating each world $w \in W$ to a subset $\phi(w)$ of atomic propositions. The mapping ϕ is called the **world truth mapping**. The model $M = (W, R, \phi)$ is said to be **based upon the frame** $F = (W, R)$, and the frame F is said to be an **underlying frame** of the model M.

The set $\phi(w)$ consists of all atomic propositions which are true at the world w. Moreover, each world w is *propositional*, in the sense that all the laws of PL hold in each world. For example, if $p \in \phi(w)$, i.e., if p is true at the world w, then $\neg p$ cannot be true at w, i.e., $\neg p \notin \phi(w)$. The new connectives $\Box$ and $\Diamond$ play roles in navigating across the worlds via the accessibility relation. We define formally how a modal proposition becomes true at (in) a world w.

Let $M = (W, R, \phi)$ be a model of K. Let x, y denote arbitrary modal propositions. Let $w \in W$ be a world. The relation $w \Vdash x$ (w **satisfies** x) is defined recursively:

(1) $w \Vdash \top$, and $w \nVdash \bot$.

(2) $w \Vdash p$ iff $p \in \phi(w)$, for any atomic proposition p.

(3) $w \Vdash \neg x$ iff $w \nVdash x$.

(4) $w \Vdash x \wedge y$ iff $w \Vdash x$ and $w \Vdash y$.

(5) $w \Vdash x \vee y$ iff $w \Vdash x$ or $w \Vdash y$.

(6) $w \Vdash x \rightarrow y$ iff $w \nVdash x$ or $w \Vdash y$.

(7) $w \Vdash x \leftrightarrow y$ iff either $w \Vdash x$ and $w \Vdash y$, or $w \nVdash x$ and $w \nVdash y$.

(8) $w \Vdash \Box x$ iff for each world $u \in W$ with wRu, $u \Vdash x$.

(9) $w \Vdash \Diamond x$ iff for some world $u \in W$ with wRu, $u \Vdash x$.

Due to unique parsing, the satisfaction relation is well defined. We may read the meaning of the mp $\Box x$ and $\Diamond x$ as follows:

$\Box x$ is true at the world w iff x is true in each world accessible from w.
$\Diamond x$ is true at the world w iff x is true in some world accessible from w.

Since satisfaction or truth at a world w depends not only on the world w, but also on the model M, we should better write $w \Vdash x$ as $M, w \Vdash x$. However, when the model M is clear from a given context, we would continue writing $w \Vdash x$. It is read in many ways such as:

the world w **satisfies** the modal proposition x,
the world w **verifies** the modal proposition x,
the world w **makes** the modal proposition x **true**, or as
the modal proposition x **is true at** (in) the world w.

When a world w does not satisfy an mp x, we say that w **falsifies** x, and write $w \nVdash x$.

EXAMPLE 11.2. Let $M = (W, R, \phi)$ be the model with

$$W = \{w, u\},\ R = \{(w, u), (u, u)\},\ \phi(w) = \varnothing, \text{ and } \phi(u) = \{p\} \text{ for atomic } p.$$

Are the mps $p, \Box p, \Box\Box p, \Box p \rightarrow \Box\Box p, \Box\Box p \rightarrow p$ true at the world w?

Look at the relation R of the model M. It says that the world w is accessible from u, and the world u is accessible from itself; nothing else. Since each binary relation can be depicted as a graph, we first represent our model as a graph. Each node of this graph is a world. A node corresponding to the world w will be written as $\textcircled{w}$. If $(w,u) \in R$, that is, if wRu, then we draw a directed edge (line segment) from the node w to the node u. That is, "u is accessible from w" is depicted by

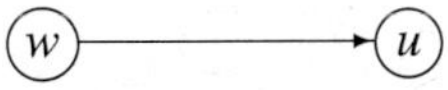

The mapping ϕ specifies which atomic propositions (mp) are true at which world. We show it in a graph by writing the satisfaction symbol, the double turnstile ($\Vdash$) as a superscript to the world (or as a subscript or just following the world) and then writing out all those atomic propositions which are true at that world. For instance,

$$\textcircled{u}^{\Vdash p} \text{ means } p \text{ is true in the world } u.$$

In our case, $\phi(w) = \varnothing$; so nothing is labelled with the world w. Since u is accessible from itself; there is a loop around u. Thus the model M is depicted as

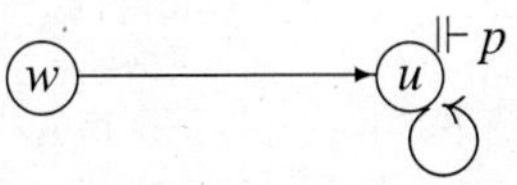

We see that $w \nVdash p$. What about $\Box p$? $w \Vdash \Box p$ iff $x \Vdash p$ for each world x accessible from w. Here, u is the only world accessible from w, and $u \Vdash p$. Hence $w \Vdash \Box p$.

Since u is the only world accessible from w, and u is the only world accessible from u itself, $w \Vdash \Box\Box p$ iff $u \Vdash \Box p$ iff $u \Vdash p$. We know that $u \Vdash p$. Therefore, $w \Vdash \Box\Box p$.

We abbreviate the iterated modality $\Box\Box \cdots \Box (n \text{ times})\ p$ to $\Box^n p$, for any $n \geq 0$, with the convention that $\Box^0 p = p$.

By induction, it follows that $w \Vdash \Box^n p$, for each positive integer n. Since $w \nVdash p$ and $w \Vdash \Box^n p$, for any $n \geq 1$, we see that $w \nVdash \Box p \to p$.

What about $p \to \Box p$? Clearly, $w \Vdash p \to \Box p$. In the model M, $w \Vdash \Box^m p \to \Box^n p$ for any $m,n \in \mathbb{N}$ with $n \neq 0$, and $w \Vdash p \to p$.

EXAMPLE 11.3. Which of the following mps are true at the world w in M?

(a) $\Box p \to \Box\Diamond p$ (b) $\Diamond p \to \Box\Diamond p$ (c) $\Box p \to \Diamond\Box p$ (d) $\Diamond p \to \Diamond\Box p$

M : 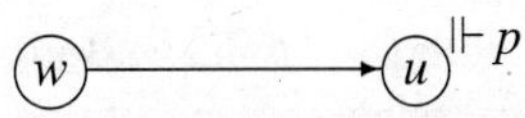

(a) $w \Vdash \Box p \to \Box\Diamond p$ iff ($w \nVdash \Box p$ or $w \Vdash \Box\Diamond p$). Now, $w \nVdash \Box p$ iff for some world accessible from w, p is false at that world. There is only one world, namely, u which is accessible from w and $u \Vdash p$. Hence $w \Vdash \Box p$. On the other hand, $w \Vdash \Box\Diamond p$ iff $u \Vdash \Diamond p$. But there is no world accessible from u. Thus, $u \nVdash \Diamond p$; consequently, $w \nVdash \Box\Diamond p$. Summing up, $w \nVdash \Box p \to \Box\Diamond p$.

(b) $w \Vdash \Diamond p$ as u is a world accessible from w and $u \Vdash p$. We have seen in (a) that $w \nVdash \Box\Diamond p$. Hence $w \nVdash \Diamond p \to \Box\Diamond p$.

(c) Since u is the only world accessible from w, for $w \Vdash \Diamond\Box p$, we require $u \Vdash \Box p$. This is so provided each world accessible from u satisfies p. As there is no world which is accessible from u, the condition is satisfied vacuously. So, $w \Vdash \Diamond\Box p$.

(d) Using (c), we conclude that $w \Vdash \Diamond p \to \Diamond\Box p$.

EXAMPLE 11.4. In Example 11.3, which mps in (a)-(d) are true at the world u?

Since each world accessible from u (there is none) satisfies p, $u \Vdash \Box p$. Similarly, $u \Vdash \Box\Diamond p$. Again, as there is no world accessible from u, we have $u \nVdash \Diamond p$. Similarly, $u \nVdash \Diamond\Box p$. Therefore, u satisfies $\Box p \to \Box\Diamond p$, $\Diamond p \to \Box\Diamond p$, $\Diamond p \to \Diamond\Box p$ but it falsifies $\Box p \to \Diamond\Box p$.

Comparing with first order semantics, a world is like a state, and a model is like an interpretation. In K, the model $M = (W, R, \phi)$ **satisfies** or **verifies** an mp x, written as $M \vDash x$, iff for each world $w \in W$, $w \Vdash x$.

For instance, in Example 11.3, $M \vDash \Diamond p \to \Diamond\Box p$. Besides, $M \nvDash \Box p \to \Box\Diamond p$ since $w \nVdash \Box p \to \Box\Diamond p$. Also, $w \nVdash \Diamond p \to \Box\Diamond p$ and $u \nVdash \Box p \to \Diamond\Box p$ imply $M \nvDash \Diamond p \to \Box\Diamond p$ and $M \nvDash \Box p \to \Diamond\Box p$.

EXAMPLE 11.5. Let $M = (\{u, v, w\}, \{(u, v), (u, w), (v, v), (v, w), (w, v)\}, \phi)$ be the model with $\phi(u) = \{q\}$, $\phi(v) = \{p, q\}$ and $\phi(w) = \{p\}$. Determine whether $M \vDash \Box(p \wedge q) \to (\Box p \wedge \Box q)$ and $M \vDash \Box p \wedge \Box q \to \Box(p \wedge q)$.

The model M is depicted by the graph in Figure 11.2. We have three worlds u, v, w in our model M, and mps p, q, $p \wedge q$, $\Box p$, $\Box q$, $\Box(p \wedge q)$, $\Box p \wedge \Box q$. We know already that $u \Vdash q$, $v \Vdash p$, $v \Vdash q$, $w \Vdash p$, $u \nVdash p$, and $w \nVdash q$.

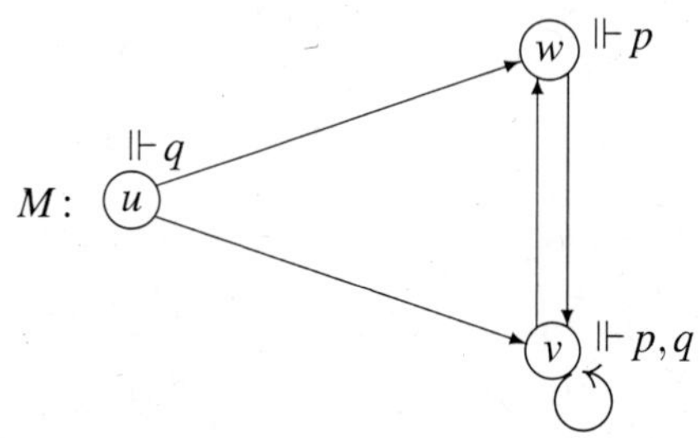

Figure 11.2: Model of Example 11.5

The worlds accessible from u are v and w, and both $v \Vdash p$, $w \Vdash p$ hold. Hence, $u \Vdash \Box p$. But, $u \nVdash \Box q$ as the world w is accessible from u but $w \nVdash q$.

The worlds accessible from v are v and w. Both $v \Vdash p$ and $w \Vdash p$ hold. So, $v \Vdash \Box p$. However, $v \nVdash \Box q$ as w is accessible from v but $w \nVdash q$.

Similarly, $w \Vdash \Box p$ and $w \Vdash \Box q$ as the only world accessible from w is v, and $v \Vdash p$, $v \Vdash q$. Since w is accessible from u, $u \nVdash \Box(p \wedge q)$. But $w \nVdash p \wedge q$. Further, $v \nVdash \Box(p \wedge q)$ since $w \nVdash p \wedge q$; and $w \Vdash \Box(p \wedge q)$ as $v \Vdash p \wedge q$. We thus have a summary in Table 11.1; where we write r for $\Box(p \wedge q)$ and s for $\Box p \wedge \Box q$.

The last two columns in Table 11.1 show that all the worlds (in M) satisfy both the mps $r \to s$ and $s \to r$. Therefore,

$$M \vDash \Box(p \wedge q) \to \Box p \wedge \Box q, \quad M \vDash \Box p \wedge \Box q \to \Box(p \wedge q).$$

Table 11.1: Table for Example 11.5, $r = \Box(p \wedge q)$, $s = \Box p \wedge \Box q$

	p	q	$p \wedge q$	$\Box p$	$\Box q$	r	s	$r \to s$	$s \to r$
u	$\nVdash$	$\Vdash$	$\nVdash$	$\Vdash$	$\nVdash$	$\nVdash$	$\nVdash$	$\Vdash$	$\Vdash$
v	$\Vdash$	$\Vdash$	$\Vdash$	$\Vdash$	$\nVdash$	$\nVdash$	$\nVdash$	$\Vdash$	$\Vdash$
w	$\Vdash$	$\nVdash$	$\nVdash$	$\Vdash$	$\Vdash$	$\Vdash$	$\Vdash$	$\Vdash$	$\Vdash$

EXAMPLE 11.6. Determine whether the following model M satisfies the mps
(a) $\Box(p \vee q) \to \Box p \vee \Box q$ (b) $\Box(p \wedge q) \to \Box p \wedge \Box q$

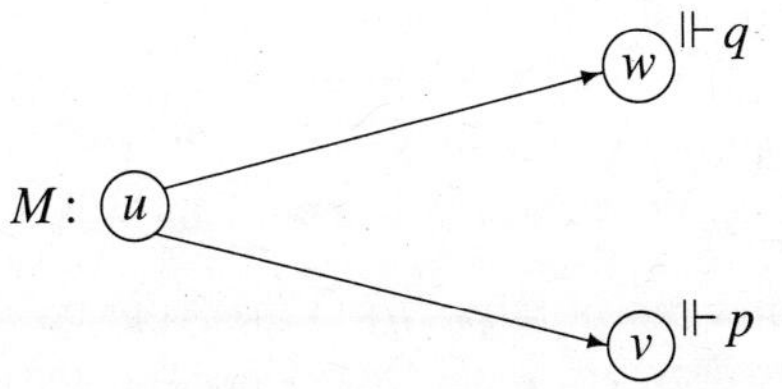

(a) Here, $u \Vdash \Box(p \vee q)$, as both the worlds v, w accessible from u satisfy $p \vee q$. But $u \nVdash \Box p$ as the world w accessible from u does not satisfy p. Again, $u \nVdash \Box q$ as $v \nVdash q$. Therefore, $u \nVdash \Box p \vee \Box q$ and consequently, $M \nVdash \Box(p \vee q) \to \Box p \vee \Box q$.

(b) $u \nVdash \Box p$, $u \nVdash \Box q$ but $v \Vdash \Box p$, $v \Vdash \Box q$ vacuously as there is no world accessible from v. Also $w \Vdash \Box p$ and $w \Vdash \Box q$. Thus, $u \nVdash \Box p \wedge \Box q$, $v \Vdash \Box p \wedge \Box q$, and $w \Vdash \Box p \wedge \Box q$. Since v is a world accessible from u, and $v \nVdash p \wedge q$, $u \nVdash \Box(p \wedge q)$. Again vacuously, $v \Vdash \Box(p \wedge q)$ and $w \Vdash \Box(p \wedge q)$. So, all the worlds satisfy $\Box(p \wedge q) \to \Box p \wedge \Box q$; consequently, $M \vDash \Box(p \wedge q) \to \Box p \wedge \Box q$.

Exercises for § 11.2

1. A says to C about B: "At least I knew he thought I thought he thought I slept." Who knew what?

2. Which of the given mps are true at the world w of the model M of the corresponding Example?

   Example 11.2: p, $\Box p$, $\Diamond\Diamond p$, $\Diamond p \to \Diamond\Diamond p$, $\Diamond\Diamond p \to p$
   Example 11.3: $\Diamond p \to \Diamond\Box p$, $\Box p \to \Diamond\Box p$, $\Diamond p \to \Box\Diamond p$, $\Box p \to \Box\Diamond p$

3. Determine whether the model M of Example 11.5 satisfies the following mps:

$$\Box(p \vee q) \to (\Box p \vee \Box q), \quad \Box p \vee \Box q \to \Box(p \vee q)$$

4. Let w be a world in a model $M = (W, R, \phi)$. Show that

   (a) $w \Vdash \Diamond\top$ iff there is at least one world accessible from w.
   (b) $w \Vdash \Box\bot$ iff no world is accessible from w.

   Conclude that $M \vDash \top$ but M may not satisfy $\Diamond\top$; and that each world in M falsifies $\bot$, though it may happen that $M \vDash \Box\bot$.

11.3 VALIDITY AND CONSEQUENCE IN K

A model has been taken as a triple (W, R, ϕ), where ϕ prescribes which atomic mps are true at which worlds. The relation $\Vdash$ of satisfaction between worlds and arbitrary mps is an extension of this ϕ from the atomic mps to all mps. The extension must, of course, satisfy the defining properties of $\Vdash$ as discussed earlier. Therefore, we write a model as the triple $(W, R, \Vdash)$ also.

There is a possible confusion in this notation and you should be aware of it. The relation $\Vdash$ changes from one model to another model. Earlier, the notation ϕ was keeping record of it. Now we must write $\Vdash$ as $\Vdash_M$ to remind ourselves of this dependence. As usual, we omit this subscript unless there is any confusion due to involvement of many models in a given context.

A modal proposition x in K is said to be **K-valid** or **valid in K**, and written as $\vDash_K x$ iff for each model M, $M \vDash x$. For simplicity, a K-valid mp x is also called as **valid** and written as $\vDash x$. We write $\nvDash x$ when the mp x is not valid.

EXAMPLE 11.7. Show that $\vDash \Box(p \wedge q) \to \Box p \wedge \Box q$.

We are not going to draw any model here since we are supposed to argue with any arbitrary model. So, let $M = (W, R, \Vdash)$ be any model (any K-model), and let $w \in W$. If $w \nVdash \Box(p \wedge q)$, then $w \Vdash \Box(p \wedge q) \to \Box p \wedge \Box q$. Otherwise, suppose that $w \Vdash \Box(p \wedge q)$. To show that $w \Vdash \Box p \wedge \Box q$, let u be a world accessible from w, i.e., $u \in W$ and wRu. Since $w \Vdash \Box(p \wedge q)$, each world accessible from w satisfies $p \wedge q$, i.e., $u \Vdash p \wedge q$. Then $u \Vdash p$ and $u \Vdash q$. This holds for any arbitrary world u that is accessible from w. Hence, $w \Vdash \Box p$ and $w \Vdash \Box q$. Therefore, $w \Vdash \Box p \wedge \Box q$.

Since w is any arbitrary world in W, $M \vDash \Box(p \wedge q) \to \Box p \wedge \Box q$. Since M is an arbitrary model, $\vDash \Box(p \wedge q) \to \Box p \wedge \Box q$.

In contrast, Example 11.6 shows that $\nvDash \Box(p \vee q) \to \Box p \vee \Box q$.

Some of the important K-valid modal propositions are listed below.

Theorem 11.2 (Laws in K). *In the modal logic K, the following laws hold:*

(1)	CONSTANTS	$\vDash \Box\top \leftrightarrow \top$,	$\vDash \Diamond\bot \leftrightarrow \bot$.
(2)	DE MORGAN	$\vDash \neg\Box p \leftrightarrow \Diamond\neg p$,	$\vDash \neg\Diamond p \leftrightarrow \Box\neg p$.
(3)	$\wedge$-DISTRIBUTIVITY	$\vDash \Box(p \wedge q) \leftrightarrow (\Box p \wedge \Box q)$.	
(4)	$\vee$-DISTRIBUTIVITY	$\vDash \Diamond(p \vee q) \leftrightarrow (\Diamond p \vee \Diamond q)$.	
(5)	$\to$-DISTRIBUTIVITY	$\vDash \Box(p \to q) \to (\Box p \to \Box q)$.	

Many K-valid modal propositions can be obtained by substituting mps in place of propositional variables in PL-valid propositions. This is so because each world in K is propositional and retains validity of PL. See the following theorem.

Theorem 11.3 (Tautological Replacement). *Let p be a propositional variable; A be a proposition (in PL); and let q be a modal proposition. Denote by $A[p := q]$ the modal proposition obtained by substituting each occurrence of p by q in A. If A is valid in PL, then $A[p := q]$ is valid in K.*

Proof. Let $M = (W, R, \Vdash)$ be a model, and let $w \in W$ be a world. Suppose that A is valid in PL. Note that A is also an mp. Since w is propositional, the world w is a PL-interpretation. Since A is valid, $w \Vdash A$.

Further, $w \Vdash A$ holds whether $w \Vdash p$ holds or not. (Imagine $w \Vdash p$ as $w(p) = 1$ and $w \nVdash p$ as $w(p) = 0$.) When p is replaced by q in A, the satisfaction of the resulting formula $A[p := q]$ would not change whether $w \Vdash q$ holds or not. Thus, satisfaction of $A[p := q]$ would be the same as that of A. That is, $w \Vdash A[p := q]$. Since $w \in W$ is any world, $M \vDash A[p := q]$. Since M is an arbitrary model, $A[p := q]$ is K-valid. ♦

Notice that you can substitute many propositional variables by the corresponding mps simultaneously as in Theorem 2.10. You now have a scheme to generate infinitely many K-valid mps using tautologies (of PL). Stretching similarity with PL a bit, we ask: does equivalence replacement hold in K?

We say that the modal propositions A and B are **equivalent** (in K), and write it as $A \equiv_K B$ iff $\vDash_K A \leftrightarrow B$. If there is no confusion, we will drop the subscript K and simply write the equivalence as $A \equiv B$. We also write $Z[A :=_e B]$ for the mp obtained from Z by substituting some or all or no occurrences of A in Z by B, when $A \equiv B$. See Theorem 2.11 and its proof for proving the statement below.

Theorem 11.4 (Equivalence Replacement). *Let A, B and Z be modal propositions. Denote by $Z[A :=_e B]$ the modal proposition obtained from Z by substituting some (or all or no) occurrences of A by B. If $A \equiv B$, then $Z[A :=_e B] \equiv Z$.*

Thus, any instance of a valid modal proposition is again a valid modal proposition. Moreover, in the calculational style, you can write $\vDash Z$ as $Z \equiv \top$, the way you did in PL. There are, of course, many differences between K and PL, the connection being that K is an extension of PL and each world in K is an interpretation in PL.

We want to define the notion of consequence in K. For two propositions (In PL) A and B, we say that $A \vDash B$ when each model of A is also a model of B. For two FL-formulas A and B, the entailment $A \vDash B$ holds whenever each state-model of A is a state-model of B. If A and B are sentences, then $A \vDash B$ holds whenever each model of A is a model of B. The first type of entailment supersedes the second type. The situation in K is similar to that in FL, albeit, we need to keep both the types of entailments.

Let G and L be sets of modal propositions. Let A be a modal proposition. We say that G **weakly entails** A, and write as $G \Rightarrow A$, iff for each model M, if M satisfies all the mps in G, then M satisfies A. You may read $\Rightarrow$ as 'implies' also.

We say that L **strongly entails** A, written as $L \vDash A$, iff for each model $M = (W, R, \Vdash)$ and for each world $w \in W$, if w satisfies all the mps in L, then w satisfies A. You may read $\vDash$ as 'entails'.

Further, A is said to be a **valid consequence with global assumption** G **and local assumption** L, written as $G \Rightarrow L \vDash A$, iff for each model $M = (W, R, \Vdash)$ satisfying all the mps in G and for each world $w \in W$ satisfying all the mps in L, $w \Vdash A$ holds.

Let M be a model, and let w be a world. If Σ is a set of mps, we write $M \vDash \Sigma$ whenever $M \vDash x$ for each $x \in \Sigma$. Similarly, if $w \Vdash x$ holds for each $x \in \Sigma$, we write $w \Vdash \Sigma$. Then, $G \Rightarrow L \vDash A$ holds iff for each model M with $M \vDash G$ and for each world w in M with $w \Vdash L$, one has $w \Vdash A$.

If $G = \varnothing$, then each model M satisfies each mp in G vacuously; the same also happens when $G = \{\top\}$. Then, the validity of the consequence with global assumption G and local assumption L reduces to the stronger entailment from L. That is,

$$\text{both } \varnothing \Rightarrow L \vDash A \text{ and } \top \Rightarrow L \vDash A \text{ are same as } L \vDash A.$$

If $L = \varnothing$, then each world w in M (with $M \vDash G$) satisfies each mp in L vacuously; the same also happens if $L = \{\top\}$. Now the consequence becomes equivalent to the weak entailment from G. That is,

$$\text{both } G \Rightarrow \varnothing \vDash A \text{ and } G \Rightarrow \{\top\} \vDash A \text{ are same as } G \Rightarrow A.$$

It is also clear that strong entailment is stronger than the weak entailment as their names suggest. That is,

$$\text{if } \Sigma \vDash A, \text{ then } \Sigma \Rightarrow A.$$

The converse does not hold, in general; see Example 11.8 below.

Moreover, if any of the sets G or L is a singleton, we will not write the braces around them while writing out the consequence relations, to save space. That is,

$$\{B\} \Rightarrow \{C\} \vDash A \quad \text{will be written as} \quad B \Rightarrow C \vDash A.$$

EXAMPLE 11.8. Show: (a) $\Box p \to p \Rightarrow \Box\Box p \to \Box p$ (b) $\Box p \to p \nvDash \Box\Box p \to \Box p$

(a) We consider all models that satisfy the mp $\Box p \to p$, and then show that any world in such a model also satisfies $\Box\Box p \to \Box p$.

So, let $M = (W, R, \Vdash)$ be a model such that $M \vDash \Box p \to p$. Let $w \in W$ be such that $w \Vdash \Box\Box p$. Let $u \in W$ be a world accessible from w (i.e., wRu). Then $u \Vdash \Box p$. As $M \vDash \Box p \to p$, for each world $v \in W$, $v \Vdash \Box p \to p$. In particular, $u \Vdash \Box p \to p$. Using the fact that $u \Vdash \Box p$, we conclude that $u \Vdash p$. But u is any arbitrary world accessible from w. Hence, $w \Vdash \Box p$. We have shown that if $w \Vdash \Box\Box p$, then $w \Vdash \Box p$. Therefore, $w \Vdash \Box\Box p \to \Box p$. This proves that $\Box p \to p \Rightarrow \Box\Box p \to \Box p$.

(b) To show that $\Box p \to p \nvDash \Box\Box p \to \Box p$, consider the model

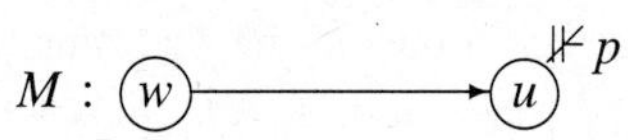

In this model, u satisfies all atomic mps except p. The only world accessible from w is u, and $u \nVdash p$; so $w \nVdash \Box p$. Vacuously, $w \Vdash \Box p \to p$. Further, $w \Vdash \Box\Box p$ iff $u \Vdash \Box p$ iff each world accessible from u satisfies p, which again holds vacuously. But $w \nVdash \Box p$. Hence $w \nVdash \Box\Box p \to \Box p$. Consequently, $\Box p \to p \nvDash \Box\Box p \to \Box p$.

EXAMPLE 11.9. Show that $\Box(p \to q) \vDash \Box p \to \Box q$.

Let $M = (W, R, \Vdash)$ be a model, and let $w \in W$ be a world with $w \Vdash \Box(p \to q)$. If $w \nVdash \Box p$, then $w \Vdash \Box p \to \Box q$, and we are through. Otherwise, assume that $w \Vdash \Box p$. We want to show that $w \Vdash \Box q$. Let u be any world accessible from w. Since $w \Vdash \Box p$, we have $u \Vdash p$. Since $w \Vdash \Box(p \to q)$, we also have $u \Vdash p \to q$. Then, $u \Vdash q$. In this case also, $w \Vdash \Box q$.

Therefore, we conclude that $\Box(p \to q) \vDash \Box p \to \Box q$.

EXAMPLE 11.10. Show that $\Box p \to p \Rightarrow \Box(\neg p \to p) \vDash p \vee \Diamond p$.

Here, $\Box p \to p$ is a global assumption and $\Box(\neg p \to p)$ is a local assumption. So, we consider all models with $\Box p \to p$, and any world w in such a model with $w \Vdash \Box(\neg p \to p)$, and then try to show that w also satisfies p.

Let $M = (W, R, \Vdash)$ be a model, and let $M \vDash \Box p \to p$. Suppose $w \in W$ is a world such that $w \Vdash \Box(\neg p \to p)$. Due to $\to$-distributivity, we have $w \Vdash \Box\neg p \to \Box p$. Then, either $w \nVdash \Box\neg p$ or $w \Vdash \Box p$. If $w \nVdash \Box\neg p$, then $w \Vdash \neg\Box\neg p$. By the law of De Morgan, $\neg\Box\neg p \equiv \Diamond p$. Hence, $w \Vdash \Diamond p$. On the other hand, if $w \Vdash \Box p$, then with $w \Vdash \Box p \to p$ (since $M \vDash \Box p \to p$), we have $w \Vdash p$. In either case, $w \Vdash p \vee \Diamond p$.

We start exploring the properties of the consequence relation in K.

Theorem 11.5 (Monotonicity in K). *Let A be an mp. Let G, G', L, L' be sets of mps such that $G \subseteq G'$ and $L \subseteq L'$. If $G \Rightarrow L \vDash A$, then $G' \Rightarrow L' \vDash A$.*

Proof. Let $G \Rightarrow L \vDash A$. Let $M = (W, R, \Vdash)$ be a model with $M \vDash G'$. Let $w \in W$ satisfy L'. Then, $M \vDash G$ and also $w \Vdash L$. As $G \Rightarrow L \vDash A$, we have $w \Vdash A$. Thus, $G' \Rightarrow L' \vDash A$. ♦

Theorem 11.6 (Deduction Theorem). *Let G and L be sets of mps. Let X and Y be mps. Then the following are true:*

(1) **(LD: Local)** $G \Rightarrow L \cup \{X\} \vDash Y$ *iff* $G \Rightarrow L \vDash X \to Y$.

(2) **(GD: Global)** $G \cup \{X\} \Rightarrow L \vDash Y$ *iff* $G \Rightarrow L \cup \{X, \Box X, \Box\Box X, \ldots\} \vDash Y$.

Unlike a single form for PL, the deduction theorem has two forms in *K*. One, where the antecedent of the conclusion comes to the local premises; and another, where it comes to the global premises in some form. The proof of the Deduction theorem is left as an exercise. Analogous to PL, compactness holds in K; see Exercise 5.

Exercises for § 11.3

1. Prove the laws listed in Theorem 11.2.
2. Using Tautological Replacement show that the following mps are K-valid:
   (a) $\Box p \vee \neg\Box p$
   (b) $\Diamond p \vee \neg\Diamond p$
   (c) $(\Box p \to \Diamond q) \leftrightarrow (\Box p \leftrightarrow (\Box p \wedge \Diamond q))$
   (d) $(\Box p \to (\Diamond q \to \Diamond p)) \to ((\Box p \to \Diamond q) \to (\Box p \to \Diamond p))$
3. Consider the cases $G \subseteq G'$ but $L \nsubseteq L'$; and $G \nsubseteq G'$ but $L \subseteq L'$. Will still the metastatement "If $G \vDash L \Rightarrow A$, then $G' \vDash L' \Rightarrow A$" hold in these cases?
4. Prove Theorem 11.6.
5. (*Compactness of* K) Let G and L be infinite sets of modal propositions, and let A be a modal proposition such that $G \Rightarrow L \vDash A$. Prove that there exist finite subsets G' of G and L' of L such that $G' \Rightarrow L' \vDash A$.

11.4 AXIOMATIC SYSTEM KC

Historically, axiomatic systems for modal logics precede the semantic characterization. Since we have discussed semantics first, we now wish to characterize valid mps through proofs. We will keep the flavour of PC in presenting an axiomatic system, called **KC (K-calculus)** for the logic K. In fact, KC is an extension of PC.

As in PC, the connectives $\wedge, \vee, \leftrightarrow$ and the constants $\top, \bot$ are defined from the basic ones such as $\neg$ and $\rightarrow$. Further, the modal connective $\Diamond$ is defined from $\neg$ and $\Box$ via De Morgan's law: $\Diamond A \equiv \neg\Box\neg A$, now, to be adapted as a definition. So, the basic symbols of KC are the propositional variables, the connectives $\neg, \rightarrow$, and the modal operator $\Box$. The following are the axiom schemes, and the rules of inference of KC:

Axiom Schemes of KC

(A1) $A \rightarrow (B \rightarrow A)$

(A2) $(A \rightarrow (B \rightarrow C)) \rightarrow ((A \rightarrow B) \rightarrow (A \rightarrow C))$

(A3) $(\neg A \rightarrow \neg B) \rightarrow ((\neg A \rightarrow B) \rightarrow A)$

(K) $\Box(X \rightarrow Y) \rightarrow (\Box X \rightarrow \Box Y)$

Rules of Inference of KC

(MP) $$\frac{X \qquad X \rightarrow Y}{Y}$$

(N) $$\frac{X}{\Box X}$$

The rule of inference N stands for **necessitation**. It allows deriving $\Box X$ from X. It means that if X is provable, then $\Box X$ is also provable. It does not assert that $X \rightarrow \Box X$ is provable!

See § 2.3 for the definitions (D1)-(D5) of $\wedge, \vee, \leftrightarrow, \top$, and $\bot$. Along with those, we have the following definition of the modal operator $\Diamond$:

(D) $\Diamond A \mathrel{\hat{=}} \neg\Box\neg A$

Such a definition is used in a proof via the rule of inference (RD), which we repeat below:

(RD) $$\frac{X \mathrel{\hat{=}} Y \qquad Z}{Z[X := Y]} \qquad\qquad \frac{X \mathrel{\hat{=}} Y \qquad Z}{Z[Y := X]}$$

A **proof** in KC is, a finite sequence of mps, each of which is either an axiom (an instance of an axiom scheme) or is derived from earlier mps by an application of an inference rule. The last mp in a proof (sequence) is called a **theorem** in KC. If A is a theorem (in KC), we also say that A is **provable** (in KC) and also that A has a proof; the proof is said to **prove** A in KC. If no other logic is involved, we will simply omit writing "in KC". The fact that an mp A is a theorem in KC is written as $\vdash A$, as a shorthand for $\vdash_{KC} A$.

We will follow the same three-column way of writing proofs. The third column shows the rule or axiom that has been used in the same line. We write 'P' when a premise is used. However, we will make a short cut.

Suppose that you want to show that $\Box p \to \Box p$ is a theorem in KC. Then, you essentially repeat the PC-proof of $p \to p$. Instead of repeating such PC-proofs, we will concentrate on the peculiarity of KC. We thus agree to use all PC theorems as axioms, documenting it as **PC**. Note that this will not affect the effectiveness of the axiomatic system KC since we can always go back to the three axioms of PC and the inference rule MP for deriving the PC-theorems.

Recall the difficulties you have encountered while constructing proofs in PC in the absence of metatheorems such as the deduction theorem and RA. So, instead of going for proofs straight away, we will have some results of this kind. We will not attempt at many such results since our interest is not in generating more and more theorems in KC, but only to show that the logic K can be captured effectively by an axiomatic system.

Theorem 11.7 (Regularity). *The following rule of inference, called regularity, is a derived rule in KC.*

(R) $$\frac{X \to Y}{\Box X \to \Box Y}$$

Proof. The following is a proof of this rule:

1.	$X \to Y$	P
2.	$\Box(X \to Y)$	N
3.	$\Box(X \to Y) \to (\Box X \to \Box Y)$	K
4.	$\Box X \to \Box Y$	MP

♦

Theorem 11.8 (Biconditional Replacement). *Let X, X', Y and Y' be modal propositions such that Y is a substring of X. Let X' be obtained from X by replacing some (or all or no) occurrences of Y by Y'. If $Y \leftrightarrow Y'$ is provable, then $X \leftrightarrow X'$ is also provable.*

Proof. Use induction on the number of occurrences of $\neg$, $\to$, $\Box$ in X. ♦

You may formulate the rule BP corresponding to the Biconditional Replacement. As noted earlier, we use all derived rules of PC as derived rules (e.g., HS) of KC in proofs. We may also use all the connectives of PL along with $\top$ and $\bot$ instead of the only connectives $\neg$ and $\to$.

EXAMPLE 11.11. Show that $\vdash \Box(p \wedge q) \to (\Box p \wedge \Box q)$.

1.	$p \wedge q \to p$	PC
2.	$\Box(p \wedge q) \to \Box p$	R
3.	$p \wedge q \to q$	PC
4.	$\Box(p \wedge q) \to \Box q$	R

5.	$(\Box(p\wedge q)\to\Box p)\to$ $((\Box(p\wedge q)\to\Box q)\to(\Box(p\wedge q)\to(\Box p\wedge\Box q)))$	PC
6.	$(\Box(p\wedge q)\to\Box q)\to(\Box(p\wedge q)\to(\Box p\wedge\Box q))$	2, MP
7.	$\Box(p\wedge q)\to(\Box p\wedge\Box q)$	4, MP

EXAMPLE 11.12. Show that $\vdash(\Box p\wedge\Box q)\to\Box(p\wedge q)$.

1.	$p\to(q\to(p\wedge q))$	PC
2.	$\Box p\to\Box(q\to(p\to q))$	R
3.	$\Box(q\to(p\to q))\to(\Box q\to\Box(p\to q))$	K
4.	$\Box p\to(\Box q\to\Box(p\wedge q))$	HS
5.	$(\Box p\wedge\Box q)\to\Box(p\wedge q)$	PC

EXAMPLE 11.13. Show that $\vdash\Box(p\to q)\wedge\Box(q\to r)\to\Box(p\to r)$.

1.	$\Box(p\to q)\wedge\Box(q\to r)\to\Box((p\to q)\wedge(q\to r))$	Ex.11.12
2.	$(p\to q)\wedge(q\to r)\to(p\to r)$	PC
3.	$\Box((p\to q)\wedge(q\to r))\to\Box(p\to r)$	R
4.	$\Box(p\to q)\wedge\Box(q\to r)\to\Box(p\to r)$	1, HS

EXAMPLE 11.14. Show that $\vdash\Diamond\Diamond p\leftrightarrow\neg\Box\Box\neg p$.

1.	$\Diamond\Diamond p\leftrightarrow\neg\Box\neg\Diamond p$	RD
2.	$\Diamond p\leftrightarrow\neg\Box\neg p$	RD
3.	$\Diamond\Diamond p\leftrightarrow\neg\Box\neg\neg\Box\neg p$	1, 2, BP
4.	$\neg\neg\Box\neg p\leftrightarrow\Box\neg p$	PC
5.	$\Diamond\Diamond p\leftrightarrow\neg\Box\Box\neg p$	3, 4, BP

Exercises for § 11.4

Show the following in KC:

1. $\vdash\Box(p\to q)\to(\Diamond p\to\Diamond q)$
2. $\vdash\Diamond(p\to q)\to(\Box p\to\Diamond q)$
3. $\vdash\Box p\to\Box(q\to p)$
4. $\vdash\neg\Diamond p\to\Box(p\to q)$
5. $\vdash\Diamond(p\vee q)\to\Diamond p\vee\Diamond q$
6. $\vdash(\Diamond p\vee\Diamond q)\to\Diamond(p\vee q)$

11.5 ADEQUACY OF KC TO K

Is the system KC adequate to the logic K? To show that KC is sound, we simply verify that each axiom of KC is valid (K-valid). Further, we must ensure that by using the inference rules of KC on valid mps, we get only valid mps.

It is easy to show that each axiom of KC is K-valid. In fact, we have already done it; find out where. Let us look at the inference rules. The rule MP is sound; it follows from the soundness of PC. But we must see this in the modal setting of K.

Suppose that $M = (W, R, \Vdash)$ is a model and $w \in W$. If $M \vDash p$ and $M \vDash p \to q$, then $w \Vdash p$ and $w \Vdash p \to q$. As each world is propositional, we have $w \Vdash q$, by MP in the world w. Since w is any arbitrary world, we conclude that $M \vDash q$. Thus follows the soundness of MP in K.

What about necessitation? We argue with accessible worlds. Let $M = (W, R, \Vdash)$ be a model and $M \vDash p$. We want to show that for each world $w \in W$, $w \Vdash \Box p$. So, let $w \in W$ be an arbitrary world. Let $u \in W$ be a world accessible from w. Since $M \vDash p$, for each world $v \in W$, $v \Vdash p$. In particular, $u \Vdash p$. It follows that $w \Vdash \Box p$; consequently, $M \vDash \Box p$. This completes the soundness of necessitation.

Finally, use induction on the length of proofs to conclude that each KC-provable mp is K-valid to complete the proof of the following metatheorem.

Theorem 11.9 (Soundness of KC). *Let X be any modal proposition. If $\vdash X$ in KC, then $\vDash X$ in K.*

As it happened for PC, completeness involves more work. We will take the approach of maximally consistent sets of modal propositions and prove the Lindenbaum Lemma.

A finite set of modal propositions $\{X_1, X_2, \ldots, X_n\}$ is said to be **KC-consistent**, iff $X_1 \wedge X_2 \wedge \cdots \wedge X_n \to \bot$ is not provable in KC. An infinite set is KC-consistent iff each finite subset of it is KC-consistent. A set Γ of modal propositions is **maximally KC-consistent** iff (a) Γ is consistent, and (b) if any superset $\Delta \supseteq \Gamma$ is KC-consistent, then $\Delta = \Gamma$.

Lemma 11.1 (Lindenbaum Lemma). *For any KC-consistent set Σ of modal propositions, there exists a maximally consistent set $\Sigma' \supseteq \Sigma$ of modal propositions.*

Proof. The set of all mps is countable. Let $X_0, X_1, X_2, \ldots$ be an enumeration of all mps. Let Σ be the given KC-consistent set of mps. Define inductively the sets Σ_m by

$$\Sigma_0 = \Sigma; \;\; \Sigma_{n+1} = \begin{cases} \Sigma_n \cup \{X_{n+1}\} & \text{if } \Sigma_n \cup \{X_{n+1}\} \text{ is KC-consistent} \\ \Sigma_n & \text{otherwise.} \end{cases}$$

As in PC, each Σ_n is KC-consistent (Show it.). Let $\Sigma' = \cup_{n \in \mathbb{N}} \Sigma_n$. Now, $\Sigma \subseteq \Sigma'$. If Σ' is not KC-consistent, then there is a finite subset, say, $\Sigma^* \subseteq \Sigma'$ such that Σ^* is not KC-consistent. Due to the enumeration of all mps, $\Sigma^* \subseteq \{X_0, X_1, \ldots, X_m\}$ for some $m \in \mathbb{N}$. But then, $\Sigma^* \subseteq \Sigma_m$ (Why?). This implies that Σ_m is not KC-consistent, a contradiction. Thus, Σ' is KC-consistent.

If Σ' is not maximally KC-consistent, then there is a proper superset of Σ' which is KC-consistent. Due to the enumeration of all mps, we get one X_k such that $X_k \notin \Sigma'$

and $\Sigma' \cup \{X_k\}$ is KC-consistent. Since $\Sigma_{k-1} \subseteq \Sigma'$, $\Sigma_k \subseteq \Sigma' \cup \{X_k\}$, and $\Sigma_{k-1} \cup \{X_k\}$ is KC-consistent, we have $X_k \in \Sigma_k \subseteq \Sigma'$. This contradicts the fact that $X_k \notin \Sigma'$. Thus, Σ' is the required maximally KC-consistent extension of Σ. ♦

Remark 11.1. In the proof of Lindenbaum lemma, we have used the countability of the set of all mps. When a modal logic is constructed basing on an uncountable alphabet, we may require to use Zorn's lemma as in the proof of Theorem 2.2. Notice that the finiteness property is included in the definition of an infinite consistent set.

Our next job is to see how to use a maximally KC-consistent extension of Σ to construct a model that would satisfy it. There can be many maximally KC-consistent extensions of the same set Σ. Generalizing a bit, we consider all possible maximally KC-consistent sets of mps. Each one of them is a maximally KC-consistent extension of some set(s). In fact, we take each such maximally KC-consistent set as a world. Let the set of worlds W be the set of all such maximally KC-consistent sets. For worlds $w, u \in W$, define the relation R (a subset of $W \times W$) by

wRu iff for each mp of the form $\Box X$ in w, $X \in u$.

Define the satisfaction ($\Vdash$) of an atomic modal proposition at a world w by

for each atomic mp p, $w \Vdash p$ iff $p \in w$.

The model $(W, R, \Vdash)$ so constructed, is called a **canonical model**. Truth or satisfaction of an atomic mp can be extended for all mps by induction. We then have the following result.

Lemma 11.2 (Truth Lemma). *Let $M = (W, R, \Vdash)$ be the canonical model. Let X be any modal proposition, and let w be any world in W. Then $w \Vdash X$ iff $X \in w$.*

We are ready to prove the completeness of KC.

Theorem 11.10 (Completeness of KC). *For any modal proposition X, if $\models X$ in K, then $\vdash_{KC} X$.*

Proof. We show the contrapositive. Suppose that X is not KC-provable. Then, $\{\neg X\}$ is KC-consistent. Lindenbaum lemma says that there is a maximally KC-consistent extension w of $\{\neg X\}$. That is, w is a world in the canonical model $M = (W, R, \Vdash)$ such that $\neg X \in w$ and w is maximally KC-consistent. Since w is KC-consistent, $X \notin w$. By the Truth lemma, $w \nVdash X$. Then, $M \nvDash X$; and X is not K-valid. ♦

Theorems 11.9 and 11.10 together show that KC is adequate to the logic K. For discussing the strong adequacy, we require to formulate the proof theoretic versions of $\Sigma \models X$ and of $\Sigma \Rightarrow X$. We will first extend the idea of a consequence in KC, via derivations, and then see whether it is adequate to strong or weak entailment.

Let Σ be a set of mps, and let X be an mp. A **KC-derivation** of X from Σ is a finite sequence of mps such that each mp in the sequence is either an axiom of KC, or a member of Σ (a premise), or is derived from earlier mps by an application of modus ponens (MP) or necessitation (N); further, X must be the last mp of the sequence. If there is a KC-derivation of X from Σ, we write $\Sigma \vdash X$ in KC (for precision, $\Sigma \vdash_{KC} X$).

In fact, KC-derivations define the notion of provability of a **KC-consequence**. If there is a KC-derivation of X from Σ, we say that "the consequence $\Sigma \,!\!\vdash X$ is

KC-provable". We often omit writing the outer braces while writing a finite set of premises, and use the same three-column style of writing a derivation. Of course, any derived rule of inference, which comes from earlier derivations, can also be used in a derivation.

EXAMPLE 11.15. Show that $\{\Box p \to p,\ \Box\Box p\} \vdash \Box p$ in KC.

1.	$\Box p \to p$	P
2.	$\Box(\Box p \to p)$	N
3.	$\Box(\Box p \to p) \to (\Box\Box p \to \Box p)$	K
4.	$\Box\Box p \to \Box p$	MP
5.	$\Box\Box p$	P
6.	$\Box p$	MP

EXAMPLE 11.16. Show that $\{\Box p \to p,\ p \to q\} \vdash \Box\Box p \to q$ in KC.

1.	$\Box p \to p$	P
2.	$\Box\Box p \to \Box p$	R
3.	$\Box\Box p \to p$	HS
4.	$p \to q$	P
5.	$\Box\Box p \to q$	HS

Since the rule of necessitation is used in a derivation, a KC-consequence captures the notion of weak entailment. Using adequacy of KC to K, and the deduction theorem, you can prove that $\Sigma \vdash X$ in KC iff $\Sigma \Rightarrow X$. Notice that $X \vdash \Box X$, but $\nvdash X \to \Box X$; further, $\vDash X \to \Box X$ is equivalent to $X \vDash \Box X$. Therefore, the notion of KC-consequence does not capture the strong entailment.

In general, there is also a notion of axiomatic version of a consequence with global and local assumption. However, we do not have "strong adequacy" in the case of a consequence with global and local assumptions.

Exercises for § 11.5

1. Prove Theorem 11.9 and Lemma 11.2.
2. Use the deduction theorem and the completeness of KC to prove that $\Sigma \Rightarrow w$ in K iff $\Sigma \vdash w$ in KC.
3. Formulate and prove compactness theorem for K in terms of satisfiability.

11.6 NATURAL DEDUCTION IN K

The situation reminds us the inference rule of universal generalization (UG) in FC. UG states that from X, derive $\forall x X$. In the case of FC and FL, we have seen that $\Sigma \vdash X$ and $\Sigma \vDash X$ coincide provided that in the proof of $\Sigma \vdash X$, UG has not been used on a free variable of any premise (just as in the deduction theorem). We have not mentioned this condition in the strong adequacy theorem of FC because, our formulation of UG in FC already takes care of this restriction. This restricted version cannot be formulated in KC since in a derivation of $\Box X$, we do not have any trace of a world. You must look at the strong deduction theorem for a modification of KC that might take care of the notion of strong entailment.

However, in a natural deduction proof, we might succeed by using a box as a book-keeping device for worlds. For a natural deduction system, we keep all the inference rules of PND, remembering that the propositions are now treated as mps. We must have some rules for $\Box$ and $\Diamond$. We plan to have an introduction rule for $\Box$, an elimination rule for $\Box$, and then regard the connective $\Diamond$ as $\neg\Box\neg$, as in KC.

The natural deduction system for K is named as **KND**. The system KND includes all the rules such as $\wedge i, \wedge e, \vee i, \vee e, \ldots$ of Section 4.2. The additional rules for handling the modal connective $\Box$ are:

$$(\Box i)\quad \frac{\boxed{\cdots X}}{\Box X} \qquad\qquad (\Box e)\quad \frac{\Box X}{\boxed{\cdots X \cdots}}$$

The dashed boxes for the connective $\Box$ are different from the solid boxes used for other rules. The contents inside the dashed boxes are written horizontally in the rules, but in an actual proof, they come vertically. In the rule $(\Box i)$, the $\cdots$ represent many mps preceding the mp X. Similarly, the $\cdots$ before and after X in the rule $(\Box e)$ also represent possibly many mps preceding and following X. These rules are intended to reason in any arbitrary accessible world.

Remember that going into a solid box means assuming the first formula in it. And after it is closed, the conclusion "first line $\to$ last line" is written on the line immediately below the box.

A dashed box serves a similar but different purpose. For the rule $(\Box i)$, a dashed box can be created with any opening line, but that line should have been justified by other rules (unlike an extra assumption in a solid box). The box begins there, meaning that from that line onwards, until the box closes, we are reasoning in a fixed but arbitrary world. Now, when we deduce X in this arbitrary world, we can close the box, showing that in any arbitrary world, X holds. Therefore, $\Box X$ must hold. We record it by closing the box and writing $\Box X$ on the next line.

Similarly, if $\Box X$ occurs as a line in a proof, then, in any arbitrary world the mp X is true. and this time the scope for going into this arbitrary world can be any fragment of the proof. This is the rule $(\Box e)$.

Read the rules for $\Box$-introduction and $\Box$-elimination as in the following:

$(\Box i)$: If X occurs at the end of a dashed box, then $\Box X$ may be introduced after (closing) the dashed box.

$(\Box e)$: If $\Box X$ occurs somewhere in a proof, then X may be introduced anywhere into a subsequent dashed box.

In general, the dashed boxes are introduced due to an occurrence of $\Box X$. In KND-proofs, both solid and dashed boxes would appear, and they may be nested without crossing, as usual. Again, for the provability of a consequence with premises in Σ and conclusion X, we write $\Sigma \vdash_{KND} X$.

EXAMPLE 11.17. The following is a proof of $\vdash_{KND} \Box(p \to q) \to (\Box p \to \Box q)$.

1.	$\Box(p \to q)$	CP
2.	$\Box p$	CP
3.	p	$\Box e$
4.	$p \to q$	$1, \Box e$
5.	q	MP
6.	$\Box q$	$\Box i$
7.	$\Box p \to \Box q$	$\to e$
8.	$\Box(p \to q) \to (\Box p \to \Box q)$	$\to e$

In the above KND-proof, we have quoted the rule $(\to e)$ from PND. Analogous to KC, we may also abbreviate KND-proofs by assuming all PND consequences as a single rule, and mention only PND. In the following example, write the exact PND rule that has been applied at each mention of PND.

EXAMPLE 11.18. The KND theorem $\vdash_{KND} \Box(p \wedge q) \leftrightarrow \Box p \wedge \Box q$ is shown by proving $\vdash_{KND} \Box(p \wedge q) \to \Box p \wedge \Box q$ and $\vdash_{KND} \Box p \wedge \Box q \to \Box(p \wedge q)$ separately.

1.	$\Box(p \wedge q)$	P
2.	$p \wedge q$	$\Box e$
3.	p	PND
4.	$\Box p$	$\Box i$
5.	$p \wedge q$	$1, \Box e$
6.	q	PND
7.	$\Box q$	$\Box i$
8.	$\Box p \wedge \Box q$	4, 7, PND
9.	$\Box(p \wedge q) \to \Box p \wedge \Box q$	PND

1.	$\Box p \wedge \Box q$	P
2.	$\Box p$	$\wedge e$
3.	$\Box q$	$1, \wedge e$
4.	p	$2, \Box e$
5.	q	$3, \Box e$
6.	$p \wedge q$	PND
7.	$\Box(p \wedge q)$	$\Box i$
8.	$\Box p \wedge \Box q \to \Box(p \wedge q)$	PND

EXAMPLE 11.19. A proof of $\vdash_{KND} \Diamond(p \to q) \to (\Box p \to \Diamond q)$ is as follows.

1.	$\Diamond(p \to q)$	*CP*
2.	$\Box p$	*CP*
3.	$\neg\Diamond q$	CP
4.	$\neg\neg\Box\neg q$	Def of $\Diamond$
5.	$\Box\neg q$	PND
6.	p	$\Box e$
7.	$\neg q$	$\Box e$
8.	$\neg(p \to q)$	$6, 7, PND$
9.	$\Box\neg(p \to q)$	$\Box i$
10.	$\neg\Box\neg(p \to q)$	1, Def of $\Diamond$
11.	$\Diamond q$	$3, 9, 10, PND$
12.	$\Box p \to \Diamond q$	$\to i$
13.	$\Diamond(p \to q) \to (\Box p \to \Diamond q)$	$\to i$

You may also dispense with the boxes and make nesting as is done in PND.

Exercises for § 11.6

Construct KND-proofs to show the following:

1. $\vdash_{KND} \Box(p \to q) \to (\Diamond p \to \Diamond q)$
2. $\vdash_{KND} \Diamond\Diamond p \leftrightarrow \neg\Box\Box\neg p$
3. $\vdash_{KND} \Box p \to \Box(q \to p)$
4. $\vdash_{KND} \neg\Diamond p \to \Box(p \to q)$
5. $\vdash_{KND} \Diamond(p \vee q) \to \Diamond p \vee \Diamond q$
6. $\vdash_{KND} (\Diamond p \vee \Diamond q) \to \Diamond(p \vee q)$

11.7 ANALYTIC TABLEAU FOR K

In KC, we have had difficulty with the rule "from X derive $\Box X$". It has led us to choose between the stronger or weaker entailments $\vDash$ or $\Rightarrow$. We have seen that this rule does not keep track of the world in which the mp X might have been satisfied so that we had to interpret the rule "from X derive $\Box X$" on the meta-level. That is, this rule has been interpreted as

> for each model M, if M satisfies X, then M satisfies $\Box X$.

A dashed box (for the rule $\Box e$) in KND says that if an mp X is satisfied in any arbitrary world, then $\Box X$ must also be satisfied in each world. This means

> for each model M, if each world in M satisfies X, then each world in M satisfies $\Box X$.

It is the same as in KC; the dashed boxes *do not* really improve the situation. We need to improve it to the level where we may assert the following:

For each model M, for each world w in M, if w satisfies X, then w satisfies $\Box X$.

This is similar to the eigenvariable condition in GFC. The idea is that the variable on which universal generalization is applied is somehow tracked in the proof. Analogously, we must have a way to represent the worlds that are accessible from these worlds; and at the same time, we should not also lose any world!

A simple way is to name all the worlds accessible from 1 as 1.1, 1.2, 1.3,... Similarly, a world accessible from 1.1 would be named as 1.1.1, 1.1.2, 1.1.3,... Remember that these numbers with dots stand for names of worlds. We plan to use these as prefixes of mps, meaning that the mp is true at the world.

A **modal prefix** is a finite sequence of positive integers, the integers being separated by dots (a single dot at a time) in between. If m is a modal prefix and X is a modal proposition, then $m\ X$ written with a blank in between is called a **prefixed modal proposition.**

For example, $1.2.1\ \Box X \to X$ is a prefixed modal proposition, with the modal prefix 1.2.1. The modal prefix 1.2.1 stands for a world accessible from a world named 1.2, which is again accessible from the world named 1. The method of analytic tableau uses the prefixed mps.

The rules for expansion of a tableau, called the tableau rules, are the same as those in PT, each coming with a prefix now. In addition, we have rules for the two modal connectives $\Box$ and $\Diamond$. Like $\wedge$ and $\vee$ the modal connectives $\Box$ and $\Diamond$ act dually.

Tableau expansion rules for K: The four types of rules, namely, Stacking rules, Branching rules, Necessity rules, and Possibility rules, are as follows.

1. *Stacking Rules*

$$(\neg\neg)\quad \frac{m\ \neg\neg X}{m\ X} \qquad\qquad (\neg\top)\quad \frac{m\ \neg\top}{m\ \bot}$$

$$(\wedge)\quad \frac{m\ (X \wedge Y)}{\begin{array}{c} m\ X \\ m\ Y \end{array}} \qquad\qquad (\neg\vee)\quad \frac{m\ \neg(X \vee Y)}{\begin{array}{c} m\ \neg X \\ m\ \neg Y \end{array}}$$

$$(\neg\rightarrow)\quad \frac{m\ \neg(X \to Y)}{\begin{array}{c} m\ X \\ m\ \neg Y \end{array}}$$

2. *Branching Rules*

$$(\vee)\quad \frac{m\ (X \vee Y)}{m\ X \qquad m\ Y} \qquad\qquad (\neg\wedge)\quad \frac{m\ \neg(X \wedge Y)}{m\ \neg X \qquad m\ \neg Y}$$

$$(\rightarrow)\quad \frac{m\ (X \to Y)}{m\ \neg X \qquad m\ Y}$$

$$(\leftrightarrow)\quad \frac{m\ (X \leftrightarrow Y)}{\begin{array}{cc} m\ X & m\ \neg X \\ m\ Y & m\ \neg Y \end{array}} \qquad\qquad (\neg\leftrightarrow)\quad \frac{m\ \neg(X \leftrightarrow Y)}{\begin{array}{cc} m\ X & m\ \neg X \\ m\ \neg Y & m\ Y \end{array}}$$

3. *Necessity Rules*

$$(\Box)\quad \frac{m\ \Box X}{m.n\ X} \qquad\qquad (\neg\Diamond)\quad \frac{m\ \neg\Diamond X}{m.n\ \neg X}$$

4. *Possibility Rules*

$$(\Diamond)\quad \frac{m\ \Diamond X}{m.n\ X} \qquad\qquad (\neg\Box)\quad \frac{m\ \neg\Box X}{m.n\ \neg X}$$

where the prefix $m.n$ is new to the branch.

In the rule for $(\Box)$ the prefix $m.n$ can have any n; however, as a heuristic, we take the prefix $m.n$ as one which has already occurred in the path. This goes in parallel to the rules $\forall$ and $\neg\exists$, where instead of 'any term', it is enough to take only those terms which already occur in the path. The appearance of $m\ \Box X$ in a branch means that "$\Box X$ is true at a world named m". Then, X must be true at each world named $m.n$ accessible from m. Also, the prefix $m.n$ in the possibility rules must be new prefixes.

The tableau proof of a modal proposition X starts with the prefixed modal proposition $1\ \neg X$. Then the rules are applied to extend the tree. A path in such a tree (tableau) is called a **closed path** when it contains either $m\ \bot$ or two mps of the form $m\ Y$ and $m\ \neg Y$. Note that both Y and $\neg Y$ should have the same prefix m. A path which is not closed, is called an **open path**.

A tableau is called a **closed tableau** if each path of it is a closed path. A closed tableau for the prefixed modal proposition $1\ \neg X$ means that there cannot be any world named 1 where $\neg X$ may be true (satisfied). However, the name 1 is an arbitrary name; thus it means that the mp $\neg X$ cannot be true at any world. Of course, we assume implicitly that there are at most a countable number of worlds. The closed tableau with $1\ \neg X$ as its root is called a **tableau proof** of the mp X. This is again a proof by contradiction showing that the mp X is K-valid. A **tableau theorem** is an mp for which there is a tableau proof. We will write $\vdash_{KT} Z$, or just $\vdash Z$ if no confusion arises, whenever the mp Z is a tableau theorem.

The tableau system with the above rules is named as **KT**.

EXAMPLE 11.20. The tableau proofs of the following are shown below.

(a) $\vdash_{KT}\ \Box p \wedge \Box q \to \Box(p \wedge q)$ (b) $\vdash_{KT}\ \Box p \wedge \Diamond q \to \Diamond(p \wedge q)$

$$\begin{array}{c}
1\ \neg(\Box p \wedge \Box q \to \Box(p \wedge q))\\
1\ \Box p \wedge \Box q\\
1\ \neg\Box(p \wedge q)\\
1\ \Box p\\
1\ \Box q\\
1.1\ \neg(p \wedge q)\\
\swarrow \qquad \searrow\\
\begin{array}{cc}
1.1\ \neg p & 1.1\ \neg q\\
1.1\ p & 1.1\ q\\
\times & \times
\end{array}
\end{array}
\qquad\qquad
\begin{array}{c}
1\ \neg(\Box p \wedge \Diamond q \to \Diamond(p \wedge q))\\
1\ \Box p\\
1\ \Diamond q\\
1\ \neg\Diamond(p \wedge q)\\
1.1\ q\\
1.1\ \neg(p \wedge q)\\
\swarrow \qquad \searrow\\
\begin{array}{cc}
1.1\ \neg p & 1.1\ \neg q\\
1.1\ p & \times\\
\times &
\end{array}
\end{array}$$

(a) (b)

Notice that in (a), the prefixed mp $1.1\ \neg(p \wedge q)$ is obtained by applying $(\neg\Box)$ on the third line and the prefixed mps $1.1\ p$ and $1.1\ q$ on the last line are obtained from the fourth and the fifth lines, respectively.

Similarly, in (b), look at the prefixes with dots; $1.1\ q$ comes from $\Diamond q$, where 1.1 is a new prefix. The next prefixed mp $1.1\ \neg(p \wedge q)$ comes from $\neg\Diamond(p \wedge q)$ by applying the necessity rule $(\neg\Diamond)$; this allows an old prefix. Other prefixed mps are obtained propositionally, i.e., by stacking and branching rules.

EXAMPLE 11.21. The tableau proof of $\vdash \Box p \vee \Box q \to \Box(p \vee q)$ is as follows.

$$\begin{array}{c}
1\ \neg(\Box p \vee \Box q \to \Box(p \vee q)) \\
1\ \Box p \vee \Box q \\
1\ \neg\Box(p \vee q) \\
1.1\ \neg(p \vee q) \\
1.1\ \neg p \\
1.1\ \neg q \\
\swarrow \quad \searrow \\
\begin{array}{cc}
1\ \Box p & 1\ \Box q \\
1.1\ p & 1.1\ q \\
\times & \times
\end{array}
\end{array}$$

Since we are able to keep track of the worlds where an mp may be true, we expect to capture the general consequence of the type $G \Rightarrow L \vDash X$. Recall that in such a consequence, G is a set of global assumptions and L is a set of local assumptions. The consequence $G \Rightarrow L \vDash X$ holds (or is K-valid) when X is true at a world of a model at which all the members of G are true, and if all the members of L are true at each world of that model.

Tableau method is a refutation method, where the negation of the conclusion is taken as an assumption, and then confirming that there is no way of constructing a world. Since the negation of a conclusion needs to concern about world and not only a model, it is required to be added as a local assumption. Therefore, the prefixes of all local assumptions and the conclusion must be same. We make it a convention to start the tableau with such a world being named as 1. That is, all members of L and $\neg X$ will have the same prefix 1 to start a tableau.

However, any member of G may be prefixed in any way we like. We will then have two additional tableau rules for handling the local and global assumptions.

Let G and L be sets of modal propositions. Let $X \in L$ and $Y \in G$ be two modal propositions. The rules are given in the following:

$$\textbf{(LA)}\ \frac{\cdot}{1\ X} \qquad\qquad \textbf{(GA)}\ \frac{\cdot}{m\ Y}$$

The rules of **local assumption (LA)** says that if $X \in L$, then add $1\ X$ to any open path of the tableau. Similarly, the rule of **global assumption (GA)** says that if $Y \in G$ then add $m\ Y$ to any open path of the tableau, for any prefix m.

In fact, the prefix m in the rule (GA) is usually taken as one which has already occurred in the path. We start the tableau with $1\ \neg X$ on the root and expand it using all the tableau rules including LA and GA. If the tableau closes, then it is called a **derivation** of the consequence $G \Rightarrow L \vDash X$. Keep it in mind that $\varnothing \Rightarrow L \vDash X$ is the strong consequence $L \vDash X$, and $G \Rightarrow \varnothing \vDash X$ is the weak consequence $G \Rightarrow X$.

EXAMPLE 11.22. The tableau derivations of the following are given below.

(a) $\Box p \to p \Rightarrow \Box\Box p \to \Box p$ (b) $\Box p \to p \vDash \Box\Box p \to \Box p$

$$
\begin{array}{c}
1\ \neg(\Box\Box p \to \Box p)\\
1\ \Box\Box p\\
1\ \neg\Box p\\
1.1\ \neg p\\
1.1\ \Box p\\
1.1\ \Box p \to p\\
\begin{array}{cc}
1.1\ \neg\Box\Box p & 1.1\ p\\
\times & \times
\end{array}
\end{array}
$$

(a)

$$
\begin{array}{c}
1\ \neg(\Box\Box p \to \Box p)\\
1\ \Box p \to p\\
1\ \Box\Box p\\
1\ \neg\Box p\\
\begin{array}{ll}
1\ \neg\Box p & 1\ p\\
1.1\ \neg p & 1.1\ \neg p\\
1.1\ \Box p & \\
1.1.1\ p &
\end{array}
\end{array}
$$

(b)

The sixth line in the tableau for (a) is the global assumption and the prefix 1.1 is used with this according to the rule (GA). Give justifications to the other lines. Since the tableau closes, it is a derivation establishing the consequence in (a).

In the tableau for (b), neither the left path nor the right path closes since the prefixes of the complementary propositions do not match. Hence the attempt fails. It is no surprise since $\Box p \to p \nvDash \Box\Box p \to \Box p$.

The difference between the consequences in (a) and (b) in Example 11.22 is that the mp $\Box p \to p$ is taken as a global assumption in (a), while in (b), it is taken as a local assumption. Check the terminology once again; when something is assumed globally, the assumption is stronger, consequently, the consequence becomes weaker. While, if the same mp is assumed locally, the assumption is a weaker assumption, and if the consequence holds, it is a stronger consequence.

EXAMPLE 11.23. The tableau in Figure 11.3(a) proves $\Diamond(p \to q) \vDash \Box p \to \Diamond q$. In this tableau, the fourth line is introduced due to the rule (LA).

The tableau in Figure 11.3(b) shows that

$$\{p \to \Box p, q \to \Box q\} \Rightarrow \Box p \wedge \Box q \vDash \Box(\Box p \wedge \Box q).$$

In this tableau, LA has been applied for introducing the first line and GA, for the ninth line.

Annotate the tableaux with appropriate justifications. Mention the suitable rule (LA) or (GA) when a premise is used.

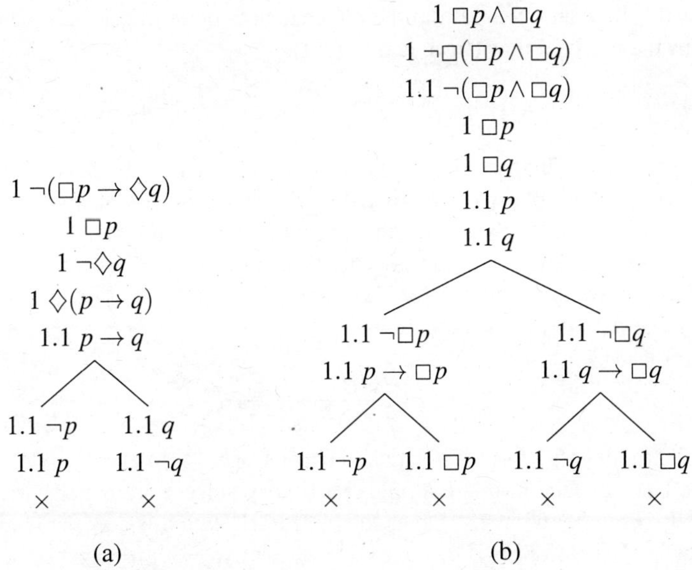

Figure 11.3: Tableau for Example 11.23

EXAMPLE 11.24. The tableau for $p \to \Box p \Rightarrow q \to \Box q$ is given below. Can you find the reason for the vertical dots there?

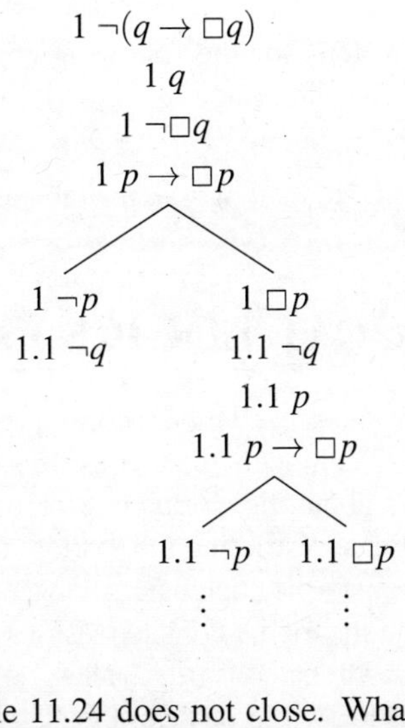

The tableau in Example 11.24 does not close. Whatever way you expand it by reusing the global assumption (one such is done on the fourth line, and again on the eighth line), the tableau does not close. In general, the tableau method is not successful in showing that a given consequence is invalid. It is very much similar to the tableaux in FL. We want to construct a model that would satisfy all the mps in an open path. Take an open path in the tableau, say, the leftmost path. The open path contains the prefixed mps (from leaf to root):

$$1.1\ \neg q,\ 1\ \neg p,\ 1\ p \to \Box p,\ 1\ \neg\Box q,\ 1\ q,\ 1\ \neg(q \to \Box q).$$

The prefixes show that we may consider only two worlds, namely, 1 and 1.1. The world 1.1 is accessible from the world 1. Since 1 q occurs in this path, the world 1 satisfies q. Again, 1 $\neg p$ implies that the world 1 does not satisfy p. Since 1.1 $\neg q$ occurs in the path, the world 1.1 does not satisfy q. Though $\neg p$ occurs with prefix 1, the literal p does not occur with prefix 1.1. Thus, 1.1 may or may not satisfy p. With the first alternative, we have the model

M : 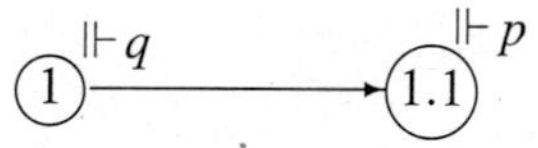

In the model M, $p \to \Box p$ is satisfied since $1 \Vdash p \to \Box p$ and $1.1 \Vdash p \to \Box p$. Note that the last satisfaction relation holds vacuously since there is no world accessible from 1.1. Now, $1 \Vdash q$ but $1 \nVdash \Box q$ as the world 1.1, which is accessible from 1, does not satisfy q. Therefore, $1 \nVdash q \to \Box q$. Consequently, $p \to \Box p \not\Rightarrow q \to \Box q$.

So, a model can be constructed from a failed attempt at proving a consequence, by taking hint from an open path. In general, any open path would not serve this purpose. This is so because, before sufficient expansion of the tableau (say, in the beginning), a path is always open. You may need the notion of a completed systematic tableau. Try it!

Exercises for § 11.7

1. Attempt tableau derivations for the following consequences and then determine whether each is K-valid or not:

   (a) $\Box p \wedge \Box q \vDash \varnothing \Rightarrow \Box(\Box p \wedge \Box q)$ (b) $\varnothing \vDash \Box p \wedge \Box q \Rightarrow \Box(\Box p \wedge \Box q)$

2. Construct a model from an open path in the tableau for Example 11.22(b).

11.8 OTHER MODAL LOGICS

Recall that in a scenario of a generalized modal consequence, the global assumptions restrict the view of models. The models to be considered must satisfy all the global assumptions. Then, we think about the worlds in each of these models and look for satisfying the local assumptions, restricting the worlds further. For the consequence to hold, these worlds must satisfy the conclusion.

What happens if you read the modal connectives in a certain way? Say, you read $\Box X$ as the modality, 'it is known that X is true'. Then certainly, we would admit that in such a world, where 'X is known to be true' the statement that 'X is true' holds. Essentially, we are admitting the truth of $\Box X \to X$ in all such worlds. Notice that $\Box X \to X$ is not as such valid in K.

In other words, if we read the connective $\Box$ as 'it is known that', then the mp $\Box X \to X$ becomes a global assumption. It is rather an assumption scheme and not just an assumption. What does it mean semantically? If in a world w, the mp $\Box X$ is true, then in the same world w, the mp X is also true. Thus, the world w must be accessible from itself.

That means, the **assumption schemes** may impose conditions on the accessibility relation. The class of frames, in turn, becomes restricted. We will have to consider various types of frames then. But remember that various types of frames correspond to various ways of reading the modal connectives of necessity ($\Box$) and possibility ($\Diamond$).

Properties of frames come from the properties of the binary relation on the worlds. Let R be a binary relation on a set W, the set of worlds, for us. The relation R is called

reflexive :	iff for each $w \in W$, wRw
symmetric :	iff for each $u, v \in W$, uRv implies vRu
transitive :	iff for each $u, v, w \in W$, uRv and vRw imply uRw
an equivalence relation :	iff R is reflexive, symmetric, and transitive
serial :	iff for each $u \in W$, there is $v \in W$ such that uRv
euclidian :	iff for each $u, v, w \in W$, uRv and uRw imply vRw
single valued :	iff for each $u \in W$, there is a unique $v \in W$ such that uRv
linear :	iff for each $u, v, w \in W$, uRv and uRw imply either vRw or wRv or $v = w$
total :	iff for each $u, v \in W$, either uRv or vRu or both.

Let W be any set of worlds, and let R be a binary relation on W having one or more of the above properties. Then, we say that the frame (W, R) has that property. Thus, a **reflexive frame** is a frame (W, R), where R is a reflexive relation, etc. Which kind of frames give rise to which assumption schemes. For instance, reflexive frames give rise to the assumption scheme $\Box X \to X$.

Our plan is to restrict our frames to satisfy certain properties so that we will have different assumption schemes. These assumption schemes can be used as axiom schemes along with those of KC, thereby giving rise to different modal logics. When we restrict all our frames to satisfy certain property, we may think of a sub-collection of frames satisfying that property. That is, properties and collections of frames can be taken as one and the same. Thus we are led to the so-called **correspondence theory** of modal logics.

Let F be a collection of frames, and let X be a modal proposition. If (W, R) is a frame in F and $\Vdash$ is a satisfaction relation specifying whether a modal proposition is satisfied (true) at a world, then the model $(W, R, \Vdash)$ is called a **model based on the frame** (W, R). The modal proposition X is **valid in the frame** (W, R) iff each model based on the frame (W, R) satisfies X. The modal proposition X is F**-valid** and written as $\vDash_F X$ iff X is valid in each frame in F.

Convention 11.1. When F is a collection of all frames (without any particular restriction or property), $\vDash_F X$ coincides with $\vDash_K X$. Due to this coincidence, we will use the symbol K for the collection of all frames.

The following theorem summarizes the correspondence of some important properties of frames in terms of axiom schemes to be added to KC. Our naming system keeps the collection of frames and the name of the axiom scheme as the same. For instance, the modal logic with reflexive frames is denoted as T; the collection of all reflexive frames is also denoted as T.

Theorem 11.11 (Correspondence). *Table 11.4 summarizes the correspondence between a frame property and the axiom scheme to be added to KC.*

Table 11.2: Correspondence Theorem

Name	Axiom scheme	Frame property
K	none	none
T	$\Box X \to X$	reflexivity
B	$X \to \Box\Diamond X$	symmetry
D	$\Box X \to \Diamond X$	serial
4	$\Box X \to \Box\Box X$	transitivity
5	$\Diamond X \to \Box\Diamond X$	euclidean
6	$\Box X \leftrightarrow \Diamond X$	single valued
7	$\Box(X \wedge \Box X \to Y)$	
	$\vee \Box(Y \wedge \Box Y \to X)$	linearity

Proof. Denote by T, the set of all reflexive frames. As you have seen, we must add another axiom scheme, namely, $\Box X \to X$ to KC for capturing $\vDash_T$.

Conversely, suppose that the mp $\Box X \to X$ is C-valid for a collection C of frames $(W, R, \Vdash)$. Then, in each world $w \in W$, we have $w \Vdash \Box X \to X$. This means that if $w \Vdash \Box X$, then we must also have $w \Vdash X$. But $w \Vdash \Box X$ means that in each world u with wRu, $u \Vdash X$. Thus, if in each world u with wRu, $u \Vdash X$, then $w \Vdash X$. This holds for each world $w \in W$. Hence R must be reflexive, i.e., $C = T$.

This proves the theorem for T. Similarly, give proofs for other logics. ♦

There is one more important modal logic which has not been considered in this naming scheme; it is the **Gödel logic G**. In addition to the axiom schemes of KC, the logic G has the following axiom scheme:

(L) $\Box(\Box A \to A) \to \Box A$

We also write T as KT emphasizing the fact that the axiom scheme T has been added to those of KC; KT4 has axioms of KC, Axiom T, and Axiom 4; similarly others. Semantically, KT4 is the modal logic of all reflexive and transitive frames. In our notation the logic G is simply the logic KL. Sometimes the axiom scheme L is also written as G.

You may read the axioms T, B, D, L as 1, 2, 3, 8, respectively to go with other axioms. But these names are historical and we refer to them this way.

Figure 11.4 shows which modal logic is a **sublogic** of another. A directed arrow from the node A to the node B means that A is a sublogic of B. It means that if an mp X is valid in A then it is also valid in B. The figure covers only some of the important logics; there are others!

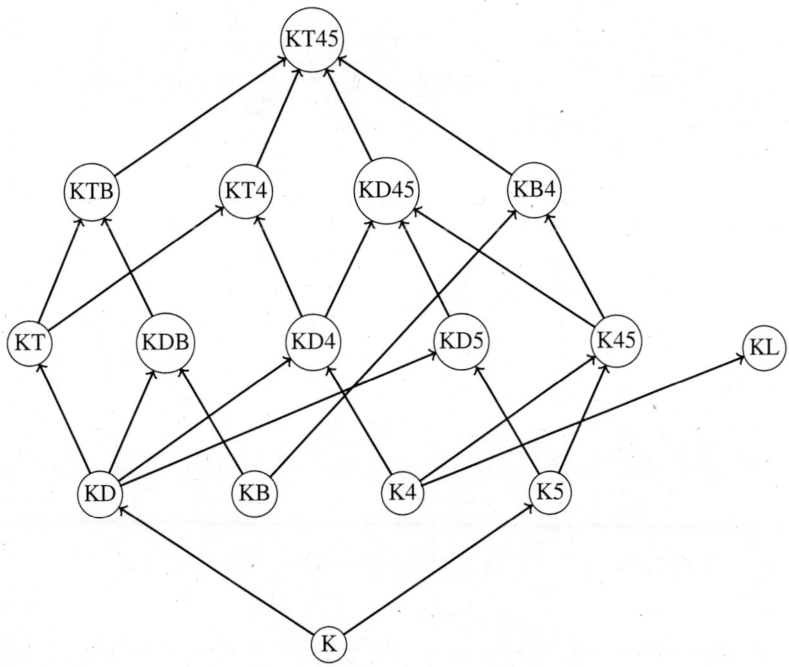

Figure 11.4: Modal logics and sublogics

The logic KT is a sublogic of KT4 as each reflexive and transitive frame is vacuously reflexive. This means that if a modal proposition X is KT-valid, then it is also KT4-valid, and each proof in KT is also a proof in KT4. The logic KT4 is also written as **S4**, and the logic KT45 is written as **S5**.

The following example illustrates how the axiomatic systems work.

EXAMPLE 11.25. Here is a proof that shows $\vdash_{K4} \Box p \wedge \Box q \to \Box\Box p \wedge \Box\Box q$.

1.	$\Box p \wedge \Box q \to \Box(\Box p \to \Box q)$	Axiom 4
2.	$\Box p \wedge \Box q \to \Box p$	PC
3.	$\Box(\Box p \wedge \Box q) \to \Box\Box p$	R
4.	$\Box p \wedge \Box q \to \Box q$	PC
5.	$\Box(\Box p \wedge \Box q) \to \Box\Box q$	R
6.	$\Box(\Box p \wedge \Box q) \to \Box\Box p \wedge \Box\Box q$	3, 5, PC
7.	$\Box p \wedge \Box q \to \Box\Box p \wedge \Box\Box q$	1, 6, HS

The natural deduction system can be extended in a very natural way by adding a corresponding rule that stems from an extra axiom to the system KND. Table 11.3 shows additional inference rules for various logics. The following examples illustrate KND-proofs.

Table 11.3: Natural Deduction:Additional Rules

System	Rule of Inference	System	Rule of Inference
KND	No extra rule	TND	$\dfrac{\Box X}{X}$
BND	$\dfrac{X}{\Box\Diamond X}$	DND	$\dfrac{\Box X}{\Diamond X}$
4ND	$\dfrac{\Box X}{\Box\Box X}$	5ND	$\dfrac{\Diamond X}{\Box\Diamond X}$
6ND	$\dfrac{\Box X}{\Diamond X}, \quad \dfrac{\Diamond X}{\Box X}$	7ND	$\dfrac{\neg\Box(X \land \Box X \to Y)}{\Box(Y \land \Box Y \to X)}$

EXAMPLE 11.26. We give natural deduction proofs of some theorems as follows.

(a) $\vdash_{K4ND} \Box p \land \Box q \to \Box\Box p \land \Box\Box q$.

1.	$\Box p \land \Box q$	CP
2.	$\Box(\Box p \land \Box q)$	4ND
3.	$\Box p \land \Box q$	$\Box e$
4.	$\Box p$	$\land e$
5.	$\Box\Box p$	$\Box i$
6.	$\Box p \land \Box q$	1, $\Box e$
7.	$\Box q$	$\land e$
8.	$\Box\Box q$	$\Box i$
9.	$\Box\Box p \land \Box\Box q$	5, 8, $\land i$
10.	$(\Box p \land \Box q) \to \Box\Box p \land \Box\Box q$	$\to i$

(b) $\vdash_{K45ND} p \to \Box\Diamond p$.

1.	p	CP
2.	$\Box\neg p$	CP
3.	$\neg p$	TND
4.	$\bot$	1, 3, $\neg e$
5.	$\neg\Box\neg p$	$\neg i$
6.	$\Box\neg\Box\neg p$	5ND
7.	$p \to \Box\neg\Box\neg p$	$\to i$
8.	$p \to \Box\Diamond p$	Def. of $\Diamond$

(c) $\vdash_{KT45ND} \Diamond p \to \Diamond\Box\Diamond p$.

1.	$\Diamond p$	CP
2.	$\neg\Diamond\Box\Diamond p$	CP
3.	$\neg\neg\Box\neg\Box\Diamond p$	Def. of $\Diamond$
4.	$\Box\neg\Box\Diamond p$	$\neg\neg e$
5.	$\neg\Box\Diamond p$	TND
6.	$\Box\Diamond p$	1, 5ND
7.	$\bot$	$\neg e$
8.	$\Diamond\Box\Diamond p$	$\neg e$
9.	$\Diamond p \to \Diamond\Box\Diamond p$	Def. of $\Diamond$

The method of analytic tableau for the logic K is also extended to other logics. The additional rules for expanding any path of a tableau are as follows.

K : No Additional Rules

T :	$\dfrac{m\ \Box X}{m\ X}$	$\dfrac{m\ \neg\Diamond X}{m\ \neg X}$		
B :	$\dfrac{m.n\ \Box X}{m\ X}$	$\dfrac{m.n\ \neg\Diamond X}{m\ \neg X}$		
D :	$\dfrac{m\ \Box X}{m\ \Diamond X}$	$\dfrac{m\ \neg\Diamond X}{m\ \neg\Box X}$		
4 :	$\dfrac{m\ \Box X}{m.n\ \Box X}$	$\dfrac{m\ \neg\Diamond X}{m.n\ \neg\Diamond X}$		
5 :	$\dfrac{m\ \Box X}{m.n\ \Box X}$	$\dfrac{m\ \neg\Diamond X}{m.n\ \neg\Diamond X}$	$\dfrac{m.n\ \Box X}{m\ \Box X}$	$\dfrac{m.n\ \neg\Diamond X}{m\ \neg\Diamond X}$
6 :	$\dfrac{m\ \Box X}{m\ \Diamond X}$	$\dfrac{m\ \neg\Diamond X}{m\ \neg\Box X}$	$\dfrac{m\ \Diamond X}{m\ \Box X}$	$\dfrac{m\ \neg\Box X}{m\ \neg\Diamond X}$
7 :	$\dfrac{m\ \neg\Box(X\wedge\Box X\to Y)}{m\ \Box(Y\wedge\Box Y\to X)}$	$\dfrac{m\ \Diamond(X\wedge\Box X\wedge\neg Y)}{m\ \neg\Diamond(Y\wedge\Box Y\wedge\neg X)}$		

We use the same symbol $\vdash$ with subscripts (for different logics) for theorems proved by tableau method.

EXAMPLE 11.27. The tableaux for the following are shown in Figure 11.5.

(a) $\vdash_{KB} \Diamond\Box X \to X$ (b) $\vdash_{KT} (\Box(X\vee Y)\wedge\neg X)\to Y$

In (a), the rule B is applied on the last line. In which line of (b) the rule T is applied?

$$\begin{array}{c}
1\ \neg(\Diamond\Box X \to X)\\
1\ \Diamond\Box X\\
1\ \neg X\\
1.1\ \Box X\\
1\ X\\
\times
\end{array}$$

(a)

$$\begin{array}{cc}
\multicolumn{2}{c}{1\ \neg(\Box(X \vee Y) \wedge \neg X) \to Y}\\
\multicolumn{2}{c}{1\ \Box(X \vee Y) \wedge \neg X}\\
\multicolumn{2}{c}{1\ \neg Y}\\
\multicolumn{2}{c}{1\ \Box(X \vee Y)}\\
\multicolumn{2}{c}{1\ \neg X}\\
1\ X & 1\ Y\\
\times & \times
\end{array}$$

(b)

Figure 11.5: Tableaux for Example 11.27

EXAMPLE 11.28. The tableaux for the following are given below.

(a) $\Diamond\Box X \Rightarrow \Box X$ in KT45

(b) $\Box\Diamond(\Box X \to \Box\Diamond Y) \Rightarrow (\Box X \to \Box\Diamond Y)$ in KT4

In the first tableau, determine where the rule of KT45 is used, and see why the prefix '1.2' is introduced. Can you close the tableau somewhere before the last line? Similarly, in the second tableau, find out where the rule of KT4 is used; and why does the tableau prove weak entailment?

$$\begin{array}{c}
1\ \Diamond\Box X\\
1\ \neg\Box X\\
1.1\ \Box X\\
1.2\ \neg X\\
1\ \Box X\\
1.2\ X\\
\times
\end{array}$$

$$\begin{array}{cc}
\multicolumn{2}{c}{1\ \Box\Diamond(\Box X \to \Box\Diamond Y)}\\
\multicolumn{2}{c}{1\ \neg(\Box X \to \Box\Diamond Y)}\\
\multicolumn{2}{c}{1\ \Box X}\\
\multicolumn{2}{c}{1\ \neg\Box\Diamond Y}\\
\multicolumn{2}{c}{1.1\ \neg\Diamond Y}\\
\multicolumn{2}{c}{1.1\ \Box X}\\
\multicolumn{2}{c}{1.1\ \Diamond(\Box X \to \Box\Diamond Y)}\\
\multicolumn{2}{c}{1.1.1\ \Box X \to \Box\Diamond Y}\\
1.1.1\ \neg\Box X & 1.1.1\ \Box\Diamond Y\\
1.1.1\ \Box X & 1.1.1\ \Diamond Y\\
\times & 1.1.1\ \neg\Diamond Y\\
 & \times
\end{array}$$

Theorem 11.11 is the soundness and completeness of various axiomatic systems appropriate to the logics. We have not proved the adequacy of analytic tableau or that of the natural deduction. In the above examples, the adequacy results have been implicitly assumed. Moreover, the strong adequacy of the tableau method follows when you have a generalized consequence with global and local assumptions. Try to prove these results. You should also attempt an extension of GPC for obtaining appropriate Gentzen systems to the modal logics.

Exercises for § 11.8

1. Attempt tableau derivations for the following consequences and then determine whether each is K-valid or not:

   (a) $\Box p \wedge \Box q \vDash \varnothing \Rightarrow \Box(\Box p \wedge \Box q)$ (b) $\varnothing \vDash \Box p \wedge \Box q \Rightarrow \Box(\Box p \wedge \Box q)$
2. Construct a model from an open path in the tableau for Example 11.22(b).

11.9 VARIOUS MODALITIES

The modal logics have been introduced by playing with axioms and frame properties. Do they actually help in representing various modalities? Modalities may express the necessity or the possibility of truth, convenience, lawfulness, certainty, agreement, acceptance, quotations, temporality, belief, contingency, knowledge, execution of programs, etc. Look at the emphasized phrases in the following sentences:

It is *necessarily true that* moon is made of cheese.
It is *possible that* the morning star is the evening star.
It is *convenient to* have your residence near your workplace.
It is *unlawful for* Indians to smoke in a public place.
It is *certain that* Plato was a student of Socrates.
It is *doubtful* whether Descartes had doubt over everything.
It is *allowed by* the authorities to park your vehicles here.
Yesterday he was in a jolly mood.
Today morning he is depressed.
Sun will rise in the east *for all time to come.*
I *believe that* you will certainly like this book.
It is *a belief that* each algorithm is a Turing machine.
It is *a fact* that Confucius was a happy and wise person.
I know it very well that Hausdorff committed suicide.
It is *common knowledge that* Bertrand Russell married thrice.
After the execution of the program P, the hard disk will burn.
It is *said by the ancients that* if you cannot decide now, then you cannot decide at all.

The emphasized phrases represent modalities of some sort. Some of them are modalities of truth (**alethic**), some are **temporal** modalities, some are obligatory (**deontic**) modalities, some are modalities of knowledge and belief (**doxastic**), etc.

Our plan is to symbolize such modalities by the two symbols $\Box$ and $\Diamond$. For example, we may translate the phrase "it is necessarily true that p" as $\Box p$; and "it is possibly true that" as $\Diamond p$. Similarly, we may translate "I believe that p" to $\Box p$. We assume implicitly that both the modalities "it is necessarily true that" and "I believe that" do not occur in the same context. Otherwise, we may have to invent new symbols for representing them.

Different modalities may follow different logics; and on deciding which logic would be more suitable for arguing about a particular modality is always debatable. However, certain modalities are well understood and their governing principles are more or less clear.

In case we represent the modality "it is necessarily true that p" as $\Box p$, we accept the mp $\Box p \to p$ to hold since it represents the acceptable assertion: "If p is necessarily true, then p is true". Thus, in the problem domain of necessarily true and possibly true, we will be translating our informal sentences to the modal propositions in the formal language of the logic K. But there can be various views.

Suppose that the necessity here is interpreted as logical necessity. Then, if p is necessarily true, so is $\Box p$. This would force us to accept the validity of the mp $\Box p \to \Box\Box p$. But if we read $\Box p$ as the physical necessity, then $\Box p \to \Box\Box p$ would no longer be valid since physical laws of the universe (as we have formulated) need not be physically necessary.

Further, if we read $\Box p$ as "I believe that" then, $\Box p \to p$ need not be valid. For example, even if I believe that $\mathscr{P} \neq \mathscr{NP}$, it need not be so. I may believe that ghosts exist, but they may not. Thus the logic of beliefs cannot have $\Box p \to p$ as a valid mp. Depending upon the problem domain, the meaning of the modal connectives $\Box$ and $\Diamond$ would change, and then you have to choose the appropriate logic. If none of the standard logics seem to be appropriate for some reason or the other, you may have to create new logics.

EXAMPLE 11.29. Use the following legend for reading Table 11.4.

$A: \ \Box p \to p$ $\qquad$ $B: \ \Box p \to \Box\Box p$

$C: \ \Diamond p \to \Box\Diamond p$ $\qquad$ $D: \ \Diamond\top$

$E: \ \Box p \to \Diamond p$ $\qquad$ $F: \ \Box p \vee \Box\neg p$

$G: \ \Box(p \to q) \wedge \Box p \to \Box q$ $\qquad$ $H: \ \Diamond p \wedge \Diamond q \to \Diamond(p \wedge q)$

Table 11.4: Different modalities

$\Box X$	A	B	C	D	E	F	G	H
It is necessarily true that X	1	1	1	1	1	0	1	0
It shall be the case that X	0	1	0	0	0	0	1	0
It should be the case that X	0	0	0	1	1	0	1	0
You believe that X	0	1	1	1	1	0	1	0
You know that X	1	1	1	1	1	0	1	0
After execution of the program P, X holds	0	0	0	0	0	0	1	0

If $\Box$ is interpreted as given in the leftmost column of the table, see that the corresponding modal propositions in the corresponding columns having entry 1 hold. You may give reasons why the mps having corresponding entry 0 do not hold.

In the following subsections, you will see some of the modalities and their formalizations. Note that we may end up at a multimodal logic if various modalities do occur in the same context. But the new modal connectives will necessarily be similar to our basic ones, possibly with different names.

A Logic of Knowledge

Suppose that we want to build up a logic for handling knowledge of an agent A. We would translate the phrase "A knows that p" to $\Box p$. Then, the dual modal operator

$\Diamond$ is read as "it is possible for all that A knows that ..." If there is more than one agent, then we have to invent more symbols. The multimodal logic would then have at least two modal operators corresponding to each agent. In such cases, we use the small letter corresponding to an agent's name as the subscript of the modal operator. The scheme of symbolization is

$\Box_x p$: X knows that p

$\Diamond_x p$: it is possible for all that X knows that p.

Then, $\Box_a$ and $\Box_b$ will be treated as two different symbols, one for the knowledge of the agent A, and the other for the knowledge of the agent B. Note that you can interpret $\Box_a$ also as "it follows from whatever A knows that" or as "A is entitled to know that", etc. What about the axioms of such a logic? The axioms of this logic will include all the tautologies of PC and three more:

(LK1) $\Box_x(p \to q) \to (\Box_x p \to \Box_x q)$

(LK2) $\Box_x p \to p$

(LK3) $\Box_x p \to \Box_x \Box_x p$

The rules of inference of the logic of knowledge are the modus pones (MP) and the rule of necessitation (N), as in K.

If you read $\Box_x$ as $\Box$, then LK1 is simply the axiom K, LK2 is the axiom T, and LK3 is the axiom 4. Hence the logic you get is simply KT4 for each agent.

In this multimodal logic of knowledge, the knower (the agent) is assumed to be logically omniscient, for, once he knows p, he also knows all the consequences of p. The axiom LK3 says that one cannot know p and yet fail to know that he knows it. This is why LK3 is called the *axiom of* or the *principle of positive introspection*.

We may take another stand by replacing LK3 by LK4 as follows:

(LK4) $\neg \Box_x p \to \Box_x \neg \Box_x p$

This says that if one (the agent X) does not know p, then he knows that he does not know p, the *principle of negative introspection*. So you see, nothing is conclusive here; it all depends upon what you want to symbolize, and which properties you want to keep and which to discard. Suppose that you want to interpret the modal operators as in the following:

$\Box_x$: the agent X believes that

$\Diamond_x$: it is compatible with whatever X believes that

Then, the same logic KT4 (for each agent) might work. However, beliefs are more problematic than knowledge. An agent is not required to be entirely consistent on the set of his beliefs. Try making a better logic than KT4 for understanding the beliefs!

A Temporal Logic

When there is a reference to time, we think of it as a linear extent, just as the real line, but with a varying reference point unlike a fixed origin. For instance, when you tell me, "Yesterday, Sam was in a jolly mood", your reference is a time interval called "today". The sentence "Sam is in a jolly mood" may be devoid of any temporal concern. To make temporality more effective you might fill the *blank-modality* with a time index. Thus you may consider the sentence:

Sam is in a jolly mood at time t.

In so doing, the sentence "Sam is in a jolly mood" is viewed no longer as a whole sentence, but just as a property of some time point, say, of t. You may universally or existentially quantify over this variable t to get one of the following sentences:

Sam is always in a jolly mood.
Sam is sometimes in a jolly mood.

Interpreting the temporality as a modal operator, the sentences above can be rewritten, respectively, as

$\Box$ (Sam is in a jolly mood)
$\Diamond$ (Sam is in a jolly mood).

This reading of $\Box$ and $\Diamond$ would naturally give way to the logic K, as you can see that the formulas $\Box p \to p$ and $p \to \Diamond p$ are true at any situation, whereas $\Diamond p \to p$ and $p \to \Box p$ are not.

If you want to operate with past and present as two connectives, instead of 'for all time' or 'for some time', then you would have to introduce two modal operators for past and future separately. Here is one such scheme:

Fp : It will sometimes be the case that p
Pp : It was sometimes the case that p
Gp : It will always be the case that p
Hp : It was always the case that p.

Here, Gp corresponds to the $\Box$-future, Hp to $\Box$-past, Fp to $\Diamond$-future, and Pp corresponds to $\Diamond$-past. This symbolization brings in a bimodal logic with two types of $\Box$'s and two types of $\Diamond$'s. However, there is a marked difference between this logic and the logic K. For example,

G(Sam is in a jolly mood)

is read as

Sam will always be in a jolly mood.

whereas the sentence "Sam is in a jolly mood" is interpreted as "Sam is in a jolly mood now". So that the mp

G(Sam is in a jolly mood) $\to$ (Sam is in a jolly mood)

is no longer valid. That is, in this logic, we cannot assert that $\Box p \to p$ holds. On the other hand, $Gp \to Fp$ (i.e., $\Box p \to \Diamond p$) holds. It says that if p will always be true then at some time p will be true. Similarly, since temporal order is transitive, $Gp \to GGp$ is also valid.

As another variant, if you take $\Box p \equiv p \wedge Gp$ and $\Diamond p \equiv p \vee Fp$, then $\Box p \to p$ holds. However, $\Diamond p \to \Box\Diamond p$ does not hold. For example, take p as the sentence "Scientists are able to discover a cure for cancer". You can imagine a world where, in some future time, p will hold, i.e., $\Diamond p$ holds (in that world), now. Then, in no future time to that time the cure can again be discovered since it would have been discovered by then. That is, $\Box\Diamond p$ does not hold.

In the next section, we will describe another temporal logic which helps in verifying the properties of a real-time system.

Exercises for § 11.9

1. The mp $\square x$ is true at a world w is interpreted as "being in the world w I know x". Similarly, interpret 'the mp $\lozenge x$ is true at a world w' as "being in the world w, I consider it possible that x holds". Assuming that I cannot know false things, explain why the mps in (a) and (b) are valid but the mp in (c) is invalid:

   (a) $\square p \to p$ (b) $\square p \to \square\square p$ (c) $p \to \square p$

2. Interpret '$\square x$ is true at a world t' as "from time t onwards, x will remain true". Similarly, interpret '$\lozenge x$ is true at a world t' as "there is an instant of time not before t when x is true". Explain why the following are valid:

   (a) $\square p \to \square\square p$ (b) $\lozenge\top$ (c) $\square p \to p$

11.10 COMPUTATION TREE LOGIC

Consider an elevator operating in a multi-storey building. We want to develop a formal language to express various states and functionality of the elevator. For example, consider representing, in our language:

> An upward going elevator at the third floor keeps on going upward when it has some passengers who wish to go to the fourth floor or higher up.

Of course, you can simply take the whole sentence as an atomic proposition in PL. Or, you may symbolize in FL by identifying the predicates. But that would not help much if you want to verify this property of the elevator after designing its switching circuit.

As a preliminary to symbolization, take the integer variables $floor$ and $direction$. Now, $floor = 2$ means that the elevator is on the second floor, and $direction = 1$ means that it is going upward. Similarly, $direction = -1$ tells that its movement is downward, and $direction = 0$ shows that it is idle. The phrase "it has a passenger wishing to go to fourth floor" would mean that someone has pressed the No. 4 button. That is, we introduce another integer variable, $buttonpressed$ so that this state is represented as $buttonpressed = 4$. Then, our sentence (quoted above) is translated as

> for all possible states of the elevator starting from any state,
> $((floor = 2 \wedge direction = 1 \wedge buttonpressed \geq 4) \to$
> (for all possible start states, $(direction = 1$ until $floor = buttonpressed)))$

The temporality in the until' cannot be omitted here. In FL, you would have translated 'until' to the connective $\vee$; in this case, it is insufficient. So, we must have a way in working with time. Here, it is enough to think of time as a discrete linearly ordered set just as the set of integers or natural numbers. (Will a finite segment of natural numbers suffice?)

Sometimes, we need to consider branching time. For example, consider a computing system where many processors are run in parallel and they might request to use certain other processes time to time. Here, once a job is submitted, it is distributed by a scheduler; the fragments, so to say, are to be worked out by many processes. Process 1 is doing its part and for it, time goes linearly in a discrete way. For Process 2, again, time goes linearly in a discrete way. For the scheduler, time goes in a branching way, looking at the different processes and their requests. In such a situation, suppose that a process has started but it is not yet ready. Then, we have a property to be verified, namely,

It is possible to get a state where *started* holds but *ready* does not.

Assume that *started* and *ready* are the propositions with their obvious meanings. Then the above sentence will be formalized as

It is possible for a state that $(started \wedge \neg ready)$.

The sentence "for each state, if a request occurs, then it will eventually be acknowledged" will similarly be translated to "for all possible states starting with any state, $(requested \rightarrow$for any starting state there will be a future state where $(acknowledged))$". To have a symbolic way of writing such sentences, we devise a scheme. We will use the mnemonics:

$A:$	for all possible states	$E:$	for some possible states
$F:$	for some future state	$G:$	for all future states
$X:$	for the next state	$U:$	for expressing 'until'

Then our connectives are:

$$AX,\ EX,\ AF,\ EF,\ AG,\ EG,\ A[\cdot U \cdot],\ E[\cdot U \cdot]$$

For propositions p, q, these connectives are used as follows:

$$AXp,\ EXp,\ AFp,\ EFp,\ AGp,\ EGp,\ A[pU\,q],\ E[pU\,q].$$

Formally, the language of **computation tree logic**, or **CTL**, for short, has the (well formed) formulas defined by the following grammar:

$$w ::= \top \mid \bot \mid p \mid \neg w \mid (w \wedge w) \mid (w \vee w) \mid (w \rightarrow w) \mid AXw \mid EXw \mid AGw \mid$$
$$EGw \mid AFw \mid EFw \mid E[w\,U\,w] \mid A[w\,U\,w]$$

where p is any atomic formula (atomic proposition in PL). For instance, the following are CTL-formulas

$$\neg EFA[pU\,q], \quad AF(p \rightarrow EGq), \quad E[pU\,A[qU\,r]],$$
$$(EF(E[pU\,((p \wedge q) \wedge A[qU\,\neg p])] \rightarrow AG(p \vee q)).$$

whereas the following are not CTL-formulas (Why?):

$$AF(pU\,q), \quad A\neg G(p \wedge q), \quad EG[(pU\,q) \rightarrow (pU\,r)].$$

We should be a bit careful with brackets larking around U. Your experience with syntax will guide you to prove unique parsing of CTL-formulas. And then, subformulas etc. can be defined in the usual way. Further, similar to any modal logic, CTL will also have a possible world semantics. A possible state of computation is taken as a world.

A model for CTL is a triple $M = (W, R, \Vdash)$, where W is a set of worlds, a set of possible states of computation; R is the accessible relation over W; and $\Vdash$ is the satisfaction relation giving details of which world satisfies which atomic formulas. A model is represented as a directed graph with nodes as the states annotated with the propositions (atomic formulas) which are satisfied there, and the accessibility relation is represented as the set of edges between the states. As earlier, whenever uRv holds, the graph has an edge from u to v:

We abbreviate it to $u \longrightarrow v$. This edge may be interpreted as follows:

> During computation, there may be a transition from the state u to the state v.

That is, v is the next immediate state to u. Given a CTL formula p, we write $M \Vdash p$ whenever $s \Vdash p$ holds for each state $s \in W$. The relation $s \Vdash p$ (shorthand for $M, s \Vdash p$) extends the definition of the given relation $\Vdash$ from atomic formulas or propositions to all formulas by the following rules:

1. For each $s \in W$, $s \Vdash \top$ and $s \nVdash \bot$.
2. For each $s \in W$ and for atomic propositions p mentioned in the model, $s \Vdash p$.
3. For each $s \in W$, $s \Vdash \neg q$ iff $s \nVdash q$.
4. For each $s \in W$, $s \Vdash q \wedge r$ iff $s \Vdash q$ and $s \Vdash r$.
5. For each $s \in W$, $s \Vdash q \vee r$ iff $s \Vdash q$ or $s \Vdash r$.
6. For each $s \in W$, $s \Vdash q \rightarrow r$ iff $s \nVdash q$ or $s \Vdash r$.
7. For each state s' with $s \longrightarrow s'$, $s' \Vdash q$ iff $s \Vdash AXq$.
   (AX stands for "in each next state")
8. For some state s' with $s \longrightarrow s'$, $s' \Vdash q$ iff $s \Vdash EXq$.
   (EX stands for "in some next state")
9. For each path of the form $s_1 \longrightarrow s_2 \longrightarrow s_3 \longrightarrow \ldots$, with $s_1 = s$, there exists an s_i such that $s_i \Vdash q$ iff $s \Vdash AFq$.
   (AF stands for "for each computation path beginning with s, there will be some future state such that")
10. For some path of the form $s_1 \longrightarrow s_2 \longrightarrow s_3 \longrightarrow \ldots$, with $s_1 = s$, there exists an s_i such that $s_i \Vdash q$ iff $s \Vdash EFq$.
    (EF stands for "for some computation path beginning with s, there will be some future state such that")
11. For each path of the form $s_1 \longrightarrow s_2 \longrightarrow s_3 \longrightarrow \ldots$ with $s_1 = s$, and for each s_i along the path, $s_i \Vdash q$ iff $s \Vdash AGq$.
    (AG stands for "for all computation paths beginning with s, and for all future states")
12. For some path of the form $s_1 \longrightarrow s_2 \longrightarrow s_3 \longrightarrow \ldots$, with $s_1 = s$, and for each s_i along such a path, $s_i \Vdash q$ iff $s \Vdash EGq$.
    (EG stands for "for all computation paths beginning with s, there will be some future state along such a path so that")

13. For each path of the form $s_1 \longrightarrow s_2 \longrightarrow s_3 \longrightarrow \ldots$, with $s_1 = s$, there exists an s_i along the path such that $s_i \Vdash r$, and for each $j < i$, $s_j \Vdash q$ iff $s \Vdash A[qUr]$. ($A[qUr]$ stands for "all computation paths beginning with s satisfy q until r")
14. For some path of the form $s_1 \longrightarrow s_2 \longrightarrow s_3 \longrightarrow \ldots$, with $s_1 = s$, there exists an s_i along the path such that $s_i \Vdash r$, and for each $j < i$, $s_j \Vdash q$ iff $s \Vdash E[qUr]$. ($E[qUr]$ stands for "some computation path beginning with s satisfies q until r happens")

Note that in this semantics, the future of a state includes the state itself. The computation paths referred to above is obtained from the (transition) graph of a model by unwinding the graph into infinite trees. For example, consider the model (the relation of $\Vdash$ omitted) given below.

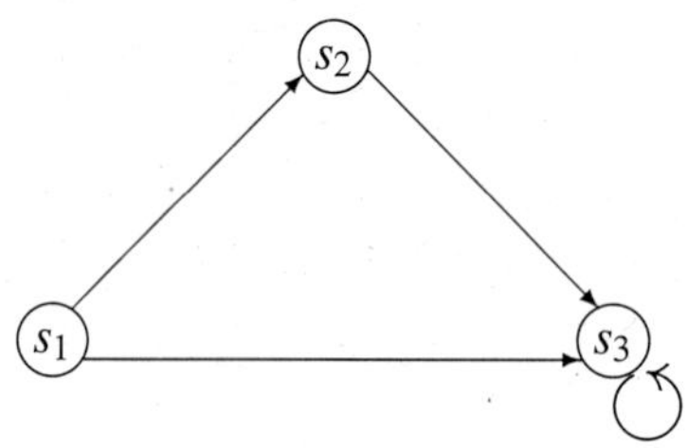

Here, a computation path beginning with s_1 is

$$s_1 \longrightarrow s_2 \longrightarrow s_3 \longrightarrow s_3 \longrightarrow s_3 \longrightarrow \ldots$$

Another computation path beginning with s_1 is

$$s_1 \longrightarrow s_3 \longrightarrow s_3 \longrightarrow s_3 \longrightarrow s_3 \longrightarrow \ldots$$

To check whether in a model, a state s satisfies a CTL formula, the computation tree is constructed. Since this tree contains all computation paths beginning with s, one has to check whether $\Vdash$ for the formula holds on these paths. The tree of all computation paths beginning with s_1 is given below.

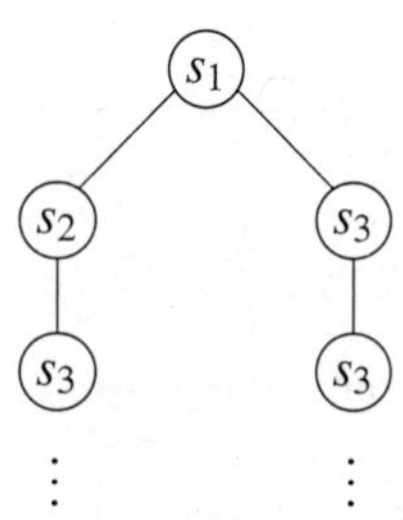

EXAMPLE 11.30. Let Y be the CTL formula $[EG(r \vee q)UAFt] \rightarrow AXr$. Let M be the following model. Determine whether $s_1 \Vdash Y$ and/or $s_3 \Vdash Y$.

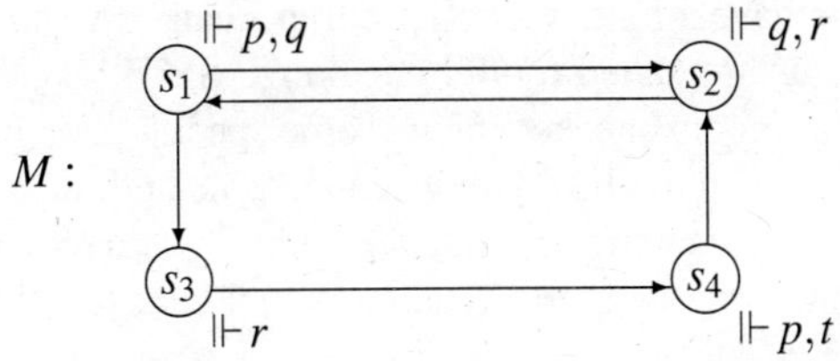

The computation trees beginning with s_1 and s_3 are given below. In the trees, the symbol τ_4 means the tree of s_4 repeated thereafter. Similarly, τ_1 means the tree for s_1 is to be appended there.

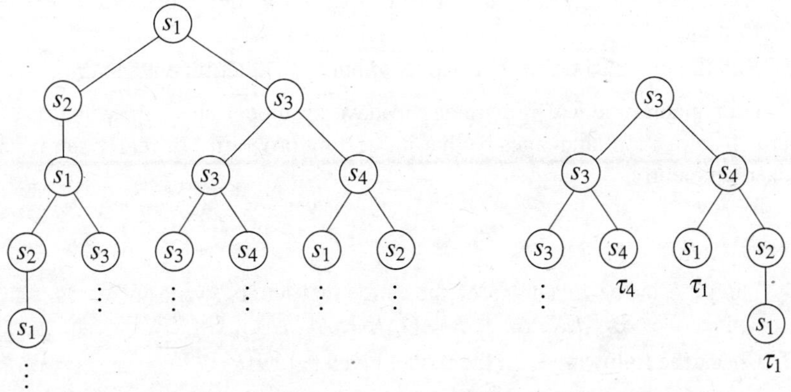

For Y to be true at the state s_1, we see that

$$s_1 \Vdash [EG(r \vee q)\,U\,AFt] \to AXr \;\text{ iff }\; (s_1 \nVdash [EG(r \vee q)\,U\,AFt] \text{ or } s_1 \Vdash AXr).$$

We take the simpler case first: $s_1 \Vdash AXr$ iff for each next state s to s_1, $s \Vdash r$. The 'next states' of s_1 are s_2 and s_3. As $s_2 \Vdash r$ and $s_3 \Vdash r$, we conclude that $s_1 \Vdash AXr$. Therefore, $s_1 \Vdash [EG(r \vee q)\,U\,AFt] \to AXr$.

For $s_3 \Vdash Y$, we consider the next states of s_3; they are s_4 and s_3. We see that $s_3 \Vdash r$ but $s_4 \nVdash r$. Hence $s_3 \nVdash AXr$.

We must check the other alternative, i.e., whether $s_3 \nVdash [EG(r \vee q)\,U\,AFt]$. This happens if there is a computation path beginning with s_3 that falsifies "$EG(r \vee q)$ until AFt".

The leftmost path in the computation tree for s_3 is $s_3 \longrightarrow s_3 \longrightarrow \cdots$. We want to check whether this path falsifies the sentence "$EG(r \vee q)$ until AFt". This means that either $s_3 \nVdash EG(r \vee q)$ or $s_3 \nVdash AFt$. (Why?) Now, $s_3 \Vdash AFt$ iff for all computation paths beginning with s_3, there is a future state satisfying t. From the computation tree of s_3, we see that s_1 is a future state, and $s_1 \nVdash t$. Therefore, $s_3 \nVdash AFt$. Consequently, $s_3 \nVdash A[EG(r \vee q)\,U\,AFt]$. Thus, $s_3 \Vdash Y$.

In fact, any model of CTL is an abstraction of any transition system like concurrent and reactive systems, networks, etc. Our aim is to verify whether such a system satisfies certain properties. These properties are now represented as CTL formulas, by looking at the satisfaction at each state (truth at each world) of the model. It is usually lengthy and too cumbersome to check this satisfaction relation manually.

However, if we have a finite model, programs can be written to do this repetitive job. These programs are called **model checkers**. SMV is one such model checker. There are also other model checkers using some specification language such as CTL. Note that it all depends upon how you visualize time and the reactions of the system components. In such a scenario of model checking, you have a real system for which some properties are to be verified. When a model checker is available, you will be doing the following:

1. Model the real system using the description language (such as SMV) of the model checker arriving at an abstract model M.
2. Translate the properties of the real system which are to be verified, to the specification language (such as CTL) of the model checker and arrive at a formula p.
3. Run the model checker with inputs M and p to determine whether $M \vDash p$.

It is of much practical importance to develop model checkers which use very general specification languages so that interesting properties of real systems can be checked efficiently.

Exercises for § 11.10

1. Plugging in the meanings of the individual letters, write in words what the connectives AX, EX, AF, EF, AG, EG, $A[\cdot U \cdot]$, $E[\cdot U \cdot]$ mean.
2. Check the following with the model given below:

   (a) $s_1 \Vdash EX(q \wedge r)$ (b) $s_1 \Vdash \neg AX(q \wedge r)$ (c) $s_1 \Vdash EF(p \wedge r)$

   (d) $s_2 \Vdash EGr \wedge AGr$ (e) $s_1 \Vdash AFr \vee A[p\,U\,r]$ (f) $s_1 \Vdash E[(p \wedge q)\,U\,r]$

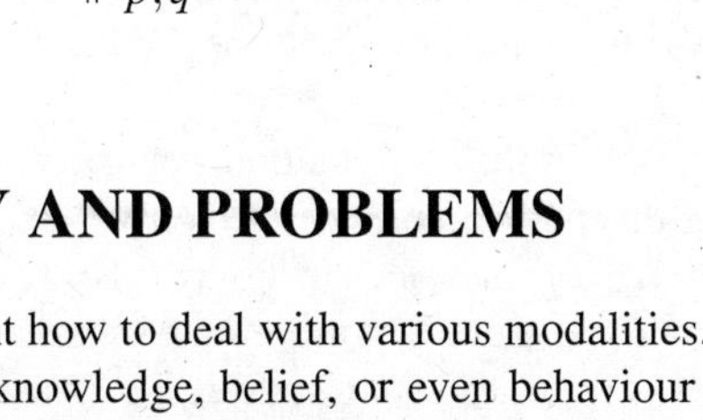

11.11 SUMMARY AND PROBLEMS

In this chapter, you have learnt how to deal with various modalities. The modalities might be pertaining to truth, knowledge, belief, or even behaviour of real systems. We have taken a simplistic approach of introducing the new modal connectives $\Box$ and $\Diamond$, which symbolize necessity and possibility, respectively. This has led us to the basic modal logic K.

The semantics of K has taken us to the relational structures called *frames*. A frame consists of a set, called the set of *worlds*, and a relation on this set, called the *accessibility relation*. Each world is assumed to be propositional in the sense that it is an interpretation of PL. A world thus comes with the information as to which propositions are true at it and which are false. The frame with this information of *truth at worlds* is called a model. The models serve the same job as interpretations in PL. The truth at each world is taken into consideration in defining satisfaction of modal propositions in models, and then the notion of validity.

Axiomatization of the basic logic K has led us to consider various properties and extensions. The extensions of KC obtained by addition of different axiom schemes have resulted in restricting frames to satisfy certain properties. This correspondence of axioms and frame properties has brought in different modal logics, which are found to address various problem domains.

As an application to real systems, you have learnt the computation tree logic which uses the idea of branching time. To understand various phenomena in computer science, you will naturally use logical models which would differ quite a bit from the ones discussed here, though this will form a basis for your future work.

Modal logic is bread and butter for a computer scientist. Once it mixes into the blood stream, it is impossible to find the source. However, one must start somewhere, and this text is meant for that. This is a mere introduction; so pointers must be given for pursuing the topics further.

You may start with the texts Epstein (2001), Lewis (1918), Lewis & Langford (1938), and Popkorn (1994). In Snyder (1971), you will get another proof procedure, called cancellation technique, a shortened form of Gentzen systems.

For a comprehensive introduction to modal logics, you may like the incomplete *Lemmon notes* as exposed in Lemmon (1977). The semantics, called the *possible world semantics*, was invented by S. Kripke; thus the name K for the basic modal logic. Some good texts exclusively meant for modal logics are Chellas (1980), Goldblatt (1987), and Hughes & Cresswell (1971). These books discuss adequacy of calculi and decidability of the modal logics via *finite models property* in great detail. You will also find the references there to be very resourceful.

You have also seen how natural deduction and the method of analytic tableau could be extended to these logics. The natural deduction system and the tableau, as presented here, have their origin in Fitting (1993).

For a modal extension of the first order logic, see Fitting & Mendelson (1998). Two good sources for applications of modal logics for reasoning about knowledge (originated by J. Hintikka) are Fagin et al. (1995) and Meyer & van der Hoek (1993).

The computation tree logic as presented here is based on the chapter on Verification by Model Checking in Huth & Ryan (2000). This text also includes discussions on two nice puzzles, the wise men puzzle and the muddy children puzzle, and more information on the symbolic model verifier SMV.

Modal logics have been extensively used in analysing the provability predicate, which first appeared in Gödel's incompleteness theorems. For such applications of modal logics, see Boolos (1979).

Problems for Chapter 11

1. Describe a model in which the given mp is false at some world:

   (a) $\Box p \to \Box\Box p$ (b) $\Box p \to \Diamond p$ (c) $\Box(p \vee q) \to \Box p \vee \Box q$

2. Prove both the local and global deduction theorems. What can you say about the following metastatements?
   (a) If $\Sigma \Rightarrow A \to B$, then $\Sigma \cup \{A\} \Rightarrow B$
   (b) If $\Sigma \cup \{A\} \Rightarrow B$, then $\Sigma \Rightarrow A \to B$
3. Let Σ be a set of mps, and let X be any mp. Show that $\Sigma \vdash X$ in KC iff $\Sigma \Rightarrow X$. Does it go hand in hand with Theorem 11.10?
4. Recall that in PND, we could forgo drawing the boxes by using artificial bracketing such as CPB and CPE. Develop similar conventions for replacing the dashed boxes in KND.
5. Prove the adequacy of KND, i.e., $\Sigma \vdash_{KND} X$ iff $\Sigma \Rightarrow X$.
6. Show that if the underlying frame is transitive, then the model satisfies the mp $\Diamond\Diamond p \to \Diamond p$.
7. Describe a model in which each world would satisfy $\Box(p \wedge \neg p)$.
8. Describe the condition on the accessibility relation of a model under which each world would satisfy $\Diamond p \to \Box p$.
9. Show that if all mps of the form $p \to \Box\Diamond p$ are valid, then the underlying frame must be reflexive.
10. Suppose the accessibility relation R in a model is such that for all worlds u, v if uRv, then there is no world w with vRw. Show that such a model satisfies $\Box\Box(p \wedge \neg p)$.
11. Show that adding the axiom scheme $\Box\Box p \to \Box p$ to KC has the same effect as adding the scheme $\Diamond p \to \Diamond\Diamond p$.
12. Show that adding the axiom scheme $\Box(p \vee q) \to (\Box p \vee \Box q)$ to KC has the same effect as adding the scheme $\Diamond p \to \Box p$.
13. Determine the frame property corresponding to the axiom scheme L of the Gödel logic G.
14. Show that K4 is a sublogic of G.
15. Define equivalence of two CTL formulas by $q \equiv r$ iff any state in any model that satisfies q also satisfies r, and vice versa. Then show that

   (a) $AF\neg t \equiv \neg EGt$ (b) $EF\neg t \equiv \neg AGt$ (c) $AX\neg t \equiv \neg EXt$
   (d) $AFt \equiv A[\top U t]$ (e) $EFt \equiv E[\top U t]$ (f) Equivalences of PL

Chapter 12

Some Other Logics

12.1 INTRODUCTION

The basic issue with logic engineering is: with a problem domain in view, what would be the most appropriate logic to use? For instance, the argument "All saints are altruistic. Bapuji was a saint. Therefore, Bapuji was altruistic" could be modelled and justified by FL, but not by PL. When a familiar logic does not fit into a problem domain, you may attempt at modifying the logic. This activity of modification of an existing logic can be of two kinds.

One approach is to extend the vocabulary and then give an appropriate semantics. These new logics talk about things that the earlier logics could not. These are called **extended logics**. An example was FL as a modification of PL. The same way, modal logics have also been obtained as extensions of PL.

The other direction in creating new logics is not by extension, but by restriction on the semantics leading to a different set of valid formulas. Equivalently, these logics can also be obtained by asserting additional (or different) axiom schemes. The logics so obtained are called **deviant logics**.

The new logics obtained either way may or may not preserve the metalogical properties of the earlier ones. By picking out different metalogical properties and then looking at various logics through the properties is yet another way of classification. One of the many such properties, namely, monotonicity, has attracted considerable attention.

Recall the definition of $\Sigma \vDash w$ in PL or $\Sigma \vdash w$ in a proof method such as PC, Calculation, GPC, PND, PT, or in resolution. All these definitions attempt at defining the consequence relation which we visualize to hold between a set of propositions Σ and a proposition w. The semantic (model theoretic) considerations or the syntactic derivations (proof theoretic) are then thought of as mechanisms for determining whether the pair (Σ, w) is an element of this relation or not.

Thus a logic may be viewed as a mechanism to define the consequence relation. Defining a consequence relation arbitrarily leads to different logics. If the new consequence relation is different from the existing ones, then the logic so obtained is also different from the existing ones.

For instance, suppose that you have a mechanism to convert each proposition to an integer. (You can have many such mechanisms since the set of propositions, in PL, is countable.) Define the consequence relation $\mathscr{C}$ by $(\Sigma, w) \in \mathscr{C}$ iff the integer corresponding to w divides the product of the integer representations of some of the elements of Σ. Taking this as the consequence relation, you can get a deviant logic of propositions.

But, do you really want any arbitrary relation between a set of propositions and a proposition to serve as a consequence relation? For ease in reading, let us write $(\Sigma, w) \in \mathscr{C}$ as $\Sigma \Vdash w$. A. Tarski and D. Scott suggested that we regard any such relation as a consequence relation provided it possesses the following properties:

Reflexivity : If $w \in \Sigma$, then $\Sigma \Vdash w$.
Transitivity : If $\Sigma \Vdash X$ and $\Sigma \cup \{X\} \Vdash w$, then $\Sigma \Vdash w$.
Monotonicity : If $\Sigma \subseteq \Gamma$ and $\Sigma \Vdash w$, then $\Gamma \Vdash w$.

Such are the **monotonic logics**. Both PL and FL are monotonic logics, in the sense that their consequence relations satisfy all the above properties. There are other logics which do not satisfy the monotonicity condition; and are known as nonmonotonic logics. A nonmonotonic logic can be an extended logic, or a deviant logic, depending upon whether it involves a nontrivial extension of vocabulary or a reinterpretation of the same vocabulary.

In this chapter, we plan to review some logics keeping in mind both the classes. The treatment is very brief, and it aims to show you how so many varieties of logics have been invented out of necessity. You will, most probably, create your own logic fitting a new situation more tightly than any of the logics known as of today.

12.2 INTUITIONISTIC LOGIC

In Example 8.19, you have seen a proof of existence of two algebraic irrational numbers a and b such that a^b is rational. Specifically, the proof uses the idea that either $\sqrt{2}^{\sqrt{2}}$ is rational, or it is not. If it is rational, then both a and b can be taken as $\sqrt{2}$. If it is irrational, then we take a as this, and b as $\sqrt{2}$. It does not exhibit, in particular, which of the two pairs, $(\sqrt{2}, \sqrt{2})$ or $(\sqrt{2}^{\sqrt{2}}, \sqrt{2})$, serves the purpose of (a, b).

Some mathematicians, now called intuitionists, object to accepting such a proof. The objection is that we do not know whether $\sqrt{2}^{\sqrt{2}}$ is rational or irrational. Therefore, we do not yet have, following this argument, a pair of irrationals (a, b) with the required property. (Of course, now we know that $\sqrt{2}^{\sqrt{2}}$ is rational due to I. Gelfand; but this is never used in the proof.)

According to this school of thought, a proposition $p \vee q$ can be true only when at least one of them has been demonstrated to be true. This implies that the law of excluded middle cannot be regarded as a law at all.

Consider the following situation. A pair of positive integers $(m, m+2)$ is a twin prime if both $m, m+2$ are primes. We know of many twin primes but we do not know whether there is a twin prime bigger than $10^{10^{10}}$. We also do not know whether there is no twin prime bigger than $10^{10^{10}}$. Hence at this stage, we cannot accept the truth of the following sentence:

> Either there is a twin prime bigger than $10^{10^{10}}$ or there is no twin prime bigger than $10^{10^{10}}$.

This is the basic insight of L. E. J. Brower who says that if the law of excluded middle is accepted, then we are assuming that every mathematical problem is solvable (in this sense), and this is certainly objectionable.

In the absence of excluded middle, the law of double negation fails. Though $A \to \neg\neg A$ would still remain valid, its converse $\neg\neg A \to A$ will no more hold. In the intuitionistic propositional logic, **INT**, negation has a different meaning. In INT the sentence $0 = 1$ is a contradiction, but for any sentence A, the proposition $A \wedge \neg A$ cannot be accepted as a contradiction.

INT has the same vocabulary as that of PL; leaving aside the symbols $\top$ and $\bot$. We do not take $\leftrightarrow$ into its vocabulary right now since this can be expressed in terms of $\to$ and $\wedge$ as in PC. INT assigns different meanings to the connectives; it is a deviant logic.

Axiom Schemes of INT:

(I1) $A \to (B \to A)$

(I2) $A \to (B \to (A \wedge B))$

(I3) $(A \wedge B) \to A$

(I4) $(A \wedge B) \to B$

(I5) $A \to (A \vee B)$

(I6) $B \to (A \vee B)$

(I7) $(A \vee B) \to ((A \to C) \to ((B \to C) \to C))$

(I8) $(A \to B) \to ((A \to (B \to C)) \to (A \to C))$

(I9) $(A \to B) \to ((A \to \neg B) \to \neg A)$

(I10) $A \to (\neg A \to B)$

Rule of Inference of INT:

(MP) $\dfrac{A \qquad A \to B}{B}$

A. Heyting gave an axiomatization of INT, in which axioms and the law of uniform replacement had been used. The above axiomatization is by M. Dummett, which uses axiom schemes.

A possible world semantics of INT uses the same idea of a frame and a model as in the modal logics, except that all our frames are now reflexive and transitive. That is, a model is a triple $M = (W, R, \Vdash)$, where W is a nonempty set of worlds, R is a reflexive and transitive relation on W, and $\Vdash$ is a relation from W to the power set of all atomic propositions. The relation $\Vdash$ is extended to include all propositions in its domain by using the following rules:

$w \Vdash \neg p$ iff for all $z \in W$ with wRz, $z \nVdash p$.
$w \Vdash p \wedge q$ iff $w \Vdash p$ and $w \Vdash q$.
$w \Vdash p \vee q$ iff $w \Vdash p$ or $w \Vdash q$.
$w \Vdash p \to q$ iff for all $z \in W$ with wRz, $z \nVdash p$ or $z \Vdash q$.
$M \vDash p$ iff for all $w \in W$, $w \Vdash p$.

As assumed earlier, the completeness and the soundness of the axiomatic system INT can be proved with respect to the above semantics. However, since we use a possible world semantics for INT, it must have some connection with modal logics. It can be verified that the following translation (due to K. Gödel) to the logic S4 (KT4) holds. Writing the translation by the map $*$, we have

$$\begin{aligned} p^* &= p \\ (\neg p)^* &= \neg \Box p^* \\ (p \vee q)^* &= \Box p^* \vee \Box q^* \\ (p \wedge q)^* &= \Box p^* \wedge \Box q^* \\ (p \to q)^* &= \Box p^* \to \Box q^* \end{aligned}$$

You can interpret $\Box$ as 'it is demonstrated that'. Now, rethink along the lines of the two introducing illustrations above (that of a^b and of the twin primes).

What is the relation between PL-validity and INT-validity? Note that all axioms of INT are PL-valid, and the inference rule is MP, which is also a valid consequence of PL. It follows (by induction?) that every INT-valid proposition is PL-valid. The converse does not hold.

The relation is best understood by noting that whenever p is PL-valid, its double negation $\neg\neg p$ is also PL-valid. But this does not happen in INT. The following result (See Glivenko (1929) for a proof.) explains the connection between PL and INT.

Theorem 12.1. *For a set of propositions Σ, let $\neg\neg\Sigma = \{\neg\neg w : w \in \Sigma\}$. Let A be any proposition. Then, $\Sigma \vdash_{PL} A$ iff $\neg\neg\Sigma \vdash_{\text{INT}} \neg\neg A$. Moreover, $\vdash_{PL} \neg A$ iff $\vdash_{\text{INT}} \neg A$.*

Notice that Theorem 12.1 does not say that $\vdash_{PL} A$ iff $\vdash_{\text{INT}} A$. This holds when the only connectives used are $\neg$ and $\wedge$. However, double negation does not hold even in this restricted language. For example, $\neg\neg p \vdash_{PL} p$ but $\neg\neg p \nvdash_{\text{INT}} p$.

Theorem 12.1 suggests that PL-theorems may have a translation into INT in some sense. The following is such a translation of PL-theorems to INT-theorems via the map $\dagger$:

$$\begin{aligned} p^\dagger &= \neg\neg p \\ (p \wedge q)^\dagger &= p^\dagger \wedge q^\dagger \\ (p \vee q)^\dagger &= \neg(\neg p^\dagger \wedge \neg q^\dagger) \\ (p \to q)^\dagger &= \neg(p^\dagger \wedge \neg q^\dagger) \end{aligned}$$

This translation preserves consequences. However, if $p^\dagger = \neg\neg p$ is replaced by $p^\dagger = p$, then only theorem-hood is preserved; see Gentzen (1936) and Łukasiewicz (1970). Dummett (1977) discusses the set assignment semantics for INT. Along with other proof procedures for INT, intuitionistic first order logic has also been well studied. Basing on this logic, intuitionistic mathematics has been created.

Exercises for § 12.2

1. Why is it that rejection of the law of excluded middle leads to the rejection of the validity of $\neg\neg A \to A$? Why does the conditional $A \to \neg\neg A$ still hold? [Hint: Use PC instead of PL.]
2. Show that the rejection of the law of excluded middle leads to the invalidity of $\neg(A \wedge B) \to (\neg A \vee \neg B)$.
3. Prove that if A is a proposition that uses only $\neg$ and $\wedge$, then $\vdash_{PL} A$ iff $\vdash_{\text{INT}} A$.

12.3 ŁUKASIEWICZ LOGICS

Consider the sentence: "There will be an earth quake tomorrow". Is it true? Is it false? Since nothing about its truth or falsity is known today, it is neither true nor false. But it is quite possible that tomorrow an earth quake may really occur. Its truth is beyond the classical bivalence. It is something like an amoral action, which is neither moral nor immoral; it is beyond morality.

To take into account such propositions, which do come up in abundance in day-to-day life, the bivalent logics like PL or FL would not suffice. What about assigning a new truth value to 'beyond true or false'?

Suppose that we agree to have one more truth value, say, $1/2$, in addition to 0 and 1. As in PL, we start with $\top, \bot$, and the propositional variables as atoms and use the connectives $\neg, \wedge, \vee, \to$ to build up a formal language of propositions. The semantics of the logic is different from that of PL. Writing the truth value of a proposition p as $t(p)$, the semantics may be specified as follows:

$$\begin{aligned}
t(\top) &= 1\\
t(\bot) &= 0\\
t(\neg p) &= 1 - t(p)\\
t(p \wedge q) &= \min\{t(p), t(q)\}\\
t(p \vee q) &= \max\{t(p), t(q)\}\\
t(p \to q) &= \begin{cases} 1 & \text{if } t(p) = t(q)\\ \max\{1 - t(p), t(q)\} & \text{otherwise}\end{cases}
\end{aligned}$$

The same is also given in terms of a truth table; see Table 12.1.

Formally, you can define an interpretation as a map from all propositions to the set of truth values $\{0, 1/2, 1\}$, obeying the conditions given in the truth table. Alternatively, you can show that the map $t(\cdot)$ is well defined on the set of all propositions (due to unique parsing), starting from a preliminary definition on the set of atomic propositions. That defines the concept of an interpretation; each such map is an interpretation. Then you can define equivalence by

$$p \equiv q \text{ iff } t(p) = t(q) \text{ for any interpretation } t.$$

Moreover, we define the connective $\leftrightarrow$ as follows:

$$p \leftrightarrow q \mathrel{\hat{=}} (p \to q) \wedge (q \to p)$$

Table 12.1: Truth table with three truth values

$\top$	$\bot$	p	q	$\neg p$	$p \wedge q$	$p \vee q$	$p \to q$
1	0	0	0	1	0	0	1
		1/2	0	1/2	0	1/2	1/2
		1	0	0	0	1	0
		0	1/2		0	1/2	1
		1/2	1/2		1/2	1/2	1
		1	1/2		1/2	1	1/2
		0	1		0	1	1
		1/2	1		1/2	1	1
		1	1		1	1	1

We call this *three-valued logic*, **L3** after the logician J. Łukasiewicz.

Though the law of excluded middle does not hold in L3, a similar law called the law of trivalence holds. To formulate this law, we introduce the indeterminate proposition in L3, written as ιp (iota p). Let p be any propositional variable. Define a proposition ιp by

$$\iota p \mathrel{\stackrel{\circ}{=}} p \leftrightarrow \neg p$$

The proposition ιp is called an **indeterminate proposition**. The truth table of ιp can be given as

p	0	1/2	1
ιp	0	1	0

Any proposition A equivalent to $\top$ is called an *L3-tautology* or an *L3-valid* proposition, and is written as $\vDash_{\mathrm{L}_3} A$. It thus follows that $p \equiv q$ iff $p \leftrightarrow q \equiv \top$.

The **law of trivalence** is the metastatement

$p \vee \neg p \vee \iota p \equiv \top$ in L3 for any proposition p.

You can also check the following for any interpretation t in L3:

$t(p \to q) = 1$ iff $t(p) \le t(q)$, and $t(p \leftrightarrow q) = 1$ iff $t(p) = t(q)$.

Let Σ be a set of propositions (in L3 now), and let w be any proposition. Define the validity of an *L3-consequence* by

$\Sigma \vDash_{\mathrm{L}_3} w$ iff for each interpretation t, if $t(A) = 1$ for each $A \in \Sigma$, then $t(w) = 1$.

You can check that the following results hold:

Modus Ponens: $\{p,\ p \to q\} \vDash_{\mathrm{L}_3} q$.

Equivalence Replacement: $p \leftrightarrow q \vDash_{\mathrm{L}_3} A \leftrightarrow A[p :=_e q]$.

Uniform Replacement: If $\vDash_{\mathrm{L}_3} B$, then $\vDash_{\mathrm{L}_3} B[p := q]$.

where $A[p :=_e q]$ is obtained from A by substituting some or all or no occurrence of p in A by q, and $B[p := q]$ is obtained from B by substituting every occurrence of p in B by q.

Moreover, J. Łukasiewicz constructed L3 for arguing about *possibility* and *necessity* by using the following truth table:

p	$\Box p$	$\Diamond p$
0	0	0
1/2	0	1
1	1	1

From the above data, it is clear that $\Diamond p \equiv \neg p \to p$ and $\Box p \equiv \neg\Diamond\neg p$. (Verify.) Though $A \to \Box A$ is not L3-valid, we have $\vDash_{L_3} A \to (A \to \Box A)$.

Theorem 12.2 (Deduction Theorem in L3). *Let Σ be a set of propositions, and let A, B be propositions. Then, $\Sigma \cup \{A\} \vDash_{L_3} B$ iff $\Sigma \vDash_{L_3} A \to (A \to B)$.*

Further, we can have a translation of PL (or PC) into L3, which preserves consequences. This is achieved via the translation map $*$ from PL to L3 by

$$p^* = p \quad \text{for atomic propositions } p.$$
$$(\neg p)^* = p^* \to (p^* \to \neg(p^* \to p^*))$$
$$\Sigma^* = \{p^* : p \in \Sigma\} \quad \text{for any set } \Sigma \text{ of propositions.}$$

Such a translation identifies PL in L3. Observe that a simplistic way of identifying both 1 and 1/2 with 1, i.e., *true*, would not result in PL. Similarly, identifying both 0 and 1/2 with 0 will also fail. (Why?) However, any L3-tautology is vacuously a PL-tautology since the truth tables of connectives in L3 restricted to the values of 0 and 1 are simply the PL-truth tables.

Observe that the truth function σp given by

σp is 1/2 for every value of p

is not definable from the connectives $\neg, \wedge$ and $\vee$. This is so because, if it were, then $\neg\sigma p$ and σp would be equivalent, forcing $\vDash_{L_3} \neg\sigma p \leftrightarrow \sigma p$ to hold. Since each L3-tautology is a PL-tautology, $\neg\sigma p \leftrightarrow \sigma p$ would also be PL-valid. But this is obviously wrong as $\neg A \leftrightarrow A$ is not PL-valid. This truth function σ is called the *Słupecki operator*. Consideration of the Słupecki operator shows that for the truth functional completeness, the connectives $\neg, \wedge, \vee$ are not enough in L3.

However, the set $\{\neg, \to\}$ of connectives is truth functionally complete in L3. An adequate axiomatic system (see Wójcicki (1998)) for L3 which uses $\neg$ and $\to$ as in PC, has the following axiom schemes and the rule of inference:

Axiom Schemes for L3

(L1) $A \to (B \to A)$

(L2) $(A \to B) \to ((B \to C) \to (A \to C))$

(L3) $(\neg A \to \neg B) \to (B \to A)$

(L4) $((A \to \neg A) \to A) \to A$

Rule of Inference

(MP) $\dfrac{A \qquad A \to B}{B}$

A generalization of Łukasiewicz three-valued logic L_3 has been obtained by him and A. Tarski. We briefly mention its peculiarity here. The idea is to view the truth values as any real number between 0 and 1, instead of the three values 0, 1/2, 1. An interpretation is taken as a map from the set of atoms to the interval $[0,1]$. This map is extended to all propositions by

$$\begin{aligned} t(\neg p) &= 1 - t(p) \\ t(p \vee q) &= \max\{t(p), t(q)\} \\ t(p \wedge q) &= \min\{t(p), t(q)\} \\ t(p \to q) &= \begin{cases} 1 & \text{if } t(p) \le t(q) \\ 1 - t(p) + t(q) & \text{otherwise} \end{cases} \end{aligned}$$

Many logics can be defined using this scheme t of truth values, depending upon what subset of the interval $[0,1]$ is fixed as the co-domain of the interpretation t. Some of the logics and their corresponding co-domains of the interpretations are given in the following table:

Logic	Co-domain of interpretations
L_n	$\{\frac{m}{n-1} : 0 \le m \le n-1,\ n \ge 2\}$
$L_{\aleph_0}$	$\{\frac{m}{n} : 0 < m \le n,\ m,n \in \mathbb{N}\}$
$L_{\aleph}$	$[0,1]$

In all cases, a proposition is called valid if each interpretation evaluates it to 1. For example, $L_{\aleph}$ has the valid propositions as all p for which $t(p) = 1$ for each interpretation t with the co-domain as the interval $[0,1]$. In this scheme, we get many logics such as

$$L_2,\ L_3,\ L_4,\ L_5,\ \ldots,\ L_{\aleph_0},\ L_{\aleph}.$$

Note that L_2 is simply the propositional logic PL. Further, $L_n \ne L_{n+1}$, and each valid proposition of L_m is also L_n-valid provided that n divides m. Again, $L_{\aleph_0}$ is the same as $L_{\aleph}$ in the sense that their valid propositions coincide. This is a non-trivial result; see Epstein (2001).

Now, in view of these many-valued logics, what do you think of INT? For a proposition p, you have $\neg p, \neg\neg p$; and $\neg\neg\neg p$ is equivalent to $\neg p$ in INT. So, is INT a three-valued logic? Is it L_3, say, in the sense that INT-valid propositions coincide with L_3-valid propositions? Or, is the converse true? K. Gödel has proved in 1932 that INT cannot be characterized as any finite valued logic L_n (for $n = 2,3,4,\ldots$). It is again a non-trivial a result.

Still there are other varieties of many-valued logics. An example is Kleene's three-valued logic which has the same three truth values $0, 1/2, 1$. Unlike L_3, in Kleene's three-valued logic, when both A, B are 1/2, the formula $A \to B$ is evaluated to 1/2. You may define other many-valued logics by playing with the truth values and the connectives.

Exercises for § 12.3

1. Verify the formulas for $t(p)$ in Łukasiewicz logic using Table 12.1.
2. Construct the truth table for $\leftrightarrow$ in L_3 by defining $p \leftrightarrow q$ as $(p \to q) \wedge (q \to p)$.
3. Show that in L_3, $p \vee \neg p \not\equiv \top$ and that $p \to q \not\equiv \neg p \vee q$.
4. Show that $\vDash_{L_3} p \vee \neg p \vee \iota p$. What are $\iota\top$ and $\iota\bot$?
5. Show the following equivalences in L_3 :

   (a) $(p \to (q \to p)) \equiv \top$ (b) $p \vee q \equiv (p \to q) \to q$

   (c) $p \wedge q \equiv \neg(\neg p \vee \neg q)$ (d) $\sigma \neg p \vee q \equiv p \to (p \to q)$
6. Prove Theorem 12.2.
7. With the translation map $*$ for L_3, show that $\Sigma \vDash_{PL} A$ iff $\Sigma^* \vDash_{L_3} A^*$.
8. Show that $L_{\aleph}$ can be axiomatized with the axiom schemes L1, L2, L3, and $(A \to B) \vee (B \to A)$, and the inference rule MP.

12.4 PROBABILISTIC LOGICS

A doctor wants to decide whether a patient has the disease D after listening to and examining the patient for symptoms. He only knows that certain symptoms and certain diseases occur with such and such probabilities. (In this section, we write $p(\cdot)$ for probabilities and not for denoting propositions.) Write $S \to D$ to mean that the symptom S implies the infliction of the disease D. To be specific, suppose that the doctor knows the following:

A1: $A \to D$ holds with probability p_1.
A2: $\neg A \to D$ holds with probability p_2.
A3: $B \to D$ holds with probability p_3.

When the patient exhibits the symptoms $\neg A$ and B, the doctor wants to determine whether the patient has the disease D. Note that the probabilities assigned to the above statements are the doctor's knowledge, i.e., they are subjective. So, the diagnosis will also be subjective; it is his rational opinion. It is rational in the sense that the final decision uses an objective procedure even on the subjective probabilities. He uses his subjective probabilities to compute the probability of the patient suffering from the disease D given that the patient exhibits the symptoms $\neg A$ and B. The doctor's interest is in determining the conditional probability

$$p(D \mid \neg A \wedge B) = \frac{p(D \wedge \neg A \wedge B)}{p(\neg A \wedge B)}.$$

Such computations become meaningful in the presence of a probability distribution of propositions, that is, a probability space of propositions and a probability measure on this space. In the diagnosis problem, we may consider the relevant propositions to be drawn from the set

$$U = \{A,\ B,\ A \wedge D,\ \neg A,\ \neg A \wedge D,\ B \wedge D,\ D,\ A \wedge B,\ \neg A \wedge B,\ D \wedge \neg A \wedge B\}.$$

Then, we go for constructing the set of *elementary propositions* (not necessarily atomic) so that a probability measure can be defined. The set $E = \{E_1, E_2, \ldots, E_n\}$ of elementary propositions will satisfy the following properties:

1. Each relevant proposition is a disjunction of some elementary propositions.
2. The elementary propositions are exhaustive: $E_1 \vee \ldots \vee E_n \equiv \top$.
3. The elementary propositions are mutually exclusive: $E_i \wedge E_j \equiv \bot$ for $i \neq j$.

Thus, in our diagnostic problem, we take the set $E = \{A, B, D, \neg A, \neg B, \neg D\}$ assuming that A, B, D are atomic. Next, a probability measure is defined on the set $\mathbb{E} = E \cup \{\top, \bot\}$. A probability measure is a function $p : \mathbb{E} \to [0,1]$ satisfying the following properties:

(a) For any $X, Y \in \mathbb{E}$, $p(X) \geq 0$.
(b) $p(\top) = 1$, $p(\bot) = 0$.
(c) If $X \wedge Y \equiv \bot$, then $p(X \vee Y) = p(X) + p(Y)$.

The probabilities are used to compute the required conditional probability. Note that the restrictions of a probability measure are imposed on the subjective probabilities of a decision-maker, here, the doctor. This is the reason that a decision-maker who uses probabilistic logic is assumed to be a rational agent. As you have guessed, probabilistic logic is rather a logical methodology for decision making than a logic. One can go further in deciding upon a consensus by taking opinions from experts for fixing the subjective probabilities of elementary propositions. One may also resort to statistical methods while arriving at a consensus. A good start on this topic may be Halpern (1990).

In a probabilistic framework, it is not possible to assign a probability to ignorance; we only assign a probability to what is known. In the presence of ignorance or insufficient information, and vagueness, probabilistic logic will not be appropriate. In the next section, we will have a rough outline of the two types of logics that deal with uncertainty and vagueness.

12.5 POSSIBILISTIC AND FUZZY LOGIC

Consider the sentence s: Sam is tall. By introducing a variable h for the height of Sam, you can translate the sentence to $h \approx tall$. If h takes values from the set { tall, medium, short }, then the truth predicate P_h can be evaluated to one value, depending upon whether h is tall, medium or short. Say, P_h is either 1, $1/2$ or 0 according as h is tall, medium, or short. Then the predicate P_h is called a *crisp predicate*, as it has definite values.

If height is allocated a value, say, any real number between 40 cm and 300 cm, then possible values for P_h will be uncountably many. In such a case, P_h has no definite value from among finitely many; it is now referred to as a *vague predicate.* The range of values, the closed interval $U = [40\,\text{cm}, 300\,\text{cm}]$, is our universe for height h, and P_h is a vague predicate defined on this universe U. Here the predicate P_h is unary; thus, when it is crisp, it is just a subset of U. What would happen if P_h is a vague predicate? It is clearly not a subset, for we do not know or we cannot know for certainty which elements of U are in P_h and which are not. In such a case, we say that P_h is a *fuzzy subset* of the universe U.

Any subset A of a set U can be characterized by its *characteristic* or *indical function* $\chi_A : U \to \{0,1\}$, by the rule that for any $u \in U$, $u \in A$ iff $\chi_A(u) = 1$. In case

A is a fuzzy subset of U, we identify this fuzzy subset with the *membership function* $\mu_A : U \to [0,1]$. Thus, any element $u \in U$ is a fuzzy member of the fuzzy subset A of U determined by its degree of membership $\mu_A(u)$. (Imagine membership to admit of degrees rather than being either 0 or 1.) If $\mu_A(u) = 1$, then $u \in A$, as in the case of a crisp subset. If $\mu_A(u) = 0$, then $u \notin A$, again as in the crisp subset case. If $\mu_A(u) = \alpha$ for $0 < \alpha < 1$, then the degree of membership of u in A is α.

When $B = P_h$ is taken as a fuzzy subset of U (as a vague predicate), we have a membership function μ_B. Then μ_B gives the idea as to how much tall Sam is, or rather, "what is the degree of tallness of Sam when his height is so and so". It gives rise to four cases as considered in the following subsections. below. The ensuing four cases are of crisp sentences and precise information, crisp sentences and imprecise information, crisp sentences and fuzzy information, and vague sentences and fuzzy information. These cases are considered in the following subsections.

12.5.1 Crisp Sentences and Precise Information

Suppose that $B = \{150\,\text{cm}\}$; we know that Sam is 150 cm tall. Here, $B \subseteq U$ is a crisp subset of U. Depending upon whether we consider 150 cm as a height to be termed as tall or not, $\mu_B(s)$ will take a value in $\{0,1\}$. That is, the truth of the sentence s is either 0 (s is false) or 1 (s is true). Here, Sam's height is exactly known. We also have a crisp sentence since we have the information whether this height is termed as tall or short. Thus the case is compared to PL, where the truth of each sentence is either 0 or 1. That is, $t(s) = \mu_B(s) \in \{0,1\}$.

12.5.2 Crisp Sentences and Imprecise Information

Suppose we know that Sam's height is within 150 cm to 200 cm, i.e., we do not have precise information here. Suppose also that the meaning of tall is crisp, i.e., if the height of a person is within a range, say, a to b in centimetres, then he is called *tall*. Symbolically, the predicate "tallness" is identified with the crisp subset $[a,b] \subseteq U$. Then, the following cases may be considered:

(a) If $B = [150, 200] \subseteq A = [a,b]$, then clearly, $t(B) = 1$; Sam is tall.

(b) If $A \cap [a,b] = \varnothing$, then $t(B) = 0$; Sam is not tall.

(c) If $A \cap [a,b] \neq \varnothing$ but $A \nsubseteq [a,b]$, then $t(B)$ cannot be fixed to either 0 or 1. The sentence "Sam is tall" is possibly true or possibly false.

These situations are tackled by introducing a possibility measure π as follows:

$$\text{for any subset } E \text{ of } U,\ \pi(E) = 1 \text{ if } E \cap A \neq \varnothing, \text{ else, } \pi(E) = 0.$$

Then the above cases correspond to:

(a) $\pi(s) = 1,\ \pi(\neg s) = 0.$

(b) $\pi(s) = 0,\ \pi(\neg s) = 1.$

(c) $\pi(s) = 1,\ \pi(\neg s) = 1.$

The case $\pi(s) = 0,\ \pi(\neg s) = 0$ leads to inconsistency; hence, it cannot occur.

12.5.3 Crisp Sentences and Fuzzy Information

Suppose that the meaning of tallness is crisp, i.e., we have a range of values for tallness, say, if the height of anyone is in $[a,b] \subseteq U$, then he is called tall. Assume also that our information on Sam's height is fuzzy. That is, $B = P_h$ is now a fuzzy subset of U, which is given by a membership function μ_B. Then, our answer to the query "whether Sam is tall" will have a fuzzy answer, i.e., tallness of Sam will have the degree of truth as $\mu_B(s)$.

12.5.4 Vague Sentences and Fuzzy Information

Here, both the sets representing tallness and Sam's height are fuzzy subsets of U. Suppose that S represents Sam's height, i.e., S is a fuzzy subset of U given by its membership function μ_S, and tallness is also a fuzzy subset B of U given by its membership function μ_B. Then the answer to the query "whether Sam is tall" will also be fuzzy. That is, the truth of the sentence "Sam is tall" will take a fuzzy truth value in the interval $[0,1]$, depending on the values of μ_B and μ_S. For example, "Sam's height is about 170 cm" is a fuzzy sentence. Such a sentence is translated to a membership function $\mu_S : [0,1] \to [0,1]$ defined as

$$\mu_S(v) = \sup\{\pi(u) : \mu_B(u) = v \text{ for } u \in U\}.$$

Here, the supremum over an empty set is taken as 0. Thus whenever $\mu_B^{-1}(v) = \varnothing$, we have $\mu_S(v) = 0$. The truth value $t(s)$ of the sentence "Sam is tall" is approximated by the numbers $N(s)$ and $\Pi(s)$ given by

$$\begin{aligned} N(s) &\le t(s) \le \Pi(s), \\ \Pi(s) &= \sup\{\min\{\mu_B(u), \pi(u)\} : u \in U\}, \\ N(s) &= 1 - \Pi(\neg s) = \inf\{\max\{\mu_B(u), 1 - \pi(u)\} : u \in U\}. \end{aligned}$$

This is the most general case, as all the earlier cases will fall into place by regarding the fuzzy subsets as crisp. The function Π is called the *possibility measure* and N is called the *necessity measure* so that the uncertainty or fuzzy measure $t(s)$ lies between the possibility and necessity.

The high rate at which work in fuzzy logic and fuzzy mathematics is growing at present prevents a non-specialist to catch up. However, it is wise to brush up some basic literature so that it will be easy for you later when some application domain demands fuzzy logic ideas. You may start with Tanaka (1996).

12.6 DEFAULT LOGIC

In this section, we briefly look at another way of dealing with certain kind of vagueness. The vagueness here is associated to limitations of knowledge or in its representation. For instance, when we say that "birds fly", we do not mean that all birds fly without exception, nor do we assert that only some birds fly. It is almost a general rule that birds fly; however, there might be exceptions, as we know that penguins do not fly and that a wounded bird may not fly. Such facts can be represented by first order consequences such as

$$P(x) \wedge \neg exception_1(x) \wedge \cdots \wedge \neg exception_m(x) \vDash Q(x).$$

In so doing, we are treating exceptions as general facts defeating the intention of a "general rule". We are also assuming that these are all possible exceptions. Tomorrow, we may discover another species of birds which might not fly! To tackle such cases, we introduce a type of rule, called *default*.

If we know that Tweety is a penguin, all penguins are birds, birds fly, and penguins do not fly, then we should be able to conclude that Tweety does not fly. We would not just dispense with the facts by telling that the facts are inconsistent. (Where is the inconsistency?) Here, we may take the following as facts:

> Each penguin is a bird. Tweety is a bird. Tweety is a penguin.

The sentence "birds fly" will be taken not as a fact, but as a default rule since this is the one that may admit of exceptions. The default rule is:

> If x is a bird and it cannot be proved that x is a penguin, then deduce that x flies.

Or, as a fraction:

$$\frac{x \text{ is a bird} : x \text{ is not a penguin}}{x \text{ flies}}$$

Thus,

> x is not a penguin

would now mean

> if it cannot be proved that x is not a penguin.

This can also be written as

> if it is consistent to assume that x is not a penguin.

Formally, a default (a default rule) looks like

$$\frac{u(x) \,:\, v_1(x), \ldots, v_m(x)}{w(x)}$$

where $u(x), v_1(x), \ldots, v_m(x)$ and $w(x)$ are well-formed formulas (of FL, in general) whose free variables are among $x_1, \ldots, x_n$, written here as a single symbol x. The formula $u(x)$ is called the *prerequisite* of the default. The formulas $v_1(x) \ldots, v_m(x)$ are the *justifications* and $w(x)$ is called the *consequent* of the default. The meaning of the default is

> If $v_1(x), \ldots, v_m(x)$ are consistent with what is already known, then $w(x)$ is inferred.

A *default theory* is a pair of sets $\Delta = (D, W)$, where D is a set of default rules and W is a set of FL-sentences.

Default logic is a nonmonotonic logic in the sense that addition of new facts may invalidate earlier established consequences. For example, consider the default theory $\Delta = (D, W)$, where $W = \{bird(tweety)\}$ and D has the single rule:

$$\frac{bird(x) \,:\, \neg\, penguin(x)}{flies(x)}$$

Here, we infer that $flies(tweety)$. If we enlarge W to $W' = W \cup \{penguin(tweety)\}$, then we cannot infer $flies(tweety)$.

EXAMPLE 12.1. Consider a universe (of constants) having two members, say a and b. Assume that an object in this universe is not an elf unless it is required to be. Moreover, at least one of a or b is an elf. Then its default theory is

$$\Delta = (D, W) \text{ with } W = \{elf(a) \vee elf(b)\},\ D = \left\{ \frac{:\neg elf(x)}{\neg elf(x)} \right\}.$$

The default rule in D says that "if it is consistent to assume that x is not an elf, then deduce that x is not an elf". You see that neither $elf(a)$ nor $elf(b)$ can be inferred from the single fact $elf(a) \vee elf(b)$. Since neither $elf(a)$ nor $elf(b)$ can be concluded, we would like to think that $\neg elf(a) \wedge \neg elf(b)$ is provable. However, this sentence is inconsistent with the fact $elf(a) \vee elf(b)$.

In order to avoid this inconsistency, default reasoning admits of many *extensions*. In the above example, we have an extension (an extended theory of Δ), where we can infer $\neg elf(a) \wedge elf(b)$, and in another extension of Δ, we can infer $elf(a) \wedge \neg elf(b)$.

Formally, let $\Delta = (D, W)$ be a given default theory. Let S be a set of FL-sentences. For any set A of FL-sentences, denote by $Th(A)$, the theory of A, i.e., the set of all FL-sentences which can be inferred from the set of premises as A. Define $\Gamma(S)$ as the smallest set satisfying the following properties:

1. $W \subseteq \Gamma(S)$.
2. $\Gamma(S) = Th(\Gamma(S))$.
3. For $u \in \Gamma(S)$, and for $\neg v_1, \ldots, \neg v_m \notin S$, if $\dfrac{u : v_1, \ldots, v_m}{w} \in D$ then $w \in \Gamma(S)$.

Finally, a set E is called *an extension for* Δ iff $\Gamma(E) = E$.

You can interpret $\Gamma(S)$ as the minimal set of beliefs that one can have in view of S, where S indicates which justification for beliefs is to be admitted. E is a fixed point of the operator Γ, just as $Th(A)$ is a fixed point of the operator Th in FL (i.e., $Th(Th(A)) = Th(A)$).

Alternatively, extensions of default theories can be defined from within. Let $\Delta = (D, W)$ be a default theory. An extension for Δ is any set

$$E = \cup_{i \in \mathbb{N}} E_i,$$

where the sets E_i are defined recursively by

$$E_0 = W,\ E_{i+1} = Th(E_i) \cup \left\{ w : \frac{u : v_1, \ldots, v_m}{w} \in D,\, u \in E_i,\, \neg v_1 \ldots, \neg v_m \notin E_i \right\}.$$

It can be proved that whenever W is consistent, every extension of the corresponding theory is consistent. The following examples will show you that a proper translation of facts and rules to a default theory can lead to the desired inference.

EXAMPLE 12.2. (Dubois et al. (1985)) Consider the following facts:

1. Generally, if Mary attends a meeting, Peter does not.
2. Generally, if Peter attends a meeting, Mary does not.
3. At least, one of Peter or Mary attends the meeting.

To have a default theory, let us use the following symbolization:

M : Mary attends the meeting. P : Peter attends the meeting.

Here,

$$\Delta_1 = (D_1, W_1),\ W_1 = \{M \vee P\},\ D_1 = \left\{ \frac{M : \neg P}{\neg P}, \frac{P : \neg M}{\neg M} \right\}.$$

This default theory has the unique extension $E_1 = Th(\{M \vee P\})$. However, it is awkward since we cannot infer from this extension that "both do not attend the same meeting". However, this sentence ought to be worth concluding. We will have another translation below, where this is possible.

This time, we take $\Delta_2 = (D_2, W_2)$, where $W_2 = W_1$, as earlier, but

$$D_2 = \left\{ \frac{: M}{\neg P}, \frac{: P}{\neg M} \right\}.$$

Here, the default translation of the sentence

Generally, if x attends a meeting, then y does not.

is taken as

If it is consistent to assume that x attends a meeting, then infer that y does not attend it.

In this translation, Δ_2 has two extensions (Verify!):

$$E_2 = Th(\{M, \neg P\}), \quad E_2' = Th(\{P, \neg M\}).$$

You see that $\neg(M \wedge P) \in E_2$ and also $\neg(M \wedge P) \in E_2'$.

A still better translation would be:

$$\Delta_3 = (D_3, W_3),\ W_3 = W_1,\ D_3 = \left\{ \frac{: M \wedge \neg P}{\neg P}, \frac{: P \wedge \neg M}{\neg M} \right\}.$$

This theory has two extensions again, and in both of them, $\neg(M \wedge P)$ can be inferred.

Further, suppose that we have the following additional facts:

4. If Bill attends the meeting, then Peter attends.
5. Bill attends the meeting.

Then, the sentence "Peter attends the meeting" can be inferred in the last two translations, but not in the first translation.

Much work on default logic have been reported in journals. If you prefer to start with a book; see Besnard (1989).

12.7 AUTOEPISTEMIC LOGICS

It is possible to have a knowledge base which has information about the scope and limitations of its own knowledge. For instance, in a database system, we often use the so-called *closed world assumption*, where "not" is interpreted as "not in the database". It is a built-in metaknowledge about the database. More flexible knowledge bases should have the ability to determine explicitly whether the knowledge of the base about a particular object in the base is in some sense complete or not. In such a scenario, we do not have to think about many agents and their knowledge or belief about facts stored in the base. We would rather have a formalization of the phrases such as "it is known that", or "it is believed that" as operators.

Writing $\Box p$ for "it is believed (known) that p", the logic K45 would be an appropriate logic. This is so because the K45 axioms

$$\Box(p \to q) \to (\Box p \to \Box q), \quad \Box p \to \Box\Box p, \quad \neg\Box p \to \Box(\neg\Box p)$$

capture the functionality of the operator $\Box$ here. However, new beliefs change an earlier conclusion; thus we require a nonmonotonic logic to deal with this operator. In this section, we briefly discuss such a nonmonotonic logic of knowledge and belief. The requirement of nonmonotonicity is made clearer in the following example.

EXAMPLE 12.3. Let p be the proposition: "Sam has died in the ongoing war". First, if p holds, then I also believe it, i.e., $p \to \Box p$. Next, suppose that I do not believe in a statement if I do not have any basis for such a belief. Hence I have the sole premise $p \to \Box p$.

Due to the absence of any information regarding Sam's death, I do not believe that Sam has died in the ongoing war, i.e., I have $\neg\Box p$. Since $p \to \Box p$ is equivalent to $\neg\Box p \to \neg p$, I conclude that $\neg p$. That is, Sam has not died in the ongoing war.

However, if I have the information that Sam has, indeed, died, then I have two premises, p and $p \to \Box p$, from which I conclude $\Box p$. Note that I have now p instead of the earlier conclusion $\neg p$, which was inferred in the absence of any information in the knowledge base.

This is the kind of nonmonotonicity involved in a logic of belief or knowledge. Such a logic is called an **autoepistemic logic**. Syntactically, the **formulas of an autoepistemic logic** are the modal propositions of K; the semantics differs.

Denote by L, the mps of K, which are now our building blocks for an autoepistemic logic. For simplicity, omit the symbols $\leftrightarrow$ and $\Diamond$; they can be introduced with the help of definitions such as $p \leftrightarrow q \mathrel{\hat{=}} (p \to q) \wedge (q \to p)$ and $\Diamond p \mathrel{\hat{=}} \neg\Box\neg p$.

A subset $T \subseteq L$ is called an **autoepistemic theory**. An **autoepistemic interpretation** of an autoepistemic theory T is a function $I : L \to \{0,1\}$ satisfying

(a) I conforms with a PL-interpretation.

(b) $I(\Box p) = 1$ iff $p \in T$.

An autoepistemic interpretation I is an **autoepistemic model** of T if $I(p) = 1$ for each $p \in T$. In such a case, we also say that p is true in I. As usual, an autoepistemic theory T is called **semantically complete** if T contains each formula that is true in each model of T. Similarly, the theory T is called **sound** with respect to a set of premises $A \subseteq L$ if every autoepistemic interpretation of T, which is a model of A is also a model of T.

Due to the absence of monotonicity, it is not easy to define the notion of a consequence. However, as in default logic, extensions would give rise to some *closure conditions* which can be used to define the set of all consequences of a theory. Instead of defining a "closure of a theory", we will give a name to a theory which is equal to its closure. A **stable theory** is an autoepistemic theory satisfying the following conditions:

1. If $q_1, \ldots, q_n \in T$ and $\{q_1, \ldots, q_n\} \vDash_{PL} q$, then $q \in T$.
2. If $q \in T$, then $\Box q \in T$.
3. If $q \notin T$, then $\neg \Box q \in T$.

It can be proved that an autoepistemic theory is semantically complete iff it is stable. However, stability is silent about what is not believed; hence, soundness with respect to a set of premises cannot be achieved under mere stability. The initial premises must be included somewhere. Suppose that A is a set of premises (formulas). A theory T is **grounded** in A if

$$T \subseteq \{q : A \cup \{\Box p : p \in T\} \cup \{\neg \Box p : p \notin T\} \vDash_{PL} q\}.$$

That is, T is grounded in A iff T is stable and it does not contain any formula which is not a PL-consequence of a *stable extension* of A.

It can be shown that a theory T is sound with respect to A iff T is grounded in A. Now, using both soundness and completeness, we arrive at the notion of a stable expansion of a theory. An autoepistemic theory T is a **stable expansion** of a set of premises A iff T is a superset of A that is stable and grounded in A, that is,

$$T = \{q : A \cup \{\Box p : p \in T\} \cup \{\neg \Box p : p \notin T\} \vDash_{PL} q\}.$$

A stable expansion contains all autoepistemic conclusions of the premises in A. This means, 'whatever that can be believed when all the formulas in A are believed' are in the stable expansion. Does there exist always a stable expansion? Is it unique?

EXAMPLE 12.4. Let $A = \{\neg \Box p \to p : p \text{ is any formula}\}$, and let T be a stable autoepistemic theory that contains the formula $\neg \Box p \to p$. If $p \notin T$, then due to stability, $\neg \Box p \in T$. Since $\neg \Box p \to p \in T$, we have $p \in T$. Hence, $p \in T$. If T is grounded in A, then T contains the PL-consequences of the set

$$\{\neg \Box p \to p : p \text{ is any formula}\} \cup \{\Box p : p \in T\} \cup \{\neg \Box p : p \notin T\}.$$

Since $p \in T$, $\Box p \in T$, we have $\neg \Box p \notin T$; otherwise, we have $p \notin T$, resulting in a contradiction. However, $\neg \Box p \notin T$ implies that $\neg \Box \neg \Box p \in T$.

Again, $\neg \Box \neg \Box p \to \neg \Box p \in A$ implies $\neg \Box p \in T$ as a PL-consequence. The contradiction $\neg \Box p \in T$ and $\neg \Box p \notin T$ shows that T cannot be grounded in A. Therefore, there is no stable expansion of A.

EXAMPLE 12.5. Let $A = \{\neg \Box p \to q, \neg \Box q \to p\}$. Let T be any stable expansion of A. The first element of A says that if p is not believed then q holds, and the second one asserts that if q is not believed then p holds.

Now, if $p \notin T$, then $q \in T$; and if $q \notin T$, then $p \in T$. Then there can be two stable expansions of T; one containing p but not q, and the other containing q but not p.

These examples show that stable expansions may not exist; and even if one exists, it need not be the only stable expansion. Note that a stable expansion in A formalizes the notion of all consequences of the premises in A. Thus, even if a theory is consistent, there may not be any conclusion, and even if there are conclusions, the set of all conclusions need not be unique. The status of theorem-hood with axioms in A is doubtful. However, this is pragmatic since belief in some statements need not conclusively guarantee other beliefs.

An alternative is to regard the intersection of all stable expansions as the set of all beliefs one may have. That is, any statement which is in every stable expansion of a theory grounded in a set of premises A can be regarded as theorems of A. This will be the view of an external observer about the agent. Also, in such a case, an empty intersection will lead to a definition of an inconsistent autoepistemic theory grounded in a set of premises.

There is a deep connection between default logic and autoepistemic logics. You may approach both the topics from applications point of view; see Baral (2003).

12.8 SUMMARY

This chapter briefly reviews some of the logics that have been in use for quite some time. You can start from the edited text Smets et al. (1998) to get an overall picture of nonstandard logics having some general frameworks and then go through the topics that interest you in Gabbay & Guenthner (2002).

We have not reviewed many logics which are in current use. One of them is the *description logic*. It is a restricted fragment of first order logic used for modelling relationships between various entities found on the web. In a description logic one uses constants, unary predicates and binary predicates, all finite in number. These are used to represent relations about the individuals named by constants, the classes named by unary predicates, and the roles or properties named by binary predicates. You may start from the introductory article Krötzsch et al. (2013) and go through the references quoted there for a comprehensive account of description logics.

References

Andrews, P. B. (1970), 'Resolution in type theory', *J. Symbolic Logic,* **36**, 414–432.

Apt, K. R. & Olderog, E.-R. (1991), *Verification of Sequential and Concurrent Programs*, Springer-Verlag, New York.

Backhouse, R. C. (1986), *Program Construction and Verification*, Prentice Hall, Englewood Cliffs, N.J.

Baral, C. (2003), *Knowledge Representation, Reasoning and Declarative Problem Solving*, Cambridge University Press, Cambridge.

Barwise, J. & Etchemendy, J. (1999), *Language, Proof and Logic*, CSLI Publications, Stanford.

Besnard, J. (1989), *An Introduction to Default Logic*, Springer-Verlag, New York.

Bilaniuk, S. (1999), *A Problem Course in Mathematical Logic*, Unpublished Note, sbilaniuk@trentu.ca.

Boole, G. (1951), *An Investigation of the Laws of Thought*, Dover, (Reprint of Walton & Maberley, 1854), New York.

Boolos, G. (1979), *The Unprovability of Consistency: An Essay in Modal Logic*, Cambridge University Press, Cambridge.

Boolos, G., Burgess, J., Richard, P. & Jeffrey, C. (2007), *Computability and Logic*, Cambridge University Press, Cambridge.

Chang, C. L. & Lee, R. C. T. (1973), *Symbolic Logic and Mechanical Theorem Proving*, Academic Press, New York.

Chellas, B. F. (1980), *Modal Logic-An introduction*, Cambridge University Press, Cambridge.

Copi, I. M. (1979), *Symbolic Logic*, Macmillan, London.

Copi, I. M., Cohen, C., Prabhakar, M. & Jetli, P. (2010), *Introduction to Logic*, Pearson, Delhi.

Davis, M. D. & Putnam, H. (1960), 'A computing procedure for quantification theory', *J. ACM* **7**, 210–215.

Dijkstra, E. W. (1976), *A Discipline of Programming*, Prentice Hall, Englewood Cliffs, N.J.

Dijkstra, E. W. (1982), *Selected Writings on Computing: A personal perspective*, Springer-Verlag, New York.

Dowling, W. F. & Gallier, J. H. (1984), 'Linear time algorithms for testing the satisfiability of propositional horn formulas', *Journal of Logic Programming,* **3**, 267–284.

Doyle, J., Sandewall, E. & Torassi, P., eds (1994), *Proc. Fourth International Conference on Principles of Knowledge Representation and Reasoning*, Morgan Kaufmann. San Fransisco.

Du, D., Gu, J. & Pardalos, P. M. (1997), *Satisfiability Problem : Theory and applications*, (Ed.) American Mathematical Society, Providence. AMS DIMACS Series : Vol.35.

Dubois, D., Farreny, H. & Prade, H. (1985), 'Sur divers problėms inhérents á l' automatisation des raisonnements de sens commun', *Congrés AFCET-RFIA, Grenoble* **1**, 321–328.

Dummett, M. (1977), *Elements of Intuitionism*, Clarendon Press, Oxford.

Ebbinghaus, H. D., Flum, J. & Thomas, W. (1994), *Mathematical Logic*, 2nd ed., Springer, New York.

Enderton, H. B. (1972), *A Mathematical Introduction to Logic*, Academic Press, New York.

Epstein, R. L. (2001), *Propositional Logics: The Semantic Foundations of Logic*, Wadsworth, Belmont, USA.

Ershov, Y. L. & Palyutin, E. A. (1984), *Mathematical Logic*, Mir Publishers, Moscow.

Fagin, R., Halpern, J. Y., Moses, Y. & Vardi, M. Y. (1995), *Reasoning about Knowledge*, MIT Press, Cambridge, USA.

Fitting, M. (1993), Basic modal logic, *in* D. Gabbay, C. Hogger & J. Robinson, eds, 'Handbook of Logic in Artificial Intelligence and Logic Programming', Vol. 1, Oxford University Press, Oxford.

Fitting, M. (1996), *First Order Logic and Automated Theorem Proving*, Springer-Verlag, New York.

Fitting, M. & Mendelson, R. L. (1998), *First Order Modal Logic*, Kluwer Academic Publishers, Dordrecht, The Netherlands.

Francez, N. (1992), *Program Verification*, Addison-Wesley, Reading, USA.

Frege, G. (1934), *Die Grundlagen der Arithmetik, Eine logischmathematische Untersuchung über der Begriff der Zahl.*, Breslau, Reprinted Marcus, Breslau.

Frege, G. (1984), 'Collected papers on mathematics, logic, and philosophy', Oxford. Ed. by M. Mc. Guninness.

Gabbay, D. M. & Guenthner, F. (2002), *Handbook of Philosophical Logic*, 2nd ed., Vol. 1-9, Kluwer Academic Publishers, Dordrecht, The Netherlands.

Gallier, J. H. (1987), *Logic for Computer Science: Foundations of Automatic Theorem Proving*, John Wiley & Sons, New York.

Garey, M. R. & Johnson, D. S. (1979), *Computers and Intractability: A Guide to the Theory of NP-completeness*, Freeman, New York.

Gentzen, G. (1936), 'Die widerspruchsfreiheit der reinen zahlentheorie', *Mathemaische Annalen,* **12**, 493–565.

Glivenko, V. (1929), 'Sur quelques points de la logique de m. brouwer', *Académie Royale de Belgique, Bulletins de la Classe des Sciences, Ser. 5,* **15**, 183–188.

Goldblatt, R. (1987), *Logics of Time and Computation*, CSLI Publications, Stanford.

Gries, D. (1981), *The Science of Programming*, Springer-Verlag, New York.

Gries, D. (1982), 'A note on a standard strategy for developing loop invariants and loops', *Science of Computer Programming,* **2**, 207–214.

Gries, D. & Schneider, F. B. (1993), *A Logical Approach to Discrete Math*, Springer-Verlag, New York.

Haken, A. (1985), 'The intractability of resolution', *Theoretical Computer Science,* **39**, 297–308.

Halpern, J. Y. (1990), 'An analysis of first order logics of probability', *Artificial Intelligence,* **46**, 311–350.

Hehner, E. C. R. (1984), *The Logic of Programming*, Prentice Hall, Englewood Cliffs, N.J.

Hoare, C. A. R. (1969), 'An axiomatic basis for computer programming', *Comm. ACM,* **12**, 576–580,583.

Hodges, W. (1993), *Model Theory*, Cambridge University Press, London.

Hughes, D. E. & Cresswell, M. J. (1971), *An Introduction to Modal Logic*, Methuen, New York.

Huth, M. & Ryan, M. (2000), *Logic in Computer Science: Modelling and reasoning about systems*, Cambridge University Press, Cambridge.

Jones, C. B. (1980), *Software Development: A Rigorous Approach*, Prentice Hall, Englewood Cliffs, N.J.

Kowalski, R. (1979), *Logic for Problem Solving*, Elsevier, Amsterdam.

Krötzsch, M., Simancik, F. & Horrocks, I. (2013), A description logic primer. arXiv:1201.4089v3 [cs.AI].

Lemmon, E. J. (1977), *An Introduction to Modal Logic*, Basil Blackwell, Oxford. Ed. N. Rescher, Monograph No.11, American Philosophical Quaterly Monograph series.

Lewis, C. I. (1918), *A Survey of Symbolic Logic*, Dover, New York.

Lewis, C. I. & Langford, C. H. (1938), *Symbolic Logic*, Century, New York.

Loveland, D. W. (1979), *Automated Theorem Proving: A logical basis*, Elsevier, Amsterdam.

Łukasiewicz, J. (1970), 'Selected works', North Holland, Amsterdam. Ed. by L. Borkowski.

Manaster, A. B. (1978), *Completeness, Compactness and Undecidability: An Introduction to Mathematical Logic*, PHI Learning, New Delhi.

Manin, Y. I. (1977), *A Course in Mathematical Logic for Mathematicians*, Springer Verlag, New York.

Mates, B. (1972), *Elementary Logic*, Oxford University Press, New York.

Mendelson, E. (1979), *Introduction to Mathematical Logic*, D. Van Nostrand, New York.

Meyer, J. J. C. & van der Hoek, W. (1993), *Epistemic Logic for AI and Computer Science*, Cambridge University Press, Cambridge.

Paulson, L. C. (1991), *ML for the Working Programmer*, Cambridge University Press, Cambridge.

Pelletier, F. J. (1999), 'A brief history of natural deduction', *History and Philosophy of Logic,* **20**, 1–31.

Popkorn, S. (1994), *First Steps in Modal Logic*, Cambridge University Press, Cambridge.

Post, E. L. (1921), 'Introduction to general theory of elementary propositions', *American Journal of Mathematics,* **43**, 163–185.

Quine, W. V. (1959), 'On cores and prime implicates of truth functions', *American Math. Monthly,* **66**, 755–760.

Rasiowa, H. & Sikorski, R. (1970), *The Mathematics of Metamathematics*, 3rd ed., Polish Scientific Pub., Warschau.

Rautenberg, W. (2010), *A Concise Introduction to Mathematical Logic*, 3rd ed., Springer, New York.

Reiter, R. & de Kleer, J. (1987), 'Foundations of assumption based truth maintenance systems : Preliminary report', *Proc. AAAI-87* .

Reynolds, J. C. (1981), *The Craft of Programming*, Prentice Hall, Englewood Cliffs, N.J.

Robinson, A. (1996), *Nonstandard Analysis*, Princeton University Press, New Jersey, USA.

Robinson, J. A. (1979), *Logic: Form and Function*, Elsevier, New York.

Robinson, J. A. & Wos, L. (1969), 'Paramodulation and theorem proving in first order logic with equality', *Machine Intelligence,* **4**, 135–150.

Schmidt, D. A. (1994), *The Structure of Typed Programming Languages*, MIT Press, Cambridge, USA.

Selman, B. & Kautz, H. (1991), *Knowledge Compilation using Horn Approximation*, (Ed.) Proc. Ninth National Conference on Artificial Intelligence, Anaheim, CA.

Shoenfield, J. R. (1967), *Mathematical Logic*, Addison Wesley, Reading, USA.

Singh, A. (1999), 'Computing prime implicants via transversal clauses', *Int. J. Computer Math.,* **70**, 417–427.

Singh, A. (2009), *Elements of Computation Theory*, Springer-Verlag, London.

Singh, A. & Goswami, C. (1998), *Fundamentals of Logic*, Indian Council of Philosophical Research, New Delhi.

Smets, P., Mamdani, A., Dubois, D. & Prade, H. (1998), *Non-standard Logics for Automated Reasoning*, Academic Press, New York.

Smullyan, R. M. (1968), *First Order Logic*, Springer-Verlag, New York.

Smullyan, R. M. (1978), *What is The Name of This Book?*, Prentice Hall, Englewood Cliffs, N.J.

Smullyan, R. M. (1983), *The Lady or the Tiger and the Other Logical Puzzles*, Penguin Books, Harmondsworth, UK.

Smullyan, R. M. (2014), *A Biginner's Guide to Mathematical Logic*, Dover Pub. Inc., New York.

Snyder, D. P. (1971), *Modal Logic and its Applications*, Van Nostrand Reinhold Company, New York.

Sperchneider, V. & Antoniou, G. (1991), *Logic, a Foundation for Computer Science*, Addison Wesley, Reading, USA.

Srivastava, S. M. (2013), *A Course on Mathematical Logic*, 2nd ed., Springer (Universitext), New York.

Stoll, R. R. (1963), *Set Theory and Logic*, W.H. Freeman, New York.

Suppes, P. (1957), *Introduction to Logic*, Van Nostrand, Princeton, N.J.

Tanaka, K. (1996), *An Introduction to Fuzzy Logic for Paractical Applications*, Springer-Verlag, New York.

Tarski, A. (1944), 'The semantic conception of truth', *Philosophy and Phenomenological Research,* **4**, 341–376.

Tennent, R. D. (1991), *Semantics of Programming Languages*, Prentice Hall, Englewood Cliffs, N.J.

Tison, P. (1967), 'Generalization of consensus theory and application to the minimization of boolean functions', *IEEE Trans. on Elec. Comp.,* **EC-16**(4), 446–456.

Turner, T. (1991), *Constructive Foundations for Functional Languages*, McGraw-Hill, New York.

van Dalen, D. (1989), *Logic and Structure*, Springer-Verlag (Universitext), New York.

van Heijenoort, J. (1967), *From Frege to Gödel: A Source Book in Mathematical Logic 1879-1931*, Ed. Harvard University Press, Cambridge, USA.

Wittgenstein, L. (1922), *Tractatus Logico Philosophicus*, Kegan & Paul, London. Translated by C.K. Ogden.

Wójcicki, R. (1998), *Theory of Logical Calculi*, D. Reidel, Dordrecht, The Netherlands.

Index